T0121965

Praise for
THE SURVIVOR

"Splendid . . . full of insight and revelation . . . No future
account of these years will be written without constant
reference to this one."
—*Chicago Tribune*

"In vivid detail, Harris leads us through the ups and downs of a
presidency that seemed to end soon after it began, only to adapt
and at times soar in the face of adversity."
—*The Christian Science Monitor*

"Smoothly readable . . . [*The Survivor*] is the first book about the
Clinton presidency that comes from an objective journalist or historian.
It is bound to set the standard for those that follow. . . . Clinton
may merely have survived, but Harris has triumphed."
—New York *Daily News*

"The definitive account so far of the Clinton White House."
—*The Economist*

"Lively and well-researched . . . [Harris] understands the subtleties of capital culture."
—*People*

"Harris is no Clinton apologist. He sees the many flaws. But he makes a powerful argument that Clinton also made many right choices on the economy, social policy and in foreign affairs."
—Baltimore *Sun*

"Important . . . *The Survivor* is a comprehensive inside portrait of the Clinton Presidency. . . . [Harris] has set the bar high for all who come after him, and written a big book that's worthy of his talents and his subject."
—*The New York Observer*

"Revealing . . . a complement and corrective to the Clintons' own memoirs, full of surprising turns that do much to explain the recent past—and the unfolding political present."
—*Kirkus Reviews*

"Harris is especially adept at creating close-ups of Clinton and his advisers at work. . . . Instead of keeping his readers behind the rope, figuratively speaking, he takes them by the elbow and drags them into the thick of the action."
—*BookPage*

"Scrupulously fair-minded . . . a modern reworking of a tragedy with a special Clintonian twist."
—*Washington Monthly*

"The best and most impartial investigation of the [Clinton] administration to date."
—*Library Journal*

The Survivor

The Survivor

BILL CLINTON IN THE WHITE HOUSE

JOHN F. HARRIS

RANDOM HOUSE TRADE PAPERBACKS
NEW YORK

2006 Random House Trade Paperback Edition

Copyright © 2005 by John F. Harris

Published in the United States by Random House Trade Paperbacks, an imprint of
The Random House Publishing Group, a division of Random House, Inc., New York.

RANDOM HOUSE TRADE PAPERBACKS and colophon are trademarks
of Random House, Inc.

Originally published in hardcover in the United States by Random House, an imprint of
The Random House Publishing Group, a division of Random House, Inc., in 2005.

Library of Congress Cataloging-in-Publication Data

Harris, John F. (John Furby).
The survivor : Bill Clinton in the White House / John F. Harris.
p. cm.
Includes bibliographical references and index.
ISBN 0-375-76084-9
1. Clinton, Bill, 1946– 2. Presidents—United States—Biography. 3. United States—
Politics and government—1993–2001. 4. Clinton, Bill, 1946-—Political and social views.
5. Political leadership—United States—Case studies. I. Title.
E886.H37 2005
973.929'092—dc22
[B]   2004062893

www.atrandom.com

Book design by Susan Turner

146119709

For Ann, with boundless love

Contents

Prologue

THE ASCENT

OCTOBER 3, 1991, ARRIVED AS RADIANT MORNING IN LITTLE ROCK, STILL more like summer than fall. The governor of Arkansas began the day with a jog through the city that had been his home for the past fifteen years. In a few hours, he was due to make his appearance at the Old State House to announce his candidacy for the presidency of the United States. The moment had arrived at last.

Clinton, promising face of America's New South, had been fantasizing about a day like this for decades. He had been organizing his life in pursuit of it for years. He had been stewing about the merits of a candidacy in 1992 for months. He had been agonizing, finally, about the precise words he would deliver this day for the past several hours—an all-nighter at the Arkansas governor's mansion. At noon, a crowd of several hundred well-wishers gathered on the lawn to hear him.

Anticipation about Bill Clinton's future was nothing new in these parts. Virtually everyone who had ever known the man—only forty-five years old as he began his ascent to national power that morning—had supposed that he would someday seek the White House. The young boy's teachers predicted it in the 1950s. Two decades later, his law school girlfriend was so sure of it that she dropped her own life plans and picked up for Arkansas, deciding to merge Clinton's life mission with her own. All through the 1980s, speculation about Clinton's career path had been a favorite parlor game of political Arkansans: When would he run? His many friends delighted in the prospect. His enemies, fewer in number but perhaps greater in passion, dreaded it. Neither camp doubted the day would come.

It said something about Clinton's capacity for drama that he could take a moment of such transparent inevitability and infuse it with a measure of suspense. Until Clinton actually uttered the words, however, there would be a pinch of doubt. The governor, after all, had summoned a similar crowd of supporters four years earlier. Old friends flew in from around the country. Then, after a night of deliberations, he shocked the crowd by announcing that he would *not* run for president in 1988. The friends and aides who knew Clinton best, aware of how little prepared he was for the personal scrutiny that would accompany a national campaign, felt sure that had been a prudent decision. Many of these same people wondered whether his impending decision this time might be a rash one. Clinton soon made their doubts moot. At noon, he delivered the words he had spent a lifetime practicing in his imagination: "Today I proudly announce my candidacy for president of the United States."

A LIFETIME OF PREPARATION HAD CULMINATED IN THE USUAL FASHION FOR Clinton: in a swirling cloud of last-minute chaos and indecision. The speech preparation had proceeded with all the ease and grace of someone passing a kidney stone. The evening was revealing in several respects. One was how Clinton, whether by design or subconscious preference, placed himself between the tug of different advisers. It was a pattern to be repeated endless times in the years ahead. He was at once conflict averse, hating personal confrontation, and drawn to conflict as a management style. Clinton found rivalries among his subordinates liberating. He found his ideas and options, he once acknowledged, "in the seams" between the clashing ideas of others. In this case the tug—civil, but spirited—for Clinton's mind was between a Washington consultant, Frank Greer, and a young speechwriter and policy aide named Bruce Reed, on hand to help Clinton from his perch at the centrist Democratic Leadership Council (DLC). Greer kept pushing more personal detail and uplifting rhetoric about Clinton's rise from humble, small-town roots. Reed kept pushing for more policy substance, the kind of details that would highlight Clinton as a new breed of Democrat, more innovative and less wedded to old liberal pieties and programs. The Washington visitors toiled away downstairs while Clinton stayed upstairs hunched over successive drafts. Hillary Rodham Clinton, the first lady of Arkansas, hovered over the proceedings with the discerning eye of the corporate lawyer she was. She softened her formidable presence with an unexpected maternal streak, appearing in the speechwriters' den with a plate of cookies. The speech was finished at dawn. The governor went to clear his mind with a morning jog through the streets of Little Rock. Clinton later told Reed that he found the announcement speech a difficult process in part because he was not used to working with speechwriters. In Arkansas, the governor simply wrote his own speeches, or more often fashioned them on the spot from scraps of jotted notes. Reed had been drawn to Clinton because of his reputation as an up-and-comer in national politics. Clinton's comment was a striking reminder that this lifelong political talent was taking his game into an entirely new arena.

The opening hours of the campaign that would carry Clinton to the presidency were notable also for their intimacy. Most Americans are familiar with the shape and size of a presidential campaign only as it nears conclusion. They see charter airplanes and motorcades, Secret Service agents and press handlers, cameras and boom mikes, bands and banners—the entire swollen enterprise revolving around a politician who by this date has become one of the most recognizable faces on the planet. At its inception, though, a presidential campaign looks more like this: four guys sitting in a hotel bar.

The bar in this instance was the lobby of the Washington Court Hotel near Capitol Hill. A college football game was playing on the television, attracting considerably more interest than the newly minted presidential candidate, who attracted none. Clinton had traveled to the capital on a recruiting trip. His campaign needed to assemble a roster of national-caliber consultants. Joined by Bruce Lindsey, his longtime friend and retainer, Clinton had arranged a barroom interview with James Carville, a flamboyant but erratic Louisianan, and his younger and more even-keeled sidekick, a Texas native named Paul Begala. The dynamic of this meeting was a bit peculiar, since it was ambiguous who exactly was interviewing whom. Begala and Carville were then very much in vogue, as the hot hands on the political circuit that year, and they were being courted by several other Democratic campaigns. It was the prospective client who was making the pitch, while the would-be employees listened inscrutably. Yet it was a pitch so expert that Begala would play over in his mind for years what had happened this afternoon. Often politicians try to make a winning impression on political operatives by demonstrating their savvy. They boast of their fund-raising potential, or likely endorsements, or sophisticated insights into the latest polls. Even at this early date, Clinton had a reputation as the consummate politician, so the operatives sat down waiting for a discussion laden with inside dope. They got nothing of the sort. Instead, Clinton launched into an impassioned discourse—nothing short of a sermon, really—about how troubled he was about his country, with its fraying social fabric and struggling economy. What kind of world would his eleven-year-old daughter find by the time she was an adult? As the meeting closed, it dawned on Begala that a presidential candidate had talked for hours with political strategists and uttered not a word about strategy. The young consultant swooned. In his crush, however, he kept enough detachment to contemplate that the session had been a put-on, and what seemed like a wonderfully guileless performance actually had been a more sophisticated brand of artifice. "Is this guy for real?" he asked Carville, who mumbled noncommittally. The consultants signed on, and Begala would soon be sharing hotels and airplanes with Clinton as a traveling aide. But he would have numerous occasions in the years ahead to return to his original question.

As Clinton's barroom sermon suggested, the 1992 presidential election arrived amid a national mood of brooding and uncertainty. The anxiety had two interwoven threads. One was a question about the state of the country. The other was a question about the state of the Democratic Party.

It was an odd moment for the United States to be feeling cheerless. One of history's monumental conflicts—liberal democracy versus communism—was just coming to an end, with a triumph for free society over totalitarianism. The United States had reason to be proud of its victory over the Soviet Union, which did not come in the cataclysmic war that people had feared so long but rather was the result of a patient, decades-long effort at containment. The country, moreover, was just months past a swift and impressive victory in a regional war against Iraq, rolling back that country's illegal invasion of Kuwait in the summer of 1990. Yet triumphalism faded with astonishing swiftness. The victories overseas seemed to belong to a closing chapter in history. As Americans looked toward the future, there was a widespread belief that the United States had lost its traditional edge in productivity and technological innovation to more competitive economies in Asia. Within a few years such fears would be proven fanciful, but the belief that the United States was a receding economic power reflected mainstream opinion in the early 1990s. There hardly seemed occasion, moreover, to celebrate the country's new status as the world's lone superpower. All the military might that had been on such dazzling display in Iraq did not seem to have much utility in the Balkans, where the end of the Cold War had unleashed ancient hatreds that led to the breakup of Yugoslavia and the killing of thousands in ethnic warfare of shocking ferocity. The emerging generation of global tests, as they were perceived in 1992, seemed to underscore American weakness rather more than power in the world.

Many Americans were not looking much beyond their borders in any event. At home, the country was mired in recession. Unemployment was near 8 percent. By historic standards, the downturn was not especially severe. Democrats dubiously called it the worst economic performance since the Great Depression. But, coming after years of prosperity beginning in the mid-1980s, its impact was indeed jarring. The sluggish growth combined with and contributed to other trends that cumulatively created a picture of a country badly offtrack—"in a ditch," as Clinton would say often that year. The trade imbalance with other countries was growing. The gap in wealth between the highest rung of society and those beneath was growing. The journalists Donald L. Barlett and James B. Steele produced an unlikely best-seller with their book *America: What Went Wrong?,* an angry indictment of the failures of the American economy. It was more than the economy that seemed to be fraying. The spring of 1992 brought the nation's worst rioting in a generation, after blacks erupted at the acquittal of police officers on trial for the beating of a suspect named Rodney King. The argument that there was something fundamentally wrong with the country's course resonated deeply.

This was distinct from a belief, certainly among Democrats, that there was much that could be done about it. Amid the general malaise, the incumbent Republican president, George H.W. Bush, began the year plainly harried by the country's domestic problems but still secure in his re-election prospects. He was, after all, a victorious war president, who held a popular reputation for a certain political clumsiness but personal decency. It was not merely Bush's advantages as an incumbent that shadowed Democratic hopes. In a much more fundamental sense, it was the Democrats' deficiencies. Over the previous several decades, the party had become anchored in the public mind as a congressional party, not a presidential one. The Democratic majority in the House of Representatives had been intact for four decades; any change in this status seemed inconceivable. At the same time, there had been six presidential elections in the twenty-eight years since Lyndon B. Johnson's 1964 landslide. The Democrats had won one of them. The South, once the engine of the party's electoral college strategy, was now overwhelmingly Republican territory. Democrats had their share of slow learners. Many of them were content with congressional power and could always find one way or another to explain why presidential nominees did not clear the bar. Jimmy Carter was hobbled by economic malaise in 1980, Walter F. Mondale was no match for Ronald Reagan's sunny spirit in 1984, Michael Dukakis was hurt by his clerkish personality and Bush's shrewd negative ads in 1988. These explanations were all true. But by 1992 there was an awakening sense among at least some Democrats that they were insufficient. A fundamental rethinking of the party's presidential strategy was needed.

Clinton loomed as a promising figure to some Democrats because his political biography suggested such a willingness to think anew. The preeminent challenge for Democrats by 1992 was to practice defensive politics. An earlier generation of Democrats had been able to run on a liberal label—standing proudly for an activist government role in regulating the economy, protecting the environment, and enforcing racial equality under the law. At its high-water mark, two decades earlier, liberalism generally and Democrats in particular became identified with the cultural movements that liberated women, empowered young people, and knocked down all manner of old taboos and conventions affecting everything from sexual behavior to what passed for humor on television. Now, the dominant forces in American politics were skepticism toward overreaching government and ambivalence about the consequences of three decades of social change—even from people who amply benefited from such change in their own lives. For a politician to be called "conservative" was something worth advertising; to be called "liberal" was an accusation to be denied.

This predicament was a new development for some Democrats, but it was a familiar one for an ambitious Democrat who had staked his future in Arkansas. Geography was central to Bill Clinton's politics. He had come of age amid people who resented from the outset the federal government's most ambitious domestic project of the 1960s, the forcible dismantlement of racial segregation. Clinton had grown up amid culturally conservative white voters, often people who were clinging precariously to their middle-class status. He knew them on the whole as decent and sensible people, who were often crippled by their prejudices and their limited horizons. They could be coaxed toward enlightened attitudes and toward progressive policies, but it was a gingerly exercise. Defensive politics—the imperative for Democrats who wanted to compete at the presidential level—was something that Clinton understood intuitively before he was even old enough to vote. Certainly he understood, with occasional remedial courses required, as he carried out his climb through Arkansas politics. That had begun with a spirited but unsuccessful campaign for a congressional seat in 1974, at the age of twenty-eight. This led the way for a successful bid as state attorney general in 1976. Two years later, he became the nation's youngest governor. Two years after that, he became the nation's youngest ex-governor, following a campaign in which his opponent portrayed him, not unfairly, as an arrogant and unseasoned young man who was out of step with his constituents. That led to his most impressive feat to date in politics, a long and shrewdly orchestrated comeback in 1982. He was secure in the capital for the next ten years, waiting for the right moment to make the jump to a national stage.

One reason Clinton had a plausible claim for a place on that stage was his affiliation with a group that was dedicated to precisely the sort of defensive politics that he had learned in Arkansas. The Washington-based Democratic Leadership Council was born in 1985, just after the debacle of Mondale's forty-nine–state loss to Reagan. Its founder, Al From, was a veteran congressional staff member and political strategist from Indiana, who would eventually figure large in Clinton's rise to power and the presidency that followed. From was a loyal Democrat, and a believer in the promise of a strong and activist national government, but from the beginning of his career he had been devoted to critiquing liberalism and its consequences. In the late 1960s, he joined Sargent Shriver's War on Poverty. His job was to investigate, in much the way a reporter or auditor might, whether the programs actually met their goals—what worked and what did not. Through the 1970s and early 1980s, From believed there was too little of that empirical-minded spirit among the Democrats. Instead, as From and his ideological confederates saw it, the party of the New Deal and Great Society had become too anchored to liberal orthodoxy, too captive of labor unions, minorities, and other special interests. The Democratic Party's roster of factions, each of them with laudable claims, did not add up to a compelling vision of the national good.

The DLC had an innovative agenda of ideas on welfare, education, and other issues, but its primary impetus was not intellectual ferment; it was fear. The founding members in 1985 came overwhelmingly from the South and Mountain West, and included such prominent Democrats as Senators Sam Nunn of Georgia and Charles Robb of Virginia, as well as less prominent ones like Clinton. Facing voters in the heart of Reagan Country, these politicians understood that the liberalism of the national party had become anathema to white voters south of the Mason-Dixon line. Of the forty-three original DLC politicians, only six had won their most recent elections with more than

60 percent of the vote. All but four came from states that Reagan had carried in both 1980 and 1984. By the spring of 1990, Clinton had become the group's national chairman, and on May 6 of that year he addressed its national convention in Cleveland. Speaking from index cards but no text, he delivered an impassioned warning to Democrats. "Too many of the people who used to vote for us, the very burdened middle class we are talking about, have not trusted us in national elections to defend our national interests abroad, to put their values into our social policy at home, or to take their tax money and spend it with discipline," he told the delegates. "We've got to turn these perceptions around or we can't continue as a national party."

It was a bravura performance, widely reported on by the national political press, and it quickly made Clinton the favorite of the party's moderate wing in 1992. Given the DLC's pivotal role in promoting Clinton's future, it is surprising that his involvement with the group was freighted with ambivalence. From sometimes surrendered to doubts about whether Clinton really believed in the DLC's agenda or was simply using it as a political pose. What's more, his personal relationship with the governor could be maddeningly noncommittal. "I realize your personal political situation is complex," From wrote in a February 23, 1990, memo, "but at the DLC we've run out of time. If you can't make a 100 percent commit to the DLC chairmanship this week, I have to recruit someone else." A year later, Clinton had become chairman, but From was no less plaintive. A March 9, 1991, memo from From to Clinton: "The purpose of this memorandum is to frame our discussion on Sunday in Detroit, which I gather will have to take place between the airport and the hotel—since, as usual, your schedule was set up without consulting us and the two phone calls I made to you in the past two weeks were not returned." He continued, "I really hate writing memos like this one, but I'm afraid if I don't, we'll have another one of those sessions where you'll charm my pants off and then nothing changes. We seem to have enjoyable discussions that never come to a conclusion."

No doubt Clinton's reluctance was partly calculation. To embrace the DLC, for all the attention this might give him before a national audience, was to risk spurning other important constituencies. African-Americans, the Democrats' most reliable voting bloc, were in particular wary of the DLC's motives and influence, which to their eyes looked like an abandonment of progressive politics. Jesse Jackson derided the group as "Southern White Boys' Caucus" and "Democrats for the Leisure Class." Governor Douglas Wilder, the first black to win statewide office in Virginia since Reconstruction, once derided the DLC for its "demeaning appeal to white Southern males."

FROM WAS LATER TOLD BY CLINTON ASSOCIATES THAT THERE WAS ANOTHER reason for the governor's oddly elusive behavior in the early 1990s: At home, his marriage to Hillary Clinton was said to be in turmoil. The speculation hinted at one of the main things that was widely believed about Bill Clinton as he made his entrance into national politics. He was a man of vagrant sexual appetites. Every political operative or journalist with even a passing knowledge of Clinton knew it. Or, more precisely, they had *heard* the gossip about Clinton's "women problem." The nature or specifics of the problem were in fact quite murky.

But the rumblings were sufficiently persistent and credible to be an essential part of the Clinton conversation in political circles. The man was defined in part by his promise—a young and articulate newcomer, winning notice for his ideas and style—and in part by the uncertain perils of his personal life.

This presented an awkward challenge for the corps of political hands, most of them recent arrivals to the Clinton enterprise, that the governor had assembled for his presidential run. What trapdoors might swing open under the pressures of a national campaign? There was obviously no way to know without some more specific understanding of the dimensions of the supposed "women problem." The matter came up at a Washington skull session with the governor—and his wife—shortly before the formal announcement of his candidacy. Questions were going to be asked, the advisers warned, that the couple had better be ready to answer. As Stan Greenberg, the campaign pollster, later recalled it, Hillary Clinton's presence at first made others embarrassed, but she seemed notably matter-of-fact about the delicate topic on the table. The governor spoke first, dismissing the political operatives' concerns with a brusque and seemingly sincere insistence that there was no problem to be concerned about. Then, it was his wife's turn. She seemed eager to show that the couple was not being naïve. "We wouldn't be having this conversation if there weren't some issues," she acknowledged. "We've been through tough times, just like other married couples." She said "kooks" and publicity seekers might well come forward. After opaquely acknowledging difficulties, she then resolutely established limits: They would not talk about the inner workings of their relationship. Impassioned now, she said their marriage was genuine. Clinton was a good husband and father, and people would just have to take that or leave it as they saw fit. Hillary Clinton's adamance seemed to embolden the governor. "*There is not a problem,*" he repeated, with emphasis. Then he railed against the prurience of the news media. "They don't seem interested in what I believe in, what kind of person I am, where I want to take the country," he protested. The matter was now closed.

While Clinton's advisers brooded over his vulnerabilities, and he bristled over the scrutiny, he hardly let the matter cramp his style. To the contrary, the candidate sometimes seemed to celebrate his indifference to the rumors. John King, then the chief political reporter for the Associated Press, sat down at a governors conference for a brief interview with Clinton as his campaign was getting under way. The interview was in the hallway of a Washington hotel. Just as Clinton launched into a discussion of welfare reform, a striking blonde woman happened to walk by. Clinton talked on, about poverty levels and work requirements, even as his gaze turned from King and fixed on the blonde's figure receding down the hallway. He halted his monologue in mid-sentence and turned back to King. "Wow," he said, without elaboration. Then back to welfare.

THE CHATTER ABOUT CLINTON'S MARITAL WANDERING NATURALLY SPARKED curiosity about the marriage itself. What was this partnership all about? The people gravitating to Clinton's nascent presidential campaign soon learned that his political career was a joint enterprise, and that the candidate's wife was a potent force to be reckoned with. She was his equal or superior in intelligence and ambition, though she did not share (or at least did not yet) his keen political intuition. There had been a frisson between them from the moment they eyed each other twenty years earlier in the library at Yale Law School, and they were soon in each other's thrall. Like nearly all her peers in New Haven, Hillary Rodham had a careerist outlook, and she had good reason for confidence about her prospects. Women were only recently breaking into elite precincts like Yale Law in the early 1970s. Anyone sizing up the student body for future world leaders would probably have been more drawn to her than to Bill Clinton. After all, she had already been featured in the pages of *Life* magazine for her 1969 graduation speech from Wellesley College, two years before their library encounter. But Arkansas and politics exerted a powerful gravitational pull on Clinton, and soon enough they tugged on Rodham, too—though not without resistance.

Her first trips there had not gone especially well. She was different from the women Clinton had dated before: more cerebral by far, less feminine in the traditional style, frightfully self-assured. Few of the important people in Clinton's life—and most especially his mother—were initially enthusiastic about her. Nor was Rodham thrilled about joining them and the world of cramped horizons they seemed to represent. Arkansas: Sometimes she would roll her eyes with droll resignation when she spoke of the place. In more serious moods, she brooded about whether she was betraying feminist ideals with the career sacrifices such a journey with Clinton would entail. Friends and mentors were dismayed by the prospect. The state was hardly the right venue for a woman aspiring to the top tiers of the legal profession. But Clinton's ambitions and Rodham's were beginning to merge in ways that only fueled their attraction. Often in politics, career and romance are in competition. In this romance—and few people who knew them at the time doubted that "romance" was precisely the right word—the opposite was true. Politics, both the idealistic calling and the thrill of the race, helped provide the heat for the relationship. By the end of law school, they were unofficially engaged, and the next year, 1974, Clinton was back in Arkansas running for Congress. It was a race the political pros expected him to lose, and he did, but he advanced his reputation even so by nearly unseating longtime incumbent John Paul Hammerschmidt. Hillary Rodham had traveled to Arkansas that fall to provide some much needed organizational ballast to her boyfriend's campaign. She arrived just in time to shoo away other girlfriends of the candidate who had landed on the campaign staff. In more ways than one, she had seen the vivid possibilities of this relationship. Her first job after law school was as a young staff lawyer on the House Judiciary Committee's inquiry into President Nixon's Watergate crimes. Once, an older lawyer who had become a mentor, Bernard W. Nussbaum, was driving his talented young protégée home one night. With earnest intensity, she made a prediction about her boyfriend: "He's going to be president of the United States." Amused, Nussbaum replied, "That's silly and ridiculous." Before slamming shut the car door, the young woman seethed: "I know this guy. You don't. He is going to be president. You think it's silly. Well, someday you'll eat your words."

HILLARY CLINTON UNDERSTOOD AS WELL AS ANYONE ELSE THAT THE POLITIcian who was introducing himself to a national public in 1992 was a man of many parts. He had been born in Hope, Arkansas. This coincidence proved to be a windfall for his speechwriters, who made great use of the metaphorical power of the "Man from Hope." The truth is the boy moved at age seven to Hot Springs, which was a larger and more complicated place, and the real crucible in which he grew to adulthood. The resort city in central Arkansas was a place of jarring juxtapositions. At mid-century, Hot Springs was at one level a place of Baptist churches, high school football games, and Middle American proprieties. It was also a place of resort spas, racing tracks, and illegal but openly tolerated gambling parlors—a place where pleasures of the flesh, the purse, and the bottle were routinely indulged by tourists and natives alike. In this vaporous environment, Clinton learned that decent and pious people could have all manner of private weaknesses. In Hot Springs, virtue and vice, sin and penitence, mingled comfortably with one another. Clinton was the pride of Hot Springs. He was a gregarious young man, not an athlete but a leader of the high school band, and a formidable mind who excelled at class work with little evident effort. This talent was his ticket into an elite world far beyond what most of his Arkansas contemporaries could reasonably aspire to. Georgetown University was followed by a Rhodes scholarship at Oxford, and then the New Haven years. He had a natural gift for moving comfortably among different classes and in different arenas and seeming perfectly comfortable anywhere—an obvious asset for an aspiring politician.

This gift for friendship and gaiety had taken root in some unhappy circumstances. Clinton grew up amid domestic chaos. The future president's biological father, William Blythe, was killed in a car accident on a rain-slicked highway a few months before his son's birth in 1946. His mother married the man, Roger Clinton, who in due course would share his last name with the youngster. A decent man when sober, Roger Clinton was an erratic and menacing figure when he drank, which was frequently. Terrible rows and even physical conflicts were common. After studying the pathology and family consequences of addictive behavior, Bill Clinton came to believe that his personality was shaped in important ways by growing up in an alcoholic household. Like many children in such circumstances, he threw his energy into personal achievement. And he became a natural conciliator—instinctually eager for people to get along and feel good, and instinctually good at getting them to do so.

This talent had a darker side. Even close friends learned there were sides of Clinton that stayed walled off. Childhood friends like David Leopoulos and Carolyn Yeldell Staley, who were in the Clinton home nearly every day, never learned until decades later—by reading articles about candidate Clinton's youth—that there was any problem in his home life. Why didn't you say something? Leopoulos asked. Everyone has to deal with his own problems, his friend replied. The father's weaknesses, moreover, seemed to echo. During the 1980s, the governor's brother, the younger Roger Clinton, was arrested for drug dealing. In crisis, the entire family went through counseling. Deeply concerned about his younger brother, Bill Clinton obliquely referred in a conversation with Staley to the vulnerabilities in his own life. "I think we're all addicted to something," he said. "Some people are addicted to drugs. Some to power. Some to food. Some to sex. We're all addicted to something."

The comment suggested a fleeting awareness to one of the paramount facts about Clinton as a politician: It was the merger of psychological function and dysfunction within the man. This was not merely the common phenomenon of a person's weaknesses being the flip side of his strengths, which is true for nearly everyone. Traits that would be regarded as emotionally unhealthy by conventional standards—a desperate need for human contact, or a heedlessness about personal risk—were in Clinton's case political assets of great utility.

His compulsive politicking was once on comic display at Disney World, where he noticed a family standing in line wearing University of Arkansas shirts and correctly presumed they were from his home state. "Thank you for coming," he enthused, as if he was the host even at Disney World. Then there was the time in 1987 when he was due at the Gillett Coon Supper, an annual rite in Arkansas. It had been snowing hard, and no one in his right mind would get in an airplane. But Clinton talked Senator Dale Bumpers, against his better judgment, into flying in with him. The small plane landed with a horrifying thud, spun around on the runway, then came to rest in a snowy pasture. Fearing an explosion from leaking fuel, the occupants leaped out and sprinted away. Instead of contemplating his brush with death, Clinton declared with delight, "Boy, I bet we never lose another vote in Gillett!"

Clinton's appetites in nearly all respects—for people, ideas, food, women—could be excessive, but this was ultimately what set him apart. Yes, he was smart, but no smarter than many other politicians of his generation. He could of course be charming, but there was nothing in his style or wit that set him far apart from others. These qualities turned into something electric only when fused with another: desire. "I knew the first time I met him—I knew that he was hungry," said Senator David Pryor, who first met the collegiate Clinton in 1966, when he was working as a volunteer driver for a gubernatorial candidate. "You could sense it. It was like meeting a jaguar that was just about to pounce."

This hunger could produce brilliant performances—such as the DLC speech in Cleveland that put Clinton in the first tier of presidential candidates. Or it could lead him into disaster, as in two days after that speech when he attended an education conference in a Little Rock hotel and noticed a young woman in the lobby. According to later testimony, he instructed one of his security officers to make an introduction and invite her up to the governor's suite. Her name was Paula Corbin; she would in time become better known by her married name, Paula Jones.

....

So here was Clinton at the outset of his presidential run. His huge potential was on bright display. His vulnerabilities were shrouded but even so unmistakable. The whole campaign seemed to be guided by opposing currents. In one direction there was the sheer implausibility of the enterprise. In the other direction was an almost mystical arc of inevitability that had been illuminating Clinton's path to the White House as far back as second grade, when his teacher announced to his mother, in all seriousness, "I promise you, if he wants to be, he will be president someday."

Such an arc, perhaps, is visible mostly in retrospect. At the time, the notion that a governor from one of the nation's smallest and most impoverished states, a man with no Washington experience, could take on a popular sitting president was downright fanciful. Even Clinton regarded it that way, at least in some moods. Just days before his announcement, the pollster Stan Greenberg was startled to hear Clinton having brooding conversations with friends about whether he should run—long after Greenberg had understood the decision to have been made. These last-minute bouts of equivocation, the pollster later concluded after witnessing many of them, were simply Clinton's way of making himself comfortable with a decision—like a bulky man tossing and turning until his sheets and pillows were just right. On the very day of his announcement, Clinton told the Washington commentator David Gergen that he basically regarded the 1992 race as a warm-up race for 1996.

The twin currents—all the positive traits that made Clinton's candidacy seem like destiny, all the troubling ones that would carry him frequently to disaster—appeared in concentrated form in the Democratic nominating contest's first showdown, in New Hampshire. Clinton started the year as the frontrunner. The first trouble came when the tabloid *Star* introduced America to a Little Rock nightclub singer named Gennifer Flowers. "My 12-Year Affair with Bill Clinton," blared the main headline, over a smaller one that promised, "The Secret Love Tapes That Prove It." Those tapes did seem to suggest a certain intimacy. The candidate appeared on CBS's *60 Minutes* to acknowledge that he had caused "pain in my marriage" but to deny involvement with Flowers. His candidacy stayed afloat, just long enough to be swamped days later by disclosures that he had been less than forthcoming about his extensive efforts twenty-three years earlier to avoid being drafted into the army. "Meltdown," warned

Greenberg, after looking at polls showing Clinton's New Hampshire lead collapsing by the hour.

It was then that a national audience first saw the instinct for survival that became the essential element of the Clinton mystique. With a prodigy of effort—he promised to keep campaigning "until the last dog dies"—he fought his way back to an eminently respectable second place. The cycle repeated itself through the winter and spring, as Clinton summarily dispatched his rivals. He beat more established Washington personalities, such as Senator Bob Kerrey of Nebraska. He withstood a challenge from the right by former senator Paul Tsongas, who ran on a deficit reduction message, as well as from the left by former California governor Jerry Brown.

"Empathy" was a word Clinton brought into political vogue that year. "I feel your pain," he told audiences, a phrase that quickly became a parody. But Clinton's gift was not simply a put-on: He did have an authentic superior sense of human dynamics. Dee Dee Myers, the campaign press secretary, saw it one day when the candidate was shaking hands on a rope line and came across a family with a disabled child. As any politician would, he stopped to give special attention to the child. Then he did something a less perceptive person would have overlooked. He stopped and focused intently on the child's brother. "Your parents have their hands full, you know that," he said. "But don't ever forget, they love you just as much."

Unfortunately, this was not the only side of Clinton his advisers saw. They were often appalled by his dissembling, as when he assured first his own campaign team and later reporters that he had shared everything there was to know about his Vietnam-era history. On first telling, "everything" did not include the story of his successful lobbying effort to join the Arkansas National Guard, a commitment he later backed out of. It later came out that his recital of the history also had neglected another small fact—that he had actually received a draft induction notice in the spring of 1969. Of receiving a letter that every young man of the 1960s era knew could change his life forever, Clinton said, "It was a perfectly normal procedural thing and there was nothing unusual about it." His own team also was repelled by his indiscipline. Under stress, the candidate ate, and there was a lot of stress in 1992. Once, campaign hands Begala and George Stephanopoulos were waiting for Clinton to arrive for a meeting at a Philadelphia firehouse. It had been another day of bad publicity about the draft. Stephanopoulos noticed a half-eaten box of stale doughnuts on the table. "Watch the doughnuts," he predicted. Sure enough, when Clinton arrived and heard the latest bleak developments from the campaign, he inhaled the doughnuts in an instant. Stephanopoulos, a slender man who was exceptionally self-disciplined about his own fitness, later described the scene to friends with revulsion.

Most of all, Clinton aides recoiled at the candidate's bouts of self-pity and flailing anger. Some aides thought the candidate was clinically depressed. Greenberg had conversations with Arkansas aides to Clinton about whether the candidate was emotionally stable enough to be president. Relax, they assured him, he's gone through cycles like this before. One night in the spring of 1992 at Doe's Eat Place, Little Rock's main campaign hangout, consultant Carville told a group of colleagues that he was "only somewhat certain" that he would vote for Clinton.

For all his troubles, Clinton persevered. By June, he had sewn up the Democratic nomination—for what it was worth, which at that point seemed rather little. He was in third place in the polls, behind George Bush and even behind the independent, Ross Perot, who was running on a message attacking out-of-control budget deficits and Washington special-interest politicians. Clinton's funk was worse than ever. The root of the problem was a clash between Clinton's perception of himself and the image that had emerged of him in the Democratic campaign. By turns, his rivals had all portrayed him as a pandering politician with no moral compass. By contrast, it was central to Clinton's self-image that he was a man of exceptionally noble purposes. "I don't think you can minimize how horrible I feel," he roared at a staff meeting that spring, "having worked all my life to stand for things, having busted my butt for seven months, and the American people don't know crap about it after I have poured $10 million worth of information into their heads."

He was saved from his slide into irrelevance by a man who, at the outset, was inclined to believe the worst about Clinton. Tennessee senator Al Gore had run for president four years earlier, but chose for personal reasons not to try again in 1992. He watched the campaign of his fellow southerner with curiosity and envy. Several times he had predicted to aides that Clinton could never become president, and he spoke disparagingly about his flawed character. When he first contemplated the possibility of running for vice president in 1992, it was as Ross Perot's running mate. Yet if Gore eyed Clinton defensively, the opposite was not true. The candidate knew that something dramatic was needed to reinvigorate the campaign. When certain dream possibilities, such as recruiting Army General Colin Powell to join the ticket, proved unattainable, Clinton's attention kept returning to Gore. The candidate had been reading a book, *Generations,* by demographers Neil Strauss and William Howe, who stressed the importance of generational symbolism. Clinton wanted his vice presidential choice to make a statement about how the generation born in the wake of World War II was now ready to assume the mantle of leadership. Instead of the usual concept of ticket balance—running a northerner with a southerner, for instance, or a conservative with a liberal—Clinton was eager for "ticket reinforcement." That meant picking a running mate who could both match and amplify the best traits of the presidential nominee. The two men spoke for hours late one evening in a secret meeting at the Washington Hilton hotel. Gore, impressed by Clinton's energy and intelligence, overcame his earlier coolness. Days later, when Clinton called his Tennessee home at midnight, Gore was pleased to accept the offer.

Ticket reinforcement had a dramatic impact. By some mysterious chemistry of politics, the two men together produced an effect that was more appealing than either by himself. Beside each other, they no longer looked like another couple of ambitious politicians—one a bit too slick and the other a bit too stiff—both trying to shimmy to the top of the greasy pole. They were two young leaders, imperfect but earnest, fresh faces on a tired national scene. The public responded. Within days of Gore's selection and Clinton's nominating convention in New York, the third-place candidate had surged into first— a position he would not surrender for the balance of the campaign.

His popular vote percentage was 43 percent, to Bush's 38, to a surprising 19 percent for the independent Perot. But the electoral college worked its desired effect of amplifying the victor's mandate. Clinton won 32 states, and 370 electoral votes. He had dethroned the last president to come of age in the World War II era, and served notice that a new generation was ready to take power.

ON ELECTION NIGHT, IT WAS AS IF SOMEBODY HAD FLICKED A SWITCH AND turned off gravity in Little Rock. Afloat on a cloud of ecstasy, exhaustion, and wonderment, the beaming president-elect once again stood on the steps of the Old State House. There was a crowd of fifty thousand on hand, swollen several dozen times over from the band of old friends and skeptical reporters who had gathered here thirteen months before. Clinton reached for higher meaning in the moment.

"This victory was more than a victory of party," he declared, "it was a victory for the people who work hard and play by the rules, a victory for the people who feel left out and left behind but want to do better, a victory for the people who are ready to compete and win in the global economy, but need a government that offers a hand up, not a hand out." In his recital of pledges, he touched on one he said was "perhaps most important of all, to bring our people together as never before, so that our diversity can be a source of strength in a world that is ever smaller, where everyone counts and everyone is part of America's family." For a twinkling moment, one could imagine Clinton becoming the national unifier he longed to be.

Gravity naturally came back on, and when it did, Clinton landed with something of a thud. A sour moment a couple of days later reflected Clinton's fatigue, as well as his accumulated grievance at thirteen months in which he was subject to one of the most personally intrusive campaigns ever in presidential politics. He went to go golfing, and snapped when news photographers were on hand to capture his first tee shot. "Goddamn it," Clinton rasped at the hapless club manager. "I thought we had an agreement that they weren't going to be up here!"

This waspish moment was the symbolic beginning to Clinton's transition from candidate to president. The interregnum between candidate to president is often a challenging period for presidents-elect. Perhaps never has the glow of victory curdled quite so quickly, and with such lasting consequences, as it did with Clinton. His arrival in Washington was eleven weeks away. In the narrow sense, his challenge during this period was administrative: to select a cabinet and fill the senior posts to serve him on the White House staff. In the larger sense, his challenge was less administrative than political and even psychological. There were two delicate and even somewhat contradictory imperatives.

The first imperative was offensive in nature. Clinton had to assert himself, before a diverse variety of audiences, as something more than just a politician. He had to establish that he was an executive who intended to be the dominant figure on the Washington landscape, and that he expected to be treated as such. The second imperative was defensive in nature. He had to adapt to the reality that as the nation's new leader, he was being watched with more care than before, and his words would land with more impact and a longer echo than they did just a few days earlier as a candidate. In his transition, Clinton failed at both imperatives.

There was an early visit to Little Rock by the Democratic congressional leaders. A three-hour beef tenderloin dinner was pleasant enough—too pleasant, in retrospect. At every turn, the president-elect let the visitors press their agenda, and seemed to retreat on his. He backed off his campaign planks urging a presidential line-item veto and cuts in congressional staff, as well as his support for campaign finance reform. This was partly a matter of temperament; Clinton always tried first to be an accommodator. But it was also a matter of strategy. The failure of Jimmy Carter, the last Democratic president, to stay on good terms with his own party's congressional leaders was a central reason his presidency foundered. Unfortunately, when word of the meeting leaked, the inevitable perception that echoed through Washington was that Clinton was a pushover. A similar phenomenon threatened to overshadow the president-elect's cabinet selections. After being out of power for twelve years, Democratic interest groups were clamoring for the spoils of victory— attention for their favored issues, and appointments. Clinton had raised expectations further with a pledge to appoint an administration that "looks like America." By making his laudable commitment to diversity so explicit, he spurred speculation that women and minority appointees were not chosen on the merits. Meanwhile, instead of the praise he expected from women and minority groups, there was even more pressure and demands that their people get not minor cabinet departments but the first-tier ones. *The New Republic* observed sourly: "Rigging certain departments for a single gender or race, tracking down an individual not for her intrinsic talent but for her ethnic makeup, is an insult to minorities and a depressing sign of the cultural balkanization of our politics. It is the old Democratic Party speaking, not the new." Clinton, too, soon snapped, when asked to counter criticism from feminist groups that he had not appointed enough women. "They're playing quota games and math games," he snarled, denouncing the groups as "bean counters." In his first encounters with Washington, the country's new leader was harried like a man with terriers gnawing at his pant legs.

Paradoxically, at the same time he was not asserting himself, Clinton was also not protecting his flanks. A week after the election, NBC News reporter Andrea Mitchell asked Clinton what sounded like a simple question that was actually quite cunning: Did he plan to implement his pledge to allow homosexuals to serve openly in the military? To the surprise and relief of Sandy Berger, a longtime friend and foreign policy adviser, this pledge had never spurred controversy during the campaign. Now, instead of allowing himself a measure of wiggle room, as he surely would have done with more experience, Clinton plunged in with a guileless answer: "Yes, I want to. My position is that we need everybody in America [who] has got a contribution to make. . . . I don't think status alone, in the absence of some destructive behavior, should disqualify people."

This sounded quite reasonable to Clinton. But quite by accident, in that instant he started a political and cultural battle that would dominate his transition and the opening months of his presidency. Social conservatives, who had been demoralized by the Bush presidency and hardly remorseful about his defeat, sprang excitedly back to life. Many military commanders, who because of Clinton's Vietnam-era history would have been a problematic constituency at best for the new president, now were sure that a man of alien values was about to become their commander in chief. Republicans in Congress vowed that they would never let the new policy take force, and would overturn it by veto-proof legislation if necessary. Gay activists, meanwhile, who had supported Clinton by large measures and been generous financial contributors to his campaign, served notice that they would regard Clinton's fealty to his promise as a critical test of his character and any retreat as a betrayal. Clinton, for all his celebrated political antenna, never saw this storm coming.

THE TRANSITION ALSO PRESENTED THE CLINTONS WITH A QUESTION ABOUT their new home that they would confront repeatedly in the years ahead: Was it their ambition to challenge the capital's established power structure and customs, or to settle in comfortably at the top of the existing order?

They had different answers in different moods. Assimilation in the Washington culture was a natural choice. Both Clintons had spent their adult lives excelling in academic and professional meritocracies. The capital was filled with similarly successful people, of the same generation, who held personal and career values that were entirely sympathetic to the ambitious couple taking over the White House. In one light, the Clintons' instinct was to like, and be liked by, the Washington elite awaiting their arrival.

But the issue was more complicated. In another light, both Clintons arrived with a vivid sense of themselves as reformers—distinctly outside the reigning Washington culture. Part of a new administration's assignment, as they saw it, was to clean up a capital cluttered by special interests, cynics, and hacks. They were understandably concerned that the capital's entrenched interests—in the Congress, in the bureaucracy, and in the offices of downtown lobbyists—represented major obstacles to the ambitious progressive agenda they hoped to pass. Could these people be charmed by engaging and well-intentioned new faces in Washington? Or was it better to move aggressively to show that their days were numbered?

Quite characteristically, the Clintons surrounded themselves with people who catered in different ways to these dueling instincts. On one side, Vernon Jordan was their ambassador to Washington. Jordan was a former president of the Urban League who had settled into a prosperous career as a Washington lawyer. Both Clintons had known Jordan since the 1970s, and the president-elect named him co-chairman of the presidential transition. As an African-

American, Jordan represented the appealing notion that the Washington establishment was fluid and open to change. The latest generation of Washington "wise men," descendants to such earlier establishment figures as Clark Clifford and John J. McCloy, could include a man who grew up as a black kid in Atlanta, raised by a mother who catered white people's parties. As a practical matter, probably no other person moved quite so comfortably through such diverse spheres of Washington as Jordan. Mark Gearan, a campaign aide now serving on the transition, recalled walking with Jordan one afternoon into the Palm, a favorite watering hole for the city's top lawyers and lobbyists. He recalled that "everyone went crazy," stretching hands to say hello to Jordan. The next stop was an African-American church where inaugural planners were preparing an event for the president-elect. Once again, Jordan's arrival sparked a frenzy. During the Clintons' visits to Washington during the transition, it was Jordan who squired them to dinners thrown by such prominent Georgetown hostesses as Pamela Harriman and *Washington Post* publisher Katharine Graham—events at which a glittering roster of senators, pundits, and assorted capital sages watched the president-elect for signs of his real feelings. As *New York Times* columnist William Safire, an invitee to the Graham dinner, put it, "Would he act like a rube on a roll or say the graceful thing?" Clinton pleased the audience when he rose without notes to deliver his toast: "Washington is a better place than most Americans think it is. I hope to bring more of the country to the capital and more of the capital to the country." The message seemed clear. Clinton wanted to get along.

Yet if Vernon Jordan was the silk of the transition, Susan Thomases was the burlap. She was a smart and combative New York lawyer who had been close friends with Hillary Clinton for two decades. During the campaign, she had moved to Little Rock and, with the deceptively pedestrian title of campaign scheduler, became a major power. Afraid of no one, fully empowered by Hillary Clinton, Thomases even clashed with Al Gore over scheduling and strategy. The fact that Thomases battled with the professional political operatives who populated the campaign was a virtue in Hillary Clinton's eyes. "She did not treat them with what they thought was the respect they were entitled to," she explained shortly after the election. "She's the consummate New Yorker as well as a woman. That may have caused some people who were there for status some difficulty." Thomases herself explained her poor reputation among Washington's political class: "The thing they resent about me is I don't know them. And I don't care if I know them. And that bothers them."

Thomases kept her title as scheduler, and her suspicions about people who might be insufficiently loyal to the Clintons, while working on the transition.

Her influence helped sever the ambitions of many experienced Washington hands who had been expected to land White House jobs. Tom Donilon, an influential lawyer and Democrat, was nixed for a top West Wing job after making a bad impression on Thomases and Hillary Clinton. He went instead to the State Department, where he performed admirably as the top aide to Warren Christopher. For her own part, Thomases returned to New York after the transition, rather than taking a government post, and precarious health made her a flickering figure during the Clinton years. Her fealty to the Clintons was admirable, but the defensive mindset she helped encourage was hardly what the Clintons needed as 1993 began. In the months ahead, there would be plenty of times when the Clinton White House could have used the kind of political experience that Donilon and others had been eager to offer.

BY NO MEANS WAS THE TRANSITION A COMPREHENSIVE FAILURE. CLINTON ASsembled a cabinet that was indeed as diverse as he promised, and contained plenty of talent as well. Among the more notable names was Texas senator Lloyd Bentsen, who became Treasury secretary. University of Wisconsin chancellor Donna Shalala took over Health and Human Services. Ron Brown, who had served ably as Democratic National Committee chairman, became the first African-American to be Commerce secretary.

On the other hand, the focus on the cabinet had come at the expense of another area that was arguably more important to Clinton's success: the White House staff. After a brief flirtation in which Hillary Clinton considered becoming chief of staff (before realizing this was prohibited by law), the president-elect turned to a boyhood chum, Arkansas business executive Thomas "Mack" McLarty, to take the top job. But few other decisions were made until early January, when the White House team was chosen amid chaos. The example of John Podesta, who took the unheralded but important job of staff secretary, was typical. One day he was summoned to Little Rock on short notice for a job interview with Clinton. Instead of drilling Podesta on his qualifications, Clinton spent most of the session bubbling with enthusiasm about his recent meeting with the president of Mexico. Podesta heard nothing for several days, and then came home one night to a message that he come to Little Rock without delay by the next morning. When he placed calls to find out what was going on, he could not get anyone on the phone. So he went to Little Rock, arrived at headquarters, discovered that everyone important was in meetings, and pleaded with an intern to give him an early peek at a press release that would be distributed at a news conference later that morning. Only then did he learn that he had gotten the job.

Another, more important staff decision did not have such a happy ending. Harold Ickes, a veteran New York lawyer and political hand, had originally been tapped to move to Washington to be the White House deputy chief of staff. He had already moved to Little Rock to help run the transition. Ickes would have been a shrewd choice that first year in the White House, providing some authentic political experience and toughness to balance McLarty's genial inexperience. But the appointment was stalled after critical news stories examined Ickes's legal work for an allegedly mob-influenced labor union. As the clock wound down on the transition, Ickes continued to receive assurances that his appointment was on track. It was not. Ickes would join the White House a year later, after his reputation was cleared. The night before Clinton was to leave for Washington, he summoned Ickes to the governor's mansion. They chatted inconsequentially for several minutes in the kitchen. Clinton would not come to the point. Finally, Ickes did. Clinton began to weep. He was so sorry, he said, but he could not offer Ickes a job. It was one of the echoing what-ifs of the Clinton years. What mistakes in 1993 might have been avoided with a more seasoned political operative by Clinton's side?

For now, time had run out. The president-elect and his harried team were headed to Washington.

Section One

Chapter One

BELLS OF HOPE

GONG! GONG! GONG! FROM COAST TO COAST, AND EVEN IN OUTER space, bells would ring for America's new leader. That was the plan. As Bill Clinton finished the grinding work of his transition in Little Rock, the impresarios of his inaugural festivities were in Washington dreaming of grand ways to launch the celebration. The result was an idea of breathtaking presumption: the "Bells of Hope." Clinton thought it was splendid.

At 6 p.m. on January 17, 1993, just after the president-elect crossed Memorial Bridge over the Potomac and into Washington, citizens of the Republic were invited to let loose with chimes. Orbiting above the earth, astronauts on the space shuttle *Endeavour* were encouraged to do the same.

The president-elect and his wife devoutly believed that the results of the 1992 election had been a cleansing event in national life, well worthy of bells. Except there was a problem. Nearly 60 percent of the American electorate had voted for someone other than Bill Clinton. Many in the 43 percent who backed him did so only after swallowing doubts. That left few who regarded Clinton's ascension to power as an occasion for a clanging continental catharsis. The Bells of Hope rang in less celebration than the Clintons had hoped. Loyal

Democrats joined in, and the National Park Service dutifully struck the Liberty Bell in Philadelphia. NASA, though, informed the inaugural planners that the astronauts would be asleep at the assigned hour. A compromise allowed them to record their bell-ringing in advance, with the video played on large screens in front of the Lincoln Memorial. Mainly, echoing gongs announced the illusions of Washington's new team. "The bell-ringing seemed a little pretentious to hail great change—when the evidence mounts that there will be precious little," wrote Mary McGrory, grande dame of liberal commentators, in her column in the *Washington Post* the next day.

McGrory's sour review reflected the oddly conflicted mood of Washington that January. The capital was charged with excitement and anticipation on the eve of the inauguration, awaiting the fresh flow of energy and ideas that inevitably accompanies a new administration. Even in a city of cynics, the formal transfer of power, democracy's most sacred ritual, commands a measure of reverence. Yet the news from recent days had made plain that Clinton was bleeding power even before he assumed it. Instead of having the clean start customarily afforded new presidents, Clinton arrived in Washington deeply stained by wounds taken during his departure from Little Rock, wounds that caused new doubts about whether the president-elect was a man of his word. This credibility crisis was not about extramarital affairs or a draft history; it was about the foundations of the agenda on which Clinton had run.

The closing days in Little Rock opened a conflict that defined Clinton's presidency for the next two years. It was a collision between the expansive promises he made in his dream days as candidate and the cramped possibilities that awaited him as president. The days before Clinton's inaugural were accompanied by an abrupt downward adjustment in popular expectations for his presidency and the changes it was supposed to herald. No one found this reappraisal more jarring than Clinton himself.

ON JANUARY 7, JUST UNDER TWO WEEKS BEFORE INAUGURAL DAY, CLINTON had sat down with his new economic team in his Little Rock living room for a budget tutorial. The meeting lasted six hours—long enough for Clinton to confront the contradictions in his own program. For all the president's reputation as a "policy wonk," his knowledge on the most pressing domestic matter confronting him was rudimentary. Most of the dozen people before him were not people Clinton knew well. They included Lloyd Bentsen, the seventy-one-year-old Texas senator Clinton had selected as Treasury secretary; Robert

Rubin, who had made a fortune on Wall Street and was joining the Clinton team to coordinate economic policy at the White House; and Leon Panetta, the California congressman whom Clinton had tapped to be federal budget director. Panetta had been startled in his job interview to discover the gaps in Clinton's understanding.

The mood in the room that day was subdued, even academic, during much of the discussion. But this was broken when Clinton suddenly flushed with a rude epiphany: "You mean to tell me that the success of my program and my re-election hinges on the Federal Reserve and a bunch of fucking bond traders?"

The president-elect's outburst captured an essential truth that he had not yet seized upon. The consuming task of his presidency would be to stanch a flow of budgetary red ink that had grown to some $290 billion a year. And these daunting numbers were growing larger still. Just the day before, the outgoing Bush administration, in a cruel welcoming gift to Clinton, announced that the projected deficit for 1997—the year by which Clinton had pledged to cut the deficit in half—was going to be nearly a third larger than earlier forecasts. Deficit reduction, as part of an appeal to common sacrifice, had been one note in Clinton's campaign message, but far from the major key. The candidate came to life talking about other things: his proposal to cut middle-class taxes, or his plan to jolt the economy with a burst of public works spending in the name of fiscal stimulus. Dearest to his heart was some $60 billion annually in education, child care subsidies, and other planned domestic programs that Clinton called his "investments"—so named because Clinton believed they were not mere spending, but catalysts for future prosperity. During the campaign it had been easy to be for it all. Now Clinton was learning that he had scarcely any choices. Lowering long-term interest rates was the key to priming the anemic economy for new growth, Clinton's tutors told him. But a president had no direct control over interest rates. They were controlled by two factors. One was the Federal Reserve, led by its mumbling, enigmatic chairman, Alan Greenspan. The other was the capital markets, the actions of which determined the long-term interest rates on the bonds the government sold to finance its debt. Interest rates would come down only if Greenspan and the markets concluded the new president was serious enough about raising taxes and cutting spending to bring the budget deficit to heel. Clinton's future indeed hinged on the Federal Reserve and a bunch of bond traders.

One casualty of this meeting was the middle-class tax cut, the status of which had already been precarious. Days later, Panetta told a congressional committee that the proposal was no longer a priority. The reversal won praise as a responsible concession to fiscal reality. But it became the most visible—and perhaps the most politically damaging—of Clinton's campaign promises to not survive in the presidency.

....

JUST AS THE BUDGET WAS FRUSTRATING HIS PROMISES AT HOME, ANOTHER rapidly building crisis was frustrating a promise Clinton had made about a problem just off America's shore. The problem was Haiti, a brutally poor island nation in the Caribbean populated largely by people of African descent. Haiti had traditions of violence and voodoo, but it also had a history as the second independent nation to take root in the Western Hemisphere. A fledgling Haitian democracy had been defied in 1991, when elected president Jean-Bertrand Aristide—leftist former priest and tribune of impoverished masses—was ousted in a military coup supported by the nation's wealthy elite. As a candidate, Clinton had attacked the Bush policy of refusing to allow refugees from the island to enter the United States. There was undoubtedly a measure of politics in his position: Because Haitians were black, their plight was an important issue to the Democratic Party's most faithful constituency. Yet Clinton's position was also sincere. Refusing passage to people who risked all by setting sail in barely seaworthy vessels to reach U.S. shores seemed a humanitarian outrage, and hardly in keeping with America's history as a refuge from tyranny.

But in early January, officers from the Central Intelligence Agency visited Clinton in Little Rock with satellite photographs showing tens of thousands of Haitians busy at work, hacking down trees and, in some cases, their own homes, to construct makeshift boats. The Haitians knew all about Clinton's campaign promise. And come his swearing-in on January 20, some 100,000 or more of them were heading for America. As many as 10,000 would likely drown at sea, Clinton was told. Those who made it would swamp the Gulf Coast with a wave of people desperately in need of food, shelter, and medical attention. In his living room, Clinton sat grimly through the briefing. Vice President–elect Gore broke the silence with his dry humor after the agency briefers departed. "Well," he said. "That's a worthy problem."

Indeed it was. And the only solution was obvious: Clinton would have to revoke his campaign promise before he was inaugurated. Sullenly, he agreed to do just that.

....

THE EQUIVOCATION ON TAXES AND REVERSAL ON HAITI HUNG HEAVILY IN THE air as Clinton met with news reporters on January 14, two days before he was to leave Arkansas for Washington. But the item that had people buzzing was a remarkable story on the front page of that morning's *New York Times:* On the same day that President Bush ordered missile strikes against Iraq to punish Saddam Hussein's latest defiance of United Nations sanctions, the incoming president said he would entertain normal relations with Iraq if the dictator mended his ways. "I'm a Baptist. I believe in deathbed conversions," Clinton told the *Times*'s Tom Friedman. Was he trying to send words of comfort to one of the planet's most odious leaders?

In fact, he was doing nothing but indulging a familiar habit—hoping to "shroud conflict in soft language and shape his thoughts by hearing how they sounded out loud," as Stephanopoulos later put it.

But when Clinton saw the story in cold type, he was convinced it had been a deliberate distortion. He said as much at the news conference. "Nobody asked me about the normalization of relations," he snapped impatiently. However, any reader of the *Times* that morning could see from the interview transcript that Clinton had been asked precisely that, twice. What did he gain by denying the obvious?

He tried the same on Haiti. There was no joy in reversing a policy that was proving untenable, nor was there dishonor in a forthright acknowledgment of change. Yet Clinton insisted that he was not reversing anything. His earlier statements offering asylum, he maintained, had hinged on a distinction between political refugees, who were entitled to stay in the United States, and economic refugees, who were not. "Sometimes people hear only half the message," he complained.

There was something to this. Reporters covering Clinton were learning to listen for the escape hatches and qualifiers incorporated, as if by subconscious instinct, into his language—placed there as insurance to preserve flexibility for later. This time he had not preserved quite enough: The previous spring he had said quite clearly that all Haitian boat people should be regarded as political refugees and given temporary asylum, absent "clear and compelling evidence" to the contrary.

The news conference continued in this peevish spirit—both the questions and the answers freighted with a suspicion bordering on contempt. A reporter noted the rumblings that Clinton was giving up plans for a middle-class tax cut and asked if there were any campaign promises that people could regard as "ironclad." During the New Hampshire primary, Clinton's ads said his economic program "starts with a middle-class tax cut." Now, he said: "From

New Hampshire forward, for reasons that absolutely mystified me, the press thought the most important issue in the race was the middle-class tax cut. I never did meet any voter who thought that." A reporter asked when Clinton's economic program would be ready, since he had once pledged to present it to Congress the day after he was inaugurated. "Well, I don't know who led you to believe that, but I'm the only one who's authorized to talk about that," he replied.

What's with those guys? Clinton fumed after he had left the podium. The session had been an exercise in mutual incomprehension, setting the tone for the contentious relationship between president and press that was to follow. Clinton saw himself as a large man pursuing large purpose amid reporters fixed on small details solely for the purpose of causing him harm. Many reporters saw Clinton as someone whose every word needed to be vetted, who possibly could not distinguish truth from evasion even in his own mind. The problem for Clinton was that the media's perception was taking hold in larger circles. On the day of the news conference, Senator Daniel Patrick Moynihan of New York was grilling Donna Shalala, Clinton's designee to head the Department of Health and Human Services. For a quarter century Moynihan had been a towering figure in the nation's political and intellectual life, and, as chairman of the powerful Senate Finance Committee, he was also one of the figures determining the fate of the new president's legislative program. He was concerned about the apparently low priority being given to welfare reform by the new team, an item of first importance to him. "This week," he observed archly, "has been rather the clatter of campaign promises being tossed out the window."

FAR FROM ENJOYING THE TRADITIONAL HONEYMOON, CLINTON AND THE Washington political class were quarreling like a couple who would have split up years ago except for the kids. He needed somehow to hit the reset button. On January 16, Clinton left his old home for his new one, hoping that the inauguration would lift the cloud of negativity over what by his lights should have been an uplifting moment in the American story.

The cloud did lift, for a time. The inaugural festivities were handled, as usual for the Clinton team, with a keen instinct for symbolism and showmanship, which, as usual, threatened occasionally to go over the top. The cochairmen of the inaugural committee were Clinton friends and Hollywood producers Harry Thomason and his wife, Linda Bloodworth-Thomason, who at the time were among television's hottest hands as producers of two hit shows, *Designing Women* and *Evening Shade*. The trip to Washington, it was decided, would be by way of Charlottesville, Virginia, where Clinton began his inaugural festivities at Monticello. Clinton and his people liked to invoke a mystical connection between the nation's third president and its forty-second, owing partly to the trivial fact that Clinton's middle name was Jefferson. More consequentially, Clinton believed that his election in 1992 was in keeping with Jefferson's admonition that in American democracy, each generation needed to revive its revolutionary impulse. After a roundtable with schoolchildren at Monticello, where Clinton allowed that if Jefferson were alive in 1993 "I would appoint him secretary of education," the Clintons and Gores drove north. They traveled by motor coach, hoping to summon anew the ebullient spirit of the previous summer's bus tours, bound for Memorial Bridge and the Lincoln Memorial.

The Jefferson and Lincoln imagery was intended to serve "as bookends," as inaugural director Rahm Emanuel put it, for the day of Clinton's Washington arrival. Clinton's invocation of predecessors, a constant practice during his presidency, was an often precarious balance between admirable and excessive. He was a genuine student of his office, and there may never have been an occupant of the White House with such a reverent understanding of who had lived there before. But there was something needy, even vainglorious, about Clinton's perpetual historical references. Citing the greatness of predecessors seemed a way of saying, I someday also will live in history as a great man. The predecessor who lived largest in the Clinton imagination—and whose legacy infused the Clinton inaugural—was not Jefferson or Lincoln but a leader of more recent vintage: John F. Kennedy.

The JFK mythology—interwoven cords of idealism and glamour, of power and sexuality—was a natural draw for Clinton, and it had been the Kennedy example more than any other that had defined his political sensibility. Accordingly, JFK's ghost hovered over the entire week. At a concert at the Lincoln Memorial upon his arrival in Washington, giant video screens played the Kennedy inaugural address in 1961; Clinton stared in wonderment and mouthed the words. A person reading nothing but the concert program would have known that a Democrat had won the election, and a baby boomer as well. Among a constellation of major talent was Bob Dylan, the bard of Clinton's generation, who rasped a barely intelligible version of "Chimes of Freedom." Aretha Franklin was in better form as she belted out "Respect." And Michael Jackson, not yet terminally eccentric in 1993, appeared at the finale to join in "We Are the World." On January 19, his last day as a private citizen, Clinton joined Edward Kennedy and others from the Kennedy clan for a pilgrimage to Arlington National Cemetery, where the president-elect placed a white rose beside the gravestones of John F. and Robert F. Kennedy. Most of all, Clinton wanted Kennedy's spirit to animate the main event, the inaugural address he would give the next day.

January 20, 1993, broke with brilliant blue skies and, with temperatures in the low forties, a crisp but tolerable bite in the air. Kennedy, Clinton believed, had delivered the last truly superior inaugural address. The theme of that address had been the synergy between generational and political change—"the torch has been passed to a new generation of Americans"—and Clinton wanted this to be the keynote of his. The speech he would deliver at the Capitol that morning had been a work in progress for several weeks. It had been, quite characteristically, a community effort. (He would begin the drafting of major speeches by throwing out, somewhat randomly, ideas and phrases.) For the inaugural, he wanted to talk about "a re-creation, a renewal," he told the collection of young aides gathered around him. He tried on lines for size: "We have changed the guard, and now each in our own way we must answer the call. . . . We have to march to the music of time but ours is a timeless mission." The real work of composition, however, would begin only after someone, or usually several people—staff, friends, and all manner of outside acquaintances—tried putting words on paper and then gave Clinton the chance to tear the work to shreds. Michael Waldman, who worked on the inaugural address and later became chief White House speechwriter, observed that Clinton "decided how to act by reacting—to our drafts, to the urgings of others. He often found his organizing principles by dissecting contrary advice."

The committee approach often served Clinton well as he was groping for the right policy option, but it was not well suited for rhetorical composition. The address was a collection of lyrical phrases, some of them tinged purple. Clinton's college friend, novelist Tommy Caplan, contributed the line, "Anyone who has ever watched a child's eyes wander into sleep knows what posterity is." Another suggestion came from beyond the grave. The Reverend Timothy Healy, former president of Georgetown University, had been working on suggestions for Clinton when he died just before the new year. An image he offered landed at the top of Clinton's speech: "This ceremony is held in the depth of winter. But, by the words we speak and the faces we show the world, we force the spring." It was a vivid, if complicated, metaphor that underscored the larger weakness of this speech, and most others when Clinton reached for oratorical heights: Lyricism simply was not his natural voice. He soared when he threw away text and spoke improvisationally, as at a late-night rally or from a pulpit.

Clinton was still working until 4:30 a.m., his swearing-in less than eight hours away. The president-elect had returned from a formal ball to his temporary quarters at Blair House, across the street from the White House, and huddled with aides around the teleprompter that contained his speech. He still did not like it, and he kept finessing the lines while speechwriters typed new language into the text. Vice President–elect Gore tried to help, but his contribution was modest. Unlike Clinton, Gore was not wired for late-night work, and he kept nodding off, head slouching on his chest. The speech finally came together in passable form as time ran out, just as Clinton's speeches always managed to do. The best line was the one that most reflected his essentially optimistic nature: "There is nothing wrong with America that cannot be cured by what is right with America." Meanwhile, much of the news media coverage focused on Clinton's admonition to Washington: "This beautiful capital, like every capital since the dawn of civilization, is often a place of intrigue and calculation. Powerful people maneuver for position and worry endlessly about who is in and who is out, who is up and who is down, forgetting those people whose toil and sweat sends us here. . . . Let us resolve to reform our politics, so that power and privilege no longer shout down the voice of the people."

Chapter Two

BEGINNINGS

I F THE INAUGURAL ADDRESS BOWED TO JOHN F. KENNEDY, THE FIRST FULL day of the Clinton administration—January 21—reached back further still for inspiration. In 1829, Andrew Jackson was the first new president to host the general public with a White House open house. He took refuge through a window when an unruly crowd devoured the food and whiskey and swept through the mansion looking for more. For Clinton, the masses were better behaved but hardly less importuning. Two thousand citizens won tickets for the open house through a mail lottery, but many more showed up with no tickets and were allowed in anyway, creating a line to shake hands with the new president that stretched from the Diplomatic Reception Room to far outside the Executive Mansion. The Clintons, joined by the Gores, stood beside a crackling log fire and a portrait of George Washington. The president's voice was hoarse and cracking from several days of little sleep.

The open house heralded a presidency with a distinctive style, leaving no doubt that the aristocratic and awkward president who had occupied the White House the four previous years was being replaced by a man of a different background and different age. One young man in line cheerfully introduced the unfazed Clintons to "my husband," and a lesbian told them her parents were not talking to her because of her lifestyle and that "I hope your administration will change that." Many people who shook his hand felt comfortable calling him "Bill."

In his presidential status and style, Clinton inclined emphatically toward the populist tradition. Accessibility was central to his conception of himself and his presidency. "This is your house, and I'm just a tenant here," Clinton boomed that day, after it became clear that so many people had arrived that he'd never have time to shake every hand and instead addressed the crowd on loudspeaker. A couple of days before taking office he fairly beseeched his fellow governors: "I ask for your prayers and your support and your true friendship, which means your constructive criticism. . . . Please, please know that the door is open, and when you think we're veering wrong, walk through it and say so." At an intellectual level, Clinton's reading of history left him well aware of the isolating nature of the presidency. At a personal level, Clinton hungered for human contact—for affirmation, naturally, but even for dissent. The throngs teased out a glimpse of Hillary Clinton's distinctive style as well. As some of the crowd were about to be turned away, the first lady rasped in her husband's ear, loud enough for the television boom mikes to hear, "We just screwed all these people!"

Long lines were far from the only chaos on that first day. The White House switchboard was busy for hours on end, and calls that did get through rang unanswered on desks as Clinton's aides wandered the West Wing trying to find offices. Clinton had begun the day with what would become a morning ritual, the national security briefing. Among the items on it was Iraq, where President Saddam Hussein evidently had been unmoved by Clinton's suggestion of a "deathbed conversion." When Iraqi anti-aircraft batteries fired on U.S. jets, the jets fired back and destroyed the batteries. The new commander in chief still sounded a bit like president-elect when he later told reporters he supported the action. The reality had not yet sunk in: Those were his jets now. Meanwhile, the lead White House spokesman, George Stephanopoulos, encountered a restive press corps at his first briefing, ending any doubt that the gaiety of the inaugural festivities was over. Among the subjects he parried were questions about Iraq, about the problems facing Clinton's nominee for attorney general, about Clinton's plans to allow gays to serve in the military, and about when the president finally would be ready to present his economic package to Congress. The queries were insistent and skeptical. On one matter—the White House's plans to bar reporters from a hallway leading to the press secretary's office—it was downright indignant. "I've been here since Kennedy," brayed

Helen Thomas, senior member of the press corps, "and the press secretary's office has never been off limits."

That quarrelsome briefing neatly summarized the many currents buffeting Clinton as he set to work. He would survive controversies that made those of his first weeks seem precious by comparison. At the time, however, the young Clinton team felt as if they were starting their presidency amid a howling gale.

Clinton's problems comprised two distinct sets of challenges. Leaders in Congress, the generals and admirals of the military, and the reporters and editors of the Washington press corps were all in their own ways testing the new president, extending him uncommonly little deference. At the same time, Clinton had emerged from the campaign less with an agenda than with a loosely bound bundle of good intentions, some of them at odds with each other. He held some vivid convictions, but a blurred sense of how and in what order to pursue them. The agony of choice—Clinton deciding what mattered most— was the drama that would unfold before a watching world in the weeks ahead.

THE CRISIS OVER ZOË BAIRD'S NOMINATION AS ATTORNEY GENERAL REACHED its closing phase within minutes of Clinton's taking power. The new president was still at the Capitol, at a ceremonial luncheon with lawmakers, when Joseph Biden, chairman of the Senate Judiciary Committee, pulled him aside. "Tomorrow," the senator said, "I will call you with one of two requests: either weigh in on her behalf and help the center hold, or take her down."

If Clinton had known the problems that would accompany Baird's nomination, he never would have named her. Yet the question of precisely what he did know, and when, was itself a source of controversy. Baird's circumstances had seemed routine. She and her husband had hired illegal immigrants, a Peruvian couple, to work in their home, the wife caring for Baird's three-year-old son and the husband serving as part-time driver. As in many such arrangements in the vast immigrant underground economy, Baird had not paid Social Security taxes on her employees. But now a commonplace arrangement had become a unique problem because the issue had never arisen in a cabinet nomination before. A vice president and general counsel for Aetna Insurance, Baird had passable credentials for the attorney general post. But Bill and Hillary Clinton had decided during the transition that the attorney general should be a woman, and transition leader Warren Christopher, who had been a mentor to Baird since they served in the Carter administration, pushed her selection after more prominent possibilities fell through. Who was responsible for this mess? Baird maintained that she had forthrightly informed the Clinton transition team about her child-care arrangements. Christopher maintained that he had told Clinton, though how clearly was uncertain. Clinton told other aides that he had not known. So when reporters pressed Stephanopoulos at the first White House briefing on whether Clinton had appointed Baird even knowing her problems, he had no choice but to dodge the question with noncommittal answers that bordered on gibberish.

In fact, no one on the Clinton team had anticipated that Baird's domestic life could be so explosive. But so it proved to be when the *New York Times* detailed the problem on its front page on January 14, three weeks after Baird was selected and six days before Clinton's swearing-in. Baird's case provoked uncommon resentment among a large group of people, who flooded Congress and talk radio programs with calls demanding to know how Clinton could name as the nation's senior law officer a woman who had ignored the law. These spasms of populist anger against the privileged were becoming familiar in the early 1990s, like the outrage that greeted the news a year earlier that hundreds of congressmen were routinely bouncing checks at no penalty off their free accounts at the House bank. During the campaign, Clinton had exploited these popular grievances to his advantage. Suddenly the anger was turning on him.

So on his first full day as president, Clinton faced a classic Washington dilemma. One option was immediate concession—throw a lamb to the wolves—based on the belief that controversies must be dispensed with quickly to not draw attention away from the president's agenda. Most of Clinton's political advisers, Stephanopoulos and legislative liaison Howard Paster among them, wanted Baird's nomination withdrawn, and it was clear that Clinton was not emotionally invested in the nomination of a woman he barely knew, in trouble for reasons he believed were not his fault. The other option was defiance. By this logic, the battle was now less about Baird's fortunes than Clinton's. Withdrawing the nomination would show to Congress and the world that a new president could be pushed around. "Fight," urged Bernard Nussbaum, the White House counsel. "Don't walk away from a nominee." What was no longer an option, as Biden made clear, was passivity.

The end came late that evening. Biden called to bluntly tell Clinton that Baird's prospects for confirmation were fading. But Baird did not want to give up, and when Christopher and Vernon Jordan met with her that evening to make clear there was no choice, the nominee insisted that the White House validate her claim that she had been fully forthcoming. The negotiations dragged past midnight. Finally, Baird wrote Clinton asking that he withdraw her nomination. He wrote back saying that he accepted her request "with sadness," and that "I realize it was your candid disclosure of the child care matter that led to the circumstances we face today." He was wearing sweatpants and eating a banana smeared with peanut butter as he signed the letter. As the whole matter was reaching a head that evening, Clinton was sitting in Stephanopoulos's office when he took a call from Senate majority leader George Mitchell, who had seconded Biden's assessment of Baird's chances. "George, does it get any better than this?" Clinton asked the senator, plainly referring not just to Baird but to the waves of controversy that had washed over him in recent weeks.

NOT FOR A WHILE, IT WOULDN'T. JUST AS THE BAIRD MATTER WAS RECEDING, another controversy that posed a choice between conflict and conciliation was rising rapidly. This time—on the question of allowing gays to serve openly in the military—the new president and his political advisers were ready to fight.

Given Clinton's retreats on the middle-class tax cut, Haiti, and the Baird nomination, there was widespread belief within the White House that he could not afford another reversal. It was an odd paradox, lost on neither Clinton nor his anxious advisers: A president who had run as a "New Democrat," sensitive to the concerns of cultural traditionalists, would wage his first defining battle on an issue that offended such people. Three days before the inauguration, Clinton met at his Blair House transition quarters with Les Aspin, the designee for secretary of defense, and produced a plan that they regarded as a sensible compromise. Instead of revoking the military's homosexual ban immediately, Clinton would wait several months, allowing a little steam to let loose from the controversy. Meanwhile, he would direct Aspin less formally to have the military stop asking recruits about their sexual orientation, and to halt discharge proceedings against people already discovered to be gay. Detailed reports of Clinton's plans were in the newspapers.

Among the readers who learned of the plan this way were the four-star officers of the Joint Chiefs of Staff. Enraged, the chiefs let loose on Aspin for ninety minutes during his first meeting with them as secretary on January 21. Allowing gays to serve openly would be devastating to morale and discipline, they told Aspin. They demanded, and won, a chance to speak with Clinton directly. And so four days later the president met with the chiefs of the army, air force, navy, and marines, as well as Joint Chiefs Chairman Colin Powell. Pictures of TR and FDR looked down on the proceedings as Clinton and his national security team stared awkwardly across a large oak conference table at the chiefs. The meeting was cordial enough, both sides speaking in soft tones designed to cushion the reality that their views were irreconcilable. "I made a campaign promise," Clinton said, his voice still raspy from the celebrations of the week before. "And I sure want to keep it." Then, he tried to round off the edges of the dispute. Clinton had no problem with rules about conduct; what he objected to was discrimination based on someone's intrinsic nature. "I don't want to see soldiers holding hands or dancing together at military posts, but that's just a matter of regulating behavior, the same as we do for heterosexual soldiers. What I don't like is barring homosexuals who want to serve, whether they're in or out of the closet." Such distinctions were lost on the chiefs, most of all Marine Commandant Carl Mundy, who made clear that he and his marines considered homosexuality a moral depravity that could not be tolerated in the ranks. Even Mundy, though, tried to end on an apologetic note: "Mr. President, I hope we don't come over here and have many more meetings like this." Powell offered Clinton an escape. Instead of ending the ban on homosexuals, the military would simply stop asking recruits about their orientation. So long as gays and lesbians kept their orientation to themselves, there would be no problem. Clinton rebuffed him, saying he was moving ahead with his own policy.

Three days later another meeting at the White House made plain to Clinton how impossible that would be. If he tried to force a change in the homosexual policy by executive order, Congress would pass, with a veto-proof majority, a bill writing the existing policy into law. On January 28, a delegation of Senate Democrats met with Clinton in the Cabinet Room to find a compromise. The chairman of the Senate Armed Services Committee, Sam Nunn of Georgia, was an ostensible Clinton supporter and a man he had considered inviting into the cabinet. But Nunn had been vocal in support of the military's positions on gays and was now proving implacable. Cameras in tow, Nunn traveled to Norfolk to visit a submarine so that people could see just how little privacy there was on board. Asserting senatorial prerogatives, he was holding up passage of Clinton's first major legislation, the Family and Medical Leave Act, until the homosexual issue was resolved to his satisfaction. What's more, Nunn seemed to be relishing the confrontation. Some Clinton aides felt sure the Georgian considered the new president an affront—that the moderate southern Democrat in the White House should have been named Nunn, not Clinton. Other Democrats were no more accommodating. Senator Robert Byrd of West Virginia rose from his seat to give a florid lecture about how the

Roman Empire fell when it began to allow moral decay, closing with a grave warning about Clinton's plan: "It will lead to same-sex marriages and homosexuals in the Boy Scouts."

Clinton had to find a compromise that was something short of a surrender. What he announced on January 29, with Nunn by his side, barely qualified. Clinton agreed to defer a final decision for six months while the Pentagon studied options. While the military would stop asking recruits their orientation during this time, personnel identified as gay during the interim could still be removed from service—a practice directly at odds with Clinton's promise. Putting it mildly, Clinton acknowledged, "This compromise is not everything I would have hoped for or everything that I have stood for, but it is plainly a step in the right direction." To which Barney Frank, an openly gay congressman from Massachusetts, replied, "I think it stinks."

In just nine days, Clinton had learned a bracing lesson in the limits of presidential authority. Two major challenges had yielded two obvious retreats. He had supposed that the election had given him a mandate, and the Constitution had given him the authority to act on it. The realities of power were more complex.

IF THESE OPENING SKIRMISHES HELD ANY VIRTUE FOR CLINTON, IT WAS THAT they were ephemeral. Zoë Baird quickly reclaimed her obscurity. Some of the unfavorable perceptions of the new president formed in his showdown with the chiefs were enduring, but the controversy itself faded. During these same early days, however, Clinton was immersed in another matter with indelible consequences. The subject was the economic plan he had pledged to present to the Congress and an expectant nation on February 17. The decisions he made in the four weeks between taking the oath of office and his first address to Congress shaped Clinton's presidency until its last day.

"The test of a first-rate intelligence," Scott Fitzgerald wrote, "is the ability to hold two opposed ideas in mind at the same time and still retain the ability to function." Candidate Clinton had passed Fitzgerald's test with ease. His agenda called for increasing social spending for the poor and near poor. It also called for ensuring universal health care coverage, cutting the deficit, and easing the tax load of an angry and burdened middle class. All these diverse aims were in the spirit of a governing philosophy that, as Clinton announced at his nomination, was not liberal, not conservative, but both. In the Clinton mind, the nation's predicament in the winter of 1993 not only invited paradoxical remedies but demanded them. "To renew America, we must be bold," he declared in his inaugural address. "We must do what no generation has had to do before. We must invest more in our own people, in their jobs and in their future, and at the same time cut our massive debt." Clinton's ability to tour the horizon, to show how seemingly discrete problems were actually pieces of a larger whole, was an impressive feature of his mind. In the presidency, however, a mind of such agility could be as much burden as blessing. What the new administration needed most was clarity of purpose. Where would it be found when the man at its center was conflicted?

Clinton was forced to settle his mind under conditions of mounting urgency. The new administration's economic plan was already overdue; he had promised to have it ready the day he took office. The new deadline, February 17, was chosen because it allowed Clinton to answer critics by noting that he presented his plan more quickly (by a day) than Ronald Reagan had done twelve years earlier. This gave Clinton four weeks to fashion concrete details for the bold, cut-here-but-spend-there program he'd promised at the inaugural. Clinton was treated to a gruesome description of the stakes on January 28, when Alan Greenspan came to the White House. Armed with columns of the latest economic data, Greenspan told Clinton he believed that the budget deficit would remain a serious but manageable problem for the next couple of years. Without radical remedies now, however, it would grow drastically by 1996, sending interest rates soaring in a way that could strangle the economy. The chairman concluded morbidly, "That's what financial catastrophe means."

Clinton and his economic team plunged into their work, meeting every day of the week, usually late into the evening, the president poring over individual lines in the federal budget and subjecting each disputed item to an extended debate. "We'd be going over the numbers hour after hour, looking at every minute program," recalled Labor Secretary Robert Reich. " 'Can we cut that? What's the consequence of cutting that? Can we get a little bit more money to do this?' It seemed to be endless, and it also did seem remarkably academic in a way. I mean, here's the President of the United States, the head of the free world, wondering about whether if we cut the Coast Guard by this much, would we have a little bit more money to go into this training program." Other participants, like budget director Panetta and economic adviser Rubin, did their best to move Clinton along. The president resisted, hungering always for more detail. The arcana of the deliberations were torture for nearly everyone but Clinton. Still hovering over the cascade of decisions were three very basic questions about the direction Clinton wanted to lead.

First among them concerned the deficit—the gap between money raised and money spent, which had been yawning ever wider since the early 1980s. That gap was now regarded widely, though not unanimously, as a grave threat to national prosperity. How much deficit reduction did Clinton need to propose in order to signal to Main Street and Wall Street alike that the new administration was serious about fiscal integrity? During the campaign, Clinton had vowed to cut the deficit in half in four years. Was his promise still attainable? How much pain would be required to keep it?

The main instrument of pain was taxes, which was the second essential question. The middle-class tax cut he had campaigned on already had been discarded as fantasy. Now it was time to consider an anguishing new prospect—the need to actually raise taxes. Every budget scenario the president was studying raised taxes significantly on the most affluent Americans, precisely as candidate Clinton said he planned to do. But it was becoming clear that he could not reconcile his diverse promises on domestic policy and deficit reduction without imposing some taxes on the middle class he had promised to protect.

And so on to the third question. Those domestic policies, so bold in concept, proved vexing from the start. Clinton presented himself as a New Democrat—moderate, innovative, detached from liberal pieties—but in an important respect the New Democrat had the soul of an old one: He wanted to spend money, lots of it. This fact was scarcely concealed in his campaign manifesto, *Putting People First,* which detailed billions of dollars of planned new programs. That was the dream. What was the reality? More precisely, if Clinton cut the deficit enough to satisfy Greenspan and the deficit hawks, how much would be left for new spending? Clinton thought his proposals— investments in education and worker training, child care, and ensuring universal health care—were as vital to the long-term health of the economy as cutting the deficit. These programs also lay much closer to his heart than satisfying the expectations of the financial markets and the Federal Reserve. One day, as he and his aides were discussing whether the plan to reform health care should be deferred while the economic plan was pending, Clinton exclaimed, "If I don't get health care done, I'll wish I didn't run for president." The frustration of the moment soon passed, but the comment was revealing. Here was a man who thought in expansive possibilities, confronting the limits of his power.

Clinton could be bleak at times, but far more striking, during the month-long marathon of budget meetings, was the positive delight he showed in the work. He would look up from the briefing books and announce, "I love this stuff" and "This is fun," and he meant it. Clinton had been dreaming of the presidency for a lifetime, and for twelve years he had been a governor with a keen understanding of national policy and its currents. No amount of dreary fiscal news could drain the essential thrill of a man, at age forty-six, doing exactly the job he always wanted.

IT CANNOT BE SAID THAT OTHERS ON HIS ECONOMIC TEAM SHARED IN THE pleasure. The crafting of the economic plan was a grinding exercise, made more exhausting by the opposing factions that immediately became evident. At the simplest level, the contest was between those who thought that taming out-of-control deficits should be the priority of the new administration and those who thought allowing this issue to dominate Clinton's agenda was an unconscionable retreat from other priorities that they regarded as more central to the reasons he was elected, and more relevant to the problems facing the nation. This second group feared that Clintonism—the specifics of his agenda and the spirit of the 1992 campaign—was in danger of being hijacked during his first month in office.

In the first group, the deficit warriors, were people like Rubin and Panetta, and the budget director's deputy, Alice Rivlin, who formerly headed the prestigious Congressional Budget Office. Their supreme commander was Treasury Secretary Lloyd Bentsen. Tall and silver-haired at age seventy-two, Bentsen was a Texas millionaire who had been enticed out of his longtime Senate seat principally by the new president's claims that he was serious about restoring fiscal soundness to the government.

Arrayed against this august group were Clinton's equally impressive deficit doves, led by Labor Secretary Robert Reich. A friend from Clinton's Oxford days two decades earlier, Reich had gone on to be a Harvard lecturer and a prominent writer and speaker on economic revitalization. Aligned with Reich, to varying degrees, were numerous young campaign aides who had landed important positions on the White House staff, including Stephanopoulos and Gene Sperling, Rubin's deputy on the National Economic Council. Outside the White House, but very much within the orbit of influence, were Clinton's 1992 political consultants, including business partners James Carville and Paul Begala, media adviser Mandy Grunwald, and pollster Stanley Greenberg. Reich and his allies had forged close relationships to the candidate in the heat of 1992. Stephanopoulos had been Clinton's brooding alter ego, helping him navigate that year's succession of personal scandals. Begala, the traveling aide, essentially lived with Clinton in airplanes and hotels for months on end. These young aides would not have been so presumptuous as to call themselves friends, but they certainly believed they had a genuine personal connection with the president. They believed they knew his core. Bentsen, Panetta, and even Rubin would never have made that claim. Clinton barely knew any of them at a personal level. They were there because of their sterling credentials on the subjects of the budget and the economy. Bentsen was a veteran of World War II, and even younger men like Panetta, then fifty-four, were not part of Clinton's 1960s generation, but of the more sober and stoical Silent Generation of the 1950s. They were respected, responsible figures and, in the case of Bentsen and Rubin, men who had made enormous fortunes before coming to government. They had all risen to the top of their professional arenas—Panetta in Congress, Rubin in business, Bentsen in both Congress and business—through understated competence and authority rather than personal flash. They were all elites, but none regarded himself as a defender of his class. To the contrary, they all viewed themselves as genuine progressives, believing in a vigorous role for government to aid and empower the less fortunate. It was no accident they were Democrats, no matter how conservative they might be on fiscal issues.

But the most important fault line running through the deliberations that February was between the self-styled populists and those who reflected an elite consensus about what was ailing the U.S. government and economy. Reich and the young political aides believed that Clinton had won the presidency by successfully indicting the established order, tapping into the widespread suspicion of working Middle Americans that they were being shafted by political and economic arrangements that neither reflected their values nor protected their interests. Clinton's success, by this reckoning, would hinge on how quickly and persuasively he responded to these grievances. This group believed the deficit was an accounting abstraction that mattered a great deal to newspaper editorialists, bond traders, and respected Washington worthies like Panetta, but meant little to most citizens. The tax increases (if they hit Middle Americans) and spending cuts would inflict new pain on the people Clinton should be trying to relieve.

The other side was made up of rationalists, all of whom believed that there was a right and logical way to run government that too often was ignored for political expediency, since sound long-term policy usually meant short-term pain. They believed Clinton had been elected largely because voters had recoiled at last from the short-term mindset, appalled by the notion of a government that could not manage its finances. To them the deficit was not an abstraction but the real-life consequence of government's dysfunction. They believed government's ravenous borrowing to fund the deficit was robbing the economy of hundreds of billions of dollars that otherwise would be available to the private sector, where businesses needed to borrow capital to invest and grow. By this reckoning, Clinton's preeminent task upon taking power was to transcend politics—to take the painful measures that would demonstrate at home and abroad that the United States could put its fiscal house in order.

IT WAS A FEATURE OF CLINTON'S GOVERNING STYLE, IN THIS DEBATE AND countless ones to follow, that he allowed factions to fester. Then, he would leave all sides with the conviction—though never a completely *secure* conviction— that they were representing his real beliefs and interests against other advisers who, for reasons of ignorance or selfishness, were tugging the president someplace he did not want to go.

The night before his swearing-in, while working on his inaugural address, Clinton said to speechwriter Michael Waldman and other veterans of the Little Rock campaign, "You know, I hired people like Leon Panetta for their technical expertise on the budget. But these people have no idea how the middle class has suffered." Later, in the midst of budget deliberations, Sperling squared off testily with Bentsen, nearly four decades his senior, over the need to include sufficient funding to expand the Earned Income Tax Credit. The program returned money to the working poor to ensure that keeping a job was more profitable than sliding into welfare. The proposal was a campaign promise dear to Clinton that Sperling wanted kept, and a $27 billion expense that Bentsen wanted trimmed. Later, with Sperling a bit shaken by the encounter, Clinton sidled up to him to say, "You stick at it. You stick at it."

However much the younger aides fighting for social spending believed they were closer to Clinton's soul, it became increasingly clear as February 17 approached that the deficit hawks were winning his mind. All those weeks of White House meetings had kept returning, insistently, to one number: $140 billion. The person insisting was Bentsen. The number represented the amount he wanted the administration to cut the budget by 1997, an amount that would approximately keep Clinton's earlier promise to cut the deficit in half over four years. To reach that figure would require a combination of steady annual squeezes in spending on existing programs, especially in defense, and new taxes on both the wealthy and middle class. It left a relative pittance for Clinton's investments, the new domestic initiatives on which he had campaigned so passionately. Other advisers said the focus on $140 billion was too high, an arbitrary figure with no economic rationale. Bentsen confidently said this was the figure that Greenspan needed to see to believe that the new administration was serious about fiscal discipline. Reluctantly, at a Saturday morning work session on February 13, Clinton agreed.

What had happened? The populist advisers were wrong to think that the side of the president they gravitated toward was the authentic Clinton, and the side that had recruited Lloyd Bentsen into his cabinet was somehow false. Both sides were real. Clinton, the kid who grew up in Hot Springs barely hanging on to middle-class status, understood average Americans. But the Rhodes scholar who went on to Yale Law School shared many elite assumptions about national policy, and the opinion of respected people like Bentsen, Rubin, and Panetta mattered greatly to him.

Toward the end of the process Begala confronted Clinton with his despair: "Mr. President, why are you listening to these people? They did not support you. It's not what you're about."

"We need them," he snapped at Begala. "We can't do anything for people unless we reduce the deficit." Of his deficit-minded budget aides, he said, "They love their country. They're working hard at this. What do you want me to do? We can't lie about the deficit."

"I agree," said Begala, though still laboring to make his point.

"Then stop," Clinton ordered.

THERE WERE TWO OTHER GRAVITATIONAL FORCES PULLING ON CLINTON IN HIS opening days. Both Al Gore and Hillary Clinton had strong opinions about what should be in the economic package Clinton was to present Congress on February 17. Their interests, however, were not solely or even principally over the question of the magic number for deficit reduction. Instead, both were preoccupied by the larger question of how to use the speech to launch Clinton's presidency—and how their own interests would be affected.

For most of the next eight years, no other advisers to the president would weigh as decisively on Clinton's politics and policies as these two principals. During much of this time, Gore and Hillary Clinton eyed each other a bit anxiously. They were rarely in direct conflict, but were often engaged in an unspoken tug-of-war. The economic plan represented the first instance of both lobbying furiously to put their own imprints on the presidential agenda.

Gore succeeded. He was the sponsor of a proposed tax increase that would have more direct impact on average Americans than any other part of the economic program. The vice president's cause was the BTU tax. Taxing energy, using an obscure measurement known as British thermal units, encouraged conservation and was good for the environment—the cause Gore was most prominently identified with—and it would help raise revenue that the government urgently needed. Under his vigorous pressure, the BTU tax was included in Clinton's economic plan. It was probably the most politically risky aspect of the program.

Hillary Clinton's ambitions were even larger. On January 25, Clinton had appointed his wife to lead his administration's efforts to overhaul the nation's health care system. The assignment was a sequel of sorts to a role she had played in the Arkansas years, when she successfully led a controversial plan to reform education. The president's confidence in her abilities was unbounded. "Of all the people I've ever worked with in my life," he told reporters in announcing her role, "she's better at organizing and leading people from a complex beginning to a certain end." One reason for her past success had been her relentless intensity and an absolute intolerance for obstacles—qualities she immediately brought to bear on the health care question. She began agitating for the White House to include significant elements of the health care overhaul when Clinton presented his budget plan. Her logic (following the advice of such lawmakers as Senate majority leader George Mitchell) had to do with the rules of the U.S. Senate. In that chamber, business can grind to a halt when a single senator takes the floor for a lengthy filibuster. It takes sixty votes to halt a filibuster, meaning as a practical matter that the Senate is run not by majority rule but by rule of sixty. An exception to this is budget and tax legislation, which are not subject to filibuster. If the health care overhaul was attached to Clinton's budget, it would need only fifty-one votes to pass and avoid the more punishing debate that would greet stand-alone legislation. This would have been an audacious move. What the Clinton administration was contemplating was the most far-reaching social legislation since the New Deal; trying to slide it through in an annual budget bill bordered on contempt for the legislative process. Moreover, many details of the health care plan, still only roughly conceived, were not remotely ready for public presentation. Heeding the vigorous objections of his economic team, Clinton reluctantly rebuffed his wife's recommendation, and health care reform was not merged with the February 17 economic plan.

What were Al Gore and Hillary Clinton thinking as they pressed such rash counsel on the new president? On the wobbly legs of Clinton's victory—

after all, 57 percent of the electorate had wanted someone other him as president—they proposed that the president, in his first major policy speech, serve notice to Americans that he would raise their taxes and give the federal government a vast new role in health care. The temptation is to suppose that they weren't thinking: a triumph of hubris over judgment. The reality is more complicated. The new Clinton team was acting on a considered analysis of how to translate that weak 43 percent into a formidable mandate.

Every presidency must settle, whether consciously or not, on a theory of presidential power. The most important text on the subject, at least for Clinton's generation of Democrats, was written by a Harvard political scientist named Richard Neustadt. In 1960 he published a book called *Presidential Power* that became celebrated the next year when it found an attentive reader in new president John F. Kennedy. Clinton had read Neustadt's book, and Gore had been a student of Neustadt's at Harvard; meanwhile, Neustadt had sent the vice president and others on the Clinton team memos on how to manage the transition. His insight into the modern presidency is that it is an inherently weak office—because the Constitution gives the president little direct power to guide domestic policy without a willing Congress—that can be made strong only with great skill. The challenge for a president is to use other means, foremost his ability to shape public opinion and expectations, to expand the office's natural limitations. Under this view, presidents should not simply draw down political power as though it were money in a savings account. Instead, they must view power as an investment: Risking power to achieve a successful result will in turn yield new power. This lesson from the world of political science combined with another from twentieth-century history to shape the mindset of the Clinton team. Clinton, like all nine presidents since 1945, labored under the shadow of Franklin D. Roosevelt, the century's most powerful president. An essential part of the FDR mythology was the first hundred days—the notion that great presidents prove their mettle with a vast rush of executive action.

Under such logic, Clinton's ability to do ambitious things would never be greater than in these early weeks after the inauguration, with Congress under public pressure to defer to a new president. By doing bold things, and quickly, Clinton would build support even among people who did not support him or his agenda, as he demonstrated that the dramatic change he promised during the campaign was coming to fruition. As it happened, the most ambitious items on Clinton's agenda, raising taxes and expanding health coverage, were the ones for which he had the hardest time garnering Republican backing in Congress. Thus a president who urgently needed to build support with independent voters instead set off on a course that stamped him as a hard-core Democrat.

There had been another path open to Clinton, which suggested that he acknowledge the weakness of his mandate expressly in his opening agenda. This did not mean that he should avoid ambitious policy proposals, but that he initially pursue ones for which he was most likely to gain Republican support. Under this theory of power, overhauling the welfare system was a shrewder first move than overhauling health care, and almost any alternative would have been preferable to tax increases on middle-class Americans. Clinton would gain leverage not in a frenetic FDR-style debut, but by slowly and methodically increasing his standing with the political center—concentrating on what was achievable now and deferring more divisive proposals for later. Eventually, nearly everyone, the president most of all, would look back with regret at the path not taken.

OF THE PEOPLE HELPING THE NEW PRESIDENT NAVIGATE THESE OPENING days, Hillary Clinton surely knew him best, but she did not know him longest. That distinction went to Thomas F. "Mack" McLarty, who first met Bill Clinton in Miss Marie's kindergarten class in Hope, Arkansas, when they were both five years old. Now McLarty was by Clinton's side again as White House chief of staff, one of Washington's most coveted and most demanding jobs.

It was more demanding than ever under this particular president. As he understood his role, McLarty was to run a White House with wide-open doors to the Oval Office. This meant the president would make decisions after weighing the advice of his wife, his vice president, his cabinet, his White House staff, and a vast circle of friends and acquaintances who might have expertise, or at least a passing opinion, on an infinite number of subjects. It also meant providing a measure of calm for a president prone to explosions, and a measure of order and efficiency to a president who never worried about staying on schedule. When Clinton first approached his old friend about becoming chief of staff, just a day after winning election, McLarty hedged for a couple of weeks. At the time he was chief executive of Arkla, a Fortune 500 natural gas concern. In the end, McLarty should have listened to his doubts, but at the time he was widely viewed as an eminently logical choice. He was a familiar face for Clinton in a White House that included many people who barely knew the president. He was a moderate business executive in an administration that wanted to send reassuring signals to the center. And McLarty, though not well known in Washington, was in his own way a political animal: He had been elected as one of the youngest men ever, at age twenty-three, to the Arkansas House of Representatives, and during the mid-1970s had been chairman of the state Democratic Party.

But McLarty did not understand the job of White House chief of staff. He especially did not understand the job of being Bill Clinton's chief of staff. This became obvious in the transition. Addressing a group of people headed for White House jobs, he said he intended to run the operation as a "confederation." He knew that everyone was talented and had the president's best interests at heart, so his job was to be a "facilitator." This was precisely what the president wanted. Therein lay the problem. Even if it was really true that everyone on Clinton's staff could be counted on to act in what he or she believed were the president's interests, each would still have conflicting notions of what those interests were. Only a powerful chief could keep those conflicts from spinning into chaos. Most of all, it was far from the case that what Clinton needed was help in keeping his options open. The people who had succeeded in his orbit in the past did so not by deferring to his instincts for more debate, but by pressing aggressively against them. In the Arkansas years, these had been people like former chief of staff Betsey Wright or political consultant Dick Morris. They told him what he should do in emphatic tones, almost as though he were a misbehaving child. Volatile though they could be, these relationships had served Clinton well.

Now he was trying something different. Steady Mack McLarty moved into the second-best office in the White House, a large suite with a garden patio, just down a narrow hallway from the Oval Office. And while McLarty and Clinton had known each other quite cordially for quite long, the truth was that they were strangers in the sense that mattered most. McLarty had never worked inside Clinton's political inner circle—the place where the publicly cheerful man would brood darkly about his options or rage against diverse frustrations or navigate the complexities of his marriage. McLarty was not especially commanding. He was of modest height, his receding hair was always closely groomed, and the soft contours of his face had a bright, freshly scrubbed quality. He spoke with an exaggerated politeness that seemed just shy of a put-on—sirs and ma'ams punctuating every clause: "I should thank you, frankly, for raising a good question." What would ordinarily be simple chores for a chief of staff, such as an interview with Democratic columnist Mark Shields or a dinner invitation from Evan Thomas, the bureau chief of *Newsweek*, would require McLarty to summon other senior staff for laborious prep sessions.

His nickname, "Mack the Nice," soon became widely known around town, at first in affection but increasingly with derision. When leaks of White House deliberations showed up in the paper one day, he summoned the staff to give his version of the riot act: "No one can be under the misimpression that this can sit well with me or sit well with the president." It sounded like a warning from Elmer Fudd.

Though miscast in his role, McLarty made contributions. In the budget deliberations the deficit hawks regarded him as an ally, but no one on the other side could complain that he had not given their side fair hearing. His sobriety and fairness were admirable, but they tended to encourage, rather than compensate for, the weaknesses in Clinton's decision-making style.

By the third week of February, President Clinton's frenzied month of work had produced a plan he was ready to present to the nation. The result was in some ways a triumph of Lloyd Bentsen over Robert Reich—the plan featured roughly two dollars in deficit reduction for every dollar in new spending—but it was by no means unconditional victory. Clintonism was still defined by contradiction. The same program that would raise taxes and tighten spending in the name of fiscal discipline would also propose some $30 billion in new spending and tax incentives, in the name of economic stimulus. As a matter of logic, it was defensible to argue that the economic growth required deficit reduction in the long run but a stiff shot of government spending to get things moving right away. As a matter of perception, the effect was jarring. One moment Clinton was serving notice that he was a tough-minded New Democrat. The next moment he was presenting himself as a latter-day Franklin D. Roosevelt.

It was appropriate that a plan with such conflicting notes was revealed to the nation not in one speech but two. The address to a joint session of Congress on February 17 was preceded by a warm-up act two nights before. Because the tax increases were the most explosive element of Clinton's program, and therefore the most newsworthy, the belief was that he should announce those first. Once the unpleasant business of taxes was cleared away, he would have a cleaner shot at attention for the entirety of his program when he actually appeared before the Congress. So, at 9 p.m. on February 15, Clinton sat at his desk in the Oval Office—the one that used to belong to John F. Kennedy and which the new president had retrieved from a government warehouse—and looked into the television cameras. He was partisan, scoring his predecessors for twelve years in which the prevailing ethic was "fairness to the middle class is less important than keeping taxes low on the wealthy." He was self-justifying, saying he had wanted to avoid middle-class tax increases and "worked harder than I've ever worked in my life to meet that goal but came up short. He was populist, warning that "defenders of decline" would be lining "the corridors of power with high-priced lobbyists" to defeat his plan.

Wall Street was listening. The next day the stock market plunged eighty-three points, the biggest one-day slide in fifteen months. Many people on Clinton's own team liked the speech no better. The keystone of the program was responsibility, as Clinton accepted the premises of academic and financial elites that the deficit mattered and bravely resolved to do something about it. But the keystone of the speech was blame-casting.

One person who agreed the night was a failure was Hillary Clinton. Whatever her personal sympathies (on the spectrum of Clinton's advisers, at least in those years, she was clearly at the more liberal end), she knew that Clinton had sounded too much like an old-style liberal, not enough like a New Democrat. She was determined that he repair the damage in the speech to Congress two nights later. On the morning of the seventeenth, she read a draft text with disgust and pronounced it unacceptable. The first lady sat down in the Roosevelt Room with the president's policy aides and speechwriters, dissecting the draft and insisting that it be recast. Clinton was away, having lunch with network news anchors (a modern custom on the day a president delivers his State of the Union address). He was unworried when he returned. The speech went through several more drafts, which Clinton casually practiced in the White House family theater, making edits of his own. He did not leave the theater until 8:40 p.m.—just twenty minutes before he was due at the Capitol. Clinton made more changes during the limousine ride, and even as he waited outside the House chamber. Within the White House, the consensus was that the text he carried to the podium was still a mediocrity.

What got delivered, however, was widely hailed as a triumph. The cycles of Clinton's life, disaster followed by recovery, had worked as ever. After the petulance of his Oval Office speech, Clinton began this one by saying: "I did not seek this office to place blame. I come here tonight to accept responsibility, and I want you to accept responsibility with me." He presented a blizzard of proposals, unified at the close of his speech with a bracing challenge: "My fellow Americans, the test of this plan cannot be 'What is in it for me?,' it has got to be 'What is in it for us?' " The masterstroke, however, was a brilliant bit of staging. The president had invited Federal Reserve Chairman Greenspan, whose approval of the package was essential, to sit in the gallery next to Hillary Clinton. Greenspan had been wary of accepting, but decided he could not turn down a president. His applause was the evening's best visual.

Clinton had survived his first month's encounter with power, and though a bit bruised and limping, he was on his way.

Chapter Three

CROWN JEWEL

THEY CALLED HIM "EAGLE." THE SECRET SERVICE GIVES EVERY NEW president a code name, and this was Clinton's. "Elvis" had been his moniker with staff during the campaign; the presidency demanded something a bit more elegant. Eagle's diverse lot of security agents and servants talked to one another through microphones buried in their sleeves and tiny speakers in their ears, and all shared different parts of the same mission: to secure the president and shepherd him through his day.

His handlers walked a treacherous line between solicitousness and suffocation. Borrowing a line from Harry Truman, Clinton liked to call the White House "the crown jewel of the federal penitentiary system." When Clinton was ready to get dressed every morning, for example, one of two navy stewards assigned to the president would discreetly arrive at the family's apartment to lay out his wardrobe. Procedures dictated that the president take the elevator, not the stairs, to the ground floor. Equipped with Clinton's daily schedule (usually simply a rough approximation of when he might actually do something), an elevator operator had long since arrived and was standing by. When the president was ready to go, the Secret Service radios would crackle to life about an impending "movement." From the ground floor, Clinton would head outside, under a covered walkway supported by white columns known as the White House colonnade, past the Rose Garden, and into the Oval Office. One Secret Service agent would walk several paces in front of him, and two or three more would walk by his side, joined by the valet who carried his papers—all this to cover a distance of perhaps fifty yards in his own home.

It was a rude challenge to Clinton's long-settled habits. As a politician for all of his adult life, he was certainly accustomed to security and handlers. But he also expected a certain flexibility, to put it mildly, with procedures. During the campaign, this meant heading out for Mexican food in Texas in the middle of the night, if the mood arose. Clinton was above all a man who prized his personal space and loathed being tethered to anyone else's schedule or expectations of how he should live. Now, as he learned on his first day in the White House, he was not even able to place a telephone call on his own. As soon as he picked up the phone, an operator came on the line to dial for him. (This long-standing arrangement, intolerable to a new president who prized his independence, was soon changed, allowing him to make his own calls when he wanted.) The White House, the destination he had fantasized so long about reaching, was indeed a kind of prison. A sense of physical and psychic confinement quickly became a dominant feature of his new life.

He fought back in different ways. Sometimes he chose passive resistance. When staff would press him on his plans so that they could prepare, he simply hedged or changed the subject. Other times he would bridle angrily at would-be handlers. On one occasion Clinton's schedule had included a possible drop-by at a book party for his friend Strobe Talbott, the former *Time* magazine bureau chief whom Clinton had placed as his top Russia expert at the State Department. The president kept hedging about whether he really planned to attend. Then, suddenly, at the end of the day, he announced cheerfully, "Let's go." Andrew Friendly, his personal assistant, said it would be quite impossible to leave now. Clinton had given his staff no time to prepare the motorcade (and, though the party was just blocks away at a downtown hotel, walking was out of the question for security reasons). After a gusher of profanity, Clinton asked plaintively, "Why can't I do what I want?"

The lumbering apparatus of the presidency is part of permanent Washington, staffed by people who stay years, even as presidents come and go. The cooks and ushers and phone operators and Secret Service agents view themselves as professionals, insulated from politics. Even so, during twelve years of Republican rule, a great many of these people had come to identify with Ronald Reagan and, especially, with George and Barbara Bush. The permanent staff did not know quite what to make of this modern new couple and the brash young team who accompanied them. Small matters stirred resentments. The ushers who stayed on call for the first family and their visitors in the White House residence had grown accustomed under the Reagans and Bushes to regular hours; the new crowd liked to stay up late. Before, someone had taken care to send word to the ushers when the family was down for the night. Clinton often neglected to do this, leaving people stewing until late into the evening, uncertain if they were free to leave. Clinton did not like deciding the night before whether he would feel like jogging the next morning, so the Secret Service would deploy two teams in the morning, one dressed in business attire, the other ready for exercise. Once, on the road in Chicago, Clinton left his hotel for a jog so quickly that agents were forced to run along in suits and ties. When he was in town, Clinton's morning jaunts through downtown Washington were a security and logistical nightmare; in due course they were deemed impractical, and Clinton agreed that he would henceforth motorcade to nearby Fort McNair to run. But he never did stop complaining about the lunacy of getting into a car to go jogging.

Within weeks, these petty irritations would escalate into something more serious. The Clintons were suspicious, with some reason, about the loyalty of the strangers hovering over their lives. One of the ushers was known to have sported a "Re-elect Bush" bumper sticker on his car. The Clintons, meanwhile, thought it was absurd that a Secret Service agent needed to be stationed immediately outside the second-floor entrance to their living quarters, within earshot of anything louder than normal conversation. Hillary Clinton soon complained to her friend and former law partner Vincent Foster, now the deputy White House counsel, about the agents' intrusiveness. Some of them seemed brusque, even hostile. Then, on February 19, a gossip columnist for the *Chicago Sun-Times* reported rumors of a terrible row between the Clintons, during which an enraged first lady supposedly hurled a lamp in the residence. The story, nasty but titillating, raced through the capital. The Clintons were mortified. The problem with the permanent staff, once an irritation, became an urgent priority. The president and first lady summoned Foster and a handful of senior aides to the residence for a discussion of cleaning house in both the security and residential staffs. The Clintons felt they knew where one problem was. Harry Thomason, the Hollywood producer who with his wife, Linda Bloodworth-Thomason, was living in the White House quarters for much of early 1993, had dinner in Washington with some reporters and told the Clintons that he believed stories about the Clintons' personal lives were leaking from staff of the residence. Allowing hostile people to be privy to the most intimate details of daily life was intolerable, Hillary Clinton believed. If subordinates were foot-dragging, then she would see to it that the White House staff was populated with Clinton loyalists.

THE CLINTONS FELT THAT THEY WERE SURROUNDED BY HOSTILE STRANGERS, not just in their private home, but in Washington at large. The most pervasive face of this perceived hostility was the national news media. At the outset of his term, the president did not like Washington reporters and resented devoting even a handful of evenings to the formal press dinners held as ritual in the capital each winter and spring. Most of all, he did not like the forced frivolity of the occasions. It was customary for the president at the press dinners to deliver a comedy routine, taking some swipes at the press but aiming the best shots at himself. Clinton by no means lacked humor, but his natural bent was toward cheerful patter and oft-told yarns. Washington humor is different—ironic and knowing, the sort of detached wit that John F. Kennedy used to beguile a generation of journalists. Sardonic was not Clinton's style. He was dead earnest about the work of his presidency, and sorely resentful of how Washington journalists seemed to reduce his noble purposes into stories about political process and tactics. Right out of the gate in February, Ann Devroy, the *Washington Post*'s lead reporter on the administration and the person whom official Washington relied on most to reveal what was really going on at the White House, published a story about the Clintons hosting a getting-to-know-you gathering of cabinet secretaries and White House staff at Camp David. She had great respect for the presidency and regarded the White House as a place of political skill, order, and maturity. Yet she quickly concluded that the Clinton White House was a place of amateurism, chaos, and insolent youth. Under the front-page headline "A Bonding Experience at Camp David," her story described with bemusement and thinly veiled disdain how the Clintons had invited professional "facilitators" to stimulate meaningful conversation. Everyone was supposed to reveal something personal; the president talked about the pain of being chubby and mocked by other children as a boy. "Don't try to make this sound weird," one source pleaded to Devroy. That was asking too much.

Clinton soon personally regarded her as chief battle-axe in the Washington press. It was with this attitude that he appeared two months into his presidency in the giant ballroom of the Washington Hilton for the annual Radio and Television Correspondents Association dinner. One of his lines noted how

Washington reporters were upset by Clinton making himself insufficiently available for questions. "You know why I can stiff you on the press conferences?" Clinton asked, "Because Larry King liberated me by giving me to the American people directly." There was some awkward laughter, but neither the audience nor the capital grapevine thought it was very funny. It was not funny because Clinton was not joking. He had stated loudly one of the preeminent early goals of the Clinton White House: to find new channels of presidential communication, using talk show hosts like King and Oprah Winfrey and satellite interviews with local TV and radio to reach voters directly and transcend what he regarded as a cynical and trivial-minded Washington press corps.

Clinton *was* on to something with his instinct to soar above D.C. media to reach his audience. Most successful presidents have been innovators in public communication, using new technology to create new politics. FDR had his "fireside chats," and JFK turned the televised news conference into dazzling entertainment. Reagan used his Hollywood stage mastery to render irrelevant the Washington consensus that he was merely an amiable dunce. While Clinton was right to seek out new forums to communicate his message, he and his young White House team would soon learn that they were wrong to assume that they could use their new leverage to bring the established news media to heel. This is because Washington's social structure is interwoven with journalists in a way that is like no other American city. Reporters feed off politicians, and vice versa. An assistant cabinet secretary might be married to a reporter for the *New York Times*. Robert Barnett, formerly the Clintons' personal attorney, was married to Rita Braver, who covered the White House for CBS News. Journalism permeates Washington culture, yet journalism was the one professional arena that Clinton neither understood nor appreciated.

Begala, Clinton's traveling aide in the 1992 campaign, came to realize that his boss fundamentally did not respect reporting. All reporters do is observe and criticize, he believed; they don't *do* anything. He actually had more respect for his political foes—at least they stood for something.

In short order there was a low-grade war under way between the Clinton White House and the veteran White House reporters who covered it, which became one of the great antagonisms to mark the Clinton years.

The tension flowed from different sources. Most obvious was the press's bridling over the new White House rules announced by then thirty-two-year-old George Stephanopoulos but inspired by Hillary Clinton to restrict access to part of the West Wing where they had previously been free to walk unescorted. An older generation of reporters bridled at the new team's style: smart and savvy, and projecting a confidence that occasionally blurred into arrogance. Brit Hume, an acerbic and respected reporter then with ABC News, used to work his crossword puzzle while sitting in the front row of Stephanopoulos's news briefings, looking up occasionally to drill the young man when he heard a contradiction or some absurd claim. David S. Broder of the *Washington Post* once said after a heated phone call with Stephanopoulos that he felt like telling him to go to his room.

The dynamic with younger reporters was a bit different. Far from being put off by the breezy, cutting-edge sensibility of the Clinton team, many were at first very attracted to it. A new and activist administration was like a gust blowing away the staid and stale Bush years. Despite the tensions of the campaign, many reporters had grown friendly with Clinton's aides on the 1992 trail. Now it seemed likely that his arrival would herald their generation's version of the Kennedy years—when Washington was a sexy place, and famous journalists like Ben Bradlee and David Brinkley jousted with the New Frontiersmen by day but reveled in one another's company by night. For their part, the Clintonites, too, had assumed that the press basically would be on their side—that journalists generally tilted to Democrats and would be generously inclined to a president trying to achieve big things.

These illusions ended quickly, as the reporters were fed a diet low on accurate information and heavy on political spin, and, as controversies mounted, many on the White House staff came to believe that there was something to the president's view of the fourth estate. To the Clintonites, the reporters seemed always to assume the worst about any set of facts. Once, Stephanopoulos was trying to assure Ann Devroy that a newsworthy rumor she had heard was untrue. Agreeing to hold off a story, Devroy—from whom threats, laughter, profanity, and cigarette smoke streamed in large measure—rasped, "George, if you are lying to me I promise I will fuck you over!" Then she put Stephanopoulos on hold to take a call from her daughter. "Sweetheart," she said, her voice metamorphosing into a lovely lilt, "how are you?"

IT SEEMED AMAZING, IN RETROSPECT, CONSIDERING ALL THE FOLLY AND heartache that followed, that the president and his wife actually believed they would win praise for taking on the mess at the White House travel office.

It was peculiar that the mess should have ever captured their attention at all. The travel office was an obscure nook in the permanent White House bureaucracy. It had seven workers whose jobs were to arrange accommodations for the White House press corps when they traveled with the president. Why would the Clintons care about something like this? The answer is that a lot of seemingly obscure matters could reach the top, given the right push. On February 17, when Clinton was not yet a month in office and the day he was presenting his economic plan to Congress, he still found time to read a memo from Darnell Martens, a friend and business partner of Clinton confidant Harry Thomason. Martens proposed that his aviation business, in which Thomason was an investor, be given a consulting contract to review use of nonmilitary government aircraft. With a backward check, the signature of a left-hander, Clinton marked a box labeled "action" and scribbled a note to Chief of Staff McLarty: "These guys are sharp. Should discuss with Panetta/[Philip]Lader," the two top officials at the Office of Management and Budget. Nothing ever came of this proposal, but all through the winter and spring of 1993 Martens and Thomason kept up a robust interest on a related subject. The travel office, according to Thomason and some other Arkansans on the White House staff, was a shoddily run outfit, and there were even suggestions that fraud or embezzlement might be taking place. Thomason raised it several times with the Clintons. Hillary Clinton in particular was attentive, pressing several White House aides for answers on what was being done. Here was yet another reason to be suspicious of the permanent White House staff, she reasoned. There surely was some good press to be had if the White House uprooted this particular nest of corruption.

This is how "Travelgate" was born, though that name is surely overblown. The decision on May 19 to fire travel office head Billy Dale and six colleagues—offering no advance notice, no opportunity to answer questions, and leveling public accusations of "gross mismanagement" and possible theft—was undeniably shabby. The decision and its aftermath were rife with improprieties and misleading assertions. Still, the whole matter was too absurdly small to justify the "gate" label. Yet the controversy would reverberate ruinously for the Clinton White House that spring and for years after. One reason was the particular target the Clintons chose. The travel office may have been obscure, but Dale and his colleagues were well known and well liked by an important constituency: White House reporters. As it happens, whatever irregularities there were in travel office bookkeeping—the place was rife with shoddy accounting, though no fraud or embezzlement was ever established—was at the expense of news organizations, not the government. The travel office workers were government employees, but it was the media that paid the travel office—handsomely, many millions of dollars each year— for the endless, dreary blur of airplanes and buses and buffets and hotels necessary while covering a president. When the firings backfired, Thomason and others maintained it was because the travel office was feathering reporters' nests, helping them evade customs by bringing back expensive gifts from foreign travels in the cargo hold of the press charter.

A procession of assertions against the travel office employees was made and then abandoned, creating a cumulative impression of a White House that was neither competent nor trustworthy. It also soon surfaced that Thomason had been involved in urging that his friend Martens's firm, TRM, be allowed to compete for the travel office bidding. On the defensive, the White House asserted that Thomason had merely "passed on information," not tried to steer business to himself. This story soon crumbled, as it became clear that Thomason's role in the housecleaning had in fact been pivotal, and that as business partner of Martens he stood to benefit. Of even greater concern, the White House had summoned FBI officials to help in the investigation of travel office accounting, and publicly trumpeted the fact that an investigation was under way. The next day Attorney General Janet Reno complained sharply that the FBI was called without her authorization, a violation of Justice Department procedures designed to keep the agency free from political interference. Publicly announcing an ongoing FBI investigation from the White House podium was another lapse of procedure. There were more frantic efforts at explanation. The White House asserted that the problems at the travel office came to light as part of Vice President Gore's "reinventing government" initiative. Then Gore's office made plain that this was the first they had heard about it. And so on. The deceptions were painful, as was the amateurism.

The president himself professed only the dimmest knowledge of the facts. The day the firings were announced, he was in the Oval Office with South African archbishop Desmond Tutu, the anti-apartheid leader. As often happened, and to Clinton's vast annoyance, reporters interrupted a joint appearance dedicated to lofty global subjects with impertinent questions about domestic controversies. Clinton said people would have to ask his staff about what happened in the travel office: "All I know about it is that I was told that the people who were in charge of administering in the White House found serious problems there and thought there was no alternative. . . . That is literally all I know about it." His wife knew more, and there were several people who knew she knew more. One of them was Vince Foster. Even before the firings, he had had forebodings of trouble, urging that more objective evidence of wrongdoing be found before proceeding with dismissals and fearing that the first lady's role would draw questions. He had spoken with the first lady several times about the travel office problems, and in notes to himself from a May 17 meeting, when he learned the firings were imminent, he jotted, "HRC problem." Then he circled it.

The HRC problem was indeed the nub of it. Divining her role would be a trip through the looking glass. David Watkins, an old Clinton hand from Arkansas and the man who actually discharged the firings, claimed that the first lady said, "We need those people out. We need our people in," and that she made it clear there would be "hell to pay" if he did not act. Hillary Clinton testified she had no recollection of that conversation. She steadfastly maintained that she did not order the firings, nor could she recall offering any "input" on the matter. She later expanded that answer to acknowledge that she did "express my concern" that any problems "should be addressed promptly." This difference—did she express concerns or order firings?—later came to occupy federal prosecutors for the better part of a decade. In 2000, with the administration just months from its conclusion, they issued a report saying that Hillary Clinton had made "false statements" about her role. No charges were filed, since the prosecutors could not establish the statements had been "knowingly false." What counted as truth anyway? The essential truth, that the first lady had been a powerful impetus for taking action, had been obvious for years. The legal truth was arrived at gropingly, through a fog, long after it had faded into irrelevance. The travel office saga was a capsule of all that was maddening about Washington in the Clinton years.

THE CONTROVERSY WAS A TOXIC MIX OF FIRST FAMILY FIXATIONS. THE FIRINGS reflected the first lady's determination to flush the White House of the old regime. The uproar that ensued, both she and the president believed with some cause, reflected the insularity of Washington and the self-absorbed nature of the White House press corps. Despite their private resentments, the Clintons and their unseasoned team had learned something in this sorry episode about the public dimensions of the presidency. Internal deliberations would not necessarily stay internal. Procedures were important, and actions that seemed small at the time could sow large trouble later. As a practical matter, there would be no more housecleanings. The Clintons would live for eight more years with a residence staff of chefs, ushers, groundskeepers, and others, all under chief usher Gary Walters. Many were of unquestionable discretion, but there were others whose loyalty and/or discretion the first family deeply mistrusted. (Although one deputy usher was fired on suspicion of having spoken about the Clintons to Republicans, both Walters and most of his staff would remain in place for both terms of Clinton's presidency.)

Every president encounters something like the question Clinton confronted in those first months: On which issues would he challenge permanent Washington to conform to his own style and purposes, and on which ones would he accommodate the capital's own rituals and expectations? Having forced early confrontations with the press and the White House bureaucracy, the Clintons quickly fell into a sullen retreat. Surely both could sympathize with their friend Vince Foster. As the controversy ground on, the lawyer sat in his West Wing office with a pen and let his feelings flow in an angry free association. Then he ripped the paper up.

Chapter Four

HIGH NOON

PRIL 22 WAS GRAY AND COLD, WITH A WIND-DRIVEN DRIZZLE THAT lashed President Clinton and an assemblage of visiting heads of state and other dignitaries. The skies this day aptly fit the occasion. Clinton was present at the official dedication of the United States Holocaust Memorial Museum, a short distance from the National Mall near the Washington Monument. He and the first lady wore overcoats but no hats and carried no umbrellas, sensing perhaps that to use them would be to shield themselves not merely from the elements but from the authentic rawness of the moment.

The twentieth century's greatest crime had weighed on Clinton's mind in recent days as he contemplated the problem of Bosnia. The ethnic warfare in the rump of Europe, following the disintegration of Yugoslavia at the end of the Cold War, had presented itself as the most prominent foreign policy challenge facing the new administration. Like Nazism, the Balkan wars of the 1990s featured mass deportations, concentration camps, and organized slaughter of hated groups. This time the killing was in the name of a scramble for land and vindication of ancient grievances known as "ethnic cleansing." The philosopher Isaiah Berlin had called the twentieth century "the most terrible in Western history." Now it was drawing to a close, murderous as ever, this time in an age of satellites and cable news, which made ignorance and averted gazes harder to sustain. Clinton and his senior foreign policy advisers had been debating options about how to respond to this crisis since the inauguration, and the deliberations in recent weeks had intensified. Clinton was buffeted by events. For weeks, the Bosnian Muslim enclave of Srebrenica had been in a tightening noose. An estimated five thousand people had been killed in a brutal artillery assault led by Bosnian Serb separatists. Clinton was buffeted, too, by his own conscience. Two days before the dedication, he had been given a private tour of the museum. He gazed at a boxcar that had hauled people to Treblinka. He stared intently at a room filled with four thousand shoes of Holocaust victims. For more than two hours he wandered the exhibits. It was after midnight by the time he returned to the White House, a haunted man.

At the dedication, Clinton was preceded to the podium by Elie Wiesel, a survivor of Auschwitz and among the most celebrated literary voices of the Nazi genocide. "Ask yourselves," Wiesel implored his audience, "how could murderers do what they did and go on living? . . . And why was there no public outcry of indignation and outrage?" Then, he pivoted to stare at Clinton. "Mr. President, I must tell you something," he said. "I have been in the former Yugoslavia last fall. I cannot sleep since what I have seen. As a Jew I am saying that we must do something to stop the bloodshed in that country. People fight each other and children die. Why? Something, anything, must be done." Clinton sat back in his chair with a noticeable jolt. The crowd applauded heartily, but the president clapped just once or twice, weakly.

A couple of hours later, a reporter asked Clinton whether he regarded "Elie Wiesel's comments about Bosnia this morning, sir, as a challenge to you personally." His composure regained, Clinton responded with his usual smoothness: "I think it was a challenge to the United States and to me and to the West to take further initiatives in Bosnia, and I accepted it as such."

IN FACT, HE HAD ACCEPTED EXACTLY THIS CHALLENGE A YEAR BEFORE, IN THE 1992 election. Candidate Clinton's aim in the race against Bush had been to fight the foreign policy debate to a rough draw, or at least something short of a rout. The incumbent, after all, had won a war against Iraq and was known preeminently as a foreign policy president. But the advantage had even become a liability, with a popular belief that Bush was so oriented to the world abroad that he let problems fester at home. Though domestic policy was Clinton's strength, Clinton and Sandy Berger, his campaign foreign policy aide, recognized that no Democratic domestic platform was good enough to win if a candidate was seen as helpless on matters of diplomacy and military force. Clinton wanted an opening to establish his own credentials by challenging Bush on the weak links in his own area of expertise. He found the opening in two places: China and Bosnia. Clinton charged that Bush, with his policy of engaging the Chinese leadership to promote commercial trade, had spurned the brave students who rallied for democracy and free expression at Tiananmen Square in 1989. He said Bush had "coddled" the "butchers of Beijing" and promised that promoting human rights, not just trade, would be the cornerstone of Clinton policy. On the question of Bosnia, the contrasts were even sharper. James A. Baker III, Bush's secretary of state, said of U.S. interests in the Balkans, "We don't have a dog in that fight." Clinton vowed he would do "whatever it takes to stop the slaughter of civilians." He added: "History has shown us that you can't allow the mass extermination of people and just sit by and watch it happen." In sum, Clinton pledged to bring a new moral dimension to the cold, interests-driven policies of Bush.

The question before him was how. What military, diplomatic, and political risks was he prepared to take on behalf of the new moralism? He already had abandoned sentimentality for pragmatism on the question of Haitian refugees. On Bosnia, the choices were even more harrowing. By the time Clinton took office, a brutal ethnic war had festered for nearly two years. A problem that might have been managed quickly at the outset, if Bush and European allies had moved aggressively, had grown infinitely more complex. One measure Western powers had taken as Yugoslavia collapsed was the imposition of an arms embargo across the region. This proved disastrous. In Bosnia, a Muslim-led government had established an independent nation but had few arms to defend itself. It was besieged by Bosnian Serb rebels, who were well stocked with arms from their sponsors in Belgrade, the capital of the Serbian republic. This imbalance led many people to advocate a solution that seemed obvious: Lift the arms embargo so that Bosnia's government could procure weapons to defend itself. This option had wide bipartisan support in Congress, but Clinton knew the solution was not as simple as it appeared. The first problem was the opposition of Europe. Several allies, including the French and British, had troops on the ground in Bosnia, serving as part of a United Nations humanitarian mission. This force was doing virtually nothing to prevent the punishing attacks on Bosnian Muslims but was at least keeping food and medical lines open. Europeans were threatening to pull out if the arms embargo was lifted, fearing their troops would be at greater risk of being taken hostage or hit by collateral fire. If Clinton unilaterally lifted the arms embargo, as some advocated, and Europeans made good on their threat to withdraw, he would transform Bosnia into an exclusive American responsibility. Even in the best light, lifting the arms embargo was a half solution. Once the embargo was lifted, there would be a naked moment before Bosnian Muslims could actually get weapons and train to use them. The Bosnian Serb aggressors doubtless would exploit this window as their last chance to crush the opposition unless the United States intervened to prevent it. This was unacceptable. What if after lifting the arms embargo the Bosnian Serbs continued their bloody assaults? Clinton had already stated that he would not send U.S. ground troops to the Balkans except to enforce any peace agreement reached by the warring parties. There was no way Clinton, or almost any other American politician in 1993, was about to send U.S. soldiers into a shooting war in a remote mountainous corner of Europe. Doing nothing was morally unthinkable for Clinton, but playing the hero and rescuing Bosnia was politically untenable. As ever, he needed to find a middle path.

In the spring of 1993 his debate focused on two such paths. The less ambitious was a diplomatic effort to pressure the sides into a ceasefire, while promising a stronger Western role in protecting Muslim enclaves. The more ambitious was an idea called "lift and strike." The arms embargo would be lifted, not unilaterally, but with the concurrence of European allies. Then, if the Bosnian Serbs tried to exploit their advantage in the interim, NATO warplanes would strike them, providing parity until the Bosnian government could fight for itself. Multilateralism was a classically Democratic instinct in foreign policy, and Clinton's personal instincts—his attentiveness to dissent and preference for consensus in all situations—made it all the more important that America not be going it alone.

Clinton's foreign policy team worked through the last week of April to present him on Sunday night with a memorandum detailing his choices. On Saturday, the first of May, the president made his decision. The killings at Srebrenica and the public lecture from Wiesel had apparently made an impact. Clinton chose the more aggressive option, lift and strike, as his policy. But he chose the more aggressive option in the most tentative way. The plan was for Secretary of State Christopher to leave for Europe that very night to sell this proposal to allies. Only if they, too, agreed would the policy go forward, and Clinton knew what a remote prospect this was. "Now you've really got your work cut out for you," he counseled, as Christopher left for the airport.

THE JOURNEY THAT FOLLOWED SOON CAME TO BE RECOGNIZED AS ONE OF THE most embarrassing episodes in American diplomacy of recent decades. At each stop, Christopher presented the supposed new policy as an idea for which Clinton was soliciting support. At each stop, he ran into a wall of opposition.

In London, the contradictions of the Christopher mission seemed layered one atop the other. The first was Christopher's dry and understated style, which imparted little sense that the American government regarded the Bosnian crisis as a matter of urgency. The second was Christopher's own ambivalence about the proposal he was selling. In internal debates he had voiced plenty of doubts over whether there was any good answer to what was happening in Bosnia. The core problem was that he was not really selling a policy, nor had he been instructed to do so. Clinton had sent Christopher to Europe to "consult" with allies and get their response. This was quite a different proposition than making clear in emphatic terms that lift and strike was what the United States wanted, and that the U.S. president expected their support. Instead, Christopher offered the new American proposal "with all the verve of a solicitor going over a conveyance deed," as Raymond Seitz, then the U.S. ambassador to the Court of St. James, later put it. In the face of Christopher's diffidence, British prime minister John Major was quite clear. He opposed any military escalation in Bosnia, an idea he said was so unpopular in Parliament that his government might fall if he were to back it. In Paris, French president François Mitterrand was equally recalcitrant. German and Italian leaders were only slightly more enthusiastic.

The secretary's real problem was back home. Clinton's agonizing over Bosnia had not stopped after the May 1 decision. The journalist Elizabeth Drew, who reconstructed Christopher's European debacle in a book the following year, reported on a conversation Clinton had with Defense Secretary Les Aspin during the third day of Christopher's trip. After presenting a trophy to the Air Force Academy football team in a Rose Garden ceremony, Clinton asked Aspin and Joint Chiefs Chairman Colin Powell into the Oval Office for a chat. The president began discoursing on the book *Balkan Ghosts,* by journalist Robert Kaplan, which chronicles the centuries of hatred and internecine conflicts that had scarred the Balkans. The implications were obvious: The region was a hopeless swamp from which the United States should stay far away. Aspin, who was himself unenthusiastic about an expanded U.S. role in Bosnia, returned to the Pentagon and got on the telephone. After trading notes with National Security Adviser Anthony Lake and Peter Tarnoff at the State Department, Aspin announced, "Guys, he's going south on this policy. His heart isn't in it." Then Aspin called Walter Slocombe, a senior Pentagon policy official traveling with Christopher. "Walt, we're going to pull the plug on it," Aspin said. "The President is going south."

Christopher came home with nothing. The trip was seen instantly for what it was, blunderbuss diplomacy, and soon became a symbol of the timidity of American power in the early Clinton years, with a president unwilling to harness his idealistic impulses to the diplomatic and military force needed to carry them out. With his old-school sense of loyalty, Christopher took the fall for the trip's failure. Still, it rankled him to do so. Years later, beneath the lines of an otherwise dusty volume of foreign policy speeches and anecdotes titled *In the Stream of History,* Christopher sought to move blame for the episode a little closer to where he thought it belonged. Upon returning to Washington, he recalled, he hurried to a Saturday morning meeting at the Oval Office. "I urge that we stay the course and try to bring the Europeans along," he told Clinton, adding that the Europeans "will only be persuaded by the raw power approach. That is, we have to tell them that we have firmly decided to go ahead with our preferred option and that we expect them to support us." Even as he was counseling boldness, though, Christopher continued to accommodate Clinton's ambivalence. "You are not publicly committed to a particular option and hence you are free to consider other options, although none seems attractive." Neither the president nor anyone else at the meeting spoke up for an assertive stance on Bosnia. "As I made my presentation," Christopher concluded, "it became evident there had been a sea change in attitudes during the week I had been away."

AT AGE SIXTY-EIGHT UPON HIS APPOINTMENT, WARREN CHRISTOPHER WAS A seasoned and honorable man—an eminently logical choice for the eminent position he held. But he misunderstood in a fundamental way what this young and uncertain president needed from a foreign policy counselor. What Clinton needed was someone who could quiet Clinton's doubts through the force of certitude. Lloyd Bentsen provided exactly this sort of rudder on economic policy. But Christopher did not try to do this. He was more like Mack McLarty, trying to read and respond to his boss's wishes and second-guessing in ways that amplified uncertainties rather than putting them to rest.

Christopher had spent a highly successful career moving back and forth between government service and his perch at the prestigious Los Angeles firm of O'Melveny & Myers. He had served as deputy attorney general under Lyndon Johnson and deputy secretary of state under Jimmy Carter. Now in the top job at last, he saw himself as a lawyer still—interpreting the client's wishes and carrying them out competently. Christopher had been in charge of the vice presidential selection process, but otherwise he had little history working with Clinton. He could not have been expected to know that the advisers who had been most influential in Clinton's orbit were people who spoke to him as advocates rather than analysts.

Christopher was not indifferent to Bosnia's agony. During congressional testimony later that year, he called the Balkans emergency a "problem from Hell." But given its hellish dimensions, and given Clinton's unwillingness to risk a rupture with Europe on the question, he and his team decided the wiser course was to try to move Bosnia off the front pages and the administration's attention on to other business. As a man of the establishment, Christopher believed that what was important in foreign policy were relations with Russia, the health of the NATO alliance, and the vibrancy of U.S. trade. An administration had only so much political and diplomatic capital. A regional war with no direct implications for U.S. security had already taken more than its share.

PRESIDENT CLINTON WAS NOT FINDING CLARITY ABOUT BOSNIA FROM THE State Department, but he was getting it from the Pentagon. The most important foreign policy adviser during that first year was actually his top military adviser, a holdover from the Bush administration, the widely admired chairman of the Joint Chiefs of Staff. Army General Colin Powell was a steadfast skeptic about Bosnia intervention. Against Christopher's diffidence, and Clinton's, Powell expressed his views with force and precision.

Clinton was entranced by the general's winning personality and impressive biography. Powell was one of the most accomplished African-Americans of his generation, which was part of his attraction to a president committed to racial progress. Powell had vaulted to prominence under Republicans, but Clinton felt intuitively that they were of like minds. Days before the 1992 election, before Clinton and Powell had ever met, Vernon Jordan dined with his friend Powell and on behalf of his friend Clinton asked, "Are you interested in State or Defense?" Powell assured him, "Vernon, I don't want either job. I don't want *any* political appointment." Powell said he wanted to stay put, serving out the balance of his term as Joint Chiefs chairman. Clinton and Powell first met a few weeks after the election, when Clinton was visiting Washington during the transition and Powell stopped by his suite at the Hay-Adams, across Lafayette Square from the White House. After a long chat (in which, among other things, Powell warned Clinton about the hazards of taking on the gays-in-the-military issue), Clinton was even more impressed. "He's very political," said Clinton to Paul Begala. This sounded like an odd thing to say about a professional soldier, but Clinton meant it as high praise—that Powell was a realist who understood the interplay of policy and personality and public opinion.

Clinton was right. Powell had excelled in the modern army not because of his command experience, which was less than many other senior officers, but because of his savvy working in a succession of politically sensitive staff jobs in the Pentagon and White House. There was a paradox to Powell's reputation that would loom large in Clinton's first year. He became a major political influence within the administration and beyond because he was widely perceived as being *apolitical*—a soldier offering strictly professional expertise uninfluenced by personal opinion. During the internal debate over Bosnia, his recommendations came wrapped always as neutral analysis. He had no opinion on what Clinton should do about Bosnia, he would say. But if the president was considering air strikes against Bosnian Serbs, he should know how ineffective they might prove to be in the mountainous and wooded terrain. What did he propose to do if the air strikes did not work? If Clinton's policy was some kind of ground force, that was one thing, but to enforce a ceasefire or peace agreement, he should know the number of troops it would take to do the job right. Then the figure always came back far higher than anything Clinton was remotely ready to contemplate. Powell's comments in any given deliberation were usually quite sensible. Over time, and after countless deliberations, however, the Clinton national security team felt the chairman was trying to set policy under the guise of neutral military recommendations. Perhaps it was subconscious or perhaps it was by design, but his comments always pointed in the direction of "no" to an aggressive policy on Bosnia, and he never offered any ideas of how to get to "yes."

The diplomat Richard Holbrooke, who watched the administration's impotence on Bosnia with mounting frustration, later summarized the relationship: "Powell simply overwhelmed the administration. He regarded the new team as children. And the new team in turn regarded him with awe."

The professional military's reluctance to take on a mission set a pattern that lasted through the administration. Sandy Berger later remarked that if *Thirteen Days*, the movie about the Cuban missile crisis, had been remade and set in the 1990s, it would have been the generals warning about the risks of confrontation, and liberals like Robert Kennedy truculently agitating for war.

This reversal was at first blush confusing. Yet there were clear historical rationales for the different positions. It was the Vietnam debacle that for twenty years turned the Democrats into the party of doves. Now, with the Cold War over, the progressives who populated a new Democratic administration returned to instincts that had far deeper roots. Historically, the Democrats, who believed instinctually in government as an instrument of good, were ready to use military force to achieve virtuous ends in the world. Franklin D. Roosevelt tried to push reluctant conservatives into arming Britain in the early 1940s. John F. Kennedy became enthralled with Special Forces and the strategy of "flexible response," so that the United States could have options for entering military conflicts in a calibrated way. If the Democratic civilians were moving beyond Vietnam, however, uniformed officers of Colin Powell's generation were not. Powell had served two tours there as a young soldier in the 1960s. He came home believing that the idea that military force could be finely tuned by politicians and delivered with predictable consequences was a dangerous delusion. Once in command, he resolved, his generation of soldiers would not allow the military profession to be so misused. From this conviction came the Powell Doctrine: Military force should always be used in a fashion overwhelming to the mission at hand, and never without clear political goals, public support, and a clearly defined exit strategy. He was especially suspicious about undue confidence in airpower, the notion that policymakers could solve problems on the ground with some well-placed bombs from the sky.

The clash between the two worldviews came one day at a White House meeting. Madeleine Albright, the U.S. ambassador to the United Nations and the administration's most vocal Bosnia hawk, challenged Powell: "What's the point of having this superb military that you're always talking about if we can't use it?" As he later recounted Albright's challenge, Powell wrote, "I thought I would have an aneurysm."

YET FOR ALL HIS DISMAY ABOUT THE BRASHNESS AND NAÏVETÉ OF THE NEW administration, Powell found the new president a surprisingly levelheaded presence. "I always felt more comfortable when the President was present at these discussions," Powell recalled. "Bill Clinton had the background to put history, politics, and policy into perspective."

Powell's sympathy for Clinton was important. Figuring in the discussions about use of force that spring was a mostly unspoken but unavoidable fact— many military officers could not stand Clinton. His avoidance of military service in Vietnam—and, even more, his prevarications about the issue during the 1992 campaign—had eroded support. So had his calls for allowing gays to serve openly in the armed services. Nor did it help that he was proposing a considerable drawdown in military spending in the wake of the Cold War. When in March the commander in chief hopped a helicopter to the aircraft carrier USS *Theodore Roosevelt* to visit his charges, who were then on the way to the Mediterranean, any positive symbolism was quickly stained by the next day's front-page account quoting sailors speaking in mocking tones. Did you hear about the protestor who threw a beer at Clinton? Not to worry, came the chortling answer, it was a draft beer and Clinton dodged it. "Maybe we can call this his military service," said Commander Bill Gortney, executive officer of one of the *Roosevelt*'s fighter squadrons. "Three hours is more than he had before."

For his part, Powell was quite troubled by such signs of disrespect for Clinton. To his mind, Clinton's Vietnam record was no more nor less distinguished than those of many of the conservatives he had served with in the Reagan and Bush administrations, who had also found a way to miss Vietnam but who never faced any grilling for it. That spring, he went with Clinton to the Vietnam War Memorial. Some thought Clinton had gall for even showing up. There were boos from protestors. No one missed the point when, taking the podium before Clinton, Powell answered these jeers by declaring in emphatic tones, "I want to introduce to you the commander in chief of the armed forces of the United States, President Bill Clinton."

Such support helped Clinton immeasurably. It also added to the vast influence that Powell already enjoyed.

SO HERE WAS CLINTON IN THE SPRING OF 1993: MADELEINE ALBRIGHT'S MORALism pulling in one direction, Colin Powell's skepticism pulling in another, Warren Christopher's caution in the middle. Clinton sympathized with Albright, feared Powell, and was getting little help from Christopher or from National Security Adviser Anthony Lake at reconciling the different interests. There was an alternative to clarity. John Deutch, a senior Pentagon official and later Clinton's director of Central Intelligence, gave it a name that stuck inside administration councils: "muddling through." Clinton would continue to rhetorically denounce ethnic cleansing, urge the warring parties to reach a ceasefire, and talk with European allies about a better solution. But he was not ready to risk a more aggressive solution.

Nor was this the only foreign policy issue that spring in which moralism yielded to practicality. The retreat on Bosnia was part of the same realism that led him to retreat earlier on the questions of Haitian refugees and, in the spring of 1993, on human rights in China. After his rhetorical valor against Bush and Beijing during the campaign, in the spring of 1993 Clinton decided the better part of discretion was to continue his predecessor's approach of insulating trade policy from human rights. Through it all, the balance between idealism and risk remained a fascinating topic to him—in foreign policy and in life. In an interview that spring with Dan Rather of CBS, Clinton suddenly turned the conversation toward his favorite movie, *High Noon,* the classic Western from 1952. "It's a movie about courage in the face of fear," he said, "and the guy doing what he thought was right in spite of the fact it cost him everything. And Gary Cooper is terrified the whole way through. So he doesn't pretend to be some macho guy. He's just doing what he thinks is right. It's a great movie."

Chapter Five

THE CLINTON STYLE

THE DAYS NEARLY ALWAYS STARTED BADLY. IT DID NOT MUCH MATTER IF the president had gotten a lot of sleep the night before or none at all. He often stayed up in the White House residence until 2 a.m. or later, and usually did not arrive in the West Wing until after nine. A West Wing aide once observed that it was as if Clinton's body clock was programmed to run on Pacific Coast time. In his morning mood, Clinton was as predictable as morning rush hour, and about as pleasant. In time the president's staff came to regard his braying as a morning ritual, a way of clearing his throat before facing the day. If he was still angry by noon, then there really was a problem.

Late nights had been Clinton's preference as a student, and as governor, too. He did not propose to change habits now. This was just one of many predilections that he carried with him to the presidency. In Arkansas, he had governed by instinct and spontaneity. Dealing with the state legislature, he would amble downstairs in the capital and collar a lawmaker when it was time to cut a deal. When his temper flared at an aide or political ally, those people would dismiss it by saying, "That's just Bill." In Little Rock he really was just "Bill," spoken of with affection or disdain but total familiarity in either event.

Clinton's city and state had long since accommodated to his diverse collection of talents and foibles. For his part, after a dozen years as governor, Clinton had the job down cold. Of all the illusions he carried to the presidency, the greatest might have been this failure to appreciate the distance between the statehouse and the White House, between the informality of Governor Bill and the rigid expectations that attach to the words "Mr. President."

Watching presidents come and go, the denizens of political Washington are quite accustomed to bowing to presidential tastes on trivial matters. On matters relating to power and its rituals, however, the capital political culture has proven uncommonly resistant to change. Presidents are presumed to have certain ways of presenting themselves, of following schedules, of making decisions and announcing them. An especially graceful president, like JFK, can discard old conventions, defy expectations, and create a new style of power. Clinton, less nimble and facing more doubts, ignored these customs at his peril.

The White House reporters had a name for his schedule, or rather his inability to keep to it: Clinton Standard Time. He acted as if he was genuinely unaware—though this was plainly impossible—of how his schedule affected the rest of the world. At any moment, vast numbers of people are waiting on a president; when Clinton was on the road, for example, hundreds of local police and emergency personnel would be kept working overtime, at local taxpayer expense. The main cost was to Clinton himself. In Washington, among the press, lawmakers, and even his own cabinet, his lateness fed a perception of an unseasoned and unsteady president.

Of the many people who labored to keep Clinton on time, one man was most important. Andrew Friendly in 1992 was just twenty-two years old, a Washington native fresh out of Middlebury College. He was the first of four young men to serve as Clinton's personal assistant. The personal assistants were uniformly known on the White House staff as "the butt boys," a phrase apparently borrowed from prison lingo. They were handsome, with polite and earnest public demeanors that made them seem, misleadingly, like Eagle Scouts. In private, these men often were raucously irreverent about their boss, whom they admired but whose shortcomings they saw at closer range than anyone. It was Friendly's job to carry the speech text and place it on the podium before Clinton spoke, to walk with him along the rope line and get the name of whoever happened to hand Clinton a gift or a note, to warn other staff members when the boss was in poor spirits. He was often more chaperone than servant. "Mr. President, it's really time to go," Friendly would say when

Clinton was lingering in conversation with an Oval Office visitor. "You're running twenty minutes behind and we've got a congressman waiting." Clinton would not respond, or even turn to acknowledge the comment. The visitor, feeling self-conscious, might make motions toward leaving. "No, no, stay, sit down," Clinton would say, leaving Friendly to stew anxiously. Even so, the aide recognized that tardiness was Clinton's way of fighting back at the regimentation the presidency had forced upon him. For all his pose of obliviousness, Clinton usually had a sixth sense of how far behind he could get before the schedule was truly beyond salvation.

Just as aides learned the idiosyncrasies of Clinton Standard Time, so too did they learn to accommodate the contours of the Clinton mind. Clinton was determined that the organizational structure of the White House not prevent him from hearing all his options. This was a laudable instinct, and also a form of rebellion. Isolation is the great peril of the modern presidency. Original thinkers are kept at bay by a staff geared toward presenting the boss with consensus recommendations. Clinton liked to hear dissenting views even when there were none. Once that first year Clinton was called to take a stand on a possible balanced-budget amendment to the Constitution. There was no doubt that he would be opposed. The idea was anathema to congressional Democrats, and the entire White House senior staff agreed. So Clinton took it upon himself to offer an impassioned argument about why the amendment was a splendid idea. "He was not for it," recalled Howard Paster, the congressional liaison, "but it drove him crazy not to hear both sides of the argument, so he made it himself."

Aides noticed that Clinton would pretend he did not know things just to get the benefit of someone else's explanation. "Did you see that article in today's paper?" an Oval Office visitor would ask. Even if Clinton had seen it he would blankly reply, "What did it say?" He did not want to know what the article said. He wanted to know what the other person thought was important about it.

Most of all, people in Clinton's White House had to learn to understand and react to his moods. His anger would roll in and crash down in powerful waves, then recede just as quickly. His explosions required translation, hard to do for someone new to his orbit. Words that sounded like emphatic orders often were not. Once in 1993 during a moment of frustration over staff failures, the president laid down the law to Roy Neel, a longtime aide to Al Gore who was then serving as White House deputy chief of staff. Clinton named five people whom he wanted gone. Break the news to them and help find them other jobs, he said. Neel dutifully went about this unpalatable assignment. Within days, he learned—though not from Clinton—that all five people had appealed directly to the president, who had reversed the firings.

From Clinton's perspective, perhaps the most surprising part of life in the presidency was the sensation of being constantly and mercilessly watched and judged. He was judged for his clothes. "The president's suit, as he stood, looked to be a couple sizes too big," read the White House pool report for January 25. "Perhaps this is one of his fat wardrobe pieces from the campaign?" He was judged for the company he kept. The Washington press said he was starstruck. At his first head-of-state summit, that spring in Vancouver, he raised eyebrows for finishing his meeting with Russian president Boris Yeltsin, then adjourning to his hotel suite for coffee and dessert with the actress Sharon Stone, the star of *Basic Instinct,* who was in town filming a new movie. (White House aides hastened to point out that Stone had not been alone in the presidential suite; co-star Richard Gere had joined her.) The parade of celebrities included Barbra Streisand, who filled in as Clinton's guest to the annual Gridiron Dinner of Washington grandees when the first lady was out of town. When Paul Newman and Joanne Woodward came to Washington, the president and Chelsea joined them for dinner at a downtown Italian restaurant. Most famously of all in those early months, Clinton was judged for his haircut. It was performed under a "personal services" contract with the stylist Cristophe, late of Beverly Hills, whose usual rate was $200 an hour. One day in May, Air Force One sat on the tarmac in Los Angeles for nearly an hour while Cristophe clipped. This forced the closure of two runways, though initial reports that air traffic was kept circling for hours turned out some weeks later to be wrong. By then, Clinton had long since apologized: "The Secret Service asked and they were told there would be no delays. It was just a mess-up." Too late—this trivial episode had already entered the anti-Clinton mythology.

In popular perception, in his first months Clinton was laboring at once with the reputation that he was a Hollywood-loving elitist as well as an Arkansas hayseed. He was by instinct a casual and accessible man. But this instinct tended to diminish the mystique on which successful presidents relied. So there was Clinton on March 9, during a morning jog on the National Mall, when a woman cried out, "I wanna jog with you!" The president waved the blonde-maned stranger over and they jogged and chatted for the remainder of Clinton's route. Often as Clinton finished these morning excursions, huffing and dripping with sweat, he'd stop to take a few questions from reporters. These encounters did not elevate the majesty of the office when replayed on the evening news. In a variety of deliberate and unconscious ways, Clinton neither invited distance from the public nor received it. The most notorious example of this came the next spring, at a televised "town meeting" with young people hosted by MTV, the music video channel. A pert teenage girl from Maryland, asserting dubiously that "the world is dying to know," challenged Clinton on his preference in underwear: "Is it boxers or briefs?" "Usually briefs," answered the commander in chief, adding quizzically, "I can't believe she did that." Others could not believe he had answered.

Even as he sometimes underestimated the value of silence, he lost his voice at moments when he needed to use it forcefully. Clinton was painfully absent from view on the horrific morning of April 19, 1993, when the FBI stormed a compound in Waco, Texas. A religious fanatic named David Koresh, wanted for possession and manufacture of illegal weapons, among other things, had resisted in an armed standoff for fifty-one days rather than surrender to authorities. When federal agents moved in, he and at least some of his followers chose mass suicide over surrender. Eighty-six people, including seventeen children, died as the farmhouse was swallowed in a blaze. Clinton had been deeply wary of the attempted assault, but ultimately consented to Attorney General Janet Reno and the Justice Department's wish to move in. When it ended in catastrophe, it was Reno who faced the cameras and even won public praise for soberly accepting responsibility. Clinton, meanwhile, was portrayed in the press as trying to dodge.

TARDINESS, TANTRUMS, TURMOIL AMONG HIS STAFF—CLINTON'S MANAGEment method could be hard to take. To focus solely on the undesirable features of his style, however, would be a mistake. Spontaneity had its pleasures. So, too, did the restless energy and search for new diversion and excitement that lay beneath it. In cheerful moods, which were more common by far than his foul ones, Clinton was a marvelously entertaining president. For most people, part of the entertainment was simply the spectacle of being with a man who was always doing several things at once, always looking to figure the angles, always loading his plate a little higher at life's buffet.

One theory among White House staff was that the ideal place to study Clinton's essential nature was at the card table. Hearts was his game. "Let's deal 'em up," he would say whenever he had a spare moment to play and partners who knew how. His games were not for amateurs. On travel days, Clinton and his staff rode by Marine One helicopter from the White House South Lawn to Andrews Air Force Base in suburban Maryland to board Air Force One. Clinton was always trying to set a new record for the number of hands that could be played during the chopper's ten-minute hop, as the cards were picked up and thrown down in a frenzy. Once aboard Air Force One, the games would continue, sometimes for hours, across the continent or across the ocean. "Why did you do that?" he might quiz another player. "You should have played a spade! Why did you lead the club? What was your strategy?" Clinton could remember the cards in his hand and everyone else's, and the precise sequence in which they had been played. A mind that instinctually categorized and analyzed political data did it for card games, too. Not that he devoted full attention to the game. He would play his hand while also reading a book, or talking on the phone, sometimes even to heads of state. The only person he reliably stopped playing for was Hillary Clinton when she came on the line.

Jake Siewert, Clinton's second-term press secretary, came to believe that the president saw cards as a metaphor for politics. Both gave him the chance to study the ways people made decisions and responded to pressure. He sometimes boomed furiously at other players, especially those who had not played with him before, if they had the nerve to drop a bad card in his hand: "You didn't need to do that! You did that on purpose!" Was this genuine anger or merely bluff? It was a bit of both. Clinton got no deference from more experienced players, veteran aides like Bruce Lindsey or Doug Sosnik. They would tell the new player not to listen to a word Clinton was saying. This president might be as hyperactive as a young boy, and sometimes no more mature. But Clinton was a life enhancer. He had a talent for bringing people more fully out of themselves.

WHETHER ONE FOUND THE CLINTON STYLE CHARMING OR MADDENING, IT soon became apparent that he had to change. The defects of trying to make decisions in a free-flowing, spontaneous way were becoming too obvious, never more so than in the tangled tale of Clinton trying to select his first nominee to the Supreme Court of the United States. It had been a quarter century since a Democratic president had had a chance to name a member of the High Court. Republican presidents had filled eight of the nine seats. Now Clinton was getting a chance to change the balance just two months into his term. On March 19, Supreme Court Justice Byron White, the lone Democratic appointee, wrote the president to tell him he was retiring from the Court. The deliberations that followed showed Clinton at his best: earnest, tireless, willing to challenge conventional thinking.

In an exchange with reporters later that day, Clinton pledged to find a nominee "who has a fine mind, good judgment, wide experience in the law and the problems of real people, and somebody with a big heart." This statement alone signaled a different approach. What did it mean? The American Bar Association had never rated judicial nominees for "bigheartedness." Clinton knew what he meant: He wanted someone in his own image, with empathy for common folk, who viewed the work of government not in abstractions but with a sense of the concrete human dimension to problems. He was rather less certain about how to meld these laudable but vague intuitions into a workable selection process. Over the next twelve weeks, no fewer than a half dozen people emerged as Clinton's favored choice to be the nominee. In all but the last case, something intervened to keep them from being announced to the public.

New York governor Mario M. Cuomo was the first infatuation. The president was captivated by the man who he had once assumed was going to be his chief competitor for the 1992 nomination. Clinton wanted a politician rather than a legal traditional jurist as his first choice to begin recentering the conservative court. Someone with elected experience, he believed, could become a leader on the Court, just as former politician Earl Warren had led the Court to a new season of activism. With his passionate oratory and liberal-minded sensibility, Cuomo represented precisely what Clinton meant when he spoke of a big heart. Likewise, the New York governor had the affection of George Stephanopoulos and Gene Sperling (who once worked for Cuomo). Clinton had given Stephanopoulos license to reach out to Cuomo; the governor's son Andrew, himself a Clinton appointee to the housing department, served as intermediary. But the Clinton team were slow learners about the sage of Albany. Just as Cuomo had wavered about running for president in 1992 and 1988, so he wavered now. Clinton called him once in early April to say he was under serious consideration. The governor, ever alert to evidence of a slight, was offended that Clinton had not made a more direct appeal. On April 7, with a call to Stephanopoulos and a public announcement, he took his name out of the running.

Now what? After Senate majority leader George Mitchell waved off inquiries about his interest, Interior Secretary Bruce Babbitt took Cuomo's place as the front-runner, and Clinton was mightily intrigued. Formerly the governor of Arizona, Babbitt had elective experience. He had another advantage, too: After the previous winter's clumsy effort to promote diversity in the cabinet, white men were back in vogue at the White House. Clinton agreed with several of his advisers (white men, as it happened) that his first court appointment was not the place to make another gesture about diversity.

But as word about Babbitt's likely promotion leaked, the administration and various special interest groups became tangled in debate about who might replace him at the Interior Department. A vacancy there likely would set off a battle between environmentalists and western senators who worried that Clinton was trampling land-use rights. With the president's economic plan still facing an uphill fight in Congress, and controversies swirling over everything from Waco to the war in Bosnia, Clinton decided he had no room for another headache. Babbitt's court prospects faded.

Once more: now what? While the deliberations over Babbitt had been unfolding, Washington's winds of conventional wisdom shifted again. Diversity was back in. The Lani Guinier debacle was the main reason. Guinier was an old law school friend whom Clinton had nominated to head the Justice Department's Civil Rights Division. She encountered a shower of bad publicity over legal writings that questioned the sanctity of majority rule and praised radical race-based "proportional representation" remedies to voting discrimination. The White House had stood by her for a time, then dropped her after deciding her writings were indefensible. Many Democrats, including Attorney General Reno, thought the matter had been handled deplorably and urged Clinton to make amends with the party's liberal base by appointing a woman to the High Court. That's when the name of Alabama Supreme Court justice Janie Shores surfaced. That Shores was a southerner was another plus. For a day or so, she was the new front-runner. It fell to White House counsel Bernard Nussbaum to douse her in cold water: No one in the national legal or political communities had ever heard of Shores. People would think Clinton had lost his mind. And so the White House search continued.

It was now mid-June, some twelve weeks since the vacancy opened. Clinton had now taken longer in filling a Supreme Court vacancy than any other modern president. Things were getting desperate. The original idea of finding a bighearted politician, or some other novelty, had been abandoned. Now Clinton simply needed a justice. Stephen Breyer, a former Harvard Law professor and chief judge on the federal appeals court in Boston, was hardly an exotic choice, but he would be an eminently respectable one, with the liberal stamp of approval of Massachusetts senator Ted Kennedy. Breyer was summoned to Washington on June 11, a Friday, for luncheon with Clinton. Thursday night, Clinton ordered White House lawyers to put together a package of

Breyer's legal writing, which the president stayed up most of the night reading in preparation for the interview. The session did not go especially well. Breyer was in pain, recovering from a bicycle accident. Clinton found him a bit cramped and cool in style—not the broad-minded humanist he was looking for. That Friday, Clinton summoned his selection team back to the Oval Office. The meeting started at 11 p.m. and continued well past midnight—a middle-of-the-night meeting for a matter that had been pending nearly three months. Breyer had been asked to stay in Washington and was instructed by White House aides to prepare an acceptance statement. But the president made plain his lack of enthusiasm. Meanwhile, there were questions about late Social Security payments on Breyer's domestic help, raising the Zoë Baird specter again. Babbitt's name re-emerged. Could they go back to him? Clinton wanted to know. Meanwhile, a new name had begun to percolate. Ruth Bader Ginsburg was a federal appeals court judge in Washington, D.C. By all means, Clinton enthused, let's bring her in. Ginsburg was reached in Vermont, where she had traveled for a wedding, and urged to come to Washington for a secret Sunday morning meeting with Clinton at the White House.

This meeting went wonderfully. During their ninety minutes, Clinton was impressed with her personal tale of graduating from law school, being rejected at blue-chip law firms, then persevering to a successful career in which she had won women's rights victories before the Supreme Court. For the time being, Breyer's prospects were over. Yet there was one more cliff-hanger to come. The day before, on Saturday, Andrew Cuomo had called Stephanopoulos with the news that Governor Cuomo had changed his mind: He would be willing to be nominated if Clinton asked. That Sunday afternoon, as Clinton's team gathered in the Oval Office, the president confided that he had made his choice. He was going to call Cuomo and offer him a spot on the High Court. "There, he had said it," Stephanopoulos later recalled. "It was really happening. But before anyone could even begin to make a counterargument, [presidential secretary] Nancy Hernreich walked into the Oval with a note for me: Mario Cuomo was on the line." Predictably, Cuomo had second thoughts. If Clinton asked him to serve, he said dramatically, the answer would be no.

Ginsburg it was. Judged by results—the standard that matters historically—the Ginsburg appointment was a success. Ginsburg proved in the years after she arrived to be precisely the kind of progressive-minded jurist Clinton set out to put on the High Court. At the time of the decision, however, the process mattered; it was one way the electorate was sizing up a young president. When it was over, Ronald Klain, a young White House lawyer who had worked on the selection team, felt he had had a revealing window into Clinton's vast potential—

and also into the habits that were hobbling this talent. "On the positive side, you could see that he was intensely engaged, and he took an incredibly intellectual approach to studying the candidates and their philosophies and searching for the right choice," he recalled. "But it was also an undisciplined process, and external influences would lead us to swing from pillar to post."

IN THE ROSE GARDEN THE NEXT DAY, CLINTON TEARED UP AT HIS ANNOUNCEment of Ginsburg's appointment, as he listened to her make a graceful statement thanking her family and various mentors who helped clear her path as a professional woman. Clinton expected praise for an inspired appointment. The first question came from ABC's Brit Hume, who quite politely asked whether Clinton could "perhaps disabuse us" of the perception that there had been a "a certain zigzag quality in the decision-making process here."

Clinton glared, clenched his jaw, then spat back his answer: "I have long since given up the thought that I could disabuse some of you [from] turning any substantive decision into anything but political process. How you could ask a question like that after the statement she just made is beyond me." He quickly wheeled off the stage and returned to the Oval Office, bringing Ginsburg's announcement ceremony to an awkward close.

While presidential flare-ups like this were common inside the West Wing, indulging in them before the outside world imposed a mighty cost. The Arkansas style Clinton brought to Washington put too much of him— his moods, his self-justifications, *a certain zigzag quality* of his own thinking about the difficult choices he was facing—on public display. The result was a failure of presidential optics. The presidency can take formerly average-seeming men, like the pre–White House FDR, and invest them with an aura of command. Clinton, however, was made to look less impressive than he was. On the cover of *Time* magazine, just four months after the inauguration, there was a tiny image of Clinton next to a devastating large-type headline: "The Incredible Shrinking President."

Chapter Six

FACES OF WASHINGTON

BY LATE SPRING OF 1993, BILL CLINTON WAS SEARCHING FOR A TONIC for his presidency. Impulsiveness and denial might be his first instincts; self-criticism and correction were his second. When the first got him into trouble, the other got him out: twin phases in a familiar cycle of crisis and survival. So it was that after midnight on May 28, the president was on the telephone making an improbable appeal. David Gergen was a magazine columnist, public broadcasting commentator, longtime Washington worthy—and, most notably, a Republican. He was also, Clinton believed, precisely the tonic he needed. "I'm in trouble," Clinton purred. "I need your help." Clinton said he wanted Gergen to join him as a new member of the senior White House staff.

It was an astonishing offer. Gergen took Clinton's call at the home of Mack McLarty. A week earlier, the chief of staff had invited Gergen to lunch in the White House mess. McLarty said he wanted to discuss ideas after reading Gergen's columns in *U.S. News & World Report* critiquing the president's shaky first months. Gergen had worked as a mid-level speechwriter and press aide in the White Houses of Richard Nixon, Gerald Ford, and Ronald Reagan before ascending into the lofty precincts of Washington punditry. After two decades in the capital, he was a quintessential product of the Washington establishment. His columns were balanced and sensible—and an accurate barometer of capital conventional wisdom. "As he nears his 100th day in office, Bill Clinton is in trouble—not deep, certainly not fatal, but worrisome all the same for a man who will be the only leader the country has for at least 1,300 days more," he warned earnestly in early May. Three weeks later: "Friend and foe alike think he can be rolled. Sadly, these perceptions are now creeping in about Clinton—one of the most gifted, dedicated men ever to serve in the Oval Office. He has a wonderful head and a big heart, but people are looking for more backbone." At the lunch, McLarty asked for some suggestions of a Washington veteran who could join the listing White House ship. Clinton, by evident pre-arrangement, stopped by the lunch to chat about his problems. Clinton and Gergen had known each other casually for a decade. Both men typically spent their New Year's holidays on the South Carolina shore with several hundred like-minded high achievers at the famous Renaissance Weekends. Gergen promised that he would come up with some names of Democrats who would fit McLarty's bill. Days later, Gergen was on the road in Louisiana when he received an urgent message to call the White House. McLarty came on the line. Clinton, he said, had decided Gergen was his choice to add some Washington wisdom to an unseasoned White House. "I damn near dropped the phone," Gergen recalled.

The lobbying campaign had just begun. Clinton said he wanted to meet with Gergen the next day—late, as the president would be returning from a day trip to Philadelphia. Next, Vice President Gore called to make an urgent pitch. Gergen, he said, would be an all-purpose counselor and wise man in the top ranks of the White House. He would have all the access to the president he needed. While waiting for Clinton at the White House residence, Gergen sat down for a searching conversation with Hillary Clinton. She gave Gergen the answers he was eager to hear. The perception that she was pulling the presidency to the left was wrong, she said, asserting that people did not understand how traditional she was in her values. After all, she noted, she had been a "Goldwater Girl" in the 1960s. She agreed that it was time for rapprochement with the Washington press and the Georgetown establishment. They needed Gergen to help. When Clinton finally arrived after 11 p.m., he was just as direct. "He thought the administration was way out of position politically," Gergen recalled years later. "He had intended to come as a New Democrat and he was perceived as being way off to the left and he had to get back to the center and he had to get back to working with Republicans and he thought I could be a potential bridge to help him get back to the center where he wanted to govern." Gergen wanted to think it all over. Clinton said there was no time for that. Gergen's appointment would be shock therapy. For maximum effect, it needed to play in the news media as a surprise. Clinton wanted to announce Gergen the next morning, a Saturday, at seven-thirty, before he left to give a speech at West Point. With his new appointee's reluctant agreement, that's exactly what they did.

An obsession with moving quickly for the sake of news coverage, a tendency to lurch from one plan to another in response to press criticism, was itself one problem in the Clinton White House; it was also a hint, though Gergen could not have known it, that Clinton's interest in him was not principally as a "bridge to the center." Before recruiting the Republican Gergen, Clinton had tried unsuccessfully to recruit Democrat Bill Moyers, another respected commentator with White House experience, but one who tilted as much to the left as Gergen did to the right. Moyers begged off the appeal, just as he had six months earlier during the transition. What Clinton was looking for was not an ideological anchor but an ambassador to establishment tastemakers. Most of all, he was looking for a swift fix to deep problems.

When Gergen arrived on the job nine days later, he was stunned by the man he found. The natural buoyancy he had known previously in Clinton had given way to tentativeness and confusion. "Here was a fellow who had lost his way and, most importantly, he had lost his self-confidence," he said. The remedy, Gergen figured, was to "get the organization tightened up, and to give him the opportunity to find himself again." For a time, the Gergen experiment worked as planned. The commentator had the high-level access he was promised. He lavished attention on the White House press corps, especially prominent reporters like Ann Devroy and Andrea Mitchell, helping soothe resentments that had festered among the networks and major papers. Clinton opened a charm offensive, inviting Washington journalists to the White House for off-the-record dinners and chats.

Gergen's problems, however, emerged quickly. He was greeted with stony resentment from much of Clinton's staff. Some of it was ideological, from liberals who did not understand the point of Democrats winning the White House only to install a Republican warhorse. Some of it was personal. Paul Begala, for example, regarded his new colleague as a self-promoting operator, showing up for meetings with Clinton with ideas and speech drafts that he had not bothered to share with others. Gergen was hardly the man to bring organizational ballast to this unruly White House. He was himself chronically tardy and overcommitted, dropping in on meetings, dispensing his nuggets of Washington wisdom, then ducking out to deal with the telephone message slips stuffed in his pockets.

The main problem with the appointment had nothing to do with Gergen. It was the contradiction inherent in a president who needed "to find himself again." Gergen had allowed himself to believe that he was recruited to the Clinton fold as a clarifying agent—a statement about the administration's essential philosophy and bipartisan approach. In truth, he was joining simply as one more voice in the chorus of advice for Clinton. As it happened, Gergen's voice began to fade nearly from the outset. Despite her protests to the contrary, the first lady soon proved herself to be something close to the liberal partisan Gergen had feared. This was the root of his undoing. He could live with the resentments of Clinton's young campaign veterans. The mounting tension with Hillary Clinton was another matter.

THE ASCENSION OF DAVID GERGEN HAD BEEN BIG NEWS THAT SPRING MORN-ing, not merely because of the oddity of a young Democratic president recruit-ing a Republican wise man into his ranks. A subplot in the Rose Garden that morning was Clinton's unspoken rebuke of the most celebrated name on the White House staff. George Stephanopoulos, indeed, was among the most cele-brated presidential aides ever. From his podium in the White House press room, Stephanopoulos had become a bona fide star. With his stylish wardrobe, shock of dark hair, and angular boyish face, he was the public symbol for the brash young team Clinton had brought with him to the White House. He was referred to in Washington conversation as simply "George." Updates on his romance with actress Jennifer Grey were a staple of the gossip columns. Like his friend James Carville, and before that the Republican Lee Atwater, Stephanopoulos represented something new on the Washington scene: the elevation of the Washington operative into a figure of glamour. He was known as a master of spin—a new name for the old art of trying to win favorable press coverage for the boss—and had become famous in the bargain.

With Gergen's arrival, the story Stephanopoulos needed to spin was his own. Clinton was moving him out as communications director, and from his prized spot at the podium, to a new and hazily defined post as presidential "senior adviser." It was not a firing, nor a demotion, but it was not a volun-tary move. Stephanopoulos later acknowledged that he had been a terrible choice as the White House spokesman. In private he was intelligent, reasonable, and reflective—one of the most impressive figures of his generation. At the podium, however, he came off as cocksure and defensive. His delivery only underlined the administration's reputation for callowness that was already one of the White House's main vulnerabilities.

Yet even as he was being dislodged, he was landing in a new spot that only added to his mystique. Stephanopoulos had first earned a place by Clinton's side during the presidential campaign. He soon emerged first as an indispensable tactician, a role that later blossomed into something like a Clinton alter ego—a protégé even. Stephanopoulos, everyone knew, was the man Clinton bellowed and complained to when he came into the office in the morning, upset about his schedule or the morning papers. But this was a sign of how close he was. "One of the reasons for this move," Clinton said, "is that I have missed very badly and I have needed the kind of contact and support that I received from George in the campaign, that I think was absolutely essential to the victory that was secured." He laid it on just as thick in private. "I need to have you close by me," he said soothingly when he first talked with Stephanopoulos about the personnel moves, during a middle-of-the-night phone call the morning before the shake-up was announced.

It was from such comments that a mythology about the Clinton-Stephanopoulos relationship was born, but the public statements only hinted at its true complexity. Among reporters, Stephanopoulos was known as the cardinal Clinton loyalist and defender. From the outset of their collaboration, however, strong currents of ambivalence flowed between Clinton and his dashing young retainer. Like other veterans of 1992 who had gone through the controversies over the draft and Gennifer Flowers and Whitewater, Stephanopoulos had found Clinton on first blush to be a thoroughly captivating and inspiring figure. On second blush, amid the crises of New Hampshire, he had discovered him to be a maddeningly unreliable and even untrustworthy candidate, so he concentrated his gaze on the appealing side of Clinton and insulated himself against the other side by concentrating on the unsavory nature of Clinton's opponents. His value to Clinton was that he was a skilled guide and interpreter of the media-political axis, the world of operatives and journalists who watched Clinton and in turn interpreted him to a larger audience. For all of Clinton's political gifts, he found this chattering class an alien and confusing constituency. As Clinton knew, however, the reason Stephanopoulos could anticipate the reactions of the media pack was that he essentially shared its values. During the draft controversy, it fell to Stephanopoulos to tell the candidate the obvious: that this was serious enough to force him from the race. Here was the paradox: Stephanopoulos gained influence by being the one who was bold and realistic enough to talk about bad news with the boss, but each time he also revealed himself in the minds of both Clintons as someone less than a true believer. Years later, the president often retold the story, but he exaggerated it to assert that Stephanopoulos had been urging him to drop out. His point was obvious—George had always been a naysayer, part of the Washington crowd, one of *them*. Clinton, with his sensitive antenna, was essentially right: Part of Stephanopoulos had always been judging him with disdain. For all his modish persona and liberal views, the young man was something of a moralist. He had grown up in suburban Cleveland as the son of a Greek Orthodox priest. He was disciplined and ascetic, tightly coiled, and possessed of rather rigid beliefs in right and wrong—a pious streak that, in the political field he had chosen, meant he was forever wrestling with matters of conscience and compromise. Clinton was the supreme relativist—he believed in right and wrong, surely, but also believed that on most questions there were all manner of ways to split the difference. Clinton always maintained the psychic edge over his brooding aide. Once, during the 1992 campaign, Clinton had gone off script during an important debate. Stephanopoulos returned to the staff van sputtering about the candidate's lack of discipline. As it turned out, the volunteer driver was a woman who was an old friend of Clinton's, and apparently a close one. Out of the blue, Clinton later surprised his young retainer by calmly asking, "George, was everything okay back in the motorcade today?" Like many overworked advisers through the years, wrestling with powerful feelings of attraction and resentment toward the boss, Stephanopoulos sometimes had the feeling that Clinton was hovering omnisciently over his life.

For the next year, at least, Clinton was true to his word and kept Stephanopoulos by his side. The young man was among the most important figures shaping Clinton's political and communications strategy. Yet Stephanopoulos, sharp and aggressive as tactician, was conventional and even timid as strategist, and putting him in such a dominant position was in retrospect one piece in a larger sequence of strategic miscalculations Clinton made in his early presidency. After winning office with a wobbly 43 percent plurality, the president found that his preeminent challenge in 1993 and 1994 was to engage the electorate's disaffected center, including the Perot voters, who were wary of partisans. Stephanopoulos, however, was a creature of Capitol Hill, where he had earlier served as a House Democratic leadership aide, and he endorsed the dubious strategy by which Clinton, in his approach to the budget and health care, deferred to the parochial demands of the Democratic caucus. Having run as a modern and tough-minded New Democrat in 1992, Clinton now had to give programmatic substance to his slogans on welfare reform and crime. Stephanopoulos, like many liberals in Clinton's fold in 1992, essentially regarded the label as a campaign ploy, and spurned the policy proposals of authentic New Democrats like Bruce Reed and Al From. The failure to settle on a consistent strategy—tacking to the center one day and back to the left the next—was most of all Clinton's. For two years, the president who was supposed to be an electoral mastermind was running an administration with only the blurriest notion of how to connect the president's daily policy battles to his larger political ends.

GERGEN AND STEPHANOPOULOS WERE IMPORTANT MEMBERS OF CLINTON'S Washington sphere. In the other sphere that dominated the president's life were the Arkansans. Inside the White House, these were two distinct cultures, each with its own claims on the president's attention. At best, the two sides viewed each other with earnest curiosity. At other times it was more like disdain. As a rule, the Arkansans believed the Washington crowd, which had gravitated to Clinton from the campaign and think tanks and law firms, was filled with operators and opportunists who little understood the moods and manners of the complicated man whom the Arkansans had known for so long. As a rule, the Washingtonians viewed the Arkansans as naïve capital tourists. Many of them could not penetrate the southern style, further widening the cultural gulf. The Arkansans spoke in chatty drawls and wore sunny dispositions that made them hard for outsiders to read—and easy for some to dismiss as hayseeds. For his part, since he was a young adult heading east to Georgetown and Oxford, Clinton had loved performing his Arkansas rhapsody to outsiders. He boasted of its colorful characters and oversized watermelons, of its decent people gamely facing the challenges of a poor state. In 1992 the best side of Clinton's Arkansas past—the progressive governor who had moved his state forward—was an appealing part of the biography he presented to the nation. Even so, for those who came into Bill Clinton's life from elsewhere, Arkansas and everything it connoted was hardly a positive association. Stephanopoulos had learned it was best to simply avert his gaze from the Arkansas past, he once confided to a reporter. Gergen had been warned by his friend and fellow commentator Mark Shields to steer clear of the Clintons' unsavory home-state connections. From this perspective, Arkansas was a perpetual trapdoor in

Clinton's presidency. It was always swinging at unwelcome moments to reveal complicated tales from the past—relationships and rivalries, alleged affairs or murky business deals, that were always just a bit hard to explain.

A benign yet fascinating example came in June when the *Washington Post* revealed that William Blythe, the father who had died on a rain-slicked highway in 1946 three months before the future president was born, had a complicated life of his own before marrying the then Virginia Cassidy. He had fathered one and possibly two children and had two previous marriages that neither Clinton nor his mother had known anything about. The president told reporters he looked forward to speaking with a man now known as Henry Ritzenthaler, his newly discovered half-brother, who was now living in California. But when he called, the man was off giving television interviews and no one was at home.

VINCENT W. FOSTER JR. WAS PREEMINENTLY PART OF THE ARKANSAS SPHERE in the Clinton White House. He was also an emphatic reminder that the Arkansas contingent in Washington included highly intelligent and accomplished individuals. Like Clinton himself, Foster was an appealing face of the New South. He had grown up with McLarty and Clinton in Hope (before Clinton moved away to Hot Springs). After graduating from North Carolina's Davidson College, he returned home to finish first in his class at the University of Arkansas Law School. Then he settled into a respectable career as a lawyer, becoming a partner at Little Rock's Rose Law Firm. Here, in the mid-1970s, his Clinton connection was revived anew. His best friend at the firm was the wife of the state attorney general, Hillary Rodham Clinton. Despite the convergences in their lives, Foster and the future president were hardly similar personalities. Friends knew Foster as proper, cautious, self-effacing. He was the kind of man who navigated discreetly among powerful and affluent people, not the sort to plunge into the fray and seek out public office himself. Behind the scenes, though, there was no doubt at all about his influence. Upon coming to Washington, the Clintons had installed Foster as deputy White House counsel even before they settled on a person to lead the office providing legal advice to the president. When Bernard Nussbaum, the powerful New York litigator who had been a mentor to Hillary Rodham two decades earlier, became the leading candidate for the top job, he met with Foster. Soon it became apparent that the deputy was interviewing him. So when Nussbaum got the job he was under no illusions that he was in any real sense Foster's boss. It was understood that Foster was working directly for the Clintons, handling significant chunks of their personal legal business that carried over from Arkansas, in addition to White House business. Most of all, it was understood that Foster regarded the first lady as his principal client. Foster and Nussbaum got along well, and early on they asked each other what their greatest vulnerability would be if the press or administration critics went after one of them. Foster gingerly explained that there had been rumors that he and Hillary Clinton were romantically involved. "It's total nonsense," Foster said, when Nussbaum asked if the rumors were true.

Even without a romantic dimension, the relationship between the two law partners was something special. Indeed, if Hillary Clinton had taken some different paths in her life, one can easily imagine she might have ended up with someone like Vince Foster. There was a side of her that wanted affluence, respectability, steadiness. Foster lived with his wife, Lisa, in a big home in the Heights neighborhood of Little Rock. He enjoyed quiet dinner parties and was a wine aficionado. He was tall, at six feet three inches, and handsome in an understated sort of way, with flecks of gray in his full head of hair. Webster Hubbell, a Rose partner and close friend of both Foster and Hillary Clinton, once observed, "He seemed like a man who had never made the stop at childhood. There was a seriousness about him that made him old beyond his years." He lived an anchored, private, prosperous life of the sort that Hillary Clinton did not, in her relationship with a hyperkinetic politician making $35,000 a year as Arkansas governor. "Why can't we lead the lives of normal people?" she vented once, when an adviser said that her hope for installing a pool in the executive mansion in Little Rock would be politically insane. In her heart, of course, Hillary Clinton wanted a life of respectable obscurity no more than her husband did. Yet perhaps because of the stresses of her life—as a modern woman in a state that preferred its first ladies on the more traditional side, working at a starched law firm where many partners were themselves ambivalent about her—the friendship with Foster was a special refuge. "I think Vince and Hillary became such friends because each recognized that the other was battling to find a viable life," Hubbell observed. "Hillary, assailed from all sides, drew into herself. Vince, assailed from inside, drew even deeper into himself." When they were together, the trio of lawyers—Clinton, Foster, and Hubbell—formed their own whimsical club. There were weekly get-togethers at the Villa, a Little Rock Italian restaurant where they drank wine at lunch and Hillary Clinton, who usually picked sparingly at meals, indulged in pasta and garlic bread with abandon. She had a rare ability to bring Foster out of his shell, mortifying him but also delighting him by ordering a belly dancer to the law offices to celebrate his birthday. She called him "Vincenzo Fosterini." Hubbell and Foster called her "Hillary Sue."

For a time, Foster was as giddy as everyone else in Clinton's Arkansas delegation about the ascension to power. This is gold, he said to Hubbell, twirling the White House pass that hung around his neck. "I could never go back," he said early in 1993. The magic wore off quickly. Within weeks, he was handling some of the White House's more delicate business. It had been Foster with whom Watkins had discussed the impending shake-up in the White House travel office, as well as the alleged importunings by the first lady that action be taken promptly. Foster was also defending the task force that Hillary Clinton had convened to draft the administration's proposed overhaul of the nation's health care system. She wanted the task force's deliberations to be private, its meetings closed to reporters and its documents privileged. It was an understandable preference for privacy—no previous administration had drafted its policy proposals in public—but also unrealistic, given that the task force included hundreds of participants who were not government employees. Soon the battle over the secret deliberations was yet another in the string of controversies buffeting the new White House. In short order, Foster began feeling pressures that were entirely new to him in his forty-eight years. He was in the public eye. The *Wall Street Journal* focused on him in part of a series of biting editorials looking at the role of Hillary Clinton, Hubbell, and other Rose partners who had arrived in senior positions in the government. A small matter drove Foster to distraction. He did not want to provide the *Journal* with an official photograph. He was aghast; lawyers, he told his friends indignantly, do their work in private. Eventually, after a lengthy delay, he relented and the photograph was sent. But not before the *Journal* published an editorial with a question mark where it would have displayed a likeness of Foster. "Who Is Vincent Foster?" read the editorial page's headline of June 17.

The editorial seemed harmless to everyone but Foster. The paper continued to fire shots at him and other Rose partners a few more times over the next month. It was the kind of criticism, especially coming from such a conservative venue like the *Journal,* that most public officials quickly learn to brush off. Foster, though, was in agony. He had revealed his own attitude on such matters in May when the University of Arkansas Law School had invited him back to speak at commencement. He told the young graduates, "dents to the reputation in the legal profession are irreparable." This was hardly an accurate description of life in Washington, where good folk and scoundrels alike suffer ethical contretemps and bounce back none the poorer. For his part, Foster warned his audience that they could expect "failures, and criticisms and bad press and lies, stormy days and cloudy days." Even as he agonized over public scrutiny, Foster was feeling beleaguered at home. Lisa Foster had spent the period from the inaugural through June back in Little Rock so that their son could finish high school there. She was unhappy and resentful about being left behind. The couple's phone conversations were sometimes snappish. Meanwhile, Foster was stunned that his relationship with Hillary Clinton had taken a quite new complexion in Washington. She was no longer a favorite colleague. She was now his client and his boss—and a demanding one on both counts. "Fix it, Vince!" she snapped at him in a conversation about the health-care task force. "It's just not the same, Hub," he told Hubbell of his friendship with Hillary Clinton. "She's so busy, Hub, that we don't ever have time to talk." Foster told him he no longer trusted his office phone, believing it might be monitored by the Secret Service, or even by Republican sympathizers burrowed in the executive branch bureaucracy.

Many people in the White House knew Foster was feeling harried and blue. What no one realized was that Foster was suffering from acute depression. He had had several long conversations with Marsha Scott, a former Arkansas girlfriend of Clinton's who had also joined the White House, in which he had spoken of his troubles. Clinton knew of these troubles, though only vaguely. He resolved to help cheer his friend up. On July 19, he invited Foster to come to the White House to watch a movie with a small group of Arkansans—Clint Eastwood's *In the Line of Fire*, about a Secret Service agent trying to thwart an assassin. Foster, who had by now been joined in Washington by Lisa Foster, begged off, saying he wanted to spend the night at home. On July 20, Foster left the White House early, around 1 p.m. The last colleague he spoke with at work—indeed very possibly the last person he spoke to on this earth—was a White House secretary named Linda Tripp.

His dead body was found shortly before 6 p.m., lying near a Civil War cannon at Fort Marcy Park, which overlooks the Potomac River in suburban northern Virginia. An antique .38 caliber revolver was in his hand. The bullet he had fired into his mouth left his face intact, exiting through the back of his skull. Two United States Park Police investigators arrived on the scene. One of them looked at the blazer Foster had left in his nearby car and discovered his White House badge—the "gold" he had boasted about to Hubbell months before. "We better notify the Secret Service," said the other. Clinton was about to hear news that would echo for the rest of his time in Washington.

The president was on live national television when White House aides learned the news. His interview with CNN's Larry King had been going so well that, spontaneously and on air, Clinton had just agreed to King's suggestion that they continue for an unplanned extra half hour. By this time, Chief of Staff McLarty—in grief over the death of a man he'd known for more than forty years—had broken the news to Hillary Clinton, who was in Little Rock visiting her mother. She broke into sobs at the news, then turned aghast with the knowledge that her still oblivious husband might learn of the tragedy on live television. During a commercial break, the chief of staff rushed into the White House library, where the interview was taking place. "Mr. President," McLarty said, "we need to quit while we're ahead." Enjoying his banter with King, Clinton plainly wanted to continue, but then he seemed to realize from McLarty's tone that something more serious was afoot. "Mack, what's wrong? What's up?" he said as they rushed out. McLarty responded: "It's not a national emergency or crisis, but it's a very serious matter. Let's go upstairs where we can sit down." Learning the shocking news, Clinton, too, began to cry. "I want to call Hillary," he said. "Have you told Hillary?"

The president immediately decided to visit Lisa Foster at her Georgetown home. Without assembling the usual limousine motorcade and press pool that ordinarily accompany the president whenever he is outside the White House grounds, he raced over to Georgetown in an unmarked Chevy Suburban. As it happened, Gergen and Vernon Jordan had been dining just a short distance away, at the home of former *Washington Post* editor Ben Bradlee and writer Sally Quinn. They, too, descended on the Foster home, along with Hubbell, Marsha Scott, and other Arkansans. Gergen, who in the two months he had been at the White House had seen how emotionally raw and harried Clinton was, worried about whether the president could withstand a tragedy this personal. What he saw that night surprised him. Clinton was poised and strong, soothing Lisa Foster and his other friends with exactly the right words. It was a revealing moment. Vince Foster had been broken by his Washington encounter, and there were friends in the room that night who would be broken, though not in the fatal sense, in the years ahead. By contrast, Bill Clinton was not someone who would break under adversity. However much he might in some moods complain about the unfairness of his critics or the hardships he was facing, the president was at bottom an accommodator. When his Arkansas habits proved untenable in Washington, he was flexible enough to adapt. He was a man of uncommon resilience, a trait that always surfaced when he needed it most.

Foster's death was more scarring for the first lady. The usual reactions to a friend's death—grief and remorse—were mixed with quite unusual ones, including a defensiveness about what might be found once investigators began looking through Foster's office. Foster had many documents pertaining to the

Clintons' personal affairs. The night of his death, Hillary Clinton acted like a stricken friend, calling confidants like Harry Thomason and Susan Thomases and her chief of staff, Maggie Williams. She talked to Tipper Gore, who had herself suffered from depression, about the need for counselors to help White House aides cope with the tragedy. Two days later, she was acting like a lawyer. The White House had reached an understanding with the Justice Department to allow a search of Foster's office as part of the death investigation. The record suggests that Hillary Clinton expressed acute interest in this. On the morning of July 22, Williams called the first lady at 7:44, and they spoke for seven minutes. Then the first lady called Thomases and talked for three minutes. A minute later, records showed, Thomases paged White House counsel Nussbaum. Later that morning, Nussbaum canceled the agreement with Justice officials. Nussbaum said he would examine the office first, then decide what documents to let the investigators see. A heated phone conversation followed between Nussbaum and Deputy Attorney General Philip Heymann, whose attorneys were cooling their heels outside Foster's office. "You are messing this up very badly," Heymann said. "You are making a terrible mistake." Several files of materials relating to the Clintons were removed from Foster's office, taken to the official residence, and then to the Clintons' personal lawyer.

And so the human tragedy of Foster's suicide became an ethical bog. Counseling his staff the next day, Clinton could not help thinking of the tragedy partly in terms of his own battles with the press and Washington. He told aides that Foster had "an extraordinary sense of propriety and loyalty, and I hope that when we remember him and this, we'll be a little more anxious to talk to each other and a little less anxious to talk outside of our family." He then faced reporters in the Rose Garden. "As I tried to explain, especially to the young people on the staff, there is really no way to know why these things happen." What Clinton intended presumably as a rumination on the imponderability of human motivation was heard instead as a defiant vow to bury the truth—"an electric prod on the press," wrote columnist Mary McGrory. This was especially so in conservative precincts. Within a few weeks of the death, conservative commentators like R. Emmett Tyrrell of the *American Spectator,* who pronounced Clinton's "the weirdest presidency I have observed," was urging greater consideration to the possibility that Foster met with foul play. "He is dead now, and from all that we have heard about him foul play cannot be ruled out," he warned darkly. The White House's own actions did nothing to discourage paranoia. Six days after Foster's death, Steve Neuwirth, an attorney working in Nussbaum's office, found torn pieces of yellow paper deep in Foster's briefcase. They had been overlooked in the earlier search. White House officials dubiously chose to wait thirty hours before alerting law enforcement officials of the discovery.

Most suicide victims leave no formal note, and Foster was not an exception. The torn-up paper seemed to be an index of grievances he wrote to himself, rather than a public explanation for taking his life. These jottings were released two weeks later, after the Justice Department and Park Police issued a finding concluding that Foster committed suicide—the first of what was ultimately five different official inquiries. Foster railed about the travel office uproar from the previous spring, saying that "the FBI lied in their report" about the matter to the attorney general, and accusing the press of "covering up the illegal benefits they received" from the travel office staff. He fulminated about Hillary Clinton's battles with the White House usher's office, saying the ushers had "plotted" to increase the costs of her White House redecoration. He said the *Wall Street Journal* editors "lie without consequence." Famously he said, "I was not meant for the job or the spotlight of public life in Washington. Here ruining people is considered sport."

There were more surprises still to come from Foster's office. Five months later, in December, the White House revealed that among the documents taken from Foster's office was a file labeled "Whitewater." New suspicions erupted. By taking his life, Foster had contributed immeasurably to the cause of those who were trying to ruin the Clintons.

Chapter Seven

WAGER

RESIDENT CLINTON BELLOWED AT HIS AIDES, WHO SAT WITH HIM IN the Oval Office like schoolchildren, cringing with a mixture of resentment at his lashings and guilt that his anger was in some measure justified. "We are losing our soul," Clinton shouted, pounding the arm of his chair.

It was the afternoon of April 7. The crafting of the Clinton economic plan had begun three months earlier in a state of panic as the new team came to grips with the magnitude of the federal budget deficit. Several times the process threatened to hurtle into disarray before magnificently coming together with Clinton's fine February 17 speech to the Congress. Chaos, near disaster, triumph: a characteristic Clinton performance. So, too, was what came next. The hours of painstaking meetings over the winter had ostensibly settled the major fiscal questions facing the administration: what to do about tax increases and the right balance between new domestic spending and deficit reduction. Now, in the spring, it was becoming clear Clinton's course was far from settled—not in his own mind, not among his quarreling subordinates.

It had been a cross day to start with in the White House, even before the

Oval Office session turned sour. Hillary Clinton's father was hours away from death in Little Rock, after falling ill from a stroke three weeks earlier. And the president had started the morning with a vivid red scratch across two inches on the right side of his face, which had been the subject of inordinate comment around the White House. He cut himself shaving, Dee Dee Myers explained to reporters. No, actually, it happened while roughhousing with Chelsea, Clinton said later. This tangled explanation had set press room gossips buzzing with another scenario: that the president was scratched in a row with the first lady, who supposedly had returned from a bedside vigil in Little Rock and learned that singer Barbra Streisand had stayed overnight at the White House. Privately, press office aides acknowledged they were not sure what the truth was; they had just repeated what others told them to say. Beset by rumors, and with Hugh Rodham's death imminent, the president was in a poor frame of mind for bad news.

Labor Secretary Robert Reich and Gene Sperling had sought the meeting precisely to deliver such news. In the six weeks since Clinton spoke to Congress, Clinton's economic package had been moving along nicely. In March, the House and Senate both endorsed the conceptual outlines of his plan. These were not the essential votes. The actual budget would not come before Congress until the summer. Importantly, however, the House and Senate actions did set the annual spending limits within which Clinton's entire five-year economic package was supposed to fall. Reich and Sperling were worried that what came dressed as victory was in truth a partial defeat. In particular, they feared the president did not understand that in passing his plan the Congress also had reaffirmed existing provisions in the law that imposed automatic caps on federal domestic spending. These caps likely would limit new initiatives, such as Clinton's coveted "investments" in education and worker training, to a small fraction of what the president wanted in 1993 and the years to follow. When Clinton found out, he blew up. How could they have spent hours and hours going through nearly every line of the budget, yet he was not aware of something as fundamental as this? It was a flashing moment of recognition for a new president. As much as he was trying to impose his values and directions on government, the wheels of policymaking had a momentum of their own.

"Where are all the Democrats?" he challenged his own team. "I hope you're all aware we're all Eisenhower Republicans. We're Eisenhower Republicans here, and we are fighting the Reagan Republicans. We stand for lower deficits and free trade and the bond market. Isn't that great?" These vivid words became famous a year later when journalist Bob Woodward recounted the episode in a book reconstructing Clinton's fateful first year. Sperling remembered recoiling at seeing words delivered in a flush of impatience invested with such significance. Clinton hardly conceived of himself or his program as in the cautious spirit of Dwight Eisenhower. The line echoed even so.

This is because the president, in his sarcasm, had appraised his circumstances rather shrewdly. How had he gotten here? It was one of the abiding mysteries of 1993, which in many ways only deepened in the years to follow. Here was Clinton, liberal by instinct, populist in style, heedless and sometimes irresponsible in his personal life. Yet he was pursuing a fiscal course that was the essence of sober responsibility. His mind had pointed him unavoidably in this direction. His heart was still tugging another way. By instinct, Clinton was a dreamer who viewed American history as a pantheon of heroic presidents he hoped to someday join. During the 1992 campaign he had read Geoffrey C. Ward's biography of Franklin D. Roosevelt, *A First-Class Temperament*. The book, he said, had lit a "burning passion" to see the Roosevelt estate at Hyde Park. A month after becoming president, he made the trip, laying a single red rose on the FDR grave. Late that year he gave a speech quoting his hero's call for "bold, persistent experimentation." He linked the New Deal's burst of big-spending innovation with the new programs in his own agenda. Clinton's frustrations mounted as he saw his grand plans grow ever more stolid, more like Ike than FDR. Clinton was first a romantic. But he was second—and more emphatically—a realist. When faced with almost any difficult policy decision, he would nearly always end up where deficit-obsessed establishment experts told him to be. The path there was often tortuous.

This tension between Clinton's dueling desires—the romance of bold government initiative versus the realism of deficit reduction—was one great source of Washington drama that first year. So, too, was the fate that met the sober-minded program Clinton had proposed. The capital's political culture had soured over the previous decade, defined increasingly by partisan anger, the quest for short-term advantage, and fundamental mistrust toward and among politicians. In this environment, the economic plan on which Clinton's presidency hinged over the next four months was never more than a few steps away from failure.

THERE WAS ONE PERSON WHOSE JOB IT WAS TO ANCHOR CLINTON TO THE POLITICAL AND FINANCIAL ESTABLISHMENT—and to its prescriptions for the American economy. Secretary Lloyd Bentsen's suite on the second floor of the Treasury

Building looked down on the White House. This was apt, for during Clinton's wobbly opening months in office it was not always apparent who was subordinate in the relationship. Tall and elegantly tailored, his profile creased with wrinkles, Bentsen was a quarter century older than the fresh-faced and fleshy president he served. World War II, not Vietnam, had been his defining experience. In his early twenties, Bentsen was awarded the Distinguished Flying Cross for the thirty-five bombing runs he piloted over Nazi-occupied Europe. He liked short meetings, not Oval Office bull sessions. Of Clinton's endless White House meetings, Bentsen noted wearily, "He's the meetingest fellow I ever saw." He wanted crisp decisions, yet like everyone else who came into Clinton's orbit he learned that any matter that seemed to be closed was sure to be reopened. This was Clinton's way of reassuring himself that all risks had been considered, all options explored; it drove Bentsen to distraction. Yet precisely because Clinton was so attuned to risk, and so in need of reassurance, Bentsen quickly became indispensable to him. For all their differences, their partnership was probably the most consequential policy relationship of Clinton's first year. The only competition in this category was Clinton's relationship with the woman in charge of his health care initiative, who happened to be his wife.

Bentsen had first come to Washington as a House member in the early 1950s, then left when he decided he wanted to return to Texas and make a fortune. He did, in the insurance industry. He returned to Washington as a senator in 1970, when he won election over Republican George Bush. In the ensuing twenty-two years, he had established himself as one of the city's quiet powers, wielding far-reaching influence over tax policy, health care, and much else as chairman of the Senate Finance Committee. However formidable his presence in Washington, he was unknown to most Americans outside of Texas until 1988, when Michael Dukakis tapped him to be the Democratic vice presidential nominee. In one of the Democrats' few happy memories that year, Bentsen in the vice presidential debate disemboweled his callow Republican opponent, Dan Quayle, with one surgical thrust: "Senator, I served with Jack Kennedy. I knew Jack Kennedy. Jack Kennedy was a friend of mine. Senator, you're no Jack Kennedy." Bentsen, however, was more content in a world of businessmen, lobbyists, and Washington elders than he was onstage. It was because his Treasury secretary was ambassador to this world that Clinton needed both his approval and the approval of others whom he could bring along. Beyond need, Clinton genuinely wanted Bentsen's approval. He was extraordinarily deferential to him, eager to impress him with his good intentions and with his understanding of economic matters. Clinton's courtship succeeded, to a degree. Bentsen *was* impressed by Clinton, by his energy and his whirring mind and his enthusiasm for governing. A year into the job, the Treasury secretary sat in his office one day reflecting on the eight presidents he had known, and concluded that Clinton was in some respects the smartest. "I think this fellow is a step above in the way of being able to correlate and see how it all works together," he mused. But Bentsen added that this very talent for seeing multiple dimensions of a problem could be a curse: "He also has difficulty making decisions." More seriously, he believed Clinton's incessantly political nature was self-defeating

Part of Bentsen's job was to curb the political advisers, whom Clinton let roam freely in policy debates but who did not support deficit reduction on substantive or political grounds. But over time his most important duty was to be confessor to a president whose faith in his own agenda often wavered. Clinton had staked his presidency on a theory that reducing the deficit would impress the Federal Reserve and Alan Greenspan that the government's fiscal house was being put in order. Once Greenspan and the Wall Street bond markets became convinced that the days of massive government borrowing were over, interest rates would come down. This in turn would spur investment by corporations and lower mortgages for homeowners. If all the gears turned as he theorized, vast suppressed potential for productivity would be unleashed and the economy would boom. But this was a big if. The theory was really just a wager. And even if it turned out to be a wise one, the payoff required the patience of an impatient man. With his calm and dignified manner, Bentsen was there to gently stroke Clinton and assure him that everything would be fine. When Clinton complained that his economic package was a "Wall Street plan" with nothing for "the people who elected me," Bentsen gave a little sermon. "Wait and see," he counseled. "It is paying off."

In many ways, the Treasury secretary lived up to his reputation as the administration's conservative counterweight. Truth be told, he was opposed to large chunks of Clinton's agenda. He thought the so-called stimulus package— the $30 billion in public works spending and tax breaks that was designed to pump up the lagging economy—was foolish. How could Clinton convince people he was serious about deficit reduction when he was pushing this liberal grab bag? Similarly, Bentsen believed the president and Hillary Clinton were making a terrible mistake by pursuing a comprehensive overhaul of health care, instead of aiming for more attainable, incremental reforms. Bentsen bristled every time Clinton lapsed into populist rhetoric suggesting he was eager to soak the rich. "Get that damned language out," he would bark. "You don't need that in this country." It was bad politics, Bentsen warned, because "there's just a lot of people out there that think someday I'd like to be rich." Certainly Bentsen understood such feelings. He remarked in passing to an aide one day that he always regretted that he never had a private jet. Even so, he was outraged at how the gulf between rich and poor had widened in the Reagan years. Of the administration's tax increases, he told Clinton, "The rich can damned sure handle it!" There was still a hint of Texas populism inside him. Furthermore, for all his gentlemanly demeanor, Bentsen knew how to settle a score. In the opening days of the administration, there was much chatter around Washington about Daniel Patrick Moynihan, the man who succeeded the Texan as chairman of the Senate Finance Committee. Moynihan was complaining publicly about not receiving sufficient attention or deference from Clinton. Then one day in *Time* magazine a quote appeared about the senator from an anonymous administration official that echoed loudly through the capital: "He's cantankerous, but he could not obstruct us even if he wanted to. . . . We'll roll right over him if we have to." The quote was widely assumed to have come from George Stephanopoulos or Rahm Emanuel or one of the other brash young men on Clinton's unseasoned staff. The words seemed to capture perfectly the impertinence of the new White House crowd, many of whom were still in diapers when Moynihan was already a towering figure in national life. Only years later, in the administration's closing days, did writer Michael Kramer reveal the name of his "senior official." It was Bentsen sending a message to Moynihan, one gray hair to another, warning him to leave this young president alone.

ROBERT REICH WAS THE OPPOSITE OF LLOYD BENTSEN IN NEARLY EVERY PARticular. Where the Treasury secretary was understated, the labor secretary was voluble and even brash. While Bentsen towered in his physical presence, Reich suffered from a congenital condition called Fairbanks disease that left him just under five feet tall. Bentsen came to his position scarcely knowing the president, yet ended up with outsized influence. Reich had known Clinton for more than two decades, but found himself that year in a lonely battle for his ideas.

He and Clinton met aboard the SS *United States,* which was carrying both young men to Oxford, England, where they had been accepted in that year's class of Rhodes scholars. The seas became too high for Reich, who retreated to his cabin with horrible nausea. Clinton knocked on the door with chicken soup and ginger ale, and a friendship was forged. After Oxford, both Clinton and Reich went to Yale Law School. Both men were high achievers, amply ratifying the judgment of the Rhodes scholar judges. While Clinton rose in Little

Rock, Reich served in the Carter administration, and after the rout of Democrats in 1980, he took refuge at Harvard's Kennedy School of Government, where he began a successful career as writer and lecturer. By the 1980s, Reich was probably a more celebrated name than Clinton, thanks to a series of popular books diagnosing the ills of the American economy and prescribing a renaissance of progressive government as the remedy. He was not an academically credentialed economist. Instead, he was more like an intellectual publicist, with a gift for promoting ideas and himself that had made him a considerable name in progressive circles. Reich thought, with reason, that he and Clinton believed all the same things about the direction progressive government needed to take in the 1990s. Reich had laid out the case in the 1991 book *The Work of Nations,* about the problems of the working class in a high-technology and increasingly globalized economy. His answer? Vastly increased public spending on education and mid-career retraining, so that the people left behind in the contracting "old economy" could contrive better futures for themselves in a high-skill new economy. This vision was precisely the one animating Clinton's 1992 platform, and after he won in November few people doubted there would be a prized spot for Bob Reich.

Reich quickly concluded he did not want to be a Clinton retainer inside the White House. Clinton often made his staff feel as if they were hopelessly inadequate. He treated outside friends and experts, however, as if they were the smartest people in the world. Reich shrewdly realized that from a plaform outside the White House, the Department of Labor, he would be part of Clinton's economic team and well positioned to implement the ideas for modernizing the American workforce that he had spent the past decade promoting.

It took Reich mere weeks to see that the reality was going to be more complicated. In February, during the long deliberations for crafting the economic plan, he fumed that the newspapers, with their emphasis on deficit reduction, made Clinton seem like Calvin Coolidge. Reich believed in an economic theory quite different from what Bentsen had offered. For him, the deficit was an abstraction, a way of counting numbers. What was real, he believed, were the problems average Americans were facing, and Clinton's economic and political success would depend on whether those problems were being met with new and better policies. Precisely because he knew Clinton, had stayed up late talking about these ideas with him, Reich felt the pang acutely as he saw Clinton embrace conventional conservative doctrine about the imperative of deficit reduction. He knew Clinton's heart was with him, but was surprised to learn how little this mattered. The president, so confident in most areas, had become tentative and deferential when it came to his own budget. "Two worlds were foreign to him: Congress and Wall Street," Reich recalled. "These were two areas where he did not feel competent, but he very much wanted to be respected by these worlds." Bentsen offered an avenue to that respect, Reich did not. "He felt he had to win a couple battles that the establishment wanted him to win."

Reich was sympathetic. He worried about the president, who during the spring of 1993 was working to the point of exhaustion. Reich felt his friend did not look at all well. And for all his frustrations, Reich realized Clinton was trying his best to play a bad hand. The description was equally true of Reich, who savored what victories he could. Clinton's economic plan included a major expansion of the existing Earned Income Tax Credit aimed at people just above the poverty line, which helped ensure that it made more sense for them to work than give up and go on welfare. This would prove to be one of the most important and tangible progressive achievements of the Clinton years. But in general, Reich lost more than he won.

THE CAUSE OF LIBERAL GOVERNMENT SPENDING, ALREADY IN RETREAT DUE TO Bentsen's ascendancy, suffered a major blow on April 21. The stimulus package, which Democrats said would revive the economy with a burst of well-targeted public works spending and which Republicans dismissed as a trough of liberal pork, was dead. The White House and Senate Democrats acknowledged that they could not break a Republican-backed filibuster preventing the bill from a vote. Many Democrats, including conservative David Boren from Oklahoma, had also made clear their opposition. Clinton struck a wounded tone at a news conference. Noting that Republicans had voted for similar measures when Reagan was president, Clinton said, "I just misgauged it. I've just been here ninety days."

The most immediate implication for the defeat was to make plain that Clinton was eminently beatable if minority leader Robert Dole and Republicans kept up a disciplined front. But the demise of the stimulus package had consequences beyond that, which became clear only over time. It marked the end of a particular Democratic faith that had endured for six decades. The economist John Maynard Keynes had been its intellectual father. He believed that modern economies could be managed by controlling the flow of government money. When times were lean, government could pump up the economy through vigorous spending, running deficits if necessary, until the private sector rebounded. Several generations of Democrats, starting with Franklin D. Roosevelt, had embraced the same notion. It was by definition a liberal theory—a splendid revelation that the social and public works spending that most Democrats supported was also the key to the broader health of the economy. The Keynesian faith reflected an era of great ideological struggles—America in wars hot and cold—in which it was natural to suppose that presidents should hold the reins of the economy in their hands and could steer with precision. Even Republican presidents like Richard Nixon accepted the premise. "We're all Keynesians now," he famously said. Two decades later, by Clinton's arrival, a competing premise reigned. It held that a vast economy could not be affected much by the items in a president's budget or what Congress chose to appropriate. Instead of fiscal policy, the key to the economy was monetary policy—the decisions by which the Federal Reserve decided how much money was in circulation, and at what interest it could be borrowed. If the Fed thought the economy needed a boost, it lowered rates. If it thought inflation was getting too high, it tugged on its money leash and raised rates. Monetarism was in its essence a conservative policy. Historically the great fear of central bankers was inflation, not weak growth. Monetarism was also anti-democratic, since the chairman and governors of the Federal Reserve were appointed and not accountable to voters. Clinton's policy in early 1993 stood on two legs that were trying to move in opposite directions. One leg was based on the primacy of monetary policy, which dictated that Clinton should cut the deficit and hope that the Federal Reserve lowered rates. Another leg was based on the primacy of fiscal policy, which dictated that Clinton should try to boost the economy with a burst of spending. Now the second leg was kicked away. For the rest of his presidency Clinton's economic priority was to accommodate Alan Greenspan's Federal Reserve.

At the time, Clinton and his policy team spoke of the stimulus package as a relatively modest proposal, just a warm-up act for the larger progressive resurgence to come once the deficit had been tamed. In fact, never in his eight-year presidency would he spend as much on a new domestic program in a single year as the $30 billion he had tried but failed to pass in his opening months with this bill. The defeat showed how Clinton's basic assumptions about presidential power were being forcibly altered. He was a progressive president acquainting himself with governance in the era of limits.

If Clinton was governing like an Eisenhower Republican, it was reasonable to assume that there might come at least one benefit of that: the support of some Republicans. He got no such thing.

Republicans at least were candid. In Clinton's first week in office, they sent word that if his economic package contained any tax increases—as of course it would, since he had campaigned expressly on raising taxes on the rich—he could expect zero Republican support. Senator Pete Domenici, a friendly Republican, told budget director Leon Panetta that the word had come down from the GOP leadership that they expected members to hold the line in voting against Clinton on all tax increases. The president was taken aback when Panetta told him. Not long after, Clinton heard it directly when Bob Dole came to the White House for his first meeting with the president. Dole growled that other presidents he had known at least served doughnuts during morning meetings. Was he kidding? Leaving nothing to chance, Clinton aides scurried to bring Dole a chocolate doughnut. It did not sweeten Dole's message. He told Clinton that Republicans planned to blame Clinton and his taxes if the economy did not improve. It was nothing personal, Dole seemed to be saying, just business.

Just as Clinton was betting on an untested theory, Republicans were placing an opposite bet. The papers that spring were filled with gaudy predictions about the calamity that would follow if Clinton's plan was enacted. Senator Phil Gramm of Texas called it a "one-way ticket to recession." In the House, Newt Gingrich warned it "will kill jobs" and "actually increase the deficit." In due course, these predictions proved ostentatiously wrong. At the time, they underlined the extraordinary risks Clinton was taking.

CLINTON'S PERFORMANCE IN BUDGET DEBATE IN 1993 HAD BEEN REPLETE with political miscalculation. The mixed messages of the stimulus package and deficit reduction reflected a larger disjunction. Clinton's public message was being crafted by consultants like Mandy Grunwald, Paul Begala, and pollster Stanley Greenberg, who basically disdained the substance of his program. Occasionally they were joined by James Carville, the leader of the 1992 "war room," but by then he was already transitioning away from domestic political consulting toward a lucrative career as a celebrity commentator. The facts gave Clinton an impressive story to tell. After a generation of fiscal profligacy, he was dutifully asking Americans to make the necessary sacrifices to clean up the mess. This was not a story his political advisers wanted to tell. Begala in particular thought the sacrifice message was sacrilege. "This is an economic growth package," he wrote in one memo to the president and cabinet in February. "It is not a deficit-reduction package, a shared sacrifice package, or a pain package." The angry and burdened middle class who, Begala believed, had secured Clinton his victory already had sacrificed under Republican policies.

The winning message, the consultants believed, should be liberation from the old regime, combined with an overtly populist message that the rich were finally going to be forced to pay their share. Begala described the message he wanted Clinton to deliver in a July memo to the president: "HALLELUJAH! Change is coming.... Your body language, attitude and confidence will be infectious," he urged the president. "If you become a merchant of pain, you'll find that the middle class isn't buying—they already have enough, thank you. Now go forth and spread the good news."

The Carville-Begala brand of populist optimism had worked well during the campaign, but it was a dubious theme for 1993. Clinton, after all, was pursuing a policy based on elite assumptions about the importance of deficit reduction. Wrapping his plan in different paper could hardly disguise its essential nature. Moreover, the idea of shared sacrifice did indeed resonate with many of the voters Clinton needed by his side—people who had voted for Perot, or who had voted for Clinton, but with reservations.

Begala and the other consultants were on more solid ground with their other great obsession—avoiding anything that looked like a tax on the middle class. If the political advisers had gotten their way—and, for all their access to Clinton, most of them felt no internal debates were breaking their way— the president would have raised taxes on the top 1 or 2 percent of taxpayers but scrupulously avoided new taxes on everyone else. This was not what happened. In February, Vice President Gore, arguing that "if you're bold, people will come around," had successfully lobbied for inclusion of his proposal to apply the BTU tax. Under Clinton's prodding, House Democrats passed the plan. But when conservative Democrats in the Senate, led by the Clinton skeptic David Boren, made clear the strength of their opposition, Clinton yielded to reality and the tax was dropped. (House Democrats, feeling that they had been pushed into a politically damaging vote only to be abandoned by Clinton, complained about being "BTUed"—soon a synonym for presidential cravenness.) The tax was replaced with a more conventional levy on gasoline. Bentsen said he could eliminate the gas tax if Clinton would scale back a proposed expansion of the Earned Income Tax Credit aimed at helping the working poor. He would not—a decision that contradicted the popular stereotype of Clinton as unwilling to pay a price for his principles. For his part, Bentsen had been in Texas politics a long time, and he allowed that he'd never seen a politician get licked over a gas tax.

SO HERE WAS A NEW PRESIDENT ELECTED WITH 43 PERCENT OF THE VOTE, pushing a plan replete with political vulnerabilities, with only tepid support from his own party and the vehement opposition from the other side. His policy advisers were at odds over substance; his political advisers thought the policy team was hijacking Clinton's presidency. Clinton had only one real asset, which was his own prodigious effort. If he had been irresolute earlier, he was now, with his political survival imperiled, a model of discipline and purpose. "Let me see the sheet!" he would say when Howard Paster, the congressional liaison, walked into the Oval Office, carrying the latest vote tallies. Paster recalled that "he'd sit there and he'd have the sheet, and he would get on the phone," talking himself hoarse. When a phone call did not work, he would summon the wavering member to the White House. If that did not work, he would schedule a trip to the lawmaker's district. It was a frenzy of activity worthy of Lyndon B. Johnson. But LBJ had known that blandishments work better when combined with a measure of fear. In Clinton's case, members of Congress learned that there was an incentive to hold back their votes. Some members wanted commitments from Clinton to help with fund-raising. Some, like North Carolina Congressman Martin Lancaster, wanted pledges that he would not single out tobacco taxes for increases as the way to pay for health care reforms. Some like Congresswoman Marjorie Margolies-Mezvinsky, a freshman Democrat from Philadelphia who rightly feared that her yes vote would be political suicide in her tax-loathing district, wanted a commitment that Clinton would visit her district and talk about the need to curb spending on entitlements like Social Security and Medicare. There was one poignant moment, however, when Clinton was visited by a House member who wanted nothing. It was Congressman Bill Natcher, a courtly Democrat from Kentucky, who came to Congress in 1953 and for the next four decades never missed a vote. As they sat side by side in two big yellow chairs in the Oval Office, the president laid it on thick. Clinton asked Natcher about his wife, and cooed over his remarkable voting record: "I suppose you're like Cal Ripken—once you got started on this thing, now you can't turn it off." Natcher soaked up this flattery, but then abruptly brought Clinton's charm offensive to a halt: "Let me just tell you something," he said gravely. "You're my ninth president, and I'm going to make sure you succeed."

Through the spring and summer of 1993, Clinton did succeed—barely. On May 27, the House backed his plan, with minor variations, by a vote of 219 to 213. Weeks later, in the early morning hours of June 25, Vice President Gore broke a 49–49 vote in the Senate to pass its version. The narrowness of these votes loudly announced the fragility of Clinton's success. The House and

Senate versions needed to be reconciled by conference committee before returning to both chambers for final passage. Clinton's economic plan would be enacted only if he lost no votes in the Senate and no more than three in the House before the final vote, which would come before the congressional recess in August. This seemed unlikely. But the alternative—a defeat on the most important item in a new administration's agenda—was unthinkable. For the next month, Clinton and his White House lived on a legislative precipice.

Chapter Eight

PARTNERS

I T WAS A CURIOSITY OF THE CLINTON YEARS THAT HE WAS OFTEN RESCUED by members of his own party who happened to regard him with disdain. So it was in the first days of August as the wild opening months of the administration reached a climax with the final vote on Clinton's economic plan.

On first glance, Bill Clinton and Senator Bob Kerrey had much in common. Kerrey was just three years Clinton's senior. Both had been governors in the early 1980s. As politicians, they were both photogenic men, handsome in somewhat unconventional ways. Both were from the generation of Democrats inspired to politics by JFK and drawn to public office by its promise of glamour melded with noble purpose.

It was in 1992, when both sought the Democratic nomination, that the profound differences between them came into sharp relief. Kerrey was a decorated Vietnam War veteran whose artificial leg was testament to his wounds in a conflict Clinton had taken steps to avoid. In his Washington dealings, Kerrey was coolly detached, with an aversion to blarney and platitudes. He prided himself on a willingness to speak hard truths. Clinton, the chatterbox pol whose instinct was to put a sunny face on unpleasant subjects, was not exactly

Kerrey's type. The diverse resentments between them were mingled with mutual fascination and, doubtless buried deep, some measure of mutual respect.

Even so, Kerrey was the last man Clinton would wish to have control over his political fate. But he had it, as all of Washington knew. Weeks of lobbying and head counting by White House officials and the congressional leadership had made clear that Kerrey was the Senate's last uncommitted vote—and the decisive one. The Nebraskan had made plain that he did not like Clinton's economic plan. He thought it did too little to attack the budget deficit and avoided the hard long-term questions of runaway entitlement spending that he believed were imperiling the country's future. He thought that the plan, like Clinton, was soft and evasive. But for all the bravado of his public image, Kerrey trembled before the implications of voting against Clinton. He would be inflicting a grievous blow on a new president of his own party. Democrats would never forgive him, and his own future as a Democrat might well be over.

After agonizing for weeks, on August 5, Kerrey picked up the phone, called the White House, and asked for Clinton, who was in the Oval Office at the uncommonly early hour of 8 a.m.—an hour that rarely found the president at his best. "Mr. President," Kerrey said, "I'm going to vote no."

"If you want to bring this presidency down then go ahead," Clinton shot back at Kerrey. Self-pity poured out as he spoke. "I was told that this was going to be the good thing to do, and I took on the most difficult problem the country faced and suddenly I'm regretting it. I wish I hadn't done it. All I'm doing is catching grief for doing what everyone knows is the most difficult problem we face."

As Clinton's anger built, Kerrey's did, too. "I really resent the argument that somehow I'm responsible for your presidency surviving," came his seething reply.

"Fuck you!" Clinton exclaimed. After more muttered recriminations—"If that's what you want, you go do it," Clinton told Kerrey—he hung up. The aides in the room, including Stephanopoulos, had expected the rage of the call to continue, and perhaps turn on them. Instead, the president was oddly subdued. "It's going to be a no," he said. Clinton realized he was going to lose on the central contest of his young presidency. For this president, however, the difference between headed for defeat and defeated was significant. He had thirty-six hours before the final Senate vote was scheduled, a long time by the never-say-die ethos by which Clinton lived. The White House senior staff, including McLarty and Gergen, raced to Capitol Hill to tend to Kerrey's bruises from the phone call and begin their importuning anew. It was to no evident avail, but Kerrey did agree to see Clinton the next morning. In the meantime, the Senate vote would be of no consequence unless the House of Representatives also gave final passage. Late that evening, after a day of frenetic presidential phone calls to the final wavering votes, it passed, 218 to 216. Kerrey arrived at the White House the next morning. He and Clinton, both calmer now, sat on the Truman balcony, looking out at the Washington Monument through a heavy summer rain. They had a searching conversation about the state of the country—Clinton felt perhaps he was breaking through Kerrey's resistance—but as Kerrey left he repeated his original stance. "I'm still a no, Mr. President," he said. Clinton, though, told aides he thought Kerry was softening.

He was right. The pressures on Kerrey were nearly as great as those on Clinton. Two of the men he respected most had urged him to vote yes. One was Warren Buffett, the Omaha investor, a constituent and friend of Kerrey's, and also the nation's wealthiest man. The other was Daniel Patrick Moynihan, the New York Democrat and among Kerrey's closest friends in the Senate. Both acknowledged that there were lots of flaws in the Clinton plan, but both said it was better than nothing—better for the country and better for Kerrey. By the end, the supposedly clear-thinking, plainspoken Nebraskan proved Clinton's equal when it came to agonizing and equivocation. He was changing his vote to yes. He called Clinton at 8:20 p.m. that evening to tell him.

That evening, August 6, Vice President Gore, presiding over the Senate, broke a 50–50 tie in favor of Clinton's plan. Clinton had averted a political debacle. The achievement, however, went well beyond that. Years later, the plan he had crafted, never mind the stumbles and clumsy improvisations along the way, was regarded by the nation's financial elite as the essential catalyst to a decade of remarkable prosperity. After years of reckless deficit spending, the country had taken a decisive step toward fiscal reason. It was a modestly progressive step as well. There were tax credits that gave low-income workers a clear incentive to keep working rather than fall onto welfare. There were all manner of other, smaller programs, such as free immunizations for poor children. Not bad for six months' work by Clinton and the Democrats. Not one Republican in either chamber had joined them.

The White House staff gathered for an uproarious celebration in the Roosevelt Room. "Lloyd! Lloyd! Lloyd!" the group chanted when Treasury Secretary Bentsen, an improbable man for chants, strolled in with his usual gravity. Clinton seemed rather detached from the gaiety. Gene Sperling gazed at his boss and saw a man oddly subdued, even a little anxious. Sperling felt he knew why. "He was glad to have won, but this was not how he wanted to govern," Sperling recalled. "He did not like the fact that this had passed with only

Democrats, and he worried the whole process had defined him in a way that was more partisan than he really was."

CLINTON WAS RIGHT TO WORRY. AS THE AUTUMN OF HIS FIRST YEAR IN OFFICE approached, the president was widely perceived as an ideologically flaccid leader. Many commentators, and a good many people in the president's own party, had concluded that the New Democrat image Clinton had fashioned in the 1992 campaign had been a fraud. A succession of controversies since the inauguration—the gays in the military fiasco, the embarrassment over the stimulus package, and now a budget that was identified in the public mind as much for its tax increases as for deficit reduction—had identified Clinton instead as a stale Old Democrat.

Who was the real Clinton? In Washington, efforts to answer this question focused on the jostling camps of advisers Clinton had arrayed around him. Conventional wisdom painted the president as a tortured figure, aiming to please all, but buffeted by irreconcilable advice. By this reckoning there were "moderates," like David Gergen, domestic policy aide Bruce Reed, and the Democratic Leadership Council's Al From, and there were "liberals," like the consultants James Carville and Paul Begala, White House aide George Stephanopoulos, and Hillary Clinton. There was enough truth in this analysis to give it resonance. But it was misleading in one essential respect.

Clinton had very few genuine Old Democrats in his inner circle. Most of the important figures in the White House had gravitated to Clinton because they believed he represented a break from the limp brand of liberalism personified by previous Democratic nominees like Walter Mondale and Michael S. Dukakis. The argument instead was over the tone and direction of a New Democrat agenda. One camp wanted it defined by combat, the other by consensus.

On the side of combat, Carville and Begala believed that Democrats had lost their way in the 1980s by allowing themselves to be sissified. Reagan Democrats had fled the party largely over issues of values and culture, including gun control and abortion rights. There was no prospect of reversing the party's liberal orientation on these issues. But Democrats could regain a tough-minded profile by de-emphasizing these issues rhetorically and re-emerging as a party "fighting for the middle class." Political definitions got forged by combat, and Begala in particular relished opportunities for the Clintons to define themselves by whom they were fighting against—greedy Republicans or profiteering drug companies. In this he was joined by the first lady, who by temperament had an instinct for the political fight. She was the principal sponsor of the political "war rooms" established in Little Rock, and again at the White House during the budget battle. Likewise, Stephanopoulos was a veteran of Capitol Hill, where the parties define themselves by legislative skirmishes and the constant battle to embarrass the opposition and "win the day" as judged by the nightly newscasts. In their instinct to rail against powerful foes and portray themselves as a friend of the average man, this side of Clinton's White House was squarely in a populist tradition in American politics.

On the side of consensus, policy intellectuals like Reed and From fit within a different tradition, one stretching back to the Progressive Era. They believed that Clinton should define himself not by being a more contentious leader, but by being a more rational and civic-minded one. Just as the Progressives wanted to rescue politics from the squalor of big-city boss politics at the turn of the twentieth century, the camp associated with the Democratic Leadership Council wanted to rescue Democrats from the increasingly heavy hand of interest group liberalism. By this reckoning, since the 1960s the party was increasingly the sum of its factions and no longer presented a compelling vision of the nation as a whole. On some questions, such as its support for deficit reduction and free trade, the group was unabashedly more conservative than congressional Democrats. But it angered these people to be portrayed as pastel Democrats, trying to win election by being almost as Republican as the Republicans. There was nothing conservative, they noted, about Clinton's ambitious AmeriCorps program, in which government paid for young people's educations in exchange for a tour of community service. Clinton would prosper by transcending partisan warfare and addressing the problems Americans worried about most— the economy, crime, a loss of community, and a decline in values—with the most sensible solutions. Every effort should be made not to insult Republicans, but to recruit as many as possible to a forward-marching cause.

From two different assumptions—the lure of combat versus the promise of consensus—two contradictory political strategies flowed. In different moods, Clinton was sympathetic to each. Little wonder that neither his Washington audience nor the public beyond yet understood who this president was and what mattered most to him.

It was in this atmosphere of strategic disarray that the president pondered, in the wake of his victory on the economic plan, what he should do for his next act. This was a critical choice. He needed to vault from one success to another, and broaden his appeal in the process.

After the exhaustion of the preceding days, the president's staff was desperate for the Clintons to do what the rest of Washington did in August—go on vacation. A Martha's Vineyard respite had been arranged, as soon as the first family gave word they were ready to depart.

They weren't ready yet. The budget vote had been on a Friday, and that weekend the president and first lady summoned senior staff to a series of meetings in their residence to discuss the battles looming after Labor Day. This grueling pace, a credit to their appetite for work, produced resentments from staff members who did not like being treated as if they had no families or interests of any kind outside the office. Not long after this, Roy Neel, Clinton's exhausted deputy chief of staff, tendered his resignation. Driving away from the White House for the last time, he took his incessantly beeping pager and hurled it into the Potomac River—free at last.

The post-budget meetings were unusually contentious. A main reason was the question of the North American Free Trade Agreement. NAFTA had been negotiated by President Bush, but never passed by the Democratic Congress. It would tear down tariffs and other trade barriers with Mexico and Canada, creating the world's largest free trade zone. Intellectually, Clinton, an adherent of free trade, supported it enthusiastically. Politically, it was agony for him. Labor, the Democrats' most powerful constituency, was adamantly opposed. A year earlier, the problem of what candidate Clinton should say about NAFTA had briefly paralyzed the campaign. He had backed the agreement, but slathered his support with a thick mayonnaise of qualifications that rendered his commitment almost meaningless. Now the problem was what President Clinton actually would do about NAFTA: Should he try to push its passage?

The debate picked up where it had left off a year earlier. Stephanopoulos, speaking on behalf of most of the political advisers, noted that even with a full-scale presidential effort, a push for passage was bound to alienate Democrats in Congress and risked a very probable legislative defeat. Why take such a risk to pass a Republican agreement?

Once again, it was Lloyd Bentsen who had the decisive voice in answering the political team's objections—and Clinton's anguished doubts. At a cabinet meeting, he slammed his fist down on the table for emphasis in front of the president. The gesture stilled the room. NAFTA was not merely good policy, he argued, it was shaping into a critical test of the president's own principles. Did he have the nerve to fight for them? Soon after, Clinton decided that he would lead a campaign that autumn to push the trade package to passage. Because it ran against the wishes of labor, this was a decision of historic magnitude for a Democrat to make.

NAFTA was not the only drama playing out as planning for the fall agenda proceeded. For the first time, Clinton's two main partners in the presidency found themselves in competition. Vice President Gore was eager that the schedule contain ample time for him to publicize a project that Clinton had assigned him: "Reinventing Government"—ReGo, in White House vernacular—a campaign to weed federal agencies of senseless rules, paperwork, and expense. Rage against bureaucratic inanity was bipartisan, and it was especially shrewd politics for a Democrat to take up what historically had been a conservative cause. Gore was determined to make the issue his own.

The talk of NAFTA and ReGo, however, left Hillary Clinton cold. The unveiling of the administration's plan for universal health coverage, her much vaunted project, had been repeatedly postponed, deferring to the imperatives of the budget battle. The first lady was hugely frustrated—and intolerant of proposals that might compete for presidential time and publicity in the fall of 1993. "We've been waiting in line," she complained at one meeting.

The emerging rivalry between the vice president and first lady was obvious but unspoken. Neither could afford to give voice to resentments, though their staffs increasingly did so without compunction. What each was battling for was primacy as the second most influential player in the administration.

In their approaches to government, they were similar in that both were synthesizers: They had minds that gravitated to unifying theories and systems to explain how the world should work. In *Earth in the Balance,* the environmental treatise he wrote as a senator, Gore called for the abolition of the internal combustion engine and urged that environmentalism should be "the new guiding principle for civilization." This was the kind of breathtakingly self-assured statement that Hillary Clinton might make, but not the president; he was a splitter: His mind seized naturally on particulars, which often did not coalesce neatly into a larger worldview. Their minds searched for consistency; his tended to fix on contradictions. It was inevitable that Hillary Clinton and Al Gore would share some of the same frustrations. Both chafed at Clinton's bouts of indecision. In internal White House deliberations, they valued clarity and closure; he cherished debate and the muddle of leaving options open. It was no accident, surely, that he had sought out these two powerful intellects. Beneath Clinton's constant whir of activity lay a passive streak. He needed people of emphatic certitudes to help sharpen his own goals, and to give him the self-confidence to pursue them. He now had two such people nearby, throwing elbows at each other.

AS JARRED AS CLINTON WAS BY THE CHALLENGES HE FACED ONCE HE ACTUALLY arrived in the presidency, the woman who had been his essential partner in the two-decade journey from Little Rock to Washington was doubly shocked. The months since the election had brought persistent personal and professional setbacks. Her father was dead; so was her friend Vince Foster. In the transition, she had dreamed of a virtual deputy presidency, with her reigning over domestic policy. Instead, the proposal to overhaul health care had been subject to repeated delays and postponements. She responded to the frustrations, she later wrote, the only way she knew how: by plunging still further into work.

Eleanor Roosevelt was the comparison everyone liked to make with this first lady. Hillary Clinton, a deep admirer of her White House predecessor, encouraged this. But there was perhaps a better analogy to the role she was fashioning in Bill Clinton's Washington. It was Robert F. Kennedy. Like Kennedy, who served as his brother's attorney general but roamed widely in the most pressing problems of the New Frontier, Hillary Clinton in those days kept an eye on many accounts beyond health care. Like him, one role she assigned herself was to impatiently poke, prod, and question an executive branch bureaucracy that often smothered ideas or fumbled their execution. Most of all, like Kennedy, she saw herself as the president's protector, skeptically judging the motives and loyalty of the staff, legislators, and other courtiers seeking his favor. She took a dim view of many of her husband's West Wing advisers, including Stephanopoulos and press secretary Dee Dee Myers, whom she regarded as too immature and too worried about currying favor with the Washington press.

The assumption in Clinton's White House was that Hillary Clinton's assignment was to do the things that President Clinton did not do well for himself. One such thing was to bring debates to a brisk conclusion. "Hillary is a closer," boasted her friend Susan Thomases. "She does not let things drag on."

Aides learned to watch her body language, the way she would hunch her shoulders and rest her elbows quite deliberately on the table at meetings when some aide had droned on too long. "She was the only person in the White House that people were afraid of," said Jake Siewert, then a young aide in the communications shop.

She had a certain naïveté about this fear. She believed, or claimed to believe, that she wished only to be treated as a professional colleague. What she regarded as constructive suggestions, her husband's aides often took as brusque orders. After meetings, she would repair to her own office with aide Maggie Williams or Melanne Verveer and ask guilelessly whether people were reacting to her suggestions on merits or simply "because I'm first lady." She was surprised and outraged when staff members did not object to things she said at meetings, but then leaked the discussions to newspapers in order to undermine her positions.

From her vantage point, she was hardly omnipotent. To the contrary, she was toiling in the face of constant small burdens and procedural indignities. She regarded her travel as important government business, so that she could speak and solicit opinions about health care. But her trips faced constant problems with logistical support. The military and Secret Service apparatus required for her to move about never seemed to materialize without an argument. The first lady and her staff suspected deliberate foot-dragging. They may well have been right. Once she summoned a young aide to Treasury Secretary Bentsen to her office for a dressing-down. Why could she not get more Treasury financial experts assigned to the health care task force? The young man apologized and said the rules did not allow it. In fact, Bentsen, skeptical of the first lady's commission, had forbidden it.

Hillary Clinton did not understand the mystique around her, and indeed she had a point. She was a novelty, certainly, as a first lady unabashedly immersed in policy. But she had hardly shrouded her goals or values. She was a woman of intense ambition and deep spirituality, who believed that the Clintons' brand of politics could have a cleansing impact on American life. In a widely noted speech at the University of Texas, she pondered, "If we ask, why is it in a country as wealthy as we are, that there is this undercurrent of discontent, we realize that somehow economic growth and prosperity, political democracy and freedom are not enough—that we lack meaning in our individual lives and meaning collectively, we lack a sense that our lives are part of some greater effort, that we are connected to one another." Michael Kelly, writing in an influential and highly skeptical 1993 article in the *New York Times Magazine* titled "Saint Hillary," observed that she seemed to be searching for a "unified-field theory of life."

"That's right, that's exactly right!" she exclaimed.

Her spiritual side had a censorious streak. Far more than her husband, she harbored deep suspicion about the motives and tactics of political opponents. One day that fall she got word that a political aide, Rahm Emanuel, who was helping to try to pass the NAFTA legislation, had planned an event for the White House East Room. Many wavering legislators would be invited to hear a bipartisan delegation, including former Republican secretary of state James A. Baker, speak in support of the measure. Emanuel expected praise for creative use of the elegant White House social room, something he believed the administration had been too shy in using to win support for its goals. Instead, he picked up the phone to hear the first lady calling from Camp David, nearly sobbing in anger. "What are you doing inviting these people in my home?" she said. "These people are our enemies. They are trying to destroy us."

IF HER PROBLEMS FORGING AN IDENTITY AS A WORKING FIRST LADY WERE unique, Al Gore's problems as vice president were thoroughly conventional. His challenges, and frustrations, were as old as the vice presidency itself. "I am vice president," said John Adams, the first to hold the office. "In this I am nothing, but I may be everything."

Like his predecessors, Gore was trying to strike a balance between loyalty and dignity. He was searching for the middle ground that would allow him to serve Clinton as an influential adviser while also preserving the independent political identity he needed for a presidential run that everyone knew was in his future.

Gore responded to this classic vice presidential quandary in a characteristic way: He insisted on a formal understanding with Clinton, in writing. One of the most important items in this contract was a regular weekly luncheon— no aides allowed, just president and vice president, with nothing said between them repeated to outsiders. Clinton was admirably sensitive to this request of his vice president. There were some weeks when the weekly meeting was simply not convenient for him, and occasionally his staff would urge that it be canceled. Clinton, one senior aide recalled, "would roll his eyes and say, 'Let's make time for Al.'" Once Clinton was running hours late for a planned departure to Europe, telling his staff he was exhausted and desperate to get some sleep aboard Air Force One during the Atlantic crossing. Gore insisted that they hold their lunch at 4 p.m. before allowing the president to slip free. He regarded this time as inviolate.

As a practical matter, he need not have insisted. Clinton liked hearing from Gore. Not only was the vice president smart, but he had actually run for office and won. Anyone who had done this could count on a deeper measure of respect from Clinton. This extended even to people like Attorney General Janet Reno, with whom the president otherwise enjoyed little rapport.

Like Hillary Clinton, Gore took it as his job to push the president. "Get with the goddamn program," Gore growled once, as Clinton succumbed to doubts during the budget battle. As Gore seemed to recognize, Clinton not only needed to be pushed—he liked it.

Gore was likewise a man with a surprising variety of sides to his personality, some of which could be frustrating. Viewed the way most Americans saw him, he seemed earnest, dutiful, square, and, the word that would become tattooed on his public image, "wooden." Reporters who spent time with him saw something different: a well-read man, shrewd, self-aware and self-mocking, and a wickedly funny observer of the chaos around him. Why, they wondered, did the vice president not reveal this appealing figure—"the real Gore"—more willingly in public? The answer was that this off-the-record figure, while authentic, was itself only a fragmentary glimpse of the real Gore.

As many White House aides knew firsthand, Gore's sense of humor sometimes curdled into acid sarcasm, sprayed casually on those around him. His intellect, while admirably searching, could sometimes be gratingly pedantic. For a while, he got on a kick about the Japanese penchant for "reverse engineering," and seemed to turn every policy discussion into a seminar on that. He was a hawk on the issue of Bosnia, which his fellow interventionist, National Security Adviser Tony Lake, appreciated. Even so, Lake commented to colleagues, the certainty Gore placed in his own views could be a little frightening.

Many West Wing aides soon concluded that Gore's abrasiveness masked a lingering insecurity. Some of this was due to the nature of his office. But in certain ways he was just another staff member, sharing the same men's room as other staff, and jostling for position and access. When members of Gore's staff, like longtime aide Jack Quinn, were recruited to Clinton's staff, the vice president was obviously resentful, "as though someone had switched teams from 'shirts' to 'skins,' " one veteran Gore aide recalled.

While Gore regularly sighed in exasperation at the managerial chaos around Clinton, in some ways he was no more organized in his own work cycles than the president. High-profile public performances in particular seemed to summon his demons. He prepared for weeks in advance of a commencement address at the Massachusetts Institute of Technology. He stood before his assembled staff—part lecturer, part inquisitor—excitedly writing diagrams and phrases on an easel, searching for the right ideas and metaphors for his address. He toured a horizon of academic concepts, such as "complexity theory," "massively parallel systems," and geometric patterns known as "fractals." Despite these long hours of preparation, the speech was still not remotely done the day before he was to speak. So Gore, guzzling Diet Cokes, pulled an all-nighter and finished his speech as the sun rose before his flight to Boston.

In November of that first year, the White House counselor David Gergen caught a vivid glimpse of the puzzling mix of brashness and self-doubt that battled within Gore. The billionaire Ross Perot, still a national figure after his strong independent bid for president in 1992, had emerged as the public face of opposition to the NAFTA trade agreement. With a vote in Congress just weeks away, the prospects for success did not look especially good. While Clinton would have a majority of Republican support, the president was having little success challenging the pro-labor, anti-trade consensus in his own party. Gore, in a bold move made without clearance from Clinton, challenged Perot to a televised debate on CNN's *Larry King Live.*

Gore burrowed into preparation for several days. On the day of the showdown, in the final practice session at the vice president's official residence at the Naval Observatory, a disaster seemed imminent. "As he stood at the podium," Gergen recalled, "he was damn near frozen . . . only hours before show time, and one of the most experienced men in politics was barely coherent."

However, the short drive, alone with his wife, Tipper, to CNN's Capitol Hill studio seemed to transform the vice president. In ninety dramatic minutes, the momentum of the NAFTA debate shifted abruptly. Gore calmly presented his argument that free trade would produce more jobs than those lost overseas. He needled Perot about contradictions in his record, including his past support for few trade barriers, and how his own businesses and those of his son had prospered from Mexican business deals. Perot, barely in control, sputtered ridiculously, "Would you even know the truth if you saw it? . . . You're lying. You're lying now," and complained about interruptions even when no one was interrupting him. The evening was effectively the end of Perot.

And it was the decisive moment in the NAFTA debate, though there would still be a need for the usual last-minute heroics by Clinton. With NAFTA's passage secure in the Senate, the House of Representatives was the focus of a furious round of lobbying. A steady stream of lawmakers went to the Oval Office with hands out. They got what they wanted—special deals for everyone from broom makers to citrus growers. But Clinton got what he wanted: NAFTA passed the House by 234 to 200. In victory came a reminder that Clinton was leading a diffuse and divided party. Only a hundred of the House's 258 Democrats voted with the president. One Ohio Democrat, Congresswoman Marcy Kaptur, said Clinton had "abandoned the real core of the Democratic Party" and was "the candidate of Wall Street, not Main Street." Such comments were a reminder of the risks Clinton had taken in support of his principles. His win, he believed, would create its own momentum for future battles ahead, including health care. A presidency that at Labor Day had seemed wobbly and unfocused was entering the holidays with new assurance.

Chapter Nine

WHITEWATER

THE GLOW OF VICTORY FROM NAFTA WOULD BE SHORT-LIVED. THAT battle had been about Clinton's policy values. In defeat, his opponents believed they might face better prospects in a battle over his personal values. Their target carried a familiar name from the 1992 campaign: Whitewater.

In the long history of presidential scandal, there was perhaps never a word freighted with more emotion and less precise meaning. In the minds of Clinton accusers, Whitewater became shorthand for cronyism, cover-up, and excess of the financial, political, and even sexual varieties. To Clinton defenders, Whitewater became a synonym for false accusations, partisan vendettas, and prosecutorial abuse. Even people well versed in the burgeoning Whitewater cottage industry soon had trouble remembering, much less explaining, how the whole mess got started. In the beginning, though, Whitewater stood for something specific, and narrow.

The word came from the name of a development of vacation homes along Arkansas's White River. In 1978, when Clinton was attorney general and had just turned thirty-two, the Clintons borrowed money to make an investment in the project. Their partner, and the man who cut them in the deal, was James McDougal. An Arkansas original, a man of bluff talk and can-do spirit, McDougal was well known in influential circles as a political and financial impresario. Clinton had met him a decade before, while working for Arkansas's most esteemed national figure, Senator J. William Fulbright. But Whitewater turned out to be a bum steer. The project languished unprofitably from its beginning, and McDougal proved to be a dubious collaborator for a couple with national ambitions. In the flush 1980s, he began dabbling in finance, becoming the proprietor of an institution called Madison Guaranty Savings and Loan. He turned it into a till. McDougal used Madison's assets, among other things, as a source of ready loans for politicians, including Bill Clinton. Hillary Rodham Clinton, while at the Rose Law Firm, performed legal work for Madison. Boom inevitably went bust, crushing both Madison and McDougal. Taxpayers bailed out the failed savings and loan at a cost of some $50 million, part of the much larger S&L scandal that tainted the decade. McDougal had a psychological breakdown and was put on trial for fraud before winning acquittal in 1990. His once close friendship with the Clintons soured. And so what? The so what, in journalistic parlance, was a suspicion that in return for campaign contributions and other favors, Governor Clinton and his wife had used their influence to curb the regulatory scrutiny that would have prevented or exposed Madison's flimflams before taxpayers got stuck with a large bill.

This was not an entirely frivolous suspicion. But the accusations had a disturbing, if little acknowledged, presumption. The Washington investigative apparatus—Congress, the Justice Department, and the media—that began churning its gears over Whitewater in late 1993 was breaking new ground by focusing on Clinton's pre-presidential career. Historically, the machinery of scandal had been aimed only at alleged corruption by a president in office.

In an earlier generation, investigators might have been kept busy for years pawing through, say, Lyndon B. Johnson's Texas laundry. Was the new standard really an improvement? Like many Clinton scandals, Whitewater was mired in slippery ambiguities. Its relevance to the pressing business of the nation was dubious at best. On the other hand, to let the matter drop required willfully averting one's gaze from genuinely troubling facts. The government agency in charge of cleaning up the S&L mess in 1993 recommended prosecution of Madison for transactions in which the Clintons had at least a tangential role. Inevitably, in the small world of Arkansas politics, all manner of other Clinton associates now serving in Washington had links of one kind or another with McDougal and his tangled financial history. "The narrow issue is simply put: Where did the money go when taxpayers were forced to pick up the tab for the failure of Madison and Capital Management [another Arkansas firm connected to the mess]?" roared the *Wall Street Journal*'s arch-conservative editorial page, "Were these institutions run as piggy banks for a self-dealing circle in Little Rock? Did some of the taxpayers' money go to cut the loss in Whitewater, or to fuel Bill's political ambitions? Why were state and federal regulators slow to curb the abuse?"

"This is a man who rode into Washington on a pledge to end politics as usual, and every time the White House dodges inquiries about the old days in Arkansas, reasonable people begin to wonder about a cover-up and Mr. Clinton's sincerity," wrote the ostensibly more sympathetic *New York Times*. "Based on what's publicly known, there's probably not a crippling scandal here. But the White House is behaving as if there were."

CONFRONTED BY THIS RUDE CHALLENGE TO THEIR INTEGRITY, THE CLINTONS in the last month of 1993 and the first of 1994 faced two critical decisions, one flowing from the other. Their choices shadowed them for the next seven years.

The first decision was whether to make a voluntary disclosure of their own financial and legal records. Reporters for the *Washington Post*, which had been pursuing the Whitewater questions with vigor, had made a written request for precisely these documents.

As the Clintons saw it, the question once again was whether to feed the Washington beast, in the hope it would go away sated, or stand on principle and bring the beast to heel. Accommodation had been chosen in earlier episodes, starting with the January decision to dump Zoë Baird as attorney general nominee. But those other matters did not hit so close to the family home.

The political advisers, including George Stephanopoulos and David Gergen, were uniformly in favor of disclosure. However irritated these men were by Whitewater inquiries, they were products of the Washington culture and subscribed to the capital's conventional wisdom as it had been understood since Watergate: Public disclosure was the only sure defense against accusation. Moreover, they argued, if disclosure was not voluntary, it would soon enough be compulsory, once the investigative machinery began churning out subpoenas—and *that* was to be avoided at all costs. On the other side were the lawyers, led by White House counsel Bernard Nussbaum and personal attorney David Kendall. They lived by the litigators' creed, by which nothing was to be yielded without a fight. During this intramural battle, longtime Clinton counselor Bruce Lindsey, who was himself an attorney, served as the first family's representative. Lindsey, a lean and handsome man with an inscrutable countenance, was far from a neutral arbiter. He was himself deeply offended by what he viewed as a niggling and irresponsible Washington press. If the Clintons released their records, all it would do was produce negative stories, which in turn would produce more questions—and demands for still more records. These were private records, he said. It was time to draw a line.

Lindsey drew exactly that line one day in a visit to the *Washington Post* newsroom. The meeting had been arranged by Gergen, who had arrived essentially to sue for peace— learn what documents the paper wanted and find a way to make disclosure happen. But while Gergen tried to be agreeable, Lindsey grew more irritable and combative with the assembled reporters and editors. When the delegation returned to the White House, Hillary Clinton was outraged that Gergen had presumed to be making disclosure commitments about her personal affairs. The moment marked the end of any effective influence of the Washington veteran she had helped recruit six months earlier. When the president precipitously canceled a meeting Gergen had requested to make his case about how to handle the growing crisis, the adviser thundered to McLarty that it was unacceptable.

Gergen had joined the White House under the promise that he would be given full access to the principals. So the next day, a meeting with Clinton was arranged. To Gergen's surprise, Clinton was accommodating. "I agree with you," he said. "I think we should turn over all the documents." Then the president revealed the passivity of his role in the unfolding drama: "You'll have to speak to Hillary and get her agreement. If she agrees, we'll do it."

The first lady refused to see Gergen. She had already made her views clear at an earlier meeting. "These are my papers. They belong to me," she said. "I could throw them all in the Potomac River if I wanted to."

Why did she feel so strongly? Theories abounded, then and later. Some took her at face value: She simply regarded the family's private papers as nobody's business, never mind the questions being raised by Whitewater. Later, as many of the papers she was shielding were indeed made public—exactly as the proponents of voluntary disclosure had predicted—there were certainly embarrassments within. These included the revelations that years earlier she had scored big through trades in the commodities markets—a fact that seemed a bit hypocritical from a couple that had denounced the 1980s as a "decade of greed." Even so, there was nothing in those documents that would have caused the Clintons anything more than passing discomfort. There was shoddiness, perhaps, but not illegality.

ONE POSSIBILITY THAT WAS WIDELY DISCUSSED WAS THAT HILLARY CLINTON did not wish the Whitewater records made public because they would spur inquiries into the relationship between the president and James McDougal's ex-wife, Susan, which was widely rumored to have been more than platonic. This prurient speculation underscored how Whitewater, for all its arcane records and impenetrable paper trails, always resided in the same neighborhood as sexual scandal.

Indeed, days after the White House had made its decision, the conservative *American Spectator* magazine and the *Los Angeles Times* each published accounts of the president's extracurricular activities as governor. Both accounts drew a lurid and detailed picture of sexual excess, and alleged that the governor regularly used his state police security detail to facilitate his exploits and shield them from his wife. They relied on interviews with state troopers arranged by Little Rock lawyer Cliff Jackson, once a friend but now an antagonist of the president. As the stories were being reported, Clinton's first instinct was to believe he could manage the situation himself. He called several of the troopers in his former detail and raised the possibility of federal jobs with them (though not, he said later, in exchange for silence). This belief that he could massage the situation to ensure a happy result only fueled more stories.

For White House aides, it was excruciating to have to discuss such controversies and their fallout in the presence of the couple. Yet the Clintons masked their own discomfort, in part by adapting the detachment of lawyers—as though it was a case they were discussing and not their own lives. Clinton, recalled press secretary Dee Dee Myers, latched on to a motive he said explained all: The troopers were simply upset because they wanted Washington jobs and did not get them. Hillary Clinton, too, seized on motives, drawing a link between the timing of the stories and the recent success on NAFTA. Both latched on to small contradictions in the stories as a way of dispensing with their contents in full.

Meanwhile, Clinton's chief aide during the Little Rock years, Betsey Wright, who had taken an inventory of the governor's potential vulnerabilities before his presidential run, told Gergen that the stories unfortunately seemed more true than not. Clinton's Little Rock life plainly had been a sprawling mess, and he would spend a long time—longer than anyone could have then predicted—trying to outrun the consequences. The *Spectator* article, in particular, with its oblique reference to a woman named "Paula," would echo.

For the moment, however, the sex stories passed quickly from view. Most of the press, and most of the public, regarded them as titillating but unworthy. Whitewater, by contrast, persisted—less salacious but vastly more worrisome in its potential to undermine the administration.

The decision not to make a voluntary document disclosure to news organizations produced one of the great what-if questions of the Clinton years. What would have happened had the Clintons listened to their political advisers instead of their lawyers or their own instinct for privacy? Might this have released the air from the rising scandal, letting Whitewater drift into obscurity? A voluntary document disclosure would not have satisfied the Clintons' Republican skeptics, of course. However, presuming that a disclosure would have yielded only embarrassments and not clear suggestions of illegality, it almost certainly would have satisfied the Democratic skeptics.

Instead, suspicions about what awkward facts the Clintons were shielding continued to mount. The revelation in late December that Whitewater files had been taken from Vincent Foster's office at the insistence of White House aides increased the frenzy. By the new year, the pressing question for Clinton was whether he would ask Janet Reno to appoint a special prosecutor to investigate Whitewater. Increasingly, the clamor for him to take such a step was ominously bipartisan.

"THIS LOOKS LIKE A MEETING I MIGHT BE INTERESTED IN," THE FIRST LADY said as she walked in unexpectedly on January 4 to a gathering of senior political aides and lawyers assembled in McLarty's spacious West Wing office, scene of now daily hours-long meetings on whether Clinton should accede to the clamor.

As she arrived, Stephanopoulos was making the case for the inevitability of an outside prosecutor. At the time, the law establishing independent counsels had expired, and the president and Congress were still months away from renewing it. But the attorney general still had the power to appoint a "special counsel," a prosecutor who would report to her but exist outside the standard Justice Department bureaucracy—thus enjoying a greater measure of independence and, in theory, public confidence. Reno, who had been resisting such an appointment, could scarcely refuse if Clinton urged her to appoint one. It was an odd circumstance to have a president initiate a criminal probe of himself, but this was exactly what the political team, and at least some of the lawyers, were urging. Stephanopoulos listed his points. As long as the issue dragged on, he told the first lady pointedly, it was going to draw media attention and political momentum from more worthy projects, like her own health care initiative. Meanwhile, even Democrats like Senators Daniel Patrick Moynihan, Joseph Lieberman of Connecticut, and John F. Kerry of Massachusetts were calling for a special counsel. The president should simply bow to the inevitable.

One person who agreed with this view was Harold Ickes, the New York lawyer. He had been blackballed by bad publicity himself a year before in Little Rock. After clearing his name, he was now back, having been appointed days earlier as White House deputy chief of staff. He was by instinct a fighter, but not in this case. "We were confronted by the iron logic of the editorial pages," he recalled ruefully, years later. "If they did not do anything wrong, why not have an investigation and clear their names?"

Hillary Clinton had a ready answer. She had served on the House Watergate committee staff, she reminded the group. She knew what a real scandal was, and she knew what the standards were. Appointing a counsel when there was no legal basis for suspecting wrongdoing was a horrible precedent and an abuse of the process. Of course, this was no matter of legal theory for her. The accusations were an almost physical assault on her own sense of virtue. As she spoke, this usually calm and incisive woman lost control. Tears welled as she turned on Stephanopoulos. As Stephanopoulos recounts in his memoir, she railed, "You *never* believed in us. In New Hampshire, it was just me and Susan [Thomases] and Harold [Ickes] who believed in us. . . . *You* gave up on us. We were out there alone, and I'm feeling very lonely right now. Nobody is fighting for *me.*"

This emphasis on the need to fight—and her impatience at her own team's instinct for concession—was a recurring theme in the days ahead. At another meeting, she contemptuously compared the aides before her to the staff of John Kennedy's New Frontier. "JFK had real men in his White House!" she taunted, as a group of advisers looked sullenly on.

The president himself was deeply torn. As a matter of strategy, he agreed with the political advisers—or at least he told them he did. People from Ickes to Secretary of State Warren Christopher were dispatched, at the president's direction, to talk with Hillary about the unavoidable next step. It was to no avail. ("The biggest fucking waste of time," Ickes reported with his usual bluntness to colleagues.) Emotionally, the president shared his wife's indignation—and was suffering from it more than anyone else. His own patience snapped later that month on his first overseas trip as president, to the Ukraine and Russia. He stormed out of a television interview when an NBC News correspondent asked questions about Whitewater. "You had your two questions," he seethed. "I'm sorry you're not interested in the trip."

But both Clintons were gradually giving up the fight against a nearly uniform front from their advisers. The president himself had little emotional energy to resist. Days before his departure for Europe, his mother, Virginia Kelley, died after a long battle with breast cancer. In a surreal scene, on January 12, Clinton got on the phone from Kiev, Ukraine. It was 2 a.m., local time. Back in Washington, the first lady and a large group of aides sat in the Oval Office with a speakerphone. It was highly unusual for people to meet in the Oval Office when the president was not there. Stephanopoulos again labored through his arguments for a special counsel. White House counsel Bernard Nussbaum offered a highly emotional rebuttal. The special counsel was an "evil" institution, he said. Prosecutors could roam freely and indefinitely, without limits or oversight, and would keep searching until they came up with something as a way to justify their efforts. Nussbaum, who had earlier resisted a voluntary document disclosure, now urged one. The Clintons should even testify publicly before Congress—anything to avoid the appointment of a prosecutor. Now it was the president's turn to get emotional. What Nussbaum proposed would be insane, he shot back; there would be nothing but Whitewater in the news for the rest of the winter.

Hillary Clinton brought the conversation to a close and ordered everyone but David Kendall out of the office. The president's disembodied voice conveyed his fatigue and depression. "Look, I think we've got to do it," he said. "We've got nothing to hide, and if this keeps up, it's going to drown out our agenda." Then, even Kendall left, and Hillary Clinton picked up the phone to talk to her husband alone. She made one last try. "Why don't you sleep on the decision," she suggested. "If you're still willing to do it, we'll send a request to the attorney general in the morning."

"No," he responded, "let's get this over with."

And so it was done. The next week, on the administration's one-year anniversary, Reno appointed a respected New York attorney and former federal prosecutor, Robert Fiske, as special counsel. Clinton soon fired Nussbaum as White House lawyer, after an accumulation of misjudgments convinced the president and his staff that this combative litigator was the wrong choice for such a politically sensitive post. Few of Nussbaum's allies disputed the judgment. But, on the question of Whitewater, the lawyer was a prophet without honor. In the months and years ahead, his dire warnings about the perils of a special counsel were vindicated beyond even his own imaginings.

Chapter Ten

HEALTH CARE

ONE OF THE MOST FOOLHARDY STATEMENTS BILL CLINTON MADE AS president was widely perceived at the time as quite clever. On the evening of January 25, 1994, Clinton went to the podium of the House of Representatives to deliver his State of the Union address. As his wife gazed on from the gallery, he toured the horizon of challenges facing the country at home and abroad with force and fluency. There was one issue above all, however, that people were waiting to hear about. This was health care. In a sense, this speech marked a debut of Clinton as president on his own terms. Deficit reduction was an essential but unpleasant task, hardly the reason he ran for president. NAFTA was a cause he believed in, but he was passing a pact that had been negotiated by a predecessor. Now came the real business. The proposal that he and the first lady had crafted to overhaul the nation's health insurance and delivery system was large and complicated. As he faced the assembled lawmakers, the president told them he was more than willing to compromise on the map by which health care reform was achieved. But, he warned, universal coverage—every American with health insurance—was his non-negotiable goal. Then, in a dramatic flourish worthy of Ronald Reagan,

Clinton brandished a pen and announced: "If you send me legislation that does not guarantee every American private health insurance that can never be taken away, you will force me to take this pen, veto the legislation, and we'll come right back here and start all over again."

Bravo! A roar of applause went up from the chamber. The cheers came particularly from the Democratic side of the aisle. And indeed Clinton's line had been aimed especially at the liberals who then still controlled the House. A year into the Clinton administration, many of these people were impatient with the president. They were a contentious lot, and many were frustrated that a progressive renaissance still had not materialized under this Democratic administration. Many were skeptical as to whether the new president had the stomach for a fight. So the veto threat was intended to allay Washington suspicions that Clinton was a patsy. For Americans watching on television, the waved pen was splendid political theater, sending a potent message that change was coming. Clinton's gesture dominated coverage of the speech in newspapers and on television, exactly as the White House planned.

But the president had embarked on a historic misadventure. The veto threat was a tactical error; it limited the president's flexibility to negotiate and compromise at the very moment he should have been expanding his room for maneuver. Much more than that, it was vividly symbolic of the debacle that unfolded in the months to come. Health care was the story of overreach. This overreach was intellectual, as both Clintons overestimated the ability of smart people to bring a hugely complicated problem to heel. It was political, as they mistakenly interpreted discontent with the status quo as a mandate for deeply intrusive remedies. And in a profound sense it was moral. Filled with confidence in their own good purposes, they raced past sensible objections as if they had been enfranchised by history itself. They saw the year ahead as filled with panoramic possibilities. In fact, 1994 would be a year of jarring limits.

HOW DID THE TWO MOST IMPORTANT POLITICAL FIGURES OF THEIR GENERAtion so dramatically misread the temper of their times? As a political matter, the mystery is how Clinton—a natural accommodator, and a person who instinctually gravitated to the ideological center—eventually came to be seen as occupying the left fringe of the health care debate. As a policy matter, the puzzle is how both Clintons came to embrace a proposal that was so complex. A densely complicated plan gave opponents avenues of attack on multiple fronts. It left supporters struggling to defend the plan with simple language that ordinary citizens, especially those who already had health care coverage and therefore needed to be persuaded that change was preferable to the status quo, could understand.

Part of the explanation for Clinton's choices during the health care episode lies in his own cycles of ambition and retreat. After a year in office, this presidency remained in its romantic phase, flush with Clinton's own lifelong dreams of standing astride great events—of earning "a little asterisk by my name in the billion pages of the book of life," as he once put it as a young man. For a president with such ambitions, health care had an obvious allure. Over the course of several decades it had become a kind of lost arc of the liberal cause. The idea of universal coverage was some of the unfinished business of FDR's New Deal. It had been part of Harry Truman's Fair Deal campaign platform of 1948. Defenders of the existing order, led by the American Medical Association, had always defeated efforts to create a comprehensive right to health coverage. Instead, there were incremental reforms, such as providing coverage for the elderly and poor through Medicare and Medicaid. History would indeed have a place for a president who could enact universal health care coverage. The problem—a recurring pattern in Clinton's life—was that his judgment was invariably clouded when he was in his romantic phase, more focused on expansive ends than on realistic means for attaining them. When the person he relied on most to provide realism and prudent judgment was herself in a vainglorious mood, it was a volatile combination—and a moment of high peril.

But excessive ambition accounts for only part of the answer. Those who would later ask why the Clintons did not pursue a centrist remedy to the nation's health care problems miss the fact that this is precisely what they and many others believed they were doing.

In the first years of the 1990s, the belief that the nation's health care system faced dire problems was nearly uniform across the political spectrum. Some 20 percent of the adult population did not have health insurance; in all, some 37 million Americans lacked it. Even those who did faced rapidly rising costs. Fourteen percent of the nation's economy was devoted to health care, as Clinton had reminded the Congress when unveiling his plan. Canada spent just 10 percent; no other nation spent more than 9. While the United States was home to the most splendid medical innovations, it also tolerated indignities—children of low-income families going without regular checkups; workers afraid to leave dead-end jobs for fear that they would lose health coverage—that most prosperous nations had vanquished. Costs rose as emergency rooms handled crisis care that could have been avoided through conscientious preventive care. Meanwhile, businesses that did offer their employees insurance were staggering under rising costs. Faced with this web of interconnected problems, every serious national politician felt obligated to offer a remedy. On the left, the remedy of choice had long been what Canada offered: a single-payer system of national health insurance. What was good for the elderly with Medicare, the thinking went, would be even better if the benefit was expanded to include everybody. The right emphatically rejected such a government takeover, but many of its solutions were also highly intrusive. Several Republicans, including Senate minority leader Dole, backed a plan sponsored by Rhode Island's patrician John Chafee that would have established an individual mandate for health insurance—opting to save money by going uninsured would be illegal—and offered various subsidies to help people comply.

Against this backdrop, the Clintons sought a middle ground. There were several distinct ideas that animated their health plan. Among its intellectual assumptions was that private insurance, not the government, should continue to finance the health care for most Americans, albeit under vastly enhanced federal supervision. Another assumption was that employers, from whom most Americans already received their health insurance, should remain the stop of first resort. Rather than the individual mandate favored by many Republicans, the president and first lady proposed an employer mandate—refusing to provide coverage to workers would no longer be an option for most businesses.

But the Clintons also introduced two more novel concepts. One was the idea of "managed competition." As it flowered among a group of health care intellectuals in the early 1990s, managed care came to describe a system in which insurance companies would compete for customers under rules strictly enforced by the government. The government would guarantee customers a minimum level of benefits; the insurance companies would be guaranteed a fixed amount of money for every participant in their plans. Within this system, competing companies would have incentives both to design the most attractive coverage packages, in order to attract more customers, and to force hospitals and physicians to find efficiencies, thus holding down costs and improving their own profits. The prophets of managed competition believed they could execute what to skeptics looked like an act of levitation. Market incentives would bring health care costs down for government and business alike; the savings would be captured to provide subsidies to bring down the number of uninsured to zero. Thus, the two most pressing problems in health care—rising cost and inadequate access—would be solved in one swoop. An essential pillar of managed competition, as Clinton proposed it, was a concept known to health care experts as "community rating." What this meant was that every person would be insured at the same cost. Companies would have to cease the long-standing practice of charging people commensurate with individual risk factors like age or pre-existing conditions. Under community rating, the young and healthy would socialize the costs of society's older and sicker population. Cumulatively, Clinton's health care proposal reflected a generous vision of society, but one that built on the status quo rather than tried to pull it up root and branch. It was not a leftist fantasy. Such certifiably non-leftist groups as the U.S. Chamber of Commerce and the American Medical Association had, for a time, endorsed the goal of universal coverage through employer mandates. In theory, the ideas in the president's health care plan were an effort of his lifelong penchant for finding a third way between traditional liberalism and the conservative alternative.

The problem was that these ideas, however coherent and defensible in theory, became enormously complicated once they were given programmatic expression. The health care bill Clinton presented to Congress was 1,342 pages long. To implement managed competition, he proposed creating a series of regional alliances that would be in charge of raising money from employers, negotiating benefit packages with insurers, and regulating the quality of care. In a nation with an ingrained skepticism of bureaucracies, this was for many people a frightening prospect. The opposition had a predictable field day. "We're going to do to health care in America what Stalin did to agriculture in the Soviet Union," brayed Congressman Chris Cox, a California Republican.

NOT SURPRISINGLY, SUCH COMMENTS TOOK THEIR TOLL ON PUBLIC SUPPORT for the Clinton plan, which still had support of a majority, though a steadily declining one. So, too, did "Harry and Louise." They were the television characters, a young couple at home, trying to make sense out of the Clinton health plan but growing increasingly alarmed as they pored over the details at their kitchen table. The insurance industry spent millions making Harry and Louise celebrities in an advertising campaign that began in the fall of 1993.

Given rising doubts in Congress, and the downward trajectory of public opinion, by the start of 1994 it was clearly time for Clinton to cut a deal and find his exit. He could have found large majorities, with substantial Republican support, for all manner of policies that would have made it harder for insurance companies to cancel policies when a person switched jobs, or increased subsidies for low-income workers to purchase insurance for themselves and their children. Such items, while a disappointment when measured against Clinton's ambitions, would have been substantial achievements, and would have improved the lives of millions of people. Why not pocket an incremental victory? The question taunts the Clinton legacy.

Some people who spent time in the Clinton orbit found an explanation in balance-of-power politics between husband and wife. At the president's moments of greatest vulnerability, Hillary Clinton achieved her moments of greatest influence. Among those who believed this was David Gergen. The White House counselor had joined such diverse advisers as Rahm Emanuel and John Podesta in suggesting that Clinton begin looking for a compromise on health care, and in particular in warning against the ostentatious veto threat in January. Presidents use their veto power to stop bad things in bills, he urged, not to support laudable things that are not in them. But Hillary Clinton thought the veto threat was a good idea, and Gergen was struck that Bill Clinton seemed entirely deferential to her on this and seemingly every question. This was just weeks after the *American Spectator*'s embarrassing sexual exposé, and just days after Clinton had acquiesced to demands for a special counsel on Whitewater. "Watching him in that time," Gergen recalled, "it was very much like watching a golden retriever that has pooped on the rug and just curls up and keeps his head down. . . . I think it put him in a situation where on health care he never challenged it in a way he ordinarily would have, had he been under a different psychological situation."

Fear was one part of the equation. But raw admiration was another. The president was dazzled by his wife. And, indeed, when she was performing at her peak she was dazzling even to her critics. Months earlier, appearing before Congress, the first lady had dispatched House minority leader Dick Armey of Texas, one of her husband's most vitriolic opponents, with a few swift strokes. Before her appearance, Armey had told reporters that the Clinton plan looked like something that might have been designed by Dr. Jack Kevorkian, the so-called suicide doctor, who put terminally ill patients to death.

When Armey greeted her by promising to make the debate "as exciting as possible," she noted with a cool edge, "I'm sure you will do that, Mr. Armey."

"We'll do the best we can," said Armey.

"You and Dr. Kevorkian," she shot back without delay, as the room dissolved in laughter and applause.

Armey sputtered, "I have been told about your charm and wit, and let me say the reports on your charm are overstated, and the reports on your wit are understated."

But that intelligence and confidence could curdle into self-righteousness when Hillary Clinton felt her high aims were being frustrated. Ralph Larsen, the chief executive of Johnson & Johnson and a member of the powerful Business Roundtable lobbying group, once observed calmly in a meeting with the first lady that the regional alliances in the Clinton plan sounded more like serious regulatory bodies and not merely benign "purchasing cooperatives" to negotiate better insurance rates, as the administration had claimed. She slammed the table and flared, "I said they were purchasing cooperatives and that's what they're going to be." Another time, in a speech before the American Academy of Pediatrics, she became so angry about the Harry and Louise ads that she threw out prepared remarks and showered vitriol on the insurance industry. Insurance companies "like being able to exclude people from coverage, because the more they can exclude, the more money they can make," she said, adding, "They have the gall to run TV ads that there is a better way, the very industry that has brought us to the brink of bankruptcy because of the way they have financed health care."

It was not merely conservative Republicans and the insurance industry that had doubts about the Clinton health plan. From the outset, it prompted deep and sullen divisions within the administration. The economic team, led by Bentsen at Treasury and Robert Rubin, then heading the National Economic Council at the White House, raised questions but soon learned to muzzle them. It was clear, they decided, that Hillary Clinton had her own mandate from the president, and her own channels for advice. She seemed uninterested in, or even hostile to, their advice, so they soon learned to stop giving it. At the Department of Health and Human Services, Secretary Donna Shalala likewise warned that the administration was on a wrong course with a plan that created an unwieldy bureaucracy. Her objections were dismissed as jealousy that she was not the one put in charge of the reform effort.

Much of the rising discontent within Clinton's own team was focused on Ira Magaziner, Hillary Clinton's deputy and chief staff member in the health care project. A former student protestor, he had spent a successful career as a business consultant, studying ways to reform large and complex organizations. He had known the president casually for twenty years, since his own days as a Rhodes scholar at Oxford.

And like Clinton, he would hold meetings at his warren in the Old Executive Office Building until well after midnight. Quite often, he spent the entire night there. His personal loyalty to the Clintons often translated as a brusque dismissal of any question or doubt about the course the Clintons were traveling.

Donna Shalala, who with mounting frustration was watching the debacle unfold, did not like Magaziner—"Ira was arrogant, rude, dismissive"—but she said he became the heavy when people should have been assigning responsibility further up the ladder. "Bill and Hillary came from Arkansas where they were always used to being the smartest people in the room," she said. "So they just naturally assumed they were the smartest people in the room in Washington, too. Anyone who had any different idea than they had was dismissed as part of the system, and part of the problem."

THE FIRST LADY'S CERTITUDES, AND THE PRESIDENT'S BRAVURA PERFORMANCE at the State of the Union, did nothing to halt the deterioration in the health care initiative's political condition over the next several months. By June, Daniel Patrick Moynihan once again chimed in with a discordant note. There was no chance of enacting Clinton's goal of universal coverage this year, he announced on NBC's *Meet the Press*. Universal coverage might take a decade to achieve. Why not, he urged, immediately pass some more modest reforms? His favored alternative of insurance reforms and subsidies would not lead to universal coverage, but experts estimated it would leave 91 percent of the population covered, a considerable improvement over the current 85 percent. Why not at least move closer to the goal? "We can do better than 91 percent, but 91 percent is not a failure. It's progress," Moynihan said. "And government is about the increments by which you move toward goals you desire."

The irony is that Moynihan had described an approach to governance that was entirely consistent with the president's own philosophy. No matter. The next day, Hillary Clinton warned publicly that the president was still ready to veto anything that fell short of universal coverage. Her refusal to acknowledge political realities was only partly bullheadedness. One signature of the Clinton plan—a defect, as it happened—was that its parts were interlocking. Its features designed to increase access to health insurance worked only if the features for controlling costs also worked, and so on. The belief among the plan's creators was that it could not be modified and scaled back without becoming incoherent.

"The argument we kept hearing was that . . . no part of the plan could work unless all of the plan was passed," said Harold Ickes, who was helping promote it from his new post as deputy chief of staff in the White House. "Maybe that was true substantively, but it was an impossible order politically."

By the summer, the Clintons' instincts—his, urgently craving a compromise; hers, grimly resolved to keep fighting—were in desperate conflict. This private tension slipped briefly into public in July, when Clinton traveled to

Boston to speak to the National Governors Association. Before his old colleagues, Clinton could not help speaking what was really on his mind: finding
some way to extricate himself from what was by now shaping up as a political
and substantive debacle. In his remarks, he backed off from his pledge to accept nothing short of universal coverage, saying "somewhere in the ballpark of
95 percent" coverage would be all right with him. He even said he was flexible
on the idea of employee mandates, a key pillar of his plan.

Clinton knew as soon as he stepped away from the podium that he was in
trouble. The anxious looks on the staff aides rushing to him confirmed it. Minutes later, the White House operator was calling, with Hillary Clinton on hold.
She was in a rage, according to a White House aide who listened to the call.
"What the fuck are you doing up there?!" she thundered. Clinton tried to explain that what he had said was not quite the way it was being reported. She cut
him off. "You get back here right away." When he returned to the White House,
Clinton immediately walked to the residence, a look of dread on his face. The
next day, he issued a humiliating retraction of his remarks to the governors,
professing that he was still committed to universal coverage.

WITHIN A FEW WEEKS, HOWEVER, EVEN THE FIRST LADY BOWED TO THE IN-
evitable, when the Clintons gave George Mitchell, perhaps their best friend in
Congress, the green light to try to negotiate a more modest compromise. This
was a desultory effort that dragged on through August and September, and
then died. By this late date, Republicans had long since made a judgment that
they were not helping Clinton find a health care compromise, and even many
Democrats had abandoned the president. The Clintons were repudiated, and
just five weeks before the 1994 mid-term election. Health care reform had
failed.

The post-mortems on one of the great liberal defeats of the twentieth century would last for years to come. In retrospect, the Washington consensus was
that the Clintons had erred by putting forward a specific health care proposal,
though they had been urged to do precisely this by the Democratic leadership
in Congress. The wiser strategy would have had the president lay down general
principles and let lawmakers of both parties fashion the precise bill. "By
putting his personal signature on health care reform," wrote Paul Starr, an academic who was part of the White House health care team, "Clinton gave the
Republicans an incentive to defeat it and humiliate him." There were other
misjudgments, including the belief that public opinion would gradually push

Republicans toward the Clinton plan, and that a compromise could be struck at the end of the legislative process without a bipartisan foundation at the beginning. "The support they imagined was never there," said Shalala. "They mistook polls saying that a majority of people were concerned about health care as though there was a majority for any particular plan of what to do about health care."

Clinton, too, reached this judgment. There were many moves he wished he could take back, both tactical and strategic. He wished he had sent Congress a set of principles rather than a specific plan, and let lawmakers work out the details. He wished he had moved first with an idea like welfare reform, on which it would have been easier to fashion a bipartisan consensus. "I set the Congress up for failure," he concluded in 1995. By then, he would be living with the painful consequences of that failure.

Chapter Eleven

SEA OF FLAMES

IT WAS COMMONLY ACCEPTED WISDOM IN THESE EARLY YEARS OF THE CLINton administration that this was a president with little spontaneous interest in foreign policy. The popular image was wrong. Clinton had a fluid mind that was curious and knowledgeable about all manner of topics. From his first days in office, he was eager to talk about and study the issue he believed would be the dominant foreign policy problem of his administration, managing the relationship with President Boris Yeltsin and a post–Cold War Russia.

Less than a month in office, he invited experts to the White House for latenight seminars on the Russia problem. He later dispatched a young foreign service officer on his staff, Nicholas Burns, to meet with the man he felt would have sage thoughts on the subject, former president Richard Nixon. The two presidents had circled each other with mutual fascination during Clinton's first year in office. The disgraced ex-president followed the Clinton controversies over Whitewater and the death of Vincent Foster with delight, and blustered to his young aide, Monica Crowley, that there was a scandal in there worse than Watergate. At the same time, he was desperate for attention from the new president, and he dispatched a longtime adviser, Roger Stone, to agitate on his behalf. Stone dutifully hectored Clinton adviser Paul Begala about why the old man was being snubbed. Nixon finally did get an invitation to the White House, a surreal meeting across the generations that even the first lady, who as a young woman loathed Nixon and served on the House Watergate Committee, later recalled fondly in her memoir. When Nixon died in April 1994, Clinton wrote an appreciative eulogy that his staff forced him to tone down. He seemed sympathetic to Nixon's tragic flaws. And, at this early stage of his presidency, he was vulnerable to believing the dubious mystique that surrounded Nixon and foreign policy. This view held that Nixon, for all his abuse of powers and temperamental unsuitability for high office, had been a maestro on the world stage.

Clinton's credulity regarding Nixon and foreign affairs highlighted his notion of foreign policy as shrouded in mystique—a kind of priesthood of which he was not yet a member. His insecurity led him to subcontract his own foreign policy to Warren Christopher at State, Les Aspin at the Pentagon, and National Security Adviser Tony Lake, whose White House suite was just steps from the Oval Office. While Clinton was indeed interested in the world abroad, and reserved final policy decisions to himself, he delegated to others the business of presenting options and worrying about the day-in, day-out implications of decisions. It was a formula destined to create unwelcome surprises.

CLINTON LEARNED JUST HOW UNWELCOME WHEN HE AWOKE TO TWO CRISES on October 3, 1993. In Moscow, Boris Yeltsin had declared a state of emergency and ordered tanks into action to dislodge armed rebels who had taken over the Russian parliament. The precarious Russian experiment in freedom seemed imperiled by the violence. At the same time, in Somalia, U.S. forces were in a horrible firefight against insurgent forces, which had downed two Army Black Hawk helicopters and killed Special Forces soldiers.

Feelings of rage and impotence swept over Clinton as the death toll rose in Mogadishu. He turned to Stephanopoulos and Lake. "We're not inflicting pain on these fuckers," he seethed, as Stephanopoulos later recounted the conversation. "When people kill us, they should be killed in greater numbers. I believe in killing people who try to hurt you, and I can't believe we're being pushed around by these two-bit pricks."

Clinton debated with aides whether he should cut short a trip to California, but the consensus was that this would only heighten the perception of events hurtling out of control. In this case, perception matched reality. By the time he returned to Washington on Thursday, the final death toll was eighteen Army Rangers. The body of one was dragged through the streets of Mogadishu, a ghastly sight that was recorded by cameras and broadcast on the evening newscasts. Clinton's feelings—the indignation that every citizen felt, combined with guilt over his own ultimate responsibility for the debacle—were intensified by the element of surprise. "How could this happen?" he kept asking.

The Somalia mission had been started by his predecessor as a humanitarian venture to open up food supply lines and prevent famine. Gradually, and without a full discussion of the implications, the ambitions had expanded to include imposing political order on behalf of the United Nations, a task that involved disarming warring tribes and eventually included an effort to capture renegade warlord Mohammed Farah Aidid. It was a classic case of what military commanders disparagingly call "mission creep." On a domestic matter, Clinton would never have been so unaware of the implications of his own policies. In foreign policy, however, he assumed the professionals knew what they were doing. In particular, he believed that Joint Chiefs Chairman Colin Powell and Defense Secretary Les Aspin were on top of the enterprise. They were not. Powell, Clinton came to conclude, was biding time until his retirement on September 30—days before the Mogadishu disaster. Clinton was resentful for years afterward. Aspin, meanwhile, shared the general Pentagon skepticism about the Somalia mission. He had denied a request from ground commanders to send tanks and armored vehicles to Somalia. In the days that followed, Clinton complained repeatedly about how he had been let down by his team. He was right.

Yet he knew the responsibility was ultimately his. Congress knew, too. In the days afterward, a bipartisan chorus called for withdrawal from a mission that most people believed had nothing to do with American vital interests. A delegation of congressional leaders arrived at the White House to barrage the president with demands that he bring an end to the Somalia embarrassment. The one thundering loudest, Senator Robert Byrd of West Virginia, was the one who could do the most about it. As chairman of the Senate Appropriations Committee, Byrd held the purse strings on military spending. Taken aback by the ferocity of the exchange and the knowledge that he was bargaining from a position of little strength, Clinton countered faintly that if the United States pulled out of Somalia precipitously, it would send a message to thugs around the world that all you needed to do was draw some blood and watch America go limp. In the end, he managed to strike an agreement that there would be a momentary surge of troops to Somalia, to restore order, followed by an exit by the end of March. National security aide Sandy Berger later recalled these days as the most painful of his eight years in the Clinton White House. The images of dead young men were searing. The spectacle of panicked legislators laying down terms about military deployments to the commander in chief was downright humiliating.

There was another humiliation coming. The thugs around the world that Clinton had warned of did indeed seem to be getting the message about the ease with which they could push around a skittish superpower. On October 11, the USS *Harlan County* steamed into the harbor at Port-au-Prince, Haiti, carrying a group of army engineers and civil affairs experts. They were going to Haiti as part of an accord reached under United Nations auspices to restore that nation's elected president, Jean-Bertrand Aristide, to power later in the month. The so-called Governors Island agreement called for the voluntary departure of the military junta that had overthrown Aristide.

If implemented, it also would rehabilitate Clinton's reputation on Haiti policy, following the embarrassment of his reversal nine months earlier on the question of asylum for Haitian refugees. Instead, Clinton's reputation was about to be further bruised, for the USS *Harlan County* was sailing into Port-au-Prince with good intentions but no power to back them. The ship was greeted at the dock by an angry mob, apparently encouraged by the Haitian military, which hurled stones and taunted, "We are going to turn this into another Somalia." There was no provision for a forced entry. For a day, the *Harlan County* sat piteously offshore. Days after Mogadishu, there was little appetite to send in reinforcements. David Gergen warned that this was a terrible image for the network news, and urged that the ship be turned around. The panicky Clinton team did not consider that being chased away by a Third World mob might be an even worse image. It was, in fact, a defining one: a picture of American impotence and irresolution, an inevitable consequence of a president searching uncertainly for his way in the world.

THESE TWIN DISASTERS FORCED A NECESSARY RECONSTRUCTION OF CLINTON'S foreign policy. One part of this rebuilding was Clinton's recognition of the bad things that can happen when he did not forcefully question and monitor his own policies. This was precisely the same discovery that his hero, John F. Kennedy, made following the failed Bay of Pigs invasion in 1961. The second part of this rebuilding involved personnel.

Les Aspin was undoubtedly a tragic figure. An uncommonly intelligent member of Congress, he was a popular figure among the capital establishment who dined out nightly in Georgetown, and was a friend and source to many of the city's top journalists. His appointment as defense secretary had been eminently logical and promised to be the capstone of a brilliant career. Yet he was made the scapegoat for the Mogadishu disaster, an irony given that he had been among the people warning about the perils of an increasingly open-ended commitment. Aspin had balked at sending armored tanks to Mogadishu, but his supporters countered that these would have had little utility in the firefight, since most of the casualties took place in the opening minutes, before tanks would have been in place. Clinton was unsympathetic, and rightly so. Whatever Aspin's personal culpability for the Mogadishu debacle, it had become painfully evident that his disheveled, mercurial management-by-seminar style—a style that was not so different from Clinton's—was totally unfit for the Pentagon. Clinton already had his problems with the military, and senior commanders were nearly in revolt over Aspin's lax leadership.

It fell to Tony Lake, another old friend of Aspin's, to break the news one afternoon in mid-December at the White House. "Les, I've got some bad news to tell you," he began gently.

"What, you're not leaving?" Aspin asked with concern.

"No, Les," Lake said, "you are."

Weeks earlier Clinton had begun recruiting his choice as the next secretary of defense: Bobby Ray Inman, a respected admiral who acted as though Clinton was lucky to get him (and indeed this was how Clinton felt) but who soon, it turned out, had been less than forthcoming with White House officials about aspects of his personal affairs. The nomination would not fly.

After a failed effort to recruit Senator Warren Rudman, a New Hampshire Republican, Clinton arrived by default at the man who should have been his choice from the outset. William J. Perry, Aspin's deputy, had initially been viewed at the White House as an ideal number-two man. Actually, he was an ideal number-one man. He had none of the partisan zeal characteristic of the Clinton team, and was not an intimate of the president. He was educated as a mathematician, and this showed in his bearing. He spoke in precise, logical, perfectly crafted sentences. Even better, he thought with this same clarity. He had a splendid ability to break a problem down to its essence and calmly lay out the options. Perry had spent an enormously successful career in the shadows of the defense establishment, both at the Pentagon and in private enterprise. While serving in the Carter administration, Perry first recognized the importance of, and gave the critical push to, "stealth" technology, a new generation of radar-defeating weaponry that was the signal advance in U.S. military power in the 1980s and 1990s. Though gentle in manner, he had the temperament of an executive, with an instinct for decision that was much appreciated by the senior officers who had been so frustrated by Aspin. There could have been no better moment for someone with Perry's clear-thinking abilities at the top of a demoralized Defense Department, or at the White House's national security table. After Perry's arrival, Clinton never again faced institutional hostility toward his presidency from the nation's military commanders. Clinton had stumbled upon this wise choice almost entirely by accident.

EVEN SO, BILL PERRY WAS AT BEST A PARTIAL SOLUTION TO THE QUANDARY OF Clinton's foreign policy. The new defense secretary had spent his career immersed in what he called "first-tier" security issues, most of all the problem of avoiding nuclear war while containing the Soviet Union during the Cold War. The problems in Somalia, as in Haiti and Bosnia, were all variations on a different theme: How could a great power exert itself as a force for good in the world? In the strictest sense, none of these places were security issues, since they posed little direct threat to America. The conservative answer was simple: Define U.S. interests narrowly and leave these countries to their fate. The challenge for Clinton, as an internationalist and a man of liberal purposes, was more complex. The United States could not do everything, but it was unconscionable to do nothing. His answer to the dilemma, like liberal internationalists before him, was to make the United Nations the instrument of U.S. leadership. But the October disaster in Somalia had vividly demonstrated the limits of this approach. The American public had little patience for performing good works under U.N. auspices, once the cost was American lives.

Even before Somalia, Clinton's retreat over the United Nations was under way. During the 1992 campaign, he had endorsed a standing U.N. army. Earlier in 1993, a draft administration policy directive that allowed U.S. military forces to be put under foreign command for U.N. peacekeeping missions caused an uproar when it was leaked to Capitol Hill. On September 27, six days before the Black Hawks went down in Mogadishu, Clinton spoke before the United Nations General Assembly and urged steps to make U.N. peacekeeping operations more professionally competent, but he also urged a new era of restraint. "The United Nations simply cannot become engaged in every one of the world's conflicts," he warned. "If the American people are to say yes to U.N. peacekeeping, the United Nations must know when to say no."

Inside the White House, Clinton launched a major policy review on peacekeeping that was aimed at coming up with precise standards that would lead to more nos and fewer yeses. The process was led by Richard Clarke, a brilliant and bullheaded man on Clinton's staff and a longtime veteran of the national security bureaucracy under several administrations. He was later to become celebrated as the man who warned most loudly and prophetically about the perils of Islamic terrorism. In this case, Clarke urged restraint, and the document he drafted that winter became Presidential Decision Directive (PDD) 25, which codified the new limits placed on humanitarian military ventures. The policy expressly rejected a U.N. standing army, prohibited putting U.S. peacekeeping troops under a foreign command, and served notice that the administration was going to reduce the percentage of U.N. costs paid by the United States from 31 percent to 25. It imposed several tests on future peacekeeping operations: They needed to be in American interests, have clear objectives, and have a definite exit date as well as the consent of the warring parties, with a ceasefire already in place. This new language of limits was aimed at satisfying congressional skeptics, but it did not work. Newt Gingrich, then leading the GOP's Republican minority, said Clinton was in the grip of a "multinational fantasy."

....

BUT THE PDD-25'S NEW PSYCHOLOGY OF SAYING NO WAS ALREADY WELL IN place, even before the document's formal announcement in the spring of 1994. The first test was in Rwanda.

On April 6, the president of this small central African country, Juvénal Habyarimana, was on a plane approaching the airport in the capital city of Kigali. The president of neighboring Burundi was also on board. They had been at a conference in Dar es Salaam, Tanzania, discussing solutions for how to end the deadly spasms of tribal warfare between Hutus and Tutsis that were gripping the region. The plane was shot down in a fiery crash, killing the occupants. The perpetrators were Hutu extremists, and their deadly frenzy was just beginning.

By nightfall, thousands had been murdered by the Hutus' methodical rampage, as they shot or took machetes to moderate leaders from their own tribe, as well as every Tutsi they came across. The killing continued the next day, and the day after, and for the next hundred days. What would the world do? What would the leader of the most powerful nation in the world do?

The answer was nothing. Later, Clinton and others fixed on the confusion of the opening days, when information on both the nature and scale of the killing was both slow and fragmentary. As rationalizations go, this was rather wobbly, for within a week there was little mistaking that a genocide was under way. The deputy to the U.S. ambassador in Rwanda had reported this back to Washington. On April 9, the International Red Cross estimated that tens of thousands of Rwandans had been slaughtered, an assertion featured on the front page of the *New York Times*. The *Washington Post* described a "pile of corpses six feet high."

Historians have searched in vain for a fateful moment of decision within the Clinton White House. There was none. The possibility of intervention in Africa to halt the genocide was never raised. The U.N. Security Council soon backed the removal of all but 270 of the 2,500-man force that had been in Rwanda. Meanwhile, the State Department labored to avoid declaring the mass killings a "genocide." Invoking that term, lawyers warned, imposed an obligation to intervene. "The use of the term 'genocide' has a very precise legal meaning," said State Department spokeswoman Christine Shelly from the press podium at Foggy Bottom. "We have to undertake a very careful study before we can make a final kind of determination." Meanwhile, the Pentagon rejected even modest measures, such as bombing the radio facilities that were spewing hateful propaganda and instructing Hutus to kill their Tutsi neighbors.

Tony Lake later searched his memory for an explanation of how unthinkable killing had been allowed to continue. "I was obsessed with Haiti and Bosnia during that period, so Rwanda was, in journalist William Shawcross's words, a 'sideshow,' but not even a sideshow—a no-show." He added: "I think it didn't arise for us because it was almost literally inconceivable that American troops would go to Rwanda. Our sin, I believe, was not the error of commission, or taking a look at this issue and then saying no. It was an error of omission—of never considering that issue. I would think, especially in the wake of Somalia, that there was no chance that the Congress would ever have authorized funds to send American troops into Rwanda."

The president, for his part, offered an occasional commentary that spring that reflected none of the anguish he later said he'd felt. On April 8, in Minneapolis, he made an oblique reference to the "situation in Rwanda," adding, "I want to mention it only because there are a sizable number of Americans there" who he promised would be evacuated to safety. On April 30, he spoke of Rwanda in a radio address—not his main Saturday morning address, which noted the imminent fiftieth anniversary of D-Day and appealed for "vigorous American engagement . . . around the globe"—but a second, shorter address taped for distribution to a smaller number of stations later in the day. "The pain and suffering of the Rwandan people have touched the hearts of all Americans," he said. "It is time for the leaders of Rwanda to recognize their common bond of humanity and to reject the senseless and criminal violence that continues to plague their country." At a news conference on May 3, a Ugandan journalist asked Clinton if the United States and United Nations might "save lives" in Rwanda. "Well, perhaps," Clinton replied, noting that "the conscience of the world has grieved" over events, but adding that the Somalia experience showed "there is a political and military element to this" that cannot be easily addressed by outsiders. On June 7: "We do want very much to try to help in Rwanda." On July 22, as he announced that the United States had finally dispatched the military to provide security and clean water at refugee camps on Rwanda's border, Clinton boasted, "From the beginning of this tragedy, the United States has been in the forefront of the international community's response."

By this time, starvation and disease were still taking lives, but the murders had finally subsided. An estimated 800,000 people were killed.

AT THE VERY SAME TIME AS THE RWANDA GENOCIDE, ANOTHER SECURITY CRISIS was building. This one, too, barely penetrated American consciousness. June 1994 was the month of O. J. Simpson's white Bronco chase and his arrest on murder charges. It was just a few weeks after a woman named Paula Jones filed a sexual harassment lawsuit against the president. Yet few people remember it as the month when the United States stood on the edge of a war that, had it erupted, would almost certainly have killed hundreds of thousands of people.

This was where the country, and President Clinton, stood on June 16 as he sat in the Cabinet Room with his national security team contemplating a crisis on the Korean Peninsula. Despite a sullen armed truce, North Korea and South Korea had remained in a state of declared war since 1954. The United States continued to station some 30,000 U.S. troops in South Korea, ready to honor a commitment to defend the nation from an attack by some one million North Korean troops positioned menacingly just over the border. In the spring of Clinton's second year, that commitment was no longer an abstraction. But this was no post–Cold War dilemma about whether to use the military as international social worker. This was a national security crisis of the old-fashioned kind.

In March 1993, North Korea's reclusive and paranoid regime, which had cloaked the nation from the outside world and ran a failing Stalinist economy that left millions of its people starving, began a purposeful confrontation. The North Koreans threatened to withdraw from the Nuclear Non-Proliferation Treaty, which allowed international inspections of North Korea's nuclear reactor at Yongbyon. Without inspections, there was every reason to suspect that the North Koreans would try to process spent nuclear fuel into weapons-grade plutonium for bombs. If so, they could have a half dozen of them within several months. This would shift the balance of power on the peninsula, possibly enticing the regime in Pyongyang into believing it could win a war against its mortal enemies to the south. Moreover, North Korea was a notorious proliferator. It previously had sold missile technology on the world black market. Clinton had already declared that allowing an outlaw country like this to have a bomb was unacceptable.

There was no way to back up his rhetoric, however, without being willing to accept the risk of an outcome that was itself virtually unthinkable: a major regional war that would be far larger and more lethal than the Persian Gulf War of 1991. Clinton was fortunate that he had settled on Bill Perry as defense secretary. But Perry was not an entirely comforting presence for the White House. With his mathematician's instinct for precision, the administration's old habits of trying to muddle through security problems without clear policies or end points were unacceptable to him. Within weeks of taking the Pentagon post, Perry began giving interviews in which he stated bluntly what until then had been left unspoken by Clinton: The administration was so determined to avoid letting North Korea build bombs that it was prepared to risk war—and soon—in order to stop it. This caused jitters in the White House and State Department, where officials wanted Perry to tone it down. He wouldn't. The defense secretary did not want war any more than Clinton did. Few people in the government understood more vividly than he did how horrible, in American and Korean lives, a war on the Korean Peninsula would be. But he was prepared to accept danger in the near term to avoid even more catastrophic danger in the long term. Clinton agreed, albeit with understandable anxiety.

One military option that the Pentagon studied was a preemptive bombing of the Yongbyon facility. But such an action might well have triggered a North Korean attack on South Korea. For this reason, Perry favored "coercive diplomacy"—a negotiated settlement backed by the threat of military force. Such a strategy, of course, could work only if the threat of force was credible. With Perry's presence in Clinton's cabinet, it became considerably more credible than before.

The North Koreans had their own ways of concentrating Clinton's mind. The administration had threatened to seek international sanctions if the north refused to consent to inspections. The North Koreans did not budge. What's more, a North Korean negotiator replied, if sanctions were imposed, his country would consider it an "act of war" and turn the South Korean capital into a "sea of flames." Many South Korean leaders and American commanders on the Korean Peninsula thought that, given the paranoia of the North Korean regime, the only responsible answer was to prepare for possible war.

This was the agenda at the White House on June 16. Perry and the new chairman of the Joint Chiefs, Army General John Shalikashvili, who had replaced Colin Powell the previous autumn, went to the White House to present military options. Eager to underscore the gravity of the occasion, Perry began his presentation to Clinton and Vice President Gore with a quote from the economist John Kenneth Galbraith: "Politics is not the art of the possible. Rather it consists of choosing between what is disastrous and what is merely unpalatable." He likewise cited the historian Barbara Tuchman, who had depicted in her famous history *The Guns of August* how leaders in 1914 had let events overtake them and drifted into world war. With this preamble, he served his unpalatable news. The Pentagon wanted to dramatically increase its troop strength in South Korea to prepare for a possible attack from the north. The risk, he noted, was that the buildup itself would be seen as provocative by the hair-trigger North Koreans, who might choose to attack immediately, before the reinforcements were in place. Clinton was grimly quiet, not the garrulous and excitable presence he sometimes was in less serious meetings.

While Perry was describing his recommended military avenue, there was simultaneously an odd diplomatic avenue being pursued—with deep reluctance at the White House. Former president Jimmy Carter, concerned the countries were lurching toward war earlier in the month, had accepted an invitation from North Korea's aging "Supreme Leader," Kim Il Sung. Most White House officials were unenthusiastic about Carter, for whom Clinton had ambivalent feelings at best, getting involved in this sensitive issue. Warren Christopher regarded Carter's foreign policy freelancing as deeply irresponsible. But Vice President Gore was more supportive. When Carter had sent Clinton a letter stating that he was going to North Korea no matter what Clinton thought, Gore intercepted it and told Carter that if he changed the wording to say he was "strongly inclined" to go, making it sound less like an ultimatum, he would try to bring Clinton on board. Carter was going as a private citizen, not an official representative, Gore told Clinton. Perhaps some good would come of it.

Back in the Cabinet Room, meanwhile, Clinton agreed with Perry about the imperative of a troop buildup. Just as Clinton was set to approve the decision, the meeting was interrupted by a phone call. Carter was on the line from North Korea. Robert Gallucci, the State Department official in charge of Korea negotiations, spoke to the former president. The North Koreans would agree to freeze their nuclear program, Carter said, pending direct negotiations with the United States. This was greeted in the room with skeptical curiosity—everything was in the details that weren't yet clear. Carter also said he was going on CNN within minutes to tell the world about his astonishing success. The room erupted: This was the hazard in dealing with that pious showboater, many of Clinton's aides believed. He was preening for the cameras while limiting the president's options. Carter went way over the line in his CNN appearance, wrongly implying that the United States had already agreed not to impose sanctions. Still, the essence of the Carter deal held, and the next month negotiations between the United States and North Korea over the fate of the nuclear program began. On that same day, Kim Il Sung suddenly died of a heart attack. His son Kim Jong Il, an even more reclusive figure, came to power.

LATER, CLINTON EXPLAINED HIS REASONING, IN WORDS THAT ILLUMINATED his broader philosophy about dealing with foreign adversaries: "Look, I knew I was going to take some heat for letting Carter go there. But I also knew we needed to give the North Koreans an escape hatch, some way to climb down without losing face. I figured if they could say to themselves that a former president had come to their country, it would allow them to do that."

Among those who were content with the awkward Carter intervention was Perry, who felt the important thing was to get North Korea's nuclear program dismantled—far better by talking than by war. But it really was Clinton who deserved the credit for averting twin catastrophes—a nuclear-armed North Korea, or a war to prevent this—even if Carter was winning the headlines. The final chapter of the Korean episode stretched out over several months. The United States negotiated an "agreed framework" in which North Korea would give up its nuclear program at Yongbyon in exchange for a rich program of assistance provided jointly by the United States, South Korea, and

Japan. The nations would build light-water reactors, which do not present a proliferation risk. This was a bitter pill for many in the United States. Conservatives, including Senator John McCain of Arizona, called it "appeasement." Unquestionably the coercion in "coercive diplomacy" worked both ways. The agreed framework became even more controversial years later, after revelations that the North Koreans had cheated on some of its provisions. The agreed framework may have been ultimately unsatisfying, but it did keep North Korea from assembling a nuclear arsenal for the next decade, and thus averted the most likely alternative policy: war. It was a classic Clinton policy—a mix of blurred lines and improvisation, with some good luck thrown in.

Clinton's foreign policy was still far from a robust enterprise, but its rehabilitation was under way.

Chapter Twelve

FLOOD LEADS
TO FORTUNE

NLIKE THE LUNATIC REGIME IN NORTH KOREA, THE STRONGMEN WHO ruled Haiti could not threaten a sea of fire. It was well within their power, however, to create a sea of despair. And so they were doing still in 1994, as desperate Haitians continued to flee poverty and torture in rickety homemade boats, and continued to be turned back by U.S. ships patrolling the Caribbean. This was the policy that Clinton had approved in January 1993, after retreating from his campaign promise of asylum for political refugees. This reversal, combined with the USS *Harlan County* debacle the previous autumn, meant that for Clinton, Haiti had become synonymous with humiliation.

"This is the same shit we've been talking about for a year!" he interrupted in exasperation in the spring of 1994, in the middle of a dispirited national security meeting about Haiti options. The ultimate solution to the Haiti crisis had been growing obvious for months. U.S. forces would need to forcibly evict the military regime and restore democracy. This was a modest military challenge, but a formidable political one. Haiti's dictatorship, however odious, posed no threat to U.S. national security. There was no clear exit strategy. How long might U.S. forces have to stay to ensure a good result? Most of all, domestic public opinion was solidly against intervention and would be intolerant of any military casualties. Under an invasion, there almost surely would be some. Even a ragtag army can fire machine guns on its way to defeat. Haiti was a prototypical example of how liberals and conservatives had reverted to their traditional pre–Cold War roles—gone "back to the womb," in historian Arthur Schlesinger's piquant phrase. Those agitating to use force in Haiti were mostly liberals, represented especially by the Congressional Black Caucus. This time it was conservatives, as in Bosnia and Rwanda, who recoiled from the assertion of American power. Among the larger electorate, polls showed considerable skepticism that the United States had any good reason to intervene in Haiti. Eager to act in Haiti, but not eager to defy such opinion, Clinton hoped for circumstances that might build public pressure to enable him to act.

This desire led to one of the oddest remarks he ever uttered as president. Randall Robinson, who had been promoting the Haitian cause as president of TransAfrica Forum, had begun a hunger strike to protest what he deemed the bankruptcy of Clinton's policy of turning away refugees. Far from taking offense, Clinton was supportive. "We ought to change our policy. It hasn't worked," the president said in April. "For the last ten days . . . I've done almost nothing but work on Bosnia and Haiti and one or two other foreign policy issues. He ought to stay out there."

Robinson, his body wasting, was incredulous. "To have the president suggest that the policy should change and I should stay out there on a hunger strike while he abdicates his responsibility is deeply disturbing," he complained to the press. "The president can make the policy effective and humane with a stroke of a pen, and he has not changed a thing. It's sad to say, but he appears to be without a moral compass."

This was a misreading. Clinton had a compass. But he had other factors to weigh. His rather transparent calculation of these factors conveyed an unfair but understandable impression of aimlessness. Robinson was confronting the paradox of the Clinton leadership style, in which his activist intentions were coiled around a curiously passive streak. This style could be maddening, no doubt, but it could also be quite useful for a politician who preferred—and needed—to preserve his options.

Perhaps the most vexing dimension of the Haiti problem was Jean Bertrand-Aristide. The radical priest and the elected president of Haiti was a democratic hero to many in the Haitian populace, and to many on the American left. The right viewed him as a fraud—a mentally unstable man whose movement specialized in necklacing (placing gasoline-soaked tires around the necks of opponents and setting them aflame) and other liberation horrors. In speech, he favored Creole proverbs and riddles. There was a 1991 CIA report, whose contents were widely publicized, suggesting Aristide had gone off the deep end, in the grip of wild and panicky mood swings. Amid these conflicting interpretations of the central character in Haiti's drama, the Clinton administration was awkwardly aligned. The president and other officials were publicly committed to Aristide; privately they harbored deep doubts about him, and discussions of his reliability occupied many Oval Office hours in 1993 and 1994.

AN EXAMPLE OF THE MISGIVINGS ARISTIDE STIRRED CAME ONE AFTERNOON that spring, April 21, 1994, when Deputy Secretary of State Strobe Talbott and Tony Lake were scheduled to meet with the deposed president and Robinson. The administration emissaries were planning to share with the exiled leader what they presumed he would regard as welcome news—that the United States would tighten economic sanctions against Haiti to put new pressure on the regime to step down from power.

An hour or so before the meeting was to begin, Talbott and Lake were aghast to read a story that had just moved on the Associated Press wire. Clinton's policy on Haiti, Aristide had hours earlier averred at a news conference, was both a "cynical joke" and "racist." Both exasperated and genuinely offended, Talbott and Lake recommended to Clinton that they call off that afternoon's meeting. Clinton was gnawing on an unlit cigar—a habit that gave him an outlet for nervous energy, while not running afoul of Hillary Clinton's no-smoking policy at the White House—as Talbott read him the wire. He grew redder in the face the more he heard, then began to vent—not so much at Aristide's rude comments as for the bind they put Clinton in. This kind of thing, Clinton said, just gives more proof to "those who say he's a whacko." He agreed that they should postpone their meeting.

Just as Talbott and Lake were filing out the door, however, Clinton summoned them back. "Wait a minute," he mused. "Let's think this through."

What he wanted to think through was how the episode would play out in the media. The press corps was rarely far from his thoughts, and concern about how stories would echo often weighed heavily on his domestic and diplomatic decisions alike. "If you postpone the meeting for twenty-four hours, people will think you've cobbled the new policy together 'cause of what he said today," Clinton mused. "If you see him today, nobody will think we did this in thirty

minutes." Clinton ordered Talbott and Lake to carry on with their plans. And
he said they should take a message directly from the president to Aristide: "Tell
him I'm the best friend he's got in this country."

FOR THE NEXT SEVERAL MONTHS, CLINTON GRADUALLY SOUGHT TO MAKE HIS
Haitian refugee policy more humane and prepare for the crisis such a policy
would inevitably yield. First, he modified the policy of immediate "direct return" to those Haitians plucked from the sea by the Coast Guard. Now
refugees would be able to have on-board asylum hearings, to see if they qualified for protection as political refugees. Soon enough, this change prompted
a human flood of would-be émigrés—the same problem that caused Clinton to waver back in January 1993. By late June, the deluge forced the administration to begin housing the refugees inside fenced camps at the nearby
U.S. naval base at Guantánamo Bay, Cuba. This was a short-term fix—and a
dangerous one. Thousands of people sweltering inside the camps was a virtual invitation for rioting. But sending the people back to an undemocratic
Haiti, where many would doubtless be tortured or killed, would be a humanitarian outrage.

On July 1, the crisis mounting, Clinton cleared his schedule to deal with
the Haitian problem. He was meeting with his national security team when an
aide walked in with a note. Bill Gray, a former congressman who had been recruited by Clinton to help coordinate Haiti policy, read it first, then slid it
across the table to the president. It read: "Coast Guard has just picked up 800
Haitians and they expect to pick up a total of 1600 by the end of the day." Clinton had been previously told that the Coast Guard and military forces in the
Caribbean could deal with a maximum of 1,000 refugees a day, and even at
that rate Guantánamo would be over capacity in a couple of weeks. Clinton
read the note with a woeful look and sighed, "I guess this is what we are up
against." Events were overtaking him.

Clinton mused that perhaps he would have to discourage the migration
by reversing course yet again and going back to a direct-return policy. Strobe
Talbott, who was taking a lead role on Haiti, warned that such a move would
be devastating to Clinton's foreign policy generally. Flip-flopping on a policy
that was already the result of an earlier flip-flop would be the new metaphor
for those who regarded Clinton as indecisive and incompetent in foreign affairs.

David Gergen, then winding down his turbulent administration tour, spoke for the other side. A Haitian intervention would be unpopular enough. If Clinton was perceived to have been forced into an invasion because his own policies let the refugee problem get out of control, he warned, "there would be political hell to pay."

At this, Clinton piped up loudly, "I know what I'd say if I were attacking me: You got yourself into this mess by letting Randall Robinson's hunger strike dictate U.S. policy. You should have let the sucker die rather than let yourself get pushed around by him this way."

This outburst illustrated an odd tic of Clinton's mind. He was never more incisive in argument than when he was critiquing his own positions. It often happened before news conferences, when he would summon his aides to practice questions and answers. To any proposed answer, Clinton would instantly seize on its vulnerabilities, jumping ahead to the two or three logical follow-up questions faster than any reporter would have managed.

He noted that the 1983 invasion of Grenada was against "a pissant country.... We took too many casualties because the military screwed up the operation, but there was no press there to know how bad it was." The 1986 bombing of Libya "was an in and out deal," and when the occupation of Lebanon went awry "he [Reagan] had enough sense to get out." Apparently no modern president had dealt with a problem quite as vexing as Haiti.

THE BALANCE OF THE SUMMER WAS A SEASON OF NOT ENTIRELY ARTFUL IMprovisation. Refugees kept flowing. The administration was forced to double capacity at Guantánamo Bay, to 23,000 refugees, and had persuaded the Caribbean nations of Antigua, Dominica, Grenada, Suriname, and St. Lucia to house refugees. Finding ever more places to house refugees was plainly not a long-term answer. The logic supporting an invasion was more obvious than ever. The political undesirability of that course remained equally obvious.

Everyone on Clinton's team was sympathetic to the reasons for his indecision, but everyone was growing increasingly impatient with it. This was especially true of the vice president.

Among Gore's roles in internal deliberations was to play the cutup. During that summer, he and Talbott could sometimes lighten the mood by engaging Clinton in parlor games about which states would be the best options if the administration was forced to start housing refugees in the United States. "Utah," Clinton responded, naming one state he was not about to carry in 1996. Gore indulged his gift for mimicry. The vice president did a devastating impersonation of Aristide, as well as of President Jimmy Carter, who by late summer was agitating with increasing persistence for a role in negotiating a settlement to the crisis that would avoid a U.S. invasion.

The bantering humor that Gore maintained with Clinton served as a tension breaker. It also helped grease the friction that might otherwise be caused by his most important role—as the person who could end debates and push the president toward closure. At an August 26 meeting, he argued that Congress would never come around to actually supporting a Haiti intervention on the merits. Congress was almost by definition feckless—ready to criticize a president but not itself able to lead. The president's role, he lectured, was to be bold and take the right action. Public support, and the necessary congressional funding for a major foreign operation, would follow in due course. The vice president, though a rather cautious politician, had a romantic view about leadership and power. "There is a tide in the affairs of men," he said, invoking the line from *Julius Caesar,* "which, taken at the flood, leads on to fortune."

Gore urged setting a precise date for invasion. "We need a pivot point" around which to plan. The vice president had recently torn his tendon while playing basketball with his former congressional colleagues in the House gymnasium. To soften the bluntness of his lecture, which stopped just a hair shy of hectoring, Gore pointed to his crutches and added ruefully, "Not that I am anyone to be talking about pivot points."

Gore had carried the day. The invasion was set for no later than September 20.

ON THE MORNING OF TUESDAY, SEPTEMBER 13, CLINTON WENT INTO THE OVAL Office after a night spent talking on the phone to congressmen dead set against invasion. "After those fucking phone calls, I guess we'll have something to show those people who say I never do anything unpopular," he groaned to his assembled aides. Indeed, a *Time* magazine poll showed nearly 60 percent of the public opposed to invasion, and nearly 70 percent opposed to military action without the consent of Congress.

That Thursday, on national television, Clinton made his best case yet for why American force would be needed to intervene in Haiti. The effort was somewhat belated in the eyes of critics who believed he should have begun weeks or months earlier to build public support for the mission. Even so, he was effective in instructing Americans to the brutality of the regime; he cited a young Haitian boy who said, "I do not care if the police kill me, because it only brings an end to my suffering." The president warned the junta: "Leave now, or we will force you from power."

It appeared a forcible entry was inevitable.

But even as Clinton spoke, another avenue was opening. It was Jimmy Carter, who once again was involved, whether Clinton wanted him or not. In the previous weeks, Carter had had several phone conversations with Raoul Cédras, the chief of the military junta that denied Aristide his elected office. Carter was proposing to the administration that he travel to Haiti to find a settlement that would have Cédras and his regime leave power voluntarily and avert an invasion he thought would be a grievous error. Hanging over this proposal, Carter made clear, was the possibility (or was it actually a threat?) that he would go to Haiti on his own if Clinton did not authorize an official mission. Clinton was supposed to call Carter after the 9 p.m. Oval Office speech. Instead, he brooded over the idea for the rest of the evening. In Georgia, Carter stewed. Try as both men might to keep appearances tidy, the reality was that they neither understood nor liked each other. Finally, around midnight, Clinton called Carter and gave the go-ahead for the mission. At Carter's suggestion, he was accompanied by former Joint Chiefs chairman Colin Powell, and Senator Sam Nunn of Georgia. It was an astonishing trio. Clinton had complicated relationships of resentment and admiration with all three; each of them, in turn, had in various ways private and public previously made plain their misgivings about Clinton. That the president would approve such a mission, by such a delegation, reflected equal measures of desperation and self-restraint. Clinton genuinely felt it was in his personal interest, as well as the public interest, to exhaust every alternative to invasion. Even so, it was a considerable gamble. All three negotiators were publicly opposed to an armed intervention in Haiti. Clinton was putting his fate in the hands of the most prominent opponents of his own policy. What if Carter announced he had a deal that made an invasion unnecessary? Even if Clinton thought the deal was bad, it would be that much harder to send troops in on an unpopular mission.

News of the delegation's trip did not break until Saturday, by which time Carter, Powell, and Nunn were already in Port-au-Prince. The three men were under instructions to conclude their talks by midday Sunday. The president was in the Oval Office that morning, joined by his secretaries of state and defense, and several others on his national security team. Would the day before them bring a last-minute peace or the first major military conflict of Clinton's presidency? Noon, the deadline, arrived—and with it a reminder of why the skeptics on his team had been right about the hazards of the Carter mission.

Instead of an answer, the negotiating team in Port-au-Prince sent a fax filled with questions. Did all three of Haiti's military rulers need to leave the country or just the leader, Raoul Cédras? Did the military triumvirate need to formally invite a U.S.-led military force into Haiti, or could this be left for their successors? Why was Philippe Biamby, who had not been the focus of the previous summer's aborted agreement at Governors Island, now being identified as someone who had to go? The question alone betrayed a certain naïveté; Biamby had a reputation for singular brutality against Haiti's own citizens.

"Apparently," said Defense Secretary Perry, after he had read the fax, "Biamby managed to convince them that he's Bambi."

Shortly after sending the fax, Carter himself called Clinton on an unsecured cell phone with a spotty connection. "He keeps beeping out on me," Clinton fumed. Carter was reporting that he was on the brink of a deal, but the details were not anything Clinton would be happy to learn. Indeed, later, when the team in Port-au-Prince faxed in a proposed settlement, there was a chorus of groans and curses in the Oval Office. "No, no, no," Clinton kept repeating, as he read through the passages.

The proposed deal was defective on multiple counts. It did not provide a specific date by which the military triumvirate would leave power, and indeed left the departure contingent on the Haitian parliament conferring amnesty on them for potential political crimes. It said nothing about the military leaders going into exile, as Clinton administration officials previously had said they needed to do. Before leaving for Haiti, Carter and his delegation had made three commitments: to discuss only the junta's departure and not enter into a negotiation about a Haitian political solution, to finish talks by noon on Sunday at the latest, and to do nothing to undercut Clinton and his options. All three commitments had been cast aside.

Clinton believed that Carter, Powell, and Nunn had been snookered, accepting Cédras's view that he was honorably trying to save Haiti from further instability and chaos. "They have been listening to nonstop shit about Aristide," Clinton said. "These guys have not seen the body parts."

But Carter, and Powell and Nunn, too, were arguing that the agreement was a good one, and it would be very hard for Clinton not to accept it. The lack of a precise exit date was the only sticking point. Clinton insisted on October 1. After hours of negotiation, the team in Port-au-Prince came back with a final offer of October 15.

Meanwhile, time was more precious than anyone in Port-au-Prince was aware. Everyone sitting around the negotiating table knew a U.S. military invasion was imminent if a deal was not struck. They did not know it had been scheduled for that very night. All Sunday afternoon, as the talks dragged on,

U.S. soldiers, sailors, marines, and airmen were in the countdown for an attack. In the Oval Office, as Clinton simultaneously worked two crossword puzzles in mid-afternoon, General Shalikashvili told Clinton that if he wished to preserve the possibility of an invasion that night, army paratroopers would have to start preparing their chutes now.

"Pack 'em," Clinton said.

Hours later, after 6 p.m., talks were still going on, even as planes were taking off from Pope Air Force Base in North Carolina, only a couple of hours from their destination. On the phone with Carter, Clinton finally made clear there was no more time for talking. Sharply, he told Carter and the delegation they needed to leave immediately.

At just this moment, there was a fortuitous breach in security. Biamby had somehow gotten word about the departing airplanes. He barged in on the talks. "The invasion is coming!" This did tend to focus the mind. At the last moment, the Haitian triumvirate agreed to voluntarily leave power on October 15. Left unstated was whether they would leave the country. The planes did a U-turn in the sky back to North Carolina. At 10 p.m., Clinton announced to the nation that a crisis had been resolved. The U.S. military was indeed arriving in Haiti the next morning, but it would be a peaceful occupation to help restore Aristide to power—a vastly safer mission.

THE WHITE HOUSE'S STORY LINE DEPICTED THE HAITI INTERVENTION AS A portrait of resolve, a diplomatic coup that had been won only by the president's steely resolve to back diplomacy by military force. The reality was that Clinton had essentially blinked in negotiations with his own negotiators. Talbott, who as a journalist had written books chronicling negotiations, remarked to Berger that he hoped no one ever chronicled this one—it would be just too embarrassing for Clinton.

Still, the Haiti episode marked an important milestone in Clinton's presidency. He had used military force in a significant way, and indeed had defied public opinion in doing so. This was an act of statesmanship. There were no U.S. military casualties, and Aristide was returned to power. As an exercise in nation building, the Haiti intervention was a modest and incomplete project; the island nation's future, like its past, continued to be marked by violence and poverty. But Clinton had at least given the Haitians a chance to govern themselves, and he had chased away the ghosts of the previous October: Somalia and the *Harlan County*. In a halting and clumsy way, he had grown.

Chapter Thirteen

"NO! NO! NO! . . ."

ARCH 14, 1994, WAS A BUSY NEWS DAY IN WASHINGTON. AT THE Justice Department, there was a stunning announcement. The associate attorney general, Webster Hubbell, abruptly announced his resignation. Hubbell was the third-ranking official at Justice, but everyone knew he was considerably more than that. He was a golfing pal of the president, a former law partner of the first lady, and the person who had been an indispensable go-to man in managing the steady flow of sensitive business back and forth between Justice and the White House. This shambling bear of a man, a former mayor of Little Rock and justice of the Arkansas Supreme Court, was well liked at the department for his easy good humor. He was also well respected for the sure-footed sense he brought to decisions. There had been concern but not panic when low rumblings of his troubles made it into the papers the first week of March. Hubbell had a complicated connection to the Whitewater case, because his father-in-law had been affiliated with the failed Madison savings and loan. In addition, there was a dispute with his former colleagues at the Rose Law Firm over allegedly improper billings. The details were murky. Indeed, Hillary Clinton, who as a Rose partner was herself a victim of Hubbell's chicanery, would not learn the truth until many months later. For now, all that was clear was a close friend of both Clintons was leaving office with a smoky odor in the air.

The president was in Boston for a political dinner when the news broke. Asked if he thought Hubbell had done anything wrong, Clinton professed "no knowledge of the facts," but added, "I find that hard to believe. . . . He's one of the most widely esteemed people I've ever known." The Hubbell case was on his mind in his remarks that night to a crowd of well-heeled Democratic contributors at the Boston Park Plaza. Clinton's theme was the need for greater cooperation between the parties. The talk started out as a historical discourse, and his mood at the outset was sad and subdued. Plenty of progress had been made under sensible Republicans like Dwight Eisenhower, he noted, and even Richard Nixon had helped create the Environmental Protection Agency. But today's breed of Republican was different, Clinton said. The Republican crowd in Washington was "dedicated just to being against everything we are for, and dedicated to the politics of personal destruction."

He warmed to his subject. The Republicans would "rather take off after" his wife than debate her on health care. Warm became hot, and hot became boiling. With the nation facing such serious problems, he asked, "Why, then, are we confronted in this administration with an opposition party that just stands up and says, 'No! No! No! No! No! No! No! No! No!' " He banged the podium harder, and his voice grew louder with each successive "No!"—nine of them in all—until at the end he was shouting. The shaken audience had just witnessed a president lose control.

His own aides were less surprised. They knew well how tenuous Clinton's grip was on his own rage. The Whitewater investigation, then still under Robert Fiske's control, was a daily assault. The intrusion into his and his wife's private dealings was a miserable burden on his marriage. Most of all, Clinton knew there was a disaster looming in his presidency. He certainly did not foresee the dimensions of the political setbacks awaiting him as the mid-term elections approached, but this most intuitive of politicians could feel the currents dragging on him. That he had no obvious solution to these problems meant there was nothing to do but seethe. John Podesta, who was then the mid-level staff secretary, observed that Clinton had not yet found the psychic space to cope with a challenge to his ethics. "Later, he could kind of put it away and deal with it as an unfair fact of life," he said. "At the beginning, he was out of his mind with anger."

INDEED, BOTH CLINTONS WERE EXPERIENCING PAINFUL ADJUSTMENTS, AS they belatedly realized that radical divergences between the way they perceived their own motives and values, and the way these were portrayed by the news media and political opposition, were now a permanent fact of life.

At the start of the year, Hillary Clinton's chief of staff, Maggie Williams, confided to Roger Altman, the deputy Treasury secretary, that the first lady was "paralyzed" by the Whitewater controversy, and that if the matter was not resolved soon, "we don't have to worry about her schedule on health care." A few months later, in a bid to reduce steam from the matter, she held what became known as the "pink press conference" (because of the bright pastel suit she was wearing) to acknowledge that her expectations of a zone of privacy in the White House had been unrealistic. "I've been rezoned," she said self-effacingly.

But no clever quip could disguise the essential grievance the Clintons felt about being the target of a political opposition that loathed them both. The hatred directed toward them was obvious. The reasons for it were not. Here was one of the essential mysteries of the Clinton years: Why did this couple inspire such animus?

At the beginning of the administration, the most common answer was that they were progressive politicians who had the audacity to be winners. The columnist E. J. Dionne noted that the right saw in Clinton a threat that it never perceived from less effective politicians like Jimmy Carter or Michael Dukakis. "In their bones, ideological conservatives know that Clinton is the toughest adversary they have faced in a long time," said Dionne, who was a Clinton favorite in part because of views like this. "He is trying to alter the country's political landscape and its assumptions about government. And he's actually doing it."

There was something to this thesis. After holding the White House for a dozen years, Republicans regarded Clinton as an intruder. "They thought these were their parking spots at the White House for life," he liked to tell aides.

But the explanation that the right viewed Clinton as an alarming ideological threat, or was simply jealous of his success, was not entirely satisfying—and became steadily less so as the years went by and the right could claim victories of its own. Gays in the military had been an offensive position to conservatives, surely, and so were the tax increases in Clinton's first budget. But no president who backed "an end to welfare as we know it," who hired Lloyd Bentsen as Treasury secretary, and who shaped his budget to please Alan Greenspan could be regarded as an apostle of the left. Clinton offended his adversaries on some more personal level.

The power he deferred to his wife was part of it. Large segments of the population remained hostile to the feminist revolution that produced Hillary Rodham Clinton. Yet this went only so far as an explanation. In the wake of health care, after all, Hillary Clinton embraced mostly traditional projects and exercised what power she had much the same way previous first ladies had—discreetly, through private advice in the family quarters. Moreover, despite their occasional flights into an airy "politics of meaning," the Clintons lived conventional lives. They doted on their precocious daughter. They went to church on Sundays. They hungered for career achievement and material success just like countless well-educated couples of their generation.

Perhaps this outward normality may have been the greatest provocation of all. The right felt certain it was artifice, a flimsy exterior that shielded all manner of unsavory secrets and hypocrisy. The rumors of Clinton's adultery were known to any American who listened to the late-night comedy shows. Surely his marriage was just for show, the critics reasoned, an accommodation that she tolerated in exchange for power.

If Clinton had been an unabashed rake, like Governor Edwin Edwards of Louisiana (who said the only way voters would turn on him was if they caught him with a "dead girl or a live boy"), he would not have left conservatives so exercised. The same would have been true if he had been a true child of the sixties and embraced open marriage. Of course, if he had been these things he never would have been president. It was the gap between the pious motives that the Clintons assigned to themselves and the crass motives the right felt sure was the reality that created such a fertile breeding dish for hatred.

And a lurid strain of hatred it was. The Reverend Jerry Falwell, a television evangelist, promoted a videotape to his flock hinting darkly that Clinton was complicit in Arkansas murders. This was nicely supplemented by a group called the American Justice Federation, which put out a periodic newsletter called *The Clinton Body Count: Coincidence or the Kiss of Death?* Floyd Brown, a veteran conservative operative in Washington, launched a daily *ClintonWatch* newsletter documenting every possible scrap of fact or tendentious rumor about the president's allegedly deficient character. "Impeach President Clinton—and her husband, too," read a favored conservative bumper sticker.

Clinton's old Oxford friend Bob Reich shrewdly observed, "The right hated the Clintons because they believed they embodied the values of the 1960s, at the same time they were a portrait of conventional success. He never paid a price, and the right could not tolerate that."

IT WAS CLINTON'S BELIEF THAT THE ESTABLISHMENT MEDIA—THE NETWORKS, and large newspapers that covered him daily—should expose the unfairness of such attacks and even the balance by illuminating for their national audiences the good work he was doing.

His brief against the news media went well beyond Whitewater coverage. He believed the national press had an unhealthy compulsion to reduce every significant story to political process. These process stories, more often than not, imparted self-serving motives to nearly every substantive decision he made. He found few things more maddening. His diagnosis was in many respects right. There was a cynical new mood in the Washington media, which reflected a cynical mood in the political culture generally that had been building since Vietnam and Watergate—national traumas that showed that a large measure of cynicism about presidents was often fully justified. Clinton had an unrealistic expectation that establishment news organs would change their tune to sing the praises of a young Democratic president pursuing a progressive agenda. In an interview with *Rolling Stone* a year into office, he complained that he had "not gotten one damn bit of credit from the knee-jerk liberal press, and I am sick and tired of it, and you can put that in the damn article."

The president did indeed generate a surprising degree of casual disdain from the rotating group of perhaps fifty writers, television correspondents, and producers assigned to the White House beat. Many reporters felt the Clinton White House had misled them purposely on an array of important and trivial controversies, ranging from Whitewater to a 1994 flap over whether a White House aide had taken one marine helicopter or two on a scouting mission to explore possible golf courses for Clinton (it was two, an expense of some $20,000 in taxpayer funds for an afternoon's recreation). More important, however, was a cultural clash between a president who, unlike most of his predecessors, was only a little older than most of the reporters assigned to him.

There is a certain kind of politician for whom journalists tend to fall. John F. Kennedy, with his cool detachment, humor, and irony, was the supreme example. Journalists of that era recall that JFK was breathtakingly candid about his political strategies, and even the contradictions between his public statements and private views. Clinton was not a man of detachment. He was immersed in his performance, utterly earnest, and offended by suggestions that his private motives were any different from his public pronouncements. At times the antagonism between president and press corps had a high school dimension. Clinton, working hard on his grades, saw the reporters as slackers and bullies—more interested in gossip and carping than anything constructive. The reporters, shooting spitballs from the back of the class, regarded Clinton as a preening apple-polisher.

On any given day, the president said things that provoked eye-rolling groans from the press. Once, currying favor with Iowa farmers, he boasted, "I am the only president who knew something about agriculture when I got there"—never mind that several of his predecessors, including Jimmy Carter, had actually been farmers. Carl Cannon, then covering the White House for the *Baltimore Sun,* wrote in *The Weekly Standard:* "This president salts his remarks with so many inventions, half-truths, and self-serving exaggerations that reporters who cover him often have to choose between truth-squadding every speech or ignoring his fibs."

It was not so bad as all this. Moreover, Clinton *was* appreciated as a wonderful ticket for reporters, who knew they were covering one of the generation's most vivid and arresting personalities. It seemed that every reporter flying on the press charter that accompanied Air Force One had a Clinton impersonation, and they regaled one another with warbling, raspy-voiced imitations of his signature lines: "I feel your pain." "This is a huge deal." Or, when angry, "May I remind you, sir . . ."

This irreverence hinted at a larger fact of Clinton's presidency. Because he was so emphatically human in his strengths and foibles, he had narrowed the gap between leader and public. In the process, he surrendered some of the aura traditionally attached to his office. His advisers worried about this. "You know, he eats too much, he loves sports too much, he talks too much," observed James Carville. "He is not remote in the way presidents have been, so you are more free to love him or hate him the way you would anyone." In part, the problem reflected the communications change. The cable networks now put a president before the public twenty-four hours a day. Clinton was overexposed.

IN THE LATE SPRING OF 1994, CLINTON WAS ABOUT TO BECOME FURTHER DISrobed. The previous year, he had faced a choice that had confronted every president since Richard Nixon: What to do about Bob Woodward?

The investigative journalist of Watergate fame was a one-man Washington institution. He had kept his affiliation with the *Washington Post,* but he was no reporter in the traditional sense. He worked on books, disappearing for a year or two at a time, then weighing in with volumes that were invariably full of sensational revelations about Washington's most powerful officials, and invariably best-sellers. Woodward was himself a member of Washington's establishment. He lived in a Georgetown mansion and was on friendly terms with cabinet secretaries, senators, and columnists. His favored form was the narrative reconstruction of presidential decisions. This type of story is called a "tick-tock" in journalistic parlance, named for the intimate minute-by-minute details of how power really works behind closed doors. Tick-tocks depend above all on access to people behind those doors, or their closest associates. No journalist was ever better at maneuvering for access, and Woodward was never shut out. Someone always talked to him, and once someone did, almost everyone else decided they had little choice but to do the same.

The Clinton White House learned in 1993 that Woodward was writing a contemporaneous history about the drafting of and effort to pass Clinton's economic plan. Stephanopoulos in particular urged cooperation. Bowing to Woodward's reputation, the aide argued that it was better to cut short the ritual mating dance over access and simply give Woodward all the entrée he sought. The reporter ended up talking to everyone, including the president, vice president, and first lady, according to Stephanopoulos and others. All the conversations were on "deep background," meaning the material was published without attribution to individual sources.

Though Woodward's reputation made him an intimidating presence, he opened up sources with modesty. "I'm humbled by what I don't know," he told Bentsen. Most of Woodward's sources, of course, remain unknown, but the evidence suggests that he benefited from the same phenomenon that the author of this history often experienced: that the closer people were to Clinton, the more voluble they were as sources—and the more critical of their president. This was doubtless a reflection of how emotionally taxing it could be to work with Clinton. People were proud to serve him, and most, with the passage of time, regard him affectionately. In the trenches, however, it was only human to feel resentment at his outbursts, and frustration at how often— whether subconsciously or by design—he pitted factions against each other. Clinton was a hard person to be around, and when people had the chance to vent to Woodward, they did so.

Clinton's moment with Woodward came one day early in 1994 in the Oval Office. The president locked on intently to his interrogator, never removing his eyes even as he slowly sipped from a glass of water. Clinton finished the session on a pleading note. "I'm worried you're going to make me look like a madman," he said.

When *The Agenda* hit the bookstands in June, it portrayed the Clinton

White House in a harsh but revealing light as a place of presidential tantrums and staff turmoil, where political consultants roamed freely in the West Wing. In historical terms, both the book and the policies it described have held up well. Woodward's reporting was a window into the personalities and pressures of Clinton's first year. The economic plan, for all the bumps that accompanied its passage, was an indispensable first step toward righting the nation's fiscal health. In the whirl of publicity that greeted the book's arrival, however, it was the bumps and not the safe arrival that got attention.

There were immediate consequences. The book hastened the inevitable. Months earlier the president and first lady had begun discussions with Vernon Jordan, Harold Ickes, and others about Mack McLarty's poor fit in the chief of staff job. Ultimately, McLarty agreed that he was not a good choice to run the White House with the mid-term elections looming. He resigned without argument. Leon Panetta, the budget director, was Clinton's choice after some others rebuffed Clinton's expressions of interest. The Woodward encounter burned the president, too, in lasting ways. Never again would he fully trust most members of his staff to protect his interests over their own. No one's stock fell more precipitously than Stephanopoulos's. Clinton also abandoned his lifelong habit of thinking aloud about policy choices except in very small meetings, so that details of his ruminations would not leak. It was a large step in Clinton's transformation from an essentially open man to a self-contained one, a change that left him with deep grievances. "That Woodward's an evil guy," Clinton said darkly to Stephanopoulos.

THERE HAD BEEN INTIMATIONS ALL YEAR OF A POLITICAL CATASTROPHE IN the offing. One of the most vivid omens came to Clinton's desk that May from pollster Stan Greenberg, who wrote a memo which he distributed solely to the president and first lady. "The administration, the Democrats in Congress and the party face a disaster in November unless we move urgently to change the mood of the country," Greenberg wrote. The news got worse as he reported back results of a recent focus group. "The voters believe Bill Clinton is struggling to handle the presidency and guide the country." When they were offered a list of descriptions of Clinton, Greenberg reported, the most common choice was "over his head," followed by "indecisive" and "immature." The good news was that almost nobody chose "dishonest" or "unethical." "This is about being young and inexperienced, from a small, backward state, and failing to master the bad forces at work in Washington. A few months ago, Whitewater was interpreted as gridlock, but now it is evidence of Clinton being over-his-head. This is about Bill Clinton personally, to devastating effect."

Hillary Clinton, from her travels to promote health care, knew there were powerful currents of discontent swirling. At an appearance in Seattle, she had been greeted by hundreds of angry protestors, most of them men. "I had not seen faces like that since the segregation battles of the sixties," she said, once back in Washington. "They had such hatred on their faces."

When faced with critics Bill Clinton's instinct was to hit the road. If he could get out of Washington, he believed, and make the case to voters directly, then he could turn things around. One problem as the mid-term elections approached was that there were very few Democrats who wanted Clinton in their districts. Approval ratings like his were not exactly a draw. But he prized the invitations he did get. "You could not pull him off the stage," said Harold Ickes. "He felt if you just gave him enough time to explain what he was doing, he could win over every voter one at a time."

But there was no time left. In September, knowing things were bad, Clinton began conversations with an old political hand who had been with him at the beginning of his career in Arkansas but later fell out of favor. Dick Morris represented Republicans now, but he was not averse to giving cutting advice to his old client. They spoke repeatedly in the weeks before the election. Stay overseas, Morris urged—anything to look like a president and not a politician. Instead, Clinton threw every punch he could at the Republicans. Few landed. Four days before the election, Morris warned, "You're going to lose the Senate and the House."

"Not the House, no way," Clinton replied.

"*And the House,*" Morris said. "And by significant margins."

"No way, no way," Clinton answered. "Not the House, not the House. You're wrong. You really think so? You're wrong."

Section Two

Chapter Fourteen

WINTER

THE DISASTER WAS EVERY BIT AS COMPREHENSIVE AS DICK MORRIS had predicted—a rout of historic proportions. Democrats lost statehouses, including in New York, where even Governor Mario Cuomo was unceremoniously dumped. Democrats lost eight Senate seats, and their majority. Most unbelievably, Clinton's party lost fifty-four House seats, giving Republicans control there for the first time in four decades. A Democratic defeat on such a scale was caused by many factors; the most important was public backlash against the young leader who was the new face of the party. The Republican Party, led by the incoming Speaker of the House, Newt Gingrich, was ascendant. A new era was at hand in Washington.

Clinton accepted the news with equanimity, for the moment. He spent election night roaming the West Wing, chatting with his shell-shocked staff, calmly dissecting the election results as though he was a neutral analyst rather than the person most directly affected by the debacle. Surveying individual House districts, he knew which members had gotten hurt by the tax increase in the economic plan, and which ones had gotten hurt by gun control. He even took a small measure of vindication in some of the results; in many cases

Democrats who ran away from the president did no better. They would have been better off forthrightly running on the good work the administration was doing, he said. Appearing before reporters the next day, Clinton insisted that the results were not a repudiation of the new administration, just a sign that voters wanted even more change, faster, than he had been able to deliver.

This was a delusion, as Clinton himself realized in more candid moments. The results were impossible to interpret except as a repudiation of the grand new design he had offered in his first two years. There were specific grievances that mattered in each race: taxes, guns, disappointment with either the substance of Clinton's health care plan or the failure of Democrats to deliver reform. But there was no mistaking the general indictment: Voters were angry at a president who offered large ambition seemingly unharnessed to good judgment or administrative competence. They took it out on anyone with a "D" beside his or her name on the ballot. Many commentators noted that Clinton's life was following a familiar rhythm. The rebuke of 1994 was eerily similar, in both cause and consequences, to the rebuke that Arkansas voters had delivered twelve years earlier, when they hurled Clinton out of office after just two years.

In the days after the mid-term elections, a mourning Hillary Clinton wept to Dick Morris, "I don't know which direction is up or down. Everything I thought was right was wrong."

THE PEOPLE WHO TOILED FOR BILL CLINTON WERE LONG SINCE ACCUSTOMED to outbursts and anger. What greeted them now was more frightening. Much of the time Clinton was literally absent from the West Wing, choosing instead to work in the residence. Even when he was physically present, he was emotionally gone.

He had entered a passive phase. He was bitterly disappointed in the political team that had carried him and the party to this end, he made clear in conversations with Morris and others. He was also bitterly disappointed in himself for what he knew were his own errors. Not ready to assign blame with precision, he simply checked out. Before the elections, he talked to Paul Begala several times a week. Now, he did not tell Begala he was fired, or even that he was disappointed in his work; he simply stopped calling. On a trip to Asia for an economic summit, the president and first lady barely spoke to George Stephanopoulos, and instead cloistered themselves in the front cabin of Air Force One with the door shut.

Harold Ickes, the deputy chief of staff, had not been around long enough to be held fully accountable for the debacle. But his conversations with Clinton were fogged and inconclusive, as if he was talking to someone just waking up from medication. Several times Ickes went to Clinton asking for some direction over whether pollster Stan Greenberg's contract, paid for by the Democratic National Committee, should be renewed. Clinton would shrug and mumble. Finally, Ickes forced the issue. If you want to fire Greenberg, just say so and I'll do it, he said; otherwise someone has to do polling and we should renew the contract.

Clinton answered with the same words he used whenever he was forced to make a decision that he was not ready to own. "Okay, Harold," he said. "If that's what you want . . ."

He felt especially bad about the departure of press secretary Dee Dee Myers. The president had always liked this intelligent and poised woman. By contrast, Hillary Clinton was of the opinion that she was too young for the job; her second-guessing undercut Myers's effectiveness in a West Wing inner circle that was already a male-dominated culture. On her last day, the president was weeping when he said goodbye, full of remorse about her departure and how terrible it was.

Myers found this flattering, and also a bit pitiful. Clinton, after all, was president; if he really wanted her to stay, he could make it happen. Like Ickes, she was struck by Clinton's passivity.

No one on Clinton's West Wing staff had known about the pre-election calls to Morris. None of them knew that those calls had now increased steadily. There was a reason Clinton did not care whether Ickes rehired Stan Greenberg. He was already in a courtship with his replacement.

Among the first to know was Clinton's trade negotiator, Mickey Kantor. During the Asia trip, Clinton invited Kantor to his suite in the ambassador's residence at Jakarta. Kantor saw a man as beaten as any he had ever seen. Clinton talked about how badly things had gone, and confided that he had been talking to Morris for some original ideas. He urged that Morris's name be kept secret, especially with anyone at the White House. "People would go crazy," Clinton said.

Kantor felt compelled to offer some blunt advice: "Stop feeling so sorry for yourself." Things aren't so bad. Clinton was not so sure. Everything would be different with a Republican Congress. But he agreed there was a sliver of hope with Gingrich. "Maybe he'll overreach," Clinton said.

The season, Clinton believed, did not call for subtle gestures. In December, with the Republicans two weeks from their official takeover of Congress, he went on national television to call for a "middle-class bill of rights," complete with a tax cut that had fallen by the wayside at the start of the administration. Under the circumstances, this looked like a craven bow to Washington's new conservative mood. Economics columnist Robert Samuelson said the speech had "all the dignity of a home shopping program."

But there *was* something nuanced—and more fundamental—going on with Clinton during this period. As 1994 reached its end, he was asking himself basic questions about his leadership style and values. In the search for answers, he was reorienting himself intellectually and emotionally.

Hillary Clinton, who enjoyed an occasional dip in the New Age pool, especially if the ideas related to feminist empowerment or liberal spirituality, encouraged this journey. She sponsored long discussions at Camp David with a variety of writers and thinkers who interested her, among them Anthony Robbins, a self-help guru whose thirty-minute infomercials ran on late-night television, and the author of the book *Awaken the Giant Within.* He got his start by showing people how they could learn to walk across hot coals. There was also Jean Houston, leader of the Foundation for Mind Research, which promoted the search for well-being through "altered states of consciousness." On the more conventional end of the spectrum there was Stephen Covey, author of the wildly successful *The Seven Habits of Highly Effective People.*

The visitors at Camp David asked the president to describe his best qualities.

"I have a good heart," he said. "I really do. I hope I have a decent mind."

Clinton, indeed, was more comfortable working through his problems intellectually than through psycho-spiritual explorations. Around this same time, he immersed himself in a subject that had fascinated him since boyhood: the history of the presidency. He read August Heckscher on Woodrow Wilson, for instance, and Benjamin Thomas on Abraham Lincoln. He did not restrict himself to famous presidencies; he studied the obscure ones, too, looking for insight. This was a sober exercise, not the vainglorious emulation of JFK and FDR that marked his early days in office. He was now in a position to really understand the office, and to think anew about how predecessors had dealt with their own challenges and limitations.

IF CLINTON NEEDED TO GO INTO RETREAT, THIS WAS A GOOD TIME TO DO IT. People were not paying him much attention anyway. All eyes were on Gingrich. Clinton's prediction to Mickey Kantor that Gingrich might go too far was not exactly clairvoyance. The Republican leader had long since served notice that he was a man of breathtaking ambition. Before the election and afterward, he boldly advertised his agenda: It was to remake the welfare state. He promised a "revolution" that would eliminate large chunks of the federal government and ensure that whatever was left operated on new premises, designed to dethrone bureaucracy and empower free markets. Gingrich believed it was his mission to execute the next and most important phase of the conservative ascendancy that had begun under Ronald Reagan.

Many commentators at the time were struck by the arresting similarities between the president and his new rival for supremacy in Washington. Both were garrulous men with outsized appetites. Both came from families dominated by doting mothers and troubled relationships with adoptive fathers. Both had endured political controversies over adultery. They were both consumed with politics in similar ways, with wonderfully retentive minds that stockpiled stories and personal encounters and data about the voting patterns in individual districts. They were peers, with Gingrich, at age fifty when he became Speaker, the older by two years.

The more vivid comparisons, though, were not with Clinton but with the president's two most important partners, Hillary Clinton and Al Gore. Like these two, Gingrich saw the individual policies he promoted as part of a larger philosophy, which he pursued with a presumption and zeal that at times bordered on messianic. Just as Hillary Clinton sermonized about a new "politics of meaning," and Gore wrote about the environment as "the new guiding principle for civilization," Gingrich wrapped his politics in missionary garb. He taught a college course, sold to the public on mail-order tape cassettes, that he humbly called "Renewing American Civilization." Without self-consciousness, he said, "I think I am a transformational figure."

Like Gore and Hillary Clinton, but unlike the president, Gingrich had a taste for partisan combat, and he often denounced opponents in highly moralistic terms. He said Woody Allen's romantic relationship with his adoptive daughter perfectly "fits the Democratic platform." He suggested that a psychotic South Carolina woman who drowned her children reflected the "sick society" that Democrats had created. He proclaimed a few days before the election that the opposition was "the enemy of normal Americans." And within days after his victory he was denouncing both Clintons as "counterculture

McGovernicks." Citing no evidence, he alleged that 25 percent of the Clinton staff had used drugs shortly before joining the White House.

Gingrich's swagger suggested another similarity with his rivals. Like the Clintons' misreading of their 1992 victory as a mandate for an ambitious brand of progressivism, Gingrich was reading the GOP victory as a mandate for his ambitious brand of conservatism, codified in the "Contract with America." This ten-point manifesto hit many of the most sacred touchstones of the right's agenda: tax cuts, welfare reform, a balanced-budget amendment, a missile defense system, and term limits for members of Congress. Boasting that the country was breaking in a new conservative direction, Gingrich noted that each item in the contract scored more than 60 percent in the polls. The year ahead would determine whether he was correctly reading the national mood.

GINGRICH COULD SAVOR HIS POLLS, BUT IT WAS IN THIS LONELY WINTER IN-terlude of his presidency that a crisis emerged that gave Clinton no choice but to ignore his own polls. The problem was in Mexico, where the peso had suddenly collapsed, as foreign investors lost confidence in the country and threatened to send its economy into a steep tailspin—with dire implications for third world economies around the world, and even the first world superpower just to the north. There were substantive questions facing the administration: Was a U.S. intervention to prop up Mexico's currency an appropriate exception to the general free-market doctrine that held that the United States should stay out of the business of trying to manage international currencies? And even if so, did the administration have effective policy remedies for the problem in Mexico?

The substantive problems were shadowed by political ones. Polls showed overwhelming public sentiment against a U.S. intervention. The pillar of economic policy in the first two years, Treasury Secretary Bentsen, had just announced his long-expected departure from the administration. His replacement, National Economic Adviser Rubin, had not by any means established the influence he would later hold. Rubin believed that a multibillion-dollar U.S. loan initiative to Mexico was called for—though in his usual laconic fashion he emphasized to Clinton that he was not at all sure his plan would work. Throughout the White House, however, there was a universal sense that the peso crisis had arrived at the worst moment for the president's domestic fortunes.

Gingrich was internationalist in outlook and favored the currency intervention, but many in his caucus disagreed, and the new Speaker reported back that he could not win passage for legislative approval of the package. Clinton would need to act on his own executive authority—and accept the attendant political risks.

"If this fails," said Sandy Berger, then the deputy national security adviser, "you'll be accused of pissing billions of dollars down a Mexican rat hole."

Clinton hardly disagreed, but responded, "We don't have an alternative."

The fact that Clinton reached this decision, at a time when he had never been weaker politically, stands as a rejoinder to those who asserted then and later that he was a slavish devotee to polls. His move on middle-class taxes in December showed that he could indeed lurch expediently on occasion. His courageous move on Mexico the next month showed that, when the stakes were highest, he was willing to risk public wrath.

By the turn of the new year, Clinton's melancholy was finally lifting. A few weeks away was the State of the Union address, always his largest audience of the year. Given that this would be the first time many Americans were giving him sustained attention since the humiliation of November, the speech was all the more important.

The White House always solicited thoughts from intellectuals and writers as it was crafting themes for these annual addresses. This year, many of the comments had a cutting edge. "Dear Mr. President," wrote historian Arthur Schlesinger, one of the nation's leading liberals. "A prime purpose of this year's State of the Union, I would think, would be to restore Bill Clinton's credibility as a President and as a man." Like many liberals, this veteran of Kennedy's White House had deplored what he took to be the "appeasing tone" of Clinton's December address calling for tax cuts. "The speech, as read by friend and foe alike, hoisted a white flag—and did so before a crowd that won't be satisfied by anything short of unconditional surrender."

Clinton's longtime friend Taylor Branch, the Pulitzer-winning chronicler of the civil rights movement, was more sympathetic. The president "should not quibble, cavil, cadge, or complain about the Republican victory. Not for this moment," he wrote. "Instead, he should graciously salute the new majority and welcome them to a positive historic view of its meaning. Don't shoot at their mountain. Show the country a bigger one."

This was in fact what the president aimed to do. Clinton tried to put himself in the place of one of those voters he knew despised him: "These white guys thought they were working harder for less money, sleeping less, couldn't even afford a vacation and now the damn guy—he didn't give me a tax cut and now he's coming after my gun." The trick, Clinton said, was to acknowledge that the old New Deal consensus in favor of big government was over, but argue that the "brave, new world" of conservatives like Dick Armey was no substitute, either. You needed a social compact which included something for everyone. The Republican plan "would be law of the jungle. So maybe you'd have 60 percent of the people that would be happy as clams, but they'd be living behind fences."

Clinton asked his speechwriters to find a way to say this—and to keep it brief. "My gut is, we ought to try to do this in half an hour—no more than half an hour."

Gore chimed in, "Shouldn't the president find a way to tick off the successes in foreign policy and the successes in economic policy?"

"Damn right!" Clinton agreed.

As it happened, Clinton would need more than thirty minutes to do all this. The address he gave ran almost three times that. That's because he gave not one speech but two. During speech preparations, speechwriters like Don Baer were puzzled when dropping by the White House residence to share the latest revisions, only to find that Clinton had full pages of ideas and suggested language written out in longhand on a legal pad. Where were these coming from? Morris, his presence still unknown to the White House staff, had faxed ideas directly to Clinton. Clinton then rewrote the faxes in his own hand. When George Stephanopoulos raised concerns with the president about some of his suggested language, Hillary Clinton, who had been hovering nearby, interjected, "It's your speech, Bill. You say what you want," shooting Stephanopoulos a peevish glare. In the end, Clinton gave the speech his White House staff recommended in the first half and the one Morris recommended in the second.

While the Washington press commentary on the 1995 State of the Union was withering—its length was seen as a perfect illustration of Clinton's inability to choose, and to explain in crisp terms what he was all about—in the chamber, Clinton was interrupted by applause nearly a hundred times. More important, the overnight polls showed that viewers loved the speech's content and did not mind the length at all. Both the cheers and the numbers were tonic to Clinton. Perhaps the year ahead would not be so bleak after all.

Chapter Fifteen

UNDERSIDE

ONE DAY DURING THE 1992 CAMPAIGN, HILLARY CLINTON AND HAROLD Ickes were lunching in New York and the subject of Dick Morris arose. Ickes had known Morris for more than twenty years, but he had not known that the political consultant had worked for his friends in Arkansas. "He's a sleazy son of a bitch," the New Yorker rasped. The future first lady made no effort to defend Morris's virtue. Instead, she patiently explained that the consultant knew the practicalities of winning elections, in particular the black art of negative advertising, as well as anyone the Clintons knew. "He understands the underside," she said.

"He *is* the underside," Ickes shot back.

Bill Clinton's ideal universe, certainly, would have no Dick Morris in it. This had been his intention for the presidency. Morris played no role in Clinton's 1992 campaign. He was a stranger to the president's inner circle, with the exception of Ickes, in the administration's early days. In truth, even then, Morris had been an occasional though spectral presence. Hillary Clinton was his point of contact, and they had been speaking once or twice a month since the presidency began. Less frequently, Morris spoke with the president. Rarely did the consultant have much good to say. He took a dim view of Clinton's course in 1993 and 1994, and his comments were received by both Clintons with polite indifference. Their last collaboration, during Clinton's final race for governor in 1990, had ended with a row that left Morris deeply resentful. During his years of estrangement, Morris worked exclusively for Republicans. He delighted in bad-mouthing his former client, and drummed up business for himself by boasting that he was the man who had Clinton's number—he knew Clinton's mind, his infirmities, and how to beat him. "Clinton is going to be indicted," he blustered in 1994 to his client William Weld, the Massachusetts governor, predicting that Whitewater would be Clinton's undoing.

Profiteering at the expense of a former client may have been dubious ethics, but it was true—Morris *did* have Clinton's number. They were not friends. They did not relate to each other at all except in one sphere of Clinton's life. But that sphere, politics, was by far the most important for both of them. With the exception of Hillary Clinton, no one knew better the story of Bill Clinton's rise, or had contributed to it more decisively, than Dick Morris. At every important turn in Clinton's political life, with the exception of 1992, Morris had been there. From the outside, little could have seemed more bizarre—a Republican strategist whispering in the ear of a wounded Democratic president. From the inside, nothing could have seemed more natural that bleak winter than for Clinton to summon the first consultant he had ever known, and for Dick Morris to come home to his first paying client.

The homecoming was a private affair, by mutual desire. Morris did not want to risk his lucrative Republican contracts if his conversations with Clinton did not result in his becoming chief strategist for the 1996 re-election. Clinton saw no point in risking an insurrection among his staff, and an inevitable flood of publicity about his odd partnership with a Republican, while still in the testing period with this rapprochement. Beneath these practical concerns lurked a curious psychological attraction. "Mystery is an integral part of power," Morris liked to say, plainly enjoying clandestine advising of a president. Clinton enjoyed it, too. "I like subterfuge," he told Morris. "That's why I like you." The subterfuge reflected not only Clinton's ambivalence about Morris, but also about his current White House team—"these kids who got me elected." His advisers had become famous on his dime, the president believed. They had spent their time cultivating friends in the press, boasting about things that went well and distancing themselves from things that went wrong. Indifferent to Clinton's views, they had pushed the White House agenda on gays, taxes, and a host of other issues toward positions that were more liberal than what the president believed.

Whatever the merits of these grievances, the president was undeniably in a strange place by 1995. He did not regard the people who worked for him as reliable instruments of his will. Nor did he feel secure enough in his political standing to simply fire aides. It was as if his staff was simply one more constituency with which to be reckoned. Morris believed that Clinton's keeping him a secret was his way of retaining a kind of power. Morris would belong to him alone. He would not dine out on Clinton's reputation. He would not be fawned over and told how brilliant his political advice was by the same Georgetown mandarins who sneered at Clinton for taking it. Since their Arkansas days, Morris had sensed Clinton's conflicted emotions about him. Clinton simultaneously prized a relationship with someone who was even more political than he was, and found the whole thing ignoble. Morris believed he reminded Clinton of the compromises and impurities in his own soul: "It was like Clinton believed, 'I'm a real scumbag, and you're the guy who's on to me.'"

When Morris called, Clinton usually dispensed no pleasantries. He simply picked up the phone with a guttural grunt and plunged into business. After Morris's involvement eventually became known, Clinton would complain to his staff—the same ones he had earlier complained about to Morris—that the consultant was ripping off the campaign with his high fees. Their collaboration carried an aroma almost of prostitution—a relationship that was thoroughly transactional, at once intimate and impersonal, driven by mutual need with an overlay of shame. Morris re-emerged in Clinton's life at a time when the romance of his presidency was, like his political fortunes, at an ebb. It had happened before in his life: Clinton's need to be rescued from the consequences of his romantic dreams by the great competing dimension of his character—realism. In a realistic mood, Clinton was governed by the imperative of survival. As 1995 arrived, the president's back against the wall, the idealism and vainglory of the early years yielded to a determination to survive Gingrich's Republican onslaught. The Clinton presidency had entered its realistic phase, and Dick Morris was the instrument—the living extension—of Bill Clinton's realism.

TWO YEARS EARLIER, AS CLINTON HAD SLOGGED THROUGH A DIFFICULT stretch in the budget battles, he lost patience at a meeting one day as his political team offered him a learned discourse on the challenges he was facing. "I know what's *wrong*," he bristled. "Give me a strategy! . . . All I get is analysis. I never get a strategy. I never get a plan."

Morris knew that this president was rightly viewed as one of the great political talents of his generation. Clinton was superb at reading an audience of one person or a crowd of a thousand. He could find the language to make a bold idea, like the Mexican currency bailout, seem routine and sensible, or make a small idea, such as urging states to toughen their regulations on driver's licenses, seem far-reaching and bold. Where he struggled was in assembling his multitude of ideas and information into a larger whole, discriminating between what was attainable and what was not, and organizing individual actions in pursuit of his larger ambitions as president. In short, Clinton was masterful at tactical maneuver, but only average as a strategic thinker. Strategy was where Morris excelled. He was well read in presidential history, as much or more so than Clinton. His conversations with Clinton were an endless flow of metaphors and historical allusions, all of them in service of the same point: No matter how dire things looked, it was possible for Clinton to use his presidential platform to transcend his present circumstances. An example came during a conversation early in 1995, when Morris blurted out a name for the strategy Clinton should follow. As Clinton looked on in bafflement, Morris shaped his fingers into a triangle and explained: "Triangulate, create a third position, not just in between the old positions of the two parties but above them as well. Identify a new course that accommodates the needs the Republicans address but does it in a way that is uniquely yours." He was conveying confidence that Clinton desperately needed to hear, at a time when everyone else in his White House was expressing despair. His message never wavered: Do not worry. This will work. You will win. Do what I say and it's guaranteed.

The early political team, men like Stephanopoulos and pollster Stan Greenberg, gave Clinton deference as president, and sympathy for how complicated his choices were. They gave him too much of what he did not really want. "Greenberg never told me what to do," he complained to Morris one day early in their latest partnership. Morris had a different philosophy. His rule was that if you did not criticize Clinton in the first five minutes of a conversation he would conclude that you had nothing of value to say and tune you out. It is not that Clinton enjoyed being lectured. To the contrary, the subordinates who left him coldest were the ones whose advice was devoid of politics. These were people like Madeleine Albright on foreign policy or budget director Alice Rivlin on deficit reduction, both of whom Clinton believed would hector him with moralistic arguments that were blind to practical realities. What Clinton prized were people who sized up his political problems, then told him—with absolute conviction and no hedging—what he should do. This was Morris to a tee. At a time when Clinton's own confidence was low, the consultant spoke in emphatic certitudes. You MUST endorse a balanced budget. Whitewater will NOT affect your re-election. You must SIGN a welfare bill. If you do your second term is GUARANTEED.

By January 1995, the advice came in streams of faxes, perhaps a half dozen a day. When the official workday was over, Morris and Clinton would talk by phone until late in the evening. They met in person on Wednesday nights, the start of the weekly political meetings that later came to define Clinton's presidency. At the beginning, they were meetings of three: the president, the first lady, and Morris. Soon, Hillary Clinton stopped attending and was replaced by a gradually expanding group, including Al Gore and Leon Panetta. At the beginning, though, even these people were only dimly aware of who Morris was and what he was doing in Clinton's life. Lower down the totem pole, the White House staff knew nothing at all. In the mania for secrecy, Morris invented a whimsical pseudonym for himself: Charlie. During meetings, Clinton would excuse himself upon getting messages that Charlie was on the line. Panetta, trying to explain a new initiative that left his senior staff baffled, would explain that it had been "Charlie's recommendation."

Morris was no less unsettling a figure once he came out of hiding. He was a short, stocky man with a dark, blow-dried pompadour. Stephanopoulos, who loathed him, took revenge in his memoir with a description of his first meeting with "a small sausage of a man encased in a green suit with wide lapels, a wide floral tie, and a wide-collared shirt," carrying a briefcase that "gave him the look of a B-movie mob'lawyer, circa 1975—the kind of guy who gets brained with a baseball bat for double-crossing his boss." He spoke in an intense metallic voice, staccato bursts of orders and opinions that sounded a little like workmen drilling.

There was a special reason Clinton found this voice so pleasing. The consultant's certitudes always came harnessed to data, to *hard numbers*. Clinton was awash in opinions. They meant little to him unless they could be supported by some evidence of what the public actually believed. Polling had always been the touchstone of the Clinton-Morris relationship, beginning with their first project together, when Arkansas attorney general Clinton was trying to decide whether he should run for governor or U.S. Senate. Both men took the customary fascination with polls among politicians and their handlers (and political reporters) to a new dimension. Many of his fellow consultants, Morris said, were charlatans, passing off their own ideologies and pet tricks to candidates as objective advice. By contrast, he asserted that by employing comprehensive survey research—more frequent and more detailed in its questions than the typical political poll—he could offer political advice that was scientific in its conclusions. Most of his competitors thought that this pose was pure bamboozle. Far from being objective, Morris's data somehow always managed to support positions for which the consultant had been arguing vociferously. (Robert Squier, a media consultant whom Morris recruited onto the 1996 re-election team despite a tense history between them, once called Morris the "Julia Child of cooked polls.") Inside the White House, though, the president and first lady made clear their appetite for what Morris was cooking. He was perhaps as influential during Clinton's 1995 season of doubt as any political hand had been in the modern presidency. He was Clinton's version of Colonel House to Woodrow Wilson or Harry Hopkins to FDR. "I have never seen such a role reversal," observed Ickes, describing Clinton's reaction when Morris presented his latest polls. "Bill Clinton dominates every other conversation I have ever witnessed, including with other heads of state. But with Morris it was almost as if he had some supernatural hold on him. He would sit for thirty minutes without saying a word." Morris, too, later reflected on the president's fascination with polling data. "In a room, he [Clinton] will instinctively, as if by a canine sense of smell, find anyone who shows reserve toward him, and he will work full time on winning his approval and, if possible, affection. . . . America is the ultimate room for Clinton. For him, a poll helps him sense who doesn't like him and why they don't. In the reflected numbers, he sees his shortcomings and his potential, his successes and his failures."

SOON AFTER MORRIS RETURNED TO CLINTON'S FOLD, THE TWO OF THEM WERE chatting privately one evening when Clinton told Morris that he was glad to have him back, but he cautioned that he had to be careful. They could not just work as if they were back in Arkansas in the old days. "Why not?" Morris asked quizzically. "This is *the country*," Clinton replied.

It was Clinton's way of saying that there were certain things he could not do in single-minded pursuit of victory. Now there were consequences. The comment spoke to Clinton's understanding of their shared past. Morris was always the guy he paid to worry about absolutely nothing but victory. For nearly two decades, Clinton believed he had gotten his money's worth.

They were an odd couple right from the outset, an Arkansas Baptist and a New York Jew, each of whom thought the other was among the oddest characters he had met. Morris initiated the introduction in 1977 by concocting a phony story that he was going to be in Little Rock on other business. He suggested a drop-by with the attorney general, who was trying to decide his next career move. Clinton, who at thirty-one was a year older than his visitor, had long hair and sideburns, and worked out of a state office that Morris thought "could have been the recreation room at the local Knights of Columbus," complete with false wood paneling on the walls, folding tables, and "the kind of metal chairs that usually have MUSIC DEPARTMENT stenciled on the back." At one point Morris visited the restroom and was shocked to find that the attorney general had a poster of a buxom blonde tacked to the door. Is that really appropriate for an officeholder? he asked. "Don't you know who that is?" Clinton asked with a disbelieving smile. As it happened, the New Yorker had never heard of Dolly Parton. Despite the chasm in cultural tastes, the two soon found they were remarkably like-minded in their view of politics. They talked that day of their mutual admiration for John F. Kennedy, and of the way that the national traumas of Vietnam and Watergate had eroded respect for politicians and left a cynical and surly electorate. The conversation lasted four hours, and Morris left Little Rock with a client.

Morris was the son of a Manhattan real estate lawyer and a professional writer, and he had inherited the liberal views that were entirely characteristic of this upbringing. (A collateral relative was lawyer Roy Cohn, *enfant terrible* of the McCarthy era, who emphatically had not inherited these liberal views.) From a young age, he was deeply engaged in politics and policy, which were invariably the topics of conversation at the Morris family table. He was vehemently opposed to the Vietnam War. The same year he began working with Clinton, he published a book, *Bum Rap on America's Cities,* which advanced a conventionally liberal view that the urban Northeast was ailing because the region was not getting its fair share of federal aid. Even as he retained his liberal faith, his idealism about the political enterprise had faded during the 1970s. By the time he met Clinton, it was gone almost completely. As a consultant, Morris was among the first practitioners of the negative television ad, which played on the public's rising willingness to think the worst about politicians. He also arrived at his signature insight as a strategist: The modern electorate could no longer be moved by gauzy biographical advertisements that tried to project an aura of heroic leadership and idealism, the kind of image associated with the Kennedys. Instead, people responded to concrete issue appeals. Tell them what you are for and what you are against—keep it simple and specific. In its way, Morris's cynicism about politics was liberating for him. He was happy to work for paying clients of either party, and his business was increasingly with Republicans. Money preceded conviction, but gradually during the 1980s, Morris found himself becoming more conservative in his own beliefs. To his mind, nearly everything he thought at the decade's beginning—against cutting taxes, for instance, and against confronting the Soviet Union—had been proven wrong by the Reagan experience. By 1990, Clinton was his sole Democratic client, and they had been together more than a dozen years. There had been some bumps along the way. The first was in 1980, when Governor Clinton failed to hire Morris until the closing days of his first re-election campaign, when polls correctly forecast that America's youngest governor was about to become its youngest ex-governor. Cast out by voters, Bill and Hillary Clinton enlisted Morris's help as Clinton valiantly crawled to an electoral comeback two years later. In 1990 there was another bump. The consultant had grown increasingly disdainful of Clinton after he declined to run for president in 1988. With some cause, Clinton believed Morris was no longer committed to his career, and during the 1990 gubernatorial campaign Clinton exploded, "You've turned your back on me. I don't get shit from you anymore. You're screwing me!"

"Thank you, thank you, thank you. You've just solved my problem," the consultant shot back, announcing he was pleased to let Clinton "go fuck" himself and allow Morris to finally become "a fifty-state Republican." As Morris stormed out of the governor's mansion, Clinton grabbed him—strongly enough to spawn years of exaggerated stories that he had decked the consultant—and only Hillary Clinton's intervention kept Morris from quitting the race three weeks before its successful conclusion.

It was against this stormy personal history that Morris arrived after the mid-term debacle in 1994. Though he was identified now as a Republican, he was an odd ideological composite. By Democratic standards, he was certainly conservative, but he was not doctrinaire. He viewed himself much the way he viewed the electorate: post-ideological, and disdainful of conventional politics with its exaggerated partisanship. He thought most voters were eager to pick and choose policies à la carte from the menus offered by both parties. Above all, voters wanted their elected officials to end petty quarrels and craft a new national consensus. His pragmatic, compromising brand of politics came in a most uncompromising package. Morris was a man of deep and diverse grievances, and he walked into the White House that winter with several chips on his shoulder. Like Clinton, he loathed Washington political culture, especially what he regarded as the insidious axis of journalists and political operatives at its core. He had always avoided the city, keeping his base in the Connecticut suburbs of New York City. Unlike Clinton, Morris also loathed the main engines of the Democratic Party. During his rightward drift of the previous decade, he concluded that the unions and the civil rights and social activists who ran the party were frauds, morally and intellectually bankrupt, more interested in preserving their power and sources of funding than in solving substantive problems. The Morris worldview was a potent stew of ideas, cynicism, ambition, and grievance. Clinton knew Morris as a brilliant man, and an erratic one. His challenge now was to exploit the brilliance and rein in the excesses.

THE PAIR STARTED THEIR WORK WITH ONE LONG POLL AND ONE SHORT MEMO. The poll, which Morris commissioned in advance of the 1995 State of the Union address, had 259 questions on it. This was so long that it had to be conducted as five separate polls, since no one in his or her right mind would stay on the phone with a caller long enough to answer so many questions. Morris and Clinton met in the White House residence on January 19 to review the results. The meeting lasted five hours. The data fortified the essential argument that a month earlier Morris had reduced to a single-page statement of principles and presented to Clinton. Morris knew Clinton had a vagrant attention span, so in the beginning he brought the page to every meeting. The first four words were the core of Morris's plan: "Fast-forward the Gingrich agenda."

What he meant was that Clinton needed to endorse the most popular premises of the new Republican majority. He should second their goals about reducing the deficit, shrinking government, pruning burdensome regulations, and overhauling welfare to demand work from recipients. Once the electorate saw that Clinton and Gingrich agreed on these broad points, his strategy held, the Republicans would have played all their best cards. Public attention then would shift to the least popular parts of the GOP agenda. These included its hostility to abortion rights and environmental protection, to federal aid for schools, and to the harsh, devil-take-the-hindmost ethic of the Gingrich revolution generally. Only then, with the energy drained from the Republican advance, would the electorate who rejected Clinton so emphatically the previous autumn again be ready to listen to him talk about his own agenda. Morris was not arguing for simple capitulation. The second point on his strategy memo was that Clinton should insist on a "Democratic way of achieving" the Republican priorities, including prudent trimming of government rather than wholesale elimination of agencies and opposition to cuts in popular entitlement programs like Medicare. The next three points were all designed to promote a perception of strength for a president who labored under the reputation for weakness. Clinton should use "executive branch actions" to promote policies without legislative approval; Morris said he should use "foreign policy situations to demonstrate your strength and toughness to the American people" and by all means never "add to the damaging perception that you have flip-flopped on issues. It is never worth the price. If we've said something before, we are bound by it.... Don't ever, ever change your mind."

Here was the essential Morris, all on one page: shrewd, confident, calculating. Clinton thought the advice was sound, but it was hard to swallow even so. For while the strategy promised a revival of his political strength and presidential stature over time, its most immediate assignment was accommodation to the new Republican majority. Seeming reasonable toward Newt Gingrich, even as a ruse, would be seen by many Democrats as a craven retreat. Many of the Democrats who believed this were on Clinton's own staff. There was Ickes, of course, who had loathed Morris since the days when they were on opposite sides of bitter feuds in Manhattan Democratic politics. But the person whom Morris and Clinton both obsessed about was not the hard-bitten Ickes, but the most famous aide on the White House staff: George Stephanopoulos. Though he had been evicted from the White House podium in 1993, he remained a key point of contact for the White House press corps. Few of these reporters knew the truth about his diminished stature: Following the 1994 election, Clinton was barely talking to his former protégé. Stephanopoulos's foes in the White House believed he used his close relationship with the press to covertly run the White House; if there was an idea floating around that Stephanopoulos and his coterie of young liberals did not like, they would shoot it down with unfavorable leaks, thus limiting Clinton's options. (These suspicions were mostly fantasy. White House reporters knew Stephanopoulos as a frustratingly discreet source.) Al Gore had been an enthusiastic backer of Morris's arrival and the changes the consultant was forcing in Clinton's political strategy. Early in Morris's run, the vice president offered him some advice: "You think your enemy here is Harold. It's not. Your enemy is George."

There was something absurd about this notion. Why would a vice president with uncurbed access to the president worry about a staff hand? Indeed, why would Clinton? But central to Clinton's explanation for his 1994 humiliation was that he had lost control of his own political strategy. If so, it was a direct consequence of his management style, encouraging competing factions on his team. Yet he disliked issuing the stern directives necessary to impose order on them. Each side felt sure that it was representing the true Clinton, and that the other side was exploiting the president's weakness for bad advice. The result was that whenever Clinton rowed in one direction, he could be sure there would be people inside his White House who felt perfectly justified in rowing in the opposite direction.

What happened in 1995 was that a White House faction that for two years had been on the margins of influence, watching Clinton's course with sullen frustration, suddenly became empowered by the 1994 debacle. What Morris did, as Ronald Klain, an aide to the vice president, aptly described it, was assemble a "coalition of the disenfranchised." These were people, like policy aide Bruce Reed and speechwriter Don Baer, who had long chafed at how Stephanopoulos and other modish young advisers had become famous, all while dispensing political advice they deemed a disaster. The first-term White House was a little like high school, with a cool crowd basking in media attention while the uncool smoldered in resentment. There was an ideological dimension to this. The famous kids were typically liberal, and the obscure kids were typically moderate New Democrats. Suddenly, they felt liberated—even before they knew who their liberator was. "Putting aside how strange he was," Reed recalled of Morris, "I was glad to have him here. I felt he was running a campaign to put Clinton back in charge of his White House."

In the middle of these internecine battles was Chief of Staff Leon Panetta. He had disapproved of how Stephanopoulos and Begala had run free in the White House for two years. Now he was even more disdainful of how Morris was running amok over the more orderly and process-minded White House Panetta had labored to create upon taking over in June 1994. His quandary was exquisite. He personally regarded Morris as odious, but also thought the chief of staff's job was to accommodate his president and indulge him in his desire to seek advice from a wider circle. Panetta occasionally found himself wondering whether he had landed in a twilight zone, running a White House in which the most influential adviser used a secret code name. Worst of all, Morris was an increasingly obvious challenge to Panetta's authority. The early episodes— the mystery speech drafts in December and January—had been unsettling. Now it was obvious that Clinton's infatuation with Morris was no passing fancy, and that the consultant was effectively running the domestic side of Clinton's presidency. There were now two executive branches. There was an official government, headquartered in the West Wing, where Panetta ruled. Increasingly this was a government of make-believe. The real government was now in the White House residence, where Clinton spent his evenings on the phone with Morris. It was in Room 205 of Washington's Jefferson Hotel, where Morris held meetings and drafted memos in his $440 a night suite. It was in obscure warrens of the Old Executive Office Building, next door to the White House, where nominally less powerful presidential aides work. There Baer, Reed, and the small handful of other aides whom Morris trusted labored to translate his manic flights of strategy and rhetoric into actual presidential proposals. Morris's belief was that a constant procession of such initiatives would demonstrate the vitality of Clinton's presidency in concrete ways—even to voters who had sworn they would never vote for the guy. In pursuit of these ideas, the consultant built his own campaign think tank, run by his brilliant deputy, Thomas Freedman, culling federal agencies and congressional staff offices for new ideas for Clinton's agenda—assuming they polled well in the campaign's weekly surveys.

BY NO MEANS DID CLINTON ALWAYS DO WHAT MORRIS SAID. WHILE SOME OF the consultant's many policy ideas over the next eighteen months were good, others were quite daft. Among the substantial ideas to make it onto Clinton's agenda were new tax deductions and credits to subsidize college tuition. Among the less substantial were widely mocked (but popular, according to Morris's polls) proclamations urging localities to adopt night curfews and school uniforms.

For all his eccentricity, Morris was an agitating and creative force within Clinton's government. He was an advocate for centrism but not for timidity. Defying more cautious and ostensibly more progressive advisers who warned about the political problems this would cause in tobacco-growing states, he was the first and most vociferous voice to urge an administration assault on the tobacco industry and the problem of youth smoking. Before Clinton could advance on intriguing new issues like tobacco he needed to retreat on nettlesome old ones. These were the issues that cut closest to Democratic bones, budget cuts and affirmative action. How much ground would Clinton yield to the Republican charge in the campaign for his own survival? This was Washington's preeminent question for the balance of 1995.

Chapter Sixteen

RELEVANCE

STAND FIRM OR BEND? NO ONE WAS MORE EAGER FOR THE ANSWER THAN the president himself. It was not true, as Bill Clinton's most jaundiced observers would have it, that he would do anything for political survival. It was true that most of his principles were sufficiently elastic that they could accommodate political realities without a crisis of conscience. Clinton could not know how far he might bend until he sized up how much leverage Republicans could exert to *make* him bend. Within months there would be negotiations between Clinton and Republicans over some of the most basic questions about government's role in American life: How big? How interventionist with its regulations on business? How aggressive in leveling the playing field for racial minorities? Before any of this, however, there would be a negotiation within Clinton himself. The partisan holy war that many congressional Democrats were yearning for looked to the president like a strategy for self-immolation in 1996. Acquiescence to Gingrich's ideological crusade was no more tolerable an option, nor any more likely to bring political success. Between self-defeating conflict and craven capitulation lay ample field for maneuver.

The spring of 1995 was Clinton's first good opportunity to explore this field—to measure Republican strength and his own. Gingrich had promised that his House Republicans would act on the ten items in his "Contract with America" within a hundred days of taking power. The hundred-days mythology, born in the New Deal, captivated FDR devotee Gingrich no less than it had captivated FDR devotee Clinton two years earlier.

Marching in disciplined lockstep behind the Speaker, the House by April 7 had voted on all ten items, and had passed nine of them. The larger political community, too, was in Gingrich's thrall. He had asked for television time to address the nation at the hundred-day mark. Astonishingly, several networks had agreed to give it to him. This was unprecedented deference to a legislative leader, offering him a platform normally given only to presidents, and only on high state occasions. The Gingrich festival was agony for Clinton, and it presented a dilemma for his White House. The president was scheduled that day to make his annual appearance before the American Society of Newspaper Editors, convening that year in Dallas. The White House staff, led by Panetta, supposed that Clinton should not do anything to give the day more prominence than it already had. They planned for the president to stay aloof from the hundred-days hype with a speech about education. Morris thought this was foolish, since Gingrich's speech would be a dominating event no matter what Clinton did. The consultant wanted the president to use the occasion to advertise that the important question was no longer the bills the legislative branch passed, but what Clinton—leading the executive branch—had to say about it. Morris urged a point-by-point recital of all the important items on the GOP agenda—where Clinton agreed and where he did not.

A well-functioning White House would have settled this dispute with a timely decision about which strategy was right. In the barely functional dual White Houses that existed now, the debate did not happen until it was almost too late. Panetta had given orders for an education speech to be drafted, and writers duly produced a text. Meanwhile, Morris and Bill Curry, an unsuccesful gubernatorial candidate from Connecticut who had recently joined the White House staff as a Morris ally, proceeded busily on their own track. The two speeches collided just thirty-six hours before Clinton was to speak. At an evening strategy session in the White House residence, each side made its case. Panetta warned that Democrats in Congress would feel betrayed by the accommodationist speech Morris was advocating. The partisan warriors on the Hill believed their drumbeat against the "Contract with America" was starting to hurt Gingrich, and a nuanced message from Clinton would stifle Democrats. But there was no contest which speech Clinton wanted to give. He was desperate to regain the initiative, "to get back in the game," as he regularly put it. Morris's speech was a way to at least engage the debate. As often happened, he let Vice President Gore deliver the news that Panetta did not want to hear. "We need now to emerge from the shadows," Gore said.

This decision marked Morris's own emergence from the shadows. Panetta and Ickes were among a handful of people on Clinton's staff who then knew the identity of the mysterious "Charlie." Having lost their fight, they turned to preventing the speech from becoming an embarrassment, as they felt sure it would be if Clinton delivered the hyperventilated rhetoric Morris had urged. The first time speechwriter Don Baer met Morris was in this period, when Ickes paged him and told him simply to get to consultant Robert Squier's Capitol Hill office by 7 a.m. There he laid eyes on "Charlie" and read his handiwork. The text was indeed far from presidential in tone. Yet the message struck Baer, who had been dismayed since joining the White House staff a year earlier by what he saw as the stale liberal tilt of Clinton's presidency, as exactly right.

But even Baer's improved text was not quite what was delivered. At the urging of Gore and Morris—both of whom felt Clinton spoke with more force and fluency when he was improvising—the president largely ignored the text he took to the podium at a Dallas hotel ballroom. The speech previewed the posture Clinton would adopt all through the coming year. The first task was to project a tone of eminent goodwill and practicality. "I do not want a pile of vetoes," he announced, "I want a pile of bills that will move this country into the future." He claimed the center, and invited his opponents to join him there: "Ideological purity is for partisan extremists. We've got to stop pointing fingers at each other so we can join hands." But this was a prelude to sterner stuff. Republicans were pushing bills that would impose "loser pays" provisions for civil lawsuits, repeal a ban on paramilitary "assault weapons," weaken regulations aimed at contaminated food and pollution, and curb the president's ability to have U.S. troops participate in United Nations peacekeeping missions. Clinton said he did plan to veto them all unless major changes were made. Then he moved to the heart of the matter, the proposed Republican tax cut. Calling it three times larger than what the government could afford, Clinton told his audience it was "not going to happen. . . . Let's get over it and talk about what we can pass."

In sum, the message in Dallas was: Let's be reasonable . . . and do it my way. Panetta was right. The most partisan Democrats, especially in the House, seizing upon the accommodating tone and not the threats beneath it, did not like Clinton's speech. Morris was right, too. Clinton at last felt he was setting the terms of debate, with arguments that were both politically and intellectually defensible. He was in fine spirits when he left Dallas.

ACCOMMODATION, RETREAT, TRIANGULATION—BY WHATEVER NAME, CLIN-ton's strategy in the spring of 1995 was necessary politics. He would abandon unfavorable ground now to fight on high ground later. The strategy was based on a paradox—he would grow in strength through moves that would be perceived, at least initially, as admissions of weakness. However shrewd the strategy, it carried a psychic cost, for it required Clinton to reprogram his internal navigation—the way he viewed history and imagined moving in its stream. Clinton worshipped the heroic, larger-than-life leaders whom he had begun reading about as a boy. Yet it was hard to assume a heroic pose while in tactical retreat. This contradiction came into sharp relief a few days after Clinton returned from California, when he traveled to a little house in a wooded grove in Warm Springs, Georgia.

The house was the cottage where Franklin D. Roosevelt had taken respite while recuperating from polio, and the place where he slumped over and died from a cerebral hemorrhage during the closing days of World War II. The date, April 12, was the fiftieth anniversary of the death. With Gingrich, the would-be dismantler of government, laying claim to the FDR legacy, Clinton and Dick Morris both conceived of the occasion as an opportunity to make the case that Clinton was the true heir to the activist tradition. The celebration included Franklin and Eleanor Roosevelt's granddaughter Anna Roosevelt and Jimmy Carter. The Georgian ex-president called it a "travesty" that Republicans "would claim the legacy of my president." Clinton struck a wistful tone, rhapsodizing about a president who managed to do something that had so far eluded him—to touch "Americans, tens of millions of them, in a very personal way. They felt they knew him as their friend, their father, their uncle. They felt he was doing all the things he was doing in Washington to help them." He concluded that Roosevelt would be in favor of precisely what he was doing—preaching the virtues of cooperation, looking for a way to reform welfare, and pushing tax credits for education.

Among the people in the audience that day were several with a better claim than he had to speculate about what FDR would be fighting for in 1995. One of them was John Kenneth Galbraith, the Harvard economist who as a young man had served in the New Deal. Another was a Roosevelt biographer, Arthur Schlesinger Jr., who later went on to serve in the White House of Clinton's other hero, John F. Kennedy. As a young man, Clinton had devoured *A Thousand Days*, Schlesinger's admiring memoir of the Kennedy years. Probably there was no historian whose high opinion Clinton valued more. But he did not have it. In the next day's *Washington Post*, Galbraith was quoted as saying, "FDR enjoyed his enemies. I'd like to see Bill Clinton enjoy them more." Schlesinger was even more pointed: "I think Clinton very much sees himself in the FDR tradition, all things being equal. Yet FDR loved a good fight; Clinton seems by temperament an accommodator. Accommodation has its uses but it can too easily become appeasement."

Clinton exploded at the White House the next morning when he read his daily clips. A White House aide called Schlesinger at home to warn of Clinton's displeasure. A letter in the president's own hand soon followed. "Those who fought me tooth and nail the last two years know well that I believed in and relished the battles," he lectured the professor. For Democrats, he added, "Now there are two choices—fight on or pile on. The latter is easier, the former right." Then Clinton did the most natural thing for him when confronted with a critic. He began his seduction. Soon came an invitation for Schlesinger, Galbraith, and a handful of other prominent 1960s-era liberals, including JFK speechwriter Theodore Sorensen, Robert Kennedy aide William vanden Heuvel, and LBJ protégé Joseph Califano. Some weeks later, over a seafood luncheon, Clinton could not have been more solicitous. "What do you fellows think I should do about Dick Gephardt's tax proposal?" Clinton asked, referring to a simplification plan the Missouri congressman had released the day before. He lamented how "everything in foreign policy is seen through the prism of Bosnia," thus obscuring other achievements. He emphasized how opposed he was to drug legalization, against which Califano was an energetic crusader, by invoking family history: "We are all prisoners of our experience, and I know that if drugs had been legalized my brother would be a dead man today." He held forth in immaculate detail about growing disparities of wealth and all manner of other subjects. But most of all he talked about how he was girding for battle with Republicans and relishing a chance to use his veto pen. The delegation of liberals nodded approvingly. But these senior citizens had encountered enough apple-polishing graduate students in their days to be wary of the president's patter. "I think all of us were both impressed and disarmed by Clinton's intelligence, vitality and charm," Schlesinger wrote that night in his journal. "I also think we all felt that if he acts the way he talked, things would improve—but still wonder about the 'if.' " Lots of people, some of them in Clinton's employ, were wondering the same thing that spring.

PRIME-TIME NEWS CONFERENCES USED TO BE MOMENTS OF HIGH DRAMA. THEY became for many a form of national entertainment during the early 1960s, the reporters serving as easy foils for John Kennedy's wit. The sessions crackled with tension a decade later, as Richard Nixon seethed at his inquisitors over Watergate. Ronald Reagan was intentionally entertaining, with his genial good humor, and unintentionally so, as when he mangled basic facts about his own policies or called on reporters who were not in attendance because his notes said they were.

The night of April 18, 1995, was the moment this particular Washington art form—news conferences as popular diversions, no matter what was happening in the news—came to an end. Of the major broadcast networks, only CBS agreed to air it. For its trouble, the Tiffany network earned ratings less than half those of *Frasier* on NBC and *Home Improvement* on ABC.

For reporters, the trick in these sessions was to frame a question in which there could not possibly be a scripted answer ready. A reporter for *Aviation Week & Space Technology* took the prize by engaging Clinton with a question that was nearly as far in orbit as the technology his magazine covered. He invited the president to discourse on the distinction between "family values" and "moral virtue in the ancient Roman or old Victorian sense" and whether 1996 might offer a chance to debate the nation's "social compact on the basis of instilling moral virtue rather than family values." ABC and NBC could hardly have been regretting their decision.

Then Clinton answered a question that he had not exactly been asked. The reporter asked whether Clinton worried about "making sure your voice will be heard" if no one was covering his words. Clinton quickly took the bait. "The president is relevant," he answered. "The Constitution gives me relevance. The power of our ideas gives me relevance. The record we have built up over the last two years and the things we're trying to do to implement it give it relevance. The president is relevant here, especially an activist president—and the fact that I'm willing to work with the Republicans." Clinton's own team cringed as the words escaped his lips. Plaintively arguing for relevance was hardly the best way to establish it. George Stephanopoulos later surmised what had happened. Clinton had spoken aloud the meditations Morris had been delivering in their private séances. This was a classic politician's foible, to deliver the stage directions rather than the actor's lines, as when George H.W. Bush had appeared in a New Hampshire diner to announce, "Message: I care." This was low tide for Clinton and his office.

THE TIDE CAME BACK IN THE VERY NEXT DAY. IN THE MIDDLE OF A PHOTO opportunity with the Turkish prime minister, Tansu Ciller, White House press secretary Michael McCurry whispered into Clinton's ear. CNN was reporting that a bomb had destroyed part of a federal building in Oklahoma City.

The news was sketchy. Stay on top of it, Clinton urged, and escorted Ciller to the adjacent Cabinet Room to continue their talks. It was there that Chief of Staff Leon Panetta slipped Clinton a yellow legal pad on which he had scrawled an alarming note: "Half of federal building in O.K. City blown up— expect heavy casualties. Called Janet Reno—she has dispatched FBI." A truism of the White House life—the constant, lurking possibility of crisis—was being proven anew. The immediate speculation was that this was an act of Islamic terrorism—plausible enough given the bombing at the World Trade Center garage two years earlier. There was speculation about the possibility of a second bomb, and misleading reports that the phones were down in another federal building in Boston. Retreating to the White House's basement situation room, Clinton rattled off questions and commands. Have the airports around Oklahoma been shut down to cut off escape? What are the death penalty provisions for such crimes? This was not the flapping, self-absorbed Clinton that aides sometimes saw. "Tight and self-contained" was how speechwriter Jonathan Prince described him in those moments. No one yet was focused on the date—the two-year anniversary of the catastrophic federal assault at David Koresh's Waco compound. But that earlier event did echo in Clinton's mind in another way. His avoidance of the public after Waco had been widely judged as an evasion of responsibility. Two years later, Clinton better understood the expectations of his job and the role the presidency played in the national psychology in moments of shock or grief. Prince came in with remarks that had Clinton vowing to catch the "cowards" who had perpetrated the act. The president wanted to go further, and when he appeared late that afternoon in the White House briefing room he called them "evil cowards." He spoke with a controlled rage. "Let there be no room for doubt, we will find the people who did this," Clinton said quietly. "When we do, justice will be swift, certain, and severe. These people are killers and they must be treated like killers." Clinton soon discovered that he knew one of the 168 people, 19 of them children, who perished inside the Alfred P. Murrah building. Alan Whicher, who weeks earlier had transferred off the president's security detail, had just gone to be second-in-command of the Secret Service office in Oklahoma City.

A blessed stroke of luck that day brought the capture of Timothy McVeigh, who was pulled over about sixty miles north of Oklahoma City for driving a car with no license plates. He went to jail on a firearms charge, and was about an hour away from being released when authorities noticed his resemblance to the "John Doe #1" who had been seen near the bombing. This break led to the arrest of fellow perpetrators Terry Lynn Nichols and his brother James. It led also to the warped explanation for this crime. The men were part of a right-wing militia movement whose members loathed the federal government and for whom the Waco tragedy was a bitter grievance. McVeigh and the Nichols brothers perversely regarded themselves as avengers. On Sunday, four days after the crime, Clinton traveled to Oklahoma City to appear before a packed auditorium of eighteen thousand. Citing a biblical verse, he said, "Those who trouble their own house will inherit the wind." His sermon underscored how the explosion had transformed Clinton's standing. It was the nature of the American system, where the president is both the administrator of government, like a prime minister, and in a more mystical sense the leader of the people. Clinton, whose emotions were the same as those of citizens everywhere, was helping the nation cope. And even the part of the nation that deplored Clinton in other contexts seemed to appreciate it. The weekend after the bombing, a poll by NBC News and the *Wall Street Journal* found 84 percent of Americans responding approvingly to Clinton's handling of the attack at Oklahoma City.

Sensing the opening, Clinton and Dick Morris methodically moved to take political advantage of the fact that the president was for the moment being perceived as above politics. That Sunday on *60 Minutes* (the last time he had been on the show was in 1992 to confess causing "pain in his marriage") Clinton proposed a package of new laws to give the government more power to investigate and prosecute terrorists. In May, he went to Michigan State University to denounce militias. "There is nothing patriotic about hating your country, or pretending that you can love your country but despise your government," he bristled. "How dare you suggest that we, in the freest nation on earth, live in tyranny?"

White House aides became indignant when reporters asked if the president was trying to reap political gain from the tragedy. But Morris had no compunction about doing exactly that. Just a week after the bombing, his agenda for Clinton's weekly political meeting on April 27 plotted how to use Oklahoma City to best advantage. "A. Temporary gain: boost in ratings," Morris wrote in the strategy paper. "B. More permanent gain: Improvements in character/personality attributes—remedies weakness, incompetence, ineffectiveness found in recent poll. C. Permanent possible gain: sets up Extremist Issue vs. Republicans." The president was relevant again.

Chapter Seventeen

BALANCE

MEMORIAL DAY WEEKEND OF 1995 ARRIVED TO FIND ALL THE WHITE House's top hands busy at the office. Their holiday assignment was to attend to presidential anxieties. Clinton had grown increasingly agitated over his strategy for confronting the year's preeminent domestic controversy. Once again, as in 1993, the subject was the federal budget: its size, and the reach of the national government in American life. Unlike 1993, when the new president had seized Washington's agenda, now he was emphatically in the role of observer and critic.

This was the heart of Clinton's problem. With the year nearly half over, he was tired of observing and criticizing the Republican budget without having a proposal of his own. As they gathered in the Oval Office, Clinton listened to George Stephanopoulos explain, as he and others had explained many times in the preceding months, the merits of continuing with the current strategy of excoriating excesses of the Republican budget plan and not muddying the debate by presenting a credible alternative. This time, however, the president turned on his young retainer with acid sarcasm: "That's fine. When people say,

'Where's your plan?' I'll say, 'Oh, I'm just president of the United States. You want me to have a plan?' "

As this outburst made plain, the "rope-a-dope" strategy that Clinton had reluctantly fashioned in concert with congressional Democrats the previous winter was no longer tolerable to him. Extracting himself from a stale strategy and its supporters, though, was complicated, with political and even psychological dimensions. Clinton desperately wanted liberation from the clammy embrace of Democrats on Capitol Hill and from his own White House team. He could get it only by an open break with ostensible friends—precisely the kind of personal conflict he would always avoid unless absolutely necessary.

In theory, the Democratic approach for the first part of 1995 had a certain smart-aleck logic. Newt Gingrich, showing admirable fealty to his promises, was leading the new Republican majority on a purposeful march to cut both taxes and spending, while putting the nation on a glide path toward a balanced budget within seven years. Democrats had responded by merrily denouncing the hardship these cuts would cause, particularly in popular entitlements like the Medicare health program for senior citizens. (The Medicare reductions were not literal cuts but reductions in the rate of growth.) As Gore put it, Republicans needed a "rendezvous with reality." In other words, they needed to confront the obvious truth that it was a lot easier to talk about balanced budgets in the abstract than to implement the specific policies needed to make them happen. Only at the end of the year, after Republicans had been softened by the rhetorical barrage, would Democrats put forward constructive ideas of their own.

Clinton had been ill at ease with this theory from the beginning, and grew ever more so as the months wore on. As a political matter, he simply did not accept the judgment of senior staff aides like Panetta and Stephanopoulos that Democrats were scoring points with the public. When presented with polls showing opposition to specific Republican budget cuts, Clinton, echoing what Morris had been urging in their private consultations, responded, "That's not right! People will forgive Republicans the details because they have a plan."

Beyond politics, the obstructionist approach offended Clinton's sense of virtue. By no means did he agree with Gingrich's prescriptions for the deficit and for the problem of rising Medicare costs, but he did agree on the diagnosis. These were large and worthy problems; the previous year's debacle over health care reform had been his own attempt to grapple with them. He deplored how Republicans then, and during the 1993 budget battle, had vilified his proposals while refusing to meet him halfway. Indeed, Clinton treasured his resentments. As Gene Sperling, who had been heavily involved in the budget debate, described the mindset, "How could he hold on to his view of how they screwed him on health care if he did the same thing to them on the deficit?"

For weeks, his White House staff had tried to restrain him. But they could not keep him corralled. The stereotype of Clinton as a supremely guileful and deceptive politician was essentially wrong. On important matters, his real sentiments always surfaced, no matter how the staff tried to keep him "on message." In this instance, he broke free in late May during a telephone interview with New Hampshire Public Radio, in which he responded to the interviewer's needling by casually endorsing the idea that the budget indeed could be balanced within ten years. Ten years was not as ambitious as the Republican target of seven. Even so, it obviously deviated from the White House official line, which was that budget balance by any precise date required grievous cuts in social services and risked sending the economy into recession. Horrified, White House aides coaxed a reluctant Clinton into walking back his interview comments during a question-and-answer session with reporters in the Rose Garden a few days later.

The president's mention of a ten-year time frame was not incidental. The administration's budget analysts had reported that balancing the budget within seven years—under the prevailing economic growth forecasts—would essentially mean rescinding most of the new Clinton domestic programs that had already been passed, and abandoning plans for anything more. (The surging economy of the late nineties, which flooded government coffers with tax revenue, would later make these deliberations seem quaint. At the time, every decision involved exquisite trade-offs between deficit reduction and the progressive domestic spending Clinton yearned for.) In May, however, Clinton learned of a Treasury Department study that showed that extending the time frame to ten years offered vastly more flexibility to accommodate both deficit reduction and some spending on new Clinton programs.

The president's gust of irritation at Stephanopoulos had a clarifying effect. It showed there was no point arguing any longer. Clinton's economic and political advisers reconciled themselves to the fact that he wanted a balanced-budget plan of his own, and it was their job to give him one. Even his anger came as something of a relief. It suggested he was voicing his genuine wishes; he was not merely taking stage direction from the dreaded Dick Morris.

As Stephanopoulos retreated from the Oval Office, his friend Sperling followed behind.

"George, are you okay?" Sperling asked.

"I'm fine, I'm fine," Stephanopoulos replied. "He wants to do this. He's never going to be able to hit the Republicans' plan until he has one of his own."

CLINTON HAD WANTED TO ANNOUNCE HIS OWN NEW BUDGET PLAN THE VERY next day, with a televised speech to the nation. Morris, with his usual fervor, had said that unless the president embraced a balanced budget immediately, Clinton's standing with the public on this issue would be lost irretrievably. But moving so quickly would have caused an insurrection. There was no way Panetta or Robert Rubin, at Treasury, could stand for releasing a plan that was not backed by credible numbers, vetted by administration budget experts. This would take another two weeks.

So the speech was set for June 13. Clinton was determined to reach a national audience, which required the cooperation of the television networks that had skipped his feeble East Room news conference two months earlier. To signal the gravity of the moment, Al Gore personally phoned the three network news anchors to make the request. They gave the president five minutes.

The brevity of the speech made the usual tussle about what to leave in and what to take out that much more delicate. Each side in the White House presumed that the first lady was an ally. Dick Morris said she had been "instrumental in the birth of this speech," and when she phoned that day with pleas that the president mention his plan to increase benefits under Medicare for mammograms and Alzheimer's care, he gladly complied. She also instructed an aide to call Stephanopoulos to tell him to "make sure the speech gives something to the Democrats." At Stephanopoulos's urging, the first lady prevailed on Clinton to take out a friendly and familiar reference to Newt Gingrich and replace it with a more austere reference to "the Speaker."

The speech itself was marinated in Morris's brand of data-driven rhetoric. Each line reflected a point that polls showed resonated with an electorate that was skeptical of government in general, but enthusiastically protective about specific items—usually the programs that benefited the middle class. Education spending was the most popular of these, leading directly to Clinton's opening: "First, because our most important mission is to help people make the most of their own lives, don't cut education." Health care was next. As Clinton and Gingrich both knew, trimming programs for the elderly and the poor was essential to finding substantial savings in the budget, even though many voters regarded the Medicare program as sacrosanct. Clinton cheerfully proposed an act of fiscal levitation: "Second, balance the budget by controlling health care costs, strengthening Medicare, and saving Medicaid, not by slashing health services for the elderly." This was a prelude to the speech's main point, which was the core of the debate in 1995, or for that matter in any year: Who should bear the burden for funding government? The president gave his answer: "Cut taxes for the middle class and not the wealthy. We shouldn't cut education or Medicare just to make room for a tax cut for people who don't really need it."

The reaction from Capitol Hill was immediate and brutal. The majority of congressional Democrats were enraged. For many, the speech confirmed what they already suspected: that Clinton was ready to save his skin and cut whatever deal he needed with Republicans. Democratic principles—and the political vulnerabilities of Democratic members of Congress—could be damned. New Jersey Democrat Donald Payne, the head of the Congressional Black Caucus, declared that Clinton's plan was "a quantum leap backward for social policy, and it will have long-lasting, explosive results." Congresswoman Patricia Schroeder of Colorado reflected the general Democratic contempt for the party's leader. Republicans, she said, were playing with Clinton "like a kitten with a string." As for Clinton's own party, she added, "I don't think he has even thought about Democrats over here. He's thinking about himself and presidential politics." Congressman David Obey from Wisconsin chimed in: "I think most of us learned some time ago, if you don't like the president's position on a particular issue, you simply need to wait a few weeks."

If it was liberation from congressional Democrats that Clinton was seeking, he now had it. Despite the discomfort the speech had caused, Clinton and Morris would soon be vindicated in their judgment, on both substantive and political grounds. On substance, the president had traded in an intellectually indefensible position for one that he could advance with a straight face. On politics, the polling over the ensuing months showed that the public, particularly the moderate independent voters on whom Clinton's fate hinged, was indeed more willing to listen to a critique of the Republican proposals when there was a credible alternative on the table.

Paradoxically, Clinton was now in an even stronger position with liberal Democrats. As Morris viewed the dynamic, the party's congressional wing was like a temperamental dog—motivated more powerfully by fear than by affection. Many Democratic lawmakers plainly had little personal regard for Clinton. The way to keep them at heel—and avoid a primary challenge from the party's liberal wing—was to be so popular in public opinion that Democrats saw no gain in defying the president. This analysis would be proven right again and again in the years to come.

CLINTON'S DECISION TO ENTER THE BUDGET DEBATE WAS AN OBVIOUS DECLA-
ration of independence from the majority of his own staff. It was also the high
watermark of Morris's influence. The consultant remained the president's
chief strategist for the next year, but the relationship lost its Rasputin-like dimension. The president's political standing was on the upswing, in some significant measure owing to Morris's advice. As Clinton's prospects rose, so did
his self-confidence—and his flexibility. He no longer wished to be in the thrall
of any one adviser. Instead, he was ready to resume his more familiar pattern
of navigating through crosscurrents of conflicting advice, fashioning a course
that was distinctively his own.

The scales began tipping within minutes of the Oval Office address. The
president had adjourned immediately after the speech to watch the television
analysis with a group that included Morris, Stephanopoulos, and Gene Sperling. Commentator Bill Schneider on CNN was describing the Democratic
backlash, prompting Clinton to agree darkly: "That's right. No president was
ever rewarded for doing deficit reduction." As Stephanopoulos later recounted
the moment, Morris sensed that Clinton needed reassurance, and chimed in:
"Remember the theory, remember the theory. We have the Perot voters out
there, lying in wait. This is the moment to strike—and watch the poll numbers
go-o *UP!*" By illustration, Morris stood on his tiptoes and wiggled his fingers
high above his head. This was all too much for the president. Two weeks before, Stephanopoulos had been in the doghouse. Now it was Morris's turn.
Clinton crushed his Diet Coke can as he barked, "I did this because it's the
right thing to do, Dick. I did this because it's the right thing to do."

The episode showed anew how the commonplace view of Clinton as
an exclusively political creature missed the mark. There was naturally an element of calculation behind the president's budget moves. But Clinton's mind,
temperament, and self-image demanded a higher standard—that the calcu-
lations also fit within a coherent intellectual framework. Was there a unifying logic behind his tactical moves? What was he really trying to achieve as
president?

The crude way of describing what Clinton was doing in early and middle
1995 was that he was lurching rightward in programs and language in order to
avoid being tattooed as a liberal in the 1996 campaign. The reality, though, is
that Clinton had learned—or, more precisely, relearned—to craft a politics
that defied easy categorization and was indeed more sophisticated than simply

embracing the most conservative position that he figured a Democrat could get away with.

For example, in mid-July, when Clinton waded into the thorny question of religion's role in public life, and especially in the public schools, his motives were, as usual in this year of Republican ascendancy, partly defensive. Conservatives had made large gains, Clinton knew, from the perception that liberals and the courts had evicted all religious observance and discussion of morality in public schools. But he felt certain the issue could be neutralized—or even turned into something more positive for the progressive side—with a more sophisticated approach. The popular perception that religion had been banished from schools was wrong, he believed, asserting that the Supreme Court rulings actually allowed administrators and students alike considerably more latitude to honor religious observance, so long as the activity was not coercive. He was eager to make a speech laying out the middle ground, in tandem with the announcement of a new Education Department pamphlet advising schools on what their rights and responsibilities really were. The plan sent his staff into a tizzy. From the right, Morris wanted to avoid the topic, fearing that any discussion of this sensitive subject would inflame conservatives and draw attention to Democratic vulnerabilities on the issue. From the left, Maggie Williams, Hillary Clinton's chief of staff, warned of another clumsy ideological retreat, as when Clinton had seemed to endorse a school prayer amendment in the wake of the mid-term elections. Jonathan Prince, the young speechwriter, was caught in the middle between these two formidable figures. The inevitable result was a bland and boring speech draft. Clinton saw the version and boiled over: "This is not what I want to say at all!" On the short drive out to James Madison High School in northern Virginia, he quickly recast the speech into a quite personal statement of his own values. He talked about the role of religion in his own life, where a daily prayer in school was "as common as apple pie in my hometown." He added, "Now, you could say, it certainly didn't do any harm; it might have done a little good." The whole process, Prince realized, showed the effort it took for Clinton to transcend his would-be protectors and simply say what he thought.

WHAT DID HE REALLY THINK? ON THAT SUMMER'S MOST POTENTIALLY DIVIsive topic—the role of racial preferences—most people around Clinton believed they knew what he *felt*. Prejudice was immoral, and helping blacks and other minorities overcome the legacy of discrimination that was deeply rooted in America's culture, economy, and government institutions was the right thing to do. But as for what he *thought*, that was a trickier proposition. How to balance the imperative of racial fairness with the political reality that affirmative action was deeply unpopular? Did he really agree with all the government was doing in the name of affirmative action? Would he try to navigate these intellectual, moral, and, above all, political shoals with clever language and better salesmanship? Or might he choose to launch a deep and substantive overhaul of affirmative action—one that would inevitably be viewed by many blacks and liberals as an unconscionable retreat? His true intentions were a puzzle even to the people with whom he was spending hours discussing these very questions.

Christopher Edley Jr., a Harvard law professor who had been tapped to join George Stephanopoulos in heading the White House's review of affirmative action, tried to help Clinton begin his intellectual journey with a large batch of articles and speeches. Clinton read the material and announced, "Most of these people don't know what the hell they're talking about." This was true enough. Clinton's own experience, as a politician bridging the color gap and as a governor and president who saw how programs were actually implemented, gave him a keener sense of reality than the abstract musings of intellectuals. Clinton saw the problem as inherently political. Most Americans, as he saw it, believed in promoting racial equality, but their emotions were easily manipulated. "The definition makes all the difference," he observed to Stephanopoulos. "Preferences we lose; affirmative action we win." Yet watching the turning of Clinton's mental gears as he solved a political problem could also be unsettling to people like Edley and Stephanopoulos. If racial justice was his lodestar, as Clinton often claimed, would not his views on the most contentious dimension of the issue be more settled? Did he have misgivings about entertaining the views of Morris, who in his Republican incarnation had helped Senator Jesse Helms win re-election in one of the most race-baiting campaigns of modern times? Morris was by no means a racist. But he and White House aide Bill Curry were eager for a form of affirmative action that moved away from race-based preferences toward what they regarded as a more intellectually and politically defensible system of preferences based on economic need. Clinton's old allies at the Democratic Leadership Council also endorsed this notion, which plainly intrigued Clinton but would have been a dramatic departure from the status quo.

If the passivity of Clinton's style could be frustrating—his penchant for study and delay and preference for contingent choices rather than final ones—

the affirmative action debate showed how useful this style could be at times. The climate changed during the five months of study on the issue. As the results of the improving economy began slowly and gradually to be more evident, polling suggested that opposition to affirmative action might be a less potent issue than Republicans had assumed and Clinton had feared. At the same time, Clinton's endorsement of a balanced budget had changed his own political calculus. He was not eager to disappoint the Democratic base again; indeed, doing so on this particular issue would have been akin to begging for a Democratic primary challenge from the Reverend Jesse Jackson. Most important, in the middle of the review, the Supreme Court had entered the issue. On June 12, in a 5 to 4 ruling, the justices ruled in *Adarand* v. *Peña* that affirmative action was constitutional only if "narrowly tailored" and served a "compelling governmental interest." The ruling suggested, though the justices left the matter maddeningly unclear, that race-based preferences would pass muster only if policymakers presented specific evidence of past or present racial discrimination—a general assertion of discrimination was not sufficient—and also demonstrated why a specific program was the proper remedy. Affirmative action had been preserved, but the threshold to invoke it had risen. Now, Clinton was in the far preferable position of announcing that his administration would comply with the ruling, even as he asserted a vigorous defense of affirmative action.

This is precisely what he said at the National Archives, where the president's podium was bracketed by copies of the Declaration of Independence and Constitution. Clinton's speech was a success, interrupted fifteen times by applause—no surprise, from a by-invitation audience—but it also won considerable praise from outside commentators. "Mend it, don't end it" was the catchphrase Clinton himself had settled on to describe his approach. He outlined the principles for any affirmative action program in his administration: "No quotas in theory or practice; no illegal discrimination of any kind, including reverse discrimination; no preference for people who are not qualified for any job or other opportunity; and as soon as a program has succeeded it must be retired."

After reciting these provisos, Clinton concluded: "But let me be clear: Affirmative action has been good for America."

The long-awaited pronouncement on affirmative action was correctly viewed as far more a defense than a critique of the status quo. As a practical matter, the administration made little effort, except as required by legal challenges, to either mend existing programs or end ones that had outlived their usefulness. Edley, though he cheered the result, reflected later that such a process could just as easily have produced a retreat from affirmative action as an affirmation. "The whole thing was very much a jump ball," he said.

SUCH DOUBTS AS EDLEY'S WERE A BY-PRODUCT OF CLINTON'S SURVIVALIST brand of politics, in which policies and personnel are constantly shifted to suit new circumstances and new emergencies. However effective, this style was destined to leave both loyalists and adversaries wondering about his character and intentions. One morning early in August, one of those loyalists met with his boss to tell him goodbye. After eight months of being cut out of the president's loop, Paul Begala told Clinton he was leaving Washington for Texas. Though he did not say so, the truth was Begala had no interest in being in Washington watching the president run for re-election under the tutelage of Dick Morris. He found the whole spectacle appalling.

The surest way to get Clinton's attention was to leave him. While people were constantly shifting between inner and outer orbits in his universe, he hated it when they left entirely. After months of distance, Clinton now urged Begala to stay and work for the campaign. Begala declined politely. Clinton then invited Begala on a morning jog; that offer the consultant accepted. As they ran, Begala noted to Clinton that Republicans seemed to be basing their budget strategy on an assumption that at the end of the day the president would buckle and sign on to a plan that accommodated Republican demands. This was not an unreasonable assumption, given Clinton's moves to date. Many on his own team, in fact, were worried that the Republicans had divined the president's likely course.

Clinton was dumbfounded. "They can't really believe that, can they, Paulie?" he said in amazement. "They can't really believe I'll cave to their demands."

The moment of confrontation still lay three months ahead. Clinton was confident of his resolve, even if few others were.

Chapter Eighteen

ROLL EVERY DIE

THE FIRST MONTHS OF 1995 HAD GIVEN CLINTON, WHO HAD ENOUGH on his plate with Newt Gingrich, a blessed reprieve from the torments of Bosnia. A temporary ceasefire among the warring Balkan parties—negotiated, inevitably, by Jimmy Carter—had halted the bloodshed through the winter. On the first of May, however, the ceasefire ended, and so did Clinton's respite. The violence, including indiscriminate shelling of civilians in Sarajevo, began immediately.

During Clinton's first two years in office, the halting and ultimately ineffectual efforts to find a solution to ethnic cleansing had yielded to an ostensibly more realistic policy of "muddling through," in the bleak phrase used at the Pentagon. This meant acknowledging there were limits to what the United States could do to halt warfare in the former Yugoslavia, and trying to move the problem to the margins of administration foreign policy. This would allow Clinton to focus on issues of larger strategic importance, like relationships with Russia and China, and his plans for expansion of the NATO alliance. But muddling through was based on a flawed premise. In the age of the satellite and twenty-four-hour news, a problem like Bosnia could not be pushed easily to the peripheries of public consciousness. Clinton was realizing that the flaccid U.S. and allied response to Bosnia was undermining even unrelated aspects of his foreign policy. It was not possible to look commanding or creative in one sphere while being ostentatiously feckless in another.

The costs of a more robust policy were as high as ever, particularly with the 1996 re-election campaign looming. From the first days of his presidency, Clinton had pledged that he would send troops to Bosnia to help enforce a final peace settlement, but would not send them into the middle of an ongoing civil war. The American people were not enthusiastic about either prospect. Polls showed that most voters did not wish to risk the lives of U.S. soldiers and airmen by sending them to a country that presented no direct threat to national security. If Clinton sent them anyway, and Americans died in even modest numbers, he could destroy his presidency. At the same time, the costs of inaction—diplomatic, political, and moral—were mounting. Clinton's efforts to weigh these costs and make an honorable choice among them represented one of the great dramas of his presidency, one that hurtled to conclusion during the remaining months of 1995.

ONE OF THE FACTORS THAT MADE THE PRESIDENT'S CHOICES IN BOSNIA SO IMpossible was that there seemed increasingly to be no way of avoiding a U.S. military commitment of some kind. Even though American troops were not currently on the ground, soldiers from many of America's NATO allies were. They were serving a dangerous and ineffective United Nations humanitarian operation in Bosnia—a peacekeeping force, allegedly. Far from keeping the peace, these forces were themselves the targets of sniper fire and hostage-taking by increasingly brazen Bosnian Serb forces. If such provocation continued, European governments had served notice that they would withdraw their lightly armed troops. Here was the rub for Clinton. A withdrawal was a potentially dangerous operation, requiring helicopter transport and ground support to ensure that the U.N. forces left Bosnia safely. Long before, Clinton had committed the United States to take the lead in extracting the U.N. troops, if it came to this. Such a pledge was the least the world's sole superpower could do for allies who otherwise were bearing all the risks in Bosnia. This commitment, however, presented a logical challenge: If the United States was willing to undertake a significant military operation to facilitate a de facto surrender, why not do the same in pursuit of success? Why not use U.S. military power to strengthen the U.N. force, punish the Bosnian Serb bullies for any further aggression, and at last push the warring parties to the peace table?

The person in the White House who hoped most devoutly for such a policy was National Security Adviser Tony Lake. He knew Clinton was not yet ready to embrace the risks a more assertive policy would entail. At the very least, however, Lake believed the president needed to make clear to the American people—and the rest of the world—that one way or the other the United States would soon confront major obligations in Bosnia. U.S. forces would be going to Bosnia to help pull the U.N. peacekeepers out, or help bring peace in. There was a hard choice looming, and the public might as well know.

Lake made this case during a long conversation with Clinton aboard Air Force One en route to Colorado Springs, where the president was addressing the U.S. Air Force Academy. By tradition, each spring presidents always deliver a commencement address at one of the nation's four service academies. On this day, the last in May, the sky was a radiant blue, offering a breathtaking view of the Rocky Mountains from the academy football stadium. Clinton made the statement Lake wanted: "We have obligations to our NATO allies, and I do not believe we can leave them in the lurch."

The actual policy changes Clinton announced seemed at first blush rather modest. In addition to restating the long-standing commitment to help evacuate U.N. peacekeepers, Clinton said he would consider sending U.S. troops in for a "reconfiguration and a strengthening" of the peacekeepers into more secure positions. To alert ears in Congress and in the national news media, this sounded like a fancy way of expanding the conditions under which the United States might go to Bosnia. The uproar was immediate and intense. Some of it came from Republicans who wanted nothing to do with putting American ground forces in Bosnia. It also came from the president's own team. "This is terrible!" exclaimed Dick Morris in a phone call after the president finished the speech. "We've got to walk this back."

Officially, the president's political consultant had nothing to do with foreign policy. Unofficially, Clinton was consulting with him on this subject as on any other that so directly affected his re-election effort. The president's injunction was that Morris should never mention foreign policy in the presence of a third person. Within this constraint, Morris never hesitated to weigh in on topics from Japanese trade to Russia policy. By no means did Clinton always take the advice, but he was eager for an outside perspective. His foreign policy team, the president believed, too often insulated him from fresh ideas. "There's a regency," Morris taunted him. "You're too young now to run your own foreign policy, so Lake and Christopher have to do it. But when you turn twenty-one they'll let you take it over."

Morris, expert on neither the Balkans nor military affairs, did at least know political history. "You don't want to be Lyndon Johnson," he warned. "It's the Democrats' disease to take the same compassion that motivates their domestic policies and let it lure them into heroic but ill-considered foreign wars." He faxed Clinton a proposed Saturday radio address trying to muffle the impact of the Colorado Springs speech. With some minor changes, the president recorded it during a stop in Billings, Montana. Clinton essentially revoked any offer to strengthen or reconfigure the U.N. force, repeating only a pledge to help in "the remote, indeed highly unlikely event" that a unit "became stranded and could not get out of a particular place in Bosnia."

If this retreat settled nerves in Washington, it rubbed them raw in Europe. Governments there already resented how little the United States was doing, even as the administration criticized the ineffectiveness of their peacekeepers. *The Times* of London observed acidly, "as so often with this most changeable of Presidents, his latest wisp of resolve evaporated halfway down Pennsylvania Avenue, blown away by Congressional muttering."

FROM THE WHITE HOUSE VANTAGE POINT, EUROPEAN OPINION WAS A NO-win proposition. Allies took flight when the United States tried to work cooperatively with them on a Bosnia solution, as during Warren Christopher's ill-fated Bosnia mission in 1993. But, equally, they enjoyed complaining about American bullying and unilateralism. Like a moody adolescent, Europe simultaneously protested Washington's heavy hand and Clinton's lack of leadership.

If Clinton was uncertain about where he wanted to lead in Bosnia, he was clear on one thing: He did not want anyone else trying to take the steering wheel. An effort by the newly elected French president, Jacques Chirac, to do precisely this was the next chapter in the year's Bosnia drama. The new French leader, formerly the mayor of Paris, had roared onto the international scene with his election in May. He combined a suave manner with an instinct for self-aggrandizement that in France caused him to be known as "Le Bulldozer." Clinton soon understood why. After Clinton's vacillating comments on an American-led rescue force in Bosnia, Chirac called the White House demanding an explanation. As Clinton tried to explain his position, with a translator on the line, Chirac interrupted the translator and interjected in English: "Bill, this is a time when we have to be tough."

Clinton did not enjoy being goaded like this. But Chirac in his way was serving a useful purpose—as a spur to action. On June 14, he came to Washington. Prior to his meeting, Clinton met with his senior foreign policy advisers for what was known in the White House as a "pre-brief," a session to review the agenda and craft talking points. The meeting focused largely on Bosnia and the Chirac challenge. Clinton snapped at his team: "We need to get the policy straight, or we're just going to be kicking the can down the road again. Right now we've got a situation, we've got no clear mission, no one's in control of events."

A BAD JUNE WAS FOLLOWED BY A FAR WORSE JULY. IN THREE YEARS OF FIGHTing, killing had become so routine that Bosnia for a time had lost its ability to shock—until a place called Srebrenica. In the early morning hours of July 6, Bosnian Serb forces began an attack on this enclave that had been declared a United Nations "safe area." Dutch peacekeepers in Srebrenica radioed for NATO air strikes to help impede the attack. Shockingly, but not surprisingly, their request was rejected. NATO's war planes were then operating under a "dual-key" arrangement, in which any use of airpower had to be approved by both NATO and U.N. commanders. The U.N. officials in Bosnia, fearing escalation of the conflict above all, regularly turned down requests for bombing or close air support, or delayed so long in approving that it was too late to do any good. In this instance, with no impediments from the air, Bosnian Serb forces quickly captured Srebrenica and executed a long-planned atrocity. Some 23,000 women and children were put on trains to Bosnian Muslim territory near Tuzla. Eight thousand men and boys left behind were executed and buried in mass graves. The scale and logistical details of this killing were not known until weeks afterward. But the general scope of horror was evident immediately to the president and his top aides from intelligence reports arriving from the CIA. For that matter, it was evident to any citizen with access to any of the major newspapers with correspondents in Bosnia.

Clinton was appalled, but a practical solution to the crisis was still not apparent. Impractical solutions continued to flow from Chirac in Paris. The French president was advocating a quick move by ground troops in a European "rapid reaction force" to forcibly retake Srebrenica and provide protection for other Bosnian Muslim enclaves in nearby Gorazde and even the capital of Sarajevo. The plan would not require American troops but would involve troop transport by American helicopters. Chirac's plan was bold, certainly, but in a phone call with Clinton he could not answer the obvious follow-up question: What next? Did he propose that troops stay on the ground indefinitely, amid the crossfire? Clinton hung up the phone and turned with disdain to his national security aides, who had been listening to the call. "Can you believe he proposed that? Then what do we do? . . . Should we take over the whole country?"

Then he turned to the young naval aide who had set up the secure line for the call. "What do you think we should do on Bosnia?" he asked.

"I don't know, Mr. President," the aide replied with bewilderment.

Chirac did not have the answer, but it was painfully clear to Clinton that he did not either.

AND YET THE HORROR OF SREBRENICA WAS CLARIFYING NOT JUST FOR THE president, but for his entire administration. For the first time, the forces that had been weighted decisively in favor of caution and muddling through shifted in favor of risk and the desire for some clear and finite conclusion.

This shift had a moral component, which Vice President Gore gave voice to at a national security meeting in the days after. He noted that the papers had all carried a photograph of a young woman, a refugee from the fallen enclave, who in agony over losing her family had committed suicide by hanging herself from a tree with a belt and floral shawl. "My 21-year-old daughter asked about that picture," he told Clinton. "What am I supposed to tell her? Why is this happening, and we're not doing anything?"

The shift also had a political component. Even Dick Morris, while terrified of putting ground troops in the Balkans a year before the election, had concluded that the growing chaos in Bosnia presented a liability of a different kind. Polls showed Americans were dead set against troops but supportive of more robust use of airpower.

Actions in Congress added political momentum toward resolution of the Bosnia problem. Prodded by Senate majority leader Robert Dole, Congress had passed by veto-proof majorities legislation mandating that the United States unilaterally end the arms embargo and let the Bosnian Muslims defend themselves. As in 1993, Clinton thought this solution was simplistic: The United States could not simply lift the embargo unless it was prepared to protect the Bosnian Muslims for several months while they had time to procure arms and train to use them. But Clinton could not sustain this position unless he could show that he had a policy of his own that was leading somewhere. He told Stephanopoulos that the administration needed "to bust our rear to get a [peace] settlement in the next couple of months—explore all alternatives, roll every die." The alternative, he said, was that a Bosnian denouement would be "dropped in during the middle of the campaign."

The third component in the shifting administration consensus toward action was military. Both Defense Secretary Bill Perry and Joint Chiefs Chairman General John Shalikashvili long had been skeptical of a Bosnian intervention. But they both also were sickened by Srebrenica and appalled at the alarming impotence of the Western powers the episode revealed. Perry had come to believe that robust airpower—"not a bomb or two, not a pinprick, but a massive air campaign"—was the only language the Bosnian Serbs or their sponsors in Serbia proper could understand. The views of "Shali," as he was uniformly known, were just as important. No figure better symbolized the transition Clinton had made in his relationship with the uniformed forces. Colin Powell, by virtue of his imposing public reputation, could effectively veto military options. He gave advice on the question of *how* to use power, on which civilians should appropriately defer to military experts, but he also did not hesitate to weigh in on *whether* to use power. Shali viewed his responsibilities differently. His job was to serve the president, which meant expanding his options and room for maneuver, not closing them off. Shali's own instincts about military strategy were in substance not so different from the Powell Doctrine, with its emphasis on overwhelming force and clear exit plans, but he cleaved to his view less rigidly. He never became famous like Powell. But his flexibility and competence in four years as Joint Chiefs chairman were a part of this young president's rising confidence as a commander in chief.

Shalikashvili was born in Poland in 1936, the son of a career soldier. He moved to the United States only at age sixteen, learned English partly by watching John Wayne Westerns, and never did fully lose his accent. He was a soft-spoken and sophisticated man, commanding but in a less luminescent way than Powell. Clinton enjoyed him immensely, and was proud of himself for appointing someone with what he saw as a uniquely American life story. When the general spoke, Clinton sometimes could be seen suppressing a half smile at this unorthodox figure in the midst of his cabinet.

THE MOST IMPORTANT FIGURE INFLUENCING CLINTON THAT SUMMER AS HE at last found his spine on Bosnia was Tony Lake. The American reaction to ethnic cleansing had so far been ambivalent—the horrible contemplation of crimes competing with the horrible realization that perhaps there was nothing reasonable that could be done about them. In this sense, Lake was the administration's emblematic figure. Ambivalence about power—the knowledge that good intentions can go tragically awry—had been woven into the whole of his adult life. The national security adviser had been a young foreign service officer. At the beginning, like others of his liberal instincts in those days, he had been a believer in the cause, then saw those idealistic purposes go sour. He had also seen the cynical side of power as a young aide on Henry Kissinger's National Security Council staff in the Nixon White House. His resignation in protest after the invasion of Cambodia defined the next two decades of his career, making him a hero of the Democratic foreign policy establishment. In his mid-career, he held the prestigious policy-planning job in the Carter State Department, and spent several years in academia—haunted all this time by the American misadventure in Vietnam. He was still haunted at age fifty-three, when Clinton gave him the job Kissinger once held.

Lake's idealistic impulses were part of a tradition dating to Woodrow Wilson, the president who was defined by his belief in the promise of international institutions and law, and in the redemptive possibilities of American power and righteousness in a wicked world. These instincts had been tempered by his generation's Vietnam experience, but not lost. Asked to define his philosophy that first year, Lake called himself a "pragmatic neo-Wilsonian." What did this mean? The incoherence of this clunky phrase aptly fit the incoherence of Clinton's early foreign policy.

Lake had all manner of problems during his first years back in the White House, mostly to do with his relationship with Clinton. They had not known each other before the 1992 campaign. Most of the time there was cordiality between them, even light banter and jokes, but little genuine comfort. Lake was a reserved and even diffident man who believed devoutly in the traditional divide between politics and foreign policy, and insisted on a thick layer of insulation. Clinton believed there was a political dimension to every important problem, and wanted someone with whom he could think and talk about this openly.

One sign of the distance between them was the fact that Clinton rarely snapped or exploded at Lake, the way he would around someone like Sandy Berger, with whom he was more comfortable. Once, on a foreign trip, Clinton did boil over at Lake over some minor irritation. Shaken, Lake sought out presidential aide Bruce Lindsey and warned, "If he ever does that again, I'll quit."

Lake was close to Stephanopoulos, but in general he did not know quite what to make of the Clinton crowd. They all seemed to breathe politics and love publicity. Lake was so averse to the latter that for the most part he refused to go on television, including the Sunday news programs where most of official Washington clamored to appear. It was not modesty that kept him away. To the contrary, it was a sense of superiority. He thought it was déclassé to go on television. A more serious issue was the priorities of Clinton's callow young staff. They believed that Clinton's predecessor had been hurt by concentrating too much on foreign policy, and, with dubious judgment, they labored to reduce Clinton's profile in this arena. As one of the most senior people in government, Lake often had to appear at meetings of junior staff in the scheduling office just to ensure that time on the president's calendar was preserved for foreign policy events.

If Lake was frustrated by his circumstances, many of his colleagues were frustrated with him. His counterparts at the Pentagon and State Department believed that, beneath his professorial demeanor, Lake was a tireless and even devious bureaucratic operator. He could be a maddeningly indirect man, and Bill Perry and especially Warren Christopher thought at times that Lake was impeding the flow of information to Clinton, rather than dispatching the national security adviser's traditional obligation to be an honest broker of policy options with the president. All sides in the rivalry tended to suspect that the others were using press leaks to undermine them.

Lake was an agonized and sometimes agonizing man. The summer of 1995, however, represented his finest hour in government. Despite his lack of personal rapport with Clinton, he had come to realize that his boss not only needed but wanted to be pushed on Bosnia policy. Beneath the surface of Clinton's complaints—his worrying about what could go wrong—he was pleading for solutions. Lake's job was to listen to these pleas, not the complaints, and help coax Clinton to act on his own best instincts.

It was in this spirit that Lake began contemplating what he called an "endgame strategy." Instead of improvising each day, and each week, the idea was to imagine what a positive outcome would be like in Bosnia, say six months in the future, then think of what risks the administration could take to get there.

THE FIRST THING LAKE NEEDED, BEFORE DEBATE COULD BEGIN ON THE SPEcifics of such strategy, was empowerment. "Mr. President," he cautioned, "tell me if you don't want to do this—stop me now because the risks are very clear." There was the risk of failure: a diplomatic initiative that fell flat. And, he noted, there was the risk of success: a peace agreement that would require the United States to commit some twenty thousand ground troops to a peacekeeping force exactly one year before the election.

Clinton, more resolute than Lake had ever seen him, urged the national security adviser to go ahead. New thinking—no matter the risks—was exactly what Clinton wanted. To varying degrees, both Perry and Christopher remained wary of greater Bosnian involvement. Only U.N. ambassador Madeleine Albright, with whom Lake's relationship was prickly, shared his determination to move more aggressively in the Balkans. On July 17, with only Lake's advance knowledge, Clinton made a surprise entrance in the national security adviser's office toward the end of a breakfast meeting of the national security cabinet. This was unusual. Normally, if Clinton wanted to see these people, he would summon them to the Oval Office. But this less formal setting was better suited to making his frustration plain. "This policy is doing enormous damage to the United States and to our standing in the world. We look weak," the president lectured his assembled team. "And it can only get worse down the road. The only time we've ever made any progress is when we geared up NATO to pose a real threat to the Serbs."

Lake's endgame strategy, about which many of his colleagues were skeptical, had just been endorsed forcefully. Within days, events moved quickly, fueled by a new sense of purpose in the ranks of American policymakers. In London, on July 21, Perry and Shalikashvili negotiated an agreement with NATO counterparts putting an end to the deplorable dual key, meaning no more U.N. vetoes of NATO airpower. Two weeks later, Lake presented a plan to the president that harnessed a more robust military threat to more creative diplomacy.

On the diplomatic front, the plan made clear to the warring parties in Bosnia, and to European allies, that the United States was ready to invest the full measure of its prestige and influence in a comprehensive solution to Bosnia. This included playing host and chaperone to negotiations to draw up a new map in which the country's three ethnic groups—Muslims, Serbs, and Croats—would divide territory and local governing authority, but remain under the auspices of a single multi-ethnic state. This was the clearest avenue yet to peace. But Lake's plan recognized that it would take significant coercion to get the parties to walk down this path. The Bosnian Serbs would be clearly warned that NATO warplanes would bomb them relentlessly for any new aggression. Meanwhile, the Bosnian Muslims, many of whom nurtured dreams that losses on the battlefield could still be redeemed if only they had access to arms, would be issued a warning, too. If they refused to negotiate in earnest, they were on their own. The United States would lift the arms embargo under which they had been suffering, but leave things at that. There would be no effort to intervene on their behalf. The message was to be plain to both sides: This is your last, best chance to end this catastrophe.

This bold new policy would require the United States to take ownership of the outcome in Bosnia in a way that Clinton had been averse to doing. Despite his frustration with a failed old policy, he plainly preferred not to be the sole owner of the new one. Would the Europeans join in the approach that Lake was now proposing? If they did not, was the administration risking a permanent rupture in the Atlantic alliance, the foundation of U.S. foreign policy for the previous fifty years? Here Clinton confronted a paradox of U.S.-European relations: The most reliable way to get reluctant European allies—Britain, Germany, and France most of all—to join him was to make absolutely plain that he was perfectly willing to act without them. What Lake proposed was to send himself as envoy to the European capitals to tell allied governments that Clinton had made a decision about a new policy and invite their support. This would be an emphatic contrast to the star-crossed mission Warren Christopher had taken two years earlier, in which he "consulted" with allies in a way that amounted to asking permission. There was one catch to this blunt new approach: Clinton had to really mean it—he had to be ready for the consequences at home and abroad alike.

"I'm risking my presidency," he told Lake.

He was ready to do so. In early August, after an intensive last round of meetings, Clinton approved the new policy. "If we let the moment slip away . . . we're history," he told his advisers. Lake flew across the Atlantic to deliver the message—part invitation, part ultimatum—that he and Clinton had discussed. The job of actually leading the U.S. negotiating team fell, with considerable reservations in the White House, to Holbrooke, then serving as assistant secretary of state for European affairs. Holbrooke's talent as a diplomat—more than this, his sense of history and gift for the theater of statecraft—was uniformly acknowledged; but his many rivals in the foreign service bureaucracy regarded him as volatile and self-aggrandizing. Lake, who had known Holbrooke for three decades, since their days together as young diplomats in Vietnam, had appreciation for both sides of the Holbrooke question. Holbrooke was godfather to one of Lake's children. Still, the friendship had curdled, in part over Holbrooke's hectoring over the administration's flaccid Bosnia policy, and partly over Holbrooke's bitterness that he was not offered a more senior position early in the Clinton administration. But in London, as Lake finished his mission, he met with Holbrooke for the official baton-passing. It was now Holbrooke's job to prod the reluctant parties to the bargaining table and, if that worked, to an agreement.

One of Holbrooke's first tasks was to resolve who would even be at the negotiating table. The Clinton administration believed the talks needed to be regional in character. This meant that the Bosnian Serbs, who were led by people under international indictment as war criminals, would not negotiate on their own behalf. Their representative at peace talks should be the man who effectively sponsored their brutal civil war in Bosnia, Serbian president Slobodan Milosevic. Enlisting Milosevic and the other major regional player, Croatian president Franjo Tudjman, to participate in the administration's new strategy was one of Holbrooke's goals as he and an administration team traveled to the Balkans that August.

On August 28, a mortar shell landed in a crowded Sarajevo marketplace, killing thirty-eight civilians. Here was a test of Clinton's new policy. Such atrocities, the administration had decided earlier that summer, were now to be met with a powerful NATO response. After a hurried round of diplomacy, during which Washington simultaneously sought to soothe and bowl over continued reservations by its allies, Operation Deliberate Force began on August 30. Warplanes flying from the Aviano Air Base in Italy and off the USS *Theodore Roosevelt* in the Adriatic Sea unleashed a punishing barrage on Bosnian Serb forces ringing Sarajevo. It was the largest military action in NATO's history.

Chapter Nineteen

FUNK

AS THE SUMMER OF 1995 CAME TO A CLOSE, CLINTON HAD PLACED huge bets on the two paramount issues—Bosnia abroad, the budget at home—then shadowing his presidency. By September, these twin dramas were on paths toward climax. On Bosnia, Clinton's gamble was that a combination of force and diplomacy could produce a settlement ending the war, without dragging the administration into an election year quagmire in the Balkans. On the budget, his gamble was that he had positioned himself to force Republicans to strike an honorable bargain with him, or, failing that, to ensure that they bore the brunt of public blame if negotiations failed and a government shutdown ensued. The autumn promised to be an extremely anxious season.

One September day, following a two-day sprint to California and Colorado, the president ambled back to the press cabin on Air Force One. There was a rotating pool of reporters always aboard in a special section at the far rear of the presidential plane. Occasionally, perhaps every tenth flight or so, Clinton would pop his head in. Usually he stayed for only a few moments. This time, though, he was in a mood to talk. Dressed in blue jeans and a denim work shirt, the president held forth for the better part of an hour. He talked about trivial subjects, like his politician's tricks for staying alert during long days on the road ("drink lots and lots and lots of water") or the right way to jog ("it depends on breathing"). He talked about consequential subjects, such as welfare reform (where he related how he had been pleading with Republican Bob Dole to help him strike a deal), education reform (including his enthusiasm for encouraging "entrepreneurialism" in the public schools through experimental "charter schools"), as well as the relationship between wage stagnation and social unrest (a phenomenon, he claimed, that he began discussing "at least eight or nine years ago, before I heard anyone else talking about it"). The president ruminated on the breakdown of journalism, in which traditional news was now competing with entertainment-driven "near news," rather like the "near beer" that people drank "when we were kids." ("There is a danger that too much stuff cramming in on people's lives is just as bad for them as too little in terms of the ability to understand, to comprehend.") He offered his explanation why many voters did not credit him or his achievements, a phenomenon he attributed to his early failures to communicate a larger vision. ("The first two years, I knew exactly what I wanted to do. . . . A lot of it required the Congress to go along. And I would have been better served if maybe we had done—even if we had done just slightly less, if people understood the big picture more.")

Here was the Clinton mind in full flight. He was facile and entertaining, self-absorbed and self-justifying, undeniably impressive. But there was peril in talking like this in the *rear* cabin of Air Force One. Despite the informal setting, the president was on the record. Under the rules of the press pool, the reporters he was chatting with had an obligation to share the quotes with dozens of other colleagues flying behind on a chartered news media plane.

Michael McCurry, the White House press secretary, thought it was useful for reporters to see the president in these kinds of settings, which showed him in a more authentic and sympathetic light. McCurry also knew it was courting trouble to let such sessions go on too long. "Time out," he interrupted at one point, gesturing to the reporters. "This is good food for thought, but these guys need some real food, too."

Unwisely, Clinton ignored him. Instead, he plunged into an analysis of the surly electorate, including his observation that many citizens were left insecure by rapid economic and technological change, making them "feel like they're lost in the fun house." He said he was "trying to get people to get out of their funk."

"Funk." In an hour's worth of words, this was the one that would cause him trouble. "Funk" sounded a bit as if Clinton thought the country was facing "malaise." "Malaise" was the word people associated with the failed presidency of Jimmy Carter, who in 1979 had warned that the nation faced a "crisis of confidence . . . a crisis that strikes at the very heart and soul and spirit of our national will."

Clinton's declaration of funk rang panicked alarms in his political team. For months, Dick Morris, as well as pollsters Mark Penn and Doug Schoen, had been urging Clinton to purge his rhetoric of any downbeat tones. Every public event, they argued, should be aimed at conveying a sense of national optimism, highlighting an activist president meeting the nation's challenges with confidence. This preference for happy talk caused considerable dismay inside administration councils. More progressive voices, such as Robert Reich, thought it was vital to emphasize the continuing problems of the economy and society. How else to build a genuine national consensus for action? The labor secretary and his like-minded colleagues were reflecting a brooding streak—an impulse for national criticism and contrition—that ran deep in the liberal tradition. Brooding, however, did not poll well with swing voters. So Clinton was forced to recant several days later, acknowledging that " 'funk' was a poor choice of words," and insisting that what he meant to say was that the public mood had been in the dumps the previous fall—when voters rashly lurched into Newt Gingrich's embrace—but now he believed voters were feeling just as up as he was. The uproar and its absurd aftermath soon passed, though the episode suggested an answer to those who wondered why politicians do not just be themselves and speak more spontaneously.

CLINTON'S PERCEPTION OF THE FUNKISH PUBLIC MOOD THAT AUTUMN WAS IN truth not so far off. The giddy boomtown spirit later associated with the 1990s did not arrive until the decade's second half. In any event, he had accurately described his own mood. Several of the topics leaving Clinton uneasy that autumn had a common theme: the vexing divisions between black and white America. His deft treatment of the affirmative action issue that summer had addressed only one of several open sores along America's color line in 1995.

This was the year of the O. J. Simpson frenzy—or, rather, the culmination of a frenzy that had begun sixteen months earlier when the former football star's ex-wife and a young male friend of hers were brutally beaten and stabbed to death outside her Los Angeles home. "The Trial of the Century" was an international spectacle of lurid exposures, angry debate, and saturating twenty-four-hour news coverage. Everyone had an opinion about this media paroxysm, which vividly anticipated a paroxysm that lay ahead in the president's own future. Clinton was no exception. Like most white Americans, he believed the evidence overwhelmingly proved Simpson guilty of the murders. As president, however, he had special reason to fear the toxic passions the case had released. Many blacks believed Simpson had been framed, according to polls, and an overwhelming majority of African-Americans believed the abuses and procedural lapses committed by Los Angeles police justified a not-guilty verdict. Black neighborhoods of Los Angeles had erupted in violence in 1992 when city police officers were acquitted in the Rodney King beating case. These riots became a metaphor for a country unraveling, and were another count in Clinton's indictment of George Bush's leadership. On the other hand, an acquittal might fuel white backlash, stoking the Middle American grievances that Newt Gingrich had exploited so effectively a year earlier. As a politician and a citizen, Clinton was deeply fearful of the approaching verdict.

Clinton actually knew the former football star slightly. In March 1994, just three months before the murders, he and Simpson had shared a round of golf while the president was vacationing in San Diego. This coincidence, though inconsequential, highlighted an aspect of Clinton's new life in the presidency. As most presidents do, he moved now in a world of wealth and celebrity in which he was usually only one or two degrees of separation from most big stories in the news. The famous faces populating *People* magazine, or *Fortune,* or the supermarket tabloids, were often as not people the Clintons knew personally.

The Simpson jury reached its verdict on October 2, but Judge Lance Ito delayed announcement of the decision until the next day, in part to give authorities time to prepare for possible riots. As with other Americans, guessing the verdict became a macabre parlor game among the president's staff. George Stephanopoulos and Leon Panetta both predicted guilty. Dick Morris, cleaving as ever to his polls, correctly surmised that the black members of the jury would never vote to convict. On October 3, however, he did sit with a group of his staff in the office of presidential secretary Betty Currie for the televised announcement of the verdict. Clinton was listening, but worked away at a crossword puzzle rather than looking at the screen. He said nothing, save for a single word: "Shit." Then he lowered his head and rubbed his palms into his eyes. His public reaction was an austere written statement, read by McCurry, in which he said "our system of justice requires respect" for a jury's verdict. Within a day or two, the public moved on with surprising alacrity, and it became apparent that the backlash Clinton feared was not coming. This seemed in the nature of the new media frenzies, in which controversies that one moment seemed all-consuming quickly faded into distant and almost hallucinatory memories.

THERE WAS ANOTHER PROMINENT AFRICAN-AMERICAN WHO WAS CONTRIBU-ting to the unsettled mood around the White House that autumn. Colin Powell had left two years earlier as chairman of the Joint Chiefs. In retirement, he had remained one of the most esteemed figures in national life. For a season, this admiration for Powell in Washington and among the general public transformed into Powell fever: a frenzy of publicity for Powell's just-released memoir and speculation about whether the soldier would follow the path of Dwight D. Eisenhower and seek the presidency. The mania for Powell was driving Clinton to distraction.

The interest in Powell was an implicit rebuke of the incumbent. It was all the more maddening for Clinton because he, too, generally respected Powell, even as he thought his reputation was overblown. He was irritated that Powell had not been held accountable for what Clinton felt was his negligence in the Somalia intervention and indifference to the Bosnia crisis. In addition, Powell was vexing for Clinton at several other levels. There was envy: Powell was in many ways what Clinton wished to be—a national unifier, respected across racial and partisan divides. There was frustration: Clinton had tried hard to win him over with public praise and private offers to join the cabinet. Powell politely turned the offers down and stayed coolly outside Clinton's psychic reach. Above all, there was fear: Powell's popularity made him perhaps the most formidable opponent to Clinton if he chose to seek the presidency as a Republican. Clinton was appalled at what seemed to be the patty-cake treatment given to Powell by the same news media that was hazing the president daily. "They're giving him such a free ride, it's ridiculous," he complained to Morris. "He comes on TV like a saint, and those white liberal guilty reporters are so awestruck that they won't ask him a damn question."

The consultant felt sure Powell would not run. The retired general could not win the election as an independent, the data showed. He could win as a Republican, but there was no chance Republican primary voters would back someone with Powell's liberal social views on abortion and affirmative action. Relax, Morris told a disbelieving Clinton, it'll never happen. The consultant's polls were right. On November 8, Powell did indeed hold a news conference to answer two mysteries: His party affiliation, never announced before, was Republican, and he would not be running for president in 1996. There was one less thing to worry about—welcome news when Clinton's list of worries needed editing.

ONE OF THE PECULIARITIES OF THE CLINTON YEARS WAS THAT THE PRESIDENT was widely regarded by his critics as an evasive man, when the reality was that he was far more often an exceptionally transparent man—sometimes to his detriment. As the "funk" comment on Air Force One showed, if a thought was on the president's mind, it was not likely to remain unspoken. Reporters soon learned that the best way to know what Clinton thought was to listen, not just to his words during the workday, but especially to the ones that came after deadlines, when he spoke at night without prepared remarks to political supporters.

On October 17, Clinton made an appearance that helped illuminate how he could be perceived as both disingenuous and guileless at the very same time. He was in Houston for an evening fund-raiser with well-heeled Democrats. Confident that no news was likely to be made, several reporters adjourned for an evening of Tex-Mex, returning to the filing center just in time for Clinton's remarks. The president was plainly in a loose mood. He noted how conservatives had "cut us a new one" in the 1994 elections by distorting his stance on gun control.

Then Clinton turned to another delicate subject, taxes. He knew, he said, that there were "people in this room still mad at me because you think I raised your taxes too much. It might surprise you to know that I think I raised them too much, too."

That few reporters—save for an alert correspondent with the Reuters news service—immediately seized on this comment was a testament to Clinton's style of argument. The balm of his language and demeanor could make startling assertions seem entirely reasonable. His claim about taxes did have a certain logic. If Republicans had joined him in a good-faith negotiation on the budget in 1993—instead of cleaving to a blanket pledge to vote against any measure with any tax increases—they could have shifted the overall balance of tax increases and spending cuts, and Clinton would have had more leverage in dealing with his own party, since he would not have needed to cling desperately to every Democratic vote to win passage. This was fair enough. But the president's implication that he had been forced to support higher taxes by his liberal caucus was deeply misleading. He had been the one who lobbied hard for the tax increases in the plan and who pushed many reluctant members of his own party to support the measure.

The next day brought a general uproar. Democratic members of Congress believed the president was abandoning his party as well as the most impressive achievement in his own record. As the anger grew, the White House staff believed the only means of escape was obvious: Clinton needed to recant his remarks and apologize. The prospect made him indignant. Clinton knew what he had intended to say in the Houston ballroom, which was criticism of the Republicans, not of his own party. Everyone in the room knew what he meant. He felt sure the reporters, too, knew what he meant, and were only distorting those comments now to help feed an uproar. The fuss seemed to him a perfect distillation of the literalism and pettiness of modern journalism.

Stephanopoulos, economic aide Gene Sperling, and deputy chief of staff Erskine Bowles collared Clinton back in Washington before he departed for an evening event. As a rule, Clinton hated confessing error—never more so than when he did not feel genuine contrition. In this case, his aides wanted him to issue an apology for an episode in which he believed he was the aggrieved party. He glared at Sperling and scoffed: "Everybody understood what I meant. Everybody who was there understood what I meant."

Sperling, holding his ground admirably, responded, "Sir, it's not just the media. It's Democrats who think we are not standing by our own plan."

Clinton was still not buying. "You are saying if I say something, and everyone understood what I mean and some reporter misconstrues it, then I ought to clarify it?"

That's exactly right, Sperling responded. Clinton pivoted and stormed off to his evening event. Then he called from his car phone and gave Sperling and Stephanopoulos permission to put out a retraction. The episode was another odd blip during a season of oddities.

CLINTON WAS IN NEED OF SOME COMIC RELIEF. IT WAS A BIT ODD, CERTAINLY, that he would find it in the person of the president of Russia. Nearly fifty years of Cold War had yielded few jolly moments between Moscow and Washington. Indeed, even now, the Cold War over, many on Clinton's foreign policy team did not find much amusing about President Boris Yeltsin and his increasingly erratic ways.

Clinton, however, had made an early and emphatic judgment that this former Communist Party operative, a man who had once helped put down a coup attempt by staring down a tank, was the coarse but authentic voice of a nascent Russian democracy. Clinton had a vast preference for people in the arena of public life—politicians who ran for office, leaders who took risks on behalf of their people—over the commentators and analysts and careerists who spent their time critiquing leaders and policies. He thought Boris Yeltsin, as a man of action and passion, was deserving of respect. Clinton approached Yeltsin with an essential human sympathy that sometimes wavered but never lapsed during the years the Russian was in power.

That sympathy would be tested on October 23, when Clinton and Yeltsin flew by helicopter from Manhattan (where a roster of 140 world leaders was on hand for a United Nations summit) up the Hudson Valley before setting down on a magnificent estate in Dutchess County. Clinton, once again, was back at Hyde Park, invoking the memory of Franklin D. Roosevelt. The setting had a special significance on this occasion. Yeltsin, like many Russians, shared Clinton's admiration for Roosevelt, and the administration's Russia experts thought a reminder of the World War II alliance between Moscow and Washington might be well timed to help spur Yeltsin's support on a contemporary problem. If the imminent start of Bosnian peace talks ended in an agreement, the administration wanted Russian troops on the ground to help enforce the peace, particularly among Serb populations with a historic affinity with Russia. At the same time, it was imperative that these Russian troops fit within a NATO command structure, and not be given exclusive authority over their own sector of Bosnia. Russian troops under their own command, forming a separate power force in this volatile situation, were unthinkable to American policymakers. At the same time, it was nearly unthinkable for the once proud Russian superpower to now be under the command of an American general. The diplomatic trick for Clinton was to persuade the Russian leader of his indispensability while gently coaxing him to accept a subordinate role. Yeltsin, for his part, had to acknowledge the obvious fact of American dominance in the Bosnia matter, while preserving enough dignity and leverage in the process that the hard-line nationalists in his own government would not accuse him of weakness or surrender.

The two began by sitting on the lawn overlooking the Hudson, in the same bentwood chairs on which Roosevelt and Churchill had sat during World War II. Easing into the day, Clinton showed his visitor the typed memo, complete with handwritten corrections, that FDR had sent Stalin, notifying him of the date of the Allied invasion of Europe in 1944. The two men gazed at a life-size bronze statue of FDR—sculpted, Clinton was quick to point out, by a Russian artist. "In such a place," Yeltsin enthused of their grand setting, "there won't be any problems that we won't be able to solve!"

Clinton began the serious talks with an appeal to Yeltsin's vanity, which also revealed a bit about his own. He played to their shared interests as two powerful leaders, spiced with a dash of their shared grievances. Their aim, he said, should be to "prove the pundits wrong. They want to write about a big blowup. Let's disappoint them."

The two made rapid progress. Yeltsin assured Clinton he would instruct his defense minister, Pavel Grachev, to strike a deal with William Perry in which Russian support troops would operate under a command structure with an American general at the top. Through some linguistic legerdemain, the official line would remain that Russians would not be under NATO command, even though the same American general would also be in charge of the NATO force.

If Clinton's mix of blandishments and rhetorical bridge-building was characteristic of his approach to a delicate negotiation, so too was the Russian leader's response. Yeltsin started drinking, heavily. Served with luncheon was a delightful white wine from, appropriately, California's Russian River. Yeltsin quickly gulped down three glasses, followed at a less urgent but steady pace by several more. This had a lubricating effect on the agreement between Clinton and Yeltsin over a treaty governing the position of Russian forces on the country's western border, which before the drinks had been a contentious issue. Then dessert wine was served. Too sweet, Yeltsin declared. Strobe Talbott was sent in search of brandy, but he came back (by his own choice) empty-handed.

The Russian leader was thoroughly stewed when it came time to face reporters at a news conference at the outdoor patio. He scowled at them, then noted sourly how he had read the predictions that his session with Clinton would be a disaster. "Now," he said, "for the first time, I can tell you that *you're* a disaster!"

One wonders how often Clinton might have fantasized about making such a pronouncement. Hearing Yeltsin's insult, the president began howling with laughter, literally throwing his head back and shaking with delight. "Make sure you get the attribution right," he said between laughs. Talbott, disgusted by Yeltsin's inebriation and concerned that the day was being reduced to a circus, later speculated that Clinton was exaggerating his reaction, to take the edge off an awkward moment and perhaps divert attention from Yeltsin's drunken condition. If so, it was a convincing performance, for Clinton was literally tearing up with laughter and was unable to resume speaking for several moments. More likely, Yeltsin's clownishness offered a break from burdens that had been weighing anxiously on Clinton all year.

THE BEMUSED APPRECIATION CLINTON HAD FOR YELTSIN WAS ONE THING. For another leader, Israeli prime minister Yitzhak Rabin, Clinton reserved something much more profound. His feelings were respect bordering on adulation. Rabin, a retired general, had taken extraordinary risks for his country's future in war. Now, in signing the Oslo accord and pledging to craft a civil coexistence with the Palestinians, he was taking extraordinary risks for a future of peace. Clinton loved citing Rabin's comment at the time of his dramatic handshake with Yasser Arafat on the White House lawn two years earlier: "You don't make peace with your friends. You make peace with your enemies." Clinton placed Rabin in an elite group, which included South Africa's Nelson Mandela, of leaders of truly historic scale. More than one of Clinton's advisers observed that the president seemed to regard the gruff Israeli as something of a father figure.

So it was with special delight that Clinton welcomed Rabin in Washington on October 26, and attended a ceremony at the State Department's majestic Ben Franklin Room at which Rabin presented Clinton with the United Jewish Appeal's Isaiah Award. The two men, friends now, met for thirty minutes before going onstage. Rabin lamented that he did not know the event he was to attend was black tie; he was not wearing a tuxedo. That is when Stephen Goodin, who the year before had become Clinton's personal assistant (the second in his string of "butt boys"), came to the rescue. He gave his bow tie to Rabin; it was frayed and a little tight, so Clinton himself helped the older man adjust the tie and trim the edges with a pair of scissors.

Clinton never saw Rabin again. Nine days later, on Saturday, November 4, the president was watching a college football game in the White House residence when National Security Adviser Tony Lake called with the news. Rabin had been shot by a fanatic right-wing Israeli nationalist who was bitterly opposed to the concessions the prime minister was making for peace. Clinton rushed to the Oval Office. A little later, the word came that Rabin's wounds were fatal. Clinton was as stricken as subordinates had ever seen him. Warren Christopher, who was with Clinton as he heard news of the death, recalled that the president fell perfectly quiet and still "for a long minute, and his silence made me feel almost as if I were inside his mind. . . . In his silence, I think the president was reflecting on his own mortality, contemplating what lay ahead for him and perhaps thinking of the price he himself had committed to pay for assuming leadership of our country." Returning from his reverie, Clinton announced quietly that he intended to go to Rabin's funeral.

Chapter Twenty

SEEDS OF TRIUMPH

CLINTON LEFT FOR ISRAEL IMMEDIATELY. TRAVELING WITH HIM ACROSS the Atlantic was perhaps the most impressive manifest ever assembled on Air Force One. There were two former presidents, Jimmy Carter and George Bush. There were dozens of senators and senior members of Congress. These included the leaders of both chambers, Robert Dole and Newt Gingrich.

The Republican leaders had been under the impression that the return trip from Israel might afford them and Clinton a good opportunity to deal with the most urgent business facing them all back home. After months of warnings by both sides that the failure to agree on a budget would result in a "train wreck"—the closure of the federal government once its spending authority expired—this scenario was now just days from coming to pass. Surely, the Republicans reckoned, Clinton would take some time on the long flight to see if the two sides could bridge differences and avert this embarrassment. The president, however, stayed in his cabin at the front of the plane, chatting and playing cards with the newspaper publisher Mort Zuckerman, while Dole and Gingrich stayed in the back. Gingrich especially was indignant after a White

House aide informed him officiously that only the president would exit the front of the plane at Andrews Air Force Base. Dole and Gingrich should get off in back with the White House staff and traveling press, the aide instructed. As it happens, this snub was no accident, nor was it Clinton's idea. His own aides, including Panetta and Stephanopoulos, had insisted upon it. They wanted absolutely no midair negotiations; they were fearful of what Clinton might do if left unchaperoned. What frightened them most was not a government shutdown. It was an agreement keeping it open on terms that would amount to a Republican victory.

The month proved to be the most climactic yet in Clinton's presidency. Two defining contests were coming to simultaneous resolution. One was the struggle over whether his vision of government or Newt Gingrich's would prevail in Washington. The other was whether the United States and its Western allies had the diplomatic, military, and moral means to end ethnic cleansing in Europe. In both contests, Clinton's own subordinates were laboring under doubts about his fortitude.

In the battle over the budget, the suspicion was that Clinton wanted a deal so badly that he would surrender important principles to the opposition. In Bosnia, the suspicion was that he did not in his heart really want the negotiations then under way in Dayton, Ohio, to succeed. Perhaps, worried State Department officials told each other, what Clinton wanted was for the talks to end without a grand bargain that would require the president to send some twenty thousand young men and women to Bosnia on the brink of an election year to enforce a fragile peace. In the end, both Clinton's adversaries and his own team underestimated the president's strength.

THE STRONG SIDE OF CLINTON'S CHARACTER WAS EASY TO MISS BECAUSE HE SO often put his accommodating side on display. In budget meetings with his Republican interlocutors, his words and body language alike conveyed an eagerness to strike a deal. Treasury Secretary Robert Rubin laid it bluntly on the line for Clinton after one session. A career in Wall Street had given him a lot of experience in negotiations, he told the president laconically. "If you were my client and we came out of this meeting, I would say, based on the way you sounded to those people, they're going to think they can roll over you," Rubin explained.

It was more than Clinton's manner that gave his staff pause. His aides all knew that he believed, as a matter of strategy, that he would be far better off politically if he could strike a grand bargain on the budget. Dick Morris had been telling Clinton this for months. It was an essential part of his theory of triangulation. A budget deal would show Clinton pragmatically transcending the bickering of the two parties and winning results. Get a budget deal and the election is functionally over, Morris kept saying. This should be easy.

It was hardly easy. All year long in public speeches, Clinton kept repeating like a mantra his determination to protect "Medicare, Medicaid, education, and the environment." Polls had shown that the public, even in an anti-government mood, overwhelmingly supported these programs. Republicans accused Clinton of demagoguery. They weren't proposing to actually cut Medicare, merely slow its rate of growth, just as Clinton himself had proposed to do the year before with his health care initiative. With just a modicum of difference-splitting, Clinton and the Republicans could come to an agreement on Medicare, give the president some token education and environmental victories, and still balance the budget within seven years. But in so doing they would impose draconian cuts on all manner of other social programs that did not poll well and were not in the headlines. Medicare was a metaphor for a large set of other worthwhile programs. Morris, they felt sure, would take such an ostensible victory even if it surrendered basic Democratic principles about the role of government and screwed the poor in the bargain. What they could not be sure of was whether Clinton likewise would go along.

The answer came on the night of November 13. The government shutdown was to start at midnight. The White House and Republican leadership were still at odds, but both sides felt the only responsible thing was to try one last bid to overcome differences. The GOP delegation arrived at the White House.

Bob Dole spoke first. He was in some ways a tragic figure in this encounter. He was a genuine conservative of the old brand. Though he wanted to curb spending, the confrontational tactics of Gingrich's "revolution" in the House were anathema to him. If he had not been running for president, perhaps he could have forced his fellow Republicans down a more responsible path. As it was, hoping to secure his party's presidential nomination the next year, he needed to prove he was a warrior in the fight against Clinton. Even so, he opened by urging both sides to settle on their bottom lines and try to respect their opponents. Gingrich, too, conveyed an accommodating tone. While no one was more brash and confrontational in a public setting, he, like Clinton, recoiled from personal conflict.

Only the House majority leader, Dick Armey, was primed to fight that day. Clinton's scare tactics over Medicare and Medicaid, he protested, had frightened old people all over the country. Even his own mother-in-law was in a panic, he said; "we could hardly get her into a nursing home, you guys have scared her so much."

Clinton, usually so genial in such settings, was in no mood for it this time. "I don't know about your mother-in-law," he shot back, "but let me tell you there are a lot of older women who are going to do pretty darn bad under your budget." Then, two years of grievances at Republican tactics tumbled out. Clinton said he had listened to them say his 1993 economic plan would strangle the economy. Not true. He had listened to them savage his 1994 health care plan and label it socialism. Not true. "So don't look for any pity from me."

He was warming up. "If you want to pass your budget, you're going to have to put somebody else in this chair," he said. He looked pointedly at Dole. Then he continued: "I don't care what happens. I don't care if I go to five percent in the polls. I am not going to sign your budget. It is wrong. It is wrong for the country."

There was an awkward silence, except from Armey, who thought Clinton's speech was grandstanding nonsense. This was supposed to be a negotiation. Instead, he said, he once again was forced to "listen to all these lies."

The meeting was beyond saving now. "Mr. Armey," the president said tightly, "at least I never, ever have and never expect to criticize your wife or any member of your family." Clinton had never forgiven Armey for suggesting Hillary Clinton was a Marxist during the health care battle. Gingrich tried to lighten the mood, but to no avail. The Republicans left as midnight approached, and the government shutdown had begun.

Clinton's defiant stand had surprised—and elated—his own team. "Mr. President, you should say that to the American people," Gore said. "It's very moving for people to hear that you are willing to lose this election for what you believe in. Just one little thing: When you said you don't care if your popularity goes down to five percent, I think it would sound a little better if you said, 'I don't care if my popularity goes down to zero.' "

Clinton put his arm around the vice president. "No, that's not right, Al," he said. "If I go down to four percent I'm caving."

The room erupted in laughter. The next morning, everything but emergency services was shut down across the federal government. And, despite Clinton's speech, it was hardly clear at this point what the public repercussions would be. The next day Clinton held a cabinet meeting, at which Commerce Secretary Ron Brown told the president about some of the services under his department, including parts of the National Weather Service, that were being curtailed. "We need to get that out," Clinton said excitedly. He turned to the rest of his cabinet. Every secretary was to compile a list of the most admired government functions under his or her domain that were not operating, for Clinton to recite at his appearances. Here was Clinton's essential insight and his political salvation: People might not like government in the abstract, but they like it in the particulars that touch their own lives.

The polls soon showed this. By large margins, voters were blaming Gingrich and the Republicans for a shutdown that they believed showed politicians at their petty and bickering worst. Clinton's cause was helped infinitely when Gingrich foolishly told a breakfast gathering of reporters that the president's rude treatment of him on Air Force One had left the Speaker in a less flexible mood, which contributed to the shutdown. "It's petty," he explained, "but I think it's human." "Cry Baby!" crowed the front page of the *New York Daily News,* with a cartoon of Gingrich in diapers and holding a rattle.

Republicans had been so certain that Clinton and Morris were eager for a deal that they had not devised a strategy for the alternative. Gingrich later confessed his error. "People feeling confident of their own strength often fail to take the proper measure of their opponents," he noted. "That was certainly the case with us and the president. Had we done our homework about this man, especially about his career in Arkansas, we never would have been quite so confident of our ability to push him into signing our legislation into law."

AFTER CLINTON, NO ONE COULD TAKE MORE SATISFACTION IN THE BUDGET triumph than Leon Panetta. The staff chief had sat through long hours of tedious negotiations with Gingrich, a man he disliked immensely. He had sat through even longer hours with Clinton, a man he admired but regarded as a near-total mystery.

Few men enjoyed more of the Washington respectability that Clinton desperately needed in his early presidency than Panetta. As a young man, he was in charge of the civil rights enforcement division of the Nixon Health, Education, and Welfare Department. He had the honor of being fired by Nixon henchman H. R. Haldeman after he insisted on rigorous enforcement. Panetta returned to his native California, where he had grown up near the Monterey Peninsula as the son of first-generation Italian immigrants. By 1976 he had switched parties and was elected to Congress, where he became one of the Democrats' top experts on budget matters, blending liberal instincts with a strong commitment to fiscal discipline. He was a hard man not to like, with his approachable manner and ready laugh, which came out as a surprisingly high-pitched giggle. But there was nothing frivolous about Panetta: He was a serious man, and deeply responsible in his approach to public service. Becoming White House chief of staff seemed a splendid pinnacle to an impressive career.

In the end, that's exactly what it proved to be. At the outset, however, Panetta was in for some rude surprises. Hired with an assignment of bringing order to the Clinton White House, he quickly discovered that the main source of disorder was the president himself. An example was Panetta's effort to remove press secretary Dee Dee Myers, acting on what he understood to be the Clintons' wishes. The chief of staff announced the move in an interview, only to have Clinton give Myers a reprieve of several months after she appealed to him directly. Myers was then offered another West Wing job, but, her own patience wearing thin and ready to leave on her own terms, she turned it down. As for the Clintons' displeasure with Stephanopoulos, Panetta took a different tack. He believed Stephanopoulos was a valuable member of the staff, so long as he was given specific assignments and no longer allowed to roam from issue to issue as a West Wing ambassador without portfolio. "What's he still doing here?" the president would occasionally ask with irritation, forcing Panetta to explain his decision yet again. The chief of staff found Hillary Clinton to be a more imposing boss than the president. At the beginning, she insisted on a weekly meeting with Panetta, for which he would prepare meticulously. It seemed plain to Panetta's own aides that their boss, so commanding in most settings, was actually a bit intimidated by the first lady. Soon enough, though, she became comfortable enough with Panetta's judgment that there was no need for a regular meeting. He never quite got comfortable with her. He was troubled, he told friends, by the anger and insecurity the Clintons showed in private moments. The couple might be chatting away on the short helicopter ride from the White House South Lawn to Andrews when suddenly the conversation would pivot to an angry discussion of some old political enemy from Arkansas. It seemed almost a touch paranoid to Panetta, who felt the Clintons needed to let go of their diverse grievances and resentments if they were going to be effective in the presidency. Like many people who had worked with Clinton, Panetta was alternately struck by Clinton's energetic and free-ranging mind, and his almost adolescent habits. On many a morning, the chief of staff was like a camp counselor, marching from the West Wing over to the residence at 9 a.m. to pull Clinton out of the shower, reminding him that he was already running behind schedule for the day.

Panetta's frustrations reached their peak during Dick Morris's ascendancy in 1995. The staff chief sympathized with Clinton's need to seek outside advice. Even so, Panetta was fundamentally offended by the consultant, and what he regarded as Morris's cynical ethic of expediency. He was also aghast at the consultant's determination to take over the policy operations of the White House by calling up aides and ordering initiatives as he saw fit. Panetta finally told Clinton he would leave if Morris was not restrained and made to channel all his White House contacts directly through Panetta's office. Clinton agreed that Morris would be kept on a tighter leash.

If Panetta was offended by Morris, he detested Gingrich, whom he had served with in the House of Representatives. He had watched Gingrich successfully take down former House Speaker Jim Wright, who was forced to resign in the late 1980s after Gingrich launched attacks on Wright's private financial dealings. In Panetta's view, Gingrich represented the devil-take-the-hindmost values of the new breed of conservative Republicans, who would damage reputations and the institution of Congress in pursuit of power. He believed Gingrich was using the budget talks not simply to reduce the deficit— a goal Panetta shared—but to dismantle important government programs and impose a dangerously right-wing vision. That Clinton, encouraged by Morris, wanted so urgently to strike a deal with this crowd had been deeply dismaying to Panetta. But as much as the president wanted a budget deal, he would not do just anything to get it. Panetta was delighted to learn that he had misread Clinton.

DURING THIS TIME, THE PEOPLE ON THE PRESIDENT'S FOREIGN POLICY TEAM enjoyed a similar epiphany. The talks under way at Dayton had come about because of Clinton's decision the previous summer to employ robust military force in support of diplomacy. Now, in a remarkable summit there, Bosnian president Alija Izetbegovic, Croatian president Franjo Tudjman, and Serbian president Slobodan Milosevic were cloistered, laboring to agree on a map for Bosnia that would end three years of killing. In some fundamental sense, these were Clinton's negotiations, though he remained in the background for much of the actual bargaining. The talks were directly supervised by the charismatic Richard Holbrooke and by Secretary of State Christopher, who traveled to Dayton at several key points. On October 31, in the last meeting before the talks began, Clinton told his team that their mission represented "the best chance for peace we've had since the war began," as well as "the last chance we have for a very long time."

For the next three weeks, Clinton waited. He got updates from Tony Lake several times a day, but his interventions were minimal, restricted to a few calls.

Clinton's detachment empowered the State Department officials. It also troubled them, since it fed suspicions that Clinton was not really rooting for success and the major U.S. troop commitment a settlement would require. It was true that some members of his political team would be content with failure.

On November 20, the talks were in fact on the brink of just that, the result of Izetbegovic's refusal to accept terms on territory, despite U.S. assurances that he had gotten the best deal for Bosnian Muslims he could hope for. After weeks of leak-free negotiations, the morning news shows now reported that the Dayton talks were in crisis and about to end with no agreement. But Clinton knew that the prospect of imminent failure might be the necessary last jolt to persuade the Bosnian leader to sign off on the pact. Clinton watched the news reports with his aides in the Oval Office. Stephanopoulos later described the scene to Holbrooke: "If Dayton failed, there would be a combination of relief and disappointment. If you succeeded, there would be a combination of pride and apprehension."

Within hours, the Bosnian president did indeed relent: Dayton had produced a deal. Clinton was eager to fly to Ohio to announce the agreement in person. Holbrooke, who knew how fanatical—and how consumed by mutual enmity—the Balkan leaders still were, urged Clinton to stay in Washington. "Mr. President, you don't want to be anywhere near these people today," he cautioned. "They are wild, and they don't deserve a presidential visit."

Success gave Clinton a daunting new assignment: convincing Congress and the American people that a Balkan peace was worth a 20,000-man troop deployment. In addition, he well knew the doubts within his own military about such a mission. At a White House meeting in the wake of a breakthrough, he addressed an assembled group of advisers, but stared directly at Joint Chiefs Chairman John Shalikashvili as he spoke: "Whatever ambiguities and uncertainties any of you may have had in the past, Dayton is done. Now we're going to make it work."

To sell the Bosnian deployment, Clinton assured the nation that it would last just a year—a naïve statement, at best, and at worst a deeply disingenuous one. American troops would still be stationed in Bosnia nearly a decade later. But it was a golden moment for Clinton in Paris the next month as he watched the three leaders formally ratify the Dayton agreement. A bloody war had been replaced by a fragile peace. Clinton met separately with all the leaders, but the usual photo opportunity for the media was canceled. The White House did not want any photos of Clinton meeting with Milosevic, who everyone knew had sponsored much of the Balkan violence, and who would in due course be declared an international war criminal.

CLINTON HAD TRIUMPHED POLITICALLY IN THE BUDGET TALKS, AND TRI-
umphed diplomatically in the Bosnia talks. Success had a transforming effect
on him. He emerged from the fall of 1995 as a vastly more self-confident and
commanding leader. The change was measured in polls. His job approval was
higher, as were perceptions of leadership traits such as strength and judgment.
The Bosnia deployment in particular illuminated a revealing paradox. While
the public was strongly opposed to sending troops to Bosnia, Clinton prospered politically by defying public opinion. For the first time, polls gave his
foreign policy majority support, and most voters said they approved of Clinton's performance as commander in chief of the military. There was an important lesson here: Voters did not want a president to cleave too zealously to their
wishes. The public preferred a leader to lead.

The gains Clinton had made in his own mood and in his political fortunes
were consolidated in January 1996. At the State of the Union address that year,
Clinton uttered one of his most famous lines ever: "The era of big government
is over."

For a Democratic president to make such a declaration was remarkable,
though the line was not the capitulation to conservative premises that some
people took it to be. Clinton had not given up on the idea of activist government, but he had changed the means by which he would achieve it. And in fact
he resented the notion that he had shifted course at all. A few days after the
State of the Union, he turned red in the face and jabbed his finger at a reporter
who compared the speech with the one he had delivered in 1993, when he
proudly boasted, "I believe government must do more." He accused the reporter of playing "word games," and said his record had shown "remarkable
consistency."

But only in his broad aims had Clinton been consistent. He survived in office by making abrupt and necessary shifts in strategy, and refocusing his ambitions to reflect the realities and limitations of the era in which he was
governing. The public appreciated Clinton not for his consistency but for his
willingness to adapt to circumstance and yet still keep fighting. From the State
of the Union until election day 1996, Clinton was never again behind the Republicans in his own polls. In one year, he had gone from being nearly irrelevant to be nearing nearly invincible.

Chapter Twenty-one

SEEDS OF DISASTER

She had fixed her gaze on him for months, desperately hoping to draw attention. He had noticed her vaguely, on the periphery of his consciousness. This shadowy flirtation continued for several months after Monica S. Lewinsky's arrival at the White House, fresh from college, for an internship in the summer of 1995. She had been recommended to the White House by Walter Kaye, a friend and major political contributor to the Clintons, and also a friend of Lewinsky's mother. Lewinsky was smitten from the outset. When the president left on trips, the interns would be invited to gather on the South Lawn to watch him board Marine One for the short helicopter ride to Andrews Air Force Base. Lewinsky would be there, always at the front of the crowd, a buxom young woman who knew how to make herself noticed. There were precious moments of eye contact, she later recalled, when she felt certain she was making a connection. Her intuition was correct. Later, there was a chance meeting in a White House hallway. She stuck her hand out and formally introduced herself to Clinton for the first time when she wasn't in a crowd. Yes, he said, I know who you are.

Under ordinary circumstances, the fantasy that was preoccupying her thoughts and was percolating at the margins of his would have remained unspoken—and unrealized. The extraordinary circumstances of the government shutdown that November gave Clinton an opportunity to get into trouble. On the first night of the shutdown, November 14, Clinton had escaped the pressures of the moment with a brisk walk around the White House grounds with Gene Sperling. Later, Sperling's friends would joke ruefully: Where were you, Gene, on the second night? For it was on the night of the fifteenth that Clinton and Lewinsky found each other alone. Because of the shutdown, the White House was operating on a skeleton staff, while most people remained home on furlough. People in the chief of staff's office, however, were considered essential workers and remained on the job. This included the chief of staff's unpaid intern, who was delighted to be put to work now answering phones in the West Wing, instead of sitting at her usual desk next door in the Old Executive Office Building. All through the afternoon, she saw Clinton several times, always with others around. They kept catching each other's gaze. That evening, Clinton walked into the chief of staff's office when there was no one there but Lewinsky. She seized her chance. In a flash, Lewinsky pulled up her dress to show Clinton the straps on the thong underwear she was wearing. She later described the moment as "a subtle, flirtatious gesture." Somehow, he interpreted this delicate signal as an invitation.

A few minutes later, he beckoned the young woman into George Stephanopoulos's darkened office, which was connected through a back door to the president's private dining room and a hallway that led past a small study and into the Oval Office. She told the president she had a crush on him. He laughed and invited her to see his study. In the hallway outside, he asked if he could kiss her. She said yes. After this embrace, she wrote down her name and telephone number, gave them to Clinton, and returned to work.

One can imagine the guilty negotiation between desire and conscience in Clinton's mind over the next hour. Around nine-thirty that night, the president approached Lewinsky in Panetta's office and invited her to meet again in Stephanopoulos's office. There was another kiss, hands wandering as the couple partially disrobed. In the president's study, as the intern later recalled, Lewinsky performed oral sex on him for the first time. Clinton did not allow pleasure to interfere with business. During the encounter, he talked on the telephone with two members of Congress. Aware of how reckless he was being, Clinton apparently rationalized his behavior by drawing arbitrary lines. As he approached climax, he stopped Lewinsky. He did not know her well enough yet for that, he explained. He complimented her, joking that it had been "a long time" since he had enjoyed anything like that. Then, turning more serious, he tugged at the pink intern pass hanging from her neck. "This could be a problem," he said.

There was another sexual encounter two nights later, when Lewinsky arrived at Clinton's suggestion with some pizza that had been ordered to Panetta's office. "I'm usually here on weekends," Clinton told the young woman, "no one else is around, and you can come and see me." But there were no more meetings for another six weeks. Then, on the afternoon of New Year's Eve, before the Clintons were to make their annual sojourn to Renaissance Weekend at Hilton Head Island, Clinton bumped into Lewinsky again in a West Wing hallway. She had by now been hired from her internship as a junior employee in the Office of Legislative Affairs. She introduced herself again, certain that Clinton had forgotten her name since he called her "Kiddo." There was another hurried furtive liaison that day, followed by another a week later, followed by another two weeks after that. Their affair, at once exhilarating and pitiful, was under way.

FEW PEOPLE WHO KNEW CLINTON, OR FOLLOWED HIS CAREER IN ANY DETAIL, were surprised eventually to learn that the president had succumbed to temptation. Rumors of his itinerant ways had followed him his adult life. Yet there was genuine surprise among many of his friends and associates that he would slip in the way he did. At a practical level, many people had assumed that there was little opportunity to carry on an adulterous affair in the confines of a modern White House, with all the staff and scrutiny that follow a president. At a more personal level, they were distraught over the particular circumstances of this affair. Lewinsky, after all, was not much older than his own daughter. She was a bright young woman, not without charm, and pretty despite her lifelong struggle with weight. But she was also immature, prone to insecurity and flights of self-absorption. That Clinton would find comfort in such company was dismaying.

It also left friends groping for an explanation. Why did this dangerous and degrading relationship happen? One answer explained the Lewinsky infatuation as a rebellion by a man against the confines of his office. This view, espoused by several old Arkansas friends, held that a sprawling and spontaneous personality had become progressively more contained and isolated under the demands of the presidency. He no longer went running when he wanted, for it had proven to be such a logistical hassle that increasingly he didn't bother. He no longer called up friends and went out to dinner on a moment's notice. He

Not yet a month into his first term, President Clinton and his staff prepare for a speech to the nation about his economic program, February 15, 1993.
(Robert McNeely, Clinton Presidential Library)

The president and first lady travel to Capitol Hill for the speech unveiling his plan for health care reform on September 22, 1993. The speech won good reviews, but Clinton's plan died the next year—a politically costly failure that echoed long afterward.
(Robert McNeely, Clinton Presidential Library)

President Clinton with *(left to right)* John F. Kennedy Jr., Caroline Kennedy Schlossberg, and Jacqueline Kennedy Onassis at the dedication of the museum of the John F. Kennedy Library in Boston, October 29, 1993. As a young man, Clinton worshipped JFK, and both the president and the first lady prized their warm relationships with the Kennedy family. *(Diana Walker)*

Clinton strikes a characteristic pose while making a point. He was often irritated by his interrogators in the White House press corps. *(Diana Walker)*

On the most sensitive political and policy questions, Clinton learned to collect his thoughts before answering. *(Diana Walker)*

President Clinton and Vice President Gore have a moment of prayer on January 16, 1997, before their weekly luncheon—an inviolate part of the West Wing schedule. For most of two terms, the two men had as close a political and policy partnership as any president and vice president in history. By 1999, as Gore sought the presidency on his own, his concern that Clinton's personal problems were imperiling his own future created an awkward chill in the relationship. *(Diana Walker)*

In the early Clinton years, no cabinet member had more influence than Treasury Secretary Lloyd Bentsen, who bolstered the president's confidence that deficit reduction was essential medicine needed to spur economic growth later in the presidency. Here he is pictured with Daniel Patrick Moynihan, his former colleague in the Senate, a Democrat who had a sometimes prickly relationship with Clinton. Of Moynihan, Bentsen told a reporter, "He's cantankerous, but he could not obstruct us even if he wanted to. . . . We'll roll right over him if we have to." (*Ray Lustig,* The Washington Post)

An inebriated Boris Yeltsin brings down the house with a lecture to reporters—"you're a disaster!"—at a news conference at the Franklin D. Roosevelt estate in Hyde Park, New York, on October 23, 1995. Clinton believed that his personal relationship with the erratic Yeltsin was vital to surmounting obstacles in the relationship between the United States and Russia in the wake of the Cold War. Over the years, this personal diplomacy yielded dividends in disputes over Bosnia and the expansion of the NATO alliance, as well as a fair share of frustrations. (*Diana Walker*)

Clinton friend and former associate attorney general Webster Hubbell. An amiable man and talented lawyer, Hubbell began the Clinton years as one of the most influential members of the Arkansas team that took power with the new president. He ended them as a convicted felon, after the Whitewater inquiry discovered fraudulent billing practices at Little Rock's Rose Law Firm. *(Dayna Smith,* The Washington Post*)*

Clinton, Gore, and the tough-minded deputy chief of staff Harold Ickes talk business during a campaign trip to Tennessee, October 27, 1996. *(Robert McNeely, Clinton Presidential Library)*

Before a major statement on affirmative action at the National Archives, July 19, 1995. For several months that year, this controversial issue loomed as a major threat to Clinton's re-election. He found the middle ground by urging a policy of "mend it, don't end it." *(Robert McNeely, Clinton Presidential Library)*

Clinton with House Speaker Newt Gingrich, December 30, 1995. Although the two were adversaries in public, their meetings were often quite cordial. *(Robert McNeely, Clinton Presidential Library)*

Clinton makes the decision to sign the welfare reform bill, July 31, 1996. After a three-hour meeting with his cabinet, Clinton adjourned with a smaller group to the Oval Office to make up his mind on the most far-reaching domestic policy decision of his presidency. *(Ralph Alswang, Clinton Presidential Library)*

The "21st Century Express" on the way to the Democratic National Convention, August 26, 1996. Huge crowds along the tracks put the president in an ebullient mood and presaged his easy ride to re-election in November. *(Robert McNeely, Clinton Presidential Library)*

On August 29, 1996, moments before accepting the Democratic nomination for president a second time, Clinton takes a deep breath. In the background are Chief of Staff Leon Panetta *(left)* and pollster Mark Penn *(right)*. *(Diana Walker)*

Political consultant Dick Morris. Adrift and afraid after the disastrous 1994 mid-term elections, Clinton brought his longtime political strategist back from exile, and for several months in 1995 made him by far the White House's most influential political and domestic policy adviser. Once Clinton regained his political footing, Morris no longer held quite the same sway. *(Shawn Thew,* The Washington Post*)*

White House political director Doug Sosnik *(left)* and press secretary Mike McCurry *(right)* at the final rally of the 1996 presidential campaign, in South Dakota, on November 5. *(Robert McNeely, Clinton Presidential Library)*

Clinton, with Oval Office secretary Betty Currie, shows off a gift from an admirer on September 23, 1996. *(Robert McNeely, Clinton Presidential Library)*

The second inaugural, January 20, 1997. The newly empowered president declared, "America demands and deserves big things from us, and nothing big ever came from being small." (*Gerald Martineau,* The Washington Post)

The first time White House intern Monica Lewinsky introduced herself to the president, in the summer of 1995, he assured her that he already knew her name. Within months, an affair was under way. The president had assumed the relationship was secret, but, in fact, gossip about the two of them was widespread among Secret Service agents and White House staff members. By 1998 the whole world knew, after the Lewinsky relationship became intertwined with the Paula Jones lawsuit and independent counsel Kenneth Starr's Whitewater investigation. *(Shawn Thew,* The Washington Post*)*

As a national security meeting breaks up, President Clinton talks with *(from left)* Deputy National Security Adviser James Steinberg, Chief of Staff John Podesta, National Security Adviser Samuel "Sandy" Berger, and National Security Council China expert Kenneth Lieberthal. *(Diana Walker)*

President Clinton in the Oval Office with British prime minister Tony Blair, who arrived for a state visit on February 5, 1998, in the opening weeks of the Monica Lewinsky controversy. Blair's success showed that the "third way" for progressive politics was not simply an American phenomenon. At the beginning, Blair seemed to enjoy playing the role of Clinton's younger brother on the world stage, but by the time of the Kosovo crisis in 1999, he became more assertive. *(Robert McNeely, Clinton Presidential Library)*

President Clinton surveys the largest crowd he faced, in Accra, Ghana, March 23, 1998. No president before Clinton had taken an extended tour of sub-Saharan Africa, but the trip came at a delicate time—not long after the Lewinsky scandal erupted. *(Diana Walker)*

A catnap on the Africa trip, March 25, 1998. At the beginning of his presidency, Clinton was self-conscious about the size and majesty of Air Force One, but, like most presidents, he came to appreciate the powerful symbolism and personal comfort of the presidential plane. *(Robert McNeely, Clinton Presidential Library)*

President Clinton and Hillary Rodham Clinton meet survivors of the Rwanda genocide on March 25, 1998, in what he later recalled as his most painful meeting as president. *(Diana Walker)*

On safari in Botswana, March 1998. All during the year of scandal, speculation about the state of the Clinton marriage was widespread among the public. Even the skeptics among their friends and advisers almost always reached the same conclusion: The Clintons' relationship, however complicated and sometimes stormy, was a genuine romance, built on intense mutual admiration and a shared sense of mission about their public lives. *(Diana Walker)*

At an East Room news conference on April 30, 1998, Clinton gets grilled by Sam Donaldson of ABC News. *(Robert McNeely, Clinton Presidential Library)*

Clinton greets supporters on the White House South Lawn on December 19, 1998, the day of his impeachment by the House of Representatives. *(Robert A. Reeder,* The Washington Post*)*

Preparation for the State of the Union address, January 13, 1999. Clinton learned to use these annual speeches as a way of organizing his agenda for the coming year, and White House policy and political aides would spend two months preparing. No other occasion affords a president such an extended amount of time speaking directly to a large national audience. (*Diana Walker*)

Defense Secretary William Cohen, President Clinton, Secretary of State Madeleine Albright, and National Security Adviser Sandy Berger clown for Diana Walker's camera in a "holding room" at the Ronald Reagan Building during a NATO summit in Washington, April 25, 1999. (*Diana Walker*)

At work in the Oval Office. Late in his presidency, Clinton said, "I've loved it. Even the bad days were good." *(Diana Walker)*

On January 20, 2001, with an hour left to go in his presidency, Clinton and new senator Hillary Rodham Clinton greet President-elect Bush. *(Diana Walker)*

hardly controlled his own schedule at all anymore. In addition, some of his Arkansas friends were regarded as intruders and potential troublemakers by the West Wing staff, who labored to keep them away. Clinton could not put his arms around an attractive woman and flirt, the way he did back in Arkansas. His staff had fits when this happened, and took pains to ensure that attractive women who might cause gossip were kept away from him. Marsha Scott, a perceptive Arkansas friend working in the White House, complained to Erskine Bowles when he was deputy chief of staff that the president, in the name of a more organized White House, was being cut off from friends and his own ebullient nature. This was not healthy, she warned. You need to open the windows and let him be himself. Bowles told her that a more orderly West Wing was for Clinton's own good, and coolly suggested that Scott leave well enough alone.

Dick Morris, too, had observed a man whose personality seemed trapped in a bottle. "He had been forced to change his basic nature, the way his mind worked," recalled Morris. Self-restraint came at a psychic cost, the consultant believed, leaving Clinton sullen and isolated.

This was particularly true when Clinton was feeling under assault. The Lewinsky relationship blossomed at a moment when the president was besieged on two fronts. In his political life, there was the pressure of the showdown with Republicans over the budget and government shutdown. In his personal life, late December and early January was an especially unhappy time for the Clintons in their confrontation with Whitewater prosecutor Kenneth Starr, who had replaced Robert Fiske. Legal records of Hillary Clinton's that Starr had long since subpoenaed were suddenly discovered, as the first lady awkwardly explained it, in a crowded storage closet in the White House residence. The circumstances did indeed smell a little fishy, and a disbelieving Starr decided it was time to get tough. Previous depositions with the Clintons had always been held discreetly in the White House. This time, he subpoenaed Hillary Clinton to appear in person before the federal grand jury to explain her story about the records—a public spectacle, the clear purpose of which was to embarrass the first lady. The Clintons could do nothing but take it.

The president had taken steps to address the isolation that people like Morris and Scott observed. Early in his first term, he set up a fax line outside his office and even a special zip code that allowed old friends to stay in touch with him without their messages being lost in the shuffle of some fifteen thousand letters a day that came into the White House. Old Hot Springs friends like Carolyn Staley and David Leopoulos regularly sent in pick-me-up notes or offered informal advice about how his policies were playing back home.

Still, Clinton sometimes confessed that his White House life left him feeling an emotional void. One day with Lewinsky he said, "I have an empty life except for work, and it's an obsession."

"Well, don't you get any warmth?" Lewinsky asked, meaning from the first lady.

Turning defensive, Clinton abruptly shut the conversation down. "Of course I do," he said.

ALL THROUGH THE WINTER OF 1996, THE PRESIDENT'S LIAISONS WITH LEWINsky continued. He was plainly guilt-stricken. On February 19, the President's Day holiday, he called her Watergate apartment, in a voice that made clear to her something was the matter. Without invitation, she soon showed up in the Oval Office. What they had been doing was wrong, he told her, and they had to stop. He hugged her, but refused to kiss her, and assured her they could still be friends. This restraint lasted a little more than a month. Late in March, Lewinsky passed the president in the hallway; he was wearing a tie she had given him. Where did you get that? she asked coyly. "Some girl with style gave it to me," he responded. Two days later, while Hillary Clinton was overseas on a foreign trip, Lewinsky was back in the Oval Office for yet another sexual encounter. There was another a week later, on Easter Sunday.

One of Clinton's illusions during this period was that he and Lewinsky were being scrupulously clandestine. They relied on Betty Currie, a kindly woman who was one of Clinton's two secretaries, to be Lewinsky's ostensible point of contact when visiting the Oval Office. Currie was purposely incurious about the nature of the visits. Beyond her, the president presumed he was being properly discreet. In fact, he was surrounded by a widening circle of people who had little doubt about what was transpiring. When Lewinsky showed up at the White House gate on weekends, Secret Service officers would amuse themselves by placing bets on how many minutes it would take until they saw their computers flash that the president was leaving his residence for the West Wing. Some West Wing personnel resented being put in what they felt were compromised positions. Harold Ickes and a uniformed Secret Service officer once entered the Oval Office, trying to alert the president that he had a phone call. The officer saw Lewinsky hastily leaving after what had apparently been an interrupted intimate encounter. She learned to sneak around such hostile staff members as Nancy Hernreich, Clinton's other secretary, and Steve Goodin, the president's young personal assistant, both of whom tried their best to keep the young woman away from the Oval Office. One Secret Service officer was so troubled by Lewinsky's frequent and plainly inappropriate appearances around the Oval Office that he complained to the deputy chief of staff, the tough-minded Evelyn Lieberman.

Lieberman tried to put an end to the Lewinsky problem in early April. Get her out of here, Lieberman ordered the staff. A devastated Lewinsky was quickly told her West Wing days were over, and she was going to take a job at the Pentagon.

In tears, she complained to Clinton, who said he was as upset as she was. "Why do they have to take you away from me?" he asked. "I trust you." He promised to investigate.

He went to Lieberman, a longtime operative for liberal groups as well as a close friend of Hillary Clinton's. Years earlier, she had been a high school English teacher on Long Island. Clinton approached her like a student nervously trying to protest a mediocre grade.

"Do you know anything about this?" Clinton asked.

"Yes," Lieberman said.

"Who fired her?"

"I did," Lieberman said.

Clinton retreated, knowing the conversation was over. "Oh, okay," he said sheepishly.

There were no more Oval Office visits for a while, but there were frequent phone calls in which the two would entertain each other with steamy conversation. "Good morning!" Clinton exclaimed, beginning a day that was to take him to the Summer Olympics in Atlanta with a six-thirty call to Lewinsky. "What a way to start the day."

The next month, Lewinsky managed to get invited to a New York fundraiser at Radio City Music Hall to celebrate the president's fiftieth birthday. As they chatted in the crowd, she later recalled, she "playfully" reached her hand to his groin. At this point, the presidential election was less than three months away. As hard as the White House staff tried to keep Clinton and Lewinsky out of trouble, the two had a way of getting back in it.

THE NERVOUS GOSSIP THAT SWIRLED AROUND THE WEST WING IN 1996 ABOUT the president and Lewinsky was not an anomaly. An abundance of other rumors echoed. There was a dazzling West Wing receptionist who had been a flight attendant on the 1992 campaign plane. Several Clinton aides and Secret

Service officers reported witnessing scenes between her and the president that strongly suggested an affair. Some agents said she had boasted to them of her presidential relationship.

Most White House aides had no direct knowledge and could only guess about the truth of various purported presidential relationships. But the fear of sexual gossip and scandal was a pervasive reality with which senior presidential advisers constantly had to reckon. Leon Panetta once got word about a scheduled presidential meeting with entertainer Barbra Streisand, who had been the subject of speculation before. He struck it from the schedule. One day in San Diego, Clinton's plane was met by Shelia Lawrence, an attractive woman whom West Wing aides called "the widow Lawrence." Before his death, her rich, elderly husband had been appointed ambassador to Switzerland. In view of the press, she embraced Clinton warmly on the tarmac and hopped into his limousine. A few moments later, White House aide Bruce Lindsey raced out of the backup car in which he had taken his seat and hopped into the president's limousine. Back in Washington, Panetta was alerted to the close call.

One of Steve Goodin's assignments was to avoid similar embarrassments. When Clinton gravitated toward an attractive woman in a crowd, or vice versa, Goodin would try to angle his way close to make sure that he was in the line of sight of any cameras. While aides fretted constantly, it often seemed to them that Clinton was intentionally, even delightedly, oblivious to appearances. The day after the incident with Lawrence, Clinton was in Santa Monica, where both Streisand and Eleanor Mondale, the former vice president's statuesque daughter, were in his hotel suite until well after midnight. The next morning Mondale, who had been the subject of rumors, went jogging on the beach with the president at 7 a.m. White House press secretary Michael McCurry scolded reporters to keep their prurient speculation out of print.

For the most part, they did. There were exceptions along the way. Early in his term, a tabloid reported that socialite Patricia Duff, who had socialized with Clinton, was boasting to friends that he was a "full-service president." Clinton was smoldering, his eyes squinting with anger, when Dee Dee Myers told him about the story. "That's a lie," he hissed.

Later, her successor, McCurry, had to delicately explain to Clinton why reporters were suspicious that he did not release his full medical records instead of just a summary. "Sir, they think you have the clap." The president smiled and shook his head, as if to say, what won't those guys think of. It was all a bit surreal—characteristically, McCurry took refuge in humor. Later, during a well-lubricated evening with reporters, McCurry rode in an open convertible through Beverly Hills shouting, "Attention, everyone! My boss does not have the clap!"

Still unknown at this early stage were stories that would have been harder to laugh off. One that did eventually come to light was the allegation of Kathleen Willey, a White House volunteer who accused Clinton of suddenly thrusting himself on her during a personal conversation in his study adjacent to the Oval Office. Clinton vehemently denied her claim. There were several women who had worked around Clinton who were shaken by the allegation and had trouble believing the denial. That is because they had heard similar stories before. One woman, a senior White House official, had heard from two colleagues who had experiences uncomfortably similar to what Willey described: innocent conversations that pivoted in an instant into fervid advances. The women were left angry and embarrassed, asking themselves if they had somehow sent a wrong signal to a man they in most respects admired. Neither of these encounters was ever publicized. But they highlighted how the controversies over Clinton and sex that did spring into public view were not strange aberrations. Concern about his behavior had been a percolating anxiety in the West Wing from the early days of the administration. There was a disaster lying in wait.

Chapter Twenty-two

WELFARE

OBSCURED BY THE PARTISAN BLUSTER AND INVECTIVE THAT FLEW BE-tween the White House and Capitol Hill in 1996 were some surprisingly cordial relationships. One of them was between Bill Clinton and Trent Lott, the new leader of the Senate Republicans. They understood each other. Although they were separated by ideology, their lives nonetheless had several points of overlap. Both were southerners. Both grew up in families headed by alcoholics and had an instinct in personal encounters to avoid conflict and find points of agreement. And both shared the same political consultant.

Dick Morris had been advising the Mississippi senator for years. Since 1995 he had been the broker for secret—and extraordinarily unusual—back-channel communications between Lott and Clinton, as they struggled to find a middle ground on the budget. These clandestine negotiations never went anywhere. Clinton liked Lott, but regarded him as a weak man. He was always suggesting in their private talks that deals could be struck, but then never delivered on his end of the bargain. Lott was not tough enough, Clinton complained, to force the conservative ideologues in the Republican caucus to march behind him.

On the evening of July 30, 1996, the two had a telephone conversation that had Clinton hissing in anger when he hung up the phone. The subject was welfare reform. A debate between Clinton and Republicans over how to overhaul the federal government's aid to the poor had dragged on for nearly eighteen months. In the wake of the Republican takeover, Clinton had hoped that welfare reform might be a rare point of agreement between the White House and Congress. Republicans wanted radical changes in aid to the poor; so, too, did Clinton. One of his most arresting—and popular—slogans was 1992's promise "to end welfare as we know it." His proposal to impose time limits and work requirements on people receiving assistance was a signature item in his New Democrat agenda, and his most important substantive and emotional break from liberal orthodoxy. He was quite sincere about it. Sincerity, however, was not necessarily a commitment to action; while Democrats still controlled Congress, there were always good reasons not to push welfare reform too vigorously. The liberals who dominated the congressional caucus hated the idea. They assumed Clinton talked about welfare largely as a rhetorical sop to conservative white voters. It was shrewd politics, perhaps, but they believed to actually enact the ideas Clinton campaigned on would be a devastating hardship on the poor and an unconscionable capitulation to the right wing. Thus, welfare reform lay dormant until the Republicans wrested control of Congress. Suddenly it sprang fiercely back to life.

There was a big difference, though, between how Clinton conceived of welfare reform and how Newt Gingrich and his revolutionary warriors tried to enact it. Clinton believed that overhauling the welfare system, though it might save money over the long run as people moved off the dole, required lots of new money at the outset to help recipients with job training and child care. Republicans resisted this. Clinton believed that legal immigrants were just as entitled to welfare as citizens. Republicans insisted the opposite. These and other divides had twice in the preceding months led Clinton to veto bills labeled welfare reform, but he had been rueful about doing so. He urgently wanted to sign a welfare bill. Most Republicans, knowing the potency of welfare as a political wedge, were thrilled at the prospect that Clinton might veto a bill again. And so the issue slouched uncertainly through Congress that summer. It was obvious to Clinton that most Republicans were trying to send him the most objectionable bill possible. But he held out hope that some Republican voices of reason, including some in Lott's Senate caucus, would push the process back toward consensus and send Clinton a measure he could enthusiastically approve. That hope died with Lott's July 30 call. The bill that emerged from the conference committee had numerous bad provisions, Clinton believed, most of all one barring legal immigrants from aid. As the Republicans had the votes to pass it, the bill would be on the president's desk within days.

Here was Washington at its worst, Clinton believed. "This is not about welfare," Clinton said bitterly to an aide as he hung up the phone. "This is about screwing immigrants and screwing me."

Republicans had indeed maneuvered Clinton exactly where they wanted him, into the kind of tight corner he hated: an either/or decision. He believed it was nearly always desirable to split differences and incorporate elements of different approaches into a new and improved composite. In this case, a crisis of definition was at hand. The legislation before him was complicated, but his choice was clear. He could sign a popular bill that contained some admirable provisions but several deeply offensive ones. Or he could veto it, paying an unknown political price and quite possibly forgoing forever the chance to make good on a central plank of his 1992 agenda. If he signed, he would thrill his main political adviser and a handful of New Democrat intellectuals on his policy team. But he would disappoint nearly all his other top advisers, and indeed stand in defiance of the mainstream of his own party. This time, there seemed to be no difference to be split.

BY THE SUMMER OF 1996, DICK MORRIS WAS BECOMING UNHINGED. HIS MANner was increasingly frenetic, and in meetings he had become even more prone to extravagant overstatement. Surely he was overstating his case that July in a memo he gave to the president and his top aides at the weekly political meeting in the Yellow Oval Room of the White House political quarters. "Welfare veto would be a disaster," the consultant warned, in the staccato prose style typical of his memos. With shrieking specificity, he said his polls showed that Clinton would soar to a lead of fifteen points over Bob Dole if he signed the bill, but drop to a deficit of three points if he vetoed it. Most of Clinton's aides rolled their eyes at Morris. Clinton himself learned to take these pronouncements *cum grano salis.* Still, there was no avoiding the political implications. A veto would give Dole at least a chance to revive his moribund candidacy, just three months away from the general election. The political consequences, however, cut in more than one direction. The Democratic National Convention in Chicago was only three *weeks* away. Signing the bill would likely produce protests at a convention that was supposed to be a celebration of Clinton's first term. The politics of welfare that summer were painfully complicated.

Those who believed Clinton's mental abacus was calculating only the politics of welfare—and this indeed was the focus of most journalistic commentary—misread him. The choice before him was no less vexing for its moral and intellectual dimensions. Signing the legislation would be the most fundamental break in the way government delivered aid to the poor in sixty years. Though his critics doubted it, the long trajectory of Clinton's involvement with welfare reform—he first began working on the issue in the 1980s—plainly suggested he was drawn to the idea as a matter of genuine principle. In any event, the current system was hard to defend. It had trapped many recipients in cycles of dependency and failure, robbing them of self-esteem and offering no clear path to self-improvement. Yet leaving the poor to their own devices, as he believed many Republicans were content to do, was likewise a moral failure. On purely substantive grounds, the bill the Republican majority had put before him was a close call: Was it better than the status quo?

This was the question on the table as Clinton, his vice president, several members of his cabinet, and his senior White House aides gathered in the Roosevelt Room on the morning of July 31. It was a Monday, and everyone was dressed for work except the president. He planned on taking most of the day off, and he arrived in casual slacks and a golf shirt. He gazed at his team and began the meeting with a simple question, "What should we do?"

HANGING OVER THIS MEETING WAS AN ECHOING MIGHT-HAVE-BEEN. BY 1996, it was established wisdom in the White House that Clinton had made a grievous error in not aggressively advancing welfare reform as soon as he came to power in 1993. The president said so frequently in private; Panetta had said it publicly. In late 1994, just after the Republican sweep, *The New Republic* published a cover story about the Democrats' failure to push welfare reform under the headline "They Blew It."

It was true. If Clinton had promoted welfare reform back when Democrats still controlled Congress, he might have achieved a bill that would have changed the program more humanely, with more assistance to people making the transition off aid, and without revoking aid to immigrants. Even more, if he had made welfare reform his signature domestic initiative upon coming to power, instead of health care reform, there very possibly never would have been a Republican majority in Congress. By pursuing an idea with a bipartisan flavor, Clinton would have immunized himself against the accusation that he was a traditional liberal hiding behind a moderate pose—the charge that Newt Gingrich hurled with lethal aim in the 1994 elections.

Clinton sometimes tortured himself about the path not taken. The truth, however, is that it was never really a close call. In early 1993, as his economic team was urgently looking for ways to meet its targets for deficit reduction, Lloyd Bentsen had blithely sacrificed the money that budget planners had dedicated to implementing welfare reform. There had been no objection from Clinton. Moreover, no one in the White House supposed for a moment that Hillary Clinton would have countenanced giving welfare reform precedence over her health care initiative.

At the time, there was a prominent voice jeering Clinton's priorities. Senator Daniel Patrick Moynihan, Democrat of New York, was a former Harvard professor who still dressed the part, with his bow ties and tweed suits. In the middle 1960s, Moynihan had been the author of a controversial government report warning of the welfare culture's devastating effect on poor families. He had devoutly hoped Clinton would push welfare reform early in his administration. When Clinton did not do it, Moynihan vented his frustration one Sunday morning in 1994 on ABC's *This Week* program. He accused Clinton of talking about welfare reform as a ploy to win over conservative white voters but lacking the fortitude to actually fix the system. Apparently, Moynihan sneered, Clinton regarded the issue as nothing more than "boob bait for Bubba." Two years later Moynihan was still jeering Clinton, only now it was for being willing to consider a Republican version of welfare reform that the senator believed would be devastating for the poor. On the very morning Clinton's team sat in the Roosevelt Room to deliberate, the papers quoted the New York senator as saying that passing this version of welfare reform would be "the most brutal act of social policy since Reconstruction." Clinton had always wanted to like Moynihan. A president who regarded himself as a serious policy student supposed he would be on good terms with the man widely regarded as the most serious policy intellectual in public life. It was not meant to be. From the early days of the administration, Moynihan's frequent taunting had left his relationship with Clinton just short of open warfare.

One person who viewed the deteriorating relations between the two men with special regret was Bruce Reed, the young policy aide who had helped draft Clinton's presidential announcement speech nearly five years earlier. Reed was an Idaho native, Princeton alumnus, and former Rhodes scholar whose boyish appearance and cheerful demeanor made him seem younger than his thirty-five years. After the campaign, Reed had landed on Clinton's domestic policy staff, where he was the White House's main ambassador to the centrists aligned with the Democratic Leadership Council. Moynihan had been one of Reed's early heroes, a brave voice who had risked liberal wrath by warning about a broken welfare system decades before such views came into fashion. It pained Reed to think that Moynihan, after being so prescient about the need for welfare reform, was now at odds with Clinton at the very moment reform was imminent. "You're here to keep me honest," Clinton flattered Reed the day of his presidential announcement in 1991. What he presumably meant was: It's your job to keep me on a centrist path. Once Clinton was elected, however, Reed was cast to the margins of Clinton's team, as more liberal people populated Clinton's inner circle. Reed watched other young aides—most notably Stephanopoulos, whom Reed regarded as something of an opportunist—vault to celebrity. Worst of all, he watched Clinton neglect welfare reform and other parts of the New Democrat agenda.

Reed did not think, as some at the DLC suspected, that Clinton had never believed in the cause of welfare reform. He harbored few illusions about the complexity of Clinton's motives and the inconstancy of his attention, but he believed his boss was ultimately committed to recasting his party around new and innovative premises.

In the summer of 1996, he was one of the few supporters of enacting welfare reform who could speak to the policy side of Clinton's mind. Reed's job was to serve as the president's intellectual lifeline each time he was swept by new doubts. One of these occasions was when Hillary Clinton's longtime friend Marian Wright Edelman of the Children's Defense Fund wrote Clinton a long and impassioned letter warning about the calamitous effects welfare reform would have on poor children. At such moments, Reed would try to untangle the hyperbolic assertions of liberal critics, and remind him of the improvements (more money for child care, for instance) that the administration had managed to wrest from Republicans.

Reed also had a superb vantage point on the way Clinton merged the mind of a theorist with an understanding of practical effects. It was a combination made possible by the president's experience as governor. Many liberals, for instance, were alarmed by the Republican plan to make federal welfare money to states a "block grant," giving states wide flexibility to spend funds as they saw fit. Clinton was not especially alarmed. As a practical matter, the welfare benefit varied widely among states anyway, with some like Texas spending virtually none of their own funds and barely giving recipients subsistence support. Other states, like New York, funded generous benefits. For all intents and purposes, welfare was already a block grant program, Clinton noted. By contrast, when Republicans, still looking for ways to put Clinton in a political box, proposed making both welfare and Medicaid programs for poor people into block grant programs, Clinton resisted vehemently. "If you do that," he said, "what will happen is the nursing home lobby in every state legislature will make sure all the Medicaid money goes to old folks in nursing homes, and poor kids will end up getting screwed." Clinton impressed Reed at multiple levels: He knew more than any congressman about the real-world impact of these programs, and at the end of the day he really did care what happened to some poor kids somewhere. He could see real faces, and real consequences, behind the clichés of Washington debate.

While Reed held up the policy side of the pro–welfare reform argument, Morris had the responsibility of offering the political appraisals, which he did with relentless predictability. All summer, the consultant had been issuing cocksure predictions to anyone who would listen that Clinton would of course sign the bill. In recent days, though, Morris had panicked that perhaps he did not know Clinton's mind as well as he supposed. On the day Clinton was set to announce his decision, Morris was close to tears when he called in by speakerphone to Leon Panetta's morning staff meeting, warning of the dire consequences of a veto. Reed, too, was alert to politics. One day in July he told Clinton that if the president rejected the bill he would probably never get a chance to sign a Democratic welfare bill, since many moderates who actually backed welfare reform would doubtless get swamped in the coming elections by voter backlash at the veto. "That's the best argument I've heard so far," Clinton said.

ON THE MORNING BEFORE CLINTON BEGAN HIS CABINET MEETING, PANETTA asked for a show of hands at the White House senior staff meeting about what the president should do. The bill would be voted on in Congress later that day, and Democrats on Capitol Hill were urgently pleading for a clear sign of Clinton's intentions. Many politically vulnerable congressmen who disliked the Republican welfare bill did not want to stick their necks on the line with a "no" vote if Clinton was going to sign it anyway. Nearly every hand at Panetta's meeting rose to say Clinton should veto the bill. A short time later many of these people braced themselves in the Roosevelt Room to make their case to Clinton directly.

Often in the Clinton White House, debates like this were roiling affairs.

Profanities flew, and people exaggerated their arguments for maximum effect. Not this time. It was as if all of them, recognizing the momentous nature of a choice that belonged to the president alone, chose to tone down their appeals. Clinton began by telling the group that he was not especially worried about the politics. He was pretty sure he could successfully argue the case with voters either way. Then, quietly, he posed the question again: What should we do?

Health and Human Services Secretary Donna Shalala argued vehemently against the bill. So did Robert Reich, the labor secretary, and Harold Ickes, the deputy chief of staff. Treasury Secretary Robert Rubin was the hero of Wall Street capitalists, few of whom knew that his social views were quite liberal. "Signing would be safer," he said, then added, "I wouldn't sign it." Housing Secretary Henry Cisneros, a Clinton favorite, concluded, "My head says yes, my heart says no." Stephanopoulos said that Democrats in Congress would be undercut by Clinton signing a Republican bill. Panetta was particularly impassioned. While in Congress, he had authored many provisions of current welfare law, which Clinton would be dismantling. "It is hard for me to be objective as the son of immigrants," he said. "I think you should veto this bill."

There were a few voices arguing for signing. Commerce Secretary Mickey Kantor was one, as was White House aide Rahm Emanuel. There were also some great unknowns. When Clinton pressed Al Gore on what he should do, he demurred, mumbling something about how the politics of the issue were complicated. It seemed that he was eager not to pressure Clinton, particularly not in a large meeting.

The most influential adviser was absent from the meeting entirely. Since the health care debacle, Hillary Clinton typically did not appear at White House deliberations like this one. No one doubted that the views of the first lady, a longtime policy advocate for poor children, were being heard. Yet no one was quite certain what those views were. Her staff, a group of mostly liberal women who were extraordinarily loyal to her, believed she was pushing Clinton to take a harder line against the Republicans. In her memoir, she describes the warnings she had given her husband before he made his decision to veto the first bill. She would speak out publicly against any bill that did not preserve Medicaid as a federal guarantee and include child-care subsidies to people going off welfare. These were his misgivings, too, of course, but the message she was sending was striking: Don't even think about signing. However, the latest bill—despite Clinton's complaints about Republican intransigence—had indeed addressed many of the administration's complaints. Hillary Clinton's aides and friends believed that privately she was keeping up the pressure on her husband, but it became obvious that her own view was softening. When Donna Shalala spoke to her about how bad the welfare bill was, assuming they were of one mind, the first lady responded, "The politics of this are really tough." The message was unmistakable: The time for fighting is over.

During the Roosevelt Room meeting, Clinton was subdued, asking questions but not speaking much. For those who knew his style well, there were clear hints of which way he was heading. The first was that he was being ostentatiously solicitous of Ickes, a fiery liberal. When Emanuel saw this, he slipped a note to Stephanopoulos: He's signing the bill. Indeed, Clinton nodded his head sympathetically as Reed laid out the case for passage. Clinton, Reed argued, had promised welfare reform, and this was his best chance to get it. The provisions eliminating aid for immigrants—a way of reducing the cost of welfare—were unquestionably offensive, Reed acknowledged. The right approach, he said, was for Clinton to say this even as he signed the bill, with a promise to reverse them later. On the basic idea of welfare reform—requiring time limits and work—Republicans had come close to delivering what Clinton campaigned on. The president should sign the bill.

Now it was Clinton's turn to speak. "This is a decent welfare bill wrapped in a sack of shit," he noted. Then, after two hours, the meeting broke up, with still nothing definitive from the president about what he planned to do.

A NEW AND SMALLER MEETING CONTINUED IN THE OVAL OFFICE. GORE, PANetta, and Reed were summoned for more discussion. Clinton pressed Gore again for his recommendation, and this time, in the smaller setting, he gave it. "You probably won't get another chance to do this," he said. "If you don't sign, the issue will just fade away and it will be a missed opportunity."

Panetta sent word to Capitol Hill, where House Democrats had kept an open line into the cloakroom waiting for a sign from Clinton, that Clinton planned to sign the bill. Then Clinton put on a business suit and went to the White House briefing room to tell reporters the news himself. Despite what he called "serious flaws," ones he pledged to remedy after the election, Clinton said he was ready to enact welfare reform. "A long time ago I concluded that the current welfare system undermines the basic values of work, responsibility, and family, trapping generation after generation in dependency and hurting the very people it was designed to help," he announced. "Today we have an historic opportunity to make welfare what it was meant to be, a second chance, not a way of life."

A years-long policy odyssey was over. His hope, Clinton said repeatedly in the days ahead, was that now the issue could move away from the old emotional arguments—conservatives complaining about welfare queens and saying the poor had only themselves to blame—to a more productive debate about the responsibility of everyone to help the poor.

Before hope, however, came a final flash of self-doubt and recriminations. Not long after his public announcement, Clinton called Morris. "I signed that bill because I trusted you," he said sullenly. He was equally short with people on the other side. Soon after his press briefing, Clinton was again in play clothes, ready to head off to the golf course during his day off. Stephanopoulos delicately suggested that the president's going golfing on the day he ended a six-decade federal guarantee of aid to the poor might be seen as bad symbolism. Clinton turned on him: "You want me to wear a hair shirt, don't you?"

This was his way of venting the accumulated pressures of a draining debate. It would be years, Clinton knew, before one could be sure whether this experiment was working. In the short term, though, the results were quick to arrive. Clinton's polling numbers did indeed rise, just as Morris said they would (if not quite as spectacularly). Then, weeks later, three of his senior appointees at the Health and Human Services Department publicly submitted their resignations. One of them was Peter Edelman, the husband of Marian Wright Edelman, and a longtime friend. With his signature Clinton had proven that he was indeed an authentic New Democrat, ready to break with old liberalism, even at personal cost.

Chapter Twenty-three

RE-ELECT

THE SIGNING OF THE WELFARE REFORM BILL WAS FOLLOWED THAT AuGust by an extraordinarily productive season of governing. Republicans in Congress, not wanting to wear the obstructionist label as they faced voters that fall, abruptly abandoned nearly two years of confrontation. A long-stalled measure to increase the minimum wage finally passed. Even more important was approval of the Kennedy-Kassebaum legislation, a bipartisan proposal that gave people the right to carry health insurance from one job to another. The measure was a far cry from the comprehensive health plan Clinton once sought. But it was a laudable reform and a welcome piece of additional evidence as Clinton made his election year case that he was solving the country's problems with progressive policies in incremental steps. He furthered the case later in the month when he signed an executive order granting new regulatory powers to the Food and Drug Administration to curb teenage smoking.

Implicit in the newly cooperative Republican strategy was that legislators were giving up on their presidential nominee, Robert Dole of Kansas, and looking out for themselves. Dole could hardly argue that the president was getting nothing done in Washington. He was left instead to warn that the election year Clinton was a fraud, and that once re-elected he would return to his old ways.

"He's a closet liberal," Dole brayed.

This was a hard charge to make stick against a president who had signed welfare reform, markedly lowered the budget deficit, and declared that the era of big government was over. Clinton simply laughed it off. "A president is too exposed," he parried. "I don't have a closet."

Voters would eventually learn about some surprising items then collecting in Clinton's closet. Who knows what might have happened if the name Lewinsky had surfaced in 1996 instead of 1998?

But Dole was hardly the man to slow the upward trajectory of Clinton's presidency as he moved inexorably to re-election. While a brave man and commendable senator, he was a miserable presidential candidate. Even though Dole and Clinton rather liked each other, as Dole faced an election blowout he was stunned that voters were rewarding a man whose character and values he regarded as flawed in obvious ways. "Where's the outrage?" he demanded plaintively.

Voters, in fact, had rather shrewdly taken the measure of both men. Clinton might be flawed, but not in ways that mattered to them—certainly not if the alternative was an aged and inarticulate figure like Dole. Still, the president was roaring to re-election on the back of an oddly ambivalent majority. A *Washington Post* poll two months before election showed that 56 percent did not believe he had "high personal moral and ethical standards," and 52 percent did not believe he was "honest and trustworthy." The same survey showed him with a fourteen-point lead over Dole. A political cartoon captured the mood of the year: It showed a pollster at the doorstep of a harried housewife, rolling pin in hand and hair in curlers. "I'm for the scumbag," she tells the pollster. Voters were fully capable of applauding the things about Clinton they liked and looking past the things they did not. Republicans would spend several more years trying to learn this lesson.

The challenge for Clinton this year was not Dole but his own expectations about his presidency and its role in history. Clinton had done some substantial things as president, deficit reduction and welfare reform chief among them. But this campaign, like much of Clinton's presidency, was now organized around the small but popular initiative. The Kennedy-Kassebaum measure was one example. So was his proposal, never enacted, calling for national drug-testing for minors before they got a driver's license. There was his plan for a national computer registry to track sex offenders. There was a call for new federal rules to discourage and punish "deadbeat dads" who failed to make their child support payments. He urged new rules on federal meat inspections, and laws allowing longer hospital stays for mothers after childbirth. He implored localities to fight youth violence by imposing curfews and adapting school uniforms. All these proposals scored well in polls, and nearly all were defensible policies. There was nothing unworthy about advocating concrete initiatives to make lives better, even if they never would be confused with the New Deal. Still, did such items really add up to a consequential presidency?

Clinton had grown up in an America that associated greatness with largeness. He was born one year after his country had mobilized on an unprecedented scale to win history's largest war. The paradigm achievements of industry in his youth were big, like the Boeing 747. The most awe-inspiring event in Clinton's early life was the Apollo moon shot of 1969. Sometime in the succeeding decade, however, history had pivoted. The frontiers of human achievement were less likely to be explored by government and more likely by scientists and technology pioneers working alone, or in university or corporate labs. Moreover, their achievements weren't big, visible things but invisible ones, like the microchip and gene splicing. This shift was accompanied by reduced faith in big organizations and big government projects. But the health-care reform effort of 1993 and 1994 reflected the values of two people who had been raised on the idea of bigness. By contrast, the values Clinton had embraced by 1996, in which government served as the catalyst for change rather than its principal engine, were far more in keeping with the spirit of the times.

For his own peace, however, Clinton needed reassurance that small measures still added up to something large. It was during this re-election campaign that he began regularly invoking Theodore Roosevelt. As he explained frequently in speeches, the challenges of the 1990s were similar to those of a century earlier, when the country made the transition from an agricultural to a large industrial economy. Now, America was making a shift from an industrial economy to a high-tech economy. Government's role was to shepherd the shift and protect people from its harshest consequences. Clinton wanted historians to write, he said in one interview that August, that under his watch "America had made a major change in the way people worked, lived, and related to each other and the rest of the world" without a major war being the catalyst. He added, "The first time, obviously, being under Theodore Roosevelt's administration."

The historical analogy was imperfect. Roosevelt's Progressive Era was a time of powerful clashes between big industry and a rapidly strengthening national government. TR himself was a confrontational personality who relished putting the federal leash on the "malefactors of great wealth." Clinton, as an accommodator, had settled on a less ambitious project. His goal was not to create a new order between government and the private economy. It was to modernize the existing government to meet the demands of the age more efficiently. His conflicts were with Republicans who felt the time had arrived to discard large portions of government altogether.

Clinton had been citing Theodore Roosevelt all year, but his notion that the Bull Moose Republican had managed to achieve greatness without a war closely echoed a remarkable conversation the president had with Dick Morris a few weeks earlier. Usually, Morris's nightly calls were brass-tacks business, devoted to going over the previous night's polling or the next day's schedule. On the evening of August 4, a Sunday, the consultant asked Clinton if they could talk a little more broadly. Morris had been thinking, he said, about how presidents make history. Clinton listened with interest as the consultant said he had ranked all forty of Clinton's predecessors. Only eighteen of these had made enough of a mark to qualify as historically outstanding. Of these, only five—Washington, Jefferson, Lincoln, Wilson, and FDR—qualified as "first tier." Beneath these were two additional tiers of leaders who managed some level of greatness.

"Right now, to be honest, I think you are borderline third tier," Morris said.

"I think that's about right," Clinton said. "What do you think I need to do to become first tier?"

There was little Clinton could do, Morris responded, unless an unanticipated event like war gave him the opportunity. But he presented a long list of other goals, from a battle to eradicate tobacco use to a global assault "to break the international back of terrorism," that could vault Clinton into the second tier.

Perhaps many presidents have had similar flights of fancy. But there is no record of a predecessor plotting a bid for history with his strategist in such self-conscious detail, as if it were a presidential campaign.

BEFORE CLINTON WAGED HIS CAMPAIGN FOR HISTORY, OF COURSE, HE NEEDED to finish his campaign for re-election. The 1996 election might have lacked suspense, but it did not lack innovation. Clinton's signal achievement that year was to fashion what counted as the most comprehensive melding of politics and domestic policy ever in a White House.

Ground zero for this project was a bright and welcoming room in the White House residency. Every Wednesday, usually about 8 p.m., a large group of White House aides, cabinet secretaries, campaign consultants, and even the deputy national security adviser would finish the day by joining Clinton and Vice President Gore in the Yellow Oval Room. Here they would engage in long discussions about the political week ahead, as well as the president's larger governing strategy.

These discussions had started small. In the beginning, there was just Clinton and Morris, sometimes joined by the first lady. Later, she dropped out and Gore came in, along with pollsters Mark Penn and Doug Schoen. Gradually, as Morris's role became more public and the re-election campaign began in earnest, the group grew still larger. By the end, a couple of dozen people had gained the coveted right of attendance. The evenings always began with Morris providing an overview of the latest polling, often followed by media advisers Bob Squier and Bill Knapp previewing the latest campaign ads. As the Wednesday night sessions grew in size, Clinton necessarily became more circumspect, for fear that his unvarnished musings would get leaked. Sometimes he would just sit quietly, working a crossword puzzle, leaving people to wonder whether he was paying attention at all until he would suddenly interrupt someone's talk by asking precisely the right question. With the exception of when the president was before an audience on the road, these evenings were his favorite time of the week. The Wednesday night group was the research-and-development department for a new brand of government Clinton had fashioned in response to the Republican takeover and the imperative of his own re-election.

After the debacle of 1994, Clinton had decided that he would never again allow his policies and public image to become so estranged from the main currents of public opinion. Never again did ideas flow from the policy operation on to the presidential agenda without being extensively tested through polling. Indeed, sometimes the pipeline flowed the other way. The political team would come back with data showing strong support for an idea, such as requiring employers to offer a choice between compensatory time and overtime pay, and insist that the policy operation come up with ideas to meet demand. Even the specific words Clinton would use to announce new proposals, or denounce the opposition's ideas, were tested in polls before he said them. When Dole unveiled his tax cut plan, Clinton repeatedly called it a "risky tax scheme"—language that polls showed was the most effective in raising public doubts. Polls themselves were nothing new. Since FDR's time, all presidents had used them, but no one before Clinton had so systematically merged his policy, polling, and communications operations.

This did not mean that Clinton always did what the polls told him to do. The interventions in Bosnia and the Mexican currency crisis demonstrated Clinton's willingness to swim against the current when necessary. But only when necessary. In the main, he had concluded that his personal fate and his ability to check the congressional Republicans demanded that he create and sustain a wide margin of public support. No more going off half cocked, intoxicated by good intentions.

Sometimes this new realism produced initiatives that did not seem quite worthy of presidential attention. There was the announcement that Clinton had persuaded the cellular industry to donate phones to neighborhood watch groups. He ordered the Education Department to mail new manuals to schools on combating truancy. Some of Clinton's moves, moreover, were nakedly defensive. In this category was his endorsement, over the objections of some Justice Department lawyers, of a new constitutional amendment to protect victims' rights (he never mentioned the idea again after the election was over). There was also his stand on the so-called Defense of Marriage Act, which said that states did not have to recognize same-sex marriages in other states. He had denounced the measure as election-year "gay baiting," then signed it at one in the morning. (Years later, Clinton kept returning in conversation to this bill, insisting he agreed with its substance even while disdaining the Republicans' motives in passing it. The fixation was a sure sign he felt guilty about what he had done.)

Yet many of the policies produced by Clinton's new style of politics were not piddling, and had little to do with moving to the right. There were new regulations for meat inspection, stalled for years by industry opposition. He expanded federal power over tobacco advertising, despite warnings this would cost him votes in border states like Kentucky. This was an important blow against the cigarette industry, which continued to attract hundreds of thousands of new young consumers annually even as its products hastened the deaths of hundreds of thousands of older smokers. In one fell swoop, he converted 1.7 million acres of spectacularly scenic but coal-rich federal land in southern Utah into the Grand Staircase–Escalante National Monument, sharply limiting mining in this wilderness expanse. This move was not popular in Utah, which Clinton had no chance of winning in 1996, but it was in neighboring Arizona, where he was running hard. So Arizona was where Clinton went to make the announcement, standing next to actor and environmental activist Robert Redford. What was notable about all these moves is that they were accomplished not with traditional legislation but through executive order—no approval of Congress needed. Facing hostile Republicans, Clinton had found a more inventive approach to governance by necessity. As Michael McCurry described it that summer, "It ain't the New Deal, but it ain't bad."

THE 1996 CAMPAIGN WAS EFFECTIVE, BUT IT WAS NOT MUCH FUN. MORRIS, never an admired figure among most of the Clinton team, had been growing increasingly rude and megalomaniacal. His emphasis on polls and small initiatives, meanwhile, had created a campaign devoid of adventure or romance. With the outcome preordained, the election became a desultory exercise.

There was a prominent exception to this, one person who was plainly enjoying himself. Bill Clinton had earned the right to feel good. After the hard work of 1993, the humiliation of 1994, and the predictions of doom in 1995, he was in command of events again. At fifty, he did not look so young anymore. The salt-and-pepper hair of four years ago was now steel gray. His appearance was more solid. He had been lifting weights, and, as one writer noted, now "fills out his suits at the chest, not just the waist." Even more than election day, the triumphant moment for Clinton came as he headed to Chicago to accept his party's nomination for a second term. He got there by train. This throwback to an earlier era of whistlestop campaigning would have him chugging for four days on the "21st Century Express," through West Virginia, Ohio, and Michigan on the way to Illinois—all heartland states critical to his re-election.

The crowds at the scheduled events were breathtaking, with thousands of people waiting for him at Columbus, Toledo, and Ann Arbor. Even more exciting were the impromptu admirers who lined the tracks to catch a glimpse of their president. He stood at the back of the train, with a loudspeaker in hand. "I like your dog!" he shouted as the train rumbled by. "Nice garden!" The trip was a blur of cornfields and corn pone. In Ohio, Clinton led the crowd in an off-key version of "Happy Birthday" to a supporter on her ninety-eighth birthday. The train ride, he told his staff, was "my idea of heaven."

Reality came roaring back as the trip neared its terminus in Chicago. Deputy Chief of Staff Evelyn Lieberman took Clinton aside to warn that there were reports of a potentially troubling story involving Dick Morris. The tabloid newspaper *Star* was reporting, with corroborating details that left little room for doubt or denial, that the consultant had been carrying on a year-long relationship with a prostitute while advising Clinton. At first, Clinton seemed not to register on the news. He was soaring too high from his train ride. By the time he arrived at his hotel suite in Chicago that evening the implications were obvious: Morris had to go.

With Clinton's acceptance speech scheduled for the next night, this was poor timing for a sex scandal. The president, however, seemed unfazed, even slightly amused, by the news, and not especially upset by Morris's departure. The consultant had played an essential role in his rehabilitation. Increasingly, however, he had become more trouble than he was worth. The president had not been enthusiastic a few days earlier, when *Time* magazine put Morris on the cover with Clinton for its convention issue. Clinton met in his hotel suite that night with Vernon Jordan and Erskine Bowles, who had then returned to investment banking between tours in government. Jordan and Clinton turned with mischievous grins to Bowles. Go talk to him, Clinton said. I don't work for the White House anymore, Bowles protested. "Why do I have to talk with him?" But Bowles was in fact the obvious choice. He had always had a smooth relationship with Morris, and soon he was making the trip downstairs to his suite, where the distraught and angry consultant was huddled with his level-headed wife, Eileen McGann, and loyal aide-de-camp, Tom Freedman. After much resistance, Morris faced the inevitable by sunrise and left Chicago before most of the national press was even aware of the blossoming scandal. Hillary Clinton was worried Morris might commit suicide. The word went out that there was to be no gloating by Morris's campaign rivals, and the Clintons and Gores both called Morris when he got home to Connecticut.

It was not until several weeks later, during the campaign's homestretch, that Leon Panetta got to raise the question he had long been curious to ask. The chief of staff and several political aides were with Clinton in the front cabin of Air Force One, chatting on a relaxed flight back to Washington. Sir, he asked delicately, how did you ever get hooked up with a guy like Morris anyway?

You have to realize, Clinton replied, when I first came back to Arkansas with Hillary, politics was our entire life. The answer was indirect, but his meaning was clear. This is a tough business. We did what we had to do.

Section Three

Chapter Twenty-four

SECOND CHANCE

THE 1996 ELECTION ENDED IN A PUNCH-DRUNK BLUR. VICTORY ASSURED, Clinton still sprinted to the end. He managed to sneak in a total of seven hours of sleep in the final three days of campaigning as Air Force One hopped across the continent. On the last day alone, he touched down in six states. Even hecklers in Denver could not dampen his giddy mood. He brushed them aside with a down-home swat. "You know what Mark Twain said about that?" Clinton jeered. "He said that every dog needs a few fleas. Now, I'll admit, I've had a few more than I wanted. But Mark Twain said every dog needs a few fleas—it keeps him from worrying so much about being a dog!"

The last stop was in Sioux Falls, South Dakota, where an arena was filled with cheering supporters even though it was nearly midnight. This was a bittersweet moment, and a man who had spent his adult life in a campaign or planning for the next one took a moment to reflect on it. This was, he told the crowd, the "last rally of the last campaign I will ever run." Clinton, though only fifty, was prone to nostalgia. In recent months, this penchant had taken a slightly lugubrious turn. Around the time of his birthday in August, he noted often how "I now have more yesterdays than tomorrows." This fatalistic streak came naturally to a man whose father had died at age twenty-eight, before the birth of his son. Waxing lyrical, Clinton now took note of the astonishing trajectory of his life. "Fifty years ago, when I was born in a summer storm to a widowed mother in a little town in Arkansas, it was unthinkable that I might have ever become president," he said. It was still unthinkable even at later dates, such as the election night sixteen years earlier in Arkansas when Clinton became the "youngest ex-governor in history." His was a dramatic story, and he knew it.

Back on Air Force One, as the plane flew toward Little Rock, the mood was pure gaiety. The stewards served mango ice cream from the Menger Hotel in San Antonio; Clinton had developed a taste for it in 1972, when he ran George McGovern's campaign in Texas. The president and first lady even performed a clumsy if exuberant Macarena, that year's dance craze. In the back of the plane, the traveling press was watching the Coen brothers' dark comedy *Fargo*. It had been on a continuous loop for the last week of the campaign. Suddenly, Hillary Clinton, who rarely wandered back to the press cabin, showed up there to earnestly tell surprised cameramen and reporters that the plane was being unexpectedly diverted. "We are making an extra stop . . . in Fargo!" she said, breaking into a smile.

But the mirth was broken in mid-flight. As the plane began to descend, Clinton turned to pollster Mark Penn and pressed him for a prediction. "What's it going to be?" he said. "How are we going to do?"

There was an awkward pause. Penn's latest overnight polling had left him confident that one of Clinton's main goals was not going to be realized. He was not going to break 50 percent of the electorate. People who knew the results held their breath, hoping Penn would keep quiet and say nothing to dent Clinton's mood. But Clinton stared intently at his pollster, who felt he had no choice but to tell the truth. Clinton's vote was stuck at 49 percent, Penn replied. The president visibly deflated. After a moment's silence, he wrapped his disappointment in noble cloth. It had been his decision to go to small states like South Dakota, where his presence might help Democrats lower down the ticket, rather than pump up his popular vote total with more visits to California, New York, and other large states where he was going to win easily. There was some truth to this. The official vote total was 49 percent for Clinton, 41 percent for Dole, and 8 percent for independent Ross Perot. The eccentric Texan had helped assure Clinton's victory four years earlier, but now robbed him of the majority he craved. It was a blowout victory, but the number rankled even so, and would for years to come. It is a reminder of the precarious state of Clinton's fortunes for most of his term that the man regarded as the most skilled Democratic politician of his generation never commanded more than a plurality in a national election.

Clinton's dreams of greatness in the second term did not depend on breaking the 50 percent threshold. They depended on staking a strong claim on public imagination, by conveying vividly that there was some compelling place he proposed to take the nation in the next four years. The campaign of poll-tested initiatives, many of them deliberately small in scale, had left this question open to doubt. But the payoff for his compromises and hard work was that Clinton now had an opportunity to answer these doubts—a second chance at making history. This second chance presented two challenges. One was to demonstrate that a president who said the era of big government was over could, even so, summon a nation to achieve big goals. The other was to demonstrate that he could pursue these lofty aims with more managerial competence and political judgment than he had shown the first time out.

He began his answer to the first of these challenges in his election night victory speech, once again in front of Little Rock's Old State House. He asserted that his re-election had ratified the "vital American center," revealing a nation that yearned for consensus and neither rejected government nor cleaved to outdated notions of bureaucracy and regulation. Frequently in the coming days he would invoke the "vital center." This phrase belonged to historian Arthur Schlesinger Jr., who had made it the title of an influential book nearly fifty years earlier to describe the place that liberal democracies occupied between the authoritarian faiths of communism on the left and fascism on the right. Schlesinger, as in the spring of 1995, played the role of Clinton's supportive but skeptical professor. He wrote soon after in the *New York Times* that Clinton still needed his brand of centrism to mean something more than "middle of the road"—there was a difference, he noted, between the vital center and the "dead center." The agenda Clinton laid out in the coming weeks included at last reaching a balanced-budget accord with Republicans, finding humane ways to implement and improve the welfare reform measure approved the previous summer, and beginning a national season of racial reconciliation. These goals were laudable, but so broad as to be almost unobjectionable by anyone. Whether they represented the vital center or the dead center would depend on details the newly re-empowered president mostly had yet to reveal.

THE SECOND CHALLENGE, THE MANAGERIAL ONE, BEGAN IN EARNEST THE DAY after the election. In public, Clinton was a steady and reassuring figure in the way he carried out the presidency. In private, there was still plenty of improvisational chaos to his decision-making style.

An illustration was Clinton's selection of a new chief of staff. Panetta had long made clear that he was leaving immediately after the election. At Panetta's recommendation, Clinton had settled tentatively on his deputy national security adviser, Sandy Berger, as his second-term chief of staff. Actually, the choice was not all that tentative. Press releases had been printed up for a Friday morning announcement. But at midnight, Clinton was on the phone to his first choice, businessman Erskine Bowles, who had left the White House a year earlier for North Carolina. "I need you here," Clinton pleaded.

Bowles, who was happy in North Carolina and had recently started a new business, reluctantly agreed. The press releases with Berger's name were thrown out. Instead, he went to the job he had wanted anyway, as Tony Lake's replacement as national security adviser. Lake was nominated as director of the Central Intelligence Agency (and later failed to win confirmation after a partisan spat). The process was messy, but Clinton was getting the results he hoped for. One person splattered in the mess was the organizational workhorse of the re-election campaign, Harold Ickes. He had known he was a long shot to be chief of staff, but had wanted to be considered anyway. Instead, he read in the papers that he was being forced off the staff at Bowles's insistence. He confronted Clinton bitterly that Friday in the Oval Office.

"I have worked hard for you and I think I deserved better than this," he said.

"You're right, Harold. I'm so sorry," Clinton replied. He said it with feeling. Ickes, who had been around politicians his entire life, found it less than persuasive.

CLINTON HAD MORE FREEDOM TO SELECT HIS OWN TEAM THAN FOUR YEARS earlier, but even as a re-elected president more confident in his powers, he was constrained in certain ways. Certainly he would have loved to be done with Attorney General Janet Reno. The same was true of FBI director Louis Freeh, with whom his relationship had steadily deteriorated since 1993. By the end of 1996, however, he did not dare touch either one.

By then, Clinton was bearing the costs of the very strategy that had brought him victory. The campaign tactics of Dick Morris, with their emphasis on paid television advertising, did not come cheap. Late in the campaign, questions had arisen about how some of the money was raised, from mysterious Asian sources. By election day, the controversy was nearly at full boil. It was becoming clear that the second term was going to be shadowed by ethical accusations just as the first term was. A decision not to reappoint Reno, with her reputation for independence, would be widely interpreted as crassly self-protective. Instead, Clinton let her fate dangle publicly for days, a virtual invitation for her to say she did not want reappointment. But she did want it. The president had little choice but to oblige.

His flexibility was constrained in a different way in his choice for second-term secretary of state, replacing the retiring Warren Christopher. The trio of contenders included former Senate majority leader George Mitchell, a Clinton favorite, and Richard Holbrooke, whose brilliance and bovine tenacity had made him the hero of the Bosnian settlement. Al Gore was strongly for Holbrooke; Clinton admired him, but warily, and wondered whether he was enough of a team player. The final candidate was Ambassador to the United Nations Madeleine Albright. She was not an intimate of Clinton's, though he was intrigued by the notion of making history by appointing the first woman to Foggy Bottom. First Lady Hillary Clinton was even more intrigued, and was backing Albright enthusiastically.

This nomination derby occasioned a peculiarly Washington episode illustrative of how Machiavellian motives are often assigned to the most random events in the capital. As invariably happens during transitions, there was a daily scramble for every scrap of information and rumor about impending appointments. The author checked in by telephone with a Clinton senior adviser, a regular source who was soon leaving his post for a career of his own in media. During this background conversation, the senior adviser—no longer particularly in the loop but trying like everyone else to read the smoke signals emerging from Clinton's private ruminations—said it seemed that Mitchell's stock was rising, and that Albright remained a contender but perhaps had fallen to the "second tier." It was a throwaway line, hardly offered as a commentary on Albright's abilities. But when this unattributed comment appeared low down in a story inside the next day's newspaper, a Washington-style uproar ensued. Feminist groups supporting her candidacy called a news conference to denounce what they interpreted as a deliberate and sexist campaign within the White House to disparage a woman's qualifications. Whether their outrage was real or artifice, it was shrewd. They had made Albright's appointment a test of Clinton's feminist commitment. Privately, the president fumed at how he had been boxed in, similar to his impatience with the diversity "bean counters" who criticized his appointments four years earlier. He blustered to Bowles and Vernon Jordan, once again helping shepherd the appointment process, that the women's groups' tactics were backfiring—he was now *less* likely to pick Albright. This was not true. She had jumped to the front of the line. Hillary Clinton herself now weighed in decisively, making it clear that the president would be facing anger at the office and at home if the choice was anyone else.

After Holbrooke learned that he was not getting the job, Bowles tried to console him. "Someone else was influencing this decision," he said knowingly.

THE RE-ELECTION VICTORY WAS A SWEET VINDICATION FOR THE CLINTONS after all the accusations and aspersions they had endured during the first term. It was also an apt occasion for them to let go of their accumulated grievances—toward the Washington establishment, toward the news media, toward their antagonists on Capitol Hill. The first family realized the wisdom of this course. Even so, they found it hard to open their grip on resentments they had clutched tightly for four years.

Michael McCurry, the White House press secretary, urged Hillary Clinton to use the second term as a chance to wipe the slate clean with the Washington media—reach out more, overcome the defensiveness, build some relationships. He'd been encouraged in this advice by Panetta, who had often been troubled by how consumed the Clintons seemed to be by bitterness toward the political establishment.

Hillary Clinton listened for a moment, then sighed impatiently. "We tried that before, Mike," she said. "It never worked." Their efforts to reach out, she explained, had been met with cynicism and more negative coverage. She was willing to try again, she said, but not optimistic that anything would change.

A couple of weeks later, the rawness of her feelings spilled out in public during a post-election trip to Australia. Meeting with a women's group at the Sydney Opera House, she noted with acid humor the controversies she had endured as an activist first lady—travails that she said predecessors as diverse as Eleanor Roosevelt and Dolley Madison would have found familiar: "There really is no way to escape the politics of one's time if you're in that position other than to just totally withdraw—perhaps, I don't know, have a bag over your head when you come out into public—or in some way to make it clear you have no opinions and no ideas about anything and will never express them publicly or privately."

The Clintons' personal grievances were just one part of a more broad-based concern about the health of civic life in the country they were trying to lead. As 1997 arrived, the president began drafting his second inaugural address. His generation had come of age amid conflict over the Vietnam War and the cultural liberation movements of the 1960s. He believed the upheavals of that decade had been on balance a good thing, bringing more equality to blacks and women and indeed more freedom for everyone to live by his or her own values. But the nation's politics had never quite recovered from the breakdown of the old 1950s consensus. As a second-term president, Clinton believed he had a singular opportunity to be a great unifier. His challenge was to purge national discourse of its penchant for needless partisan conflict, its addiction to conspiracy theory, and the constant questioning of the motives of opponents.

As he labored to give voice to these thoughts, Clinton came upon an unlikely collaborator. The Reverend Robert H. Schuller was the host of television's *Hour of Power,* a platform that had made him one of the best-known evangelists. He was personally conservative, but was also quite receptive to Clinton's attention when the president sought him out for consultations in early 1997. Schuller told him, "I wish you could see yourself with a pastoral heart, not a political heart." One of the minister's favorite biblical passages was Isaiah 58:12, "Thou shalt be called, The repairer of the breach."

Clinton seized on the quotation, and the injunction to transcend political differences, both of which found their way into the inaugural address. Like most of this president's formal rhetoric, this speech did not especially resound. Clinton's own head speechwriter, Michael Waldman, later cringed at the triteness of one of the speech's signature lines. Noting that Americans surely did not elect a Congress of one party and a president of another with the expectation that they would pursue petty bickering, Clinton said, "Nothing big ever came from being small."

As ever, Clinton was more impressive when he spoke spontaneously—and personally. This was the case two weeks after the inauguration, when he made his speech to the National Prayer Breakfast, an annual Washington event that presidents had been addressing for decades. The capital, Clinton said, "is ripped with people who are self-righteous, sanctimonious and hypocritical," and went on to confess, "I plead guilty from time to time."

Clinton recalled being stunned when he took office at how "mean" Republicans were to him and how the spirit of "payback" had infected the government. "So then pretty soon I was behaving that way," he admitted. "I'd wake up in the morning, and my heart was getting a little harder. And I thought, 'Now, who can I get even with?' "

Politicians and the news media had fallen "in a deep hole" of cynicism, he told the audience of clergy. "So I ask you to pray for us."

A few hours later, it was Hillary Clinton's turn at confession to the same audience. She said that the night before a man had come up to her and asked for her forgiveness. "For most of the last four years, I have worked very hard to destroy you," she quoted him as saying.

"Of course I forgive you," she responded. "What I should have said is, 'I don't know you and I don't know anything about you, but I want you to forgive me also, because I am sure that in my moments of frustration and anger I have said terrible things about people like you—and I have thought even worse.' "

These were heartfelt statements. But the hope that a second term would spell the end of the mutual animosities between the Clintons and their foes was a forlorn one, as would become abundantly clear in the year ahead.

Chapter Twenty-five

THE QUIET YEAR

As Bill Clinton embarked on a second term, his White House was run by a man who professed that he really wanted to be someplace else. Erskine B. Bowles told everyone who asked and even those who didn't that he planned to return as soon as he could to his native North Carolina. A Charlotte investment banker and a millionaire many times over from his business dealings as well as the family fortune into which he married, Bowles fairly boasted of his indifference to capital customs. "I'm a creature of the private sector," he liked to say. "It's my natural habitat." On the wall of his office was a framed *New Yorker* cartoon of a fellow who had been sent to hell to roast in eternity. "On the other hand," the character says, "it's great to be out of Washington." These protests were partly genuine, partly performance. Bowles did indeed dislike partisan warfare and modern Washington's obsession with scandal. Even so, in a city of cynics, it was natural to suspect that Bowles's anti-political pose was itself a political contrivance. Colleagues grew a bit weary of his talk about the awesome burden he was carrying by accepting the president's offer to fill what was typically regarded as one of Washington's most coveted jobs.

To the White House, he brought an obsession with organizational process. Unlike Panetta, who wanted in on anything important, Bowles was happy to delegate most things. He was fluent in management jargon, often invoking "goals, objectives, and timelines." To the negotiations with Congress, Bowles likewise brought his business values. He wanted to establish a "common buy-in to the goal," and build a "framework to get to yes."

But his real stock was his relationship with the president. They had not known each other long, but their bond was nearly fraternal. Bowles met Clinton in 1992, when the candidate went to North Carolina for a fund-raiser. They began talking about the problems of Bowles's eldest son, who suffered from juvenile diabetes. Bowles vented his frustration about the Bush administration's ban on using fetal tissue (obtained during abortions) for research on diabetes cures. Clinton listened raptly. Later, as president, Clinton overturned the ban by executive order and sent Bowles the pen he used to sign it. In that gesture, a powerful friendship was struck. Bowles told Clinton he was ready to go to Washington and do any job Clinton wanted. First it was as administrator of the Small Business Administration, then later as deputy chief of staff. Within the first months after Bowles's arrival in late 1994, it was clear he had a sway with the president far beyond his official duties. Panetta might have been the chief of staff, but it was Bowles who spent the long hours chatting with Clinton on the golf course. The president was clearly entranced, seeking his comments on all manner of questions about politics, policy, and the operation of the White House. More than once, Clinton told Bowles he thought of him as the kind of brother he always wished he had.

In part it was the similarities that explained the attraction. Bowles and Clinton were separated by just a year in age, both progressive-minded sons of the New South. Both men were faces of the prosperity and national achievement that was possible once the region became liberated from its old hateful obsessions. It was surely the differences, however, that provided more fuel for the friendship. The Clintons had organized their lives around politics, not money, yet they were fascinated with people who had made money and understood it, especially when these people were not conservative Republicans. Clinton knew he was just as smart as and usually more experienced than almost any political operative giving an opinion. But an investment banker like Bowles—now, there was someone worth listening to.

Bowles was fascinated by the performer in Clinton. "He had more personal magnetism than anybody I'd known in my life," he recalled later. He also believed that Clinton had taken bum raps in his first term because of his failure to implement some basic rules. "I think he's the best decision maker I ever saw," Bowles once said. "He could analyze all the factors, all the risks and opportunities, and weigh them brilliantly." All he needed was a way to get the information before him in an orderly form, and a process for evaluating it so that he would not be influenced by the last old friend whom he happened to talk to on the phone. Establishing such a process was a natural for Bowles.

The new staff chief was an emblematic figure for a presidency settling in 1997 into a kind of mature middle age. The helter-skelter of the early years, in which meetings might start at 11 p.m. and drag past midnight, was over. So too, it seemed, was the contest for Clinton's soul. There were no more pitched battles to define the ideological direction of the Clinton presidency. The Gingrich challenge of 1995 and 1996, and Clinton's survival of it, had set the president securely on a centrist course from which he had no interest in deviating. Though Washington remained divided, with a Democrat in the White House and Republicans still in control of Congress, Clinton correctly believed that he had emerged from the election with the upper hand. The continuing strength of the economy validated the bold and politically costly plan he had pushed to passage in 1993. As the president declared a few days before the inaugural, he proposed to use his position of strength to bring the unresolved battles of 1995 and 1996 to a close on his terms. The fact that Republicans had retained a hold, however weak, on Congress was seen as a good thing. "Gingrich's victory can be the Republican Party's undoing," pollster Mark Penn wrote in his weekly memo to Clinton. "On the one hand, the need for Gingrich to rehabilitate his image may drive him to agree to a balanced budget and other legislation, giving us a more workable Congress. On the other hand [voter] dislike of Gingrich provides the 1998 target."

When he arrived in Washington, Bowles's mandate from Clinton was to launch negotiations with the Republican majority and strike a comprehensive budget deal. Like Bentsen and the other deficit hawks of the first term, the new chief of staff regarded Washington's inability to balance its books and find sensible compromises as an embarrassment to democracy—the kind of failure that would never be tolerated in the business world.

Bowles knew one thing it would take to close a deal—keeping Clinton out of the negotiations. This was a dramatic change from the pattern of 1995 and 1996, when Clinton and Gore were often dealing face-to-face with Gingrich. "Clinton will say yes to anyone," Bowles told colleagues.

The chief of staff firmly told his boss that he would do the negotiating. The president would give him the goals and then step away. "If they call you, you can't take their calls," Bowles warned. "Tell me what you want and we'll find a deal. But if I say yes, it's got to mean 'yes,' not 'yes, but I've got to talk to the president.' " Bowles rarely saw the temper fits that others told him were so common with Clinton. On the few occasions he did, his response was noteworthy. One sour morning Clinton dressed down two of Bowles's deputies in the chief of staff's presence. Taken aback, Bowles asked his aides to leave the Oval Office, then served notice to the president: "If you ever do that again, I'll leave."

On the Republican side, Gingrich, for his own reasons, had decided to absent himself from day-to-day talks over the budget. Thus began a months-long exercise in Washington shuttle diplomacy. Bowles and his White House team, including budget director Franklin Raines, economic adviser Gene Sperling, and congressional liaison John Hilley, were traveling up to Capitol Hill daily to square off with their GOP counterparts, including Congressman John Kasich of Ohio and Senator Pete Domenici of New Mexico. These talks were everything that the 1995 negotiations were not. It was far from a game of patty-cake—frustrations and tempers flared regularly—but there was an essential respect between the two sides that had been missing before. There was also an understanding that differences were going to be split—no "train wrecks" this time.

For once, Washington was working the way most Americans said they wanted it to work, valuing achievement over ideological purity. Many congressional Democrats liked this scarcely better than the GOP fire-breathers did. Here, too, Bowles served a purpose—as lightning rod for thunderbolts that otherwise might have hit Clinton. The chief of staff was disliked by partisan Democrats, especially in the House, where there was widespread suspicion that Clinton might sell out the party in his haste for a deal. The regular sessions in which Bowles would brief the party caucus became brutal affairs, with legislators whacking the White House ambassador like a piñata. Once, David Obey, an irascible Wisconsin liberal, flayed him so aggressively that the mild-mannered Bowles finally struck back in his own defense: "I'm a pretty damn good Democrat, too!"

The negotiation-by-proxy strategy worked. When Bowles called to say that the two sides had finally reached a deal, Clinton was on a Las Vegas golf course playing a round with some governors and basketball star Michael Jordan. The president hit par the next three holes. "If you heard what I just heard, you'd be playing like that, too," he beamed. Back in Washington on August 5, the grand bargain that had eluded Clinton and his antagonists for two years was finally signed into law at a ritual ceremony in the White House Rose Garden. An unknowing observer would scarcely have guessed at the toxic feelings flowing between Clinton and the Republicans—or that these streams would flow again within months. Gingrich lavished praise on Clinton for his willingness to "reach out" to Republicans; Clinton hailed Washington's new spirit of cooperation. The event showed how comfortably Clinton had trimmed his sails from the ambitious dream days of his early presidency. He had bent to Republican demands that he cut taxes and trim the growth of Medicare spending. In return, he won gains that earlier he and Hillary Clinton would have dismissed as trifling half measures. Nearly 40 percent of House Democrats, including minority leader Richard Gephardt, refused to vote for the deal. (Many conservative Republicans were similarly aggrieved, believing Gingrich had acquiesced to too few tax cuts.) Judged on its own terms, however, rather than against the fantasies of 1993, the deal Clinton had struck was impressive. He was relearning lessons he had first encountered fifteen years earlier, following his defeat and comeback in Arkansas: Scrappy, incremental victories were better than noble defeats.

THE MOMENT ALSO OFFERED A HIGH PLATEAU FROM WHICH TO OBSERVE ALL that lay behind. The gamble Clinton took four years earlier that deficit reduction would spur the economy was paying off extravagantly. Annual growth in 1997 was 8.2 percent. The tax revenue this growth produced was erasing the deficit far faster than anyone had projected—it was $22 billion in 1997, compared to $290 billion when Clinton took office. The deficit would be gone entirely by the first week of 1998—a milestone the *New York Times* called "the fiscal equivalent of the fall of the Berlin Wall." Republicans, of course, were not giving Clinton credit for this. Nor were they advertising their own bogus 1993 predictions of economic doom if Clinton's program passed. Surely few in the GOP's own business constituency yearned to turn back the clock and try a different course. The 1993 package, passed with no Republican support, and this 1997 agreement, a model of bipartisan comity, had left the government on far sounder footing. Clinton deserved credit for both.

With Bowles running the White House staff and negotiations with Congress, the hope was that Clinton would be liberated to cast his gaze on the large issues facing America on the brink of a new century. During the re-election campaign, part of his strategy was to speak frequently on "values issues"—carefully selected and intensively polled—such as the moral content of television and film entertainment and the desirability of school uniforms. What had begun as a campaign stunt had now grown into something more ambitious: the presidency of exhortation. It was based on Clinton's belief that many of the nation's most profound challenges had little to do with bills pending in Congress. Instead, they were issues of national character and values. A president's greatest influence could be as moral tutor, so the theory went, using his White House pulpit to lead a searching national conversation.

The presidency of exhortation was engaged on numerous fronts. At the beginning of 1997, Clinton's aides put out word that he would be canvassing the nation to lobby state legislatures, urging them to participate in national standards tests for schoolchildren. Rather than engage the controversy over whether education was properly a national or local responsibility, Clinton said he was happy to let the tests be voluntary and leave the rest to moral suasion. "I want to create a climate in which no one can say no," he told Michigan legislators in Lansing, "in which it is voluntary but you are ashamed if you don't give your kids the chance to do this." On a similar theme, Clinton proselytized on behalf of community volunteerism. In April, he and Gore appeared with retired general Colin Powell at a "summit" in Philadelphia, where Clinton donned jeans and picked up a roller to paint over graffiti along the city's blighted Germantown Avenue. After having declared the year before that the era of big government was over, Clinton pledged here to usher in a new (and infelicitously phrased) "era of big citizenship."

Most of all, the presidency of exhortation was to concentrate on America's original sin, racial prejudice. The plan was for the president to lead a sustained year-long campaign of discussion, travel, study, and finally recommendations about the challenges of diversity. The White House called it "the race initiative." Clinton liked to note its unprecedented nature. Always before, such efforts had been prompted by crisis—angry protests, burning cities—but he was launching an effort in a time of relative racial quiet. "This is a huge deal," he explained one night to a group of Democratic contributors. "We can't hold America together and we can't maintain our position of moral leadership to be for peace in a world that is coming apart around racial, ethnic, tribal, and religious differences unless we can deal with this. And we need to start now, before we have to figure out what we're going to do when things start to fray." Here, in plainspoken language, was a true statement of Clinton's core beliefs.

The race initiative did have some moments of high symbolism. In May, Clinton issued a formal apology on behalf of the nation for the federal government's sponsorship of the egregious "Tuskegee experiment," in which black men were allowed to suffer from advanced syphilis so that scientists could study the effects of untreated disease. In September, Clinton returned to his home state for an anniversary ceremony honoring the Little Rock Nine, the black students assigned to Central High School, where the gaze of a reproachful world had been fixed forty years earlier, when Governor Orval Faubus defied an integration order and forced a reluctant President Eisenhower to send in the National Guard.

Such events had their value. Increasingly, however, they served only as reminders of how the race initiative hurtled off into abstraction and substantive irrelevance. The effort had bogged down earlier on organizational issues: Should the campaign focus on race alone or include such questions as treatment of gays and the physically disabled? (Clinton eventually settled on a narrower focus.) Should the president appoint a high-profile body like the Kerner Commission of the 1960s to issue a report to the nation? (He chose instead a lower-profile advisory board, whose recommendations were made directly to him.) These logistical tussles only skirted the larger problem: What was Clinton really trying to achieve? By the end of 1997, even before the nation was introduced to the charms of Monica Lewinsky and public attention moved to other subjects, the race initiative was a dawdling and aimless exercise that was drawing criticism even from participants on Clinton's advisory board.

The presidency of exhortation had lost its voice elsewhere as well. After promising to visit state legislatures across the nation, Clinton ended up speaking to just three, and his campaign for educational standards trailed off. Little more was heard about volunteerism. What was the problem? One was the expectations the nation had for him. His approval ratings were high, registering regularly in the upper 60 percent range; but his personal ratings were low, usually scoring in the low 40s. A solid majority of Americans, prosperous and satisfied, had come to a utilitarian view of their president. His job was to run the government and keep watch on the Republicans, who in turn were to keep watch on him. For all the noble purposes Clinton envisioned for himself, moral tutor was not one the public bought. These placid times ill suited his personal and political strengths. A curious passivity had settled upon his presidency by late 1997. For once, he was in flat water. Clinton's essential personality was intact—he was still a vexing mix of enthusiasm and grievance—but the highs and lows were both more subdued. *Time* magazine noted disapprovingly how he was spending more and more time on the golf course. The whole presidency had grown just a bit thick around the middle. The chaos and ineptitude of the early days had been replaced by steady competence and clear lines on Bowles's organizational chart. But it was almost as if order had come at a psychic cost for Clinton: He needed a crisis to engage at the highest level. If so, he would not have to wait long. There were several in the offing.

Chapter Twenty-six

THE SULLEN YEAR

THE FACTS SWIRLING AROUND THE SAD CASE OF WEBSTER HUBBELL certainly had a ripe odor. Since his resignation in 1994, when his former Rose Law Firm partners were reporting that Hubbell had bilked the firm and its clients out of hundreds of thousands of dollars through fraudulent billings, he had pleaded guilty and been sentenced to twenty-one months at the federal penitentiary in Cumberland, Maryland. But in the fifteen months between plea and incarceration, Hubbell had done rather better for himself than the typical high government official who leaves office under a cloud. He made hundreds of thousands of dollars in consulting fees. To provide what services? This was not at all clear, and Hubbell refused to say. Most tantalizing of all was the source of this money. One of his largest contracts, for $100,000, came from the mysterious Lippo Group of Indonesia. This was the very same outfit that was then in the thick of controversy for making illegal foreign contributions to the Democratic National Committee to fund Clinton's 1996 re-election campaign. Commentators were not delicate in voicing their suspicions. "Hush money," thundered William Safire in the *New York Times*. The Clintons, he felt sure, had arranged a comfortable exile for Hubbell to ensure his silence before prosecutors on topics that might spell trouble for the White House, including Hillary Clinton's work at the Rose Law Firm on matters related to the Whitewater investigation.

As aides prepared the president in late January to face questions about Hubbell, Clinton's first response was to dismiss the suspicions airily. It was only natural, he explained, to suppose that old friends might try to help out Hubbell, a man with four children, when he hit a patch of bad luck. The president's lawyers assured him the matter was deadly serious. Clinton said he was in no danger: He had known nothing about the Lippo Group's hiring of Hubbell until he read about it in the papers. This was the answer he rehearsed carefully the morning of January 28, as he and his team did their ritual "pre-brief" before meeting reporters. That afternoon, though, as he met with reporters in the East Room, Clinton became oddly flustered. He was not asked the expected question, Did you know about the Hubbell payments? Instead, the reporter backed into the matter by inquiring whether Clinton himself did not think it was just a bit "unusual or suspicious" for a man who had resigned in scandal to suddenly be showered with lucrative business contracts?

Clinton, usually so fluent, fumbled for an answer. He began with an almost solicitous tone. "Well, first of all, I did not know about it," he explained. "To the best of my recollection I didn't know anything about his having that job until I read it in the press. And I can't imagine who could have ever arranged to do something improper like that and no one around here know about it. It's just not—we—we did not know anything about it." Still stammering, he repeated himself. "I knew nothing about it. None of us did before it happened." Then, in a moment, Clinton seemed to fix on the challenge to his integrity implied by the question. His jaw clenched and eyes narrowed as he glowered at the reporter. "I think when somebody makes a charge like that there ought to be some burden on them to substantiate their charge instead of saying, we'll make a charge, see if you can disprove it. That's not the way things work."

Defensiveness, anger, defiance: The cycle of moods displayed in that one answer neatly captured the spectrum of Clinton's reactions throughout 1997, as he entered his second term and discovered that he would be under no less accusation and suspicion than he had been in the first.

It was a year of quiescence and compromise in Washington only when it came to policy. When it came to politics, the battles over Bill Clinton were as sullen and unrelenting as ever. For reasons of self-interest, Newt Gingrich and the Republicans had decided they needed to find common ground with Clinton over the budget. They had hardly given up the dream, however, that his ethical failings would lead to his ruination. If anything, the opposite was true: As the Republican leadership compromised with Clinton over once inviolate principles on taxes and spending, there was even greater imperative to intensify the fight elsewhere—or risk charges of appeasement among the rank and file. Whitewater's prospects as the magic bullet seemed to be receding. A year had passed since Hillary Clinton's grand jury appearance—the one that fueled so much talk about her imminent indictment—and still Kenneth Starr's team labored away with no clear bead on the first family. As ever, Clinton provided his adversaries with promising new ammunition. The campaign finance scandal of 1997 faded with remarkable speed in public memory. It looked pale in retrospect only after being overtaken by a more florid scandal of 1998.

At the time, all manner of dark possibilities loomed. Had Clinton, in his frantic pursuit of cash for the re-election campaign, let shadowy foreign agents infiltrate his political operation, and thus the top levels of the executive branch? What to make of the strange payments to Hubbell from some of these same people? As the controversy blossomed, the roster of mysterious characters became ever longer and more confusing. The linkages between Clinton and these characters and suspected misdeeds were murky but tantalizing. For a time, it seemed to Republicans that they might indeed have discovered a unified field theory of scandal—a pattern that linked Arkansas cronyism with Washington corruption in ways that had compromised national security. With his usual light touch, Gingrich predicted, "What we're seeing here is the opening phase of what will turn into being the largest scandal in American history."

BEHIND ALL THE SHOUTING WAS A BYZANTINE MAZE OF ALLEGATIONS AND bizarre characters, organized around three main themes. The first avenue of suspicion was that Clinton may have intentionally—or, more likely, through gross negligence—encouraged foreigners to contribute illegally to the Democratic National Committee to help pay for his re-election campaign. This stream of foreign money, it was in turn suspected, might have been exploited by agents of the People's Republic of China eager to influence U.S. policy. As ever with Clinton, the origins of the controversy reached back to Arkansas. It was in Little Rock that Clinton first became acquainted with the Riady family, ethnic Chinese in origin and the principals of a powerful Indonesian financial conglomerate called the Lippo Group. The family patriarch was named Mochtar Riady. The scion, James Riady, had run a branch of the business in

Arkansas in the mid-1980s and became a financial supporter of Clinton. Clinton knew the Riadys to be generous folk during times of need. During the 1992 campaign, following a limousine ride with the candidate, James Riady made a $200,000 contribution to the Democratic National Committee. Unknown to most people in Washington, the family had come to command considerable attention at the White House. At the family's urging, a veteran Lippo employee, John Huang, was appointed to a senior position at the Commerce Department. Meanwhile, James Riady was a frequent visitor to the White House, and he and Huang both had received numerous personal audiences with the president. By 1997, this high-level access had taken on a menacing aura. Justice Department and congressional investigators believed that the Lippo Group had been infiltrated by, and was possibly an agent of, the Chinese intelligence service. In the meantime, John Huang, who had left his job at Commerce but retained his high-level security clearance, became one of the Democratic National Committee's top fund-raisers, a switch that James Riady personally recommended to Clinton. Huang proved superbly effective at his work. The problem came late in the 1996 campaign, when it was disclosed that millions of dollars that had been raised by Huang and others mining the Asian connection had come from illegal foreign contributions. In many cases, the money had been funneled through the U.S. subsidiaries of Asian firms, including vast sums from the Lippo Group. The money path was painfully hard to follow. The most extreme interpretations drawn by Republicans seemed far-fetched: The White House penetrated by agents for China? Yet it seemed equally hard to conjure a benign explanation, as the DNC recognized when it returned millions of dollars of suspect funds after the election.

In the meantime, new revelations about Hubbell formed a second avenue of suspicion. Clinton's indignant assertions of January that "no one around here" knew anything about Hubbell's lucrative employment were soon exposed by investigators and reporters as false. Clinton's loyal aide Bruce Lindsey had known shortly after the Lippo contract was made. Mack McLarty, then the chief of staff, had called business friends on behalf of Hubbell in the spring of 1994, and later testified that he told Hillary Clinton about his efforts. Bowles, then serving as the administrator of the Small Business Administration, had likewise made calls to business contacts recommending Hubbell. So had Vernon Jordan. Just two days before James Riady had hired Hubbell, Riady had met with Clinton at the White House. It remained possible that the president had not been informed of any of this activity on Hubbell's behalf until he "read it in the press." Yet to believe that required giving Clinton the benefit of the doubt in the face of suspicious circumstances. Few in political Washington—not the press, not the Republicans in Congress, or even many Democrats—were of a mind to do that anymore.

The scandal's third line of inquiry was less about specific violations of law than of simple decorum. In 1995 and 1996, Clinton had been a desperate man. The pursuit of campaign cash had been a matter of survival. In this urgent atmosphere, the procedures and restraints that would have saved later embarrassment came tumbling down—and all manner of unsavory figures came waltzing in. There was Johnny Chung, whom Clinton's own national security aides had described as a "hustler" who should be kept away from the White House. Instead, he went to the White House some fifty times. On one occasion he arrived in Hillary Clinton's office with a $50,000 check. "You take, you take!" he urged in broken English to the first lady's aides. Her chief of staff did exactly that, passing the money on to the DNC. It turned out some of the money had come from an executive in a Chinese aerospace firm. Chung later told an interviewer that he viewed the White House "like a subway: you have to put in coins to open the gates." Others viewed it similarly. There was Charlie Trie, a Little Rock restaurateur whose Chinese joint Governor Clinton had enjoyed. When Clinton became president, Trie set up shop in Washington as a fund-raiser and as a for-hire facilitator of export deals to Asia. He showed up in the offices of Clinton's legal defense fund—established to help pay the president's Whitewater bills—with $460,000 in sequentially numbered money orders, ostensibly from different people but all filled out in the same handwriting. Among those Trie escorted to the White House in twenty-three visits was a Chinese arms dealer for a meet-and-greet with the president. That had been at one of the White House "coffees" in which prospective donors were treated to sweet rolls and hour-long sessions with the president, usually a day or two before the DNC moneyman called. Also joining Clinton for coffee were a New Jersey stock swindler with a recent conviction and ties to the Gambino crime family, and Roger Tamraz, a controversial Lebanese-American businessman who was trying to win administration backing for his Caspian Sea oil pipeline project. Once again, national security aides waved flags, saying Tamraz was trouble and should be kept out. Instead, after $177,000 in contributions, he was let in four times. "Good to see you again," Clinton cooed in a videotape of the coffee later made public.

More than the hustlers, more than the coffees, what seemed to ignite public outrage that year was the Lincoln Bedroom. In Clinton's term 938 guests stayed in the Executive Mansion, including in the historic Lincoln Bedroom and the Queen's Bedroom, directly across the hall. More nights than not in the

White House, the Clintons had houseguests, people staying literally just down the hall from their own bedroom. Many were longtime friends from Arkansas. Some were celebrities whom the Clintons wanted to get to know, like Tom Hanks, Chevy Chase, and Steven Spielberg. But dozens of others seemed to have had little or any previous relationship with the Clintons other than that they gave significant contributions to the Democratic Party. Clinton had raised the money he needed to pay for Dick Morris's ads in 1995 and 1996. In the process he had left a flatulent air—the scent of garishness and greed—wafting over his White House.

When the watchdog group Center for Public Integrity first alleged in the summer of 1996 that Clinton had turned the White House into a "Fat Cat Hotel," Clinton spokeswoman Ann Lewis said the suggestion that contributions and overnight invitations were linked was an "outrageous accusation, without one shred of evidence." But evidence, in Clinton's own hand, was soon unearthed. A subpoena of Harold Ickes's political papers forced the disclosure of a note Clinton had scrawled after his December 1994 meeting with fundraiser and future DNC chairman Terry McAuliffe. The fund-raiser had told the president he needed to be more attentive to the party's most generous donors, some of whom had felt neglected since 1992. Clinton agreed, and days later scribbled a note on a memo to his staff. Now his words were in cold daylight: "Ready to start overnights right away." He admonished his staff, "Give me the top ten list back, along with the 100, 50,000" dollar donors.

The response to this latest revelation brilliantly illuminated an unbridgeable gulf. It was the difference in how Clinton perceived himself and his motives, and how he and they were perceived by others, in particular by the press. Even the imperturbable Lewis, who would point to the sunny skies shining on Clinton no matter what storm was raining down, had to modify her defense in light of inconvenient new facts. Yes, she acknowledged, the Clintons had invited friends to stay with them, and also people who "weren't friends yet." Clinton, by contrast, was not prepared to yield at all. On February 25, the day the White House released his handwritten note to McAuliffe, Clinton was asked to explain why he had used the White House residence for fund-raising. "That's one more false story we've had to endure." Clinton was not lying. He was not even trying to deny the facts of his memo. Instead, he was employing his singular ability to blend facts and language into a description of reality that felt true to him. Charles Krauthammer, the conservative commentator, aptly summarized the view of Clinton prevailing that year among establishment Washingtonians of all ideological stripes: "Richard Nixon was laid low by his enemies list. How fitting that Bill Clinton should be laid low by his friends list. . . . Has there ever been a president so lacking in discrimination in his choice of friends, associates, liaisons, partners? So willing to embrace, engage, exploit, transact with anyone? So 'ready to start overnights right away'?"

AL GORE HAD SPENT YEARS IN THE HOUSE AND SENATE WITHOUT ANY TAINT of scandal. As vice president, he had long worried that the bubbling pot of Clinton's ethical controversies might splatter on him. When Whitewater first reached a boil, he nervously asked a top aide, "How many times do I have to stand up for them? Do you think my credibility is being hurt by this?" Whitewater had not splashed on Gore, but the "Funny Money scandal" (as the *New York Post* dubbed it) was indeed lapping at the vice president's office. This was fair. Ever the loyal soldier, Gore had plunged into the job of raising money with his usual discipline. In so doing, he had found himself in circumstances both absurd and indefensible. One of the indelible images of the 1996 campaign had been a sober-faced Gore wearing a necklace of flowers as he was escorted to speak at the Hsi Lai Buddhist Temple in Los Angeles, where monks take vows of poverty. That did not prevent John Huang from raising $140,000 at the event, including some in envelopes from monks filled with $5,000 in cash. The money, plainly from other sources and therefore illegal, was returned by the DNC. Meanwhile, Gore was learning to cleave to Clintonesque distinctions. At first he explained that he had thought the event was "community outreach." When documents he had viewed cast doubt on this, he allowed that the temple was a "finance-related event" but not a fund-raiser, apparently since no money was raised until afterward. This level of pettifoggery required an expert, but Gore was an amateur. He was in palpable agony.

Gore and Clinton had at first tried to defend themselves by saying that the fund-raising problems had been at the national party, not the Clinton-Gore re-election campaign—overlooking the fact that the DNC was under the White House's direct control. The *Washington Post*'s Dan Balz, in a January 1997 interview, pressed Gore on this seemingly spurious distinction. His answer began with a four-second pause. "Uh," he finally began, followed by another four-second pause, "well," and here a two-second pause, "the DNC is a, uh, uh, different entity from the campaign, uh, and uh." The sentence trailed off, followed by a twelve-second pause. "That, that's a fact," he finally concluded.

This paralysis under pressure did not bode well for the vice president, who had been planning to steadily raise his profile in the second term, in preparation to be Clinton's successor. An even more anguishing moment came in early

March, when questions were raised about Gore's making fund-raising solicitations from his White House office. If so, this was possibly a violation of federal law, though a seemingly trivial one, since if Gore had walked to a pay phone across the street the calls would have been perfectly legal. Gore decided he needed to address the controversy at once, and hurriedly called a news conference in the White House briefing room to offer his defense. In preparation, Charles Burson, Gore's lawyer, told him there was "no controlling legal authority" about the calls—in other words, no legal precedent that suggested what Gore did was wrong. The vice president had a mind that fixed on precise facts and phrases, and somehow he fixed on this one. Over and over, seven times in a twenty-four–minute encounter with reporters, he invoked the term about "no controlling legal authority."

Clinton, watching in mounting dismay on television in the Oval Office, moaned, "What is he saying? This is horrible, this is horrible."

Upon the vice president's return to the Oval Office, Clinton beamed and told him, "Al, you did great!"

DESPITE THE PRESIDENT'S PROTESTS, THE CAMPAIGN FINANCE FUROR OF 1997 was not an invention of the news media or the Republicans. What responsible reporter or opposition would ignore reports of mysterious hustlers showing up at the White House with envelopes of campaign cash? Clinton's evasive response was characteristic, too, as he described strangers as friends and acted as if he could change facts by proclamation. Still, what happened in 1996 was about sloppiness and excess, no more. No criminal wrongdoing was ever uncovered. The Democratic moneymen, including Huang and Chung, pleaded guilty to fund-raising violations, but no link to espionage or Chinese government infiltration was ever established. And like so many of the Clinton scandals before it, it faded slowly away.

Chapter Twenty-seven

MY KIND OF GUY

BILL CLINTON HAD EVERY RIGHT TO SUPPOSE THAT HE WAS THE BEST-informed man on the planet. He had at his disposal the most sophisticated and far-flung intelligence apparatus in human history—a vast network of satellites, spies, and eavesdropping technology that employed countless thousands of people and cost tens of billions of dollars a year to maintain. All of this, comprising the work of several government agencies, ultimately was in service to one man, the commander in chief. Each morning, he received the PDB, the president's daily briefing. Sometimes the Central Intelligence Agency director was present to deliver information in person, but Clinton generally preferred to receive his intelligence in writing, so that he could digest it on his own schedule. Each day he received a binder, usually ten pages or so, of the most interesting secrets from around the world collected by the intelligence community during the previous twelve hours. With all of this at his command, a president is not supposed to learn interesting news about national security in the morning newspaper.

The story on the front page of the *Washington Post* on March 9, 1997, was interesting all right—and it was definitely news to Clinton. The article ran under one of his least favorite bylines, Bob Woodward. The reporter revealed that nearly a year earlier, in the midst of the 1996 elections, the FBI had gone to a half dozen members of Congress to warn of law enforcement intelligence suggesting that their campaigns might have been targeted by China to receive illegal campaign contributions. In the current political environment, this was a stunning fact. In the wake of the election, after all, the possibility that Clinton's re-election effort had been tainted by Chinese money had mushroomed into a major controversy. If the White House had known that China might be making such efforts, the information would have had serious ramifications for U.S.-Sino diplomacy. What's more, the Democratic National Committee would have been on alert to ensure that any money from suspicious sources was caught as it arrived. The FBI, however, apparently had never seen fit to give the president the same briefing it gave to members of Congress. For Clinton, the implications were obvious: "That bastard was trying to sting us!"

That "bastard" was otherwise known as Louis J. Freeh, the director of the FBI. Clinton had long since come to regret appointing him. Now, tensions that had simmered for years between the two men boiled over in a painfully public dispute. The next day, reporters naturally wanted to press Clinton about the apparent rupture between the White House and the FBI over China. How could a president tolerate being kept in the dark by one of his own appointees? As he understood it, Clinton explained, the FBI had in fact briefed two lower-level officials at the White House National Security Council about the China suspicions. Then the FBI had mysteriously—and improperly, he alleged—requested that these officials not share the information up the chain of command. "The president should know," Clinton said. He had been raging a day earlier, but his public demeanor was now composed. When a reporter noted that Clinton did not seem especially angry, the president noted archly, "What I seem and what I feel may be two different things." By day's end, there would be no mistaking that a civil war had broken out within the executive branch. The FBI released a statement contradicting the president: Its briefing to the NSC officials did not include any restrictions on sharing the information with superiors, the agency insisted. That assertion in turn sent White House press secretary Michael McCurry racing to the briefing room to allege that the FBI statement was "in error."

The truth, as it later emerged, was somewhere in the middle. The FBI had indeed been reluctant to share information about its mounting suspicions over China. By 1996, Deputy Attorney General Jamie Gorelick had become the administration's main point of contact with Freeh on this issue. Gorelick got this job by default. The White House long ago had given up on Attorney General Reno asserting oversight over Freeh. She seemed to lack either the interest or the nerve to do so. No one in the White House, meanwhile, had relations with Freeh that were more than coolly civil. In a meeting with Gorelick at the time the China suspicions first came to light, Freeh indeed had resisted providing the White House a briefing over China. Doing so, he warned darkly, could compromise an ongoing investigation. Gorelick told him that to brief members of Congress while snubbing the White House was out of the question. The FBI needed to alert officials at the White House. The briefing that the agency reluctantly did provide, however, was apparently so opaque—and so freighted with cautions about the sensitivity of the information—that its recipients wrongly assumed they were not supposed to alert superiors that a briefing even took place.

Freeh felt so strongly about insulating his investigations from any possible taint of political interference that, just a few weeks before the Woodward revelations, he had refused a direct request from the White House that Secretary of State Madeleine Albright be given a briefing before an official trip to China. Understandably, Albright might wish to know whether the Chinese officials she would be meeting with had been involved in an improper attempt to influence U.S. elections. Freeh apparently believed that diplomacy between the United States and the world's most populous nation could wait.

The relationship between Clinton and Freeh had an almost chemical instability, an acid reacting with a base. Personal animus, however, was framed by a larger institutional tension that long predated the administration. There was an ambiguity at the core of the relationship between any president and the FBI. The agency was part of the executive branch, its director appointed by the president and supervised by the attorney general. Yet a substantial measure of independence was presumed. Under law, the FBI director could be fired by a president only for cause. Otherwise, the appointment was for ten years, meaning the director was supposed to outlast any president who appointed him. The director had a dual role. On matters of criminal investigation, there was no question the FBI director had a right to full independence from the White House, especially when the investigations involved the president or his associates. Other matters between the White House and FBI, however, concerned national policy. A question of increasing importance during the Clinton years was the problem of investigating—and, if possible, interdicting—terrorist activity at home and overseas. On matters like these, a president had a right to assume that the FBI director was as much his servant as any other senior appointee of the executive branch. As the president is accountable to the electorate, so should the FBI on questions of policy be accountable first to the attorney general and ultimately to the president. While the dual roles were clear in theory, in practice they were inevitably in tension. The only way to manage them was with a certain amount of professional trust and respect between the FBI and the White House, starting at the top. What blossomed instead was one of the mortal antagonisms of the Clinton years. There simply was no working relationship at all, only profane contempt. In conversation with the president, said John Podesta, "Freeh's first name became 'Fucking,' " as in "Fucking Freeh has screwed us again."

YET THIS RELATIONSHIP HAD STARTED SPLENDIDLY. IN 1993, SIX MONTHS INTO his presidency, Clinton had pushed out the FBI director he had inherited, William Sessions, a Reagan appointee who still had five years left in his term, after a Justice Department report found he had misused travel privileges and other perquisites. Clinton wanted a replacement ready to announce at the same time as Sessions's ouster. Freeh came to his attention as a possible replacement via Bernard Nussbaum, then the White House counsel. Nussbaum had known Freeh in New York, where he had fashioned a formidable reputation as a federal prosecutor and had been appointed to a federal judgeship by George H.W. Bush at the comparatively young age of forty-one. He was only forty-three when Clinton tapped him for the FBI. Announcing the appointment, Clinton called Freeh an "amazing man," and "my kind of guy." Nussbaum's last words to Vincent Foster Jr., on the morning of Freeh's appointment and the day Foster took his life, were to remark about how the pick was a "home run." Clinton chose Freeh after a warm two-hour White House interview that left both men thinking they had hit it off wonderfully. Freeh was a devoted Catholic and family man. One misgiving he had about the job, he told Clinton, was whether it would leave him with enough time to spend with his growing brood of young sons, who then numbered four. Clinton assured him that he, too, was a family man, and that the administration was eager to help him balance his commitments. Later, after the complexities of Clinton's private life came into public view, Freeh would recall this conversation with acid indignation. There might have been no one in America, Freeh's colleagues believed, more offended by Clinton's sexual frailties. Perhaps there was no one in America, meanwhile, more offended by what he saw as Freeh's arrogance and sanctimony than the man who had appointed him.

The first signs of a rift did not involve Clinton's personal failings, but rather those of a cabinet member. Housing and Urban Development Secretary

Henry Cisneros had acknowledged a sensitive personal matter during the FBI background check that preceded his confirmation. During his time as mayor of San Antonio, he had had an extramarital affair, and agreed to make payments to his former lover. Evidence later emerged that he had understated the amount of these payments, possibly to mislead investigators about the degree of his financial exposure. The Justice Department's own Public Integrity Section recommended dropping the matter as trivial. Freeh did not think it was trivial. Lying to the FBI was a serious offense, and he urged Reno to trigger the appointment of an independent counsel. She did so, in March 1995. Clinton thought this was a travesty. Meanwhile, it had not escaped White House notice how closely Freeh was cultivating relationships with the new Republican majority on Capitol Hill. He was fawned over in public hearings; his budget requests sailed to passage. Many of the same Republicans who hated Clinton treated his FBI appointee as a golden boy. Which side was Freeh on?

The answer became obvious the next year. In June 1996, in the midst of answering a congressional inquiry, White House lawyers stumbled upon something truly interesting in a basement office: more than four hundred raw FBI files, many of them of prominent Republicans, including former secretary of state James Baker. It was flagrantly improper for the Clinton White House to have such material, and not hard for suspicious minds to imagine the worst: The Clintons might be running a Nixon-style intelligence operation against their political enemies. The president offered an alternate explanation. It appeared to have been "a completely honest bureaucratic snafu," he told reporters when the matter erupted, during a campaign fund-raising stop in Las Vegas.

At a moment of acute vulnerability for the White House, Freeh's self-protective instincts kicked in. The FBI put out a statement in his name announcing, "The prior system of providing files to the White House relied on good faith and honor. Unfortunately, the FBI and I were victimized."

Freeh's statement was not only gratuitous; it was wrong. The White House security office had requested the FBI files for permanent White House employees who were holdovers from the Bush administration. This was a proper request. What came back from FBI headquarters were the files not only of the permanent employees but of the political appointees who had left with the change of administrations. No doubt it was sloppy for the Clinton White House not to notice this immediately and return the wayward files. It was sloppier, and more troubling, for the FBI to have sent over errant files in the first place. At Justice, Gorelick blew up in a conversation with Freeh, who responded with a dubious claim that he had not known about the initial statement in his name. He issued a second one later in the day, saying he took responsibility. In the meantime, the matter of the FBI files was added to the growing brief of independent counsel Kenneth Starr. Four years later, his inquiry would find no criminal violation by the Clinton White House. Clinton's explanation of a bureaucratic snafu had been correct.

From this time forward, from Clinton's vantage point, the relationship with Freeh was beyond salvage. Others in the White House, meanwhile, did their best to work with a man who seemed to view it as a point of professional pride that he would not work with others. Sandy Berger, who prided himself on maintaining a civil working relationship with Freeh, found his patience tested even so. Once Freeh mentioned, seemingly in passing, that the bureau later that week planned to arrest a Caribbean leader on drug charges as he switched planes in Miami. "Gosh, Louie," Berger inquired sarcastically, "do you think this is the kind of thing the White House might want to know?" Among the people who were most frustrated with Freeh and his agency was one of Berger's deputies, Richard Clarke, who was the White House's official in charge of counterterrorism. Colleagues regarded him as a man possessed by convictions of an imminent threat. Clarke was trying to coordinate, across several agencies, the government's efforts to identify, track, and react against terrorist threats abroad and domestically. The FBI was invariably the most resistant.

It was extremely difficult for the FBI to coordinate with a White House against whom, on other fronts, it was in increasingly open warfare. On the campaign fund-raising controversy, Freeh had drafted a memo to Reno asking her to appoint an independent counsel to investigate potential abuses by the Clinton White House. For once, she resisted. After several years' experience with open-ended and expensive independent counsel probes, Reno had become more skeptical. Freeh's memo soon found its way to Republicans on Capitol Hill and to the press. In December 1997, McCurry was asked at his daily briefing whether Clinton still had confidence in Freeh. He responded with a masterpiece of a quote: "The president has great confidence that Louis Freeh is leading that agency *as best he can.*" When reporters noted that this was not exactly full-throated praise, the press secretary noted, "I am pretty careful on how I choose my words." A couple of weeks later, the question was put directly to the president, who declined his endorsement. "On this confidence business," he noted, "I think there's been too much back and forth on that, and I don't want to get into it." Freeh made plain this did not bother him at all. After all, he was a man who refused to accept a badge giving him White House access, believing it would send the wrong message to the public. Instead, he needed to be cleared in by security each time he came to the White House, visits that were increasingly infrequent, and included zero one-on-one visits with the president in the second term. "My job is not to make people happy or please them or be a loyal subordinate," he explained, "when that conflicts with what I think my job is."

THE DISJUNCTION BETWEEN THE FBI AND THE REST OF THE EXECUTIVE branch had an obvious and troubling precedent. From 1924 until his death in 1972, J. Edgar Hoover had presided with little accountability over an FBI empire. With his thick dossiers of gossip and damaging personal information, he kept presidents and Congress at heel. With a sure instinct for public relations, he turned himself into a national hero. Only after his death did the world learn about a long record of agency abuses. Clinton regarded Freeh as very much in the Hoover tradition. This was a stretch. Freeh was by most accountings an honorable man, yet one who many colleagues believed had become so gripped by self-righteousness that his judgment suffered. And he was far from a skilled administrator. Clinton was right that the FBI was operating without effective oversight. The director ignored and intimidated his superiors at the Department of Justice. At the same time he was the toast of Capitol Hill, where his Republican patrons fully shared his disdain for the president.

Clinton had cause to fire Freeh after the China briefing debacle, but there's no evidence it was considered. One can sympathize with the president's dilemma. Such a move would have unleashed a thunder of denunciation by those who said Clinton was purging an enemy. There would have been inevitable comparisons to Nixon's "Saturday Night Massacre" firing of the Watergate special prosecutor. "No one in the press or Congress would have believed we were doing it for any reason other than to protect the president," one of Clinton's chiefs of staff later recalled ruefully.

The comment underlined a paradox of Clinton's presidency. In 1997 he stood astride the world, a newly re-elected president whose job approval ratings measured far above those for any other American politician. Yet this imposing exterior was held in place by some weak beams. Clinton was harried from inside his own government, and neither his temperament nor his political circumstances gave him any choice but to take it.

Chapter Twenty-eight

ALLIANCE

RESIDENT CLINTON HAD NEVER MADE A LESS IMPRESSIVE ENTRANCE. In March 1997, Air Force One had just touched down in Helsinki, Finland, after a long flight over the Atlantic for a summit meeting with Russian president Boris Yeltsin. The president's doctors had pleaded with him not to make the trip. Days earlier, while on a trip to Florida, Clinton had badly wrenched his knee in a late-night stumble while staying at the estate of professional golfer Greg Norman. He was still in pain from surgery. Presidential physician Connie Mariano had urged him not to go, warning that a long plane ride ran the risk of blood clots. Clinton responded that his attendance in Helsinki was non-negotiable. When he landed, however, he was in too much discomfort to hobble down the stairs off the plane. So the president of the United States, sitting in his wheelchair, was unceremoniously lowered in a Finnair catering platform.

Clinton might have looked lame, but the reality was quite different. He was arriving for the first overseas trip of his second term as the most commanding figure on the world stage. In the early years of his presidency, he had been a figure of derision in Europe, mocked for his vacillation on the Balkans, and what was perceived as his obsession with domestic politics at the expense of exerting global leadership. But the successful if belated intervention in Bosnia had transformed European perceptions of the administration. Success had also transformed Clinton's perception of himself. No longer intimidated by the arcana of foreign policy, he had learned to trust his own instincts. Clinton at last felt at home in the world.

He was determined to promote the preeminent item in his second-term agenda for U.S. foreign policy. The collapse of the Soviet Union and the ensuing liberation of its former satellite states in Eastern Europe had created a signal opportunity. The dream, as he often stated it, was for the United States to take the lead in building a "free, peaceful, undivided Europe." His proposed means of doing this was an expansion of the North Atlantic Treaty Organization—the alliance that had won the Cold War. By taking in new members, NATO could provide security to the anxious states of Eastern Europe, just learning to walk on their own, and tether them to the mature free-market democracies of the West.

Quite understandably, however, leaders in Russia regarded the proposed NATO expansion with alarm. This was an organization that for fifty years had been defined by its opposition to Moscow. Now, at a moment when Russian power was at an ebb as it made the transition from communism, Clinton was proposing to bring NATO to Russia's doorstep. In many Russian eyes, this was at best a humiliation, at worst a dangerous provocation. The president's challenge in Helsinki was to persuade Yeltsin to see NATO expansion as Clinton himself did—not as a threat but as an opportunity for new cooperation between Moscow and Washington.

Clinton's policy of NATO expansion had provoked similarly intense feelings back home. This issue was hardly the stuff of popular debate in bars or pool halls, but in elite think tanks and newspaper editorial pages, the strong consensus was that Clinton's policy was a grievous error. No issue was more important than coaxing a new relationship with Russia, many experts warned. So why risk it by expanding a Cold War alliance that, truth be told, had probably already outlived its useful life? Even within the administration, such clear-thinking voices as the Pentagon's Bill Perry had been urging a go-slow approach to NATO expansion. Clinton listened intently to Perry's objections, but made it clear he planned to move ahead anyway. When he did, among those thundering their dissent were the *New York Times* editorial page and Senator Sam Nunn, who was among the Democratic Party's most respected voices on national security. George Kennan, then in his nineties and a revered sage of foreign policy, warned ominiously that NATO expansion was a "strategic blunder of potentially epic proportions."

Most charitably, his critics accused Clinton of naïveté. Less charitably, he was accused of naked cynicism by people who believed that his real motive was winning support from the ethnic eastern Europeans in key electoral states like Ohio and Illinois. But the election was over, and Clinton was still pursuing NATO expansion on an accelerated schedule. The reason had nothing to do with politics. Clinton's policy on the alliance was an expression of his naturally enveloping personality. He prized human relationships—the more, the better. Optimism and cooperation were basic values, and he believed that there were few human conflicts that could not be resolved if people would simply approach them with reason.

WOULD YELTSIN BE REASONABLE? AS HE ARRIVED IN HELSINKI, CLINTON'S four-year cultivation of the volcanic Russian leader was facing its most important test.

The president placed considerably more faith in Yeltsin than most foreign policy professionals, including many in his own administration. In the best light, Yeltsin was the proud and colorful embodiment of the new Russia: still a bear, as in the old days, but now a benign one. This view saw Yeltsin as a vital life force. He was full of human frailties—his drinking, his swaggering outbursts at news conferences—but these were offset by wonderful virtues: his bravery in standing up to the hacks in the communist old guard in the closing days of the Soviet Union and, most of all, his imagination in wanting Russia to break at last from the sad grip of its autocratic past and emerge as a prosperous and peaceful nation in a post–Cold War world order. There was, however, a darker interpretation: that Yeltsin was a blustering alcoholic crank who was willing to trample Russia's emerging civil liberties, relight old conflicts with the West, and do whatever else he needed to preserve his tenuous hold on power.

Time and again, Clinton embraced the benign interpretation. They called each other Boris and "Beeeel" at summits. When Yeltsin played the bully, as in his blustering denunciations of NATO, Clinton was always forgiving. Yeltsin, he reminded colleagues, was the proud leader of a troubled country. And, just like Clinton, he had rivals on the right to worry about. "We keep telling Ol' Boris, 'Okay, now, here's what you've got to do next—here's some more shit for your face,' " Clinton told a sympathetic Talbott. "We've got to remember that

Yeltsin can't do more with us than his own traffic will bear. . . . I've got some domestic politics of my own—stuff that I can't do that I'd like to do, stuff I've got to do that I'd like not to. But he's got a much harder deal than I do."

This insight led to Clinton's evolution on the diplomatic stage. He had realized that a subject he once thought he did not know well—foreign policy—was inseparable from politics, the subject he knew best. The key to his relationships with other leaders, and to negotiations from the Middle East to Northern Ireland, was understanding the political pressures and the realistic alternatives those leaders faced.

In 1996, Clinton was all but openly rooting for Yeltsin as he sought re-election—a contest considerably more competitive than the president's battle with Bob Dole. Russia at the time was being uniformly denounced around the world for its ugly crushing of rebels in the breakaway republic of Chechnya. On a visit to Moscow, Clinton was urged by staff members not to let his sympathy for Yeltsin get in the way of an appropriately measured statement of concern about Chechnya. Instead, the president caused his traveling delegation to wince by comparing Yeltsin to Abraham Lincoln, who had also stood for the proposition that "no state had a right to withdraw from the Union."

The occasional gaffes aside, Clinton in the main had been proven right that he could finesse his relationship with Yeltsin in ways that were productive for the rest of the world. Russian troops, for example, played an essential role in helping enforce the Dayton peace agreement—all the while serving in Bosnia under an American commander. This was astonishing cooperation between two nations that a few years earlier had been mortal foes, and it set a precedent that would prove useful several times in years to come.

At their first dinner in Helsinki, however, the bad Yeltsin was on display. He had been in frail health and looked like a cadaver. But Yeltsin's parlous condition did not prevent him from hitting the sauce with his usual vigor. He downed four glasses of wine and a glass of champagne in rapid succession.

Amazingly, though, Yeltsin always managed to bounce back in the morning. Clinton's agenda for the summit was to get Yeltsin's agreement to back a formal charter outlining NATO's new relationship with Russia. At the same time, Russia would swallow its objections to NATO expansion, which was set to begin with the first wave of invitations to new countries that summer: Poland, Hungary, and the Czech Republic. Yeltsin's concern was over future waves. Clinton had been warned that the Russians would push for commitments that the three Baltic states that had once been part of the Soviet Union—Estonia, Latvia, and Lithuania—would never be invited to join

NATO. This would be simply too much of a provocation for Russia. Clinton, though he knew NATO had no intention of including the Baltic states in the near term, had already decided there was no way he could make such a commitment without fatally undermining his vision of an undivided Europe. This conflict consumed the rest of the summit.

Yeltsin said he understood that Clinton could not give a formal commitment. But give me something, he pleaded, a gentleman's agreement between us. Clinton recognized this was an absurd distinction: A private commitment would soon leak and be the same as a public one. Now it was his turn to plead. The whole idea of the new NATO was that the alliance would no longer be defined in opposition to Russia. What Yeltsin was proposing would keep the old division, just move the lines around a bit. "Look, Boris, you're forcing an issue that doesn't need to drive a wedge between us here," Clinton said. ". . . I don't want to do anything that makes it seem like the old Russia and the old NATO."

Finally, Yeltsin stopped arguing. It was the same pattern he had shown before: bluster in public, argue more reasonably in private—then give in. "Well," he said, "I tried."

The Russian was scowling when he and Clinton went to face reporters. Yeltsin said the expansion of NATO was "a mistake and a serious one at that," but it was his job to "minimize the consequences for Russia."

Talbott later speculated on the bond between Clinton and Yeltsin—a bond that survived even when such sober-minded voices as Warren Christopher and Vice President Gore had run out of patience with the Russian. "Yeltsin combined prodigious determination and fortitude with grotesque indiscipline and a kind of genius for self-abasement. He was both a very big man and a very bad boy, a natural leader and an incurable screw-up," Talbott wrote in his memoir of Russian diplomacy. "All this Clinton recognized, found easy to forgive and wanted others to join him in forgiving."

TWO MONTHS LATER, IN MAY, CLINTON RETURNED TO EUROPE FOR THE SIGNing in Paris of a charter formally offering Russia a consultative voice in NATO policymaking. While he was in Europe he stopped in London to meet with England's newly elected leader, Tony Blair.

Blair had been voted in on the strength of his Labour Party's victory just four weeks earlier. This was a victory for Clinton as well, and not only because several of his current and former political advisers were also consulting with Blair. The new prime minister was a living rebuke to the cynical interpretation

of Clinton, which regarded him as a supreme improviser, a man of fancy foot-
work and changing fashions, but with little core philosophy. It took a little distance to see the reality more clearly: The American president was now the
leader of a political movement that transcended national boundaries. What
Clinton was slowly, if fitfully, doing to the Democrats—stripping a progressive
party of old and outdated orthodoxies—Blair was trying to do also. In Germany, Italy, and the Netherlands, other progressive party leaders were doing
the same thing and, like Blair, were citing Clinton as their role model.

A remarkable news conference, on a sunny day in a garden at 10 Downing
Street, illustrated the uplifting effect Blair's victory had had on Clinton's own
stature. The session came just two days after a major development in the Paula
Jones case—the Supreme Court ruled unanimously that a sitting president
was not immune from civil lawsuits—but this news did not prompt even one
question from either the American or British press corps, who under ordinary
circumstances were each other's match in impertinence and might have been
expected to feast on such a gossipy development. Instead, the afternoon turned
into a virtual seminar on the future of progressive politics. "This is the generation that prefers reason to doctrine, that is strong in ideals but indifferent to
ideology, whose instinct is to judge government not on grand designs but by
practical results," explained Blair. "I would pay tribute to the way that Bill Clinton blazed the trail in this area."

Blair and Clinton had met casually during the Briton's Washington visits,
yet Clinton seemed instantly to assume a kind of big-brother manner with the
prime minister, who was seven years his junior. Blair seemed to accept the role,
even to the point of obsequiousness. "I like that," he fawned after one Clinton
answer. "I like that very much indeed."

Beneath the surface of this mutual admiration society, though, one could
discern differences in the nature of their minds and characters. It was Clinton's
instinct to smother the contradictions or shortcomings in his record or the
Democratic philosophy with pillowy language. Blair was a man of sharper intellectual edges. When a reporter asked the pair to explain the difference between their new centrism and old-fashioned expediency, Clinton responded
with a recital of his policy achievements. Blair engaged the question directly,
acknowledging in a way Clinton never would that certain parts of their "third
way" progressivism were indeed a concession to the conservative cause. "There
were certain things the 1980s got right—an emphasis on enterprise, more flexible labor markets. Fine, accepted—they got it right," Blair said. His party's
move to the center, the prime minister acknowledged, was "electorally necessary, but it was also the right thing to do."

In the years to come, it would become clear that this instinct for speaking more clearly was married to an instinct for acting more decisively. For all the similarities between Blair and Clinton, there would be an element of complexity—and frustration—to the relationship.

IF CLINTON WAS BLAIR'S BIG BROTHER, THEN GERMAN CHANCELLOR HELMUT Kohl had a relationship with the president akin to a gruff great-uncle watching over a talented but wayward nephew.

They were neither ideological confederates nor generational contemporaries. Kohl's Christian Democrats were, by German standards, the conservative party. Sixteen years Clinton's senior, a man forged by Cold War politics, and one of the heroes of German reunification at the Cold War's end, Kohl was secure with his own large role in European history. Perhaps as a result, he found it easier to offer support to a young American president when other European leaders were watching Clinton's tentative early foreign policy with anxiety and disdain. Kohl liked Clinton, and the feeling was mutual. They were both outsized men, and neither got that way by accident. Kohl had published a celebrity cookbook in Germany, featuring his famous recipe for Saumagen, a stuffed sow's stomach. The chancellor's Washington trips became famous for the visits he would insist on taking to Filomena's, an otherwise unexceptional Georgetown restaurant that was known for its giant servings. The two leaders would feast on heaping plates of carpaccio, calamari, ravioli, and zabaglione. Once, in Milwaukee, the two men stopped in at a diner for a six-course lunch, prompting White House press secretary Michael McCurry to tell reporters waiting outside, "It's ugly in there." Time zones helped facilitate the relationship. Clinton, with his night-owl metabolism, would often call to chat with Kohl long after midnight Washington time—morning in Germany. They closely followed each other's political situations, and enjoyed giving one another advice. "Are you going to be okay against this guy?" Kohl would ask when Clinton was enduring Bob Dole's broadsides in 1996. Commenting on their settled routines of conversation and dining out, Clinton remarked in one phone conversation, "We are like an old married couple, Helmut."

By the summer of 1997, Clinton no longer needed Kohl as a tutor in the intricacies of European diplomacy. Still, he had one last occasion to be glad the German was on his side. The culmination of the administration's four-year effort to expand NATO was a July meeting in Madrid. Several of the sixteen NATO nations, led by France, were bridling under the U.S. insistence that the first wave of expansion be limited to Poland, Hungary, and the Czech Republic. In particular, Jacques Chirac was agitating on behalf of Romania and Slovenia. The administration was adamantly opposed. NATO membership was not a frivolous military commitment; lowering the standard of membership could irreparably weaken the alliance's utility. In addition, if Romania and Slovenia entered now, there was little logic to delaying the hopes of the long-suffering Baltic nations for admission, even though Russia remained intensely opposed to putting those countries under NATO's umbrella. Clinton knew it was crucial not to let Chirac's grandstanding hijack the Madrid summit, but equally critical not to let the event degenerate into recriminations at American bullying. As the sixteen leaders of NATO countries met privately, Kohl put an end to the conversation. "One miracle has already come true," he stated. A few years earlier, no one could have imagined that the Cold War would be over, and that Warsaw Pact nations would be joining NATO. Going slow was the right approach, and did not prevent other nations from joining later.

Clinton's Madrid summit was a success, but the public manifestation of this came in the succeeding days. Throngs greeted him in Warsaw, Poland. Even more remarkably, they did the same in Bucharest, Romania, even though everyone in the crowd knew Clinton had been opposed to letting them join NATO immediately. He reassured a crowd of over a hundred thousand that stretched back for many blocks that Romania was an excellent candidate to join NATO later, as in fact happened. These people, though, were not there to hear the finer points of alliance management. They were there to see an American leader who had plainly emerged as the leader of Europe, and indeed of free and modern people in many lands. The crowd waved Romanian and American flags, swayed rhythmically, and let loose chants of "Bill! Bill! Bill!"

Chapter Twenty-nine

UNSETTLED

Good luck, Chief Justice William Rehnquist had growled at the second inaugural. Four months later, it turned out Clinton would need it. On May 27, 1997, the High Court rejected his argument that presidents should be immune from civil lawsuits while they are in office. Perhaps it was not, after all, just jittery nerves that had made Rehnquist's good wishes sound so sarcastic and menacing to the Clintons. They regarded him as a conservative ideologue, and felt sure he would happily harm them. If so, Rehnquist had enlisted some unlikely allies in his vendetta, for the Court's decision was unanimous, supported even by the two justices Clinton had nominated. On legal grounds, the president's argument that a civil lawsuit would be a distraction from official duties had been quite flimsy. On practical grounds, Clinton had no idea how right he was. In any event, the sexual harassment case of *Jones* v. *Clinton* was moving forward, and quickly.

For three years, the case had hovered in a middle zone of public consciousness. Jones's allegations were too troubling to be dismissed as pure farce. They were too absurdly lurid, and too obviously linked to conservative partisans, to be treated by most of the national press and indeed by most voters as if they were on the level. Jones, after all, had first made her accusations public at a Washington convention of conservative political activists. The alleged encounter that began the whole saga was now six years old. As Jones and others described it, in May 1991, then-governor Clinton had spotted the twenty-three-year-old state worker as she staffed an information booth in Little Rock's Excelsior Hotel, where a conference was being held. Clinton then allegedly enlisted a member of his security detail to invite the woman, then still single and known as Paula Corbin, up to his suite. ("The governor said you make his knees knock," state trooper Danny Ferguson said he told her.) So far, this all had a ring of plausibility, given what had long been rumored of Clinton's itinerant libido. But what of what Jones said happened next: Would Clinton simultaneously dispense both with small talk and his trousers, and feverishly urge the young woman to "kiss it"? This parade of prurient detail and allegation all contributed to the sense that the Jones case was a carnival freak show. And what about the testimony of Ferguson? He was already established, through his cooperation with the December 1993 *American Spectator* article, as hostile to his former boss. Yet even he said Corbin, far from scurrying in horror from the suite, had expressed interest in being Clinton's regular girlfriend. In any event, could Jones lay any reasonable claim to having suffered damage to her reputation or her career? She never saw Clinton again. She continued to receive scheduled raises at her $23,000-a-year job. The *Spectator* article that offended Jones had made a reference to the supposed encounter, mentioning a woman named "Paula." The obscurity that she supposedly craved was hers to enjoy before she filed her suit. A majority of the public seemed to put the allegations in a particular place—fit for joking about on the late-night talk shows, not fit to take seriously in judging presidential fitness.

Pollster Mark Penn's numbers made the point. In a confidential memo to Clinton as the Jones case reached a boil a few months later, he reported that 94 percent of voters were aware of her allegations. Roughly a third believed Jones, a third believed Clinton, and a third said they did not know. But 61 percent believed Clinton would win the case, and half believed "this is just an effort to undermine the president funded by the right wing with no other purpose." Only a third of voters believed she had a "real and just cause and case that deserves to be heard."

On this last question, the High Court had the only votes that mattered. Clinton was in the Netherlands for a commemoration of the fiftieth anniversary of the Marshall Plan when he got word of the ruling, in a call from his lawyer Robert Bennett. Clinton knew he needed to respond, even if he had nothing much to say, or the traveling press corps would be preoccupied with the matter for the rest of his European tour. While shaking hands with awe-struck Dutch citizens on the streets of The Hague, Clinton ambled over to the press pool to say he had seen Bennett's comments on CNN that morning and had nothing to add, though he did express concern about "what might happen to future presidents" because of the precedent.

THE JONES CASE NOW POSED GRAVE DANGERS TO CLINTON'S PRESIDENCY, though this was not obvious immediately. Bill Clinton was the only person who knew the full facts about his complicated private life. His lawyers could speculate, and did at great length, but he was the only one who could appreci-ate the true hazards of letting the Jones case proceed along a path to deposi-tions and trial, proceedings at which opposing lawyers could question him under oath about his sexual history. The question echoed through his presi-dency: Why did he not settle this case? In retrospect, it is plain that virtually no demand Paula Jones could have imposed as terms for settling this case would have been an unreasonable price to pay from the vantage point of Clinton's self-interest.

Vernon Jordan was in favor of settling, as was Bruce Lindsey. Even before the case was filed in 1994, and several times after that, there seemed to be win-dows of opportunity for settlement. Each time they slammed closed. In May 1994, there was a deal on the table that would have had Clinton read a state-ment saying merely that he had no recollection of meeting Jones at the Excel-sior but that he did not challenge her claim that they did. He would have stated that she did nothing improper or sexual, and that "I regret the untrue as-sertions which have been made about her conduct." No money would have changed hands. But the Jones team wanted a "tolling agreement" that they could renew the case within six months if any Clinton associates made dis-paraging remarks about Jones after the settlement. They had some reason for concern. A few weeks earlier, James Carville, Clinton's loyal defender, had an-nounced, "You drag $100 bills through trailer parks—there's no telling what you'll find." The tolling agreement was a deal-killer for Clinton's side, and the case got filed. Bennett announced, "The president adamantly denies the vi-cious and mean-spirited allegations in this complaint."

Bennett, a stout, pugnacious bulldog of a man, loved high-profile cases and expressed a zeal for combat that both Clintons appreciated. Hillary Clin-ton had interviewed him before he signed on to the Jones case. For a time, President Clinton wanted him to take over the Whitewater defense, believing that Bennett was more of a fighter than the mild-mannered (though equally tenacious) David Kendall. Bennett's real strategy for Jones over the next two years was neither combat nor settlement but delay—get the thing past the 1996 re-election campaign. He succeeded in that. Now, in 1997, the original question was revived: What was the price of settlement? An apology, which Jones wanted, remained out of the question. By August, however, Bennett had offered a settlement that would have had Clinton pay $700,000 to Jones and make a statement she had done nothing improper. This was a lot more expensive than 1994. Given what lay ahead, it would have been a bargain still.

By no means did Clinton see it this way. Most of the people around him believed he was just as happy to see the case head for trial. He was hugely embarrassed by the Jones allegations, and indignant whenever the subject arose. He himself discussed it selectively—he virtually never raised the case with Erskine Bowles, yet he would bring up the subject with another close friend, Terry McAuliffe—in order to emphatically deny that anything untoward had happened between him and Jones. In a curious episode, Clinton once got on the phone with *Washington Post* reporter Ann Devroy to welcome her back to the White House beat after a long illness (one that took her life within a few months). When she remarked sarcastically about how thrilled she was to be coming back to cover matters like the Jones case, he seemed to take her seriously. Interestingly, his comment was not a denial that he had ever met her. "I wish I could tell you everything about this," he said cryptically. "What happened is not what she said."

There seemed to be two great impediments to settlement, Clinton's legal team believed. Hillary Clinton was adamantly opposed to any deal with the likes of Jones. What would have been an embarrassment for him would have been a searing insult to her. The second was Clinton's own sense of righteousness. He viewed himself as a man of great virtue. The moral ambiguities of his private life, and the vulnerabilities these imposed on his public life, seemed beyond his range of vision.

Blind spots like these are one reason people hire lawyers. Though he was paying Bob Bennett more than $400 an hour, Clinton was serving as his own lawyer on the most sensitive questions. John Podesta, then serving as Clinton's deputy chief of staff, recalled an Oval Office meeting in the summer of 1997 at which Bennett coolly laid out the various arguments over settlement. Bennett made plain his own belief that settlement was desirable, so long as the terms were not so severe that people would assume that Clinton was guilty, as opposed to simply chasing away a political albatross. Then, however, he laid out the other side: Surely the case was winnable if it went to trial. The bottom line of the presentation seemed to be "It's up to you, sir. Tell us what you want." Podesta, who was himself a lawyer, would later cite the case as an object lesson in how lawyers can let clients down by being too respectful. There are times, and this was one, where somebody needed to grab the client by the lapels, shake him, and scream, "Are you out of your goddamn mind?" No one said this to the president of the United States.

CLINTON WAS NOT THE ONLY OBSTINATE CHARACTER IN THIS DRAMA. It was plainly now also in Jones's interest to settle. Her legal bills were rising; her legal case was weak. On August 19, 1997, her lawyers, dismayed by her refusal to accept a $700,000 settlement they thought was a superb deal for her, pleaded with her to reconsider. "Your focus has . . . changed from proving that you are a good person, to proving that Clinton is a bad person," wrote lawyers Gilbert Davis and Joseph Cammarata. Two weeks later, the lawyers dropped out of the case. Whatever Jones's real focus, the former lawyers had described precisely the motives of a growing circle of conservative warriors advising the young plaintiff and her husband.

A zealous new set of attorneys, based in Dallas and funded with help from a conservative advocacy group, took over that autumn. For the next several months, Jones's legal team used the discovery process to systematically pry open Clinton's sexual history. This was a different exercise than the prurient exclusives of the *American Spectator* or the *Star,* which had plowed this ground years earlier. This time, a record was being established in testimony taken under oath in a federal court case.

Clinton's exposure was grotesquely literal. When she first made her allegations, Jones had promised corroborating detail, making a cryptic reference to an "identifying characteristic" of the president's genitals. What she said she saw was later disclosed to be an alleged curvature to the presidential member that experts said might be Peyronie's disease, a previously obscure condition that produces marked curvature. This now became a subject of chortling journalistic inquiry: Did Clinton suffer from it? Bennett assured the press that "in terms of size, shape, direction, whatever the devious mind wants to concoct, the president is a normal man." To prove the point, Clinton underwent a detailed examination by urologists during a physical at the National Naval Medical Center in Bethesda, Maryland, where all presidents go for their medical care. The examination showed no sign of curvature, though the conservative *Washington Times,* which broke the story of the exam, scrupulously cited sources noting that "definitive diagnosis is possible only when an erection is induced . . . and it was learned that this was not done at Mr. Clinton's examination."

His humiliations only multiplied as the case churned dangerously forward. The testimony being compiled in depositions and sworn statements in late 1997, all of which would come tumbling out publicly in early 1998, was drawing a portrait of a man lacking in sexual scruples or even self-control. Much of this evidence was of dubious relevance to the specific allegations in the Jones case. Most of it had a familiar ring to anyone who had even in passing followed the gossip about Clinton for the previous six years. Moreover, any individual allegation was subject to the familiar challenges from Clinton defenders: This person was lying, and was known for having a vendetta against Clinton. This person was fantasizing, and was known as emotionally unbalanced. Yet it would soon be impossible to maintain that everyone, under oath, was inventing such excruciating revelations. Among the descriptions of excess was testimony from state troopers that, in the months after Clinton's 1992 election, his friend Marilyn Jo Jenkins made several mysterious 5 a.m. visits to the president-elect at the governor's mansion, meeting him in the basement. The woman, an Arkansas utility executive, would arrive dressed in a long coat and baseball cap. Her last visit was on the very day Clinton left Little Rock for his inauguration. Then there was the statement of Dolly Kyle Browning, who had known Clinton since high school. She claimed that she had had a long-term sexual relationship with the governor, and recounted an alleged conversation in which he agreed with her suggestion that he was a "sex addict." The troopers also repeated their 1993 allegations about repeatedly approaching women on Clinton's behalf. They recounted stories about lying to Hillary Clinton about the governor's whereabouts, or the time she woke up to find her husband had left the mansion. "Where's Bill?" she asked trooper Roger Perry. "Hillary, he had insomnia. He couldn't sleep, so he went for a drive," he responded. She cursed furiously. When the trooper alerted him by cell phone, Clinton exclaimed, "Oh my God! Oh, God! Oh, God!" and he came right back. There was testimony about an alleged affair with an administrator of the mansion. Gennifer Flowers told her story of a twelve-year affair. And Kathleen Willey, who had resisted efforts to make her testify, gave her story of Clinton's lunging advance in his study off the Oval Office in the fall of 1993. It was a devastating recital of self-destructive behavior.

Clinton had been confronted with many of these allegations before. On December 6, 1997, he learned that he was about to confront a brand-new one. In a meeting at 5 p.m. with Robert Bennett and Bruce Lindsey in the Oval Office, Clinton learned that one of the women the Jones attorneys had on their witness list was Monica S. Lewinsky.

"Bob, do you think I'm fucking crazy?" Clinton asked incredulously. "I . . . know the press is watching me every minute. The right has been dying for this kind of thing from day one. No, it did not happen . . . I'm retired."

As it happened, Lewinsky had left the Oval Office, where she sat on the floor while Clinton sat in a rocking chair and stroked her hair, only hours before Bennett arrived.

BENEATH HIS PERFORMANCE, WHAT COULD CLINTON HAVE BEEN THINKING? There was a lot he did not know on December 6. He did not know that Lewinsky had been telling the story of her affair to a presumed confidante named Linda Tripp. He did not know that Tripp, filled with disdain for Clinton, had been taping these confessions. He did not know that she had been sharing these revelations with a gossipy New York literary agent named Lucianne Goldberg, in hopes that Tripp could secure a book contract for what she knew about Clinton's sensational indiscretion. He did not know that Goldberg had shared the news about Lewinsky eagerly with the Jones attorneys. Most of all, he did not know that there would soon be an intersection between the Jones case and Kenneth Starr's independent counsel probe that still, almost quaintly, went by the name of Whitewater.

Clinton *did* know that a White House affair that he thought had been a closely held secret was somehow so well known that the Jones attorneys had thought to put Lewinsky on their witness list. He knew that, if events followed their current course, he would be asked about her while under oath in a deposition. The president was at a crossroads. He was the only one who knew the perils. The logic that had been plain since May—that it would be better for Clinton to take a bold step to dispense with the Paula Jones case, no matter how painful—was now screaming to be followed.

Instead, Clinton let circumstances drift, apparently confident that he could manage the complexities of this situation with charm and guile and good luck. He had been in many jams in his life, but very few that he was not able to maneuver out of.

In truth, Clinton and Lewinsky both had begun their maneuvering months before. Lewinsky began 1997 under the illusion that Clinton, safely reelected, would bring her back to a White House job from her Pentagon exile. Clinton apparently was ambivalent about the prospect. He did press his secretary Betty Currie to help bring Lewinsky back to the White House. Currie in turn sent Lewinsky to Marsha Scott, an old Arkansas friend of Clinton's who now worked in White House personnel. When Scott resisted Lewinsky's importuning for a job, apparently in an effort to protect Clinton from himself, he did little to help Lewinsky's cause. The whole situation was comical—a president making furtive and fruitless gestures to get someone hired in his own White House.

Lewinsky began to suspect she was getting the runaround. She pressed Clinton repeatedly about why he could not simply snap his fingers and bring her back to the White House. He would tell her that Robert Nash, his personnel director, was working on it, or that Marsha Scott was, or others, and that "We just sort of need to be careful."

Finally, she got tired of waiting. On July 3, she sent Clinton a letter that didn't call him "handsome" or any of her usual diminutives. Instead, it began "Dear Sir," and warned darkly that since she could not get a job back at the White House she might have no choice but to tell her parents about the affair. The next day, Independence Day, Clinton began the meeting with his twenty-three-year-old paramour sharply, reminding her, "it's illegal to threaten the president of the United States." Yet Lewinsky's threat had its effect. After she broke into tears, he stroked her arm, kissed her neck, and suggested that perhaps they might be together once he left the White House. "I don't know, I might be alone in three years," Clinton purred. The lovers were each other's match in both adolescent immaturity and adult manipulation. Clinton later told an Arkansas friend that his only goal throughout 1997 was to keep Lewinsky within his fold, realizing that he had been stupid to have the affair but fearful of leaving her embittered. As Lewinsky left the Oval Office, she later recounted, "I just knew that he was in love with me."

She became more clear-eyed later that year. Realizing the affair was going nowhere, she had decided to leave Washington for New York. She wanted Clinton's help finding a job, and soon got it. Soon she had John Podesta, enlisted by Betty Currie, setting up interviews for her with U.N. ambassador Bill Richardson. She was meeting with Vernon Jordan, one of America's best-connected men, who told her that she came highly recommended from the president and promised to help her cause. Did Jordan and Podesta wonder why the president and his secretary were taking such an intense interest in the fortunes of such a young woman of such modest professional attainment? If so, they apparently squelched curiosity and averted their gazes from the obvious. Both later testified that they did not know of any sexual relationship between Clinton and Lewinsky. It is notable, given later allegations that Clinton's efforts to secure

Lewinsky a job were part of an effort to obstruct justice, that these efforts began in the fall of 1997, well before Lewinsky's name came up as a possible witness in the Paula Jones case.

The case, needless to say, did instill new urgency in Clinton's efforts to manage the Lewinsky relationship. After Lewinsky complained that Jordan was not devoting much effort to her search, Clinton promised to take it up with him again. Around 2 a.m. on December 17, Clinton called Lewinsky at home to inform her that she was on the Jones witness list and might be subpoenaed. If she was subpoenaed, he noted, she could sign an affidavit stating that she had not had any sexual relationship with him. He reviewed with her their established cover stories—that she had come to the Oval Office bringing official papers or to visit Betty Currie. Lewinsky was indeed served with a subpoena at her Pentagon office just two days later. Ominously, the subpoena asked her to produce all gifts and correspondence between her and Clinton, specifically making reference to "hat pins." Clinton had given Lewinsky a hat pin. How would they know to ask for that?

Lewinsky, with judgment rather more sound than Clinton's, had urged him to settle the case. Instead, he continued to drift toward catastrophe. He and Lewinsky discussed—at her initiative, she later testified—her returning his gifts via Betty Currie, rather than producing them for the Jones attorneys. On December 28, Lewinsky went to the White House, where Clinton gave her what she at first thought was a soulful kiss, though when she opened her eyes she noticed he was staring vacantly out a window.

There was a reason, of course, that Jones's lawyers knew to ask for a hat pin. Lewinsky had told Linda Tripp. It would be another few weeks before she learned that her confidante was also her betrayer. Late in December, the two had a conversation that showed how well Lewinsky had learned Clinton's number.

"He won't settle," Lewinsky told Tripp. "He's in denial."

Tripp replied, "I think if he fucking knew, he would settle."

Chapter Thirty

TRAPPED

As HE ENTERED 1998, THE SIXTH YEAR OF HIS PRESIDENCY, CLINTON'S life was surrounded with an air of expectancy. Certainly the looming Jones case and the Lewinsky entanglement shadowed his thoughts and occupied many hours of his time at the turn of the year. His deposition in the case was scheduled for January 17, less than three weeks away. This matter, though, occupied only one corner of the president's psychic space. Other corners were fixed on the promise, not the hazards, waiting in the weeks ahead.

His presidency had awakened from the lassitude of 1997. Late in December, Clinton held forth about his future plans at a news conference for a full ninety minutes, the longest such encounter of his presidency. After years on the defensive, when incremental gains in his agenda were the best he could hope for with a constrained budget and a hostile Republican Congress, he announced he was now eager to pivot to the "long-term problems of the country, the long-term challenges." He vowed to enact an international agreement on pollution aimed at combating global warming. He pledged to push forward on free trade, an issue about which, he acknowledged, many in his own party had misgivings. Democrats had doubts, too, about another of his announced priorities: fixing the Medicare and Social Security programs, in recognition that these popular entitlement programs were too expensive to be sustained at current levels as the baby-boom generation retired. All these were indeed long-term problems, and addressing them would require leadership of a sort Clinton seemed well positioned to offer. In the near term, as a run-up to the 1998 State of the Union, Clinton and his aides had fashioned and previewed a flurry of policy initiatives, on issues as diverse as AIDS prevention, expanding the Peace Corps, and improving federal food inspections. There was much more to come, they promised, in the January 27 speech. All this left an impression, accurately, of a still young and still creative president eager to make the most of the remaining three years of his presidency.

His personal life seemed settled in a comfortable place as well. With the Clintons now firmly in middle age—he was now fifty-one and she was fifty—they had reason to be content with the trajectory of their life together. The ordeals they had suffered, political and personal, were more than outweighed by the achievements. The daughter they had raised in such unusual circumstances, amid the glare of a political life, had reached young adulthood as an intelligent and appealing young woman, though Chelsea Clinton's public reserve made her still little known to the nation. She had enrolled the previous fall at Stanford University. The void in the household was filled in part by a pet, a chocolate Labrador retriever named Buddy. The first family repaired to a four-day Caribbean vacation in the U.S. Virgin Islands. In St. Thomas, Clinton slept late, ate out only once, and even golfed only once. He told reporters he was lying low because he wanted to spend time with his family and reflect on the balance of his presidency. He curled up with a new book by journalist Robert Kaplan, the same writer who earlier had influenced his thinking on Bosnia, entitled *The Ends of the Earth: A Journey at the Dawn of the 21st Century.*

One afternoon, the first family walked down to frolic at a secluded beach near their borrowed home. The president and first lady, both in swimsuits, began dancing playfully on the beach. Across a lagoon, an Agence France-Presse photographer, hidden among some bushes, shot an image that was beamed around the world. The White House protested what it called an invasion of privacy. Cynics presumed the dance and the protest were a deliberate put-on, a way of presenting the Clintons as a loving couple in the days before the Jones deposition. Hillary Clinton, however, seemed authentically outraged, and noted plausibly that not many women in their fifties are eager to be photographed in a swimsuit. The president, aides said, seemed to regard the whole fuss as rather amusing. Even if the dance itself had not been intended as a publicity shot, the doting on Hillary Clinton was well timed. He surely knew the weeks ahead, in which news of the impending deposition would reach a crescendo, would be hard for her. As he had lavished attention on Lewinsky before leaving town, he now lavished attention on his wife.

As the year began, this president was well established in the public mind as a man of contradictions. Polls consistently showed solid majorities believed Clinton "does not have high personal moral and ethical standards." The toll, however, was on balance rather modest. At the New Year, Gallup took a poll that put Clinton atop the list of the public's "most admired" men. Another survey found that nearly 80 percent of the public said the Jones allegations had not affected their opinion of Clinton. When asked about the Jones case a few days before his deposition, Clinton told an interviewer, "I just try to put it over in a little box and go and do my work."

CLINTON, UNDISCIPLINED IN SOME SETTINGS, WAS FANATICALLY DISCIPLINED in others. In the days before his Jones deposition, he was a methodical man, carefully practicing his answers again and again. He and his lawyers spent six hours in rehearsal on the Friday night before the deposition, January 16, then Clinton insisted that they practice another ninety minutes the next morning. He had decided he would lie, under oath, rather than answer embarrassing questions about his sexual history.

He had been warned, bluntly, about the dangers of this. On Friday night, Bennett had told Clinton he found the president's answers about his relationship with Marilyn Jo Jenkins, the Arkansas utility executive who had paid 5 a.m. visits to the governor's mansion after the 1992 election, "frankly unbelievable." If Clinton lied, "The crazies will come after you. They will try to impeach you if you lie. That's the only thing to worry about."

"I hear you," Clinton said.

Perhaps, but instead he chose to listen to his inner counsel. Clinton believed, with reason, that Paula Jones's suit was spurious. A little more than two months later, the federal judge in the case, Susan Webber Wright, a Republican appointee, agreed. He believed that questions no one had a right to ask were not entitled to a truthful answer. In any event, when it came to Monica Lewinsky—just one of seven women he knew he would be asked about in the deposition—he might have believed he was telling the truth in some rough sense of the word. Several of his lawyers and political aides reached this conclusion. Several weeks before Clinton testified, Lewinsky had seized on the same insight. In surreptitiously taped conversations with Linda Tripp, Lewinsky noted: "The way that man thinks, I don't think he thinks of lying under oath. . . . He doesn't think about it in those terms. Okay?" In Clinton's mind, forever navigating between desire, guilt, and rationalization, he believed he had stayed on the right side of an important line with Lewinsky by never indulging in intercourse. So no matter the lurid specifics of what he might be asked in the deposition, he felt justified in denying a sexual relationship. He also felt confident in this deception. On January 7, Lewinsky had signed an affidavit saying she had "never had a sexual relationship with the President." The young woman was heading to New York. With Vernon Jordan's assistance, she had been offered a job at Revlon. Clinton's efforts to massage this delicate problem seemed to have worked out just fine.

What Clinton did not know was that on the same Friday he was rehearsing his testimony, other people were equally busy in anticipation of the next day's deposition. In suburban Virginia, at the Pentagon City mall, agents for Ken Starr's Whitewater prosecution surrounded Monica Lewinsky as she arrived for a meeting with Linda Tripp and detained her for several hours in a partially successful effort to interrogate her. They had learned of her false affidavit and Vernon Jordan's efforts on her behalf. Starr's team was convinced, though the lawyers could never prove it, that similar efforts by Clinton and Jordan had helped buy Webster Hubbell's silence on Whitewater. The day before, ecstatic over a chance to prove a pattern, Starr had sought and received authority from the Justice Department to expand his probe to examine possible obstruction of justice in the Jones case. This represented a breathtaking merger of the criminal investigation that was Clinton's longest-running torment and the civil suit that was his longest-running embarrassment. The story's multiple lines were tangled in other ways. Under the orchestration of Lucianne Goldberg, Tripp had told her story to Michael Isikoff, a reporter at *Newsweek* magazine. That very night, in a meeting with Tripp's lawyer, they heard her surreptitiously recorded tapes of conversations with Lewinsky, in which she talked of her affair and the efforts she and Clinton had taken to avoid disclosure in the Jones case. At the same time, Isikoff's editors debated whether the story of this alleged affair—and the late-breaking intervention of Starr—was nailed down solidly enough to report by the magazine's Saturday deadline. Meanwhile, Tripp, eager to help Clinton's adversaries, met late in the evening with the Paula Jones attorneys who would be questioning Clinton that morning. The plot and its spiteful cast of characters were becoming hard to follow. The president and his wife had complained for years about a conservative conspiracy to undermine them. His suspicions did not prevent him from waltzing into what surely was, if not necessarily a conspiracy, then certainly a well-orchestrated trap. Lewinsky had confided to Tripp, who, in her disdain for Clinton and eagerness to sell a book about her Clinton adventures, had violated the confidence by telling Goldberg, who with relish saw to it that both *Newsweek* and the Paula Jones lawyers knew about the affair with Lewinsky. Paula Jones's attorneys, meanwhile, were tapped into a network of conservative lawyers who were delighted to ensure that Ken Starr's team knew everything.

The deposition took place at Robert Bennett's law firm, the offices of Skadden, Arps, just two blocks from the White House. Clinton's motorcade arrived through a basement garage, and around ten-thirty he arrived in the conference room. The two sides sat across a large, oval-shaped wooden table. Paula Jones was already waiting in the room when Clinton arrived. This was only their second encounter, or possibly even their first. For nearly four years, Clinton had maintained publicly that he had no recollection of even meeting Jones in 1991. He gave her no acknowledgment now. Knowing Clinton's garrulous penchant, and his tendency to charm even adversaries, his lawyers had warned him to stay coolly distant during the deposition, which would last the next six hours. On this most unfortunate day for Clinton, he did get a couple of lucky breaks. The first was that Bennett had succeeded in persuading Judge Wright to preside over the deposition in person. She had not been at other depositions. In this case, Bennett persuaded her that she should be present, in deference to the unusual circumstances and to protect the dignity of the institution of the presidency. Her attendance meant she could make rulings on the relevance of certain inquiries, as well as provide a general restraining presence, that prevented the questioning from being even more wide-ranging and intrusive than it would have been. The second stroke of luck was that the Jones attorneys, evidently hoping to impress Wright about their eagerness to maintain decorum, proposed that they not ask Clinton direct questions, such as whether a particular woman had performed oral sex on him. Instead, they arrived at the hearing with a written, clinically worded three-part "definition of sexual relations." Wright was skeptical, noting that she had long since reached a point in this case where awkward subjects were no longer so embarrassing. Perhaps he should just ask his questions directly, she suggested to James Fisher, a Jones lawyer. Bennett cautioned that an elaborate definition might be an effort to confuse his client. Finally, Wright forced the Jones attorneys to narrow their wording and approved an official definition of sexual relations for purposes of the deposition: "contact with the genitalia, anus, groin, breast, inner thigh, or buttocks of any person with an intent to arouse or gratify the sexual desire of any person." This contorted definition, far from confusing the witness as Bennett had protested, would in time be seen as his salvation.

⋯⋯⋯⋯⋯⋯

THE DECEPTIONS CONTINUED EVEN AFTER THE DEPOSITION ENDED. WHEN Clinton returned to the White House, Rahm Emanuel, a senior political adviser, asked how things had gone. "It went great," the president enthused. "I did really well."

Clinton's actions that evening made plain he knew the day had been a disaster—and that the days ahead would likely bring still more disasters. The White House functions as a kind of satellite dish on political Washington; when bad news is building, the president's aides usually hear the static even before they can make out the precise words. Friday evening and Saturday, while Clinton was trying to bluster his way through the deposition, the senior political hands on his staff were being bombarded with frantic calls from reporters at *Time* magazine who had heard vague rumors that *Newsweek* was preparing some kind of sensational report. John Podesta decided to call Michael Isikoff directly to ask what was happening. Isikoff was not forthcoming, but he did ask Podesta whether he knew a young woman named Monica Lewinsky. Now Podesta realized why Betty Currie had been so concerned about that young woman's job hunt. Podesta told lawyer Cheryl Mills about *Newsweek*'s interest in Lewinsky, and she in turn called Bruce Lindsey, who was waiting in an office just outside where Clinton was giving his deposition. The president and Lindsey spoke several times during breaks in the questioning.

The two spoke again in the Oval Office when the deposition was over, to review it and its troubling focus on Lewinsky. His agitation mounting, the president canceled plans to have dinner with the first lady and Erskine Bowles and his wife. Instead, he called Currie at home and instructed her to come to the office the next day, a Sunday. By the next morning, the first confusing fragments of the story were public. *Newsweek* editors had chosen not to run Isikoff's story that weekend, but the internal debate at the magazine about this decision was splashed onto the *Drudge Report,* a then little-known Web site. The item, which did not mention Lewinsky by name, had been leaked to Drudge by the scandal's impresario, Lucianne Goldberg. When Currie arrived at the White House that afternoon, an anxious Clinton came to her desk outside the Oval Office to tell her that the deposition had included pointed questions about Lewinsky. "There are several things you may want to know," Clinton said, as Currie later recalled it. What followed was a series of questions that sounded more like statements, and statements that sounded really like questions, since it was obvious to Currie that Clinton was desperately seeking her assent.

"You were always there when she was there, right?

"You remember I was never really alone with Monica, right?

"Monica came on to me, and I never touched her, right?

"You can see and hear everything [in the Oval Office], right?"

Clinton had enlisted Currie as a helper in his tangled relationship with Lewinsky. Still, the plain fact was that he had misused her loyalty, leaving her in an exposed and embarrassed position when the Lewinsky mess became public. For the next two days, the White House carried on its business under an eerie half-light, with everyone waiting for a storm that was sure to arrive. Vernon Jordan tried a last-minute push to persuade Clinton to settle the case. His loyalty, too, had been pushed to the brink, and the sinking feeling in the White House that the presidency might be genuinely on the verge of collapse was driven in large measure by fear that either Currie or Jordan might cooperate with Starr's probe. On Monday, January 19, the president placed some thirty calls to White House lawyers and Currie. Meanwhile, the secretary was leaving her own urgent messages and pages with Lewinsky, none of which were returned. Currie soon left the White House, and even her own house, checking into a hotel and ignoring a stream of frantic messages from White House aides urging her to call. At the advice of her lawyer, she would recount to prosecutors Clinton's conversation with her in which he appeared to be trying to coach her to agree that he and Lewinsky had never been alone.

The inevitable happened on Tuesday night, January 20, while Clinton was in a meeting with Israeli prime minister Benjamin Netanyahu. The *Washington Post* and ABC News simultaneously reported the story that Isikoff had been on the verge of breaking the previous weekend. The president first got the news from his lawyer David Kendall, which itself was a sign that the expected news had an unexpected twist. Bennett represented Clinton in the Paula Jones matter; Kendall represented the first family in the Whitewater investigation. It was during Kendall's call that Clinton first learned that his nemesis Kenneth Starr was now pursuing obstruction of justice in the Jones matter. The implications were instantly obvious. This was the most severe crisis of a crisis-prone career. Clinton's presidency was on the precipice.

As the Netanyahu session finished shortly before midnight, Clinton's evening was just beginning. He talked with Vernon Jordan, who was in New York. The story being published in the *Post* was not true, he told Jordan, who did not know all the facts but knew enough from his conversations with

Lewinsky to know the facts were not exactly favorable. "He said he was aware of the seriousness of it, and serious, in his mind, because, according to him, it was not true," Jordan later testified. From 12:08 a.m. to 12:39 a.m., Clinton spoke with Bennett. He then immediately called Lindsey and spent a half hour with him. Then he called Betty Currie, at 1:16 a.m., and in a twenty-minute call warned her that her name would be in the morning newspaper. Then he called Lindsey again. He told his aides later that he never did go back to sleep. Those hours, from 2 a.m. on, with no one left to call until the harsh glare of morning came, gave Clinton ample time to contemplate the folly of his actions with Lewinsky. He was in a contrite mood by 6:30 a.m., when he phoned Jordan again. Jordan himself was already caught in the frenzy. He had been awakened in the middle of the night, he told the president, by David Bloom, an NBC News reporter seeking comment on the *Post* story. "I've gotten you involved in this because you're my friend and I'm sorry about it," Clinton told Jordan.

Jordan gave Clinton the assurance he was looking for: "Mr. President, you don't need to apologize. We're friends and let's get on with it."

The question was whether Hillary Clinton would be as understanding. She was still sleeping while the president talked to Jordan. When Clinton awakened her, as she recounted the morning on national television a few days later, he said he had something to tell her. "You're not going to believe this but . . . ," he began.

"What is *this?*" she answered quietly.

". . . but I want to tell you what's in the newspapers."

THE NEXT PERSON CLINTON SPOKE WITH WAS HIS AIDE RAHM EMANUEL, WHO had taken over George Stephanopoulos's old job. The president had a casual rapport with Emanuel, compared to his edgy relationship with Stephanopoulos. Emanuel greeted him in the residence after reading that morning's *Washington Post*. "Is this story fucking true?" he exclaimed.

"No," replied Clinton weakly.

"Then you better be ready to fight," Emanuel said.

The president, though, was not yet in a fighting mode. He was in shock, for now trying merely to find some solid ground. While he was not by instinct a truthful man about his personal life, flatly untruthful statements were not his first instinct either. His preference was for qualified and equivocal language that could give reassurance to audiences who needed it. The first such audience was his senior staff, to whom Clinton said: "I want you to know I did not have sexual relationships with this woman, Monica Lewinsky. I did not ask anybody to lie. And when the facts come out, you'll understand." With his restrained manner and careful wording—there were no indignant denunciations of the press or Starr this morning—he left participants in this meeting with the belief that he was communicating not a full denial but a partial one. Surely something had happened, and it was by no means a good thing, but perhaps not as bad as it seemed.

This kind of nuance was easier to convey to a private audience than a public one. As luck would have it, the president was scheduled to give three interviews that day to promote the State of the Union address, which was then six days away. Canceling the appointments would only contribute to an air of crisis and impending doom. The interviews would have to go forward, and Clinton would have to talk about the Lewinsky controversy in some fashion. These interviews were pitiable performances. The first was with Jim Lehrer of PBS's *NewsHour* program. Clinton tried to appear calm and relaxed. He chatted amiably with the host, and brought in Buddy, the dog, to show off for his visitors. It was obvious he was stalling for time. Lehrer, displaying no interest in the dog, finally reminded the president firmly that they needed to get started.

Clinton denied to Lehrer that he had told anyone to lie under oath. He spoke of the controversy as if he, like the rest of the country, was monitoring it from afar, like an unexplained plane crash: "I think it's very important that we let the investigation take its course." While declining to address many of the specific questions, he cast himself as the injured party, saying he had been warned upon becoming president that the opposition was "going to go after me because they thought I represented a new direction in American politics and they thought we could make things better.

"You know," he continued, "I didn't come here for money or power or anything else. I came here to spend my time, to do my job, and go back to my life."

What was most striking about this session, however, was the way the president denied untoward involvement with the former intern. He repeatedly used the present tense: "There is no improper relationship." What does that mean? Lehrer asked. "Well, I think you know what it means," Clinton replied. "It means that there is not a sexual relationship, an improper sexual relationship, or any other kind of improper relationship."

This wouldn't fly. After the session with Lehrer, press secretary Michael McCurry delicately told Clinton that people would be expecting him also to deny the Lewinsky relationship in the past tense. This escape blocked, Clinton dutifully broadened his denial in a later interview with National Public Radio's Mara Liasson. By now, however, everyone was on high alert for weasel words. Might Clinton be invoking a narrow interpretation of "sexual relations" that included intercourse but not other kinds of intimacy? Between the PBS and NPR chats, in a telephone interview with *Roll Call* newspaper, questioner Morton Kondracke asked if the relationship was "in any way sexual." "The relationship was not sexual," Clinton replied. "And I know what you mean and the answer is no." Another exit closed. The sequence of interviews gave the impression of a man trapped in a room with a locked door, desperately trying to pry open the windows and finding that none of them opened either.

In the whirl of the day, Clinton had not lost his intuition about who could be told which story. To White House aide Sidney Blumenthal, who was close to the first lady, he explained, "Monica Lewinsky came at me and made a sexual demand on me." Naturally, Clinton added, he rebuffed her: "I've gone down that road before, I've caused pain for a lot of people, and I'm not going to do that again." Still, he had not lost his caring nature, so he continued to minister to the troubled young woman. When Blumenthal said the president simply had to cut himself off from such disturbed people, Clinton protested, "It's very difficult for me to do that, given how I am. I want to help people." Blumenthal later surmised that he was given this absurd invention (which was slanderous of Lewinsky) on the assumption that it would be relayed back to Hillary Clinton, since it was what the president wanted her to believe.

The president knew he could be more candid with Dick Morris. The consultant was someone Clinton always had reached for instinctually in times of crisis. "You poor son of a bitch," Morris said when Clinton's voice came on the line. "I know just what you're going through. I've been there."

"Oh God," Clinton replied. "This is just awful."

In 1997, in the year after the consultant's career had derailed in a sex scandal, Morris had spoken fairly regularly with the president. For the first time, he felt a personal, not just a professional, connection. Morris shared details of his own spiritual awakening as he sought to battle a history of compulsive behavior. Clinton had listened attentively. What had been implicit in those earlier conversations Morris now brought in the open: "It occurred to me that I may be the only sex addict you know, and maybe I can help you."

"Ever since I was elected," Clinton responded, "I've tried to shut my body down, I mean, sexually, and sometimes I just failed. This woman, I didn't do what they said I did, but I did do something and I don't know if I can prove my innocence."

Morris believed the best course for the president was to "play this thing outside the foul lines"—by which he meant going over Starr's head to address the nation, confess error, and rely on the country's innate sense of forgiveness. Morris volunteered to take a poll on how this would play. When the consultant called back to the White House late on the evening of the twenty-second, however, his recommendation had changed. The poll, though rudimentary because of a comparatively small sample size, showed that voters would be tolerant of sexual indiscretions but censorious toward any hint of lying under oath. Some 35 percent, indeed, thought Clinton should go to jail if he had lied. This news prompted an admirable flash of gallows humor. "You didn't ask them about capital punishment, did you?" the president asked.

But Morris was not joking back. "They're just too shocked by this," he said. "It's just too new, it's just too raw. They're just not ready for it."

"Well, we just have to win then," Clinton replied.

That flat denial, not clever evasions, would be necessary to save his presidency left him badly demoralized. On Friday afternoon, Podesta greeted Clinton in his study off the Oval Office. The president's face was heavy and drawn, his frame almost physically deflated as he slumped in a chair. For the first time, it seemed entirely possible to Podesta that this presidency might be over. Clinton's mood was desultory but his words blunt as he offered Podesta another denial about his relationship with Lewinsky. There had been nothing between them, no intercourse and no oral sex, Clinton insisted, describing these acts in locker-room language.

In addition to Morris (who later had to be cut loose *again* after he speculated in an interview that perhaps the president had strayed because his marriage was chaste), Clinton was being pressured from other directions to take a more defiant stand. Harry Thomason, the Hollywood producer and longtime friend of the first family, had watched Clinton's interview with Lehrer in horror. The impression was one of evasion and tentativeness. The president was not acting like a man who had been wrongly accused. Thomason urged a more forceful statement. Most of the president's political advisers, including Emanuel and Paul Begala (who had rejoined the Clinton team as White House counselor in 1997), had been pushing for the same thing, and felt it was essential to do something dramatic before the State of the Union address, or risk having the speech drowned out in a storm of speculation. The problem was that Clinton's attorneys, Kendall in particular, were sticking to the traditional legal maxim that it was best for an accused person to keep his mouth shut. The debate continued for a couple more days. The Sunday morning talk shows, in which presidential surrogates urged people not to rush to judgment but could offer no effective defense of the president, made the arguments of the political team that much more compelling. On Sunday evening, the old warrior Harold Ickes—still ready to come to the Clintons' defense despite what he regarded as his shabby treatment by the president—flew back from a speech at his alma mater, Stanford University, and headed to the White House. In a midnight meeting in the solarium of the Executive Mansion, Ickes and Thomason persuaded Clinton that his situation was too grave to leave his fate to the lawyers. "You know," said Thomason, "we shouldn't wait any longer. You should make a strong statement at the first opportunity."

There was an opportunity scheduled for the next morning. It was an appearance in the Roosevelt Room with the first lady and Vice President Gore to talk about child-care policy. At the close of his remarks, Clinton glared directly at the cameras. His jaw clenched visibly, and he pointed his fingers. "I want you to listen to me," he ordered. "I'm going to say this again. I did not have sexual relations with that woman"—and here he paused for an instant— "Miss Lewinsky. I never told anyone to lie, not a single time—never. These allegations are false. And I need to go back to work for the American people."

This was the performance his advisers had been hoping for, but it was not strictly a performance. His rage was real. As he finished speaking, he pivoted almost violently away from the lectern and out the door. His body was literally shaking. The one flaw in the statement had been the note of contempt conveyed by referring initially to "that woman." It was not intentional, Clinton explained to an adviser immediately afterward: "I blanked out on her name."

Chapter Thirty-one

LOYALISTS

THE FINGER-WAGGING PERFORMANCE IN THE ROOSEVELT ROOM HAD several effects. The most immediate was to freeze what had been a dangerously fluid story. Before, there was a sense of events hurtling to an unknowable destination, the airwaves filled with speculation about a Clinton admission or even a resignation. Now, there was a standoff. Kenneth Starr had his tantalizing investigation; Clinton had his unqualified denial. This is how things would remain for the indefinite future.

The purpose of Clinton's denial had not been persuasion in the literal sense. While the president's tone was more adamant, he offered no new facts or rebuttals beyond what he had said the day the Lewinsky story erupted. Only someone prepared to willfully suspend disbelief could put full faith in Clinton's denial. Even without evidence the allegation was consistent with the president's existing reputation. Moreover, nearly a week into the scandal there was already a wealth of evidence on display. Vernon Jordan had publicly acknowledged providing extensive job assistance to Lewinsky. Some portions of Linda Tripp's tapes had been widely publicized, featuring verbatim quotations in which the former intern described her Oval Office visits, her conversations with Clinton, and clinical details of their intimate relations. The White House had refused to release records documenting her visits, but there were numerous independent news reports, undisputed by Clinton's side, corroborating claims on the tapes about the dates of Lewinsky's trips to the Oval Office. If there was an innocent explanation for all this activity, surely the president would provide it now.

Yet an explanation rapidly was becoming beside the point, for Clinton was not asking people to have faith in the veracity of his *denial.* He was really asking them to have faith in *him.* The statement was his way of pleading to his supporters, and to a discomfited but undecided constituency in the middle, for some time and space to work his way out of this jam. He was asking for the benefit of the doubt for the sake of his presidency. A clear majority of Americans were willing to oblige him.

The next night, January 27, Clinton offered a good example of why. His State of the Union speech was a polished and steely performance. There had been a debate among the White House staff about whether to make even a glancing reference to the evening's unusual context. The argument for was that it seemed bizarre not to at least nod to the obvious. The argument against was that even an elliptical mention would dominate coverage of the speech and undermine the argument that Clinton was not letting the controversy interfere with the work of the nation. In the end, Clinton made no mention of his problems. Clinton was relieved when Mark Penn, his pollster and the man who had emerged as his foremost political adviser in the second term, said the data made clear that Americans did not want the president mentioning the furor. Substantively, the speech offered a clear picture of what the capital's 1998 agenda might have looked like had the scandal not interfered. Clinton called for enacting comprehensive legislation aimed at youth smoking and overhauling the practices in the tobacco industry. He urged an increase in the minimum wage and a bill protecting consumer rights for participants in health maintenance organizations. The catchphrase of the speech was four words: "Save Social Security First." This was Clinton's answer to what should be done with budget surpluses. He wanted no tax cuts until he and Congress agreed on legislation protecting the long-term solvency of the retirement program, and he vowed to lead a bipartisan effort toward that. The speech's most striking feature was stylistic. Clinton looked robust, calm, and confident—not at all like the withered and sullen man who had greeted Podesta in his study a few days earlier. Podesta was in the crowd, sitting with Sylvia Mathews, the other deputy chief of staff. "Can you believe this?" he whispered. The president was interrupted for applause 104 times. Most of this was from Democrats, but even a House Republican leader, Congressman Bob Livingston of Louisiana, called the speech "a very strong performance. . . . He has every reason to be proud."

If one effect of the Roosevelt Room denial was to freeze the public into not rushing to judgment, another effect was to polarize it. The question *had* been: Did Clinton do it? Now, he wanted people to ask, were they with Clinton or with his enemies? Framing the matter this way helped assure the president that he could retain his most important ally, Hillary Clinton. On the day he awoke the first lady with the bad news in the morning paper, he could not have known for sure whether her inevitable anger would be directed against him or outward against his accusers. The information that led most people to assume that an affair with Lewinsky had happened, leaving aside the truth about obstruction of justice, was available to her. But the human mind seizes on what it wants to believe. The Clintons' shared grievances toward their conservative tormentors was a powerful bond. Even more, if his presidency was doomed, their shared project of nearly a quarter century was doomed, too. From the first moments of the scandal, she was privately rallying supporters. And within a few days, she was doing so publicly. On the same day as the State of the Union, she appeared on NBC's *Today* show for a previously scheduled interview with Matt Lauer. It was here that she invoked a phrase that later became famous, saying that the investigation was part of a "vast right-wing conspiracy, that has been conspiring against my husband since the day he announced for president." That line, in isolation, conveyed a more paranoid tone than the interview in full context. Her general points were entirely defensible, including that the Lewinsky allegations were promoted by those "using the criminal justice system to try to achieve political ends in this country."

Moreover, she was closer to the truth in her complaint—alleging secret coordination between the independent counsel and right-wing Clinton opponents—than all but a few people knew at the time. Presidential aide Sidney Blumenthal, a former journalist who had joined the White House staff the previous summer, had made a career following the machinations of conservative political activists. His spirited denunciations of those making the Whitewater allegations—both the formal investigators and the journalists covering the story—were a principal reason he had grown close to the first lady. They had a shared interest, to say the least. During the opening days of the story, Blumenthal had been conversing regularly with David Brock, the author of the notorious *American Spectator* story in December 1993. Four years later, Brock was in the opening stages of his disillusion and eventual break with his right-wing confederates. He was close enough to the conservatives to know the basic outlines of how Linda Tripp and her tapes had come to the attention of the Jones lawyers and the Starr team. He was enough of an apostate to happily share this with Blumenthal, who shared it with Hillary Clinton, who in her *Today* appearance tried to goad the political press to cover "the great story here, for anybody willing to find it and write about it and explain it." For now, exploring the motives and methods of Clinton's opponents was more favorable terrain than answering questions about his own conduct.

WHICH SIDE ARE YOU ON? NOW THAT THE PRESIDENT HAD HIS WIFE'S ANSWER, he could turn his attention to others. Vice President Gore had been sickened by the charges, and was far less prone to believe that they were a malicious fabrication. As he understood his responsibilities, however, unconditional support was his only option. The day after the State of the Union address, he and Clinton went on the road together. The president traditionally made a road trip the day after the speech to Congress, though not usually with the vice president. This time, White House political strategists decided that, as in the 1992 campaign, the two of them together made a more winning impression. There was a strange and awkward moment between the two of them as they stood in a holding room before walking out to the stage of a giant auditorium at the University of Illinois in Champaign. In what was apparently their first extensive conversation about the allegations, Clinton momentarily lost control of himself.

His face red and his finger jabbing the air, he nearly shouted at Gore, "This is a fucking coup d'état!" The vice president looked back at Clinton blankly, neither agreeing nor disagreeing.

Whatever his private ambivalence, in public Gore rose to the occasion. The vice president gave a roaring defense of the Clinton record that had the audience of twenty thousand out of their seats cheering, and prompted Clinton to comment, "I wish I had people walking the aisles passing the plate."

The enthusiastic crowds at Champaign were not an anomaly. A *Washington Post* poll taken in the days after the State of the Union registered the highest approval ratings for Clinton of his presidency. Six out of ten Americans believed the country was "headed in the right direction," and 67 percent endorsed his job performance. As for the sex scandal, a majority believed that something had happened, but similar numbers also accepted the Clinton thesis—that political enemies were "conspiring" to bring down the presidency, and that Starr was more interested in hurting Clinton than determining whether crimes were committed. Not every finding was good news for the president. While two-thirds of voters said they thought Clinton should stay in office even if an affair was proven, a slight majority said he should resign if he had lied under oath.

This reaction was not what most in the Washington journalistic and political class had expected. On ABC, Sam Donaldson had predicted in the opening days of the scandal, "Mr. Clinton, if he's not telling the truth and the evidence shows that, will resign, perhaps this week." On the same program, conservative commentator George Will declared that Clinton's presidency "today is as dead, deader really, than Woodrow Wilson's was after he had a stroke." Even George Stephanopoulos, now himself a commentator for the network, could not offer a much better prognosis for his former boss: "Is he telling the truth, the whole truth, and nothing but the truth? If he is, he can survive. If he isn't, he can't." It was a stark example of a pattern that would pervade the year: elite Washington opinion falling far out of step with the nation.

In late January and early February, Starr's chances of locking down a powerful legal case against Clinton were fast receding. Vernon Jordan had told an associate, "I'm a loyal friend, but I'm no damn fool." But neither his testimony before the grand jury nor even Betty Currie's proved particularly helpful to Starr, or unduly damaging to Clinton. Moreover, lawyers for both were sharing information about what their clients were being asked and what they were saying with Clinton's legal team. Jordan, for his part, left his grand jury appearance and headed straight for the frenzied press area outside Washington's E. Barrett Prettyman Courthouse, which had become the ground zero for the hundreds of domestic and foreign news organizations now covering the Lewinsky scandal. Fixing a cool gaze at the cameras and speaking in a slow baritone, Jordan said: "As to those of you who cast doubt on my friendship with President Clinton, let me reassure you that ours is an enduring friendship, based on mutual respect, trust, and admiration."

Even so, in the days and weeks following January 17, many of Clinton's most important friendships had been reshaped in sad ways. Jordan, while remaining loyal, could hardly maintain the joshing rapport that had once given the president such comfort. Their constant phone conversations and regular golf outings were over, at least for now.

Erskine B. Bowles, the chief of staff and the man whom Clinton once said he regarded as a brother, was further removed from the scandal, but he was in no position to serve as Clinton's emotional crutch. It was all he could do to remain in Clinton's physical presence. He had been sickened and outraged by the allegations. Bowles was loyal enough not to quit—it would have been a devastating gesture to Clinton's own staff and the wider political community in those fragile early days. Instead, Bowles stayed but announced to the staff that he would have nothing to do with managing the response to the scandal. He did this on the reasonable principle that only a select group of lawyers and political advisers should be worrying about the legal uproar; the rest of the White House should go about its business. In truth, however, Bowles seemed to retreat even from conventional duties, and this once commanding figure was now presenting a wan and worried face before the staff he ostensibly led. Some senior Clinton aides resented Bowles for this, believing he had gone soft in battle. But Bowles felt personally used by Clinton. Knowing nothing about the circumstances of the president's relationship with Lewinsky, Bowles had followed Clinton's orders and instructed Podesta to help with the job hunt for her, and instructed other subordinates to arrange favorable recommendations for her less than superb job performance during her White House employment. This meant that the chief of staff would also be heading to the grand jury, with uncomfortable questions to answer. Friends did not ask friends to clean up their personal messes this way, Bowles believed. So he essentially adjourned his friendship with Clinton. He never golfed with him again during the White House years. The easy banter with the president was over. From now on, the chief of staff was coolly correct around his boss, confining their relationship strictly to business.

Other senior Clinton associates were less judgmental. One of these was Emanuel. He was perhaps the most flamboyant White House figure of the second term, and also one of the shrewdest.

"Look, I know what went on," Emanuel said to his boss one day in the Oval Office. "This was less than sex, but more than kissy-face." The aide said the moral implications were between the president and his wife, though he rapped his boss good-naturedly on the political implications of his indiscretion.

"You got it backwards," joked Emanuel, a devout Jew. "You messed around with a Jewish girl, and now you're paying a goyish lawyer. You should have messed around with a goyishe girl, and gotten a Jewish lawyer."

Clinton smiled quizzically at Emanuel, but said nothing.

Around this time, the president found that he was still standing after the initial shock waves of scandal, and his mood was gradually improving. In a meeting with his young scheduling assistants, who did not think it their place to bring up anything about the controversy, he brought up the matter himself. "If they want me out of this office," he said in a chipper voice, moving his head rhythmically from side to side for emphasis, "they are going to have to carry me out feet first."

There was one area of his life where the mood remained dark. Chelsea Clinton, then in her freshman year at Stanford, was dealing with all the customary concerns of a young adult away from home for the first time, at the same time she was coping with seeing her father at the focus of an embarrassing scandal. It was an especially heavy burden. In late February, Hillary Clinton took an unannounced trip to Stanford to be with her. The plan was for the president to meet up with them both later when political business brought him to nearby San Francisco. But then Chelsea made plain that under no circumstances did she want her father near her campus. A backup plan was hastily hatched—the Clintons instead would retreat to the borrowed Park City, Utah, ski chalet of Hollywood producer Jeffrey Katzenberg. But now Clinton had been confronted with the fact that his daughter was embarrassed to be in his presence.

Chapter Thirty-two

AFRICAN JOURNEY

THE CAPITAL OF GHANA IS A RELIABLY SWELTERING LOCALE. ACCRA IS on the Atlantic, just north of the equator, with humidity that hovers in the high nineties even as the temperature often soars to the low hundreds. For Clinton, in March 1998, such a climate seemed rather appealing compared to the fevers of Washington.

Clinton's journey to Africa in the first week of spring was not in response to the Lewinsky explosion. It had been planned long before as a centerpiece of the second term. Indeed, Clinton had been yearning to visit sub-Saharan Africa since he was a boy. Still, as Kenneth Starr's investigation had settled into what promised to be a long sullen phase of daily trench warfare, the president and a large delegation were happy to leave a gossipy, hyperventilating capital and take refuge on a world stage. This was a trip quite unlike any predecessor had taken. Clinton was now taking the longest trip of his presidency—six nations in eleven days—on an itinerary designed to highlight progress and potential in a continent that tended to make news in America only for its horrors.

The stop in Ghana was to celebrate President Jerry Rawlings, a former dictator who twice came to power in coups but then led his country to democracy. On Accra's Independence Square, the visiting president was greeted almost as if he were the Messiah. The crowd had begun gathering at 5 a.m., even while Air Force One was far over the Atlantic, and by the time Clinton arrived there were hundreds of thousands of people in wait; it was by several times the largest crowd ever to greet Bill Clinton. The heat was unbearable for the visitors, including Clinton, whose face turned beet red as his clothes became drenched with sweat. Even many Ghanaians collapsed in the tightly packed throng. Those still standing could not hear much; the outdoor sound system was tinny and could not carry. But few people cared. People craned their necks and jumped up, or created human towers just for a glimpse of Clinton. This friendly scene turned briefly menacing when Clinton stepped down to do what he always did at the end of speeches, shake hands along the security line separating the crowd from the stage. The crowd surged. Suddenly, a woman steps from the president was being crushed between people and a fence. Fearing he was about to witness a tragedy, Clinton shouted angrily to the mob, "Get back! Back off!"

It was a long minute of chaos before the crowd was subdued, and the woman was saved. Afterward the president was exhilarated, telling aides what a fabulous morning it had been. At home, Clinton was being systematically disrobed in the most personally embarrassing investigation in American political history. Here, he was revered. The throbbing mass of Ghanaians understood that in taking this trip, Clinton was showing himself as a different kind of leader, possessed of a larger vision, who wanted to take American diplomacy— and America's reputation among common folk around the world—in new directions.

For much of the past year, as Clinton had been trying to lead a "national conversation" on race relations, he and his staff had been wrestling with the question of whether the president, on behalf of the nation, should issue an apology to African-Americans for slavery. Some black leaders had been pushing for such a symbolic gesture. Others were demanding more than symbolism, calling for financial reparations to the descendants of slaves. Clinton ultimately decided against such an apology, judging that it might be divisive rather than unifying. The Africa trip, however, presented a related question: How should the United States recognize and express remorse for its role in the slave trade? The discussion of whether and where to make some carefully modulated statement was still going on while the trip was under way.

Then, Clinton simply preempted the issue. In the village of Mukono, Uganda, after watching schoolchildren perform a charming dance with colored scarves and listening to Ugandan president Yoweri Museveni recite in a long speech Africa's troubled history, Clinton plunged into the issue extemporaneously. "Going back to the time before we were even a nation, European Americans received the fruits of the slave trade," he said. "And we were wrong in that." Warming to his subject, Clinton continued, "Perhaps the worst sin America ever committed about Africa was the sin of neglect and ignorance. We have never been as involved with you, in working together for our mutual benefit, for your children and for ours, as we should have been."

Reactions at home and in Africa varied toward the president's comment, a division that paralleled how people reacted to Clinton generally. Skeptics heard Clinton preening for acclaim with words that sounded brave but were actually empty. Admirers found an appealing modesty and candor in his words, reflecting Clinton's instinct for human connection.

THE NEXT STOP TOOK HIM TO A PLACE WHERE A GREAT CRIME WAS MORE RECENT, and Clinton's own connection to events was more direct.

Rwanda, the scene of a genocide just four years earlier, had not been on the itinerary as White House planners originally conceived the trip. But as the president's departure loomed, they reconsidered. On a trip to Africa, how could he credibly avert his gaze from such a recent horror?

His visit to this blood-soaked nation lasted just three hours. Air Force One landed at the same airport President Juvenal Habyarimana's plane was approaching when it was shot down in 1994, the start of the killing. Clinton did not leave the airport grounds at Kigali. Instead, he and Hillary Clinton walked across the tarmac to an airport lounge. Inside were several dozen people—friendly, welcoming faces, just as he had seen elsewhere on the trip. A closer look revealed more. Many had visible scars or missing limbs. The Clintons sat beside each other in gold-upholstered armchairs. He sipped a can of Diet Coke. Then, for the next hour, he listened.

He heard the story of Gloriosa Uwimpuhwe. Her father and mother had been killed, she explained calmly. So had four of her siblings.

He listened to Josephine Murebwayire. Her family had taken refuge with hundreds of others in a Catholic seminary. The Hutu soldiers dragged them outside and began swinging their machetes. She was badly cut. Her husband, two brothers, and six children were all killed. "Thank you," the president whispered when she finished speaking.

There was Venuste Karasira, who had fled with some four thousand others to a local college where they had been told that United Nations peacekeepers would protect them. When the U.N. forces left, fearing for their own safety, a wild gang rampaged through, killing all but four hundred people. "I lost my right hand," Karasira said. "We died because we were left by the United Nations soldiers." Clinton swallowed but said nothing. He simply nodded for the next speaker to begin.

Probably no other president had ever confronted the consequences of his decisions—or, in this case, his non-decisions—on such intimate grounds. After this wrenching session adjourned, Clinton addressed a larger group of Rwandans. He said he accepted his share of responsibility for not intervening in the most rapid "slaughter in this blood-filled century we are about to leave." Never, he said, should the "international community" have dithered in rhetorical debate about whether the killing amounted to "genocide." The pace of killing with machine guns and machetes, he noted, was "five times as fast as the mechanized gas chambers used by the Nazis.

"It may seem strange to you here," he said, "but all over the world there were people like me sitting in offices, day after day, who did not fully appreciate the depth and speed with which you were being engulfed in this unimaginable terror."

This was a questionable assertion. The scale of the killing, if not the precise numbers, was available to any subscriber of the *New York Times*. Intervention was never on the table. The terror might have been unimaginable, but so too, in 1994, was the notion that the United States would commit its military forces in far-off Africa to stop it. This visit, Clinton later told friends, was the most emotionally searing moment of his presidency.

THE NEXT STOP WAS SOUTH AFRICA, WHERE CLINTON WAS CONFRONTED again with the unpleasant task of balancing affairs of high state in the midst of a low-minded scandal. At his hotel in Cape Town, the president grimaced sadly as he sat with aides to run down the list of Lewinsky questions that might come up at a news conference later that day with President Nelson Mandela. The brave and long-suffering Mandela, imprisoned for two decades during the long struggle against apartheid, was the world leader Clinton respected more than any other. To stand beside this heroic figure, only to be peppered with questions about an investigation into sex and perjury, was beyond humiliation. Mercifully, there were no questions about the Lewinsky matter at the news conference. It was as if Mandela's luminescent presence had an inhibiting effect on the traveling press. Without prompting, though, Mandela made what some interpreted as a glancing reference to the ugly matter brewing in Washington. The South African said President Clinton and his wife "have the correct instincts on the major international questions facing the world today," and added pointedly, "I fully accept his integrity and his bona fides."

One potentially awkward aspect of the Africa trip turned out not to be a problem at all. To the vast relief of their traveling aides, Bill and Hillary Clinton seemed to be getting along fine. Even before the scandal broke, this was often not the case during foreign travel. Hillary Clinton was often crabby when accompanying her husband abroad, or so it seemed to his aides. She loved travel, but did not like the second-fiddle role that was inevitably assigned to her when she traveled with him. Her own foreign trips were impressively substantive. On presidential travel, by contrast, she was at the mercy of his schedule, and was subjected to all manner of teas, receptions, and other ceremonial functions. On this trip, however, she was a useful guide for her husband. She had already visited many of the African cities and countries they were stopping in, and local officials and activists greeted her like an old friend.

There was even a mini-vacation for the first family built into this trip. For two days in Botswana, the Clintons dropped most of their traveling delegation in the capital, Gaborone, and flew several hundred miles north to the Chobe National Game Park. They spent a magical time together on safari, seeing hippos and lions and a pair of elephants. They snuggled together on a boat ride as the sun set on the Chobe River. No matter the storms back home, the pleasure they took in each other's company was plain.

IT WAS AT A PRESIDENTIAL APPEARANCE IN BOTSWANA THAT ONE MEMBER OF Clinton's traveling party ventured to try a local specialty: boiled worms. With a gaggle of reporters and locals looking on, White House press secretary Michael McCurry popped one in his mouth and announced, "Tastes like a dead worm."

This was a typical moment of whimsy for Clinton's spokesman. When he took the job in January 1995, his mission was to open the windows on what had become a fetid relationship between Clinton and the Washington news media. "I want to have some fun around here," he announced. Once he showed up in the White House briefing room with a paper bag over his head and announced that he was an "anonymous official." Another time he jumped, fully clothed, into a fancy swimming pool at a Democratic fundraiser on a $100 bet.

The press secretary was not a Clinton intimate. To the contrary, both the president and first lady well remembered that he had worked in the 1992 primaries for Bob Kerrey, who had gotten personal toward the end of his failed bid. McCurry was eventually welcomed into the West Wing, where people appreciated his poise at the podium and his sound judgment about communication strategy. But he never made it—or tried to make it—into Clinton's inner circle. There was always an unspoken reserve between them. Clinton had a keen intuition, and he seemed to separate people into those who were with him as a job and those who were with him in their hearts. McCurry was in the first category. Now, three years after taking his post, his goals of having more fun and forging a happier relationship between the president and his press corps were in a shambles.

He was bitter about it. A veteran Washington operative, McCurry had grown up with a respectful view of reporters. He longed for the old-school days of hard-drinking, card-playing hacks who worked hard to get important stories but did not try to get on television and had no interest in a politician's sex life. The new breed of reporters, he complained often to his West Wing colleagues and to the reporters directly, were a preening bunch, who substituted a pose of sneering cynicism for professionalism and genuine tough-mindedness. McCurry was uniformly described in newspaper profiles and Washington chatter as "a nice guy"—true words in normal times—but in these feverish days the description did not always apply. He had turned belligerent almost daily in his telephone calls with reporters, indignantly refusing to answer questions or sometimes even listen to them, and demanding to speak with editors. One night on the Africa trip, at an off-the-record dinner with reporters, he reduced a network correspondent to tears with an angry attack on her coverage.

McCurry's job might have been easier that year if he could have retreated into blind support for Clinton. But that was not his feeling, either. The president's behavior with Lewinsky—whatever the details of the relationship—plainly had been egregious. It put the press secretary in a ludicrous position when each day he had to stand at the podium and repeat the official line that nothing improper had happened when it was clear that something had. Shortly before the Africa trip, he got sent to the doghouse for stating the obvious in an unguarded moment to the *Chicago Tribune:* "Maybe there'll be a simple, innocent explanation. I don't think so, because I think we would have offered that up already."

McCurry was angry at Clinton for acting rashly. He was angry at the White House lawyers, who were hoarding information and sending him out to deliver increasingly lame talking points. He was angry at reporters for their relentless small-mindedness. This genial professional was the embodiment of how frayed Washington relationships had become in this age of scandal.

························

THE AFRICA TRIP CAME TO AN EXHAUSTED AND ECSTATIC CONCLUSION ON April 1 in Dakar, Senegal. The president was finishing up an interview with ABC's Sam Donaldson when White House aides got word from Washington that presidential attorney Robert Bennett was eager to talk to Clinton the moment the interview was over. Bennett represented Clinton in the Paula Jones case. For once, urgent news on this subject actually meant good news. In Little Rock, federal judge Susan Webber Wright had dismissed Jones's lawsuit—the very one in which Clinton was asked under oath about Monica Lewinsky, and the precipitating event for Starr's perjury investigation. "Is this an April Fool's joke?" an elated Clinton asked Bennett. Not a chance, the lawyer replied. Still incredulous, the president called back ten minutes later just to be sure.

Top aides immediately sent word down through the ranks: no gloating. The decision was to be acknowledged with quiet solemnity. One person did not get the word. Clinton himself was ecstatic. That night in his Dakar hotel, after Hillary Clinton and Chelsea went to bed, he popped an unlit cigar in his mouth and surveyed a room full of gift merchandise that local officials had arranged for sale to the presidential delegation in a top-floor suite. Whimsically, Clinton picked up a drum and began banging good-naturedly on it as he stood near the balcony door—near enough that a Fox News camera crew captured his impolitic celebration from the parking lot below.

Clinton was happy because, as the *New York Times* wrote in its news pages the next day, "While the relentless machinery of investigation may grind on for many months, it is now politically inconceivable that Congress will consider impeachment—for President Clinton's alleged lies and obstruction in a case that no longer exists." This was indeed the conventional wisdom in the spring of 1998. The Reverend Jesse Jackson, a member of the traveling delegation as Clinton's special envoy to Africa, said that the judge's decision, coming while the president was completing a historic trip, was "a convergence that could only be planned by God."

But some of Clinton's aides had seen enough to know that the conventional wisdom was not accounting for the zeal of Starr and Republicans against the president. As they saw it, the president had lied under oath. That the case that inspired his testimony was later judged to be without merit was beside the point. One Clinton adviser tried to remind the president of this point as the Africa trip ended just as it had begun, with a long ride over the Atlantic: "Sir, the ruling is great news," the aide began delicately, "but you know this business may not be over."

Clinton looked surprised for a moment, then irritated, as if he had been interrupted with business in the middle of a party. He stared for a moment. "I know that," he said finally. "It's never over."

Chapter Thirty-three

SURVIVOR

LIFE WENT ON. MUCH OF THE TIME, IN FACT, IT WENT ON LIKE NORMAL, at least by outward appearance. The president would show up in the Rose Garden to talk about his "Patients' Bill of Rights" for consumers of health maintenance organizations. He would be smiling cheerfully at a party on the South Lawn to salute U.S. athletes who had competed in the previous winter's Olympic Games. In public, there was no nod to the reality that his own top aides were cycling steadily through the federal courthouse twelve blocks away to testify to Kenneth Starr's grand jury, or that he himself often spent several hours a day huddled with attorneys.

Foreign policy, in particular, rolled on, seemingly unshaken by the potholes of scandal. There were two preoccupying issues on Clinton's overseas agenda in 1998. One of them was Iraq, where the dictator Saddam Hussein had persistently defied U.S. demands that he allow United Nations inspectors access to search for weapons. This was a requirement that had been imposed on him by the world after the Persian Gulf War, and that winter Clinton described the standoff with Saddam in dire terms: "What if he fails to comply, and we fail to act, or we take some ambiguous third route which gives him yet more opportunities to develop this program of weapons of mass destruction? Well, he will conclude that the international community has lost its will. He will then conclude that he can go right on and do more to rebuild an arsenal of devastating destruction. And someday, some way, I guarantee you, he'll use the arsenal."

For the next several months, a military confrontation with Iraq looked to be inevitable.

Clinton was far more hopeful about the year's other top foreign priority. In late June, he made his first presidential trip to China. The visit was a milestone in Clinton's long effort to coax a more constructive relationship with China, which had made laudable steps toward a market economy but remained an old-style dictatorship when it came to human rights. As part of the visit, Chinese president Jiang Zemin insisted that Clinton submit to the traditional arrival ceremony for foreign visitors at Tiananmen Square, where authorities nine years earlier had slaughtered pro-democracy student protestors. Clinton accepted this indignity in pursuit of his larger goal, which was to convince the Chinese that their own interests were emphatically on the side of internal reform and cooperation with the external world. There were signs of progress, including a remarkable visit to Beijing University, in which the visiting president parried questions from students and urged them to make "common cause" with Americans. He ended the trip in Hong Kong with a valentine for Jiang, calling him a man of "vision and imagination and courage" who will "put China on the right side of history"—an appraisal that was a bit more effusive than Clinton's own China experts thought wise. Still, the adrenaline-fueled man striding across China that week certainly did not look like someone burdened by doubts about his survival in office. There was a valor to it.

These impressive displays of discipline and focus put a new word in Washington currency: "compartmentalization." This was supposedly the president's great skill. "In the gaudy mansions of Clinton's mind, there are many rooms," explained *Time* magazine. The seamy private problems in one room were not allowed to mingle with the vital public problems in the others. Around the capital, legislators, diplomats, and commentators all marveled: How did he do it?

He did it by illusion. As the group of West Wing aides who worked closest with him knew, the president's mind worked like most people's. A problem that threatened to destroy his career and marriage lapped at his consciousness. His anger toward his accusers, and recriminations toward himself, hovered constantly. When his national security advisers arrived to give the president his morning briefing, they would wait patiently for his venting over the latest Starr outrage in the morning papers to exhaust itself. Erskine Bowles would arrive in the Oval Office and find Clinton oblivious to his presence. He was lost in space, absently fussing with the collection of campaign buttons he kept in the Oval Office. James Wolfensohn, a Clinton friend and head of the World Bank, returned from a meeting with Clinton and called back to a White House aide, "It's like he isn't there." These aides weren't surprised to get calls like this. "It's almost as if the government adjusted to his limping," recalled Donna Shalala, the head of the Department of Health and Human Services. "If this had happened in 1994, it would have been disastrous. It was the maturity of the government that saved the year. We all knew how to do our jobs."

Senior advisers like Rahm Emanuel and Doug Sosnik would take the president's mood each day. On bad days before the morning meeting they would pull aside a trusted cabinet member like Treasury Secretary Robert Rubin and warn, "He needs a little help today. You're going to have to pick up the slack in there."

FACING THE MOST SEVERE EMOTIONAL AND POLITICAL TEST OF HIS LIFE, CLINton was in a state of isolation from the people who had been his pillars for most of the previous five years. Hillary Clinton, while she had rallied to her husband's side, was obviously not someone he could speak candidly with about his particular problems now. There was an awkward new constraint in the friendship with Vernon Jordan; their dealings were at the heart of Starr's investigation. A new chill, likewise, settled into the relationship with Erskine Bowles. Even Dick Morris, who had been intimately involved in Clinton's politics for two decades, was also out of the picture—banished after foolish conjecture he offered in a radio interview several days into the scandal about the sexual dimension of the Clinton marriage. The president continued to have a narcotic attraction to the consultant. When Don Baer, a former White House communications aide, went to see Clinton in March, he told the president that he had been in touch with Morris. "What did he say?" Clinton asked eagerly. "I wish I could talk to him, but I can't trust Dick to keep his mouth shut."

With his old pillars no longer bearing weight, Clinton's presidency depended on finding new ones.

One of the most important was Bob Rubin at Treasury. As Mary McGrory had noted before the Lewinsky affair broke, "It's the Dow Jones, not Paula Jones, that determines his standing."

With the stock market soaring and unemployment near modern lows, the president's private morals were of little relevance to most citizens. Yet Clinton never would have lasted were it not for the competence voters credited to the administration on its handling of the economy. The public face of that competence, the hero of the day even to many who deplored Clinton, was Robert Rubin.

Clinton and his Treasury secretary were not social intimates. Rubin was not on the president's late-night call list when he was in the mood to chat. Rubin was almost eight years older—just enough to be of a different generation. Indeed, Rubin, like Leon Panetta and Bill Perry, was a classic Silent Generation type: responsible, understated, unapologetically square in his manner and tastes. For all these exterior differences, however, Rubin and Clinton had similar habits of mind, and it was on this basis that they established their remarkable communion.

Rubin, since his Wall Street days, had been a devotee of "probabilistic thinking." In the world of finance, he believed, the best minds understood that the future was imponderable. The most one could do was try to shrewdly reckon risks and rewards, and accept that even smart decisions sometimes produced bad results. Only over the long haul could performance be honestly measured. Washington, by contrast, too often imposed a false certitude on policy debates, as though there was one correct answer to problems that hinged on countless variables, some of which were outside policymakers' ability to control. Rubin had an appreciation for shades of gray and a disdain for absolutes that were very much like Clinton's. What skeptics often described as the president's tendency to equivocate about decisions, Rubin viewed as Clinton's instinct for complexity. Early in their collaboration, Clinton earned Rubin's lasting trust. On the problems of deficit reduction in 1993, when Rubin was the White House's economic policy adviser, and in the Mexican currency crisis of 1995, during Rubin's first month as Treasury secretary, he had always seen Clinton take the responsible course. Who cared how much to-and-fro it took to get there?

In 1998, the Treasury secretary was equally indifferent to certain other matters in the news. People who knew him were sure that adultery was not part of Rubin's moral code. But he seemed stoically devoid of judgment about

Clinton's lapse, or even of curiosity about what happened. "His view was that the bottom line was all that mattered," recalled Gene Sperling, who advised Clinton on economics, "and everything else was noise."

There was some irony in the fact that a man who had run on a "putting people first" platform had retained the support of those people by following Wall Street's favored economic policies. So be it, Clinton had long since decided. As 1998 churned on, Rubin's account grew larger still. In late 1997, Asian economies began to flag, in what Clinton initially called "a few little glitches in the road." By 1998, the so-called Asian flu had become what he now called "the biggest financial challenge facing the world in a half-century."

From his perch at the Treasury Department, Rubin worked with Fed chairman Alan Greenspan and finance ministers around the world to try to contain the problem. Characteristically, Rubin wanted to keep the mood as low key and panic-free as possible. Several times he had to dissuade Clinton from his instinct, shared by Tony Blair, to convene an international summit on the problem. Too risky, Rubin decreed, while Clinton champed at the bit. Still, more than once in the crisis Rubin remarked to colleagues how fortunate it was that he was working for a president who actually understood currency flows—what Clinton knew, he had learned from Rubin—and appreciated the large stakes at risk. If a Republican president had pursued such responsible economic policies, Rubin told colleagues, "they'd be building a monument to him on the National Mall."

If Clinton had any complaint about Rubin, it was that his Wall Street life had left him with no sense of the concrete human dimensions of Washington decisions. Each Thanksgiving, Clinton liked to remind his staff to "get out and talk to real people" over the holiday.

"You say talk to real people," Rubin bridled. "Am I a real person?"

"No, Bob," Clinton said with a smile. "You weren't before and you are even less of one now."

<hr />

ANOTHER MAN HELPING HOLD UP A PRESIDENCY UNDER SIEGE WAS MARK Penn, the presidential pollster. A few weeks after the Lewinsky story broke, he sent a confidential memo to Clinton based on his latest survey results. "The drip of rumor still has more people believing the story of an affair" than the president's denials, he reported.

But Penn had some good news, too: All of the questions showed conclusively that "it is not the belief of an affair, but the belief in an illegal cover-up that would give the issue traction." These numbers suggested a strategy. "All of this shows that we should continue to issue periodic denials, and wait until there is a clear story to respond to. . . . Such a response will turn on people believing that there is a stand-off on whether they had sex and agreement [Lewinsky] was not asked to lie. This will create the dominant view that the investigation was a diversion that should go nowhere."

Here, in Penn's note, was the strategy that the president followed for seven months in 1998. Deny the charge, let the world see Clinton hard at work, and wait it out until Starr finished his investigation and showed his best cards.

What Bob Rubin was to Clinton's domestic policy, Mark Penn was to his political life: the man who knew the numbers. The White House strategy for Clinton's survival in 1998 was based on several premises. The facts about the president's relationship with Lewinsky and lies in the Paula Jones case, though still not proven, were bad enough that Republicans in Congress would surely want to impeach him. Congressional Democrats, self-protective by instinct and not unduly supportive of the president, would probably turn tail if the going got tough. The only way to avert this was by maintaining a wide buffer of popular support. Who would want to take on a president with approval ratings at 66 percent, as they were in Penn's polls through the month of February? The furious attention to survey data that began under Dick Morris was now more urgent than ever.

It was Morris who first recruited Penn and his longtime partner, Doug Schoen, into the Clinton fold. Penn accepted many of the same premises that Morris had. Values were what drove political behavior, he believed, but the way for a politician to communicate values was not with the old campaign baloney. Gauzy ads showing a candidate's smiling face and attractive children did not work. What communicated values were policies—discrete, concrete positions that signaled for voters whether a politician was on their side. After the re-election, Penn moved to Washington, set up an office a block from the White House, and essentially institutionalized the Morris brand of campaign governance even when there was no more campaign to run. By any reckoning, Penn as a private citizen on contract to the Democratic National Committee was one of the most important members of Clinton's domestic policy team. In the fall of 1997, when the White House was worrying about how to prevent Republicans from spending the new budget surplus on tax cuts, it was Penn who sealed the argument. The idea of "saving Social Security first," by refusing to cut taxes until the long-term solvency of the retirement program was secured, scored off the charts—82 percent. Clinton was astonished by the numbers.

Presidential phrases always got "tested" by Penn before big speeches. His data had surprises. Anti-poverty programs could be popular, but not by employing the usual rhetoric emphasizing poor children. That sounded too much like a sentimental liberal. Clinton began emphasizing his plans for "working families." When Penn's polls showed that privacy concerns were scoring high in surveys, the Treasury Department was ordered to come up with some policies to meet demand. The policies Penn favored did not need to be sweeping. In March, he sent Clinton an alert that frustration over ATM fees was "an issue missile that concerns 75 million Americans or more." On some issues, he had close to veto power. In April, the Health and Human Services Department was set to approve a program allowing federal funds for locally sponsored "needle exchange" programs. Junkies could get clean new needles, thus discouraging the spread of HIV. But Clinton had been worried that the issue had the potential to be another cultural flashpoint, like gays in the military years before. Penn's polls showed 57 percent of Americans were strongly opposed. The morning that HHS Secretary Shalala was preparing her news conference to announce the program, Bowles called to reverse her. Clinton had changed his mind.

In some ways, the nerve center of the Clinton presidency was an obscure office park in Denver, where Penn and Schoen—paid handsomely by the Democratic National Committee—ran a phone bank of operators calling randomly selected Americans. And at least weekly in 1998—sometimes several times a week—those operators were asking about the president and Lewinsky. Has Starr gone "too far"? (Fifty-eight percent of Penn's respondents said yes in February.) What if Clinton lied under oath about not having an affair, should he resign? (Sixty percent said yes in the first weeks of the scandal.) What about this business of whether something is an "affair"—does oral sex count? (Certainly yes, said 74 percent.) There were some encouraging signs for Clinton in these ludicrously detailed questions as the year went on. The country was becoming more likely to believe the worst—an affair and some deception about covering it up—but gradually more tolerant of this possibility.

The pollster did not cut the most dashing figure in Washington, with his flyaway hair and chronically untucked shirts. Once he showed up for a weekly political meeting with the president wearing shoes that did not match. Nor was he the most popular member of Clinton's teams. He displayed Jeeves-like attention to the president, but could be rudely dismissive of colleagues. But Penn's clients were not grading him on style. During the same time he was working for Clinton, he had also been hired by Microsoft. For a time, Penn's late-night calls were as likely to be from Bill Gates as from Bill Clinton. This gave Penn an arresting vantage point on the 1990s: an adviser to the decade's preeminent innovator in the realm of politics, and to the preeminent innovator in the realm of business and technology.

WITH RARE EXCEPTIONS, CLINTON'S HOURS WITH RUBIN OR PENN WERE working hours. When he spent time with Terry McAuliffe, it was usually for play. They were together on the golf course at least once a week. They were together at Camp David, where McAuliffe and his wife had become regular guests. Most of all, they were together on the phone several times a week in conversations that usually began at midnight and stretched into the early hours of the morning.

Clinton and the smiling curly-haired man more than a decade his junior had not known each other when the president came to Washington. But in certain circles of the capital McAuliffe was already famous for a particular skill: There was no one who knew more rich Democrats or had more success in loosening up their wallets than this young native of Syracuse, New York. With his boundless energy and ingratiating personality, McAuliffe had been raising money for nearly two decades, since his early twenties. It was during the re-election campaign that Clinton learned the charm of working with McAuliffe. He performed exactly the way he promised—rare enough in the blustery world of fund-raising. Early in 1995, fresh off Clinton's mid-term rout, McAuliffe met with a demoralized president and struck a deal: You need to pledge me this many dates for presidential fund-raisers, he told Clinton. Just show up and I'll raise you every dime you need for re-election. Then McAuliffe did exactly that. A bond was struck.

By 1998, McAuliffe was known in Washington as the president's new best friend. Longtime friends of Clinton found this odd, and even a little sad. Why would the president be spending so much time with a relative stranger? There was no real mystery. Clinton liked McAuliffe because, at a time when there was bleakness all around him, McAuliffe offered pure optimism. If Clinton was feeling down, McAuliffe would pick him up with reports of his latest chats with contributors. "They love you out there, Mr. President," he said. "The enthusiasm is unbelievable." With men like Jordan and Bowles now in an outer orbit, McAuliffe offered an uncritical, undemanding brand of friendship. If Rubin and Penn were the pillars helping Clinton sustain the public dimension of his presidency, McAuliffe was the pillar of the private dimension.

One advantage he had is that he mixed equally well with both Clintons, which not many people did. This made him welcome in their home even at moments of great sensitivity. During the February vacation in Utah, when Chelsea Clinton was not even sure she wished to see her father, White House aides told McAuliffe, "Terry, you have to get out there." McAuliffe went, and he and a lonely president talked in the living room of the ski condominium through the night.

McAuliffe did not mind playing the jester. Sometimes during their weekly golf games, usually played at the Army Navy Country Club just over the Potomac in Virginia, Clinton would be interrupted with calls from foreign leaders. Before the military aide handed the president his secure phone to talk to, say, Tony Blair or Ehud Barak, McAuliffe would hoot, "Let me have the phone, I'll solve this problem!"

In their conversations that year, Clinton and McAuliffe would tour all the byways of that year's scandal. McAuliffe would listen sympathetically while Clinton railed at Starr, or offer his latest intelligence on the mood of congressional Democrats like Dick Gephardt (another old McAuliffe friend) about the unfolding story. But they always steered clear of the matter at the heart of it— the foolish relationship with Lewinsky that started the whole thing.

Not until much later, after the controversy had cleared, did Clinton bring the subject up. You've never asked me about this, he noted gingerly. Can I explain? McAuliffe did not really want to hear. "Mr. President," he said cheerfully, "we all make mistakes."

Chapter Thirty-four

ROCK-BOTTOM TRUTH

"**M**R. PRESIDENT," NEWT GINGRICH SAID, "WE ARE GOING TO RUN you out of town."

Gingrich offered his barbed prediction as he was leaving an Oval Office meeting and a group of foreign policy advisers was arriving. One of them asked Clinton: Did he say what I thought he said? Clinton nodded his head, with an expression that said, See what we're up against?

Gingrich would have been well advised to recall a conversation with Clinton during the government shutdown when, in a moment of confidence, Clinton asked the Speaker, "Do you know who I am?

"I'm the big rubber clown doll you had as a kid, and every time you hit it, it bounces back." He paused, as though pondering the significance of his own words. "That's me—the harder you hit me, the faster I come back up."

Three years later, as spring turned to summer and Starr's investigation churned remorselessly ahead, Clinton was being hit harder than ever.

Several more hits came in rapid succession in late July and early August 1998. The moment Mark Penn had forecast in February—when the "standoff" would break and there would be "a clear story to respond to"—was now at hand.

On July 28, Lewinsky reached an agreement with Starr and his prosecutors to provide the story of her relationship with Clinton under oath in exchange for immunity from prosecution on possible perjury charges. For the prosecutors, her agreement came with an invaluable bonus. The long-percolating rumors that she had saved a dress with the president's "genetic material" on it turned out to be true. Lewinsky's dark blue dress from the Gap left her closet and arrived in Starr's evidence locker. The prosecutor chose to tip his hand. He let Clinton's attorney David Kendall know that he needed a presidential blood sample. Arrangements were made that very night for a prosecutor and federal agents to meet the president in the White House Map Room to draw blood. What looked at first blush like a rite of humiliation was in an odd way a gentlemanly gesture. By seeking the blood sample, Starr was serving fair notice of his evidence. In the wake of Lewinsky's grand jury appearance, Clinton now faced his own date with the jurors. He now knew that if he tried to lie about the Lewinsky relationship, he would be confronted with irrefutable physical evidence and a rock-solid perjury charge.

This roundabout favor hardly blunted the indignity of the evening. Clinton's face was flushed with anger as he sat in a chair and rolled up his sleeve while one of his navy physicians drew the sample. A prosecutor and federal agent fixed their gaze on the vial the entire time, fearful that Clinton's team might try a surreptitious switch. Kendall was no more trusting of the prosecutors. As soon as they left, he ordered a second sample taken for his own side, in case Starr later resorted to fraud. The whole morbid evening was a metaphor for the invasiveness and mistrust that pervaded this year of scandal.

Several choices now confronted Clinton. Before the grand jury, he could assert his Fifth Amendment right to avoid testifying against himself. In any normal criminal defense case, this would be the obvious path. But congressional Democratic leaders, who would have Clinton's fate in their hands in an impeachment proceeding, had made clear this path was politically unacceptable for a president. Yet if he did testify, there was the even more acute dilemma of what to say. Simply coming clean was not an attractive option, since he had uttered several falsehoods months before at the Paula Jones deposition. Sticking with his existing story was an even more perilous path. Many Americans had regarded the Jones case as a burlesque, and could easily forgive Clinton his deceptions there. Lying in front of a federal grand jury was a different matter—that kind of thing sent people to prison.

Beyond the legal consequences were awesome political uncertainties. After the immediate shock of the January disclosures, much of the public had placed the drama in a middle zone between politics and entertainment. Late-night viewers could get their fill of the story on either *Nightline* or the *Tonight Show*. Clinton might not have been a compartmentalizer, but in the main the public was: Many people could laugh or argue about Lewinsky in one part of the brain, even as they did not actually conceive of the story as something that could or should topple a president. Clinton realized that events in August could shift that uneasy balance—from tolerance to a public conviction that this president was more trouble than he was worth. Interwoven with all these choices was still another factor, in which Clinton faced a constituency of one. Peace had been preserved between Clinton and his wife by his January denials and her decision to accept them at face value. That peace, he knew, could not easily withstand an admission that he had lied.

PERHAPS IT IS A FEATURE OF ANY MODERN PRESIDENCY THAT CRISES NEVER arrive in isolation, but it was supremely a feature of this one. On August 5, Saddam Hussein again announced that his country would not submit to United Nations weapons inspections. A similar clash the previous winter had been resolved when the dictator backed down—only after Clinton had assembled a large naval and air armada on Iraq's doorstep. Now it was plain the retreat was only temporary. A new test of wills was under way.

Still another came two days later. The president was woken up at five-thirty by a call from Sandy Berger telling him that the United States had suffered two nearly simultaneous terrorist strikes on its embassies in Nairobi, Kenya, and Dar es Salaam, Tanzania. Hundreds were dead, it became clear within hours, including dozens of American foreign service personnel. There was an obvious suspect immediately, and within days U.S. intelligence would confirm the culpability of a man whose name was until then unfamiliar to most Americans: Osama bin Laden.

Amid the crush of news, Clinton mostly kept to his schedule. As his legal troubles mounted that summer, he responded by pushing himself at an even more exhausting pace than usual. Within the past few weeks, on a return trip to Arkansas, he summoned his old boyhood chum David Leopoulos and other friends for a late-night card game that lasted until 5 a.m. He and Hillary Clinton had spent the previous weekend in the Hamptons, at the summer home of director Steven Spielberg. For two days, they sprinted to several fund-raisers, and soaked up support from a long roster of celebrities and tycoons, including screen stars Julie Andrews, Alec Baldwin, Kim Basinger, and Chevy Chase; fashion designer Vera Wang; pop music stars Billy Joel and Hootie and the Blowfish; and publishing mogul Mort Zuckerman. "If it weren't for the 22nd Amendment, I'd give the American people another chance to elect or defeat me because I believe in what we're doing," Clinton said to laughter and exuberant applause.

After the bombings, Clinton continued with a trip to California—as usual, a mix of policy announcements and fund-raisers. He knew that everyone who saw him secretly wondered how he was holding up. "No matter what you read, every day has been a joy for me, and I have loved it," he assured one group of contributors. This remarkable exuberance in the face of adversity was something he had grown up with. Around this time, Hillary Clinton recalled the little sign that the president's mother had kept in her home: "Lord help me to remember that nothing is going to happen to me today that I can't handle."

On August 13, however, the accumulated pressures mounting on the president from nearly every direction did, for a moment, become more than he could handle. He was at Andrews Air Force Base, just outside Washington, for a ceremony to greet ten flag-draped caskets returning from Nairobi. The president who had so often been a comforter to the stricken was now himself the stricken one. A tear's path was streaked down his face. When he spoke, his voice was barely able to rise above a whisper. The first lady kept looking at her husband with a look of obvious concern. Then, when it was time to leave, the president sat in the back of his limousine, his head bowed, rubbing his hand into the bridge of his nose.

CLINTON'S DATE WITH THE GRAND JURY WAS NOW FOUR DAYS AWAY, ON August 17. Starr had withdrawn a subpoena in exchange for Clinton's agreement to testify voluntarily.

He had reached the inevitable: He had no choice but to tell his wife that his testimony to Starr would be different from what he had told her and the nation.

There were efforts to till the soil in advance of the president's change of story. The *New York Times* and *Washington Post* both ran banner front-page stories, citing unnamed sources, disclosing the president's plans. The first lady had long maintained that she had stopped reading the papers since they left her so upset. These stories would have been hard to miss.

The president had tried to recruit Linda Bloodworth-Thomason, the director, to talk with his wife. She begged off, noting that this unpleasant task was his duty. Some lawyer friends, including Kendall, were more willing to at least nudge Hillary Clinton about what was coming. Kendall's partner Robert Barnett—a longtime friend of the Clintons who no longer represented them after his wife, CBS correspondent Rita Braver, began covering the White House—also gave it a stab.

"You have to face the fact that something about this might be true," he warned.

"Look, Bob," Hillary Clinton responded. "My husband may have his faults, but he has never lied to me."

Her response was characteristic. She had built a wall of disbelief around herself the previous January and never looked out from behind it. She had been in constant contact with her close Arkansas friend Diane Blair during this period, but their conversations always steered wide of Lewinsky. The same was true with close staff members, who revered their boss and felt deeply protective of her. People like Melanne Verveer, her chief of staff, and scheduler Patti Solis Doyle would take each other aside and whisper, "How do you think she's doing? Have you talked to her?" The answer was always no.

THE PRESIDENT'S HOPE OF RECRUITING PROXIES TO TALK WITH HILLARY CLINton was hardly a profile in courage, but on the most important decision facing him during these awful weeks of August he did not waver. August 14 was a Friday, and Clinton's schedule was largely cleared so that he could spend several hours huddled with Kendall and fellow attorney Nicole Seligman for the grand jury appearance. One item that stayed on the schedule was a meeting with his national security team, at which CIA director George Tenet reported an exciting intelligence lead. On August 20, bin Laden was expected to appear with his top lieutenants at a camp in Afghanistan. With a little luck, Clinton could avenge the embassy bombings by killing the leader of the al Qaeda network that carried them out. The downside was that Clinton's motives were sure to be challenged, especially if the attack was unsuccessful, by people suspecting that he was using a military intervention to divert attention from his legal problems.

Irresponsible in his private life, Clinton had a deep sense of responsibility in his public life. The Lewinsky scandal had shown that private failures had public consequences, but not in this instance. "Do not give me political advice or personal advice about the timing. That's my problem. Let me worry about it," he told his national security team.

He dealt with his other worry the next morning.

As Hillary Clinton later recounted the painful moment, he paced back and forth by the bed before coming to the point of his confession. She was as angry as he feared. "What do you mean?" she gasped. "What are you saying? Why did you lie to me?"

"I'm sorry. I'm so sorry. I was trying to protect you and Chelsea."

BY HILLARY CLINTON'S RECKONING, THE BEDROOM ENCOUNTER THAT MORN-ing had left the future of their marriage in doubt. The encounter two days later in the White House Map Room threatened to do the same to the future of his presidency. Under his agreement with prosecutors, Clinton was allowed to testify in the presence of his lawyer, and was spared the indignity of having to appear at the federal courthouse.

That was the only shame he was spared that day. The session began with one of the prosecutors, Sol Wisenberg, reminding the president that he was "under oath" and asking him if he understood that if he gave false or misleading answers, "you could be prosecuted for perjury and/or obstruction of justice."

"I believe that's correct," Clinton replied.

This set the tone for what followed the rest of the afternoon—stern and literal-minded prosecutors trying to pin down a cool and opaque defendant. The problem for Clinton was to find words that could reconcile his version of what happened with Lewinsky with the irrefutable evidence prosecutors had assembled, without acknowledging that he had lied during his deposition in the Jones case. Little surprise, if this contest was going to hinge on mastery of words, that Clinton quickly took command of the session.

He began by refusing to answer directly prosecutor Robert Bittman's blunt query, "Mr. President, were you physically intimate with Monica Lewinsky?" Clinton responded by reading a written statement acknowledging "inappropriate intimate contact" with the young woman, but specifying that the encounters "did not consist of sexual intercourse" and did not "constitute sexual relations" under the definitions he was presented in January at the Jones deposition. He was not going to answer questions in clinical detail, he said, "in an effort to preserve the dignity of the office I hold."

With prosecutors prizing every minute of what was agreed would be a strict four-hour time limit, Clinton then spent much of the session running down the clock with lengthy answers denouncing his political opponents. Lewinsky had nothing to do with the Jones case, he said reasonably, and the Jones case had little to do with sexual harassment. "They just thought they would take a wrecking ball to me and see if they could do some damage."

He mocked the obsessiveness of the prosecutors, who were disbelieving of his claims not to remember key dates and meetings. "I say, sir, just from the tone of your voice and the way you are asking questions here, it's obvious that this is the most important thing in the world." Later in the session, he snapped, "I'm not going to answer your trick questions."

Acknowledging the clear pattern of evasions and concealment he had followed with Lewinsky, he explained himself in commonsense words that no doubt resonated with many on the grand jury, just as they did when a videotape of the session was released to the public a month later. "I did what people do when they do the wrong thing," he said. "I tried to do it when nobody else was looking."

Most of all, he masterfully obscured what prosecutors believed were the clear facts of the case in a cloud of verbiage. Some of it was prim and punctilious, as when he explained that the legalistic definition of sexual relations in the Jones case meant that Lewinsky had had sexual relations with him, but not vice versa. "If the deponent is the person who has oral sex performed on him, then contact is not with anything on that list, but with the lips of another person."

The Starr team was furious at what it regarded as the president's pettifogging. Bittman recalled that in the Jones deposition, Robert Bennett had assured the judge and the plaintiff's lawyers that "there is no sex of any kind in any manner, shape, or form" between the president and Lewinsky. Wouldn't you agree, Bittman sneered, this "was an utterly false statement"?

Clinton smiled and said, "It depends on what the meaning of 'is' is. . . . If 'is' means is and never has been, that is one thing. If it means there is none, that was a completely true statement." A few minutes later, he added, "I was not trying to give you a cute answer to that."

Of course, he had been doing that—and he paid for his cuteness. That throwaway line turned out to be one of Clinton's entrants in *Bartlett's Familiar Quotations.*

In an important way, Clinton was honestly describing his worldview. The grand jury session, like the entire eight-month battle, was a contest between Starr's absolutism and Clinton's relativism. The prosecutor believed there were truths and lies. Any adult should know the difference and realize that the duty to tell the truth in a court proceeding is inviolate—even if the questions are personal. This was Starr's moral code. It was just as much a part of Clinton's code to believe that truth is often not black and white. Human behavior, motives, and language are subject always to many interpretations. Since no one could possess absolute truth, judgment should always be tempered by generosity and tolerance. This might have been self-serving in his present circumstances, but, in fairness, he brought these same values to most decisions in his private and public life. This penchant for ambiguity was central to who he was.

THE STARR PROSECUTORS LEFT THE SESSION FEELING THEY HAD ACCOMPLISHED their objectives. They had shown, beyond any reasonable doubt, that Clinton had lied in both the Jones deposition and again before the grand jury. What Clinton was asking people to believe was absurd—that during a sixteen-month affair he had received sexual favors but scrupulously avoided touching Lewinsky in a sexual way. His version was directly contradicted by Lewinsky, who had described in lurid detail sexual favors he had performed for her. Her account had been corroborated so frequently on other particulars—the dates of her White House visits, the phone calls Clinton received in her presence—that there was no reason to doubt her on this one. Simply put, the former intern was a more credible witness than the president.

Clinton, however, had achieved his goals in the testimony, in ways that the Starr team did not appreciate. With his frequent rhetorical excursions and hair-splitting distinctions, the president had subtly shifted the legal and political contest to more favorable terrain. The case was no longer about a large question: Is the president a truth-teller? Clinton had successfully framed it around a series of ridiculously small ones: Is a president "alone" with a woman if there's a Secret Service agent standing outside the door? Did people believe Lewinsky that the president had fondled her breasts and genitals, or Clinton that he had not? Starr's team regarded these distinctions as worth fighting about. A majority of Americans, it would soon become clear, did not find such questions as worthy of a democracy's attention, and certainly not worth removing a president over.

IF THE DAY WAS A RELATIVE SUCCESS FOR CLINTON, THE EVENING THAT FOLlowed was an extravagant failure. With admirable discipline, Clinton had kept his cool throughout the testimony. As soon as it was over, however, he let down his guard. When he walked out of the Map Room and met his political team in the hallway, Clinton was in a shaking rage.

He was in no frame of mind for the day's next big assignment: a nationally televised speech to the nation. Clinton needed to tell the American public what he had told the prosecutors, that he had indeed had an improper relationship with Lewinsky. He would also need to acknowledge that he had misled the public for months with his steadfast denials. It was obvious, of course, that Clinton needed to break this news with an apology, and a profession that he deeply regretted his initial lie. The reality of his feelings was more complicated. He told several people that he did not regret his initial evasion. If he had told the truth in January, the public furor might have been such that he would have been forced from office. By August, the public had had time to come to terms with the Lewinsky matter. Most voters had long since reached the conclusion that some kind of improper relationship had taken place, but were willing to keep the matter in perspective.

"The lie saved me," Clinton told one close friend.

The question confronting him on the evening of August 17, two days before his fifty-second birthday, was how to acknowledge the truth in a way that engendered sympathy for his plight, rather than anger at his recklessness and deception. Clinton was a politician who operated with natural intuition for his audience. His intuition for the right words and right tone rarely failed him as critically as it did on this evening, when his judgment was warped by a toxic combination of fatigue and anger.

Paul Begala was a natural wordsmith who had set aside his own considerable resentment at Clinton's behavior to write a statement with the appropriate mix of confession, contrition, and commitment to move on. There was one problem: Clinton did not believe it. It was another reminder of an essential fact about the man: Supposedly full of artifice and guile, he was in fact quite transparent, especially about matters close to his heart. There were few closer than this one, and he was determined to say what he really believed. He had written this out in longhand over the previous several days. His words dripped, not with remorse, but with fury at Starr and his investigation.

The drama of this evening—the contest between what was sensible for Clinton to say and what he really wished to say—reflected a familiar tension. There were different poles to his personality, and within his circle of friends and advisers, different sorts of people gravitated to one pole or the other. There was a set of people who he knew would sympathize with and feed his instinct for grievance, and his belief that the forces arrayed against him were deeply illegitimate. Harry Thomason fit into this camp. So did the former journalist

Sidney Blumenthal. There was another set of people whom the president depended on to ignore his grievances and give him a clear-eyed view of political realities. Advisers in this category, like Rahm Emanuel and Doug Sosnik, tended to roll their eyes at Blumenthal's incessant conspiracy theorizing, and the way he would recite all manner of obscure but dark connections between Starr's team and various right-wing financiers and zealots. This understanding of the conservative shadow world was a principal reason Blumenthal was in the White House. Both Clintons had a huge appetite for it. "I know you all make fun of Sid, but he's on to something here," the president would say to more conventional minded aides like Emanuel or Sosnik.

Blumenthal's colleagues did not think his views were wrong so much as beside the point. Yes, they believed, Clinton's enemies were out to get him, but the fixation on this was unproductive. The president's task was to transcend the right's viciousness by assuring that he stayed attuned to the politics of Middle America, where most people did not care about ideological crusades or political vendettas and simply wanted Clinton to go about business that mattered to them. Under ordinary circumstances, Clinton liked to vent with people like Thomason or Blumenthal, even though in the end he usually chose the more practical approach of people like Emanuel or Sosnik. But this night, just hours after his grueling testimony, was no ordinary night.

Just a couple of hours before Clinton was due to speak to the nation, his lawyers and political advisers gathered in the solarium of the White House residence to discuss the competing drafts. The lawyers rather liked Clinton's plan to denounce Starr; tell that SOB where to get off, they agreed. Without exception, the political advisers felt this was a huge mistake. What the public wanted from the president was accountability and contrition; surrogates could take the fight to the prosecutor.

"Mr. President, that's why God invented James Carville," said Sosnik, while the Louisiana consultant, who loathed Starr and delighted in saying so publicly, nodded his head in agreement.

Clinton said that mere contrition would let his own supporters down. His people needed something to hang on to, he explained, and a Starr-bashing message would give it to them. Emanuel countered bluntly: "People don't care about you or your problems, they only care about what you are doing for their problems." As Clinton argued with his staff, it seemed to several people in the room that the president's words were directed at one person in particular. He kept looking over to Hillary Clinton, seeking validation. This was not by itself unusual. Advisers had long since learned, in political and policy discussions alike, to give the president arguments that they knew would resonate with her.

What was unusual on this occasion was that the first lady had absented herself, psychically if not physically, from the discussion. She sat quietly, with a sullen countenance and an air of total exhaustion. As the debate swirled and the president's political advisers continued to plead with him to soften his language, she said with impatience: "It's your speech, Bill. Say whatever you want." To some in the room, it sounded more like a taunt than advice.

Whatever her intent, Clinton took his wife's words to heart. His four-and-a-half-minute address, from the same room in which he had testified earlier in the day, started out with an obligatory apology and confession. Then, halfway through, the tone of his voice changed abruptly. So did his appearance, as he narrowed his eyes and stiffened his jaw. Explaining why he had deceived the country about his illicit relationship, he suggested that the prosecutor drove him to it. "I had real and serious concerns about an independent counsel investigation that began with private business dealings twenty years ago, dealings, I might add, about which an independent federal agency found no evidence of any wrongdoing by me or my wife over two years ago," he protested. "It is time to stop the pursuit of personal destruction and the prying into private lives and get on with our national life."

THE REVIEWS BEGAN ARRIVING WITHIN MINUTES. EMANUEL, OBSERVING THE network commentary after the speech, warned Clinton that it was overwhelmingly negative. Soon, though, pollster Mark Penn called with more reassuring news. A clear majority of viewers thought Clinton's remarks were fine. They were desperate for closure on the scandal, and Clinton's confession, however grudging, offered that promise. It was only hard-core Republicans and political "elites"—the kind of people quoted by the networks—who were dissatisfied with the speech, Penn reported. It was a vivid example of the dichotomy in public opinion that had existed all year.

But the complaints raised about the speech could not be dismissed as mere static from the "chattering classes." There were several potential threats. Many of the elites infuriated not just by Clinton's behavior but by his sullen speech were congressional Democrats. Sosnik had warned the president back in January: If you get brought down, it will be by your own party, not by the opposition. There was also the problem of liberal women, including some prominent examples in his own administration. If an accomplished woman like Health and Human Services Secretary Donna Shalala or Secretary of State Madeleine Albright suddenly announced that she could no longer in conscience serve a president who would carry on a sexual relationship with a young woman on his staff, the public impact would be sensational. In addition, there was already a medium-size chorus of voices—from such people as respected former Georgia senator Sam Nunn and the writer Garry Wills—suggesting the honorable thing for Clinton to do was resign.

He left the next morning for a scheduled vacation to Martha's Vineyard. In a striking image, Chelsea Clinton stood between her parents and took their hands as they walked, a wounded family still together, across the South Lawn to board Marine One. Observing Clinton during these next days was like watching a man under the pulse of a strobe light. In public, in his sporadic appearances, he presented a flickering image of presidential normality. He still had his planes and motorcades; when he landed at Martha's Vineyard, he bounded over to greet a crowd of locals gathered behind a rope line, just as ever. Yet there was no disguising—his own spokesmen did not try—that this was a surreal moment for both the public figure and the private man. In both spheres of his life, he had been exposed and humiliated. At their borrowed vacation compound, the Clintons spent most of their time apart. He spent his days in a cottage adjacent to the main house. And when they were together, Hillary Clinton made no effort, even in the presence of staff, to hide her cold rage toward her husband. Indeed, it seemed to some of his advisers that she was publicly orchestrating his punishment—that he be seen as paying her price.

He had been at Martha's Vineyard for only a day when he made a sudden appearance in the elementary school gymnasium at Edgartown that served as the filing center for White House reporters. The cruise missile strikes he had ordered several days earlier against Osama bin Laden's training camp had been carried out, the president told the startled reporters, most of whom were slumped over their computers in T-shirts and shorts for what they had assumed would be a barely working vacation. In addition, U.S. forces had hit a pharmaceutical plant in the Sudan at which it was suspected that bin Laden's al Qaeda network had made chemical weapons. After making a brief statement, Clinton flew back to Washington so that he could make a formal statement explaining his action to the nation in an Oval Office address that evening. The explanation fell flat with some.

Three years later, in the wake of September 11, there would be undying controversy over whether the president's missile strikes were a feckless response to a threat as dangerous as bin Laden. At the time, however, the questions were of a quite different nature. Immediately, there were questions—never satisfactorily resolved—about whether the intelligence evidence was sufficient to justify hitting the Sudan facility. More pointedly, there were questions about Clinton's motivation in ordering any attack at all. Earlier that year, Hollywood churned out an improbable movie called *Wag the Dog*, in which an embattled president goes to war with Albania in order to distract the nation from a sex scandal. A few weeks later, the Lewinsky scandal broke, and some people thought the plot was not so improbable after all. "There is a cloud over this presidency," said Republican John Ashcroft, then in the Senate representing Missouri. His colleague Arlen Specter, Republican from Pennsylvania, was even blunter in casting doubt on the president's motives: "There's an obvious issue that will be raised internationally as to whether there is any diversionary motivation."

Comments like these made plain that the president was not the only one distracted by scandal from the pressing business of the age.

CLINTON RETURNED TO MARTHA'S VINEYARD FOR ANOTHER WEEK. THE COUple joined in the island's social scene, pasting on a mask of gaiety as they attended dinner parties in their honor, giving their well-heeled companions a chance to whisper and stare as they looked for any clues about what was really going on with the marriage. The Clintons did not show much affection toward each other, but no overt anger either. Back at the house it was different, as the first lady continued to give her husband the deep freeze. During his many spare hours, he worked the phones—and learned more about just how badly he had stumbled in his televised Lewinsky confession. Some Democratic members of Congress refused to take his calls. Those who did told him how inadequate his speech was, failing to give any sense of what he had put the nation through. Clinton was starting to understand how badly his anger had warped his political judgment. He was also realizing that he would need to show the nation some of the remorse he insisted to friends he genuinely felt.

Over the next several days he tried, haltingly, to do that. "All of you know I'm having to become quite an expert in this business of asking for forgiveness," he told an African-American church congregation at Oak Bluffs, a village on Martha's Vineyard. "It gets a little easier the more you do it. . . . But I have to tell you that in these last days it has come home to me again—something I first learned as president, but it wasn't burned in my bones—and that is that in order to get it, you have to be willing to give it. The anger, the resentment, the bitterness, the desire for recrimination against people you believe have wronged you—they harden the heart and deaden the spirit and lead to self-inflicted wounds." This was a start, though close listeners noted that he never used a simple word, "sorry." In fact, anger and remorse were still competing with each other inside Clinton, anger clearly winning. As his vacation ended he left for a planned trip to Moscow, infuriated that the controversy was still shadowing him during an overseas visit. After a news conference in the Kremlin, where an American reporter asked about Lewinsky, he repaired to a back room and erupted at his staff. "Can you believe he's asking that kind of shit over here! Can you believe it!" An aide frantically waved his finger across his throat and pointed to the chandelier. It was well known that the holding rooms the Russians supplied visiting leaders were bugged, and Kremlin officials were no doubt busy translating Clinton's tirade even now.

Clinton needed to convince the doubters that his remorse was indeed as deeply felt as his resentment. This was urgent business. By September, Clinton's political situation had deteriorated badly. Senator Kent Conrad, a North Dakota Democrat, told Gregory Craig, an old Clinton family friend who had joined the White House legal team, "You are about three days from having the senior Democrats come down and ask for the president's resignation." Meanwhile, soundings by White House aides Sosnik and Podesta made plain that the administration's women had grown only angrier over the August vacation; a feminist mutiny was by no means implausible. What Clinton genuinely felt inside himself—did he regret his misdeeds or just the public exposure of them?—was a mystery even to some of his closest aides, but his political needs at the moment were obvious. He needed to prove, as ostentatiously as possible, that he had learned his lesson. In so doing, the hope was that he could persuade people to look at his crisis in a personal context, rather than a political one. In this situation, self-restraint was not called for; groveling was.

It began with a meeting with his cabinet, which assembled not in the West Wing but in the White House residence. Clinton began with a remarkable soliloquy in which he apologized for the difficulty and embarrassment his conduct had caused them all. His eyes welling, he said he had turned to Scripture for strength during his ordeal, and then offered his explanation to the essential mystery of the Lewinsky saga: How could he have done something so self-destructive? The answer, he said, was that he had been a deeply angry man for much of his presidency. Frustration at his opponents, rage at Starr, had thrown off the internal balance that people need to be successful in both their private and public lives. He had long wrestled with personal demons. In his emotionally vulnerable state, those demons had gained the upper hand. After this, the rest of the room got a chance to speak. The speeches that followed fell into three distinct groups. Many of Clinton's African-American cabinet members, including Transportation Secretary Rodney Slater and Labor Secretary Alexis Herman, rushed to their president's defense, and themselves quoted Scripture on the universality of sin and the power of forgiveness. By contrast, many of his white male appointees mumbled uncomfortably when it was their turn to speak. Treasury Secretary Robert Rubin told Clinton that he had "screwed up," but everyone did from time to time, and it was time to move on. As Agriculture Secretary Dan Glickman later recalled his embarrassment, "I think a lot of us just wanted to end the meeting and get out of there." The principal purpose of this session, though, was to provide a vent for several of the administration's most prominent women to let loose their frustrations. Shalala, in particular, thought that Clinton's bit about anger and personal weakness was self-justifying nonsense. She did not think his lapse—an affair with a much younger woman who worked under him—was either trivial or a strictly private matter. In her previous job as chancellor of the University of Wisconsin, she had fired faculty for the same. To her, Clinton seemed blind to the moral implications of what he had done, and was taking solace in his conviction that he was an effective president. "I can't believe that is what you're telling us, that is what you believe, that you don't have an obligation to provide moral leadership," she said. The room tensed up, with colleagues taken aback by the pointedness of Shalala's challenge and Clinton's visible anger. "By your standard, Richard Nixon would've beaten John Kennedy," he snapped in retort.

Clinton had never confronted so directly the ambivalence some of his own subordinates felt toward him.

The president did not sleep that night, but stayed up writing on a legal pad for an appearance the next morning. A group of ministers had been previously scheduled to join him in the East Room for a prayer breakfast. The event was open to news cameras, and the breakfast was the occasion to give the larger public what he had given to his cabinet the day before. He spoke in a quiet voice, his body stooped with fatigue. "As you might imagine, I have been on quite a journey these last few weeks to get to the end of this, to the rock-bottom truth of where I am and where we all are," he told the ministers. ". . . I don't think there is any fancy way to say that I have sinned."

Clinton told the ministers he would begin "pastoral counseling" to help him confront personal weaknesses. And he drew a distinction between his legal defense and his personal sense of right and wrong. That legal defense, it was now clear, would rest on tedious and sometimes galling distinctions—the difference between misleading answers and flatly false ones in his testimony. But Clinton wanted people to know that he knew "legal language must not obscure the fact that I have done wrong."

Then he took his sermon further—a bit too far for some listeners. Perhaps something good could come of this sordid scandal for America's families, he explained, and that by his example "the children of this country can learn in a profound way that integrity is important and selfishness is wrong," Clinton explained. "But God can change us and make us strong at the broken places."

Chapter Thirty-five

AGE OF EXTREMES

A FEW HOURS AFTER CLINTON'S PRAYER SERVICE CONFESSION, KEN-neth Starr and the congressional Republicans who were his sponsors took their best shot against the president. The prosecutor's 445-page report to Congress detailed what he called a record of "abundant and calculating lies" under oath, obstruction of justice, and manifold other transgressions that he alleged were an abuse of power that "may constitute grounds for impeachment."

It was not the solemn pronouncements on constitutional theory and precedent that sent the document racing across the Internet within minutes to millions of eager readers. It was Starr's lurid recitation of the president's sad relationship with Lewinsky, narrated in near-pornographic detail. The logic behind Starr's approach was that the public would be so shocked by the perversions of a president who employed cigars in sex play or practiced phone sex in hotel rooms while traversing the country in his re-election campaign that public demands for his removal from office would be overwhelming. The pressure for resignation would rise, and, if Clinton resisted, impeachment and forcible removal from office would be inevitable.

At last, they had him—or so it seemed to Republicans that fall. Newt Gingrich, who had no reason to suspect that he was then in his last weeks as Speaker of the House, assured people that it was Clinton's perjury, not his sexual adventures, that was at issue. He promised to discuss the president's mendacity at every speech he gave until the matter was resolved. The release of the president's videotaped grand jury testimony ten days later, it was presumed, would accelerate Clinton's demise. Leaks from the prosecutor's office warned that the nation was about to see the real and unvarnished Clinton—a snarling, evasive figure, it was said, trapped in the glare. As millions watched the testimony—which the networks ran on a thirty second delay in case they needed to excise any dirty parts—what they actually saw was an entirely familiar Clinton. He was articulate and clever, sometimes too much so for his own good, but basically a reasonable-sounding fellow. Clinton's testimony the month before contained plenty of evasions, but they seemed to most Americans like the efforts of a man to preserve his dignity in the face of a ghoulish ordeal.

If humiliation was the object, Clinton's pursuers had achieved their goal. The president's daughter, with whom his relationship was then nearly as frayed as it was with his wife, read the report on the Internet at Stanford University. "This is killing me," he told Terry McAuliffe one night. "I know what this is. This is about trying to destroy me as a person."

If shifting the political balance was the object, it became clear within days the opposition had failed. Polls showed disappointment with Clinton, but disdain for the effort to humiliate him with the effluvium of the Starr report. These polls, however, did not give Republicans pause. George Santayana, the philosopher, had anticipated Gingrich's team by several decades. "Fanaticism," he wrote, "consists of redoubling your effort when you have forgotten your aim." For the next several weeks, House Republicans defied public opinion with a series of mostly party-line votes authorizing an impeachment inquiry.

There was a curiously self-defeating dimension to the GOP strategy. If the goal was simply to damage Clinton, Republicans had many opportunities to do so effectively. Several times during this period the president and his surrogates virtually pleaded with Congress to pass a resolution of censure against him. Even Clinton recognized there was a considerable public appetite—and widespread support among Democrats—for some kind of measure registering official disapproval of his conduct. The Constitution has no provision for such a resolution, and it would have had no formal impact on presidential power. Even so, a resolution might well have diminished Clinton severely in public opinion had it been passed with an overwhelming bipartisan vote, as it would have if Republicans had agreed. But their goal was to destroy Clinton, not simply damage him, so they rejected this compromise and several others that would have garnered significant Democratic backing. Republicans pressed on, either oblivious or indifferent to the fact that they were hurting themselves as much as Clinton by administering such a solemn constitutional procedure as impeachment through heavily partisan votes.

The president's success since 1995 had been based on the fact that the electorate was less partisan in nature than it had been in decades. The capital, by contrast, was more partisan than it had been in decades. America was yearning for an age of moderation; Washington was governing in an age of extremes.

THE PRESIDENT HAD LONG SINCE LEARNED HOW TO LEVERAGE HIS INFLUENCE in such a climate. Ever since they had been burned by the government shutdowns in 1995, Republicans had followed a similar pattern. They would bluster for months, stall in negotiations with the White House over spending—then cave at the end by giving Clinton substantially what he wanted.

The only thing notable about the pattern this year—in which Clinton won big increases in spending to subsidize localities for hiring new teachers, as well as major appropriations for the International Monetary Fund—was the context. "The Republican Congress had more caves than Okinawa," chortled Begala. They would yield on spending bills but not on their determination to remove Clinton from office.

The day of his budget victory, the president flew by helicopter sixty miles east of Washington to the Wye River Plantation along the Chesapeake Bay. The aim was to revive a flagging Middle East peace process. A schedule of commitments made by Israel and the Palestinian Authority was in shambles, and a summit under U.S. auspices was aimed at reassembling the pieces. Over the next nine days, the president spent some eighty-five hours shuttered with Israeli prime minister Benjamin Netanyahu, Palestinian Authority chairman Yasser Arafat, and Jordan's King Hussein, who was suffering from cancer that would take his life within months. Nearly every night Clinton's helicopter returned to the White House several hours after midnight. On the final night of the summit, he stayed in Maryland until sunrise, and coaxed an agreement just minutes before the leaders, ready to declare the summit a failure, were prepared to depart. Clinton's physical powers, and his persuasive ones, were at a peak.

The visiting leaders sang hosannas to their host at a ceremony back at the

White House. What was striking was how they praised precisely the traits that in other contexts critics found so maddening—his instinct to unite opposites with fancy rhetorical formulations, and his penchant for last-minute tightrope maneuvers. Even Netanyahu, who kept ties to Gingrich and was no admirer of Clinton, marveled: "I mean, he doesn't stop. He has this ability to maintain a tireless pace and to nudge and prod and suggest and use a nimble and flexible mind."

At a gathering of African-American religious leaders that evening, Jesse Jackson observed with wonder, "This man's survival skills are of a different order."

It was at this event that Clinton, who had spent months saying that his personal problems had no bearing on his public business, suggested they might be linked after all. His frenetic efforts at Wye River, he explained in a hoarse voice that conveyed equal measures of satisfaction and exhaustion, had been part of his "personal journey of atonement."

Redemption of a more secular nature was just days away. Gingrich had predicted gains in his House majority of some thirty or forty seats. On election night, November 3, Clinton awaited returns in the White House with aides while eating sausage pizza. Hillary Clinton, who was superstitious about watching early returns, stayed away and instead watched a movie, *Beloved,* in the residence. The evening brought an epiphany to Clinton. While he had often extolled the wonders of computers and the Internet, he had never actually used either one. He was busy with the presidency and had lots of people at his service, so there was no point in learning. Now, standing over the shoulder of political director Craig Smith, Clinton was excited to discover that the Internet could be used to track election returns in real time, even faster than they were reported on television. What he saw on the screen was even better news. Far from gaining dozens of seats, Gingrich's Republicans actually lost five, leaving them only barely in the majority. There was also a sweet vindication in a Senate race in New York: The powerful Republican Alfonse D'Amato, one of the Clintons' chief Whitewater tormentors, had lost to Democrat Charles Schumer.

There were two more arresting developments in the days ahead. Gingrich, facing deep disaffection in the Republican caucus, resigned from the speakership and the House. It had been just four years from revolution to Thermidor. This was an immensely gratifying moment for the Clintons, but the more consequential event was on the Democratic side. New York senator Daniel Patrick Moynihan, with whom the president had such a turbulent relationship, announced he was giving up the Senate seat he had first won in 1976. Within days, New York congressman Charles Rangel of Harlem was on the phone with the first lady with a wild idea. The first lady should run for Moynihan's seat. One reason this was wild was that she had never lived in the state and had no historic connection to it at all. As Hillary Clinton later recounted the story of her Senate bid, for this and other reasons she at first dismissed Rangel's suggestion as flattering but absurd, and only months later began to take it seriously. But there is reason to believe she was more purposeful in her pursuit of this seat than her recollections suggest. One senior West Wing political aide said the Clintons were discussing the likelihood of Moynihan's retirement and the possibilities that would open up even in advance of his announcement. Within a couple of days of Rangel's call, Hillary Clinton was discussing with political aides what she would need to do to freeze the field of potential Democrats and keep her options open while she decided whether she was ready to make the race.

CLINTON'S SUCCESS WITH THE BUDGET, AT THE WYE RIVER TALKS, AND IN THE mid-term elections created the surface impression that his governing influence had emerged from the Lewinsky uproar unscathed. It had not.

One person who knew the truth well was Erskine Bowles. At the beginning of the year, just days before the scandal erupted, Clinton had convinced him to stay on as chief of staff with the promise of an enormously productive year ahead. Clinton would push Congress to grant him expanded authority to negotiate free trade agreements on an accelerated basis. He would pass major legislation expanding the government's ability to regulate tobacco and putting cigarette smoking on the path to extinction. Most of all, he would push both parties to compromise and make major reforms to the nation's expensive entitlement programs, like Medicare and Social Security.

Every item on this ambitious agenda had a common theme: It would require Clinton to push his own party against its liberal grain. A politically prospering president might have been able to do this. A president fighting for survival—and thus dependent on every last Democratic vote in order to avoid being herded out of office by Republicans—proved virtually impotent to challenge his party's orthodoxies. The promised bid for "fast-track" trade authority never materialized; the party's union base would not countenance it. Nor was there any sustained effort to reform and trim the rising costs of entitlement programs. In the best of times Democrats had no appetite for this; in 1998 few Democrats, Clinton included, wanted to lay down the argument that

Republicans would cut benefits for seniors if Democrats were not there to stop them. Clinton did make a spirited campaign for tobacco legislation, but the only way this measure was going to pass was to give cigarette makers a measure of immunity from class-action lawsuits for past damages in exchange for tougher anti-smoking rules in the future. Clinton supported this bargain. Most Democrats, heavily funded by trial attorneys, did not. In the end, the president was not able to stake out a sustainable middle ground, and his tobacco bill died. Clinton, the centrist New Democrat, was the leader of his party; but congressional Democrats, most of whom retained the uncompromising souls of Old Democrats, called the shots on the president's agenda with no fear of reprisal.

Bowles, who had been the hero of 1997, was demoralized and diminished in 1998. He had made it clear at the beginning of the scandal that he would play no role in legal strategy or political damage control. Someone had to stay busy working on substance, he explained. But there was precious little substance to work on. He stayed on for much of the year as a spectral presence, resigning in October to return to North Carolina.

It was not simply on the legislative front that Clinton's ambitions had been pruned. A deeper loss was the dream he had announced at the beginning of his second term, to be a "repairer of the breach." All of 1998 had been a reminder of how right Clinton had been in his diagnosis. The country did need to drain the malice and distrust from politics, leave behind the old arguments from the 1960s, and find common purpose for the challenges of a new century ahead. Under different circumstances, Clinton might have had the skill and imagination to be this supreme national unifier, but not now. Far from repairing the breach, Clinton came to rely on it during his battle for survival. Castigating Republicans was the best way to unite his own party and maintain sufficient public support to stay in office. That Clinton was often right in his accusations did not absolve his own culpability in the deterioration of the nation's civic life. He had compromised his ability to speak to the nation not simply as a political leader but a moral one.

THE POISONOUS ATMOSPHERE PERMEATING WASHINGTON THIS AUTUMN WAS not restricted to relations between the president and his Republican tormentors on Capitol Hill. The estrangement between Clinton and certain precincts of permanent Washington had never been more stark. The mutual suspicion and resentment between Clinton and the capital's elite Georgetown culture had begun six years earlier with the first family's arrival from Arkansas. Ill will had ebbed at times, but never went away. Now, in Clinton's hour of maximum embarrassment, it was at a peak.

The personification of this Georgetown culture of prominent journalists, senators, arts patrons, and former high government officials was writer Sally Quinn. She had arrived in Washington a quarter century earlier and fashioned a fearsome reputation on the pages of the *Washington Post*'s "Style" section, where she penned acidly sketched profiles of the capital's most powerful and socially connected citizens, filled with gossip and insight. Her own personal life had sparked a certain amount of gossip when she began dating and eventually married the *Post*'s dashing editor from the Watergate era, Benjamin Bradlee. Her marriage and her rising reputation had gradually changed Quinn's vantage point on the capital. Now she did not just chronicle the capital establishment; she viewed herself, and was unquestionably viewed by others, as a preeminent representative of the establishment. Many of its denizens were regular guests at her dinner table.

In early November, Quinn produced a story for the *Post* that was exhaustively reported, full of quotations from many of Washington's most eminent citizens. It was Quinn's answer to the mystery of why Clinton was so unpopular in the capital, even as most Americans did not seem to care much about his sexual failings and the resulting deceptions. "With some exceptions, the Washington Establishment is outraged by the president's behavior in the Monica Lewinsky scandal," she explained. The reason was that Washington was essentially a small town—full of decent and principled people, she insisted—where Clinton's transgressions were not an abstraction or the stuff of jokes but a personal affront. Quinn quoted Ronald Reagan's social secretary about how Washington was a "demoralized little village." There was a comment from David Gergen on how it was not sex, but deceit and indiscretion, that was Clinton's sin: "That is a cardinal rule of the village. You don't foul the nest."

One could hardly imagine a more well-timed morale booster at the White House than Quinn's article. Begala went to the Oval Office waving the article in his hand. "This is perfect," he exclaimed. "This is the best and most accurate article you will ever read about Washington." Quinn, as Begala saw it, had accurately chronicled the smug insularity of establishment Washington, as well as its preciousness and hypocrisy. Clinton could not agree more. The article stayed on his desk for weeks, and on his mind even longer. Some time afterward the president was going over papers with his staff on the upcoming Presidential Medal of Freedom awards. Spontaneously, he launched into a little riff for his assembled aides. His nominee for the prestigious award this year would be none other than the famous Ben Bradlee, husband of Sally Quinn.

The aides looked on in puzzled amusement.

"Anyone who sleeps with that bitch deserves a medal!" he explained.

AS THE YEAR SLOGGED TO A CONCLUSION, THE PREVAILING ASSUMPTION HAD been that the Republicans' poor performance in the mid-term elections would cool their ardor for driving Clinton out of office. At last, it was thought, the time had arrived for a sensible conclusion to the Lewinsky episode.

And Clinton's lawyers, with their client's grudging permission, acted on this logic in the weeks following the election. The president approved a settlement of the Paula Jones case, agreeing to pay her $850,000 to dispose of the case. Jones got no apology, but she did get more money than she had ever sought. It appalled Clinton to pay, but this was a time for closure.

But Republicans did not want closure. Instead, the GOP engine rumbled down the impeachment track that had been laid months earlier. In December, articles of impeachment accusing Clinton of obstructing justice and lying under oath raced through the House Judiciary Committee on a party-line vote. Soon after, they did the same before the full House of Representatives, again on nearly party-line votes. Why did no one on the Republican side reach for the brakes, when the evidence was so overwhelming that solid majorities did not regard Clinton's transgressions as an impeachable offense? The answer to this question illuminates not only the impeachment riddle, but much else about political life in the age of Clinton, and in the years afterward. Members of Congress were not driven by the logic of national majorities, but by two other imperatives: One was the politics of individual congressional districts; the other, the politics of the party caucus.

By the 1990s, few members of Congress in either party needed to worry much about their re-election prospects, at least in the general election, in any given year. The ancient practice of gerrymandering—drawing legislative districts to maximize partisan advantage—had grown more brazen over the years. It had even obtained a certain moral and legal imprimatur, due to civil rights laws that, as interpreted over time, virtually required district lines to be drawn to create majority African-American districts where possible. However well intended, these policies had the effect of reducing political competition. Democratic-leaning districts became even more Democratic, and Republican-leaning districts more Republican. The result was that any individual legislator did not worry much about finding the political center; his or her seat was not endangered by a general election challenge. To the extent politicians felt peril, it came from within parties—from the threat of primary challenge, or from the fear of being ostracized by leaders in the party caucus for failing to show adequate devotion to the party line. In such an environment, few incentives promoted moderation, self-restraint, or compromise across party lines. To the contrary, the incentives were for ideological purity and remorseless combat against political enemies.

No legislator was more emblematic of the power of the Republican leadership to impose its agenda on wavering members than Jack Quinn, a veteran Republican congressman from Buffalo. Quinn, from a Democratic-leaning district, often voted with Clinton and was even on friendly personal terms with him. Everyone who knew him was aware he had no appetite for impeachment, and he had indicated to reporters that he was planning to vote no. White House officials believed he had given similar assurances. If so, Quinn was not as good as his word. Faced with a choice of voting against his own instincts and the preferences of his district, or facing political oblivion with his Republican House colleagues, Quinn decided in mid-December that he would vote yes on impeachment.

The implications of Quinn's defection were self-evident to the White House aides, who had been conducting an intensive head-counting operation on Capitol Hill. They knew they had no votes to spare. Quinn's "yes" vote meant that Clinton was almost certainly going to be impeached, only the second U.S. president in history to meet such a fate. Clinton knew the implications, too. He was in Israel when his press secretary Joe Lockhart (who had replaced Mike McCurry in October) and Doug Sosnik, the White House senior adviser, arrived in his hotel room early in the morning with the news. He hung his head and prepared for a day of meetings with Prime Minister Benjamin Netanyahu, as well as a press conference that was certain to be dominated by one topic. Clinton's manner, as with Lockhart, was flat and subdued as he and the prime minister met with reporters. "It's out of my hands," Clinton said.

He flew back across the Atlantic to await his humiliation in the House. In addition to impeachment, Clinton's years-long confrontation with Saddam Hussein's Iraq was reaching denouement. The dictator was again refusing to admit United Nations weapons inspectors into his country, and the United States was again threatening serious consequences for this refusal. This produced a bizarre scene on Air Force One, as described by author Peter Baker. In one section of the plane, National Security Adviser Sandy Berger and Secretary of State Madeleine Albright huddled and talked by secure air phones with Vice President Gore, Defense Secretary William Cohen, and White House Chief of Staff John Podesta (who had taken over from Bowles in October) about a pending missile attack against Iraq. In another part of the plane, Sosnik and Lockhart were on the phones with Washington colleagues gathering news on the imminent impeachment vote. Every few minutes, one of the political aides would poke his head into the national security room to give Clinton the latest updates. Inevitably, the two conversations merged at times. White House aides and Clinton brooded, as they had in August during the missile strikes against bin Laden, whether people would believe that he was not ordering the strikes simply to divert attention from his domestic embarrassments.

Many lawmakers did believe exactly that. The man slated to be the new Republican Speaker of the House, Louisiana's Bob Livingston, agreed to postpone the impeachment vote by a day, after meeting with Clinton and receiving assurances from Cohen that the military action was not politically motivated. The four-day bombing that made up Operation Desert Fox was aimed at "degrading" Hussein's suspected weapons of mass destruction facilities and other military installations. Yet the attacks were not coordinated with any broader plan for either forcing weapons inspectors back into Iraq, or forcing Hussein from power, or coming to grips in any long-term way with what to do about his regime. Operation Desert Fox did inflict some considerable damage on its targets, then ended. Clinton essentially ended his confrontation with Saddam Hussein and left the dictator to bide his time. Months earlier, in February, the president had warned about the hazards of taking an "ambiguous third route" toward this outlaw regime. Now he was taking precisely such a route. As a weakened president who had no stomach in any event for an extended conflict in the Middle East, Clinton apparently believed he had no other choice.

There was little dissent on this from Republicans. They, too, were happy to be done with the Iraq distraction and return to their real target, which was Clinton himself. The impeachment brand was seared on his brow on December 19. It was an extraordinary day on many counts. That morning, Speaker-designate Livingston took to the House floor to insist that Clinton should do the honorable thing and resign. "You resign! You resign!" came the outraged response from Democrats in the chamber. To everyone's astonishment, Livingston did precisely that. *Hustler,* the pornographic magazine, was preparing a story detailing Livingston's extramarital affairs. Rather than fight to stay in power, the veteran congressman said to hell with it and publicly apologized to his family and colleagues. At the White House, Clinton was aghast—both at what he considered Livingston's unnecessary capitulation to smear tactics, and at an unwelcome example that some people would urge the president to follow. He immediately issued a public statement urging Livingston to reconsider. A couple of hours later, the House of Representatives passed two articles of impeachment against Clinton on mostly party-line votes. One article alleged that Clinton lied in his grand jury appearance. The other alleged that he obstructed justice and tampered with witnesses in the Paula Jones case and Starr's investigation by encouraging Lewinsky to lie in exchange for help getting a job, and by coaching secretary Betty Currie to give incorrect answers.

While the Republicans' move did not have majority public support, their votes were not only a humiliation for Clinton but an acute new threat as well. The danger was that the public, which had stayed with Clinton this long, would conclude that he was simply too weakened to continue serving, and that he should join Livingston in voluntarily stepping down. To counter this, the White House's political team, led by Sosnik, recommended an unusual response. Clinton would greet the news not with remorse but with exuberant defiance. The White House summoned House Democrats, who had been on the losing side of the vote, to the South Lawn of the White House for what amounted to a pep rally. The world would see Clinton not as a solitary and embattled figure like Richard Nixon walking the beach in his wingtips at San Clemente, but surrounded by friends. As the president and first lady waited in the Oval Office before walking past the Rose Garden out to the cameras, the mood between them seemed tense. They hardly spoke. But as soon as they stepped out, their hands were held tightly, and Clinton flashed a resolute smile.

It was a brave gesture, but also a sad one. The impeachment came a year to the day after Monica Lewinsky received her subpoena to testify in the Paula Jones case. The twelve months that followed put the image of Clinton as a bold and even impulsive man in an odd light. Certainly he was heedless in his personal affairs. But as a leader he had shown himself to be self-defeatingly cautious when it came to his own defense. At every turn, he took the step that would preserve options, and keep him alive for another day. At every turn, he rejected more emphatic steps that would have carried more risk but might have spared him the impeachment humiliation. He could have settled the Paula Jones case, or told the truth in the Paula Jones deposition, or thrown his predicament to the court of public opinion back in January, rather than letting the matter drag on for endless months. He had a survivalist ethic that was focused on maneuvering through whatever circumstances challenged him in the here and now—not on trying to take command of his circumstances in a decisive way.

The president repeated his familiar and heartfelt lament against the "poisonous venom of excessive partisanship, obsessive animosity, and uncontrolled anger," and vowed to stay in his job "until the last hour of the last day of my term." He had rarely spoken more sincerely.

The next two months were a slow-motion drama, to the extent they were a drama at all. The outcome of the Senate trial was never in doubt in any fundamental way. Clinton professed that he was too busy with his work to watch the proceedings, and for the most part this was true, though he got regular briefings and was intimately involved in his defense. Acquittal came on February 12, 1999. The obstruction of justice article was rejected on a vote of 50–50, and the perjury article by 45 to 55—both far from the two thirds necessary to force removal from office. Memorandums from the pollster Mark Penn to the president described the White House strategy as the impeachment ordeal drew to a close. "When we lost the impeachment vote," the pollster told Clinton, "the impeachment 'pep rally' and speech was perfect—it turned a seeming defeat into a victory, catapulting our ratings. The resignation sentiment they hoped to build was totally blunted by the afternoon." Two months later, the political task was different. "The Republicans will have lost and we will be in the position of commenting on our own victory. It is a no-win proposition. . . . We should speak softly and quietly so that the world will be focused on the acquittal, not criticizing our reaction to the acquittal. There is no greater victory than winning itself." A subdued reaction, Penn noted, would "draw out the differences so that resolution of the conflict is again seen as capitulation by the Republican Party."

Two days later, Clinton took this advice. Shortly after the Senate votes, Clinton appeared in the Rose Garden. "Now that the Senate has fulfilled its constitutional responsibility," he said, "bringing this process to a conclusion, I want to say again to the American people how profoundly sorry I am for what I said and did to trigger these events and the great burden they have imposed on the Congress and on the American people." The statement lasted just a minute, and Clinton turned to walk away. From the assembled press corps, the stentorian voice of ABC's Sam Donaldson boomed: "In your heart, sir, can you forgive and forget?" Clinton paused, as if weighing whether to disregard his own plan to take no questions. Then he turned back and spoke once more: "I believe any person who asks for forgiveness has to be prepared to give it."

Section Four

Chapter Thirty-six

KOSOVO

CLINTON SURELY WAS ENTITLED TO A SEASON OF QUIET IN THE WAKE OF his impeachment victory and the tumultuous thirteen months that had come before. He did not get it. Instead, with frightening velocity, a new and quite different crisis was upon him. It was unfolding in a place called Kosovo.

Kosovo is a province of Serbia, still ruled then by the strongman of Belgrade, Slobodan Milosevic. The emergency that sprang upon the Clinton White House in March 1999 had been building in plain view for a year. But the latest problems of the Balkans had occupied a rather small space in the peripheral vision of a president whose gaze had been focused on political survival. Most Americans, whose news had been saturated with the Lewinsky opera, could be forgiven for wondering how it was that the United States was suddenly in a war. But war it was—for seventy-eight days that spring, an ordeal just as intense, and with human consequences that were vastly more far-reaching, than the scandal Clinton had just endured.

War came that spring when Clinton concluded this was the only way to enforce an obscure but long-standing U.S. commitment, dating to the closing days of the Bush administration, to protect Kosovo and its population of ethnic Albanians from aggression by the Serb majority just over the borders of this largely autonomous province. Serbs had deep historic hatreds of Kosovar Albanians, and Belgrade had long coveted direct control of the province, which was filled with religious and cultural landmarks with deep symbolic resonance in Serbian history. Hatred and territorial ambition flowed both ways. The Kosovar Albanians equally loathed ethnic Serbians. The violent and popularly supported Kosovo Liberation Army wanted nothing short of independence, something Washington did not support. The Kosovo problem was replete with parallels with the confrontation Clinton had faced at the beginning of his term in Bosnia. The question now was whether the administration could live up to its pledge to deter a Bosnia-style campaign of ethnic cleansing and slaughter in Kosovo.

The escalation of the Kosovo confrontation during 1998 was still another example of how the administration's energy and attention had been sapped by the Lewinsky scandal. In early March of that year, Serb atrocities in a Kosovo village left dozens of Kosovar Albanians dead. The administration pronounced this unacceptable, and sought to deter Belgrade from further violence with a combination of economic sanctions and negotiations. Several diplomats with long experience in the Balkans, including Madeleine Albright and Richard Holbrooke, warned that this strategy alone was insufficient. Milosevic would respond only to a formal threat of military intervention. NATO ambassador Alexander Vershbow, a veteran foreign service officer who had been heavily involved in Bosnia policy, wrote a long memo in the summer of 1998 urging a push for a comprehensive Dayton-style solution to the Kosovo problem. This would mean putting another international peacekeeping force, with more U.S. troops, on the ground in the Balkans. He found no takers in the White House, where national security officials knew that Clinton had no room for any more problems on his plate. For now, containment of the Kosovo problem was his goal.

By January, however, it had become clear that Kosovo's perils could be ignored no longer. On the fifteenth, while the Senate was busy with opening arguments in Clinton's impeachment trial, Milosevic's security forces broke a ceasefire agreement and killed fifty civilians, including women and children, in a village called Racak. Never again, Clinton had said after the horrors of Rwanda and Bosnia. Did he mean it?

He did. On January 27, Clinton agreed to a vigorous strategy to push toward resolution of the Kosovo problem before it became a full-fledged crisis of ethnic cleansing. Albright would launch negotiations at Rambouillet, France. These negotiations would be carried out with a powerful stick. If Serbia failed to pull back the ground forces it was currently massing around Kosovo and accept a negotiated settlement guaranteeing autonomy for the province, then NATO would forcibly intervene with air strikes against Serbia. (At the same time, the Kosovar Albanians were warned that unless they relinquished dreams of independence and also forswore violence, they would have no NATO protection and would be left to their own fate.) Albright crossed the Atlantic and negotiations began at a turreted fourteenth-century castle nestled in snow-covered woods around Rambouillet. The hope was that this magical environment would produce another breakthrough like the one four years earlier at Dayton. Instead, it produced a stalemate. By late March, Milosevic remained defiant, while his forces continued to build menacingly around Kosovo. The implication was inescapable: The dictator *wanted* a test of wills with Clinton.

On March 20, the Serbian forces swarmed into Kosovo. There was a final sprint by Holbrooke to Belgrade to warn Milosevic that he was guaranteeing a bloody confrontation. He professed indifference. So acting on Clinton's ultimatum, on March 24, NATO war planes began dropping bombs on Serb military targets. It was the start of the first full-fledged war in NATO's fifty-year history. That night Clinton spoke from the Oval Office, with a large map of Serbia on his desk as a visual aid to explain to a largely baffled public what Kosovo was and why it mattered. The Serbs, he explained, had launched "an attack by tanks and artillery on a largely defenseless people whose leaders already have agreed to peace." Noting that genocide had plagued this region before, he implored, "Ending this tragedy is a moral imperative."

In this speech, one could see the shape of a bolder and more purposeful leader. Clinton did not equivocate, as in Bosnia, or avert his gaze, as in Rwanda. This was a different man, tested by experience and more confident in his own judgments. At the same time, the new boldness was still interwoven with the old caution and sensitivity to political risk that was always in Clinton's nature. He made clear that NATO would fight this war from the air only. As for U.S. ground forces, he announced, "I do not intend to put our troops in Kosovo to fight a war."

An air war was most sensible for a variety of reasons. It was safer by far for NATO forces, which made it easier to sustain support for the Kosovo intervention with both a skeptical U.S. Congress and NATO allies, many of whom were deeply anxious about going to war against Serbia. What was unwise, however, was for Clinton to appear in his Oval Office address to be *ruling out* the possibility of ground troops. The effect was to telegraph to Milosevic that there were clear limits to what NATO would do in pursuit of a "moral imperative." If the Serbs could simply wait out the air campaign and wait for NATO's resolve to weaken, the dictator could fairly presume, he might be able to set his own terms for Kosovo.

Another misjudgment became glaringly evident in the opening days of the air war. One rationale for the bombing campaign, as Clinton explained it, was that it would "deter" the Serbs from waging an even more aggressive campaign against the Kosovars. The assumption was that Milosevic, like bullies in other settings, would back down quickly in the face of NATO's show of force. This had been the best guess of the Central Intelligence Agency, and it had been Madeleine Albright's argument in internal deliberations. This assumption proved dead wrong. Far from being deterred, the Serb forces dramatically accelerated their campaign of ethnic cleansing in Kosovo. Within several days, several hundred thousand Kosovars were forcibly expelled from their homes and transported under gunpoint out of Kosovo. Refugee camps in neighboring Albania and Macedonia were quickly swamped. A humanitarian and military catastrophe was in the offing. NATO had laid down promises of protection to Kosovar Albanians and threats of reprisal to Serbs that it lacked the military might to deliver on.

But in these bleak opening days of the Kosovo war Clinton revealed he was a different and much stronger character than the man who took office six years before. In those early years, when events went badly, Clinton would stammer and second-guess his own judgment and others'. He would tell visiting lawmakers that his advisers had given him bad information. Now the old roles were reversed. It was Clinton's foreign policy team—whose members were being pilloried daily in the press and beginning to cast accusing eyes at one another—who had lost confidence. And it was the president who was telling them to take a breath and realize that everything was going to work out in the end. There was no point of having high poll numbers if you were not prepared to spend capital on something like this, he said.

In the Oval Office one morning after a particularly brutal day of news from Kosovo, Clinton looked around the room and "could see fear in the whites of the eyes," as one participant recalled.

"Guys, let's not lose sight of why we did this," the president urged. "Let's not forget what prompted us to do this and who is responsible."

The prospect of failure was very real. So was the poise with which Clinton confronted this prospect and resolved to avoid it.

THAT SPRING *TIME* MAGAZINE PUT THE KOSOVO CONFLICT ON ITS COVER WITH an arresting image. It was Albright, standing on a tarmac wearing a flight jacket and holding a cell phone to her ear. "Madeleine's War," read the headline.

More than Clinton even, the secretary of state had become the public face of the Kosovo intervention. She was the first woman to preside at Foggy Bottom, but her celebrity sprang from her great theatrical presence and charm, which allowed her to dominate a room. Most beguiling of all was her biography. She was not yet two when her family whisked her out of their native Czechoslovakia to escape the Nazi occupation. In America, she had married a newspaper heir, and, while raising her children, began a career in diplomacy. After a jarring divorce that left her well set financially, she turned her Georgetown home into a Democratic foreign policy salon. This history, a flight from fascism and a climb up America's ladders of opportunity, helped inform a deeply idealistic view of America's benevolent role in the world. It was an attitude that many foreign policy traditionalists, including some who now worked under her at the State Department, regarded as naïve. Her admirers believed it gave her voice a deeper timbre. "History is watching us," she told fellow foreign ministers at a conference in Kosovo in London.

Clinton himself put it aptly that spring when he publicly thanked Albright "for being able to redeem the lessons of your life story by standing up for the freedom of the people in the Balkans."

Clinton genuinely was drawn to Albright's life story, and was proud that he had appointed her. Just as genuinely, he found her a difficult woman, and on occasion regretted that he had been pressured into her appointment. In Clinton's view, in internal deliberations Albright was less likely to bring realistic analysis than sententious pronouncements about the morally right course. Clinton vastly preferred solutions over sermons from his own aides. In her public role, Clinton regarded Albright as a strong voice, but also a grandstander. Once she allowed herself to be the star at a ceremony at the Truman Library in Independence, Missouri, to celebrate NATO expansion. A presidential friend and foreign policy adviser told Clinton how curious this seemed—the president should be the one representing the United States at an occasion like this. With some real heat in his voice, Clinton replied, "Madeleine will screw me every time."

Albright might have been the face of the Kosovo intervention, but by no means was she Clinton's most important aide as he executed the policy. That role belonged to a man who enjoyed less publicity but vastly more influence. Sandy Berger was one of the Clinton White House's long-haul players. Berger was himself a shrewdly political man who had known Clinton since the 1970s—long enough to understand the president's idiosyncrasies. When Clinton barked, Berger was comfortable barking right back. When Clinton worried about the political implications of a foreign policy decision, Berger was a sympathetic ear. He had bided his time patiently, albeit with growing frustration, as Tony Lake's loyal deputy in the first term. Now that he had achieved his goal of being national security adviser, managing difficult personalities was still part of his job.

One of those personalities was Albright. She and Berger had been friends for twenty years. In their public postures, they rarely betrayed signs of the traditional tensions between national security advisers and secretaries of state. But those tensions were there, and were often the theme of the half dozen or more phone conversations a day between Berger and Albright. Their relationship was based on mutual affection, but overlaid by bickering and sighs and eye-rolling resentment. She believed, with some cause, that the heavily male team at the White House privately condescended to her and sought to hoard influence at her expense. He believed, with some cause, that she worried as much about massaging her public image and getting on the Sunday talk shows as about the substance of policy.

Berger's credentials in the priesthood of foreign policy intellectuals had themselves been challenged on occasion. He had been a deputy to Lake in the State Department's Policy Planning Staff in the Carter years, but he was more of a speechwriter than a strategist. Most of Berger's career had been as a successful Washington lawyer, with a practice specializing in international trade. This was a fine background for understanding the new world of foreign policy, with its emphasis on commercial markets, but it was not a résumé to impress the elitists. "I really like him," said Henry Kissinger. "But you can't blame a trade lawyer for not being a global strategist."

Clinton and Berger both had reason to resent that remark. They did have a strategy. It was a worldview—different from the one Kissinger and national security traditionalists had espoused—that put a premium on updating and expanding alliances for a post–Cold War world, opening up commercial markets, curbing weapons proliferation, and trying to limit humanitarian catastrophes as long as this could be done at acceptable political and military cost. These spacious themes allowed a lot of room for improvisation. And it was here that Berger was superbly well equipped for his job. He worked inhuman hours, arriving at the White House by 7 a.m. and staying invariably to 9:30 or 10 p.m. and often much later. He was a worrywart, by temperament and legal training, and he immersed himself in virtually every problem, large and small alike, that moved through the sprawling National Security Council bureaucracy beneath him. He was an intelligent and good-hearted man, though sometimes a short-tempered one. All of this, combined with his intimate rapport with Clinton, had made him the most powerful national security adviser since Kissinger in the Nixon White House. The top foreign policy advisers called themselves the "ABC Club," for Albright, Berger, and Cohen. No one inside the State Department or Pentagon or White House doubted that it was Berger who was the dominant member.

It was Berger who crafted the composite policy on Kosovo that emerged from the ABC Club's deliberations. While Albright brought aggressive instincts, pushing always for the most robust intervention and wanting a revocation of the no-ground-troops pledge, Cohen reflected the Pentagon's usual reluctance to commit its forces, particularly in humanitarian ventures. Berger shared Secretary of State Albright's moralism and Defense Secretary Cohen's caution. By April, several weeks into the air war, ground troops remained off the table, at Berger's insistence, even as there was precious little evidence that the air campaign was achieving the war's stated objectives. Clinton's policy continued to reflect a paradoxical mix of lofty aims pursued with limited means.

IN THE THIRD WEEK OF APRIL, WASHINGTON PLAYED HOST TO AN EVENT THAT was originally conceived of as a celebration: the fiftieth anniversary of NATO. Instead of a party, heads of state from across Europe arrived for a war council. Allied confidence was justifiably shaken by the poor course of the Kosovo intervention so far. But there were serious splits between nations about what to do.

Tony Blair, who approached the crisis with the same crusading instincts as Albright, was agitating with rising impatience for NATO to prove its will to win. That meant preparing for a possible ground invasion of Serbia. On the other hand, Germany's newly elected chancellor, Gerhard Schroeder, was warning that his government would likely fall if NATO pursued a ground option. His public was already deeply ambivalent about NATO waging an air war, even for laudable purposes. It was more than domestic politics that caused Clinton to avoid committing U.S. ground troops; he was caught in the crosscurrents of deeply contradictory views within the alliance.

Remarkably, Clinton was enjoying these crosscurrents. He was again liberated by his central insight into foreign policy: It was just like domestic politics, but in a different forum. As leaders descended on Washington, Clinton was working them as if he was trying to pass an education bill in the Arkansas legislature.

Blair, who had been having almost daily phone conversations with Clinton, was the first to arrive in Washington. Their meeting at the White House was unusually tense. Two years before, at their first Downing Street meeting in 1997, it was the similarities of the two men that had been so striking: two young leaders, both tugging progressive parties into a more modern era. Now, the crisis had put their differences in sharp relief. Blair valued action and clarity of purpose; Clinton, flexibility and consensus. As the stakes rose in the Kosovo crisis, the two men viewed each other with mounting frustration. While still close to the president, after two years in office Blair was no longer willing to play the subordinate to Clinton. Nor was the prime minister so flush with admiration. As he watched the American equivocate on whether he would commit the political and military resources to guarantee victory, he began to understand why some people regarded Clinton as an unreliable leader. For his part, Clinton was irked by Blair's impatience. It should have been obvious to Blair, Clinton thought, how delicate relationships in the alliance were. In their White House meeting, Clinton implored the prime minister to give it time. Air strikes might yet make a ground intervention unnecessary, he reasoned, and in the meantime the paramount goal had to be allied unity. We can't let Milosevic wait us out and divide NATO, Clinton said.

Later, Clinton met with the prime minister of Spain, José María Aznar López, in the White House residence. The conversation offered a vivid glimpse into how Clinton had come to excel at massaging his relationships on the world stage. In this case, Clinton's goal was to prevent French president Jacques Chirac from disrupting the NATO summit, as was his wont, with a grandstanding French proposal for resolving the Kosovo conflict. Clinton knew that Chirac had been enlisting other European leaders. Gleefully, the president suggested lines for Aznar that could show sympathy for Chirac but keep him at bay. "You tell him, 'These damn Americans! They won't give me any room to breathe. I'm sorry, Jacques, I can't be with you.' "

Clinton's energetic maneuvering at the NATO summit—insisting that hawks like Blair agree to keep faith with the bombing campaign, while also keeping dovish nations like Germany from losing nerve and seeking a premature compromise with Milosevic—was a masterpiece of diplomacy. The week ended with the alliance intact, if precariously united in strategy for Kosovo.

All nineteen nations agreed to a resolution in support of the air war, and declaring to Serbia that no action short of withdrawal from Kosovo was acceptable. Artful diplomacy, however, could not make up for the failure, so far, of the military campaign. Serb forces remained inside Kosovo; a million Kosovar Albanians remained outside, in refugee camps. The allied bombing had grown more aggressive. It was no longer aimed principally at Serb military forces in Kosovo; instead, the target list steadily expanded to include bridges, power plants, military headquarters, and other strategic locations across Serbia, especially in the capital, Belgrade. A more robust campaign had its perils. On May 7, NATO accidentally bombed the Chinese embassy in Belgrade, killing three Chinese citizens. The bombers had hit the building they intended, but outdated CIA maps did not show that the building was no longer a Serbian military office. Clinton was appalled that such an egregious error could be committed by the world's most technologically advanced military. He tried to call Chinese premier Jiang Zemin to apologize, but for several days Jiang would not even accept his call. For the moment, it looked as if Clinton's carefully plotted march to a more cooperative relationship with China would be a victim of Kosovo. Meanwhile, Milosevic remained defiant. He did indeed believe he could wait out NATO—and Clinton, too.

If Clinton was going to prove Milosevic wrong, it was increasingly obvious that he needed to acknowledge that Blair had been right. The insertion of ground troops into Kosovo, once unthinkable, would have to be put on the table. After weeks of agonizing internal debate, Clinton announced a dramatic policy shift almost as an aside during a brief exchange with reporters. "I and everyone else has always said that we intend to see our objectives achieved and that we have not and will not take any option off the table." Characteristically, the White House insisted that this important reversal actually represented no change at all. At the same time, Clinton was of no mind to give any nod to Blair for his prescience on this key question. Instead, a few hours later, the two leaders had their most difficult conversation ever. Clinton was furious that the British had been openly advertising their position in favor of the ground troop option in the American papers, and not so subtly underscoring the weakness of the U.S. position. Clinton had reason to be sensitive. Both public polls and Mark Penn's surveys showed that the American public was losing confidence in Clinton's handling of the war. A majority, however, did not want escalation—they preferred an immediate negotiated settlement. Clinton was losing the war, and his public; the last thing he needed was his closest ally shooting spitballs at him from across the Atlantic. After clearing the air over the media question, the two settled into a tense discussion of strategy that lasted hours. While ground troops were on the table, Clinton said, they still were not the right option. Blair reminded him that a ground operation might take several months to be successful. If they did not move soon, then the first autumn snows would be falling in the mountainous Balkans before a NATO victory was at hand—inviting a serious humanitarian crisis for refugees living in open-air tents, and making an already dangerous military venture much more complicated. Preparations for ground troops needed to begin immediately. Only at the end of the conversation was a sense of common cause regained. In a tone that conveyed both defiance and reassurance, Clinton told Blair, "Let's be clear about one thing. We're not going to lose."

THE PRESIDENT NEEDED TO SEND THIS MESSAGE NOT ONLY TO BLAIR, BUT down through his own administration, which remained sharply divided on the question of ground troops. Albright continued to press hard for any means to victory. She was joined in this by the nation's top military commander in Europe, General Wesley Clark, the supreme allied commander at NATO headquarters outside Brussels. Clark was an Arkansas native who had known Clinton casually for years. Brilliant and highly ambitious, Clark had a legion of critics within the army who regarded him as vainglorious and opportunistic—a latter-day Douglas MacArthur. But Clark was a favorite at the White House, where he kept in touch regularly with senior officials throughout the Kosovo war. These back-channel communications only increased the commander's friction with his superiors at the Pentagon. Defense Secretary William Cohen, reflecting the institutional skepticism of most of the military, was deeply wary of expanding the Kosovo commitment. It fell as usual to Berger to resolve this bureaucratic tussle, all the while trying to discern Clinton's calculus of risks: What costs was he really prepared to bear?

Berger well knew the hazards. The military planning had made clear the ground troop option was going to be costly and dangerous, far beyond anything the American public had been prepared to expect. For instance, it turned out NATO tanks were too wide to fit in the maze of mountain road tunnels in Kosovo. American forces would be fighting a Serb army on its own territory. Casualties would be in the thousands, far exceeding what the armed forces had incurred in the 1991 Persian Gulf War. Yet if Clinton meant what he said—anything short of victory was unacceptable—this was the path before him. In early June, Clinton resolved to start down it. Berger, at the president's instruction, recommended an immediate deployment of 100,000 American troops to the Balkans, in preparation for invasion.

Here, as if by some mysterious cycle in Clinton's life, was when fortune broke his way. After weeks of defiant resolve, Milosevic buckled in early June. To the surprise of the administration and its allies, the Serbian dictator yielded to NATO's demands for a withdrawal from Kosovo and the arrival of an international peacekeeping force in the province. The war was over. The previous three months had been harrowing, and hardly a textbook exercise in military strategy. "Winning ugly" is how military scholars Ivo Daalder and Michael O'Hanlon described the Kosovo episode. But if Clinton's victory was not a thing of beauty, neither was it simply a stroke of good luck. For most of the bombing campaign, Milosevic had enjoyed the sympathies of Russia, historically an ally of Serbia. Boris Yeltsin had been so appalled by what he regarded as NATO's illegitimate war that for weeks he refused even to take Clinton's calls. But the careful bridge-building that the Clinton administration had pursued over two terms with Yeltsin's Russia paid dividends. In the end, the Russian leader made clear his nascent relationship with the West was more important than his grievances over Kosovo. He appointed his prime minister, Viktor Chernomyrdin, to negotiate the details of an ultimatum that NATO and Russia jointly presented to Serbia. Milosevic folded only after realizing the full extent of his isolation. Clinton's victory, no matter how ugly, reflected his own seasoning as a leader and the fruition of a strategy for cooperatively engaging the world that he had begun seven years earlier.

Chapter Thirty-seven

EMPIRE STATE

IN THE MIDST OF BILL CLINTON'S WORST YEAR IN OFFICE, THERE HAD BEEN flashes of a bright future awaiting Hillary Rodham Clinton.

In the summer of 1998, a few weeks before the president's grand jury testimony, she toured upstate New York as part of a campaign to promote historic preservation. The reception was more like those of her overseas travels. Thousands awaited her appearance in the small town of Auburn, in New York's Finger Lakes region, when she visited the Harriet Tubman house. The next day, on a sweltering morning in Seneca Falls, the crowd was even larger to hear the first lady mark the anniversary of the Women's Rights Convention held there 150 years earlier. The modern generation of women, she implored, needed to "finish the work" of feminist pioneers like Susan B. Anthony and Elizabeth Cady Stanton.

From the moment she moved to Arkansas, Hillary Clinton had experienced a persistent paradox. One of the most ambitious and intelligent women of her generation, she stirred her greatest controversy when she tried to give expression to those traits; she received her greatest public acclaim when she played the loyal wife who persevered to keep her dignity and marriage intact in the face of her husband's disloyalties.

That upstate tour had been the first indication that she might finally be able to marry the public adoration and her personal feminism as a senator from New York, the Empire State. The idea at first blush seemed absurd—running for office in a place she had never lived. But one unexpected consequence of the Lewinsky humiliation and the public sympathy it engendered was that the first lady had at last been liberated to pursue her own political career independent of her husband's.

The juxtaposition was even more obvious on February 12, 1999—the same day the Senate acquitted the president in his impeachment trial. All that day, she had been meeting with her old friend Harold Ickes, their conversation in the White House residence interrupted by occasional reports on the latest vote tallies. Ickes's account with the Clintons was the same as ever: the man to deliver hard truths. With both of them, Ickes had always enjoyed license to express unvarnished opinions of the sort that less familiar advisers would dare not utter. On this occasion, the first lady had summoned Ickes, a New Yorker, for an appraisal of what it would take to successfully run in New York. In his usual blunt fashion, Ickes laid out all the problems. For all the public sympathy that had accrued to her during impeachment, there was no telling what the backlash would be once she actually began running in a state where she had not lived. One had to assume the carpetbagger factor would be formidable, he warned, and possibly insurmountable. Then there was Hillary herself. "You might not be any good as a candidate," Ickes warned. He reminded her that as a candidate she would have to deal regularly with reporters. The first lady took the advice as dispassionately as he gave it. Her deliberations about running would continue for weeks more, but during the session with Ickes the main current of her thinking was obvious: She was going to run.

Among those most surprised, and troubled, by this were her closest aides. The first lady's chief of staff and old friend, Melanne Verveer, had urged her not to. So did Verveer's predecessor, Maggie Williams, who remained a close confidante. Hillary Clinton was already an international figure, with a voice and reputation that carried around the world, they reasoned. Why plunge into partisan politics, especially in a race that she could conceivably lose? Several people who raised objections felt a chill from her that lingered long after their conversations. It was clear she was looking for people to give her reasons to get to yes, and she seemed impatient and even dismissive of those who were repeating the reasons to say no. Still, the loyal sorority that made up the first lady's circle remained full of foreboding. No one who really cares about you, Williams pleaded, wants you to do this.

There was a prominent exception. Bill Clinton was enthralled with the idea of his wife in the Senate. Always in awe of her abilities, he had thought she belonged there from the first days of their relationship. Beyond that, in the wake of the Lewinsky ordeal, in the long-running balance sheet of their relationship he was now deeply in debt. Whatever she wanted, he wanted. A few days after the Ickes meeting, reporters covering his state visit to Mexico asked him about her potential candidacy, an idea that in public was still being treated like a lark. The president enthused, "She would be great if she did it."

BY JULY SHE WAS UNABASHEDLY RUNNING. THE 2000 ELECTION PROMISED A titanic clash, pitting arguably the planet's most famous woman against the larger-than-life mayor of New York City, Rudolph Giuliani. Her announcement of a statewide "listening tour," an obvious preface to a candidacy, was remarkable in part for where it occurred: at Moynihan's farm upstate in Pindars Corners. There had been no love lost between the senator and the Clintons over the previous seven years, and Moynihan's wife, Liz, who was the senator's political majordomo, had even less affection for the Clintons. Yet Moynihan also had a sense of history and vanity alike about his Senate seat, which had previously been held by another newcomer to New York, Robert F. Kennedy. He believed his seat should be held by a large and consequential figure. Hillary Clinton certainly qualified. Moreover, he knew the political world would be watching and judging him by what he did to help her. Still, he could not muzzle all his ambivalence. In an interview about her candidacy, he sang her praises by noting the "Illinois-Arkansas enthusiasm" she would bring to the Senate—not exactly helpful words for a candidate facing accusations of carpetbagging.

The moment it was clear she was running, public sympathy for her as a loyal and long-suffering political wife curdled in an instant into skepticism about her motives. What looked like loyalty in 1998 now looked to many like opportunism. And so the other contradiction: A candidacy Hillary Clinton hoped would give her a political base of her own, independent from her husband, was, for the moment, inextricably linked to him. This prompted questions that had little to do with her Senate qualifications, but everything to do with who she was as a person: What was it that kept the two of them together?

This question seemed to weigh especially on women. Mark Penn's polls in

New York showed her running lower than historic voting patterns with the women's vote, which in turn was causing her to underperform with Democrats generally. Interviews and focus groups made it clear the reservations were not political but personal: Women simply did not understand what made Hillary Clinton tick, and remained deeply skeptical about her marriage and her motives in coming to New York.

This was the subject on the table in the White House residence during a political meeting at which the president, now playing the role of campaign consultant, was vigorously participating. Perusing the polling data, he turned to his wife and observed, "Women want to know why you stayed with me."

There was an awkward pause in the room. Marital troubles were not the usual stuff of campaign skull sessions. But Hillary Clinton did not seem embarrassed. Instead, a half smile crossed her face. "Yes," she responded. "I've been wondering that myself."

The president gave his answer: "Because you're a sticker! That's what people need to know—you are a sticker. You stick at the things you care about."

THIS WAS TRUE. PERSEVERANCE WAS AMONG HER MOST ADMIRABLE TRAITS, AS it was his. But it only partly answered the mystery: Why did she stick with him through so many trials? What was the glue?

Even the cynics in the Clinton fold almost invariably arrived in the end at the same noncynical answer: She loved him, and felt loved by him in return. Over the course of a decade covering the Clintons, one found very few people who worked or socialized closely with them who did not in the end believe this. Their marriage, like many enduring marriages, was built on romance. That they had a genuine love affair did not mean, of course, they had a conventional one. It was exotic in its passions and daily routines. Bill Clinton and Hillary Rodham Clinton shared a powerful love of politics, and they loved also the sense of shared mission that a career together in public service gave them. In important ways, politics was the heat for this relationship—and never more so than in 1999 and 2000.

Her Senate campaign provided a project upon which they could rebuild their marriage and remind themselves anew what it was that drew them to each other. They had been happiest together when they had separate endeavors, and unhappiest, as on overseas trips, when ceremony or public expectations forced her to play a secondary role to him. Now, they were like a couple that had separated. She was on the road in New York most nights; they might get an evening a week together. Yet the affection between them was more evident than it had been in years. She lit up when he called her while she was on the road. Her draft speech texts would fly back and forth between New York and Washington.

"B—what do you think of this?" she would write at the top.

He would fill up the margins with comments and suggested edits, and at the end write a note: "I love you, B."

This melding of work and giggly banter suggested the dynamic that propelled their marriage. Maggie Williams once tried to explain it to a dumbfounded Ickes. Hillary was a more traditional girl than people realized, Williams said. She'd been the hard-working class brain with thick glasses, with a crush on the most popular boy in the class.

The relationship, by some reckonings, rested on mutual astonishment. He truly believed that she was a better and smarter person than anyone else he had ever known—more committed, more passionate, more idealistic. She truly believed that he was the most impressive leader of his generation—a handsome and energetic man with a gift at human connection that to her mind was beyond comprehension. Paul Begala told friends he had figured out the secret of their relationship: Hillary and Bill both looked at each other and could not believe that the other person had married someone so undeserving.

Ickes, in fact, felt certain that her appreciation for her husband grew during this period. There were certain things he was good at—getting up in front of a crowd at the end of a fourteen-hour day, walking off a stage into a throng of reporters—that she had come to take for granted over the years. She told Ickes: "I never realized how good Bill was at this until I tried to do it."

She was good, too—eventually.

At the beginning, she was a novice candidate with a problem that no office-seeker had ever confronted: how to handle a controversy-generating spouse who happened to be president. There were clumsy moments. He issued clemency to sixteen convicted Puerto Rican terrorists, apparently out of a belief that this would help her with a critical Empire State constituency. The move backfired with a barrage of negative publicity, prompting her to repudiate the president's action and assert that they had never discussed the matter before—despite her claim in an interview that "we talk in the solarium, in the bedroom, in the kitchen; it's just constant conversation."

As 1999 turned to 2000, she learned to avoid these kinds of stumbles. More than that, she began to show actual grace on the campaign trail. She no longer avoided the press pack, as she had in the White House years, or seethed at their impertinent questions. She faced the supposedly fearsome New York press corps daily, and handled the encounters well. There was likewise an interesting change in her interaction with crowds. For her, large audiences demanded an emotional and physical energy that left her depleted. Bill Clinton was the rare person who actually drew energy from crowds. During the White House years, when the Clintons appeared onstage with each other, she would usually retreat to the limousine and wait—sometimes for an hour or more—while he hopped down from the stage and shook hands. In New York, however, she, too, learned the art of working a rope line—perhaps not with his ease, but with striking results even so. The results were most dramatic in upstate New York. This was historically Republican territory, but with nearly constant visits she was soon running nearly even with Giuliani here. This was partly a reflection of the mayor's snobbery; he did not like leaving the city for the upstate backwaters. But it was even more a reflection of her gift at human connection. People in the economically dying small towns of rural New York, as well as in the decaying industrial cities like Buffalo, appreciated the attention of a bona fide celebrity, and she soon managed to convince them that her interest was genuine.

Once, her loyal aide Patti Solis Doyle exclaimed, "You could be in Paris! Why do you want to go to Poughkeepsie?"

"I like Poughkeepsie," she responded, with feeling.

As she grew more comfortable, there was a subtle reversal of roles between the Clintons. She still cared about his advice, but was becoming less dependent on it. Accustomed to thinking he knew the most when it came to politics, the president did not realize at first that he was becoming something of a fifth wheel in his wife's campaign. "He just did not understand what was going on as well as she did, and so at times his presence was more of a nuisance," recalled a close political adviser to her. "Sometimes there would be a political meeting scheduled at the White House when she was home on weekends, and we'd all roll our eyes and stall and say, 'Let's just have it in New York.' It's not that he wasn't brilliant; it's just that what he had to say was less relevant."

This seemed to pain him a bit, but he took it manfully. In May 2000, as she was to speak to the Democratic nominating convention in Albany, her campaign was paralyzed for days over the question of what to do with the president. At one level, it would be a lot easier if he would stay home: Presidents have a way of overshadowing everything. The decision was made and he accepted it, with obvious disappointment. Only the day before the event did Hillary Clinton change her mind. She wanted him there. Howard Wolfson, her steady, taciturn press secretary, had encouraged the reversal. In any normal marriage, of course, the spouse would be present for a partner's big day. It looked weird for Clinton to be absent. It's a rare event for a president to get on a public stage and say nothing, but that was what happened.

Whether he spoke or not, the fact was that her campaign was made in his image. This surprised some people close to her. Many of them had believed that the two of them represented distinct poles in the Clinton enterprise. In this formulation, she was the ideologue, eager to win but motivated principally by the higher cause. He was the compromiser, eager to do good but motivated principally by the imperative of victory. The New York race revealed that, after eight years in the White House and the debacle of the health care reform effort, her brand of politics was in spirit and practice the same as his. She was a liberal, though not a liberal crusader. Like her husband, she placed pollster Mark Penn at the center of her operation, and practiced a steely brand of centrist politics that was designed to advance progressivism but do so in modest steps. After eight years in Washington, she had become ever alert to the perils of overreach.

One way that she was not like her husband was in how she responded to the rigors of political combat. Criticism might make him indignant in the moment, but he regarded it as part of the game; he was resilient. She, however, was sensitive. Beneath a tough exterior, criticism was personal and painful to her. During one sordid moment in summer 2000, a character from the president's Arkansas past surfaced, leveling charges of anti-Semitic utterances by Hillary Clinton. The alleged episode was more than a quarter century old, from Clinton's unsuccessful 1974 campaign for Congress. Hillary Rodham, not yet married to Clinton, supposedly hurled the epithets at a campaign staff aide in an argument. An angry dressing-down was certainly plausible; crude religious epithets were not. After denying them heatedly in public, she privately began to sob to an aide, "Why do I keep having to prove to people that I am not a liar?"

She pushed on. Her perseverance, along with some good luck, had produced a remarkable effect. A campaign that was supposed to be high drama had become almost boring. A bout with prostate cancer and a slew of personal and political problems had persuaded Giuliani to drop out of the race almost at the last minute. No longer a battle of titans, the race now featured Hillary Clinton, running a cautious by-the-numbers campaign, against a pleasant but hardly commanding congressman from Long Island, Rick Lazio. Voters faced a choice between a large and controversial Democrat and a bland and life-size Republican. At least in a state like New York, with its clear Democratic tilt, such a contest favored Hillary Clinton.

She grasped control of the race for good one September evening in Buffalo. It was the first televised debate between her and Lazio. Buffalo native Tim Russert, the NBC newsman, was on hand to moderate. It was a crackling evening of charge and countercharge, of the conventional political sort, when Russert took the debate in a personal direction. He recalled the day, nearly three years back, when she had blamed the newly erupted Lewinsky scandal on a "vast right-wing conspiracy." Since the Lewinsky allegations had turned out to be true, he asked her, did she regret having misled the nation? Seemingly taken aback by the bluntness of the question, she grabbed a breath and slowly and deliberately answered. "That was a very painful time for me, my family, and our country," she said. "Obviously, I didn't mislead anyone; I didn't know the truth. Obviously, there's a great deal of pain involved with that."

Lazio thought he had an opening. Her conduct before and answers after, he said, revealed how she believed "it only matters when you get caught," and reflected a penchant for "blaming others every time . . . when you have responsibility."

But this moment was not an opening for Lazio; it was a trap. His taunts, and Russert's effrontery, had delighted the throng of reporters covering the debate in a large holding room adjacent to the studio but caused a backlash with actual voters. While Russert asked the question that many New Yorkers were curious about, that did not mean they wanted it asked in a televised debate. Hillary Clinton came off the stage nervous, and uncertain of how she did. Within minutes, Penn's instant polls showed that she had won overwhelmingly, particularly with women voters. The evening was the past three years in microcosm: She prospered by maintaining dignity in the face of humiliation.

A little after 11 p.m. she was on the phone to the White House. Clinton had been watching the debate on cable television. "You did great!" he told her.

Chapter Thirty-eight

"AL JUST NEEDS TO BE HIMSELF"

ON THE DAY THE HOUSE OF REPRESENTATIVES IMPEACHED BILL CLINton, in December 1998, Al Gore joined his boss and a large delegation of congressional Democrats on the White House South Lawn and uttered perhaps the day's most memorable words. The vice president said he was proud to stand with a "man I believe will be regarded in the history books as one of our greatest presidents."

For nearly seven years, Gore had never flashed a public hint—and only rarely private ones—that this was not exactly what he believed. He expressed loyalty in the same way he expressed other values important to him: with emphatic certitude.

The exaggerated affect with which Gore dispatched the obligations of the vice presidency only heightened the curiosity. What did this discreet and self-contained man really think about the president he served with such deference? There were, once in a while, fleeting glimpses that suggested he might harbor more complex feelings about the man who had placed him in his job.

Clinton, for his part, was irritated by Gore's chronic neediness and inflexibility over the routine business of politics, such as public schedules and agency appointments. "That is just like Al Gore—just like Al Gore!" Clinton fumed one day late in the first term as Gore was angling to install more of his loyalists in jobs. Gore would have the presidency to himself soon enough, Clinton complained, but he wanted it all now. "We are going to have real problems with him in the second term, I'll tell you that."

In his own way, Gore had been plotting a path to the presidency for much of his adult life, just as Clinton had. Now he had concluded that the biggest obstacle in that path was Clinton himself.

GORE HAD SEEN POLLING THAT TO HIS MIND SHOWED IRREFUTABLY THAT PUBlic disdain over Clinton's conduct in the Lewinsky affair, and his ethics generally, was creating a serious headwind for Gore's own candidacy. He found the surveys on public discomfort with Clinton entirely plausible. They mirrored the feelings he found in his own family, where his wife and daughters in particular had been disgusted by 1998's year of scandal. Moreover, after seven years of discretion and self-discipline, Gore was no longer of a mind to contain his own real feelings. It was as if an inner dam had burst.

At one skull session with his advisers, Gore noted the long-standing public doubts about Clinton's character and gave his appraisal of the political dynamic between them. "In 1992, I provided the moral energy for Clinton to win," he said. "This year, he's sapping the moral energy of my campaign."

There was an irony in Gore's predicament, though he was in no mood to appreciate it. By the spring of 1999, polls showed that a majority of the public, and certainly most Democrats, were eager to move on from the Lewinsky obsession—if not necessarily to forgive, certainly to forget, and to accept Clinton for what he was: an imperfect but talented man. Gore was more judgmental, and more mired in the past, than the voters he brooded over.

This is not to say that the vice president was imagining the Clinton problem. A critical portion of culturally conservative independent voters, people any national Democrat needs to win election, were indeed angry with Clinton and inclined to take it out on Gore. It was a genuine problem, but one a politician like Clinton could have dispatched easily. For a less nimble politician like Gore, the problem was almost paralyzing. It should not have been so hard for him to declare that he was running on the policy record of the previous eight years and his own platform for the next four, while inviting voters to judge his character on its own, not in the shadow of Clinton. But Gore oddly came to believe that to embrace any part of the Clinton record was to embrace all of it.

Clinton was in Europe at the time Gore officially launched his presidential campaign with an announcement in his hometown of Carthage, Tennessee. The speech was laced with references to personal values that seemed by implication an indictment of Clinton: "I say to every parent in America: It is our own lives we must master if we are to have the moral authority to guide our children." If his subtlety was lost on anyone, Gore made it explicit in an interview with Tennessee reporters in which he recalled "that awful year we went through. . . . I felt what the president did, especially as a parent, was inexcusable."

In his Paris hotel suite, Clinton had gotten word of Gore's comments from his traveling staff. He was angry—and incredulous. "What is this about?" he boomed. He calmed down a few minutes later and placed a call to Gore. Making no mention of his irritations, Clinton said he had watched a replay of the announcement speech. "Nice job!" he said.

Then, putting down the phone, he returned to his mystification at Gore's efforts to put distance between them. "I don't get it," Clinton said. "Is this some kind of strategy? What the hell is this about?"

IN PART, IT WAS ABOUT THE PARADOX OF THE VICE PRESIDENCY. THROUGH much of American history, the job had been a backwater, occupied by a parade of historical obscurities. In the twentieth century, however, it had transformed into the principal launching pad to the presidency itself. Since World War II, five vice presidents had become president (Truman, Nixon, Johnson, Ford, and Bush) and three more missed but managed at least to secure their party's presidential nominations (Hubert Humphrey, Walter Mondale, and Gore). Yet the office also had a diminishing effect on its occupants, who were regularly humiliated by the presidents they served and at the very least were seen in the public as servants rather than masters of their own fate. Clinton never sought to humiliate Gore, as Lyndon Johnson did Humphrey. Indeed, he relied on Gore and gave him more substantive influence than any vice president had ever before enjoyed. Even so, Gore continued the historic pattern: He seemed a less vibrant, less self-confident, and, most of all, less independent figure at the end of his tenure. Years of self-effacing service had taken a powerful emotional and political toll.

Like most people who worked closely with Clinton, Gore was impressed by his energy and intelligence and broad good intentions, even if sometimes erratically executed. Moreover, as someone who in 1988 had sought the presidency and failed, Gore had as keen an appreciation as anyone else of Clinton's political skills. For Clinton's part, he genuinely liked Gore and wished him well. But the two men had not become personal intimates over the course of seven years. When a Gore aide once remarked about an evening of movies the Clintons had hosted in the White House theater, Gore had said coolly, "They have never once invited us."

Under other circumstances, these small fissures would have remained inconsequential. In the wake of the Lewinsky scandal, they became glaring. By 2000, Gore's travel meant that he and Clinton often went weeks at a time without seeing each other. When they were together, Gore seemed to physically shrivel in Clinton's presence.

An especially awkward episode occurred one evening at a fund-raiser in New York City, a Democratic double billing featuring both the Clintons and the Gores. For big-dollar donors, there was a small reception before the main event at which the couples were scheduled to appear. At the last minute, there was a crisis. Tipper Gore announced that she would not attend. She was of appealing vivacity and charm, but in some moods the vice president's wife could be a fearsome presence. Gore's staff learned to walk on tiptoes around her. A staff hand tried to gently remind her that donors were waiting. She was not especially fond of Hillary Clinton, and now refused even to be in the president's presence.

"No, I'm not doing it," she snapped at an aide. "I'm not going out there with that man."

The vice president, in anguish, realized she meant it. He went to the reception by himself. When it was over, the Clintons and both Gores spoke to a larger audience in a hotel ballroom. The president entertained the crowd with his usual polish, gushing with superlatives for his vice president. But when Gore took the podium, his words were slow, lifeless, and meandering. One felt the room grow limp. When it was over, Democrats in the crowd were whispering to themselves, asking what was wrong with Gore. The answer was that Clinton's very presence imposed a psychic burden on him that was a major hidden factor in the politics of 2000.

CLINTON WAS MYSTIFIED BY WHAT HE REGARDED AS GORE'S POLITICAL CLUMSINESS. Routine political tasks that for Clinton required no more effort than breathing or blinking—dodging a curveball question at a news conference or warming up a crowd of Democrats—were a heavy lift for the vice president.

Back in 1992, in the bright first light of their partnership, it was the similarities that were most striking: They were young, intelligent, moderate southern Democrats. It was by now clear that their differences were more numerous and profound. Gore was a vastly more complex public figure than Clinton.

One reason that Clinton found it easy to speak in public was that he was essentially a transparent man. There was a narrow difference between the man at the podium and the man with his shoes off and feet up on Air Force One. Clinton in private was surely more expressive, more profane, but the opinions and perspective he expressed were the same in both settings. Clinton was, by the standards of politicians, free of artifice.

In his frustration with Gore's awkward performances, Clinton would say to friends like Terry McAuliffe, and even to Gore's campaign operatives, that "Al just needs to be himself." It was not so easy as that. Gore, for all his moderate Democrat packaging, had the intellectual instincts of a radical. He had revealed himself as such in his environmental tract, *Earth in the Balance*. He had written the book in 1991 at a time when he was not calculating presidential politics, and indeed had grown contemptuous of what he described in its pages as his own tendency to be a "finger-in-the-wind" politician. There was a utopian streak to his mind, manifested in the book's calls to banish the internal combustion engine and to make environmentalism the "new guiding principle for civilization."

If Gore had spent a career just being himself and saying what he really thought, he never would have made it into office in Tennessee, much less to the vice presidency.

CLINTON MEANT WELL WITH HIS ADVICE. WHEN IT CAME TO HELPING OTHERS, he was an uncommonly generous politician—certainly by the standards of presidents, who historically have not been notably helpful to vice presidents trying to succeed them. Dwight Eisenhower, when asked in 1960 about Richard Nixon's contributions to his administration, answered, "If you give me a week I might think of one." Lyndon B. Johnson scarcely lifted a finger to help Hubert H. Humphrey in 1968. Ronald Reagan lifted a finger, but no more than that, to help George H. W. Bush. Clinton, however, genuinely believed that Gore had been the best vice president in history, and would have done anything to make Gore his successor.

Clinton's reputation for political selfishness was a consequence of the necessary steps he had taken in 1995 and 1996 to put distance between himself and congressional Democrats. But the reputation was in the main unfair. Long after he had raised enough money for himself, the president kept up a punishing schedule of evening and out-of-town fund-raisers to help the Democratic National Committee and all manner of other party candidates. He wanted nothing more than to hit the campaign trail on Gore's behalf. All Gore wanted Clinton to do was go away.

Ordinarily a perceptive man, the president was nearly the last person to see the reality that his relationship with Gore was broken. When his own West Wing advisers fumed about Gore, Clinton always made excuses for him. Gore's strategists were the problem, Clinton would say, adding that they had embraced a bogus notion that voters suffered from "Clinton fatigue." He would not accept the fact that Gore himself was rejecting Clinton, for reasons that were personal as well as political.

Clinton's interest in the matter, of course, was not completely selfless. He wanted Gore to run on the Clinton record—job growth, deficit reduction, environmental enforcement—and believed that the vice president's election would be an important validation of his own legacy. He was genuinely stumped that Gore would not do so, and blind to the fact that for some voters Gore needed to reach, the Clinton legacy was more about personal failings than public accomplishments. Clinton had long been worried about the election. Watching cable television early in 1999, he had seen Texas governor George W. Bush speak to a group of Republicans. Bush was laboring under a reputation for being a lightweight, but Clinton instantly recognized a formidable politician. As he saw it, Bush's promise of "compassionate conservatism" was a brilliant formulation. It was a way of taking the old right-wing agenda and dressing it up so that it sounded like something Bill Clinton would say—high praise indeed in the president's book.

In the summer of 2000, as the problems between him and Gore became too obvious to ignore, Clinton tried to patch things up. Run on the record, he urged, and stop worrying about Clinton fatigue. "Al, there's not a single person in this country that thinks you messed around with Monica Lewinsky," he said.

On another occasion, he tried to make light of things. If it would help, Clinton said, he would be delighted to stand on the front step of the *Washington Post* and let him "lash me with a bullwhip."

"Maybe we ought to poll that," Gore replied. For a moment, the old banter between them returned.

It was not, however, enough to heal the rift. If Clinton had trouble seeing this, his wife did not. In August, Gore chose as his running mate Senator Joseph Lieberman of Connecticut. Clinton had known Lieberman since he campaigned for him during his days at Yale, and both were leaders in the New Democrat movement to remake the party. Nationally, however, Lieberman was most famous as a Clinton critic. He had been the first and most vocal to denounce Clinton's conduct as "immoral" in the wake of the Lewinsky confession.

White House press secretary Joe Lockhart walked in on the Clintons on the day Gore announced his choice. What do you think? the president asked.

"I think it's a way of saying 'screw you' to Bill Clinton," he replied.

A look of satisfaction crossed Hillary Clinton's face. "I'm glad someone agrees with me," she said.

The president would hear none of it. "No, no, you're wrong," he said. "It's a great choice."

Chapter Thirty-nine

SPRING TERM

IT HAD BEEN A TRUISM OF MODERN PRESIDENCIES THAT THEY DO NOT END well. The Oval Office occupants in Clinton's own lifetime were a parade of tragedy and defeat. Truman left the presidency a despised man. Kennedy was killed, Johnson crushed, Ford and Carter both soundly defeated. Even Reagan by the end was drifting into senescence, and Bush was staggering from forces he neither anticipated nor understood.

In late 1999 and 2000, Clinton emerged as the grand exception. This was a remarkable feat, given what he had endured. His ordeals were less momentous than Johnson's war or Nixon's scandal, but they were more searingly personal. Yet Clinton's face was not creased with wrinkles; his eyelids did not hang heavy. It was not a shock to compare a photograph of the president from 1993 with one from 2000. If anything, the later image was more reassuring. His hair was whiter but his features were leaner and more commanding. The camera revealed a cool and self-confident man but not a relaxed one. With the end of his presidency now in sight, Clinton was not slumping to the finish line; he was sprinting.

Even so, he was exhausted much of the time. On a helicopter tour over forest fires in Idaho, he rattled off questions to the Forest Service official who was narrating the smoking, charred landscape below. But in the middle of the ranger's answer, the president's eyes shut and mouth hung open: He had fallen asleep. Minutes later, he came to and rejoined the conversation midstream. "I can sleep on January 20, 2001," he liked to say when asked about his punishing pace.

Clinton's sense of urgency—the schedule packed with more executive orders, more evening fund-raisers, more travel than ever—was at odds with the rest of his White House, which seemed palpably to be slowing down. The frenetic, anxious young team of the early first term had for the most part already moved on, and even those who stayed—like the tireless Gene Sperling at the National Economic Council or Bruce Reed at the Domestic Policy Council— were now in early middle age. Pizza boxes and coffee-fueled all-nighters—all the alarums and excursions of the first several years—were mostly in the past. Indeed, the whole orientation of the White House changed. In the early days, the marker of status was how close an aide's office was to the Oval Office. Now, the measure of prestige was the quality of an aide's White House good-bye party. A so-so party was crackers and cheese in the Old Executive Office Building. A more important official might merit shrimp and lamb chops in the White House East Room. Protein equaled power: Every week usually brought several receptions at which to make such invidious comparisons. The whimsical mood of Clinton's staff was revealed on a presidential visit to New Zealand. The schedule included a down day—something that would not have happened in the early years—during which dozens of Clinton's traveling party went bungee jumping off a bridge high over a river gorge. For perhaps the last year or so of Clinton's presidency, his White House had the feel of high school seniors enjoying their spring term.

THE COUNTRY ITSELF WAS ENJOYING AN EASY TERM. AS THE MILLENNIUM AP-proached, the markets were soaring, driven by white-hot technology stocks. The usual problems of the world—famine, war, recession—that had shad-owed much of Clinton's terms seemed for the moment at bay. In Afghanistan and elsewhere, people were plotting to disrupt this peace, but most Americans did not know this.

Clinton did know, and he talked regularly about the perils of terrorism, but Americans were not listening, for the most part, to his words on this or other problems. Clinton was aware of how little his voice was carrying. The prosperity that had been his savior was also an obstacle. Americans reveled in the fact that the economy was humming, and were finally ready to give him the credit. But they were of little mind to heed his exhortations about new challenges. Acute frustration over what he saw as a precious moment slipping away was a dominant theme of this last phase of his presidency.

"What have you done in the times in your life when you thought everything was hunky-dory?" he asked a crowd of supporters one night. "After things have been tough—and they were tough for America for a long time— the natural thing to do is to sort of say, 'Man, I've been working like crazy. This is great. Leave me alone. Give me a break.' " In dozens of speeches over the next two years, he told audiences the moment reminded him of his youth, the prosperous America of the early 1960s, before the nation was ripped apart. "We believed that our economy would grow on forever, we believed we would meet the challenges of civil rights in a lawful, peaceful way, we believed we could win the Cold War without what ultimately happened in the dividing of our country in Vietnam," he told a rally of congressional Democrats in February 2000. "We thought it would go on forever.

"I have waited for thirty long years to see my country in a position to pull together and move forward together, and build the future of our dreams," he pleaded. "We dare not blow that chance."

He tried to put poverty back on the agenda. He toured Appalachia and inner cities to promote his "New Markets" plan. Here was a classic New Democrat idea: Rather than try to revive large Great Society–style welfare programs, this used tax incentives to draw businesses into depressed areas and spur job growth. Even the new Republican Speaker of the House, Dennis Hastert, was a supporter. The country, though, was dreaming of private gains, not public missions.

The president found it harder to craft consensus on more ambitious projects. The World Trade Organization went to Seattle in the fall of 1999. The aim was to strike an agreement between developed and Third World nations on the next wave of trade liberalization—a first principle of Clinton's since he bravely pushed NAFTA to passage six years earlier. While angry anti-trade activists rioted in the streets, the talks collapsed with no agreement. Clinton himself was one of the reasons. Rather than use his bridge-building gifts at Seattle, he arrived making threats against developing countries that they should face trade sanctions if they did not improve labor standards. Labor unions hailed the president's support. But the developing countries, business groups, European nations, and virtually anyone with an interest in moving forward on free trade were dismayed. The suspicion was that Clinton had sabotaged the talks to curry favor with unions. In the wake of impeachment and his devout hope for Al Gore's election the next year, a weakened Clinton was no longer in a position to challenge his party's most powerful constituency. On this issue, at least, his effort to remake the Democratic Party had fallen short.

AS CLINTON PURSUED MORE MODEST AIMS IN HIS FINAL TWO YEARS, HE DID SO surrounded by more professional skill than ever before. Over eight years, the Clinton White House had gone through several distinct phases. The dewy-eyed idealism of 1993 and 1994 had fallen victim to disillusion and incompetence. The survivalist ethic that pervaded the Dick Morris years of 1995 and 1996 ran its course, as did the corporate model that Erskine Bowles imposed before the Lewinsky explosion. Now, on the homestretch, Clinton was no longer surrounded by old friends like Mack McLarty, or young retainers with a political crush like George Stephanopoulos. This was the season of the Washington operative. Shrewd, wisecracking men like Doug Sosnik, Steve Ricchetti, and Joel Johnson now dominated the West Wing. They all had established careers on Capitol Hill as political hands before coming to the White House. None of them had known Clinton before he was president, and none claimed to be his social intimate. They saw themselves as professionals serving a client. This detachment made their relationships less complicated and more competent.

Another group in the West Wing mix had been viewed as talented youngsters when they arrived in the early or middle Clinton years and now were running the White House. In addition to Sperling and Reed, there were press operatives like Joe Lockhart and Jake Siewert, both of whom eventually served as White House press secretary, and Jennifer Palmieri, a former assistant to Leon Panetta who stayed until nearly the end of the term.

Clinton's staff now was an irreverent bunch who regarded him with respect and affection but few illusions. While an earlier group tended to shudder and brood over his tantrums, this crowd laughed them off. They regaled themselves with the story of his annual physical in 1999. Clinton had been trying to diet with what he assumed were impressive results. But the scale at the National Naval Medical Center at Bethesda, Maryland, was less impressed—it showed the president weighing five pounds more than he thought he weighed. This is wrong, he stammered, insisting that the lower figure be released in the public statement about the checkup. The president's naval physicians averted their gaze to the deception.

Another episode during this same time revealed Clinton's occasional need to take flight from watching eyes. In the summer of 1999, he and Hillary Clinton were in the market for a new home in suburban New York. This was personal business, Clinton believed, and he did not wish to be shadowed by the press pool that was supposed to be with the president whenever he left the White House grounds, even if these people would sit in a van at some distance from whatever property he happened to be visiting. But to not take the pool along when Clinton traveled from Washington to New York on a Sunday morning would be a flagrant violation of a compact that had been reached between the White House press corps and successive presidents since the Kennedy assassination. Clinton knew that his aides would never approve such a plan, so he tried to play a game of hooky. He told his military aides to prepare for a trip, but not to tell anyone on his political staff. His plan was to sneak out of town and back in without anyone knowing. This plan was averted when one of the military aides, shrewdly sensing trouble, alerted the West Wing staff to the brewing plot. Sosnik congratulated the president on a nice try, but explained that there was no way a president could sneak out of town.

The hunt for a post-presidential residence revealed the Clinton family's dependence in more fundamental ways. With massive legal bills, the Clintons were deep in debt—despite his strong earning prospects upon leaving office—and in no position to put up the collateral for the kind of home suitable for an ex-president and a would-be senator. They had expected Erskine Bowles to guarantee their bank loan, but a couple of days before they planned to make an offer on a new home in Chappaqua, he backed out with little explanation, leaving the Clintons hurt and distressed. Bowles told others he decided the arrangement had a bad odor about it. The Clintons were able to buy the house they wanted only when Terry McAulifffe—also a wealthy man, though his fortune was considerably smaller than Bowles's—stepped in at the last moment to back the loan.

THERE WAS NO ONE WHO EXEMPLIFIED THE HOMESTRETCH ETHOS OF CLINton's last year in office more than the fourth and final man to serve as his White House chief of staff. John Podesta would have been an unlikely figure for this post earlier in the term, when people might have questioned whether as a veteran Washington staff man he had the necessary public stature. He had never served in Congress like Panetta or run a business like McLarty or Bowles. As it was, Clinton at first had been skeptical of the Podesta appointment. It had taken long effort by Bowles before stepping down in late 1998 to assure Clinton that Podesta was by far the best choice. It was a recommendation that Clinton never had occasion to regret accepting.

There was a curious pattern to Clinton's choices for his top staff job. One set was the WASPs, wealthy personal friends of the president who had little appetite for partisan politics. McLarty and Bowles were in this group. The other set was the highly political men, sons of immigrants who were initially less close to Clinton personally, and better at surviving in the hurly-burly of the White House.

Podesta had an ascetic streak. He was a regular runner who ate dinner but usually not breakfast or lunch. His arms and legs were like pencils. He tended to mumble in conversations, and would occasionally start laughing in mid-sentence. What's so funny? One rarely knew, except that Podesta had thought of something that amused him. At age forty-nine, when he became chief of staff, he had retained his obsession for roller coasters and *The X Files*. However, he was not always jolly. He had a fearsome temper that he had learned over time to control, albeit with occasional lapses that West Wing aides attributed to "Skippy," the chief of staff's evil twin.

Podesta was one of the lifers of Clinton's White House. In the first term, he had served as staff secretary, managing the voluminous flow of official paperwork into the Oval Office—"secretary of shit," he sometimes called it. He had spent some time in the Hillary Clinton deep freeze after leading an internal investigation in 1993 of the travel office affair that was a bit more candid than she might have preferred. He and Leon Panetta did not click, and in 1995 he left the White House to teach law, before returning in 1997 as Bowles's deputy. During 1998, when Bowles was functionally incapacitated by the Lewinsky scandal, Podesta became indispensable.

He brought several assets to Clinton now. Years on Capitol Hill had given him vast knowledge of policy, including of arcane subjects like the regulation of encryption technology. Most of all, he had close relationships with the congressional Democratic leadership. House minority leader Richard Gephardt and Senate minority leader Tom Daschle had resented the Bowles era of cooperation with Republicans, and they had resented Clinton for squandering a year during the Lewinsky scandal. No one could have been better positioned than Podesta to rebuild this wobbly bridge between Clinton and his own party.

Podesta well understood the need for Democrats to modernize their message and capture the political center. By temperament and instinct, however, he was an old-style urban liberal. He had grown up in Chicago, and his political values remained rooted in that city's brand of politics, in which people remembered their friends and fought to protect their turf. Podesta believed in loyalty—and holding grudges against those who betrayed it.

Once toward the end of the term there was a White House reunion for people who served throughout the administration. Podesta saw to it that former labor secretary Robert Reich, who had left his job to write a memoir that was somewhat critical of Clinton, was stricken from the invitation list. Wounded, Reich wrote Clinton a lengthy letter of protest. In distress, Clinton waved the letter at Podesta: "Bob thinks I hate him."

"You should hate him!" Podesta replied.

BUT AS THE END OF HIS TERM APPROACHED, CLINTON SEEMED TO NOT WANT to let himself be defined by grievance. He was in the end a forgiving man, and a practical one.

He had no more fierce an opponent than Tom DeLay, the whip and chief shock trooper for the House Republican majority. DeLay, a leader of the impeachment crusade, had expressed his contempt for Clinton many times publicly, and Clinton had reciprocated the sentiment many times privately. But he made DeLay a guest of honor at a White House ceremony promoting adoption. DeLay, who with his wife had adopted two foster children from troubled backgrounds, had recently been quoted in a newspaper article accusing Clinton of being a habitual cheater, even at golf. At the ceremony, Clinton recalled reading the article: "He started grinding on my golf game and saying that I didn't count my scores and all this, and I was getting really angry. And then I get to the next part of the story, and it talks all about his experience and his commitment to adoption and to foster children, and the personal experience that he and his wife had. And my heart just melted." This belief that there was no hostility that could not be overcome was an essential part of Clinton's character.

An earlier example came when the Republican Congress, in a fevered campaign to name as much of the country as possible for Ronald Reagan, passed a bill adding Reagan's name to Washington National Airport. This was a particular affront: Reagan celebrated local autonomy over federal intrusion, and Washington-area governments had announced their opposition to the renaming. In any event, Clinton's policy had in many ways been about reversing what he considered the most damaging parts of Reagan's domestic legacy. Presidential aide Paul Begala waved a sign urging "VETO!" when the bill reached Clinton's desk. He smiled and signed the bill. Perhaps earlier Clinton might have had interest in such a symbolic battle. Now he had no time.

There was a change in his public demeanor during this last year as well. He was more relaxed and less guarded. His most embarrassing secrets exposed, he had been impeached, and still he survived. What could anyone do to him now? He was meeting once a week with the pastors whom he had begun seeing in the midst of the Lewinsky scandal. In addition, he and Hillary Clinton were in marriage counseling. Carolyn Staley, an old friend from Arkansas, said she saw a man who was "asking himself who he is when he is at his best."

He was quite willing to share his answers. An appearance before a gay rights group in New York turned into a sermon on the foul moods Clinton said sometimes overtook him: "It has occurred to me really that every one of us has this little scale inside, you know. On one side there's the light forces, and the other side there's the dark forces in our psyche and our makeup and the way we look at the world. And every day we wake up and the scale is a little bit tilted one way or the other. And life is a big struggle to try to keep things in proper balance. You don't want to have so much light that you're just a fool for whatever comes along. But if the scale tips dark even a little bit, things turn badly for people and those with whom they come in contact."

These were not words that any other president would have spoken. Some of this willingness to talk about interior life perhaps was generational, a signature of the baby boomers. Some of it was unique to Clinton, who believed, with good reason, that he had an interesting story to tell. In any event, as his term wound down, people seemed ready to accept and appreciate him on his own terms.

An illustration came in late April 2000, when Clinton attended the annual White House Correspondents Association dinner. The year before he had come close to skipping the event, because the group was presenting an award to Michael Isikoff, the *Newsweek* reporter who had made a specialty of the Paula Jones case and had led the pack on the Lewinsky story. At the last minute, he decided this would look small, so he attended the dinner—after the awards had been presented. A year later, this contretemps was long since forgotten. Joe Lockhart and other aides prepared for Clinton's valedictory appearance as if it were a state summit. The format—sardonic, insider humor—was still not a natural for Clinton, but his irreverent and sardonic staff was born for the occasion. Among their gags was a job-seeking president, writing his résumé, taking care to use pithy, active verbs: "Designed, built, and painted bridge to the twenty-first century."

Clinton would squint his eyes in a skeptical expression as his chortling aides brought their latest material to him. "You could tell he did not really think it was funny," recalled Lockhart, "but then he'd see everyone else laughing and he'd join in." No matter whether he enjoyed the jokes, he had, over eight years, become a skilled comedic performer, delivering his lines with perfect pitch and timing.

The highlight of the routine they prepared for Clinton was a video, prepared with the help of a Hollywood producer, purporting to show what his life in the White House was like as his term wound down and his wife spent most nights on the Senate campaign trail in New York. There was the president washing his limousine, answering the White House switchboard, doing laundry, and bicycling the halls of the Old Executive Office Building with Terry McAuliffe.

There were gales of laughter from the crowded hotel ballroom of journalists and celebrity entertainers, and a standing ovation when the houselights came back on. "You like me, you really like me!" Clinton mugged, mimicking the actress Sally Field's infamous Oscar acceptance line. Then he turned a bit more serious: "Let me say to all of you, I have loved these last eight years. You know, I read in the history books how the other presidents say the White House is like a penitentiary. . . . And they all say they can't wait to get away. I don't know what the heck they're talking about!"

There had been few people over eight years toward whom Clinton had been more consistently aggrieved than the people in this room. But they finished the night with toasts for a survivor, and an American original.

Chapter Forty

TERROR

EVERY PRESIDENCY HAS ITS MOMENTS OF STARK CLARITY. ONE OF BILL Clinton's naked moments before history's gaze came nine months after he left the office. The former president was on a speaking tour in Australia when the first plane struck the World Trade Center. As it happened, his old confidant Bruce Lindsey was just a couple of miles from the disaster. He was visiting the downtown office of Cheryl Mills, Lindsey's former colleague in the White House counsel's office and herself one of the Clinton family's most trusted aides. They quickly called Clinton to tell him about what seemed to be a terrible and freakish accident.

As they were speaking, Lindsey suddenly exclaimed, "My God! A second plane has hit the tower!"

All over America, people experienced similar moments of horror and bewilderment. On the other side of the world, Clinton shared the horror but not the bewilderment. He reached his conclusion in an instant. "Bin Laden did this," he said with disgust, while the sound of sirens rose in the New York streets outside Mills's office.

In a day of countless tragedies, Clinton's reaction that morning hinted at still another. As president, he perceived acutely the threat of terrorism. He had spent his final two years in office focused intently on the threat of Osama bin Laden. Little wonder that he scarcely needed to think before realizing that the Saudi exile was the man behind the great crime of September 11, 2001. Yet in his time in power Clinton never succeeded in conveying the urgency he felt. He sat atop a government populated with subordinates who did not embrace—or responded inadequately to—his understanding of the danger. He stood before a citizenry that slumbered while this danger grew, and could hardly be roused by a president who was himself conflicted about how to respond.

Like many tragedies, this one was laced with irony. One thought back to five years earlier, as Clinton and Dick Morris spent a whimsical Sunday evening playing a historical parlor game, speculating where he would someday rank among the presidents. Only leaders who govern in times of great conflict can vault to the first tier, Morris gently told his client. Yet even then a mortal conflict was building, its early signs visible even as its dimensions were still obscure.

The conflict with Islamic terrorism was a clash of ideologies just as surely as World War II or the Cold War had been. A world of modernity and pluralism, in which people embraced tolerance and accepted the unfathomable distance between God and man, ended the century on what seemed like a triumphant note. In truth, it was in an escalating war with a world of absolutism and violent faith. These new prophets believed themselves enfranchised by God in the same way that Nazis and Bolsheviks earlier in the century believed themselves enfranchised by history and, like fanatics of all eras, felt certain the killings they sponsored served a noble end.

These two worlds had found emblematic leaders in Clinton and bin Laden—one man in the Oval Office, his adversary shuffling between high desert camps in Afghanistan. The contest pitted a man of diverse purposes and vagrant attention against a man of single-minded purpose. One man had an instinctual commitment to moderation and peace, the other an instinctual commitment to zealotry and violence. Clinton was by no means naïve about human character and its darker corners. He had grown up in a region laboring under the yoke of racism, and had seen brutish behavior in his own home. Yet Clinton had emerged from his circumstances with a belief in the essential benevolence of human nature and indeed of history itself. In a characteristically American way, he saw the planet's story flowing broadly from dark to light, toward ever greater prosperity and tolerance. These convictions—the opposite of the absolutists' creed—shaped his approach to the world in most arenas, including the problem of Islamic terrorism.

These pages are not the home for a comprehensive discussion of the Clinton record on terrorism. The aim instead is to suggest the common threads that tied his approach to this problem to the larger story of his presidency. In the four years since he left office, the argument about Clinton's role in confronting terrorism centrally occupied two major governmental inquiries, both of which produced thousands of pages of documentary evidence and conclusions. The debate has been further enriched by numerous memoirs and journalistic investigations. This vast record tells a complicated story. It shows a president through the 1990s growing steadily more aware of the terrorist threat, and responding with policies that devoted substantially more money and effort to the challenge. Those policies yielded some successes. The catastrophe of September 11, in any event, cannot be placed principally on a former president's ledger. Still, the record shows that all during Clinton's time in office, the terrorist threat grew steadily. The response of the federal government did not grow with commensurate effectiveness. The understanding among most Americans that they were living in a dangerous new age grew hardly at all. A leader's task is to perceive the character of one's times, describe it in vivid terms, and summon people to meet the challenges. As the twin towers burned that day, this aspect of Clinton's leadership could only be judged a failure.

This judgment should be rendered with restraint. Few people—and very few among Clinton's partisan and ideological critics—viewed terrorism on September 10, 2001, with the vivid comprehension that they would the next morning. Even more, no one can know where paths not taken might have led. The principal indictment against Clinton's terrorism record is that he did not give preeminence to the fight against bin Laden and the Taliban regime in Afghanistan that gave him and his al Qaeda network safe haven. Instead, Clinton let this fight compete with and often fall subordinate to other priorities. But those other priorities were hardly casual affairs. Clinton reasonably perceived the bin Laden menace as linked to two other urgent problems in a troubled neighborhood: the challenge of fashioning peace between Israel and the Palestinians, and preventing the escalation of a frightening conflict between two nuclear-armed foes, Pakistan and India. For reasons of both strategy and temperament, Clinton gravitated to the task of waging peace in these places more than he did to the task of waging war against bin Laden.

Clinton's terrorism record bore all the signatures of his leadership style as it had emerged from his earliest days in office. One reason Clinton was a survivor is that he lived by an ethic of contingency and improvisation. By no means did he see himself this way. He regarded himself as a strategic thinker, pursuing large goals with clear principles. As a practical matter, however, his goals were so spacious, and his principles so often in tension with one another, that governance and political survival were usually matters of day-by-day maneuver. Here was a president who came into office leaving both the spenders and the deficit hawks wondering which side he was really on, deep down. Amid this ambiguity he maneuvered to one of his administration's greatest successes. He was also a man who resisted opportunities to dispatch the Paula Jones controversy while it was still a nuisance. Here the preference for ambiguity and improvisation carried him to disaster. Now, his presidency nearing its close, contingency and improvisation were again his guideposts as he pondered the problem of Osama bin Laden. Clinton wanted the man dead or in American custody, if the right opportunity arose. But as he contemplated the risks this pursuit demanded, there were always reasons to wait for a better day.

THESE REASONS SEEMED ALL THE MORE COMPELLING IN THE AFTERMATH OF Clinton's first and boldest stroke against bin Laden and his network, the August 1998 missile strikes in Afghanistan and Sudan. These strikes missed bin Laden, and ignited controversy over whether the White House had been right to strike the al Shifa pharmaceutical plant in Khartoum, which it maintained—on disputed evidence—was involved in the production of chemical weapons. The failure of that strike did not end the desire to kill bin Laden. With a series of memorandums of notification, Clinton sought to steadily expand the authority under which the United States would be justified in killing or capturing bin Laden in a covert action or a direct assault. Two navy submarines were on permanent station on the shores of Pakistan, able to land a cruise missile anywhere in Afghanistan within six hours of a White House order. Even so, the disappointment of that first strike—and the speculation it inspired over whether an embattled president was acting in part to draw attention away from his sex scandal and imminent impeachment—did chasten Clinton and his chief subordinates. The national commission investigating the 9/11 attacks perceived "a cumulative effect on future decisions about the use of force against bin Laden."

There were several such future decisions, some of which prompted agonizing deliberations at the White House, all of which ultimately were made against another attempt. Clinton knew the threat had not receded. Though he rarely mentioned bin Laden's name in public—not wanting to raise his international profile any further—he began receiving frequent reports specifically about bin Laden after the embassy bombings. Several times a week, the intelligence briefings given to National Security Adviser Sandy Berger would include the latest information about the al Qaeda network, and the most provocative reports would also go directly to Clinton in his own PDB—the president's daily briefing. Clinton was an avid consumer of intelligence, though he generally preferred to get it in written form, so he could assimilate it on his own schedule, rather than the oral briefings that some other presidents have preferred. On December 4, 1998, a Friday while the impeachment controversy was still churning, the PDB included a particularly alarming item. "SUBJECT: Bin Ladin Preparing to Hijack US Aircraft and Other Attacks." Noting that some members of al Qaeda had received hijack training, the memo asserted that the apparent aim was to hold hostages in order to demand the release of terrorists in U.S. custody. These included Ramzi Yousef, the man behind the first terrorist attack on the World Trade Center, a car bombing just five weeks after Clinton took office in 1993. (Yousef and his confederates were not then linked directly to bin Laden and al Qaeda, but they later would be.)

Amid these alarms, from time to time the CIA also would bring promising information to the White House: intelligence about bin Laden's expected whereabouts. Each time, these reports would prompt debate about whether the information was reliable enough to allow another attempt to kill him with cruise missiles. These decisions were made vexing by multiple layers of uncertainty. The first was the fragmentary nature of intelligence itself. The CIA often produced information about where bin Laden had been, or even where they thought he might be at a given moment. But information about where he would be next—to allow the several hours to land a missile—was rare, and even then was freighted with speculation and doubt. Berger was of the view, shared by Clinton, that to attempt to kill bin Laden and fail would only make the leader stronger and more attractive to many eyes in the Islamic world. And if a strike also killed innocent civilians, as was probable in any strike, the backlash against the United States across the world could be severe.

Clinton was keenly sensitive to this last factor, for both strategic and humane reasons. Once, he later explained, he rejected an option for missile strikes on Kandahar, Afghanistan, upon learning that its chance of killing bin Laden was 40 percent, at a compound where many families lived. "I could just imagine the news report: 'US bombs Kandahar, hundreds of women and children killed; Bin Laden press conference to follow,' " Clinton said.

Clinton's caution on this and other matters echoed through the bureaucracy, even in ways that he apparently did not intend. An example was the question of whether the president had authorized covert action that would allow Afghan tribes working with the Central Intelligence Agency to kill bin

Laden if a capture operation was deemed infeasible. Clinton and Sandy Berger, as they later testified, believed that the president had signed a memorandum of notification on Christmas Eve 1998 that made clear their intent: They wanted bin Laden stopped, and would have been quite satisfied if CIA-supported Afghans did the job by bullet rather than by capture. Yet the White House's evident squeamishness about anything that might be interpreted as a presidentially authorized assassination remained obvious to the Central Intelligence Agency. Years later, both CIA director George Tenet and others in the agency testified to the 9/11 commission that it was their clear understanding that there was no authority to kill bin Laden except in the context of a genuine capture attempt.

Little wonder there was confusion. Two months later, in February 1999, Clinton was presented with a nearly identical memorandum of notification extending the new rules—kill bin Laden, don't worry about a capture—to the Northern Alliance insurgents who for years had been battling the Taliban. Clinton took his own pen to the draft and softened the language to make it more ambiguous. Later, the former president testified that he had no recollection of this episode. His editing might indeed have been done with little conscious deliberation; his discomfort with violence and his political sensitivity about being perceived in the Islamic world as personally responsible for the killing of bin Laden were so ingrained as to be automatic.

No covert operation ever reached the point that the language in Clinton's memorandums was given a real-world test. But the discomfort radiating from the White House was itself one reason that the sporadic efforts to have Afghan locals carry out the deed against bin Laden never reached full flower.

By no means should Clinton's caution be confused with complacency.

Far from averting his gaze from terrorism, as some critics later contended, Clinton was at an intellectual level deeply drawn to the issue. There was a professorial bent to his approach to the presidency. He believed—quite rightly— that one of his strengths was an ability to explain complicated subjects in ways that ordinary citizens could understand. He loved holding forth on the wondrous new possibilities of globalization, which trade and immigration and the Internet made possible, but he rarely failed to warn audiences that these changes also carried a "dark side."

Clinton was drawn to the subject mostly as a matter of authentic conviction. "Terrorism is the enemy of our generation, and we must prevail," he declared at George Washington University on August 5, 1996, within days after the explosion of a pipe bomb marred the Atlanta Olympic Games, and a TWA jumbo jet disintegrated off the Long Island coast, a disaster that was originally presumed to be the work of Iranian terrorists. He observed presciently, "I want to make it clear to the American people that while we can defeat terrorists, it will be a long time before we defeat terrorism."

He was also drawn to the subject as a matter of politics. In an age when activist government was on the defensive, terrorism offered an opportunity to make the case for a robust federal role in meeting the problems of a new age. Clinton regularly chided Gingrich's Republican majority for responding with insufficient haste in passing measures to increase funding and expand law enforcement power to combat emerging terrorist threats.

Finally, Clinton was drawn to the subject as a matter of intellectual imagination. In 1998 the president was transfixed upon reading a fiction thriller with a disturbingly realistic premise. Richard Preston's *The Cobra Event* depicts a madman terrorizing New York City with a genetically engineered virus. Not long after, the president gave an interview to the *New York Times* in which he explained his obsession with the new terrorist threat: "But to me, it's money well spent. And if there is never an incident, nobody would be happier than me 20 years from now if the same critics would be able to say, 'Oh, see, Clinton was a kook; nothing happened.' I would be the happiest man on Earth. I would be the happiest man on Earth. If they could say, 'He over-exaggerated it; nothing happened. All he did was make a bunch of jobs for scientists and build the Pentagon budget,' I would be elated 20 years from now to be subject to that criticism because it would mean that nothing happened and in no small measure because of the efforts we've made."

Alas, Clinton hardly anticipated the line of criticism. But his heartfelt words that day suggested a paradox: He had the mind of an activist, but this intellect was harnessed to a governing style that was marked by a certain curious passivity. One of the people who noticed this paradox was the chief official dealing with terrorism on the National Security Council. Richard A. Clarke, a career government official with a fixation on terrorism that many colleagues thought obsessive, was deeply impressed by Clinton's mind. But on several occasions he puzzled at the way Clinton seemed to issue his commands—an odd combination of complacency and deference to the subordinates who were supposed to be deferential to him. "Clinton would make requests, and just assume these were being done, or that the people around him knew best," Clarke later recalled. "Perhaps that's a reasonable thing for a president to expect." But the reality, as Clarke well knew, was that in government nothing really happened unless somebody at the top was riding herd and imposing his will on the bureaucracy, which would otherwise continue to follow its own institutional interests and rhythms.

Clarke's method was simply not Clinton's style. Even when Clinton had strong convictions, he could yield with surprising ease in the face of bureaucratic objections or competing interests. People concerned foremost about terrorism felt it was imperative to use intelligence and technological means to disrupt terrorist finances by covertly freezing suspect accounts. Robert Rubin at Treasury protested that the United States could not in any way be seen as undermining the international financial system, and the proposal died.

Clinton regularly pressed for more imaginative military options against bin Laden, including use of U.S. commandos to make a strike. This would have given more flexibility than launching cruise missiles from hundreds of miles offshore, and more reliability than employing local tribes to covertly do American dirty work. To General Hugh Shelton, the chairman of the Joint Chiefs in the late 1990s after the retirement of John Shalikashvili, Clinton once said excitedly, "You know, it would scare the shit out of al Qaeda if suddenly a bunch of black ninjas rappelled out of helicopters into the middle of their camp."

But Shelton and Defense Secretary William Cohen patiently explained that such an operation was high risk and not very practical. The military nearly always had such objections at hand for things that ran against its preferred customs and priorities, and they were usually sensible in any given case. Cumulatively, they represented a refusal to carry out Clinton's plea for more urgency and more options. Rather than keep pushing, Clinton withdrew.

The most vivid example of Clinton's willingness to yield rather than confront obstacles within his own government was also the most inexcusable. The relationship between the White House and the FBI—and specifically between Clinton and director Louis Freeh—had turned rancid in the mid-1990s. By the late 1990s, this dysfunction was having serious and adverse consequences on national security. Both Clinton and Freeh regarded themselves as vigilant defenders against the problem of terror, and each regarded the other as thwarting his efforts through arrogance or incompetence. In particular, Freeh believed that the White House was letting its desire for a rapprochement with Iran stall the pursuit of justice for a terrible truck bombing in 1996 that killed nineteen U.S. service personnel at the Khobar Towers military barracks in Saudi Arabia. (Clinton indeed hoped to improve relations with Iran and nudge forward a moderation of the radical theocracy that ruled the country, but he maintained this wish did not hinder the search for justice over Khobar

Towers. In any event, Clinton's desire was frustrated, as what looked like tentative signs of moderation in Iran proved ultimately to be a mirage.) From the White House vantage point, Freeh was increasingly a renegade force within the executive branch. He rarely shared information and was a sullen or absent presence from White House policy meetings. He made only the barest nod to being responsive, much less subordinate, to Attorney General Janet Reno.

On this last question—the problem of FBI accountability—Freeh was emphatically in the wrong. The FBI director's traditional independence was for the purpose of preserving the integrity of criminal investigations, not for absenting himself from the coordination of federal policy or ignoring a president's priorities. In the case of terrorism, moreover, better coordination and more effective oversight were sorely needed. For whatever his strengths in some arenas—Freeh was by most accounts a dedicated law enforcer—the record suggests he was overwhelmed as an administrator. The official inquiries in the wake of 9/11 found the defense against terrorism was undermined in the FBI by poor information-sharing both within the agency and between other relevant agencies, antiquated computers and other technology, and rampant diversion of resources intended for counterterrorism to other purposes as local offices deemed fit.

Clinton and his aides have offered as a defense the argument that Freeh had so devoutly cultivated Republicans in Congress, and so effectively positioned himself in the public mind as a watchdog against alleged Clinton corruption, that the president had no ability to either rein in the director or dismiss him without creating a Watergate-style firestorm. Ultimately, this was no defense at all. Freeh's suspicions to the contrary, Clinton was not a corrupt public servant. But, on matters ranging from Whitewater to fund-raising to Monica Lewinsky, he had followed a pattern of limited disclosure, evasive or false public explanations, and shabby personal conduct that made suspicion far from unreasonable. It would not have been possible for an FBI director to hold hostage a president with a scrupulous personal reputation. Nor should a responsible president have allowed himself to be held hostage—no matter the firestorm that would have resulted. The president's refusal to assert the authority that belonged to him over the FBI and insist that the agency become a fully cooperative partner in the campaign against terrorism was a critical abdication of leadership.

As Clarke, who despised Freeh and regarded him as a serious obstacle to an effective counterterrorism policy, later concluded, "He should have fired Freeh and just taken the shit it would have caused."

A MORE CAPABLE FBI OR MORE CREATIVE THINKING AT THE JOINT CHIEFS might well have yielded important tactical improvements in the fight against bin Laden, but these would not have been a remedy to the essential strategic problem. This was the existence of the radical Islamic regime in Afghanistan known as the Taliban, which harbored bin Laden and his training camps. If an outlaw regime was the fundamental problem, the critics asked, why did Clinton not address it in a fundamental way?

One part of the answer is that he would have found precious little sentiment for doing so from any quarter—not within the administration, nor within the Congress, nor among American allies around the world. In the Middle East and through the Muslim nations of Central Asia, an aggressive U.S. effort to topple the Taliban prior to September 11 likely would have produced a backlash more worrisome than the original problem.

The main part of the answer, though, is that Clinton and his top advisers did *not* regard the Taliban and its links to al Qaeda as the fundamental issue. It was secondary to the problem one country over—in Pakistan. The Islamabad government, particularly its military and intelligence services, was a key supporter of the Taliban regime. Pakistan was a historic ally of the United States, but relations had been troubled for many years, mostly over the problem of weapons proliferation. A U.S. effort to intervene in Afghanistan, the White House and State Department believed, would have turned trouble into crisis. This was not an attractive prospect under any circumstances, but it became much more frightening in May 1998. That was when India, Pakistan's bitter enemy, surprised Clinton and the rest of the world by conducting underground nuclear tests. This was a critical step in turning its long-standing theoretical capability into a working nuclear arsenal. In a series of urgent meetings and phone calls, Clinton pleaded with Pakistan's prime minister, Nawaz Sharif, not to reciprocate by letting the Pakistani military perform nuclear tests of its own. These appeals were to no avail; Pakistan tested. Suddenly, the rivalry between India and Pakistan, which previously had been a bothersome regional issue, was a global security problem of the first order—a contest between two belligerent nuclear-armed powers in which the actual use of such weapons in a conflict was all too easy to imagine.

Clinton's efforts to manage this problem in the late years of his presidency merit attention, both as context for the terrorism issue and as an illumination of his leadership style. The record on bin Laden revealed a leader recoiling from a conflict that deserved escalation in order to defeat a menace before it grew. The record on the India-Pakistan conflict showed a man reveling in the task of conflict de-escalation. As anyone who had known Clinton from a young age could have testified, he was by talent and temperament a peacemaker. It was in his nature to get along and try to coax others to do the same. In the spring and summer of 1999, he had occasion to put these traits to use.

For fifty years, India and Pakistan had staked competing claims to the province of Kashmir. This was no mere argument; there were constant fire-fights along a tense line of control between two militaries, and there had been three full wars over the decades. Over time, however, the conflict had settled into certain routines and expectations. One of them was that each winter the militaries would draw back from their most forward positions, high along ridgelines in the Himalayas, which were difficult to maintain amid blizzards and avalanches. It was understood that both armies would return in the spring, and in the interim neither side would try to take advantage of the seasonal change in deployment patterns.

In the winter of 1999, however, Pakistan violated this custom by moving Kashmiri militants and regular army units into the evacuated Indian positions above the small Kashmiri town of Kargil. The Pakistani cheating was curious, as Sharif previously had been regarded in Washington as a benign force who had responded productively to moves by Indian prime minister Atal Vajpayee to begin a thaw in relations with Pakistan. Why would Sharif do something like this? The answer, it seemed evident, was that Sharif was only nominally in control of his own government, and that the Pakistani military—led now by General Pervez Musharraf—was really steering the conflict. Outraged, India fought back hard, and by the spring a furious military campaign—replete with air strikes and artillery fire—was under way. Confronted with the prospect of a full-scale war that Pakistan was likely to lose, in late June a panicked Sharif appealed to Clinton for help. Clinton had to intervene to prevent a catastro-phe, the prime minister pleaded, proposing that he come to Washington im-mediately to meet with Clinton and discuss a negotiated resolution of the conflict. This was an awkward request. The administration did indeed want a peaceful settlement, but Pakistan was plainly the culpable party in this dispute. Clinton replied that he was happy to see Sharif, but there would be nothing to talk about unless Pakistan was prepared to unilaterally withdraw forces back to the original line of control. Sharif, Clinton suggested, needed to think hard be-fore coming. Without committing to withdrawal, Sharif said he was on his way. The summit between Clinton and Sharif was scheduled at Blair House, across the street from the White House, on the Fourth of July. As Sharif traveled, the situation grew more dire. For one thing, the prime minister had brought his wife and children with him on the plane. This was a clear indication that his grip on power was so tenuous that he might be overthrown before he could return. Even worse, the administration received intelligence indicating that Pakistani military forces were preparing their nuclear missiles for possible use. On the streets outside the White House, hundreds of thousands of Washingtonians and tourists were heading in droves on a sun-drenched day for the National Mall for the annual Independence Day festivities. Inside the White House, Clinton's briefing for the Sharif meeting began with a dire comment from Sandy Berger. This meeting might be the most important of his presidency, the national security adviser warned, since hundreds of thousands of lives would surely be lost in the increasingly plausible event that the India-Pakistan conflict went nuclear. Clinton had a delicate balance to strike. He needed to push Sharif to withdraw his troops, while offering enough dignity and political cover to avert a revolution in Pakistan and allow Sharif to actually implement a withdrawal when he returned home.

Sharif appeared for his session with Clinton as a pathetic figure—plainly aghast at how events were hurtling out of his control, but just as plainly hobbled by his own weakness. Clinton was warned not to allow Sharif to press for a one-on-one meeting. Bruce Riedel, the National Security Council's expert on the region and the official note-taker, was to always remain present, lest Sharif or his more belligerent ministers later try to claim Clinton made commitments that he did not. Likewise, Clinton was urged not to speak too candidly around the Pakistani foreign minister, since this official would leak everything to the Pakistani military intelligence service, which was hostile to the prime minister. Clinton began by showing the prime minister a political cartoon from the *Chicago Tribune* depicting Indian and Pakistani soldiers fighting atop two nuclear bombs. This showed the real danger, Clinton told his guests.

The meeting did not start well. Sharif began as Riedel had earlier predicted he would, with a long rote defense of Pakistani grievances over Kashmir, and an admonishment to Clinton that if he had spent just one percent of the amount of time on this conflict as he did on the Israeli-Palestinian negotiations, the whole problem would have long since been solved. Clinton responded that the United States was happy to help Pakistan but could do so only after a full and immediate withdrawal. It was essential, he added, that the world believe Pakistan got no reward for its nuclear threats, otherwise the signal would go out around the world that this was the best way to command the attention of the world's sole remaining superpower. "I'm not—and the Indians are not—going to let you get away with blackmail, and I'll not permit any characterization of this meeting that suggests I'm giving in to blackmail."

The meeting was stuck in a sullen and inconclusive mood when Clinton reached for a historical analogy. The president had been reading military historian John Keegan's book on World War I, he explained. The India-Pakistan conflict reminded him of 1914—both sides drifting thoughtlessly toward catastrophe. If Sharif was moved, he could not show it in this larger meeting. Sharif asked for time alone with Clinton, who replied that everyone else could go but Riedel had to stay to keep a record of the conversation. Sharif, sounding by turns confused and afraid, pleaded with Clinton to allow Pakistan some kind of concession in exchange for its withdrawal. Otherwise, he insisted, the military and Islamic fundamentalists at home would revolt, and this would be his last meeting with the American president. Ominously, Sharif seemed caught unaware when Clinton mentioned the advanced state of Pakistani nuclear preparations—quite likely he had known nothing of it. Referring to the Cuban missile crisis, which Clinton remembered well from his own teenage days, he started to tell Sharif that if even one missile fired . . . The prime minister interrupted to finish the sentence: "it would be a catastrophe."

Soon it became Clinton's turn to do the imploring. Sharif had requested this meeting, Clinton reminded him, fully aware that the price was unilateral withdrawal, and the Pakistani's intransigence was setting the session up for failure. If that happened, Clinton was fully prepared to tell the world what had occurred. Then he linked the administration's foremost priority in the region, averting nuclear catastrophe, with its secondmost, stopping bin Laden. Despite promises, Pakistan had still done nothing to help capture bin Laden. To the contrary, Pakistani intelligence remained supportive of the Taliban and al Qaeda. The meeting showed Clinton in a kaleidoscopic display of different moods and tactics. One moment brought flattery, as he praised Sharif for his earlier gestures toward peace, another brought a raised voice, red-faced anger at the way Sharif had cornered Clinton and himself in such a dangerous place. Above all, the president conveyed sympathy for the political dilemma Sharif was facing, while making clear that he too had political requirements. It was Clinton using every instrument in his toolbox of persuasion.

None of them worked at first. Sharif's mind was elsewhere. He denied that he had ordered the nuclear preparations, but explained that he was worried not just for his job but for his very life in Pakistan. The two men then took a break. During this time Clinton placed a call to Indian prime minister Vajpayee. Deeply angry at Sharif, who he felt had betrayed him, and suspicious of Clinton's involvement, Vajpayee responded stonily. When the call was over, the president needed to rest from the day's tension. He lay down on a couch and closed his eyes.

The day ended happily. During the meeting Berger, Riedel, and Deputy Secretary of State Strobe Talbott had crafted a proposed joint U.S.-Pakistani press statement that announced the desired U.S. conclusion. The statement called for the prime minister to agree to an immediate withdrawal behind the line of control, urged a ceasefire once the withdrawal was complete, called for the resumption of the India-Pakistan peace process, and took note of Clinton's long-standing plans to visit the region. That last item was important. Pakistan had long been eager for the prestige of a presidential visit. Sharif read the statement several times slowly, staring at a precipice in either direction. In the end, he decided the risks of retreat were less than those of confrontation. After some minor tinkering with the language, Sharif accepted the statement. Clinton was effusive. They had tested their relationship this day, he told his visitor, and passed.

Things did not end so well for Sharif. He returned to Pakistan to implement the withdrawal, but within just three months he was overthrown—by General Musharraf. He spent the next year in prison before going into exile.

The Pakistan relationship continued to be tugged by competing alternatives after Musharraf's arrival. Within several months, Clinton would need to decide whether to travel to Pakistan during a tour of South Asia that would take him to India. One school of thought said that Pakistan should not be honored with a visit so soon after a coup d'état, and after so little progress had been made on the twin goals of counterproliferation and counterterrorism. The consensus on Clinton's foreign policy team, particularly Berger and Talbott, was that a brief stop in Islamabad after a much longer tour in India would be productive. This was emphatically Clinton's preference. He nearly always wanted engagement over isolation. In the end, the biggest obstacle was not diplomatic but practical. The Secret Service pleaded against a Pakistan trip, warning in the strongest language they had ever used with Clinton that he risked assassination. Two weeks before the South Asia trip was set to begin, a group gathered in the Map Room to discuss the trade-offs. Berger said he recognized the merits of the Secret Service's caution but on balance thought the risk was worth taking. Clinton agreed. Then he added, with a wicked smile, "But you, Berger, are definitely coming with me."

CLINTON DID GO TO ISLAMABAD, THOUGH HE LEFT HIS WIFE AND DAUGHTER behind for this portion of the South Asia trip. He also resorted to subterfuge. He landed fast and low in a small, white unmarked jet—after the officially marked air force plane landed and a man who looked like Clinton hopped out, surrounded by a retinue of Secret Service agents who also hopped out. There were five black limousines, instead of the usual two, as the motorcade headed from the airport into town, an added measure to foil would-be assassins.

The president's meeting with Musharraf proceeded by rote—right down to its unsatisfying conclusion. Nuclear proliferation and the conflict with India dominated the agenda, though Clinton repeated the long-standing American plea for more cooperation in pressuring Pakistan's Afghan allies into cracking down on terrorism and turning over bin Laden. "I offered him the moon," Clinton later recalled, "in terms of better relations with the United States, if he'd help us get bin Laden and deal with another issue or two."

Musharraf responded with bland and noncommittal bromides. And Clinton's frustrations continued. He well knew his administration was not responding adequately. The threat remained obvious to him, as indeed it would have been obvious to anyone who read the papers and had the imagination to contemplate that a group which wanted to destroy U.S. embassies in Africa was not likely to stop there. In February 2000, Berger sent the president a memo outlining what was being done on al Qaeda. Clinton sent it back with a scrawl across the top—unsatisfactory, he wrote.

But the old obstacles—bureaucratic sluggishness, competing priorities, just plain bad luck—stayed in place. There was a brief rush of excitement in the late summer when the CIA brought back results from a new tool—an unmanned Predator flying drone which could beam back intelligence images and ultimately be armed with weapons. CIA director George Tenet played a two-minute video clip for Clinton and Berger, showing images of a tall bearded man, fitting bin Laden's description, surrounded by a large security team crossing the street to a mosque. But the Predator's promise in trials ended for the balance of the Clinton term when one of them crashed.

Then, on October 12, 2000, the enemy struck again. Seventeen American sailors died when a boat loaded with explosives drove into the USS *Cole* in Aden, Yemen. The probability that this was the work of bin Laden was immediately recognized in the White House. But there was no retaliation, nor effort to reorder al Qaeda's place among U.S. strategic priorities, as would happen after the attack on American soil now just eleven months away. Clinton and

Berger later testified that they would have taken action, but the intelligence services could not establish with sufficient certainty during Clinton's last weeks in office who was responsible for the attack on the *Cole*. After he left office, the initial suspicions about bin Laden's involvement were confirmed. At the time, it seemed to some people laboring elsewhere in the administration that the White House was not particularly eager for confirmation. There was no desire to confront the implications—and launch a military campaign—in the closing days of the 2000 presidential campaign, or in the weeks that followed between election day and the administration's exit. Clinton believed that a central cause of Islamic rage was the unresolved Israeli-Palestinian conflict. A new war in Afghanistan would no doubt set back the search for peace there. Clinton was determined to use the falling light of his presidency to keep searching.

Chapter Forty-one

CAMP DAVID

TWO POTENT IDEAS DROVE THE FOREIGN POLICY OF CLINTON'S FINAL year in office. The first was Clinton's notion of the unique power of the American presidency as peacemaker on a troubled planet. Over the course of two terms, he had seen the effect of this power firsthand in several places. Bosnia was an example. Northern Ireland was another. Here Clinton and his special envoy, former senator George Mitchell, had helped broker the so-called Good Friday accord, which established a path (though imperfectly followed in the years since) for ending four decades of sectarian violence between Catholic Nationalists and Protestant Unionists. From these experiences and others, Clinton had developed a general theory of peacemaking.

The theory was built on several assumptions. Most important was that crafting peace agreements was fundamentally a task of public persuasion for which politicians like himself were well suited. People needed to be coaxed, prodded, and flattered into making an existential choice in favor of hope for the future over grievances rooted in the past. Usually, the only way this could happen was for the outside world to convey legitimacy on leaders who—since they had emerged amid war—invariably had bloody pasts, shrouded in moral ambiguity and even criminality. This is what Clinton had done for Gerry Adams, the leader of Northern Ireland's Sinn Fein, the political arm of the terrorism-sponsoring Irish Republican Army. By this logic, such legitimacy gave leaders the influence and moral authority they needed to push their own publics to make difficult decisions for peace. Common folk needed to support leaders who made concessions to enemies they loathed, and who were willing to yield some historic claims on property or cherished principles as the only practical way to make good on other claims. Clinton had found this revelation wonderfully liberating: Most difficult international problems were in essential ways really problems of domestic politics, a subject he knew plenty about. He also believed that the United States, personified by the president, could play a crucial role in helping world leaders surmount their domestic problems. America's superpower status, as he conceived it, was partly about military and economic might but often just as much about psychology. People were flattered to have the attention of the world's most powerful leader, so long as that attention was respectful and not overbearing. Clinton was superb at conveying such respect. In conversations with foreign leaders, no matter how small the country, he always let the other leader speak first and at length about his problems, before Clinton made any pronouncements on U.S. policy.

These general notions about peacemaking were focused most urgently on a specific conflict: the long and seemingly endless clash between Israelis and Palestinians. Clinton did not believe it was endless. This was the second idea driving his foreign policy as his last year came to be measured in months and weeks: It was his belief that he personally had a rendezvous with destiny in helping bring peace to this defining conflict of the Middle East. Through the years, Clinton came to feel an intimate connection with the problems of this land. Part of it was his affection for Yitzhak Rabin, the old man who had sacrificed his life in pursuit of peace. Clinton believed Rabin could have achieved his goal if he had not been assassinated by one of his own countrymen, a right-wing fanatic opposed to the peace the prime minister was trying to deliver. Of the assassin, Clinton told Sandy Berger, "That young man sure knew what he was doing."

Clinton had been present at Rabin's seminal moment, when he shook hands with his mortal enemy, Palestinian leader Yasser Arafat, on the South Lawn of the White House in September 1993 during the signing of the so-called Oslo peace agreement. Clinton had helped stage-manage the handshake, but he did not have much to do with the actual agreement. It had been negotiated in secret directly by Israelis and Palestinians, without American auspices. The promise of 1993, however, had not come to fruition. The Oslo agreement had placed its faith in incrementalism. Israelis and Palestinians, with their warring claims to the same land, would each take a series of limited and concrete steps toward resolving their disputes, each move serving as a "confidence-building measure" toward eventual resolution of the wider conflict. This resolution would involve statehood for the nation-less Palestinian people, in exchange for acknowledging Israel's right to peaceful and permanent existence. The problem was that these proposed gradual steps, far from building confidence, further inflamed mistrust and resentment. The plan for reconciliation envisioned under Oslo was far beyond schedule, and a deadline was looming. Arafat had declared that he would unilaterally proclaim statehood for his Palestinian Authority by September 2000. This would provoke a thunderous response in Israel; Clinton realistically feared the two sides were headed for a new wave of violence. Amid this fear, there was in the Israeli and U.S. governments alike new sympathy for a different solution to the Palestinian problem. Instead of contemplating incremental steps, the aim of negotiations should be more ambitious: "final status." This meant trying to resolve the outstanding claims and reach a permanent settlement in one bold swoop.

The new prime minister of Israel, the Labor Party leader Ehud Barak, supported this. And the idea had obvious appeal to Clinton. In the midst of the Monica Lewinsky scandal, he had called searching for Middle East peace part of "my personal journey of atonement." It was not solely a quest for glory and redemption, but it was partly such a quest that inspired Clinton to put his full weight behind a final push for peace. If such a push worked—ending one of the world's most remorseless conflicts, one with a loud echo across the Muslim world—he would be due all the glory he wanted.

It was in this spirit that Clinton invited Arafat, Barak, and their negotiating team to cloister themselves away for days at Camp David, the rustic presidential retreat sixty miles from the White House, deep in the woods of the Catoctin Mountains of Maryland. Such a summit, among these particular players, was almost by definition fraught with risk. Most gatherings of foreign leaders are planned carefully in advance, with at least some concrete agreement already decided upon in order to give leaders a guaranteed success to announce. There was no such guarantee here. Indeed, a few months earlier, an effort to craft a peace agreement between Israelis and Syrians under U.S. auspices at Shepherdstown, West Virginia, had fallen flat. But the dramatic possibilities of a fluid, unscripted gathering at Camp David appealed to Clinton. Moreover, the risks of doing nothing—and drifting toward the September deadline—seemed larger than the risk of a failed summit. Over the July 4 weekend, Clinton summoned his own foreign policy team to Camp David.

He turned to Berger. "We have no choice, right?"

Berger, warning that the conflict "is heading toward an explosion," replied, "I think that's right."

Invitations went out to both sides to join Clinton back at the camp in a week.

THE SUMMIT OPENED ON JULY 11. IT WAS SCHEDULED TO END NO LATER THAN nine days later, when Clinton needed to leave for Japan and a meeting of the Asia-Pacific Economic Cooperation forum, a group near to his heart and which he had elevated to head-of-state status. There were three issues at the core of a final settlement between Israel and the Palestinians. One was the borders of Israel and a new Palestinian state. Israel had expanded its territory in the 1967 war, and any settlement would shrink the country. But this would not be back to its original size, since Israeli settlers had already built homes outside the original boundaries, and the political right in Israel was determined to protect the claims of these settlers. The second was the right of return for Palestinian refugees who wanted to resettle in old homesteads. This right had to be strictly limited, since a large influx of Palestinians would undermine both Israel's security and its essential identity as a Jewish state. Most sensitive of all was Jerusalem, home to the holy Old City, capital of Israel, and the place where Palestinians were determined to establish their own capital. Historically, this had been an issue on which both sides had been unmovable in asserting claims that were mutually exclusive. There was a lengthy roster of other issues— security guarantees, control of airspace, the division of municipal services— but these three were the ones on which the Camp David drama would pivot. They touched basic nerves of identity and day-to-day existence in ways that were virtually impossible for most Americans, in an established nation in which mortal foes did not live within shooting distance of each other, to conceive.

Camp David was fundamentally a story about three leaders and what they were willing and unwilling to do in the name of peace.

Arafat, who had spent decades as the face of Palestinian grievance and aspiration as head of the Palestinian Liberation Organization, in earlier years had been an outcast on the world stage because of the PLO's terrorist tactics. But over time he had come to enjoy legitimacy and even an aura of celebrity, particularly with European publics sympathetic to the Palestinian cause. He was now head of an autonomous "authority" that governed the stateless Palestinians. After the Oslo agreement, Arafat was even awarded a Nobel Peace Prize—rather prematurely, as it turned out. His emergence in the international mainstream was given the full imprimatur of the Clinton administration. He had been to the Clinton White House more than any other foreign leader. This attention reflected Clinton's belief that Arafat was in a basic way on the level: that he was the genuine leader of his people, and had the capacity to move them toward peace. In some moods, Arafat had a bluff charm. But as Clinton had learned, and would have occasion to relearn, Arafat's brand of leadership thrived in ambiguity, in which the unsettled nature of the conflict and Palestinian grievances were his greatest source of power. The possibility of black-and-white decisions—in which Palestinians would let go of grievance—was frightening to him. Arafat had not been enthusiastic about going to Camp David, as he let the Americans know beforehand. He did not trust what he regarded as Barak's record of falling through on earlier commitments, and he believed the time was not right for a comprehensive deal. The summit could end in failure, embarrassing everyone, he warned. But, feeling under pressure from the Americans and with no real choice, he was here.

Barak, on the surface of things, was the kind of leader to whom Clinton should have been drawn. Like Rabin, he was a military man and an Israeli hero. He was a former military chief of staff. Once, on a mission for the army special forces, he had donned a dress and wig and slipped into Beirut to assess Palestinian movements. And, like Rabin, he seemed ready to place a historic wager that his country's security could be better protected through reconciliation than more conflict, a judgment Clinton deeply respected. Barak, moreover, had won election over a man Clinton disliked, the conservative Likud leader Benjamin Netanyahu. To top it off, Barak's political consultants were none other than James Carville, Stan Greenberg, and Robert Shrum, all intimates of the Clinton circle. These points of similarity, however, were clouded by a lack of personal warmth between the two men. Barak could be an exasperating and inscrutable man, as would be on vivid display in the days ahead.

Finally, there was Clinton himself. His negotiating style reflected his personality. He had an addiction to detail that was quite useful in the Camp David setting. He pored over detailed maps of Jerusalem, trying to gain a block-by-block understanding of the potential solutions. His own team had long since learned his strengths and weaknesses in moderating peace talks. One weakness was to win vague or preliminary agreements from one side and oversell them to the other side, presenting tentative movements as dramatic breakthroughs, which only led to disappointment later. Dennis Ross, the Mideast envoy, later wrote that he learned not to brief Clinton too early on the critical bottom lines and trade-offs for each side: Clinton would want to rush in with his ideas, instead of letting negotiations mature and build a natural momentum. But the president's weaknesses, in Ross's view, were amply offset by his strengths. Foremost among them was a superb ability to articulate the issues in ways that highlighted the advantages of peace and sympathized with the pain involved in the sacrifices.

The mood at Camp David was shadowed in ways large and small by the sense of time running short. Clinton was taking advantage of a last chance to enjoy a presidential lifestyle he loved. Chelsea Clinton, on summer break from Stanford, was present for much of the negotiations. This was their last chance to soak up the splendid Camp David setting together, and for her to be a witness to history in the making with her father. There were numerous all-nighters, but Clinton plainly did not mind. And even during the long down times, when negotiations paused while the teams went into private huddles, Clinton did not try to rest. Instead, he played nonstop cards with his press secretary, Joe Lockhart, or personal aide Doug Band, the last of his presidential "butt boys."

GIVEN ARAFAT'S AMBIVALENCE AT LAUNCHING FINAL STATUS TALKS, ROSS urged Clinton to lift the Palestinian's sights. The president rose to the challenge with a meditation on history, telling Arafat how eager he was to be present when the flag was raised for the first time on a new state of Palestine.

But inspiration soon gave way to a desultory mood, which pervaded Camp David for the next several days. Both sides were doing nothing productive, but Barak's position was perhaps more infuriating. The Israeli prime minister had pressed hard for the negotiations, but now that he had them he was showing no initiative or flexibility. To the contrary, he told U.S. negotiators that he did not expect anything to happen for days—pressure needed to build up on Arafat, Barak reasoned, to get him to show flexibility. The Americans were galled. Stalling as strategy was hardly calculated to please his American host, who wanted the parties to respond to the obvious urgency of the calendar. Barak's approach, the White House team believed, was characteristic of his aloofness and even arrogance.

The summit dragged on inconclusively, Clinton's frustration growing. The Palestinians were the first to feel his lash. On the fifth day at Camp David, Clinton was meeting jointly with the two negotiating teams under Arafat and Barak, while the top leaders remained in their cabins. In a discussion of the borders between Israel and a new Palestinian state, one of Arafat's negotiators, Abu Ala, began a recitation of historical grievances over the 1967 war, rather than responding to Clinton's urging to make realistic proposals on a new map. While the Palestinian lectured, Clinton's face grew red. Sensing an explosion, Ross quickly suggested a break, but it was too late. The explosion came.

Clinton reminded Abu Ala about the political risks he had taken in hosting a summit. What the Palestinians were doing now was a waste of his time and everyone else's. This, Clinton shouted, was an "outrageous approach." Then he stalked out of the cabin.

This outburst was startling. Clinton threw fits of temper all the time back at the White House, in the company of his own staff. But rarely did he show that side with others, least of all in a diplomatic setting. Was this authentic anger or a performance? The different reactions of his own team reflected how opaque the president's own thinking could be even to close subordinates. Clinton's anger, believed Ross, "was always genuine, not done for effect." Berger, who knew Clinton far more intimately, believed that "he used anger in a very calculated way."

There would be occasion for more of that anger later in the day, this time for Barak. You pressed for this summit, Clinton reminded the prime minister, but the truth was he was not doing anything to make it a success.

This would change, but not before Barak's mood got worse. The next evening, day six, Barak sent Clinton a note that reflected his grim outlook. Arafat was manipulating the process, he said, trying to draw Israel out to show its bottom line, then pocketing any gains while giving nothing in return. He would never do such a thing unless he felt the Americans were behind him. "I do not intend to allow the Israeli state to fall apart physically or morally," he wrote. "There is no power in the world that can force on us collective national suicide." This was chilling stuff—the words, Ross believed, of a leader who was feeling cornered.

The breakthrough came on day eight. Barak asked to see Clinton alone. The president was ebullient when the meeting adjourned, but would not say why in front of the larger team. He cleared everyone out except for Berger, Ross, Chief of Staff John Podesta, and Secretary of State Madeleine Albright. "I finally have his bottom line," Clinton said with delight. Indeed he did have it. After giving nothing away for days, Barak had finally come through in an instant with more concessions than most Israelis had ever contemplated. On borders, Barak would give back the West Bank territory it had seized in 1967, except for a relatively small 9 percent annexation, which in turn would be compensated with a land swap in nearby Palestinian areas in Gaza City. On

Jerusalem, Barak had agreed to give the Palestinians sovereignty over the Muslim and Christian quarters of the Old City, as well as several other neighborhoods. On the other questions, including right of return for refugees, Israel's needs were met in ways that fell entirely within what had been the reasonable expectations before the summit. An international presence would help maintain security.

The immediate question—how did Barak go this far?—was immediately overtaken by another: How would Arafat react? Could he take yes for an answer? The feeling, widely though not universally shared on the American team, was that the moment of final decision had arrived. If Arafat would not take this, he would not take anything. The Palestinian went to Clinton's headquarters at Aspen Lodge. The two of them were alone in the living room. Clinton's team strained to keep abreast of the meeting by listening at a kitchen door or watching the body language from outside through the windows.

Berger recalled seeing his boss, a large man, give the diminutive Arafat "the full Lyndon Johnson treatment"—towering over the object of his persuasion, hands cupping the shoulder, fingers jabbing the chest. Clinton raised his voice again, this time not so much in anger as pleading: "This is the best deal you're gonna get. For God's sake, don't turn this down. It'll never get better."

Arafat saw things differently. He came back with questions and requests for meetings. Only the next morning did he come out and say no. The summit continued for five more days, a full two weeks in total. There were more heroics to keep the process alive. At one point, the summit seemed over as Clinton prepared to leave for Japan. The bags of the Israeli and Palestinian negotiators were packed, and the cars were lined up for a motorcade. Then, at the last moment, the two sides agreed to stay until Clinton flew back from Japan. But when he flew back, the answer was still no.

Clinton bluntly told Arafat that if the summit failed, he would tell the world that it was because the Palestinians would not negotiate in good faith. Arafat was shocked and told Albright, "I can't lose my friend Clinton." Berger saw a man trapped somewhere between panic and paralysis.

The summit at Camp David had seemed at the time achingly close to a historic breakthrough. The implications of Arafat's intransigence, however, soon began to take shape. Perhaps they had not been close at all, many of the Americans would conclude. Arafat had spent his life in opposition, defined by struggle. He might not have wished ever to be a conventional leader, worried about administrative tasks like schools and water quality. In all likelihood, there was no result he would have accepted at Camp David other than an abject Israeli capitulation. This possibility was too cheerless to contemplate. As the summit broke down, the Americans turned the focus to somehow keeping the peace process alive. Clinton gave a pep talk to Barak that was revealing of how Clinton saw himself. "You are smarter than me and you are experienced in war and I am not," the American said. "But I am more experienced than you in politics and there are several things I have learned. The most important is don't corner your adversaries and don't corner yourself; always leave yourself a way out. Don't lock yourself into a losing option."

The unilateral declaration of Palestinian statehood that the Americans feared did not come, but a new outbreak of violence did. Clinton and his aides would keep their efforts to strike a peace accord alive for another six months. Ross had once told Clinton that Arafat would wait until five minutes before midnight to make a deal. Clinton related this conversation to Arafat with an observation: "I am afraid your clock is broken. It's already midnight."

But Arafat might have been less the leader of his people than Clinton had first supposed. What looked to Americans like an excellent deal would be regarded by many Palestinians as ignoble retreat. Arafat protested, "You're asking me to sign my death warrant."

Chapter Forty-two

EXIT

THE CLINTONS BEGAN ELECTION DAY 2000 AT THEIR NEW HOME IN CHAP-paqua, in the Westchester County suburbs of New York. It was a su-premely satisfying morning. Barring some huge error in the polls, Hillary Clinton was going to win her Senate seat with ease. The president of the United States, meanwhile, huddled in a study with her staff, fussing over the victory speech she would deliver later that night. The candidate stayed away, trying to stay relaxed and rested for the night ahead. This was their new life together—she was the star and he was the adviser. The roles they had played in their thirty-year relationship had been reversed.

Later that afternoon, they flew into the city on Marine One, the helicopter that was his for another couple of months. They sat comfortably by each other's side. He stroked her affectionately. She read a *New York Times* profile of Daniel Patrick Moynihan, the man she was set to replace in the Senate. Jake Siewert, Clinton's final White House press secretary, noted an odd paradox in this scene. They lived some of the most exposed and even exotic lives of any couple on the planet. Just two years earlier, their marriage had been teetering amid the scandal. Yet at certain moments, even while flying into Manhattan accompanied by a retinue of aides, they could seem the picture of domestic conventionality.

After they arrived at their suite in the Hyatt next to Grand Central Station, it proved to be a longer night than they expected. Hillary Clinton won early and went to bed after midnight. But Al Gore's fate remained unclear all the way through a wild night, during which he first called Texas governor George W. Bush to concede defeat, then revoked his concession when it turned out network television projections that Bush had won Florida proved premature. The president stayed up all night watching the drama, making regular phone calls with advice for the vice president's team in Tennessee.

If only one of the president's two main partners of the previous eight years could win election on this night, this surely was the outcome Clinton preferred. He was more vested in his wife's future than his vice president's. But Clinton devoutly wanted them both to win—and felt sure they would have if Gore had run anything near as competent a campaign as his wife. The president was equally frustrated with Gore's performance during the thirty-six days in which the Florida recount battle dragged on. He believed Gore had plainly won Florida, if the genuine intent of voters could be registered, just as he had won the popular vote nationwide. From Clinton's vantage point, the vice president was quite characteristically treating the recount as if it was on the level, some kind of pristine legal proceeding. Instead, he should be mobilizing public opinion, pulling out all stops to prevent a miscarriage of democracy. Clinton shared this belief with anyone who would listen. As for Gore, he had long since stopped listening to Clinton's freelance strategizing. On December 12, 2000, a 5–4 decision of the U.S. Supreme Court stopped the recount, and Gore's chances ran out, and with them Clinton's eight-year hope that he would be succeeded by his vice president.

Left to his own devices, Clinton likely would have continued to stew privately over his disappointment in Gore, and in the deterioration of their relationship. But the vice president was more assertive—and had more to get off his chest. A few days after he conceded the race, Gore sought time on Clinton's schedule. It was their first significant conversation in eighteen months. The two men were alone in the Oval Office, but both subsequently described the session to friends. For more than an hour, in uncommonly blunt language, Gore forcefully told Clinton that his sex scandal and low personal approval ratings were the major impediment keeping him from the presidency. Clinton was taken aback at first. Soon, anger rising, he pushed back. It was Gore's failure to run on the administration's record that hobbled his ambitions.

Gore left feeling satisfied that he had spoken truths that needed to be said.

Clinton was in a foul temper when the session ended. The more he talked about the conversation with friends, however, the more at ease he became. Perhaps the meeting had served some kind of psychological purpose for Gore, for whom Clinton continued to feel more sorrow than resentment. Their relationship—once so close and so consequential during the previous eight years—was hardly repaired. But at least the broken pieces were put squarely on the table.

CLINTON DID NOT HAVE TIME TO LINGER ON THE SUBJECT. THERE WAS AN-other, more urgent business of reconciliation on his table. After the collapse of the Camp David talks in July, he and his national security team continued to nurture hope that he could prod Israelis and Palestinians into a final settlement before leaving office. Perhaps he could even use the ticking clock of his presidency to his advantage. Both sides knew he was much more invested in the peace process than President-elect Bush, who had already made clear that he thought it was unproductive to expend his capital in the bog of Middle East talks in the way Clinton did. If ever the moment was right for peace lightning to strike, this was it. In that spirit, in late December, Clinton summoned negotiators from both sides to the White House and presented a U.S. plan for peace—Clinton's judgment of the best deal possible for both sides. Dennis Ross, the longtime Mideast negotiator, later recalled that Clinton was as stern as he had ever seen him in years of meetings as he slowly read the terms of a final settlement. It dealt with all the outstanding issues that had been wrangled over for years: the borders of a Palestinian state, a Palestinian capital in East Jerusalem, security guarantees for Israel, and the status of refugees. The two sides would have five days to say yes or no. Any answer other than an unconditional acceptance of Clinton's premises for final settlement would be taken as a no.

What happened next followed the same sad routine established at Camp David. Ehud Barak said yes for Israel. The prime minister was facing a tough re-election battle just weeks away. Having taken huge risks for peace with nothing so far to show for it, he was almost certain to lose his job unless he could finally produce a settlement. Arafat, meanwhile, continued his usual exasperating ways. Ignoring the instructions to say yes or no, he instead came back with questions and suggestions for modifications and various delaying tactics, as if there was any time left to delay. Clinton, desperate for a deal, tolerated this routine one more time. He even offered to fly to the region the last week of his presidency if it was to announce a settlement. But Arafat rebuffed this offer, and the prospects for peace receded one last time.

·······························

INSTEAD OF FLYING TO THE MIDDLE EAST IN HIS FINAL DAYS IN OFFICE, CLINton was tending to some other unfinished business. On January 19, 2001—literally his last full day in office—his battle with the independent counsel over his statements in the Paula Jones and Monica Lewinsky matters came to an end. His encounter in Little Rock was a decade in the past. Paula Jones had filed her lawsuit nearly seven years earlier. It had been three years since he had testified in the civil suit, two years since he was acquitted in the impeachment trial. Even Kenneth Starr had moved out of his job as independent counsel. Still, the criminal case chugged on. Starr's replacement, Robert Ray, was offering a settlement that would ensure Clinton would not face post-presidential prosecution.

Reluctantly, Clinton took the deal. It came at a steep cost. He had to agree not to seek reimbursement for millions in legal fees, as allowed under the independent counsel statute. In a separate deal with Arkansas authorities, he agreed to pay a $25,000 fine and accept a suspended law license for five years. For the first time, he offered a forthright statement that he had testified falsely under oath. "I tried to walk a fine line between acting lawfully and testifying falsely, but I now recognize that I did not fully accomplish this goal and that certain of my responses to questions about Ms. Lewinsky were false," the president said in a statement, which closed by saying, "I hope my actions today will help bring closure and finality to these matters."

The problem was that Clinton did not really believe this. Though no fair reading of his statements could support this conclusion, he devoutly believed that he had told the literal truth in all his dealings—in the Jones deposition, before the Starr grand jury, and in his answers to congressional inquiries. It galled him to make such an admission, just as it had earlier galled him to pay a fine to Judge Susan Webber Wright for his false answers in the Jones case.

Clinton's worst decisions were often the result of two factors: grievance and fatigue. Both were weighing heavily on his last night in the White House, a virtual all-nighter. He had resolved in his final weeks in office to use the presidential pardon power aggressively.

There were a great number of people that last night eager to benefit from Clinton's instinct for forgiveness and his conviction that zealous prosecutors sometimes trampled individuals. In the light of day, many of these people would hardly be seen as sympathetic or politically defensible pardon recipients. Thus was born the last controversy of the Clinton years. Among the claimants were Webster Hubbell and Susan McDougal, both of whom had been ensnared by the Whitewater investigation. There were a number of people who had put the president's brother, Roger Clinton, on retainer in the hope that he could promote their cause. Most troubling was the claim of Marc Rich, a millionaire tax fugitive who had chosen to renounce his citizenship and flee to Europe nearly twenty years earlier rather than face federal charges of tax evasion. At first blush, he seemed to be the last person to deserve a favor from the president. But Rich had important people in his corner. His pardon plea was being pressed by a top Washington lobbyist, Jack Quinn, a former Clinton White House counsel. Even more important, Rich had the energetic support of his ex-wife, Denise Rich, who had become an important Democratic fundraiser and a friend to the president. His case also won an endorsement—how heartfelt it was later came under dispute—from Ehud Barak of Israel, where Rich now claimed co-citizenship and where he was a major charitable benefactor.

The experienced hands at the White House were not naïve about the hazards Rich's case posed. Clinton's longtime aide Bruce Lindsey argued against a pardon. Chief of staff John Podesta worked energetically those final hours trying to quash Rich's pardon, as well as several others he believed were politically toxic. Late on the evening of the nineteenth, Podesta believed he had succeeded. Not until the next morning did he find that the night-owl president had outlasted him: In the middle of the night, Clinton had signed the Rich pardon. McDougal, too, was granted presidential mercy, though Clinton, to his dismay, decided the storm from a Hubbell pardon would be too great. Apart from the dubious merits of the Rich pardon, there was something horribly dispiriting about this final performance. Over the course of eight years, Clinton had grown steadily more sure-footed, mature, and organized in the technical execution of the presidency. In his final hours, it was as if he reverted to the worst excesses of 1993—making consequential decisions in the dead of night, pulling end runs around staff, acting on personal impulse instead of considered judgment.

IT HAD BEEN A TERRIBLE NIGHT IN HIS PRESIDENCY. ONLY WHEN THE SUN came up the next morning did Clinton rise to the appropriate level of solemnity for his last day in power. Following a long-standing tradition, he left a note to George W. Bush on the desk of the Oval Office. The West Wing was nearly empty now, and most aides had cleared out. Clinton stood for a moment with John Podesta, his chief of staff, the two of them lost in reverie. Podesta put his arm around his boss and said, "We did a lot of good."

Clinton then walked over to the East Wing for another tradition: a reception thrown by the outgoing president for the president-elect on the morning of the inauguration. The occasion was a little stilted, with both the elder Bush, the man Clinton had defeated, and his son, the man who would succeed him, in attendance and making awkward small talk. But Clinton was in a fine mood. His winter coat was on, and he sat down on the bench with the Marine Corps piano player, who was playing "As Time Goes By." Clinton sat for a moment lost in thought. Then an aide came over to tell him that Bush's inaugural procession needed to leave. It was time to go.

Chapter Forty-three

ARGUMENT WITHOUT END

CLINTON HAD MADE IT TO THE END—STILL STANDING AFTER EVERY-thing, his political fortunes and personal dignity intact, if a bit scuffed by the long ride. There had been many seasons during the preceding decade when this result was in doubt. From the moment he sprang to national notice in the 1992 campaign, Clinton was identified with crisis—and recovery from crisis. The victory that year was followed by a stumble-prone transition and an opening two years that were among the most tumultuous encountered by any modern president. He persisted. Following the Democratic repudiation in the 1994 elections, Clinton bested the Republican efforts to render him irrelevant in 1995 and 1996, and in the process won the argument Newt Gingrich had provoked about the role of the federal government in national life. Clinton defied the effort to evict him from power in 1998, then thwarted the predictions that he would hobble through his final two years as a political cripple. In his closing days in office, Clinton himself pondered the mystique surrounding his gift for survival. "I had a high pain threshold," he explained. "I remember once I was in an accident in a car in high school, and my jaw hit the steering wheel real hard, and it was the steering wheel that broke, not my jaw."

The subject demands a less mystical explanation. Clinton survived the crises of his presidency for three principal reasons.

Foremost among these is that he assembled a competent policy record. As ever in his life, there were contradictions and frustrating excursions. In the main, however, it was a record defined by responsibility. However heedless he could sometimes be in his personal life, Clinton brought a dutiful sensibility to his public life. His governing values were informed by the elite side of his character. He gravitated instinctually to the worldview and policy prescriptions of a certain breed of progressive-minded expert. His policy anchors were people like Bob Rubin at Treasury, Donna Shalala at Health and Human Services, Bill Perry at the Pentagon, and Al From at the Democratic Leadership Council. By the end of Clinton's term, the issue that had been in doubt at the beginning—whether Democrats had credible ideas about the role of government in a rapidly changing global economy—was put to rest on favorable terms. Clinton had implemented a mild but innovative brand of liberalism that favored economic growth over redistribution, insisted that government pay its way rather than rely on budget deficits, and embraced free trade rather than taking refuge in protectionism. One can argue over how much credit any president deserves, but the larger picture of American life at the end of the Clinton years was unmistakable. Twenty-two million jobs had been created over eight years. The budget was in surplus. Crime was down; so were welfare rolls and teen pregnancies. Home ownership was on the upswing, as were median incomes for African-Americans and Hispanics. These changes were the result of the productive energies of Americans, but no one who recalled the sense of national drift in 1992 could fail to credit the Clinton administration for at a minimum serving as an essential catalyst. Lapsing into down-home blarney, Clinton often liked to say, "My old daddy used to say, if you find a turtle on a fence post, chances are it didn't get there by accident." Clinton survived his challenges in part because at the end of the day his policies were seen by most Americans as succeeding.

But this is not the only reason. If elite values nurtured in Georgetown, Oxford, and New Haven shaped one side of his presidency, other values nurtured in Hot Springs and Little Rock shaped another. Clinton's presidency was anchored to an authentically populist spirit and animated by a genuine connection between a politician and common folk whose support he needed. Countless times Republicans believed they had Clinton cornered. The reality was that they never really told voters anything about the president—about his diverse excesses and vulnerabilities—that the voters had not long since supposed to be true. Nor could opponents break the bond of affection between

Clinton and many followers who saw him fondly as a leader who fundamentally liked people and wished to be liked. During the impeachment drama, if blacks, women, or labor unions—all Democratic constituencies who on various occasions had reason to be aggrieved with Clinton—had ever abandoned the president, he might very well have been sunk. They did not abandon him. His presidency survived because most citizens accepted him as he was, and wished him to stay where he was.

Finally, one must note the phenomenon seen so often in his story: the blurring of function and dysfunction in the Clinton style. Voluminous appetites got him into trouble. Voluminous appetites carried him out of trouble. No president had a greater capacity for the work of politics and governance— it was often hard, even physical, work, across long hours and multiple time zones—or any greater emotional and intellectual attraction to his job. Clinton was not a conventional figure in his lifestyle or psychology. But, across a lifetime, he had settled on personal and professional habits that worked effectively when he most needed them to—the essence of the survivor's ethic.

The survivalist approach to life and to the presidency imposed certain costs. Clinton's presidency was largely a defensive project. He spent six of his eight years devoting as much energy to halting what he regarded as the excesses of the Republican congressional majority as advancing his own agenda. As a politician, he prospered much more in those years when he could respond to the Republicans and position himself in opposition than during the opening years, when Democrats controlled Congress and Clinton could set Washington's agenda. Many of his largest achievements, moreover, had a defensive character. Balancing the budget and overhauling the welfare system—two consequential accomplishments—were historically conservative goals. Clinton's task was to implement these goals with a more progressive cast. The imperative of survival also forced Clinton to limit his reach. One mission of his presidency had been to force the Democratic Party to reconsider and refashion the liberal agenda, a task that necessarily involved some discomfort to traditional constituencies and to protectors of the party's old order in Congress. Come 1998, when Clinton needed every Democratic vote possible in order to survive the Republican attack over Monica Lewinsky, the work of challenging his own ground to a halt. He had no political latitude to push for reform of the entitlement programs for the aged, Medicare and Social Security, both of which faced soaring and unsustainable long-term costs, or to continue to push his party on the issue of trade, as he had done bravely during the passage of NAFTA at the outset of his presidency.

The trade-off he made between ambition and necessity was consistent with a larger theme of his politics. One of the continuing dramas of his presidency was the contest between competing strains of romance and realism in the Clinton character. The romantic in Clinton was a politician of florid imagination who viewed himself on history's stage in a line of heroic presidents who left large imprints on their times. In such a mood, he was scornful of limits, less attuned to political hazards, the most devout believer in his own abundant possibilities. It was this spirit that had pervaded 1993 and came crashing down with the failure of health care reform and the mid-term elections of 1994. The realist in Clinton was an accommodator who accepted political limits and tried to work within them. One irony of this tension, as it played out over eight years, is that Clinton in the end proved to be a more effective and more consequential president during those times when he was disciplined by political caution than when he was motivated by vainglorious dreams.

For his undeniable competence in many arenas, Clinton left office with a weak claim on membership in the elite gallery of truly large presidencies. All presidents must react to circumstances and play the hand they are dealt. The greatest presidents, however, manage simultaneously to create their own circumstances—to impose their own values and purposes on the age. Clinton was a hyperkinetic man, and a president of undeniably activist intentions. Yet beneath the flurry of activity he frequently displayed a certain passivity. It was often his habit to let matters drift before choosing, after agonizing debate, his ultimate course. This was his pattern in the Balkans in 1993 and 1994, in the confrontation with Republicans in 1995, and in deciding what to do about welfare reform in 1996. Those episodes all ended to his advantage. The same passivity was on display as he confronted the Paula Jones case in 1997, with disastrous results. A presidency that spent so much of its time operating on defensive premises, and recovering from self-inflicted wounds, was ill suited to presidential greatness as conventionally defined.

Perhaps the times in which he governed were ill suited as well. There were great engines of energy and change at work in American life in the 1990s. These engines were found on Wall Street, where markets amassed and distributed capital in unprecedented sums. They were in Silicon Valley, Seattle, and northern Virginia, where technology entrepreneurs created a revolution in how people work, learn, and communicate. They were in Hollywood, where the entertainment industry made American popular culture a saturating influence around the planet. In the best light, Clinton was a brilliant modernist who understood the transformational character of his times and helped prepare his country to take advantage of them. Even in this light, the fact remains that the 1990s was one of those eras when the great currents of history did not flow primarily through Washington and the national government.

All this is not to say that Clinton will not have a long historical echo. He was too vital and too vexing a character to be easily forgotten or dismissed. He was one of the great personalities to occupy the White House. It seems likely that, decades from now, his personality will be producing arguments—about his character, about his enemies, and about the long-term consequences of both—that would be entirely familiar to a contemporary audience. There's no reason to suppose that a man who caused so much debate in his own time will have a settled and stable reputation in posterity. "History," said the historian Pieter Geyl, "is an argument without end."

Indeed, what is most striking about the argument over Clinton's legacy so far is its volatility. Four years out of office, he has already seen his reputation go through several cycles of decline and revival. The controversy over the pardons he issued during his last hours in office prompted predictions at the time that he had permanently shattered public sympathy and would never be embraced even by Democrats. But this storm receded soon enough, and by the summer of 2001 Clinton nostalgia was at full flood, as he opened his post-presidential office in Harlem before an ecstatic crowd of thousands and wall-to-wall cable news coverage. The attacks of September 11, 2001, sent Clinton's historical stock down anew, as commentators cast a censorious gaze on the failure of his campaign against Osama bin Laden and his willingness to tolerate the continued reign of Saddam Hussein in Iraq. Yet his successor's record on these same problems—bin Laden still at large in early 2005, and a war in Iraq filled with unforeseen complexities—put Clinton's caution in a better light. And the failure of two successive Democratic nominees to match his election successes seemed to speak for itself about the forty-second president's political skills. For demoralized Democrats trying to figure out how to respond to the political challenges of the Bush era, the most common question was "What would Clinton do?"

It is a sign of the diverse strands of his political appeal that the question would produce quite different answers among different groups of Democrats. By the end of his presidency, he had transcended the ideological fissures within his party that earlier caused him such difficulty. The centrist "New Democrats" claimed him as their own, but so too did the traditional liberals. A politician sometimes criticized for trying to be all things to all people ultimately succeeded in being just that, at least for his own party. In the end, what unified Democrats around him may have been less specific programs or ideological touchstones than a certain native faith in progressive government that Clinton exemplified. In the final year of his presidency, Clinton often cited to his aides and public audiences two books that had deeply engaged him. One was *The Tipping Point,* by *The New Yorker*'s Malcolm Gladwell. The other was *Nonzero: The Logic of Human Destiny,* by Robert Wright. His attraction to both revealed something about how he saw the world, and his role in it. *The Tipping Point* was an illumination of how incremental efforts can produce cascading changes in society. One did not need radical reforms to make a difference; it was enough to chip away at problems with persistence and intelligence, much as he had tried to do. The argument in *Nonzero* was more sophisticated. It was that the instinct for social progress was inherent in the human species, and that progress is achieved by human interactions that are not zero-sum propositions, propositions, that is, in which one side's gain must be someone else's loss. The imperative for the modern world was to promote relationships and social endeavors in which all sides win. Clinton was enthralled by the book. With academic language and high-concept metaphors, it articulated a kind of idealism and progressive faith that Clinton had felt at an elemental level his entire political career. The world could do worse than to possess more of this faith.

Another irony of history awaited Clinton upon his exit. This president had little patience for his successor in office. Clinton regarded George W. Bush as an amiable man, and he was early to comprehend—as far back as 1999— that the Texas governor was a more effective politician than most Democrats realized. But Clinton regarded Bush as an incurious and smug man who seemed to think that the White House was an inheritance belonging to the Republican Party generally and his family specifically. For his part, Bush ran against Clinton while never mentioning his name. Even many voters who happened to like Clinton nodded in affirmation at Bush's pledges in 2000 to "restore honor and dignity to the White House" and to "change the tone in Washington." Whatever their personal feelings, however, Clinton and Bush are likely to be tethered to each other historically. Their presidential styles are such distinct opposites that it is hardly possible to talk about one without invoking a contrast with the other.

As a politician, Clinton made it preeminently his task to capture the center while trying to tame the more ideological elements of his party. Bush has celebrated ideology, and has worried less about placating the center than about rallying the enthusiasm of his party base. On the world stage, Clinton was a pluralist who believed the United States in most instances was better served exerting influence by persuasion and by acting in a community of nations. Bush has been devoted to American exceptionalism, believing in the supremacy of force over persuasion and serving regular notice that the United States is ready to act alone to protect its self-interests. The starkest contrast is in the nature of their minds. The philosopher Isaiah Berlin famously invoked the Greek fable about the hedgehog and the fox to classify the intellectual habits of artists and statesmen: "The fox knows many things, but the hedgehog knows one big thing." Clinton was a classic fox. He was driven less by ideology than by experience and contingency. His words and his actions could at times seem contradictory, his true intentions and priorities opaque even to the people closest to him. Bush proved to be a classic hedgehog. In the wake of the September 11 attacks, he tended to see all decisions through the prism of security and the terrorist threat. The challenge of leadership, as Bush framed it, was above all a matter of conviction, in which the hard part of governance was not deciding right from wrong but pursuing right with sufficient devotion in the face of setbacks and criticism. In the Clinton and Bush presidencies, history has crafted an experiment of sorts about which model of leadership is more productive.

The experiment may not be over for a long time. Just fifty-four years of age upon leaving office, Clinton may have decades left in the public arena. What projects lie ahead? Some of his own advisers have urged a campaign to position Clinton to be secretary-general of the United Nations. It is an arresting (if still implausible) possibility: Clinton as a kind of "president of the world." This prospect no doubt generates more enthusiasm in some precincts than in others, though Clinton himself is said to be intrigued.

There is another large figure on the political stage whose fate will help shape how Bill Clinton is remembered. Hillary Rodham Clinton counts with her husband as one of the most arresting personalities of her era. In the Senate, with her own power and liberated from the derivative roles she played during most of her husband's career, she has proved to be a vastly more appealing and effective politician than she was as first lady. Though she now has more independence, the Clintons' relationship remains as symbiotic as ever. She has the potential to come to her husband's aid in the court of history just as she did so often in the political arena. If Hillary Clinton were to become president, or even to remain as a leader of the Senate for a sustained tenure, she could help determine how history views Bill Clinton's presidency. With a longer lens, the flamboyant personal dramas of those eight years might well recede, and the remarkable fact of one talented couple dominating Democratic politics over a period of decades would move to the foreground. The story remains unfinished, as do the controversies these two leaders inspire. Here, truly, is an argument without end.

Acknowledgments

My relationship with the Bill Clinton story has been driven by serendipity. Like anyone with an interest in politics, I was fascinated by this arresting new figure who arrived on the national stage in the 1992 presidential campaign, and I watched his tumultuous first two years in office with curiosity.

Professionally, however, I was content with my job in 1994 covering the military for the *Washington Post.* Unexpectedly, one of the paper's two positions on the White House beat opened up at the beginning of 1995. My editors suggested I spend a couple of years working with (and, as a practical matter, for) Ann Devroy, the *Post*'s indomitable senior White House correspondent.

As it happened, a couple of years stretched to six—the balance of Clinton's tenure in office. Tragically, Devroy fell ill in 1996 and died the following year at age forty-nine, leaving me and a succession of partners to try to match her high standards. When I first started reporting on Clinton, in January 1995, the Republicans had just taken over the Congress and Clinton looked to be a beaten man. The leader who later came to be seen widely as one of the world's larger-than-life personalities at that moment loomed rather small—almost physically diminished, to my eye, and demoralized and tentative in his manner. Over the next two years, I witnessed his remarkable comeback as he triumphed in his confrontation with Newt Gingrich and the Republican Congress and won easy re-election. It continued to be a wild ride. After following the Clinton story through the Lewinsky scandal, impeachment, acquittal, the Kosovo war, the Camp David talks, and Hillary Clinton's Senate campaign—along with overseas trips that took me to some forty countries—it was with satisfaction and relief that I left the White House beat when Clinton's second term ended in January 2001.

It turned out I was not quite through with Clinton. Again the unexpected happened, this time in the form of a call in the summer of 2001 from an editor at Random House asking whether I might be interested in writing a history of this controversial presidency. That call and subsequent conversations led to this book. I undertook this project with a sense that the history of the Clinton presidency has a certain paradoxical quality. On the one hand, I feel sure that fascination with Clinton and his legacy will continue for decades. On the other, I know perhaps more acutely than most how perishable much of this history is. Even in younger people, memories recede with surprising speed. Recollections tend to get edited by the mind into a few polished anecdotes. The millions of documents stored in the impressive presidential library that Bill Clinton built on the banks of the Arkansas River in Little Rock—now owned by the federal government and managed by the National Archives—will be an invaluable resource for scholars for decades. However, it seemed to me as I undertook this project that time was running short to capture what day-to-day life was really like in the Clinton White House—the personalities, the political maneuvers, the hopes and anxieties of people who lived through history. Thus, *The Survivor* is an interview-driven book, written immediately in history's wake.

For this reason, the first acknowledgment I owe is to the many dozens of veterans of the Clinton White House who helped me in this project by sharing their recollections. Bill and Hillary Clinton attracted many very talented and interesting people to work with them. Most of them are justifiably proud of their public service. Getting to know these diverse people, as I did while covering the White House and while working on this book, was the fun part of the job. Thanks very much to everyone who helped.

I must also be extravagant with thanks to my friends at the German Marshall Fund of the United States. This wonderful organization, dedicated to the promotion of transatlantic relations, is part foundation, part think tank. GMF housed me during my leave from the *Post* and helped fund the foreign policy research for this history. The time I was there, 2002 and 2003, was a period of intense debate over the role of the United States in the world. European perspectives on Bill Clinton are often quite different from conventional wisdom in America. Talking about Clinton and his legacy in the world amid the fertile intellectual atmosphere GMF sponsors was a terrific opportunity. Thanks especially to Bill Antholis, Craig Kennedy, and Phil Henderson for making this happen.

Thanks also to the folks at the Brookings Institution, where I briefly hung my hat and where I have many valued personal and professional relationships. E. J. Dionne, Tom Mann, Mike O'Hanlon, and Strobe Talbott have all given valuable advice on this project.

Any historian of the Clinton presidency must be especially grateful to several participants in the administration who have written memoirs of their experiences. These include Bill Clinton and Hillary Rodham Clinton, of course. But there are several other indispensable works, including those by George Stephanopoulos, David Gergen, Dick Morris, Sidney Blumenthal, Dennis Ross, Strobe Talbott, and Michael Waldman.

My job in reconstructing the Clinton years would have been vastly harder—and impossible in places—were it not for outstanding work written contemporaneously. The Washington writer Elizabeth Drew deserves special notice for her two richly reported books on Clinton's first term.

Then there is the giant in the room: my colleague Bob Woodward. One of the advantages of working at the *Washington Post* is the privilege of knowing some of the legends of journalism, and of working with them in a commonplace, everyday sort of way. But there is nothing commonplace about Woodward. Only someone who has worked to understand the Clinton presidency in retrospect can truly appreciate the magnitude of Woodward's achievements in capturing so many essential facts and truths about the political and policy dramas of those years at the very moment they were unfolding. His 1994 book, *The Agenda,* tells the story of the passage of Clinton's first-term economic program better than it will ever be told; his next book, 1996's *The Choice,* is essential reading for anyone who wants to understand Clinton's personal evolution on the problem of Bosnia. Of course, these are routine achievements in the context of his career. Bob has worked similar miracles during every presidency since Nixon's. He was uncommonly generous with advice to me on this project, just as he has been for countless other colleagues over the years. In addition, he helped facilitate with Mrs. B. A. Bentsen the release of his 1993 and 1994 interviews with former Treasury secretary Lloyd Bentsen, who was too infirm to participate in interviews for my book.

While on the subject of legends, there are a couple of others here in the newsroom to whom I'm indebted. David Maraniss's *First in His Class,* now a decade old, remains the best source for the story of Bill Clinton's rise to power in Arkansas. Like everything David writes, this biography is also a delight to read. On the sad story of the Clinton administration's failed effort to reform health care in 1993 and 1994, David S. Broder wrote the best book, *The System,* with Haynes Johnson. For four decades now, David has been the anchor and conscience of the political staff at the *Washington Post,* and he is a lodestar for journalists throughout the business. What a privilege it is to work beside him.

It is the nature of being a White House correspondent that one works constantly with many colleagues on the story of the moment—it might be politics one day, social policy the next, and foreign policy the day after, or sometimes all three on one day. Only the assistance of other beat reporters on this improvisational work saves the White House reporter from embarrassment (at least usually). Of necessity, this list of colleagues to whom I am grateful in the *Post* newsroom is only a fraction of what it should be. At the top, executive editor Len Downie and his deputies in the Clinton years, Bob Kaiser and Steve Coll, set a standard of excellence, and were all encouraging of this project. I'm grateful also to national editors Karen DeYoung, Jackson Diehl, and Liz Spayd. In the trenches, where the hard work of White House and political journalism takes place, I was incredibly fortunate to have two wise friends as my boss, Bob Barnes and Maralee Schwartz. In Washington, Schwartz is so well known for her commitment to the *Post,* her reporters, and first-rate coverage of politics that people all over town refer to her simply by her first name. Other colleagues and friends who helped me immeasurably during my time at the White House or in the drafting of this book include Mike Abramowitz, Mike Allen, Jo-Ann Armao, Chuck Babington, Don Baker, Dan Balz, Tom Edsall, Bill Hamilton, Al Kamen, Ruth Marcus, Robert Melton, Dana Milbank, Ellen Nakashima, the late Richard Paxson, Sue Schmidt, and Jim VandeHei.

I mentioned above the famous Ann Devroy. For nearly a decade now, in both Clinton's second term and the presidency of George W. Bush, the community of journalists and political operatives in Washington has asked, "I wonder how things would be different if Devroy were still around." It's quite a fair question; she was that good a reporter. After Ann was stricken with cancer, I was joined at the White House by Peter Baker, with whom I had been working since we were both young reporters covering Virginia. After publishing a book that is the essential history of Clinton's impeachment, and a tour as Moscow bureau chief, Peter returned to the White House beat in 2005 to cover George W. Bush. I have watched his work with admiration and awe for nearly two decades, and I can say that Peter deserves the highest praise I know how to give a reporter: He is as good as Devroy.

As people can see from the photographic pages of this book, I'm indebted to the expertise of the people who captured these images. From the *Washington Post* photo department, thanks especially to Joe Elbert, Mary Lou Foy, and Katherine Frey. Diana Walker is one of Washington's most talented and fascinating photojournalists; I'm very grateful to her for allowing me to reproduce some of her work. Several photos also come from the Clinton Presidential Library. Thanks to archivist John Keller, and to Robert McNeely, who took most of these images as a White House photographer. People who want to see more arresting images of the presidency should see two books, McNeely's *The Clin-*

ton Years: The Photographs of Robert McNeely, and Walker's *Public & Private: Twenty Years Photographing the Presidency.*

It would probably surprise outsiders to know how people covering the White House can simultaneously be competitors and friends with colleagues from other news organizations. Among the many people in this group, I owe special thanks to James Bennet, John Broder, Josh Gerstein, Mara Liasson, Bill Nichols, Bill Owens, and Todd Purdum for their wisdom and friendship.

Thanks also to Mark Halperin and Karen Avrich for their friendship and advice during several stages of this project, as well as to my friend and teacher Steve Schier of Carleton College. It was also my honor while undertaking this book to receive advice from Arthur M. Schlesinger, Jr., who shared some of his notes from his own encounters with Bill Clinton. Arthur, of course, is among the greatest historians and writers America has ever produced. His work as a public intellectual, public servant, and advocate for a liberalism that lays claim to the "vital center" makes him one of the most outstanding and consequential citizens of the twentieth century. To know and receive encouragement from this generous man was an incomparable privilege.

My friend Scott Moyers was the first to see promise in this project and the notion of my undertaking it. Toward the end of the process, Lisa Chase gave wise advice for tightening the text. Dave Ohls, a 2004 graduate of Carleton, came to my rescue by helping tackle the endnotes and some final research with vast intelligence and diligence. Kayeen Thomas, a current Carleton student, also lent a hand.

For most of my time away from the *Post* on book leave, I was joined by a research assistant, Will Bohlen. Will is everything an author would want: smart, conscientious, curious, well organized, independent-minded, funny, and uncommonly decent. More than a helping hand, Will quickly became a valued friend, which he remains.

The sheer logistics of book publishing, I've found, are dizzying. Fortunately, I have been in good hands. Thanks to my agent, the creative and loyal Andrew Wylie. And thanks to all the folks at Random House. These include Jonathan Jao, a shrewd and patient editor (or at least he learned to be patient working with me), and Jonathan Karp, the brilliant editor in chief of the Random House Publishing Group. I first worked with Karp in the summer of 1985, when we were both summer interns at the *Washington Post.* Anyone might have guessed that he was a future big shot. Being reunited with him after many years has been a delight.

I did not know what I was getting into by writing a book, but most of my family and friends—more aware of my habits than I am of my own—surely had a hunch. My best friends—Tom and Karin Kullman Freedman, and Rick and Jane Ward—have my thanks for making sure that fun and laughter stayed in my life even during periods of frustration. My sister, Catherine Harris, and brother, James Harris, likewise kept my spirits high during the long march. My mother, Nancy Hamlin, gave me a love of language from an early age. It is one of life's disappointments that my father, Carl M. Harris, who died in 1995, is not here to see this book. My three wonderful children—Liza, Griffin, and Nicola—suffered through a grumpy and behind-schedule father with their usual good cheer. And Ann O'Hanlon, to whom this book is dedicated, brought a huge heart and a wise mind—not to mention quite a good editor's eye— to this project. She has brought the same rare qualities to everything we have done together since our first date in 1994.

JOHN F. HARRIS
March 25, 2005

Notes

This is an interview-driven history. The pillars of my research were hundreds of interviews with people who know Bill Clinton or intersected with his presidency in various ways. This group includes people at all levels of the Clinton White House during both of his terms. Most of these interviews were on the record. Because both Bill Clinton and Senator Hillary Rodham Clinton remain active figures in public life, some of their current or former aides and associates said they could share recollections only on a "background" basis, without being identified by name. These notes aim to reflect sources with as much precision as these conditions allowed.

The notes also make clear my debt to numerous other writers who have added in essential ways to the record of the Clinton presidency. These include daily journalists, book writers, and veterans of the Clinton administration who published memoirs of their experiences. I am also indebted to several people who shared contemporaneous notes or other documents about key foreign and domestic policy decisions.

Finally, this book draws on my decade of covering the Clintons for the *Washington Post*. Over the course of those years, including during the period I was researching this history, I have had numerous on-the-record and less formal conversations with both Bill Clinton and Hillary Rodham Clinton. These interviews were in my capacity as a political reporter for the *Post*, not as author of this book, but they do inform this book's understanding of these two vital personalities and their impact on American life.

Prologue THE ASCENT

xi Clinton later told Reed: Interview with Bruce Reed.

xi The bar in this instance: The description of this meeting comes from an interview with Paul Begala.

xv Instead, as From and his ideological confederates saw it: Interview with Al From.

xvi What's more, his personal relationship with the governor: These memos come from the files of a 1992 Clinton campaign adviser.

xvii As Stan Greenberg, the campaign pollster: Interview with Stan Greenberg.

xviii John King: Interview with John King.

xix With earnest intensity, she made a prediction about her boyfriend: James B. Stewart, *Blood Sport*, pp. 238–39.

xxi "I think we're all addicted to something": David Maraniss, *First in His Class*, p. 422.

xxi "Thank you for coming": John Brummett, *High Wire*, p. 3.

xxi "Boy, I bet we never lose": Dale Bumpers, *The Best Lawyer in a One-Lawyer Town,* pp. 244–45.

xxi "I knew the first time": Interview with David Pryor.

xxii In the other direction was an almost mystical arc: "Bill Clinton: Born to Run . . . and Run . . . and Run," *Washington Post,* July 13, 1992.

xxii Just days before his announcement: Interview with Greenberg.

xxii On the very day of his announcement: David Gergen, *Eyewitness to Power,* p. 255.

xxvi "I thought we had an agreement": Al Kamen, "Clinton Shows Quick Temper While Golfing," *Washington Post,* Nov. 8, 1992.

xxvii "Rigging certain departments for a single gender or race": George Will, "Grievance Groups' New Sovereignty," *Washington Post,* Dec. 27, 1992.

xxix "everyone went crazy": Interview with Mark Gearan.

xxix As *New York Times* columnist William Safire: William Safire, "Working the Room," *New York Times,* Dec. 14, 1992.

xxix "Washington is a better place": Ibid.

xxix "She did not treat them": Lloyd Grove, "She's the Consummate New Yorker . . . ," *Washington Post,* Mar. 2, 1993.

xxix Thomases herself explained: Ibid.

xxxi Only then did he learn that he had gotten the job: Interview with John Podesta.

Section One

One BELLS OF HOPE

4 NASA, though, informed the inaugural planners: Felicity Barringer, "Live on Inaugural Stage, Symphony of Diversity," *New York Times,* Jan. 11, 1993.

4 "The bell-ringing seemed a little": Mary McGrory, "And the Rockets' Red Glitz?," *Washington Post,* Jan. 19, 1993.

4 On January 7, just under two weeks: Bob Woodward, *The Agenda,* p. 84.

5 The reversal won praise as a responsible concession: "Breaking the Right Promises . . . ," *Washington Post,* Jan. 17, 1993.

6 In his living room, Clinton sat: Interview with Sandy Berger.

7 "I'm a Baptist": Thomas L. Friedman, "Clinton Backs Raid but Muses About a New Start," *New York Times,* Jan. 14, 1993.

7 "shroud conflict in soft language": George Stephanopoulos, *All Too Human,* p. 158.

7 "Sometimes people hear only half": Transcript, Bill Clinton news conference, Jan. 14, 1993.

7 "From New Hampshire forward": Ibid.

8 What's with those guys?: Interview with adviser to Clinton during the transition.

8 "This week," he observed archly: "More Clear Sailing for Cabinet Picks," Associated Press, Jan. 14, 1993.

9 The Jefferson and Lincoln imagery: Michele Norris, "Populist Inauguration Could Mean Ulcers for Police," *Washington Post,* Dec. 3, 1992.

10 He would begin the drafting: Michael Waldman, *POTUS Speaks,* p. 30.

10 Michael Waldman, who worked on the inaugural address: Ibid.

10 Clinton's college friend, novelist Tommy Caplan: Ibid., p. 35.

10 An image he offered: *Public Papers of William J. Clinton,* 1993, vol. I, p. 1.

Two BEGINNINGS

12 Two thousand citizens won tickets: Richard Berke, "Thousands Show Up to Greet White House's New Tenants," *New York Times,* Jan. 22, 1993.

12 One young man in line cheerfully introduced: Ibid.

13 "This is your house": Ibid.

13 "We just screwed all these people!": Martin Kasindorf, "Well, Bill, There's This Problem," *Newsday,* Jan. 22, 1993.

13 "I've been here since Kennedy": Howard Kurtz, "News Media Hammer Soft Tosses," *Washington Post,* Jan. 22, 1993.

14 The new president was still: Elizabeth Drew, *On the Edge,* p. 38.

15 So when reporters pressed Stephanopoulos: George Stephanopoulos, *All Too Human,* pp. 110–11.

15 But so it proved to be: David Johnston, "Clinton's Choice for Justice Dept. Hired Illegal Aliens for Household," *New York Times,* Jan. 14, 1993.

15 "Fight," urged Bernard Nussbaum: James B. Stewart, *Blood Sport,* p. 245.

15 Biden called to bluntly tell Clinton: Drew, *On the Edge,* p. 41.

16 He was wearing sweatpants: Stephanopoulos, *All Too Human,* p. 120.

16 "George, does it get any better than this?": Interview with David Leavy.

17 "I made a campaign promise": Colin Powell, *My American Journey,* p. 572.

17 "Mr. President, I hope we don't": Drew, *On the Edge,* p. 47.

17 Senator Robert Byrd of West Virginia: Stephanopoulos, *All Too Human,* p. 127.

18 Putting it mildly, Clinton acknowledged: *Public Papers of William J. Clinton,* 1993, vol. I, p. 21.

18 To which Barney Frank: Ruth Marcus and Helen Dewar, "Clinton Compromise Delays Showdown Over Ban on Gays," *Washington Post,* Jan. 30, 1993.

19 "To renew America, we must": *Public Papers,* p. 1.

19 Armed with columns of the latest: Bob Woodward, *The Agenda,* p. 106.

19 "We'd be going over the numbers": Robert Reich interview by Chris Bury, PBS *Frontline,* September 2000.

20 "If I don't get health care done": Woodward, *The Agenda,* p. 124.

20 "This is fun": Drew, *On the Edge,* p. 68.

23 The night before his swearing-in: Michael Waldman, *POTUS Speaks,* p. 36.

23 Later, with Sperling a bit shaken: Woodward, *The Agenda,* p. 127.

24 Toward the end of the process: Ibid., p. 126.

25 "Of all the people": *Public Papers,* p. 15.

27 He was a familiar face: Michael Tackett and William Gaines, "Mack McLarty, Clinton's Alter Ego," *Chicago Tribune,* Dec. 19, 1993.

28 Addressing a group of people: Interview with Dwight Holton.

28 What would ordinarily be simple chores: Background interview with former McLarty aide.

29 So, at 9 p.m. on February 15: *Public Papers,* pp. 105–6.

30 Within the White House: Waldman, *POTUS Speaks,* p. 43.

30 "I did not seek this office": *Public Papers,* pp. 114, 121.

Three CROWN JEWEL

33 On one occasion Clinton's schedule: Interview with Andrew Friendly.

34 Then, on February 19, a gossip columnist: Bill Zwecker, " 'Hot' Rumors Dog Clintons," *Chicago Sun-Times,* Feb. 19, 1993.

34 The president and first lady summoned: Interviews with Clinton advisers.

34 The Clintons felt they knew: Background interview with Clinton family adviser.

35 he appeared two months into his presidency: Roxanne Roberts, "Clinton & Company Dish Scraps to Press," *Washington Post,* Mar. 19, 1993.

36 Begala, Clinton's traveling aide: Interview with Paul Begala.

37 David S. Broder of the *Washington Post*: Thomas Rosenstiel, "POTUS and the Posties," *Los Angeles Times,* May 16, 1993.

38 On February 17: *Final Report of the Independent Counsel In Re: Madison Guaranty Savings & Loan Association, In Re: William David Watkins and In Re: Hillary Rodham Clinton,* Oct. 18, 2000, p. 62.

38 With a backward check: Ibid., p. 63.

38 The decision on May 19: Dee Dee Myers, transcript, White House press briefing, May 19, 1993.

39 On the defensive, the White House asserted: Ann Devroy, "Staff Denies Clinton Ally Had Role in Firings," *Washington Post,* May 21, 1993.

39 "All I know about it": *Public Papers of William J. Clinton,* 1993, vol. I, p. 705.

39 He had spoken with the first lady several times: Toni Locy, "Foster Journal Shows Worry About Travel Office," *Washington Post,* July 29, 1995.

40 "We need those people out": *Final Report of the Independent Counsel In Re: Madison,* pp. 14, 36.

40 She steadfastly maintained: Ibid., p. 28.

40 She later expanded that answer: Ibid., p. 33.

40 In 2000, with the administration: Ibid., p. 17.

Four HIGH NOON

42 April 22 was gray and cold: White House pool report, Apr. 22, 1993.

43 "Ask yourselves," Wiesel implored: Henry Allen, "Holocaust Museum Dedicated with Hope," *Washington Post,* Apr. 23, 1993.

43 The crowd applauded heartily: White House pool report, Apr. 22, 1993.

43 A couple of hours later, a reporter: *Public Papers of William J. Clinton,* 1993, vol. I, p. 481.

44 He said Bush had "coddled": Mary Jo Layton, "Asian-Americans Jockeying for Clout," *The Record* (Bergen County, NJ), Oct. 15, 1992.

44 James A. Baker III: J.F.O. McAllister, "Atrocity and Outrage," *Time,* Aug. 17, 1992.

44 Clinton vowed he would: Walter Mears, "Clinton and Gore, 'On the Road Again,' Rip into Republicans," Associated Press, Aug. 5, 1992.

45 "Now you've really got your work": Elizabeth Drew, *On the Edge,* p. 156.

46 Instead, Christopher offered the new American proposal: Raymond Seitz, *Over Here,* p. 328, and David Halberstam, *War in a Time of Peace,* p. 227.

46 The journalist Elizabeth Drew: Drew, *On the Edge,* p. 157.

47 Years later, beneath the lines: Warren Christopher, *In the Stream of History,* p. 346.

48 Days before the 1992 election: Colin Powell, *My American Journey,* p. 561.

49 "He's very political," said Clinton: Interview with Paul Begala.

49 The diplomat Richard Holbrooke: Interview with Richard Holbrooke.

49 Sandy Berger later remarked: Interview with Sandy Berger.

50 The clash between the two worldviews: Powell, *My American Journey,* p. 576.

50 "I always felt more comfortable": Ibid., p. 577.

51 "Maybe we can call this his military service": Barton Gellman, "Warship Gives Clinton a Not-So-Hail to the Chief," *Washington Post,* Mar. 13, 1993.

52 "It's a movie about courage in the face of fear": *Public Papers,* pp. 760–61.

Five THE CLINTON STYLE

54 "Mr. President, it's really time to go": Interview with Andrew Friendly.

55 "He was not for it": Interview with Howard Paster.

55 Once in 1993 during a moment: Background interview with senior White House adviser.

56 "The president's suit, as he stood": White House pool report, Jan. 25, 1993.

56 This forced the closure: Glen Kessler, "Bill's Coif: The Myth," *Newsday,* June 30, 1993.

56 By then, Clinton had long since apologized: *Public Papers of William J. Clinton,* 1993, vol. I, p. 751.

56 So there was Clinton on March 9: White House pool report, Mar. 9, 1993.

57 A pert teenage girl: Transcript, MTV "Enough Is Enough" Forum on Crime, Apr. 19, 1994.

58 Jake Siewert: Interview with Jake Siewert.

59 In an exchange with reporters: *Public Papers,* p. 325.

59 Clinton had given Stephanopoulos license: George Stephanopoulos, *All Too Human,* p. 166.

59 On April 7, with a call: Ron Fournier, "Cuomo Out of Supreme Court Picture," Associated Press, Apr. 7, 1993.

60 But as word about Babbitt's likely promotion: Interview with Ronald Klain.

60 Clinton had now taken longer: Ibid.

61 The day before, on Saturday: Stephanopoulos, *All Too Human,* pp. 170–73.

61 When it was over: Interview with Klain.

62 The first question: *Public Papers,* p. 844

62 On the cover of *Time:* Michael Duffy, "That Sinking Feeling," *Time,* June 7, 1993.

Six FACES OF WASHINGTON

63 So it was that after midnight: The next several paragraphs, describing David Gergen's recruitment to the Clinton White House, come principally from his description in *Eyewitness to Power,* pp. 264–71.

63 "I'm in trouble": Ibid., p. 251.

63 A week earlier, the chief of staff: Ibid., p. 265.

64 "As he nears his 100th day": David Gergen, "After 100 Days, a President in Distress," *U.S. News & World Report,* May 3, 1993.

64 "Friend and foe alike": David Gergen, "Looking for More Backbone," *U.S. News & World Report,* May 24, 1993.

64 "I damn near dropped the phone": Gergen, *Eyewitness to Power,* p. 265.

64 "He thought the administration": David Gergen interview by Chris Bury, *Frontline,* PBS, June 2000.

65 "Here was a fellow": Ibid.

65 Paul Begala, for example: Jeffrey H. Birnbaum, *Madhouse,* pp. 212–13.

67 "One of the reasons": News conference, May 29, 1993; *Public Papers of William J. Clinton,* 1993, vol. I, p. 776.

67 He laid it on just as thick: George Stephanopoulos, *All Too Human,* p. 149.

69 Gergen had been warned: Gergen, *Eyewitness to Power,* p. 267.

71 Foster gingerly explained: James B. Stewart, *Blood Sport,* p. 243.

71 Webster Hubbell, a Rose partner: Webb Hubbell, *Friends in High Places,* p. 40.

71 "Why can't we lead the lives of normal people?": David Maraniss, *First in His Class,* p. 428.

71 "I think Vince and Hillary": Hubbell, *Friends in High Places,* p. 64.

72 Hubbell and Foster called her "Hillary Sue": Ibid., p. 169.

72 The *Wall Street Journal* focused: Robert L. Bartley, ed., *Whitewater: From the Editorial Pages of The Wall Street Journal,* pp. 41–88.

72 "Who Is Vincent Foster?": *Wall Street Journal,* June 17, 1996.

72 He had revealed his own attitude: Stewart, *Blood Sport,* pp. 254–56.

73 "Fix it, Vince!": Hubbell, *Friends in High Places,* p. 212.

73 His dead body was found: Stewart, *Blood Sport,* pp. 25–27.

73 The president was on live national television: Ibid., pp. 27–30.

74 Clinton was poised and strong: Gergen, *Eyewitness to Power,* p. 319.

75 The night of his death: Hillary Rodham Clinton, *Living History,* p. 176.

75 On the morning of July 22: *Final Report of the Independent Counsel In Re: Madison Guaranty Savings & Loan Association,* vol. III, Mar. 20, 2002, pp. 212, 227–28.

75 A heated phone conversation: Ibid., pp. 207–10.

75 He told aides that Foster: Stewart, *Blood Sport,* p. 298.

75 "an electric prod on the press": Mary McGrory, "The Fog After Foster," *Washington Post,* Aug. 8, 1993.

75 Within a few weeks of the death: R. Emmett Tyrrell, "Questions Begging Answers," *Washington Times,* Aug. 1, 1993.

76 Foster railed about the travel office uproar: Michael Isikoff and Dan Balz, "Foster Note Reveals an Anguished Aide," *Washington Post,* Aug. 11, 1993.

76 Five months later, in December: Michael Isikoff "Whitewater Files Were Found in Foster's Office, White House Confirms," *Washington Post,* Dec. 22, 1993.

Seven WAGER

77 President Clinton bellowed at his aides: Bob Woodward, *The Agenda,* pp. 161–62.

78 Labor Secretary Robert Reich: Ibid., pp. 160–61.

78 "Where are all the Democrats?": Ibid., p. 165.

79 Sperling remembered recoiling at seeing words delivered: Interview with Gene Sperling.

79 During the 1992 campaign he had read: *Public Papers of William J. Clinton,* 1993, vol. I, p. 137.

81 A year into the job, the Treasury secretary: These quotations come from background interviews Bentsen gave journalist Bob Woodward for his 1994 book, *The Agenda.* By 2002, Bentsen was too infirm to give interviews for this history. His wife, B. A. Bentsen, and Woodward graciously gave permission for transcripts of his earlier interviews to be placed on the record for this book. This quotation comes from a March 11, 1994, interview.

81 "He also has difficulty": Ibid.

81 Bentsen was there to gently stroke: Ibid.

81 Bentsen bristled every time Clinton lapsed: Bentsen interview by Woodward, Mar. 31, 1994.

82 "The rich can damned sure handle it!": Ibid.

82 Then one day in *Time* magazine: Michael Kramer, "The Political Interest; Still Waiting for Bill's Call," *Time,* Feb. 1, 1997.

82 Only years later, in the administration's closing days: Michael Kramer, "Headache Awaits W.," *New York Daily News,* Dec. 17, 2000.

82 Robert Reich was the opposite: Interview with Robert Reich.

82 He and Clinton met aboard the SS *United States*: David Maraniss, *First in His Class,* p. 123.

83 "Two worlds were foreign to him": Interview with Reich.

84 Clinton struck a wounded tone: News conference, Apr. 21, 1993; *Public Papers,* p. 485.

86 Senator Pete Domenici: Interview with Leon Panetta.

86 Not long after, Clinton heard it: Interview with Howard Paster.

86 Senator Phil Gramm: Paul Bedard and J. Jennings Moss, "Democrats Hope for Accord on Economic Package Today," *Washington Times,* July 29, 1993.

86 In the House, Newt Gingrich: "The Clinton Budget: Georgia Delegation," *Atlanta Journal and Constitution,* Aug. 6, 1993.

86 Begala in particular thought the sacrifice message: Woodward, *The Agenda,* p. 116.

87 Begala described the message: Ibid., p. 261.

87 In February, Vice President Gore: Ibid., p. 91.

87 For his part, Bentsen: Interview with Sperling.

88 "Let me see the sheet!": Interview with Paster.

88 There was one poignant moment: Ibid.

Eight PARTNERS

91 After agonizing for weeks: Bob Woodward, *The Agenda,* p. 287.

91 Clinton realized he was going to lose: George Stephanopoulos, *All Too Human,* pp. 175–76.

92 "He did not like the fact": Interview with Gene Sperling.

95 At a cabinet meeting, he slammed: Interview with Lloyd Bentsen conducted by Bob Woodward. Shared with the author with the permission of B. A. Bentsen.

96 "We've been waiting in line": Woodward, *The Agenda,* p. 314.

97 "Hillary is a closer": Margaret Carlson, "At the Center of Power," *Time,* May 10, 1993.

97 "She was the only person": Interview with Jake Siewert.

97 She was surprised: Interviews with advisers to Hillary Clinton.

98 In a widely noted speech: Clarence Page, "First Couple's Vision Quest Is Leaving Us Stranded," *Chicago Tribune,* May 26, 1993.

98 Michael Kelly: Michael Kelly, "Saint Hillary," *The New York Times Magazine,* May 23, 1993.

99 "These people are our enemies": Interviews with West Wing aides.

99 "Get with the goddamn program": Woodward, *The Agenda,* p. 281.

100 In November of that first year: David Gergen, *Eyewitness to Power,* pp. 282–85.

101 The evening was effectively the end of Perot: "NAFTA Debate: Gore vs. Perot," *Larry King Live,* CNN, Nov. 9, 1993.

101 One Ohio Democrat: Michael Duffy, "Secrets of Success," *Time,* Nov. 29, 1993.

Nine WHITEWATER

102 The word came: The best overview of the factual predicates and political pressures that burgeoned into Whitewater remains James Stewart's *Blood Sport.*

103 "The narrow issue is": "On Ethics: Arkansas Anxieties," *Wall Street Journal,* Dec. 15, 1993.

104 "Based on what's publicly known": "Open Up on Madison Guaranty," *New York Times,* Dec. 20, 1993.

105 It was time to draw a line: Both David Gergen and George Stephanopoulos offer

personal recollections of the Whitewater debate in their respective memoirs, *Eyewitness to Power* and *All Too Human.*

105 When the president precipitously: Gergen, *Eyewitness to Power,* p. 288.

106 Indeed, days after the White House had made its decision: William Rempel and Douglas Frantz, "Troopers Say Clinton Sought Silence on Personal Affairs," *Los Angeles Times,* Dec. 21, 1993; and David Brock, "Living with the Clintons," *American Spectator,* January 1994.

106 The troopers were simply upset: Interview with Dee Dee Myers.

106 Meanwhile, Clinton's chief aide during the Little Rock years: Stewart, *Blood Sport,* p. 356.

107 "This looks like a meeting": "Hearing of the Senate Special Whitewater Committee; Witness—Mark Gearan," Federal News Service, Jan. 15, 1996.

108 "You *never* believed in us": Stephanopoulos, *All Too Human,* pp. 231–32.

108 "JFK had real men": Interview with senior White House aides present at the meeting.

109 "I'm sorry you're not interested in the trip": *Nightline,* ABC, Jan. 12, 1994.

109 The special counsel was an "evil" institution: Stewart, *Blood Sport,* p. 374.

109 "No," he responded: Hillary Rodham Clinton, *Living History,* pp. 215–16.

Ten HEALTH CARE

110 As his wife gazed on from the gallery: *Public Papers of William J. Clinton,* 1994, vol. I, pp. 126–35.

112 After a year in office: David Maraniss, *First in His Class,* p. 67.

114 "We're going to do to health care in America": "Republicans Begin Attacks on Clinton Health Plan," transcript, CNN, Sept. 15, 1993.

115 "Watching him in that time": David Gergen, *Eyewitness to Power,* pp. 308–9.

115 "I'm sure you will do that, Mr. Armey": Haynes Johnson and David S. Broder, *The System,* p. 185.

115 Ralph Larsen: Ibid., p. 319.

116 Donna Shalala: Interview with Donna Shalala.

117 "We can do better than 91 percent": Robin Toner, "Moynihan Sees Danger in Delay on Health," *New York Times,* June 20, 1994.

117 "The argument we kept hearing": Interview with Harold Ickes.

118 "What the fuck are you doing up there?!": Background interview with senior White House official.

118 "By putting his personal signature": Paul Starr, "What Happened to Health Care Reform?" *American Prospect,* Winter 1995.

119 "The support they imagined was never there": Interview with Shalala.

119 "I set the Congress up for failure": Johnson and Broder, *The System,* p. 609.

Eleven SEA OF FLAMES

120 The two presidents had circled each other: Interview with Nicholas Burns.

120 The disgraced ex-president followed: Monica Crowley, *Nixon Off the Record,* p. 218.

120 At the same time, he was desperate for attention: Interview with Paul Begala.

121 "We're not inflicting pain on these fuckers": George Stephanopoulos, *All Too Human*, p. 214.

122 Powell, Clinton came to conclude: Bill Clinton, *My Life*, p. 553.

122 Taken aback by the ferocity of the exchange: Interviews with White House advisers and members of Congress at the meeting.

123 National security aide Sandy Berger later recalled: Interview with Sandy Berger.

123 The ship was greeted at the dock by an angry mob: Howard French, "Haitians Block Landing of U.S. Forces," *New York Times*, Oct. 12, 1993.

123 David Gergen warned that this was a terrible image for the network news: Stephanopoulos, *All Too Human*, p. 217, and interview with Berger.

124 "Les, I've got some bad news to tell you": Interview with Tony Lake.

124 After a failed effort: Elizabeth Drew, *On the Edge*, p. 373.

125 "The United Nations simply cannot": *Public Papers of William J. Clinton*, 1993, vol. II, pp. 1612–18.

126 Clarke urged restraint: Samantha Power, *"A Problem from Hell,"* p. 342.

126 Newt Gingrich: Ann Devroy, "Clinton Signs New Guidelines for U.N. Peacekeeping Operations," *Washington Post*, May 6, 1994.

127 The *Washington Post* described: Keith Richburg, "Westerners Begin Fleeing Rwanda; 170 Americans Leave by Convoy," *Washington Post*, Apr. 10, 1994; and Robert McFadden, "Western Troops Arrive in Rwanda to Aid Foreigners," *New York Times*, Apr. 10, 1994.

127 the State Department labored to avoid: Power, *"A Problem from Hell,"* pp. 359–64.

127 "I was obsessed with Haiti and Bosnia": Ibid., p. 364.

127 "I think it didn't arise": Interview with Anthony Lake, "Ghosts of Rwanda," *Frontline*, PBS, April 2004.

127 On April 8, in Minneapolis: *Public Papers*, 1994, vol. I, p. 643.

128 "It is time for the leaders of Rwanda": Ibid., pp. 806–7.

128 "Well, perhaps," Clinton replied: Ibid., p. 830.

128 "We do want very much to try to help": Ibid., p. 1057.

128 On July 22, as he announced that the United States: Ibid., p. 1298.

129 Within weeks of taking the Pentagon post: R. Jeffrey Smith, "U.S. Tough Talk Rattles Nerves in Asia," *Washington Post*, Apr. 5, 1994.

129 For this reason, Perry favored "coercive diplomacy": Interview with William J. Perry; and "Remarks of Former Secretary of Defense Perry to the Brookings Institution," Federal News Service, Jan. 24, 2003.

130 What's more, a North Korean negotiator replied: J.F.O. McAllister, "Pyongyang's Dangerous Game," *Time*, Apr. 4, 1994.

130 Perry and the new chairman of the Joint Chiefs: For a thorough reconstruction of this episode, see Don Oberdorfer, *The Two Koreas*, pp. 305–68.

130 "Politics is not the art of the possible": Ashton B. Carter and William J. Perry, *Preventive Defense*, p. 123.

130 He likewise cited the historian Barbara Tuchman: Joel S. Wit, Daniel B. Poneman, and Robert L. Gallucci, *Going Critical,* p. 227.

130 Most White House officials: Oberdorfer, *The Two Koreas,* p. 318.

130 When Carter had sent Clinton a letter: Interview with Jimmy Carter, "Kim's Nuclear Gamble," *Frontline,* PBS, April 2003.

131 The North Koreans would agree: Oberdorfer, *The Two Koreas,* pp. 330–33.

131 "Look, I knew": Wit, Poneman, and Gallucci, *Going Critical,* p. 240.

132 Conservatives, including Senator John McCain: John McCain interview with Martin Smith, "Kim's Nuclear Gamble," *Frontline.*

Twelve FLOOD LEADS TO FORTUNE

133 "This is the same shit": Interview with Sandy Berger.

134 "For the last ten days": Elaine Sciolino, "Haitian Impasse—A Special Report," *New York Times,* Apr. 29, 1994.

135 The administration emissaries were planning to share with the exiled leader: This anecdote, like many in this chapter, comes from the contemporaneous notes, shared with the author, of one of the senior participants in the policy debate.

138 Indeed, a *Time* magazine poll showed nearly 60 percent: George Church, "Good Cop, Bad Cop," *Time,* Sept. 12, 1994.

138 Even so, he was effective in instructing Americans: *Public Papers of William J. Clinton,* 1994, vol. II, pp. 1558–61.

139 In Georgia, Carter stewed: Douglas Brinkley, *The Unfinished Presidency,* p. 420.

141 "Pack 'em," Clinton said: John Farrell, "Haiti Invasion Averted," *Boston Globe,* Sept. 20, 1994.

141 "The invasion is coming!": Colin Powell, *My American Journey,* p. 601.

Thirteen "NO! NO! NO! . . ."

143 Asked if he thought Hubbell had done anything wrong: *Public Papers of William J. Clinton,* 1994, vol. I, p. 446.

143 The Republican crowd in Washington: Ibid., pp. 450–53.

143 "At the beginning": Interview with John Podesta.

144 At the start of the year: "Capitol Hill Hearing with White House Personnel," Federal News Service, Aug. 2, 1994.

144 "I've been rezoned": "Press Conference by First Lady Hillary Rodham Clinton," Federal News Service, Apr. 22, 1994.

144 "In their bones": E. J. Dionne, "Why They Can't Stand Clinton," *Washington Post,* Dec. 28, 1993.

144 "They thought these were their parking spots": Interviews with Clinton aides.

145 And a lurid strain of hatred it was: Ann Devroy, "Clinton Foes Voice Their Hostility, Loud and Clear," *Washington Post,* May 22, 1994.

145 "The right hated the Clintons": Interview with Robert Reich.

146 In an interview with *Rolling Stone:* Jann S. Wenner and William Greider, "The *Rolling Stone* Interview with President Bill Clinton," *Rolling Stone,* Dec. 9, 1993.

147 "I am the only president": Todd Purdum, "Clinton Pledges to Defend Farm Subsidies," *New York Times,* Apr. 26, 1995.

147 "This president salts his remarks": Carl Cannon, "Bill Clinton's Pathetic Lies," *Weekly Standard,* Oct. 2, 1995.

147 "You know, he eats": Devroy, "Clinton Foes Voice Their Hostility."

148 "I'm humbled by what I don't know": Bentsen interview by Woodward.

148 Most of Woodward's sources: For a description of the White House's interactions with Woodward, see George Stephanopoulos, *All Too Human,* pp. 280–88. In addition, the author interviewed several senior White House officials who acknowledged speaking with Woodward.

148 "I'm worried you're going": Interview with a source familiar with the Woodward-Bentsen interviews.

149 "That Woodward's an evil guy": Stephanopoulos, *All Too Human,* p. 325.

149 "The administration, the Democrats in Congress and the party": Memorandum from Stanley Greenberg to the president, shared with the author.

150 "I had not seen faces like that": Hayne Johnson and David S. Broder, *The System,* p. 461.

150 "You could not pull him off the stage": Interview with Harold Ickes.

150 "You're going to lose the Senate and the House": Dick Morris, *Behind the Oval Office,* p. 16.

Section Two

Fourteen WINTER

153 He spent election night roaming the West Wing: Interview with Don Baer.

154 Appearing before reporters the next day: *Public Papers of William J. Clinton,* 1994, vol. II, pp. 2045–52.

154 In the days after the mid-term elections: Interview with Dick Morris.

154 On a trip to Asia: George Stephanopoulos, *All Too Human,* p. 322.

155 Finally, Ickes forced the issue: Interview with Harold Ickes.

155 On her last day: Interview with Dee Dee Myers.

155 He urged that Morris's name be kept secret: Interview with Mickey Kantor.

156 Economics columnist Robert Samuelson: Robert Samuelson, "The Nadir of His Presidency," *Washington Post,* Dec. 21, 1994.

156 She sponsored long discussions: Bob Woodward, *The Choice,* pp. 55–57.

156 "I have a good heart": Ibid., p. 56.

156 He read August Heckscher on Woodrow Wilson: Interview with Brian Lamb of C-SPAN, Feb. 17, 1995.

157 "I think I am a transformational figure": Dan Balz, "The Whip Who Would Be Speaker," *Washington Post,* Oct. 20, 1994.

157 He said Woody Allen's romantic relationship: David Broder and Ruth Marcus, "Bush Charges Democratic Platform Ignores God," *Washington Post,* Aug. 23, 1992.

157 He suggested that a psychotic South Carolina woman: Maureen Dowd, "G.O.P.'s Rising Star Pledges to Right Wrongs of the Left," *New York Times,* Nov. 10, 1994.

157 He proclaimed a few days before the election: Ibid.

158 Citing no evidence: Thomas Lippman and Ann Devroy, "Gingrich Takes Aim at Clinton Staff," *Washington Post,* Dec. 5, 1994.

159 "Dear Mr. President," wrote historian Arthur Schlesinger: Letter from Arthur Schlesinger to Clinton, Feb. 6, 1995, obtained by the author.

159 Clinton's longtime friend Taylor Branch: Letter from Taylor Branch to Clinton, obtained by the author.

159 Clinton tried to put himself: A transcript of this rehearsal session was given to the author by a participant.

160 During speech preparations: Interview with Baer.

160 "It's your speech, Bill": Stephanopoulos, *All Too Human,* p. 336, and interview with Baer.

Fifteen UNDERSIDE

161 Ickes had known Morris for more than twenty years: Interview with Harold Ickes.

162 "Mystery is an integral part": Eric Pooley, "Who Is Dick Morris?," *Time,* Sept. 2, 1996.

163 "It was like Clinton believed": Interview with Dick Morris.

163 "I know what's *wrong*": Bob Woodward, *The Agenda,* p. 172.

164 As Clinton looked on in bafflement: Dick Morris, *Behind the Oval Office,* p. 80.

164 "Greenberg never told me what to do": Ibid., p. 41.

165 Stephanopoulos, who loathed him: George Stephanopoulos, *All Too Human,* p. 331.

166 Robert Squier: Richard Stengel and Eric Pooley, "Masters of the Message," *Time,* Nov. 6, 1996.

166 "I have never seen such a role reversal": John F. Harris, "Policy and Politics by the Numbers," *Washington Post,* Dec. 31, 2000.

166 Morris, too, later reflected: Morris, *Behind the Oval Office,* p. 11.

166 Soon after Morris returned: Interview with Morris.

166 They were an odd couple: Morris, *Behind the Oval Office,* pp. 45–48.

168 The consultant had grown increasingly disdainful: Ibid., pp. 64–65.

169 The poll, which Morris commissioned: Ibid., p. 93.

169 The data fortified the essential: Ibid., p. 37.

170 Early in Morris's run: Interview with Morris.

171 What Morris did: Interview with Ron Klain.

171 "Putting aside how strange he was": Interview with Bruce Reed.

Sixteen RELEVANCE

174 Morris thought this was foolish: Dick Morris, *Behind the Oval Office,* p. 119.

175 "We need now to emerge from the shadows": Ibid.

175 Having lost their fight: Michael Waldman, *POTUS Speaks*, p. 81.

175 There he laid eyes on "Charlie": Interview with Don Baer.

175 "I do not want a pile of vetoes": *Public Papers of William J. Clinton*, 1995, vol. I, p. 482.

176 The house was the cottage: John F. Harris, "Among New Deal Believers, Clinton Has His Skeptics," *Washington Post*, Apr. 13, 1995.

177 In the next day's *Washington Post:* Ibid.

177 "Those who fought me tooth and nail": Letter to Arthur Schlesinger Jr., Apr. 20, 1995.

177 "What do you fellows think": Schlesinger notes from meeting, July 7, 1995.

178 Then Clinton answered a question: *Public Papers*, p. 547.

178 George Stephanopoulos later surmised: George Stephanopoulos interview by Chris Bury, *Frontline*, PBS, June–July 2000.

179 In the middle of a photo opportunity: James Carney, "Measure of a President," *Time*, May 1, 1995.

179 "Tight and self-contained": Interview with Jonathan Prince.

180 Citing a biblical verse: *Public Papers*, p. 573.

180 The weekend after the bombing: Gerald Seib, "Terrorism Fears Running Deep, U.S. Poll Finds," *Wall Street Journal*, Apr. 27, 1995.

180 That Sunday on *60 Minutes:* John F. Harris, "Clinton Lashes Out at Terrorists, Seeks Expanded Powers," *Washington Post*, Apr. 24, 1995.

180 Just a week after the bombing: Morris, *Behind the Oval Office*, p. 419.

Seventeen BALANCE

181 This time, however, the president turned on his young retainer: Interview with Gene Sperling. For a slightly different recollection of Clinton's quote, see George Stephanopoulos, *All Too Human*, pp. 345–46.

182 As Gore put it: Elizabeth Drew, *Showdown*, p. 217.

182 When presented with polls showing: Interview with Sperling.

183 As Gene Sperling, who had been heavily involved: Ibid.

183 In this instance, he broke free in late May: *Public Papers of William J. Clinton*, 1995, vol. I, pp. 713–16.

183 Horrified, White House aides coaxed: Ibid., pp. 735–39.

183 In May, however, Clinton learned: Interview with Sperling.

183 As Stephanopoulos retreated from: Ibid.

184 Dick Morris said she had been: Dick Morris, *Behind the Oval Office*, p. 169.

184 "make sure the speech": Stephanopoulos, *All Too Human*, p. 358.

184 At Stephanopoulos's urging, the first lady: Ibid., pp. 358–59.

184 The speech itself was: *Public Papers*, pp. 878–79.

185 New Jersey Democrat Donald Payne: David Broder and John F. Harris, "Choosing Conciliation Over Confrontation," *Washington Post*, June 14, 1995.

185 Congresswoman Patricia Schroeder: Adam Clymer, "Whether Friend or Foe, Most Think Clinton Is Playing Politics on Budget," *New York Times*, June 16, 1995.

185 Congressman David Obey: Ibid.

186 Commentator Bill Schneider: Stephanopoulos, *All Too Human,* pp. 359–60.

187 Jonathan Prince: Interview with Jonathan Prince.

188 Clinton read the material and announced: Christopher Edley Jr., *Not All Black and White,* p. 16.

188 "The definition makes all the difference": Stephanopoulos, *All Too Human,* p. 365.

189 On June 12, in a 5 to 4 ruling: Linda Greenhouse, "Justices, 5 to 4, Cast Doubts on U.S. Programs That Give Preferences Based on Race," *New York Times,* June 13, 1995.

189 Clinton's speech was a success: *Public Papers,* 1995, vol. II, pp. 1106–14.

189 Edley, though he cheered the result. Interview with Christopher Edley Jr.

190 One morning early in August: Interview with Paul Begala.

Eighteen ROLL EVERY DIE

193 Lake made this case during a long conversation: Interview with Tony Lake.

193 "We have obligations to our NATO allies": *Public Papers of William J. Clinton,* 1995, vol. I, p. 767.

193 "We've got to walk this back": Interview with Dick Morris.

193 "There's a regency": Dick Morris, *Behind the Oval Office,* p. 246.

194 "You don't want to be Lyndon Johnson": Ibid., p. 253.

194 Clinton essentially revoked any offer: *Public Papers,* p. 805.

194 *The Times* of London observed acidly: "Fireflies in June," *The Times,* June 5, 1995.

194 "Bill, this is a time when we have to be tough": William Drozdiak, " 'Bulldozer' Heads for Halifax," *Washington Post,* June 14, 1995.

195 "We need to get the policy straight": Bob Woodward, *The Choice,* p. 255.

196 "Can you believe he proposed": Derek Chollet, *The Road to Dayton,* p. 17.

196 "What do you think we should do on Bosnia?": Woodward, *The Choice,* p. 260.

196 "My 21-year-old daughter": Ibid., p. 262.

197 The alternative, he said: George Stephanopoulos, *All Too Human,* p. 383.

197 Perry had come to believe that robust airpower: Chollet, *The Road to Dayton,* p. 19.

197 Shalikashvili was born in Poland: For a portrait of Shalikashvili, see David Halberstam, *War in a Time of Peace,* pp. 319–21.

198 "If he ever does that again": Interview with Lake.

199 He could be a maddeningly indirect man: Interviews with former Defense Department and State Department officials.

199 "Mr. President," he cautioned: Woodward, *The Choice,* p. 258.

200 "This policy is doing enormous damage": Ibid., p. 261.

201 "I'm risking my presidency": Ibid., p. 265.

201 "If we let the moment slip away": Ibid., pp. 265–66.

Nineteen FUNK

203 Dressed in blue jeans: White House pool report, Sept. 22, 1995.

204 He talked about trivial subjects: *Public Papers of William J. Clinton*, 1995, vol. II, pp. 1455–63.

205 More progressive voices, such as Robert Reich: Robert B. Reich, *Locked in the Cabinet*, pp. 276–77.

206 Clinton was no exception: George Stephanopoulos, *All Too Human*, pp. 392–94.

206 Clinton actually knew the former football star: Jill Zuckman, "Clintons Slow the Pace; Calif. Vacation Long on Relaxing," *Boston Globe*, Mar. 31, 1994.

206 On October 3, however, he did sit: Stephanopoulos, *All Too Human*, p. 393.

206 His public reaction was: "Clinton Tells Americans to Respect Simpson Verdict," Associated Press, Oct. 3, 1995.

207 "They're giving him such a": Dick Morris, *Behind the Oval Office*, p. 156.

208 On October 17, Clinton made an appearance: *Public Papers of William J. Clinton*, 1995, vol. II, pp. 1616–25.

209 Sperling, holding his ground admirably: Interview with Gene Sperling.

210 The two men gazed: White House pool report, Oct. 23, 1995.

210 "In such a place," Yeltsin enthused: Strobe Talbott, *The Russia Hand*, p. 180.

211 Yeltsin started drinking, heavily: Ibid., pp. 182–83.

211 The Russian leader was thoroughly stewed: Ibid., p. 184.

212 Rabin lamented that he did not know: White House pool report, Oct. 26, 1995.

212 Nine days later: Michael Putzel and John Aloysius Farrell, "Clinton Calls Peace Rabin's 'Lasting Legacy,' " *Boston Globe*, Nov. 5, 1995.

212 Warren Christopher, who was with him: Warren Christopher, *Chances of a Lifetime*, p. 208.

Twenty SEEDS OF TRIUMPH

214 His own aides: George Stephanopoulos, *All Too Human*, p. 404.

214 "If you were my client": Robert E. Rubin, *In an Uncertain World*, p. 167.

216 Even his own mother-in-law: David Maraniss and Michael Weisskopf, *"Tell Newt to Shut Up!,"* pp. 147–48.

216 "No, that's not right, Al": Ibid., p. 149.

216 The next day Clinton held a cabinet meeting: Interview with Gene Sperling.

217 "It's petty": Lars-Erik Nelson, "Gingrich Shows Pique & Volleys, Crisis Reveals Newt Depths of Pettiness," *New York Daily News*, Nov. 16, 1995.

217 "People feeling confident": Newt Gingrich, *Lessons Learned the Hard Way*, p. 55.

217 He had sat through even longer hours with Clinton: This section is based on a long acquaintance with Panetta beginning during his years as White House chief of staff, and numerous interviews with Clinton advisers who worked closely with him.

218 "What's he still doing here?": Interview with a White House senior adviser.

219 On October 31, in the last meeting before the talks: Richard Holbrooke, *To End a War,* p. 227.

220 "If Dayton failed": Ibid., p. 307.

220 "Mr. President, you don't want to be": Ibid., p. 309.

220 "Whatever ambiguities and uncertainties": Tom Morganthau and John Barry, "On the March," *Newsweek,* Dec. 11, 1995.

221 At the State of the Union address: *Public Papers of William J. Clinton,* 1996, vol. I, p. 79.

221 A few days after the State of the Union: Interview with the author, for *Washington Post* article in late January 1996.

Twenty-one SEEDS OF DISASTER

222 She had fixed her gaze on him for months: *The Starr Report Narrative,* Part II: 1995 Sexual Encounters, Section B: First Meetings with the President.

223 Where were you, Gene: Interview with Gene Sperling.

223 She later described the moment: Monica Lewinsky interview with ABC's Barbara Walters, *20/20,* Mar. 3, 1999.

223 She told the president she had a crush on him: *Starr Report.*

224 "This could be a problem": Ibid., Section C: November 15 Sexual Encounter.

225 Marsha Scott: Interview with former aide to Erskine Bowles.

225 "He had been forced to change": Interview with Dick Morris.

225 Early in his first term: Peter Baker, "With a Private Fax Pipeline, Friends Help Clinton Keep in Touch," *Washington Post,* Jan. 20, 1997.

226 "I have an empty life except for work": Transcripts of taped conversations between Linda Tripp and Monica Lewinsky, Oct. 3–Dec. 22, 1997.

226 "Of course I do": Ibid.

226 Harold Ickes and a uniformed Secret Service officer: Gary Byrne grand jury testimony, July 17, 1998, p. 18 (p. 347 of *Starr Report, Supplemental Materials,* vol. 1), and John Muskett grand jury testimony, July 17, 1998, pp. 13–17 (p. 2966 of *Starr Report, Supplemental Materials,* vol. 2).

227 "Do you know anything about this?": Evelyn Lieberman, grand jury testimony, Jan. 30, 1998, p. 62 (p. 2340 of *Starr Report, Supplemental Materials,* vol. 2).

227 "What a way to start the day": The *Starr Report Narrative,* Part V: No Private Meetings, Section C: Telephone Conversations.

228 Some agents said she had boasted: Transcripts of Secret Service interviews in the *Starr Report,* supplemented by author interviews with Secret Service agents.

228 Leon Panetta once got word: Leon Panetta, grand jury testimony, Jan. 28, 1998, p. 144 (p. 3235 of *Starr Report, Supplemental Materials,* vol. 3).

228 A few moments later: The author witnessed the episode.

228 The day after the incident with Lawrence: White House pool report, June 10, 1996.

228 Early in his term: Mickey Kaus, " 'Full Service' Chatterdump," *Slate,* Jan. 29, 1998.

228 "That's a lie": Interview with Dee Dee Myers.

229 "Attention, everyone!": The author was present for the occasion.

229 One woman: Interview with a former senior White House official.

Twenty-two WELFARE

231 On the evening of July 30, 1996: Interviews with Clinton advisers who spoke with him immediately after his conversation.

231 There was a big difference: For readers interested in a comprehensive and rigorously reported overview of the welfare reform issue, see Jason DeParle's *American Dream.*

232 "This is not about welfare": Interview with Clinton adviser.

232 "Welfare veto would be a disaster": Dick Morris, *Behind the Oval Office,* p. 595.

233 This was the question on the table as Clinton: The reconstruction of this meeting comes from interviews with several Clinton administration officials present. Foremost among them was domestic policy adviser Bruce Reed, who was the White House's most important advocate of welfare reform and kept careful notes and records of the deliberations. Other interviews include Health and Human Services Secretary Donna Shalala, Deputy White House Chief of Staff Harold Ickes, and political adviser Rahm Emanuel. Their accounts are broadly consistent, and vary only in detail. The narrative description of this fateful day represents an amalgamation of these interviews.

233 In late 1994, just after the Republican sweep: Mickey Kaus, "They Blew It," *New Republic,* Dec. 5, 1994.

234 Apparently, Moynihan sneered: Jason DeParle, "Moynihan Says President Is Insincere About Reforming the Welfare System," *New York Times,* Jan. 8, 1994.

234 On the very morning Clinton's team sat in the Roosevelt Room: Senator Daniel P. Moynihan, congressional press release, Mar. 4, 1996.

235 "You're here to keep me honest": Interview with Bruce Reed.

236 "That's the best argument I've heard so far": Ibid.

237 She would speak out publicly against any bill: Hillary Rodham Clinton, *Living History,* pp. 367–68.

238 "The politics of this are really tough": Interview with Shalala.

238 "Today we have an historic opportunity": *Public Papers of William J. Clinton,* 1996, vol. II, p. 1233.

239 "I signed that bill because I trusted you": Morris, *Behind the Oval Office,* p. 304.

Twenty-three RE-ELECT

241 "He's a closet liberal": John F. Harris, "Clinton Says He Is No Liberal," *Washington Post,* Sept. 24, 1996.

241 "A president is too exposed": Ibid.

241 "Where's the outrage?": Katharine Seelye, "Politics: The Republican," *New York Times,* Oct. 26, 1996.

241 A *Washington Post* poll: John F. Harris, "Clinton Backers of Two Minds," *Washington Post,* Sept. 13, 1996.

242 "The first time, obviously": "My Election Will Be Overwhelmingly Focused on the Future," *Washington Post,* Aug. 25, 1996.

243 On the evening of August 4: Dick Morris, *Behind the Oval Office,* pp. 305–8.

244 Ground zero for this project: Richard Berke, "After Hours at White House, Brain Trust Turns to Politics," *New York Times,* July 21, 1996; and James Barnes, "Burning the Midnight Reelection Oil," *National Journal,* July 22, 1996.

245 Years later, Clinton kept returning: Interviews with numerous Clinton advisers.

246 As Michael McCurry described it: Eric Pooley, "The Last Action Hero," *Time,* July 22, 1996.

246 He had been lifting weights: David Maraniss, "The 'Comeback Kid' Is Back—Again," *Washington Post,* Aug. 29, 1996,

246 "I like your dog!": John F. Harris, "A Swing from Partisan to Presidential," *Washington Post,* Aug. 29, 1996.

246 The train ride: John F. Harris, "Next Stop, Campaign Heaven," *Washington Post,* Aug. 27, 1996.

247 At first, Clinton seemed not to register: Interviews with Clinton advisers.

247 Jordan and Clinton turned with mischievous grins: Ibid.

247 Sir, he asked delicately: Interview with Clinton adviser.

Section Three

Twenty-four S E C O N D   C H A N C E

251 "You know what Mark Twain said": *Public Papers of William J. Clinton,* 1996, vol. II, p. 1986.

251 This was, he told the crowd: Ibid., p. 2072.

252 In the back of the plane: White House pool report, Nov. 4, 1996.

252 "What's it going to be?": Interview with Mark Penn.

252 People who knew the results: Interview with Jonathan Prince.

253 He asserted that his re-election: *Public Papers,* p. 2081.

253 He wrote soon after in the *New York Times:* Arthur M. Schlesinger Jr., "The Ultimate Approval Rating," *New York Times Magazine,* Dec. 15, 1996.

254 At Panetta's recommendation: Interview with an aide to Leon Panetta.

254 "I need you here": Interview with Clinton adviser.

254 "I have worked hard for you": Interview with Harold Ickes.

256 Hillary Clinton herself now weighed in decisively: For Hillary Clinton's own version of this episode, described somewhat more delicately, see *Living History,* pp. 392–93.

256 "Someone else was influencing this decision": Interview with Clinton adviser.

256 Michael McCurry, the White House press secretary, urged: Interview with Michael McCurry.

256 Meeting with a women's group at the Sydney Opera House: John F. Harris, "First Lady Still Interpreting Her Role," *Washington Post,* Nov. 27, 1996.

257 "I wish you could see yourself": Peter Baker, "President Finds Power in Preacher of the 'Hour,' " *Washington Post*, Feb. 12, 1997.

257 Clinton's own head speechwriter: Michael Waldman, *POTUS Speaks*, p.156.

257 "Nothing big ever came from being small": *Public Papers*, 1997, vol. I, p. 46.

257 "is ripped with people": Ibid., p. 125–27.

258 "For most of the last four years": John F. Harris, "Applying the Salve of Prayer," *Washington Post*, Feb. 7, 1997.

Twenty-five THE QUIET YEAR

259 "I'm a creature of the private sector": John F. Harris, "As Clinton's Deal-Maker, Bowles Means Business," *Washington Post*, May 12, 1997.

260 He wanted to establish: Ibid.

260 "He had more personal magnetism": Gary Robertson, "Senate Candidate Bowles' Political Run Started with a Jog," Associated Press, Oct. 23, 2002.

260 "I think he's the best decision maker": Interview with Erskine Bowles.

261 "Gingrich's victory can be": Weekly memo from Mark Penn to the president, Jan. 8, 1997.

261 "Clinton will say yes to anyone": Background interview with senior White House official.

262 One sour morning Clinton dressed down: Ibid.

262 "I'm a pretty damn good Democrat": Harris, "As Clinton's Deal-Maker, Bowles Means Business."

262 When Bowles called to say that the two sides: Peter Baker, "Mount Rushmore or Bust: Clinton's Quest for a Legacy," *Washington Post*, Aug. 3, 1997.

264 "I want to create a climate": *Public Papers of William J. Clinton*, 1997, vol. I, p. 246.

264 In April, he and Gore appeared: James Bennet, "Presidents Call for Big Citizenship, Not Big Government," *New York Times*, Apr. 29, 1997.

264 "This is a huge deal": *Public Papers*, p. 752.

265 *Time* magazine noted disapprovingly: James Carney, "The White House Adrift," *Time*, Oct. 20, 1997.

Twenty-six THE SULLEN YEAR

266 "Hush money": William Safire, "Practice to 'Deceive,' " *New York Times*, Sept. 26, 1996.

267 As aides prepared the president: Interview with White House official who participated in the discussion.

267 That afternoon, though, as he met with reporters: *Public Papers of William J. Clinton*, 1997, vol. 1, p. 81.

268 With his usual light touch: Ruth Marcus and R. H. Melton, "DNC Donor Controversy Widens as Republicans Step Up Criticism," *Washington Post*, Oct. 18, 1996.

269 In the meantime, new revelations: Jeff Gerth, "White House Aides Helped Job Hunt of Clinton Friend," *New York Times*, Apr. 2, 1997.

270 There was Johnny Chung: Francis Clines, "First Lady's Ex-Aide Denies Soliciting Campaign Money," *New York Times*, Nov. 14, 1997.

270 He showed up in the offices: John F. Harris, "President Decides to Close Money-Losing Defense Fund," *Washington Post,* Dec. 31, 1997.

270 Instead, after $177,000 in contributions: George Lardner Jr., "White House Video Crew Taped Coffees," *Washington Post,* Oct. 6, 1997.

270 In Clinton's term 938 guests stayed: Charles Babcock and Sharon LaFraniere, "Hundreds of Contributors Enjoyed an Overnight Stay at White House," *Washington Post,* Feb. 26, 1997.

271 Some were celebrities whom the Clintons: Charles Babcock, "The Overnight Guests," *Washington Post,* Feb. 27, 1997.

271 When the watchdog group: Ruth Marcus, "Many Backers Spent Night at White House, Study Says," *Washington Post,* Aug. 25, 1996.

271 Yes, she acknowledged, the Clintons: Babcock and LaFraniere, Hundreds of Contributors."

271 Charles Krauthammer: Charles Krauthammer, "A Thousand Friends," *Washington Post,* Feb. 28, 1997.

272 When Whitewater first reached a boil: Interview with a former senior Gore aide.

272 The *Washington Post*'s Dan Balz: Dan Balz, "Out of Clinton's Shadow, Vice President Finds Heat Withering," *Washington Post,* Mar. 4, 1997.

273 Clinton, watching in mounting dismay: Interview with senior Clinton aide.

Twenty-seven MY KIND OF GUY

274 The story on the front page: Brian Duffy and Bob Woodward, "FBI Warned 6 on Hill About China Money," *Washington Post,* Mar. 9, 1997.

275 "That bastard was trying to sting us!": Interview with John Podesta.

275 The next day, reporters naturally: *Public Papers of William J. Clinton,* 1997, vol. I, p. 272.

275 That assertion in turn sent: Peter Baker, "Clinton, FBI Clash Publicly Over China Probe Briefing," *Washington Post,* Mar. 11, 1997.

276 In a meeting with Gorelick: Interview with senior Clinton administration official.

276 Freeh felt so strongly about insulating: David Johnston, "F.B.I. Denied Data the White House Sought on China," *New York Times,* Mar. 25, 1997.

277 In conversation with the president: Interview with Podesta.

277 One misgiving he had about the job: John F. Harris and David Vise, "With Freeh, Mistrust Was Mutual," *Washington Post,* Jan. 10, 2001.

278 Clinton thought this was a travesty: Interview with senior Clinton administration official who discussed the matter with Clinton.

278 The president offered an alternate explanation: Neil Lewis, "Clinton Apologizes Over Use of F.B.I. to Get G.O.P. Files," *New York Times,* June 10, 1996.

278 The FBI put out a statement: George Lardner and John F. Harris, "FBI Chief Says Request for Files Was Unjustified," *Washington Post,* June 15, 1996.

278 At Justice, Gorelick blew up: Interview with senior Clinton administration official.

279 Sandy Berger, who prided himself: Interview with Sandy Berger.

279 In December 1997, McCurry was asked: Michael McCurry, transcript, White House press briefing, Dec. 4, 1997.

279 "On this confidence business": *Public Papers,* 1997, vol. II, p. 1782.

280 "My job is not to make people happy": John F. Harris and Peter Baker, "Clinton Vows an Activist '98 Agenda," *Washington Post,* Dec. 17, 1997.

280 "No one in the press": Interview with former Clinton chief of staff.

Twenty-eight ALLIANCE

281 Presidential physician Connie Mariano: Hillary Rodham Clinton, *Living History,* p. 399.

281 So the president of the United States, sitting in his wheelchair: Thomas Lippman, "Hale Yeltsin, Lame Clinton Open Summit," *Washington Post,* Mar. 21, 1997.

282 George Kennan: "A Fateful Error," *New York Times,* Feb. 5, 1997.

283 "We keep telling Ol' Boris": Strobe Talbott, *The Russia Hand,* p. 201.

284 At their first dinner: Ibid., p. 237.

285 "Look, Boris": Ibid., p. 241.

285 "Yeltsin combined prodigious determination": Ibid., pp. 185–86.

286 "This is the generation that prefers reason to doctrine": *Public Papers of William J. Clinton,* 1997, vol. I, pp. 672–82.

287 Once, in Milwaukee: Sandra Sobieraj, "Clinton, Kohl Chat Over Italian Feast," Associated Press Worldstream, June 4, 1997.

287 "Are you going to be okay against this guy?": Interview with a senior administration official who read transcripts of the Clinton-Kohl calls.

288 "One miracle has already come true": Ronald D. Asmus, *Opening NATO's Door,* p. 243.

Twenty-nine UNSETTLED

290 "The governor said you make": Michael Isikoff, Charles Shepard, and Sharon LaFraniere, "Clinton Hires Lawyer as Sexual Harassment Suit Is Threatened," *Washington Post,* May 4, 1994.

290 Pollster Mark Penn's numbers: Mark Penn's weekly memo to the president.

291 While shaking hands with awestruck Dutch citizens: White House pool report, May 28, 1997.

291 In May 1994: Michael Isikoff, *Uncovering Clinton,* pp. 90–92.

291 James Carville: *New York Daily News,* Apr. 7, 1994; "Carville: He's Not Just for Breakfast Anymore," at Hotline, Apr. 7, 1994.

291 "The president adamantly denies": Stephen Labaton, "Suit Accuses President of Advance," *New York Times,* May 7, 1994.

291 Hillary Clinton had interviewed him: Jeffrey Toobin, *A Vast Conspiracy,* p. 48.

291 For a time, President Clinton wanted him: Interview with White House official who served on Clinton's legal team.

292 By August, however, Bennett had offered: Toobin, *A Vast Conspiracy,* p. 121.

292 In a curious episode: Ann Devroy recounted the conversation contemporaneously to the author.

292 There seemed to be two great impediments: Descriptions of the president and first lady's positions come from numerous background interviews with lawyers and other family associates.

292 John Podesta: Interview with John Podesta.

293 "Your focus has . . .": Kelly Kissel, "Letters from Jones Lawyers Released," Associated Press, June 10, 1998.

293 The examination showed no sign of curvature: Frank Murray, "Is This the President's 'Distinguishing Characteristic,' " *Washington Times,* Oct. 15, 1997.

294 Among the descriptions of excess: Deposition of Danny Ferguson, conducted Dec. 10, 1997, released Mar. 13, 1998, at http://www.washingtonpost.com/wp-srv/politics/special/pjones/docs/ferguson031398.htm.

294 Then there was the statement of Dolly Kyle Browning: Deposition of Dolly Kyle Browning, conducted Oct. 28, 1997, at http://www.cnn.com/ALLPOLITICS/1998/03/16/jones.clinton.docs/dolly.browning.deposition/.

294 "Where's Bill?" she asked: Deposition of Roger Perry, conducted Nov. 11, 1997, released Mar. 13, 1998, at http://www.washingtonpost.com/wp-srv/politics/special/pjones/docs/perry031398.htm.

295 "Bob, do you think I'm fucking crazy?": Toobin, *A Vast Conspiracy,* p. 167.

295 As it happened, Lewinsky had left: Ibid., p. 169.

296 He would tell her: Monica Lewinsky, grand jury testimony, Aug. 6, 1998, pp. 86–87 (*Starr Report* appendices, part 1, pp. 806–7).

296 On July 3, she sent Clinton: *Referral to the United States House of Representatives Pursuant to Title 28, United States Code, §595(c), Submitted by the Office of the Independent Counsel, September 9, 1998,* p. 66.

296 "it's illegal to threaten": Monica Lewinsky, grand jury testimony, Aug. 6, 1998, p. 75. (*Starr Report* appendices, part 1, p. 795).

296 After she broke into tears: Monica Lewinsky, grand jury testimony, Aug. 26, 1998, pp. 54–55. (*Starr Report* appendices, part 1, pp. 1334–35).

296 As Lewinsky left the Oval Office: Ibid., p. 56. (*Starr Report* appendices, part 1, p. 1336).

297 Around 2 a.m. on December 17: Monica Lewinsky, grand jury testimony, Aug. 6, 1998, pp. 121–26. (*Starr Report* appendices, part 1, pp. 841–46).

297 On December 28, Lewinsky went to the White House: Ibid., p. 36. (*Starr Report* appendices, part 1, p. 756).

297 Late in December, the two had a conversation: Transcript, phone conversation between Monica Lewinsky and Linda Tripp, at http://www.washingtonpost.com/wp-srv/politics/special/clinton/stories/newsweek012498b.htm.

Thirty T R A P P E D

298 Late in December, Clinton: *Public Papers of William J. Clinton,* 1997, vol. II, p. 1791.

299 The first family repaired: Peter Baker, "Return Trip to 'America's Paradise' Lets Clintons Master Art of Relaxing," *Washington Post,* Jan. 5, 1998.

300 At the New Year, Gallup: *Inside Politics,* CNN, Dec. 30, 1997.

300 Another survey found that nearly 80 percent: John F. Harris, "Jones Case Tests Political Paradox," *Washington Post*, Jan. 19, 1998.

300 "I just try to put it over": Kenneth Walsh and Ronald Brownstein, "Just Applying Old Principles to 'A New World Out There,' " *U.S. News & World Report*, Jan. 26, 1998.

300 He and his lawyers spent: Jeffrey Toobin, *A Vast Conspiracy*, pp. 215–16.

300 On Friday night, Bennett had told Clinton: Bob Woodward, *Shadow*, p. 374.

300 If Clinton lied, "The crazies": Toobin, *A Vast Conspiracy*, p. 216.

300 "I hear you," Clinton said: Woodward, *Shadow*, p. 374.

301 In surreptitiously taped conversations: Transcript, phone conversation between Monica Lewinsky and Linda Tripp at http://more.abcnews.go.com/sections/us/StarrReport/starr_report_119.html.

301 What Clinton did not know: There are several accounts of the drama preceding Clinton's Jones deposition. Among the best are Toobin, *A Vast Conspiracy*, pp. 200–6, 214–15; and Michael Isikoff, *Uncovering Clinton*, pp. 309–23.

302 Knowing Clinton's garrulous penchant: Background interview with Clinton associate.

303 When Clinton returned to the White House: Interview with Rahm Emanuel.

303 When Currie arrived at the White House: Betty Currie, grand jury testimony, Jan. 27, 1998, pp. 70–75 (*Starr Report Supplemental Materials*, vol. 1, pp. 559–660).

304 It was during Kendall's call: Alexis Simendinger and James A. Barnes, "A Day Clinton Would Like to Forget," *National Journal*, Jan. 24, 1998.

305 "He said he was aware": Vernon Jordan, grand jury testimony, June 9, 1998, p. 76 (*Starr Report Supplemental Materials*), vol. 2, p. 1975).

305 "I've gotten you involved in this": Ibid., p. 80.

305 When Clinton awakened her: *Today*, NBC, Jan. 27, 1998.

305 The next person Clinton spoke with: Interview with Rahm Emanuel.

305 The first such audience was his senior staff: Erskine Bowles, grand jury testimony, Apr. 2, 1998, p. 84 (*Starr Report Supplemental Materials*, vol. 1, p. 239).

306 Clinton denied to Lehrer: *Public Papers*, 1998, vol. I, pp. 89–99.

306 This escape blocked, Clinton dutifully: Ibid., pp. 100–1.

307 Between the PBS and NPR chats: Ibid., p. 100.

307 To White House aide Sidney Blumenthal: Sidney Blumenthal, grand jury testimony, June 4, 1998, pp. 48–49 (*Starr Report Supplemental Materials*, vol. 1, pp. 184–85).

307 Blumenthal later surmised: Sidney Blumenthal, *The Clinton Wars*, p. 342.

307 "You poor son of a bitch": Dick Morris, grand jury testimony, Aug. 18, 1998, p. 14 (*Starr Report Supplemental Materials*, vol. 2, 2926).

307 For the first time, he felt: Interview with Dick Morris.

307 What had been implicit: Dick Morris, grand jury testimony, Aug. 18, 1998, p. 15 (*Starr Report Supplemental Materials*, vol. 2, p. 2926).

307 "Ever since I was elected": Ibid., p. 93 (*Starr Report Supplemental Materials*, vol. 2, p. 2946).

307 Morris believed the best course: Ibid., p. 15 (*Starr Report Supplemental Materials,* vol. 2, p. 2926).

308 "You didn't ask them about": Ibid., pp. 28–30 (*Starr Report Supplemental Materials,* vol. 2, pp. 2929–30).

308 Clinton's mood was desultory: John Podesta provided a sanitized version of this episode to the grand jury, June 16, 1998, pp. 92–93 (*Starr Report Supplemental Materials,* vol. 3, p. 3311). He has recounted the blunter version to associates.

308 Harry Thomason, the Hollywood producer: Harry Thomason, grand jury testimony, Aug. 11, 1998, pp. 13–17 (*Starr Report Supplemental Materials,* vol. 3, pp. 3730–31).

309 On Sunday evening, the old warrior: Harold Ickes, grand jury testimony, June 10, 1998, p. 100 (*Starr Report Supplemental Materials,* vol. 1, p. 1566).

309 In a midnight meeting in the solarium: Harry Thomason, grand jury testimony, Aug. 11, 1998, p. 39 (*Starr Report Supplemental Materials,* vol. 3, p. 3736).

309 "I want you to listen to me": *Public Papers,* 1998, vol. I, p. 111.

309 His rage was real: The author was in the room for this event.

309 It was not intentional, Clinton explained: Background interview with Clinton associate.

Thirty-one LOYALISTS

311 The catchphrase of the speech: *Public Papers of William J. Clinton,* 1998, vol. I, pp. 112–21.

311 Podesta was in the crowd: Interview with John Podesta.

311 The president was interrupted for applause: John F. Harris, "Clinton Pledges Activist Agenda," *Washington Post,* Jan. 28, 1998.

312 It was here that she invoked: *Today,* NBC, Jan. 27, 1998.

313 There was a strange and awkward moment: Background interview with Clinton political aide.

313 "I wish I had people walking the aisles": *Public Papers,* p. 123.

313 A *Washington Post* poll: Richard Morin and Claudia Deane, "President's Popularity Hits a High," *Washington Post,* Feb. 1, 1998.

314 On ABC, Sam Donaldson had predicted: *This Week,* ABC, Jan. 25, 1998.

314 "As to those of you who cast": Peter Baker and Toni Locy, "Jordan Reaffirms Clinton Friendship," *Washington Post,* Mar. 4, 1998.

315 "Look, I know what went on": Interviews with Clinton advisers familiar with the episode.

316 There was one area of his life: Interviews with Clinton advisers.

Thirty-two AFRICAN JOURNEY

318 Fearing he was about to witness a tragedy: John F. Harris, "Clinton Hails 'African Renaissance,'" *Washington Post,* Mar. 24, 1998.

319 "Going back to the time before we were even a nation": *Public Papers of William J. Clinton,* 1998, vol. I, p. 426.

319 Inside were several dozen people: White House pool report, Mar. 25, 1998. See also Jodi Enda, "Clinton: U.S. Fell Short on Rwanda," *Philadelphia Inquirer,* Mar. 26, 1998.

320 He said he accepted his share of responsibility: *Public Papers,* pp. 431–34.

320 At his hotel in Cape Town: Interview with Clinton adviser.

321 The South African said President Clinton and his wife: *Public Papers,* p. 448.

322 "Maybe there'll be a simple, innocent explanation": Roger Simon, "Telling the Truth Slowly," *Chicago Tribune,* Feb. 17, 1998.

323 "Is this an April Fool's joke?": Peter Baker, "*Jones* v. *Clinton* Suit Dismissed," *Washington Post,* Apr. 2, 1998.

323 Whimsically, Clinton picked up a drum: James Bennet, "Clinton Marks a 'Vindication' with a Guitar," *New York Times,* Apr. 2, 1998.

323 Clinton was happy: John Broder, "A Change in the Political Dynamic," *New York Times,* Apr. 2, 1998.

323 "a convergence": John F. Harris, "Coming Out of Africa with a Double Boost," *Washington Post,* Apr. 3, 1998.

324 "Sir, the ruling is great news": Interview with Clinton adviser.

Thirty-three SURVIVOR

326 There were signs of progress: *Public Papers of William J. Clinton,* 1998, vol. I, pp. 1080–89.

326 He ended the trip in Hong Kong: Ibid., vol. II, p. 1174.

326 "In the gaudy mansions of Clinton's mind": Nancy Gibbs, "Twin Perils of Love & War," *Time,* Mar. 2, 1998.

327 He was lost in space: Interview with Clinton adviser.

327 "It's like he isn't there": Peter Baker, *The Breach,* p. 36; and interview with Clinton adviser.

327 "It's almost as if the government adjusted": Interview with Donna Shalala.

327 On bad days: Interview with Clinton adviser.

328 "It's the Dow Jones": Mary McGrory, "Of Bombs and Bulldozers," *Washington Post,* Aug. 10, 1997.

328 Rubin, since his Wall Street days: For Rubin's explanation of his decision-making philosophy, see Robert Rubin's *In an Uncertain World.*

328 What skeptics often described: As explained by Rubin in interviews during Clinton's tenure.

329 "His view was that the bottom line": Interview with Gene Sperling.

329 In late 1997, Asian economies: *Public Papers,* 1998, vol. II, p. 1647.

329 If a Republican president had pursued: Interview with Sperling.

329 Each Thanksgiving, Clinton: Ibid.

329 "The drip of rumor": Memo by pollsters Mark Penn and Doug Schoen, Feb. 12, 1998, in documents shared with the author.

330 In the fall of 1997: John F. Harris, "Policy and Politics by the Numbers," *Washington Post,* Dec. 31, 2000.

331 Has Starr gone "too far"?: Memo from Penn and Schoen, Feb. 18, 1998, shared with the author.

332 Early in 1995: Interview with Terry McAuliffe.

333 "Let me have the phone": Ibid.

Thirty-four ROCK-BOTTOM TRUTH

334 "Mr. President": Interview with Clinton foreign policy adviser who heard Gingrich's comment.

335 A prosecutor and federal agent: Susan Schmidt and Michael Weisskopf, *Truth at Any Cost,* p. 219.

335 As soon as they left: Interview with Clinton adviser.

336 The president was woken up at five-thirty: *The 9/11 Commission Report,* p. 115.

336 Within the past few weeks: John F. Harris, "On the Road, Away From Crisis," *Washington Post,* Aug. 11, 1998.

337 "If it weren't for the 22nd Amendment": *Public Papers of William J. Clinton,* 1998, vol. II, pp. 1386–88.

337 "No matter what you read": Ibid., pp. 1436–40.

337 "Lord help me to remember": Harris, "On the Road."

337 A tear's path: John F. Harris, "At Ceremony, Grief Overtakes Weary Clinton," *Washington Post,* Aug. 14, 1998.

337 The *New York Times* and *Washington Post:* Richard Berke, "President Weighs Admitting He Had Sexual Contacts," *New York Times,* Aug. 14, 1998; and Bob Woodward, "President's Lawyers Brace for Change in Story," *Washington Post,* Aug. 16, 1998.

338 The president had tried to recruit Linda Bloodworth-Thomason: Jeffrey Toobin, *A Vast Conspiracy,* p. 310.

338 Some lawyer friends: Peter Baker, *The Breach,* p. 24.

338 "You have to face the fact": Hillary Rodham Clinton, *Living History,* p. 465.

338 She had been in constant contact: Diane Blair died of cancer in June 2000. Both an aide to Hillary Clinton and her husband, James Blair, told the author around the time of her death that she reported that her conversations with a woman she regarded as her best friend touched only obliquely on the scandal and its stresses.

338 The answer was always no: Interview with adviser to Hillary Clinton.

338 "Do not give me political advice": Richard A. Clarke, *Against All Enemies,* p. 186.

339 "What do you mean?": Hillary Clinton, *Living History,* p. 466.

339 The session began with one of the prosecutors: President Clinton's grand jury testimony was released to the public by Independent Counsel Kenneth Starr's *Referral to the United States House of Representatives Pursuant to Title 28, United States Code, §595(c), Submitted by the Office of the Independent Counsel, September 9, 1998.*

342 "The lie saved me": Interview with Clinton friend.

342 There were different poles to his personality: The account of the White House deliberations that night comes from interviews with a half dozen participants. See also Baker, *The Breach,* pp. 30–33.

343 "I know you all make fun of Sid": Interview with Clinton adviser.

343 "Mr. President, that's why God invented James Carville": Baker, *The Breach*, p. 32.

343 "People don't care about you or your problems": Interview with Rahm Emanuel.

344 Explaining why he had deceived the country: *Public Papers*, pp. 1457–58.

346 "There is a cloud over this presidency": Guy Gugliotta and Juliet Eilperin, "Tough Response Appeals to Critics of President," *Washington Post*, Aug. 21, 1998.

346 "There's an obvious issue": Ibid.

346 "All of you know": *Public Papers*, pp. 1472–75.

347 An aide frantically waved his finger: Interview with Clinton adviser present on the trip.

347 "You are about three days": Al Kamen, "United He Falls," *Washington Post*, Apr. 28, 1999.

347 Clinton began with a remarkable soliloquy: The account of this cabinet meeting relies on interviews with more than a half dozen participants. See also Baker, *The Breach*, pp. 72–76; and Robert Kaiser and John F. Harris, "Shalala's Remarks Irk President," *Washington Post*, Sept. 11, 1998.

348 "I think a lot of us": Interview with Dan Glickman.

348 Shalala, in particular: Interview with Donna Shalala.

348 "As you might imagine": *Public Papers*, pp. 1565–66.

Thirty-five AGE OF EXTREMES

350 The prosecutor's 445-page report to Congress: *Referral to the United States House of Representatives Pursuant to Title 28, United States Code, §595(c), Submitted by the Office of the Independent Counsel, September 9, 1998.*

351 "This is killing me": Background interview with Clinton friend.

352 "The Republican Congress had more caves than Okinawa": Peter Baker, "Clinton Celebrates a Victory Made Possible by Reduced Expectations," *Washington Post*, Oct. 16, 1998.

353 "I mean, he doesn't stop": *Public Papers of William J. Clinton*, 1998, vol. II, pp. 1836–38.

353 "This man's survival skills": John F. Harris, "Clinton Ambiguity Proves a Strength in Summit Role," *Washington Post*, Oct. 25, 1998.

353 His frenetic efforts at Wye River: Ibid.

353 Hillary Clinton, who was superstitious: "Clinton Takes Heart in Results," *New Orleans Times-Picayune*, Nov. 9, 1998.

353 Within days, New York congressman: Hillary Rodham Clinton, *Living History*, p. 483.

354 Within a couple of days of Rangel's call: Interview with senior White House adviser.

356 Quinn quoted Ronald Reagan's social secretary: Sally Quinn, "Not in Their Back Yard: In Washington, That Letdown Feeling," *Washington Post*, Nov. 2, 1998.

356 "This is perfect": Interview with Paul Begala.

357 "Anyone who sleeps with that bitch": Background interview with senior White House aide.

358 No legislator was more emblematic: For a description of Jack Quinn and his maneuvering regarding impeachment, see Peter Baker, *The Breach*, pp. 208, 221–22.

358 "It's out of my hands": *Public Papers*, pp. 2161–65.

358 This produced a bizarre scene: Baker, *The Breach*, p. 227.

359 "You resign!": Eric Pianin, "Clinton Impeached: House Approves Articles Charging Perjury, Obstruction," *Washington Post*, Dec. 20, 1998.

360 To counter this: Interview with Doug Sosnik.

361 "When we lost": A copy of Penn's Feb. 10, 1999, memorandum to the president was made available to the author.

361 "I believe any person who asks for forgiveness": *Public Papers*, 1999, vol. I, p. 189.

Section Four

Thirty-six K O S O V O

366 NATO ambassador Alexander Vershbow: Ivo H. Daalder and Michael E. O'Hanlon, *Winning Ugly*, pp. 54–55.

367 The Serbs, he explained: *Public Papers of William J. Clinton*, 1999, vol. I, pp. 451–53.

368 In the Oval Office one morning: Interview with Clinton adviser.

368 "Guys, let's not lose sight of why we did this": John Broder, "Crisis in the Balkans: White House Memo," *New York Times*, Apr. 1, 1999.

369 It was Albright: *Time*, May 17, 1999.

369 "History is watching us": Barton Gellman, "The Path to Crisis: How the United States and Its Allies Went to War," *Washington Post*, Apr. 18, 1999.

369 Clinton himself put it aptly that spring: *Public Papers*, p. 688.

369 With some real heat in his voice: Interview with Clinton foreign policy adviser.

370 "I really like him": Elaine Sciolino, "Nuclear Anxiety: The Point Man," *New York Times*, May 18, 1998.

372 While still close to the president: Interview with two senior advisers close to Prime Minister Blair.

372 "You tell him, 'These damn Americans!' ": Interview with Clinton foreign policy adviser.

373 "I and everyone else": *Public Papers*, p. 801.

374 In a tone that conveyed both defiance and reassurance: Tony Blair interview, *Frontline*, PBS, February 2000, and interviews with Clinton foreign policy advisers.

Thirty-seven E M P I R E S T A T E

377 Ickes's account with the Clintons: Interview with Harold Ickes.

378 "She would be great if she did it": *Public Papers of William J. Clinton*, 1999, vol. I, p. 192.

378 In an interview about her candidacy: *Meet the Press*, NBC, Feb. 14, 1999.

379 Perusing the polling data: Interview with two advisers to Hillary Clinton, one on her staff and the other working on the White House staff.

380 "B—what do you think of this?": John F. Harris, "The Last Chance Presidency," *Washington Post,* Sept. 10, 2000.

380 She'd been the hard-working class brain: Interview with Clinton adviser.

380 "I never realized how good Bill was": Interview with Ickes.

380 "we talk in the solarium": Christopher Goodwin, "Why Hillary Stands by Her Man," *Ottawa Citizen,* Aug. 1, 1999.

381 "I like Poughkeepsie": Interview with Hillary Clinton advisers.

382 "Why do I keep having to prove to people": Interview with Hillary Clinton adviser.

383 "Obviously, I didn't mislead anyone": "New York Senate Debate," Federal News Service, Sept. 13, 2000.

383 "You did great!": Interview with Clinton family adviser.

Thirty-eight "AL JUST NEEDS TO BE HIMSELF"

384 The vice president said he was proud: Vice presidential statement on White House South Lawn, Dec. 19, 1998.

385 "We are going to have real problems": Interview with Dick Morris.

385 "This year, he's sapping the moral energy": Interview with a political adviser who served closely with Clinton and Gore, and was present at the meeting.

386 "I felt what the president did": Andy Sher, "Gore Officially Announces Today," *Chattanooga Times Free Press,* June 16, 1999.

386 Making no mention of his irritations: Interview with Clinton adviser present in the room.

387 "They have never once invited us": Interview with Gore adviser.

387 "No, I'm not doing it": Interview with Gore adviser.

388 He had written the book in 1991: Al Gore, *Earth in the Balance.*

389 Watching cable television: Clinton has recounted this anecdote on several occasions, including at the dedication of his presidential library on November 18, 2004.

389 "Al, there's not a single person in this country": As described by a source familiar with Clinton's thinking.

389 If it would help: Bill Clinton, *My Life.*

390 What do you think?: Interview with Joe Lockhart.

Thirty-nine SPRING TERM

393 "After things have been tough": *Public Papers of William J. Clinton,* 1998, vol. II, pp. 1425–29.

393 "We believed that our economy would grow on forever": Ibid., 2000–2001, vol. I, p. 225.

394 The president's naval physicians averted their gaze to the deception: Interviews with Clinton aides.

395 Another episode during this same time revealed: Interview with Clinton aide.

397 "Bob thinks I hate him": Interview with John Podesta.

397 "He started grinding on my golf game": Remarks announcing the Adoption Bonus Awards, Presidential Hall, Sept. 24, 1999; *Public Papers,* 1999, vol. II, pp. 1583–85.

398 Now he had no time: Interview with Paul Begala.

398 Carolyn Staley: John F. Harris, "His Term Fading, a Wistful Clinton Loosens Up," *Washington Post,* Oct. 18, 1999.

398 "It has occurred to me": Remarks at an Empire State Pride Gala, New York City, Oct. 7, 1999; *Public Papers,* 1999, vol. II, pp. 1720–24.

399 No matter whether he enjoyed the jokes: Interview with Joe Lockhart.

399 "Let me say to all of you": *Public Papers,* 2000–2001, vol. I, p. 793.

Forty TERROR

400 As they were speaking: Clinton related this anecdote in an interview on CNN's *Larry King Live,* Sept. 3, 2002.

403 The national commission investigating the 9/11 attacks: *The 9/11 Commission Report,* p. 118.

404 "SUBJECT: Bin Ladin Preparing to Hijack US Aircraft": Ibid., pp. 128–29.

404 "I could just imagine the news report": "Clinton Defends Decision Not to Strike at Bin Laden Compound," PR Newswire, Feb. 5, 2002.

405 Years later, both CIA director George Tenet: *The 9/11 Commission Report,* pp. 132–33.

405 His editing might indeed have been done: Ibid.

405 "Terrorism is the enemy of our generation": *Public Papers of William J. Clinton,* 1996, vol. II, pp. 1257–59.

406 "But to me, it's money well spent": Judith Miller and William Broad, "Clinton Describes Terrorism Threat for 21st Century," *New York Times,* Jan. 22, 1999.

406 "Clinton would make requests": Interview with Richard Clarke.

407 "You know, it would scare the shit out of al Qaeda": Daniel Benjamin and Steven Simon, *The Age of Sacred Terror,* p. 318.

408 As Clarke, who despised Freeh: Interview with Clarke.

410 In the winter of 1999: The material on the Kashmir crisis comes from two sources: Strobe Talbott, *Engaging India;* and Bruce Riedel, *American Diplomacy and the 1999 Kargil Summit at Blair House* (http://www.sas.upenn.edu/casi/reports/RiedelPaper051302.htm).

413 "But you, Berger, are definitely coming with me": Talbott, *Engaging India,* p. 192, and interview with Sandy Berger.

414 "I offered him the moon": *The 9/11/ Commission Report,* p. 183.

Forty-one CAMP DAVID

The account of the Camp David summit is drawn principally from two sources: envoy Dennis Ross's comprehensive memoir, *The Missing Peace: The Inside Story of the Fight for Middle East Peace;* and an interview with Clinton national security adviser Sandy Berger, also a key participant, who took contemporaneous notes while the summit was under way. An important account also is to be found in Madeleine Albright's *Madam Secretary: A Memoir.* For an illuminating account more sympathetic to Arafat than Ross or most U.S. officials, see that of Robert Malley and Hussein Agha's series of articles in the *New*

York Review of Books, "Camp David: The Tragedy of Errors" (Aug. 9, 2001), and "Camp David and After: An Exchange" (June 13, 2002).

419 "We have no choice, right?": Interview with Berger.

420 But, feeling under pressure from the Americans: Malley and Agha, "Camp David."

421 Foremost among them was: Ross, *The Missing Peace,* p. 651.

421 The president rose to the challenge: Ibid., p. 653.

422 The explosion came: Ibid., p. 668.

422 Clinton's anger, believed Ross: Ibid., p. 684.

422 Berger, who knew Clinton far more intimately: Interview with Berger.

422 "I do not intend": Ross, *The Missing Peace,* pp. 676–77.

422 "I finally have his bottom line": Interview with Berger.

423 An international presence: For descriptions of Barak's offer, see Ross, *The Missing Peace,* pp. 688–89.

423 "This is the best deal you're gonna get": Interview with Berger.

423 Berger saw a man trapped: Ibid.

424 "You are smarter": Ross, *The Missing Peace,* pp. 694–95.

424 "You're asking me to sign my death warrant": Interview with Berger.

Forty-two EXIT

425 Yet at certain moments: Interview with Jake Siewert.

426 It was Gore's failure to run on the administration's record: Interview with associates of both Clinton and Gore. See also John F. Harris, "Clinton and Gore Clashed Over Blame for Election," *Washington Post,* Feb. 7, 2001.

427 Any answer other than an unconditional acceptance: Dennis Ross, *The Missing Peace,* p. 751.

428 "I hope my actions today will help bring closure": "Statements of Clinton and Prosecutor and Excerpts from News Conference," *New York Times,* Jan. 20, 2001.

430 His winter coat was on: Interview with John Podesta.

Bibliography

Albright, Madeleine. *Madam Secretary: A Memoir.* New York: Miramax, 2003.

Aldrich, Gary. *Unlimited Access: An FBI Agent Inside the Clinton White House.* Washington, DC: Regnery, 1996.

Allen, Charles F., and Jonathan Portis. *The Comeback Kid: The Life and Career of Bill Clinton.* New York: Birch Lane, 1992.

Anderson, Christopher. *Bill and Hillary: The Marriage.* New York: Morrow, 1999.

Anonymous (Klein, Joe). *Primary Colors.* New York: Random House, 1996.

Asmus, Ronald D. *Opening NATO's Door: How the Alliance Remade Itself for a New Era.* New York: Columbia University Press, 2002.

Baer, Kenneth S. *Reinventing Democrats: The Politics of Liberalism from Reagan to Clinton.* Lawrence: University Press of Kansas, 2000.

Baker, Peter. *The Breach: Inside the Impeachment and Trial of William Jefferson Clinton.* New York: Scribner, 2000.

Balz, Dan, and Ronald Brownstein. *Storming the Gates: Protest Politics and the Republican Revival.* Boston: Little, Brown, 1996.

Bartley, Robert L., ed. *Whitewater: From the Editorial Pages of The Wall Street Journal.* New York: Dow Jones, 1997.

Benjamin, Daniel, and Steven Simon. *The Age of Sacred Terror.* New York: Random House, 2002.

Berman, William C. *From the Center to the Edge: The Politics & Policies of the Clinton Presidency.* Lanham, MD: Rowman & Littlefield, 2001.

Birnbaum, Jeffrey H. *Madhouse: The Private Turmoil of Working for the President.* New York: Times Books, 1996.

Blinder, Alan S., and Janet L. Yellen. *The Fabulous Decade: Macroeconomic Lessons from the 1990s.* New York: Century Foundation, 2001.

Blumenthal, Sidney. *The Clinton Wars.* New York: Farrar, Straus and Giroux, 2003.

Bowden, Mark. *Black Hawk Down: A Story of Modern War.* New York: Signet, 2002.

Brinkley, Douglas. *The Unfinished Presidency: Jimmy Carter's Journey Beyond the White House.* New York: Viking, 1998.

Brock, David. *The Seduction of Hillary Rodham.* New York: Free Press, 1996.

Brummett, John. *High Wire: The Education of Bill Clinton.* New York: Hyperion, 1994.

Bumpers, Dale. *The Best Lawyer in a One-Lawyer Town: A Memoir.* New York: Random House, 2003.

Burns, James MacGregor, and Georgia J. Sorenson. *Dead Center: Clinton-Gore Leadership and the Perils of Moderation.* New York: Scribner, 1999.

Campbell, Colin, and Bert A. Rockman, eds. *The Clinton Presidency: First Appraisals.* Chatham, NJ: Chatham House, 1996.

Carter, Ashton B., and William J. Perry. *Preventive Defense: A New Security Strategy for America.* Washington, DC: Brookings, 1999.

Carville, James. *. . . And the Horse He Rode In On: The People v. Kenneth Starr.* New York: Simon & Schuster, 1998.

Chollet, Derek. *The Road to Dayton: U.S. Diplomacy and the Bosnia Peace Process, May–December, 1995.* Declassified State Department history of the Bosnia peace settlement, scheduled to be publicly available from Palgrave Macmillan, New York, November 2005.

Christopher, Warren. *Chances of a Lifetime: A Memoir.* New York: Scribner, 2001.

———. *In the Stream of History: Shaping Foreign Policy for a New Era.* Stanford, CA: Stanford University Press, 1998.

Clark, Wesley K. *Waging Modern War: Bosnia, Kosovo, and the Future of Combat.* New York: PublicAffairs, 2002.

Clarke, Richard A. *Against All Enemies: Inside America's War on Terror.* New York: Free Press, 2004.

Clinton, Bill. *Between Hope and History: Meeting America's Challenges for the 21st Century.* New York: Times Books, 1996.

———. *My Life.* New York: Random House, 2004.

———, and Al Gore. *Putting People First: How We Can All Change America.* New York: Times Books, 1992.

Clinton, Hillary Rodham. *It Takes a Village.* New York: Simon & Schuster, 1996.

———. *Living History.* New York: Simon & Schuster, 2003.

Communications from Kenneth W. Starr, Independent Counsel. Washington, DC: United States Government Printing Office, 1998. (This is the official message that Starr sent to the U.S. House of Representatives on Sept. 11, 1998, reporting his findings in the Monica S. Lewinsky investigation.)

Conason, Joe, and Gene Lyons. *The Hunting of the President: The Ten-Year Campaign to Destroy Bill and Hillary Clinton.* New York: St. Martin's, 2000.

Coulter, Ann. *High Crimes and Misdemeanors: The Case Against Bill Clinton.* Washington, DC: Regnery, 1998.

Crowley, Monica. *Nixon Off the Record: His Candid Commentary on People and Politics.* New York: Random House, 1996.

Daalder, Ivo H. *Getting to Dayton: The Making of America's Bosnia Policy.* Washington, DC: Brookings, 2000.

———, and Michael E. O'Hanlon. *Winning Ugly: NATO's War to Save Kosovo.* Washington, DC: Brookings, 2000.

Davis, Lanny J. *Truth to Tell: Notes from My White House Education.* New York: Free Press, 1999.

DeParle, Jason. *American Dream: Three Women, Ten Kids, and a Nation's Drive to End Welfare.* New York: Viking, 2004.

Drew, Elizabeth. *On the Edge: The Clinton Presidency.* New York: Simon & Schuster, 1994.

———. *Showdown: The Struggle Between the Gingrich Congress and the Clinton White House.* New York: Simon & Schuster, 1996.

Edley, Christopher, Jr. *Not All Black and White: Affirmative Action and American Values.* New York: Hill and Wang, 1996.

Flowers, Gennifer. *Sleeping with the President: My Intimate Years with Bill Clinton.* New York: Anonymous, 1996.

Gergen, David. *Eyewitness to Power: The Essence of Leadership, Nixon to Clinton.* New York: Simon & Schuster, 2000.

Gingrich, Newt. *Lessons Learned the Hard Way: A Personal Report.* New York: HarperCollins, 1998.

Greenberg, Paul. *No Surprises: Two Decades of Clinton-Watching.* Washington, DC: Brassey's, 1996.

Greenberg, Stanley B. *Middle Class Dreams: The Politics and Power of the New American Majority.* New Haven, CT: Yale University Press, 1996.

Greenstein, Fred I. *The Presidential Difference: Leadership Style from FDR to Clinton.* New York: Free Press, 2000.

Guinier, Lani. *Lift Every Voice: Turning a Civil Rights Setback into a New Vision of Social Justice.* New York: Simon & Schuster, 1998.

Hager, George, and Eric Pianin. *Balancing Act: Washington's Troubled Path to a Balanced Budget.* New York: Vintage, 1998. Also published as *Mirage: Why Neither Democrats nor Republicans Can Balance the Budget, End the Deficit, and Satisfy the Public.* New York: Times Books, 1997.

Halberstam, David. *War in a Time of Peace: Bush, Clinton, and the Generals.* New York: Scribner, 2001.

Halley, Patrick S. *On the Road with Hillary: A Behind-the-Scenes Look at the Journey from Arkansas to the U.S. Senate.* New York: Viking, 2002.

Harpaz, Beth J. *The Girls in the Van: Covering Hillary.* New York: St. Martin's, 2001.

Holbrooke, Richard. *To End a War.* New York: Random House, 1998.

Hubbell, Webb. *Friends in High Places: Our Journey from Little Rock to Washington, D.C.* New York: Morrow, 1997.

Hyland, William G. *Clinton's World: Remaking American Foreign Policy.* Westport, CT: Praeger, 1999.

Institute of Politics. *Campaign for President: The Managers Look at '96.* Hollis, NH: Hollis, 1997.

Isikoff, Michael. *Uncovering Clinton: A Reporter's Story.* New York: Crown, 1999.

Johnson, Haynes. *The Best of Times: America in the Clinton Years.* New York: Harcourt, 2001.

———, and David S. Broder. *The System: The American Way of Politics at the Breaking Point.* Boston: Little, Brown, 1996.

Jordan, Vernon E., Jr. *Vernon Can Read!: A Memoir.* New York: PublicAffairs, 2001.

Kelley, Virginia. *Leading with My Heart: My Life.* New York: Simon & Schuster, 1994.

Kessler, Ronald. *Inside the White House.* New York: Pocket Books, 1996.

Klein, Joe. *The Natural: The Misunderstood Presidency of Bill Clinton.* New York: Doubleday, 2002.

Kurtz, Howard. *Spin Cycle: Inside the Clinton Propaganda Machine.* New York: Free Press, 1998.

Lake, Anthony. *6 Nightmares: Real Threats in a Dangerous World and How America Can Meet Them.* Boston: Little, Brown, 2000.

Levy, Peter B. *Encyclopedia of the Clinton Presidency.* Westport, CT: Greenwood, 2002.

Lyons, Gene. *Fools for Scandal: How the Media Invented Whitewater.* New York: Franklin Square, 1996.

Maraniss, David. *The Clinton Enigma: A Four-and-a-Half-Minute Speech Reveals This President's Entire Life.* New York: Simon & Schuster, 1998.

———. *First in His Class: A Biography of Bill Clinton.* New York: Simon & Schuster, 1995.

———, and Ellen Nakashima. *The Prince of Tennessee: The Rise of Al Gore.* New York: Simon & Schuster, 2000.

———, and Michael Weisskopf. *"Tell Newt to Shut Up!"* New York: Simon & Schuster, 1996.

Matalin, Mary, and James Carville. *All's Fair: Love, War, and Running for President.* New York: Random House and Simon & Schuster, 1994.

Morris, Dick. *Behind the Oval Office: Getting Reelected Against All Odds.* Los Angeles: Renaissance, 1999.

Morris, Roger. *Partners in Power: The Clintons and Their America.* New York: Holt, 1996.

The 9/11 Commission Report: Final Report of the National Commission on Terrorist Attacks Upon the United States. Washington, DC: United States Government Printing Office, 2004.

Oberdorfer, Don. *The Two Koreas: A Contemporary History.* New York: Basic Books, 2001.

O'Hanlon, Michael, and Mike Mochizuki. *Crisis on the Korean Peninsula: How to Deal with a Nuclear North Korea.* Washington, DC: Brookings, 2003.

Pollack, Kenneth M. *The Threatening Storm: The Case for Invading Iraq.* New York: Random House, 2002.

Powell, Colin. *My American Journey.* New York: Random House, 1995.

Power, Samantha. *"A Problem from Hell": America and the Age of Genocide.* New York: Basic Books, 2002.

Public Papers of the Presidents of the United States: William J. Clinton, 1993–2001. Washington, DC: United States Government Printing Office, 1993–2001.

Reeves, Richard. *Running in Place: How Bill Clinton Disappointed America.* Kansas City, MO: Andrews and McMeel, 1996.

Reich, Robert B. *Locked in the Cabinet.* New York: Knopf, 1997.

Renshon, Stanley A. *High Hopes: The Clinton Presidency and the Politics of Ambition.* New York: Routledge, 1998.

———, ed. *The Clinton Presidency: Campaigning, Governing, & the Psychology of Leadership.* Boulder, CO: Westview, 1995.

Rosenstiel, Tom. *The Beat Goes On: President Clinton's First Year with the Media.* New York: Twentieth Century Fund, 1994.

Ross, Dennis. *The Missing Peace: The Inside Story of the Fight for Middle East Peace.* New York: Farrar, Straus and Giroux, 2004.

Rubin, Robert E. *In an Uncertain World: Tough Choices from Wall Street to Washington.* New York: Random House, 2003.

Schmidt, Susan, and Michael Weisskopf, *Truth at Any Cost: Ken Starr and the Unmaking of Bill Clinton.* New York: HarperCollins, 2000.

Sigal, Leon V. *Disarming Strangers: Nuclear Diplomacy with North Korea.* Princeton, NJ: Princeton University Press, 1998.

Starr, Kenneth. *The Starr Report: The Official Report of the Independent Counsel's Investigation of the President* (including volumes one through five of the supplemental materials). New York: Prima Lifestyles, 1998.

Stephanopoulos, George. *All Too Human: A Political Education.* Boston: Little, Brown, 1999.

Stewart, James B. *Blood Sport: The President and His Adversaries.* New York: Simon & Schuster, 1996.

Talbott, Strobe. *Engaging India: Diplomacy, Democracy, and the Bomb.* Washington, DC: Brookings, 2004.

———. *The Russia Hand: A Memoir of Presidential Diplomacy.* New York: Random House, 2003.

Tomasky, Michael. *Hillary's Turn: Inside Her Improbable, Victorious Senate Campaign.* New York: Free Press, 2001.

Toobin, Jeffrey. *A Vast Conspiracy: The Real Story of the Sex Scandal That Nearly Brought Down a President.* New York: Random House, 1999.

Turque, Bill: *Inventing Al Gore: A Biography.* Boston: Houghton Mifflin, 2000.

Waldman, Michael. *POTUS Speaks: Finding the Words That Defined the Clinton Presidency.* New York: Simon & Schuster, 2000.

Wit, Joel S., Daniel B. Poneman, and Robert L. Gallucci. *Going Critical: The First North Korean Nuclear Crisis.* Washington, DC: Brookings, 2004.

Woodward, Bob. *The Agenda: Inside the Clinton White House.* New York: Simon & Schuster, 1994.

———. *The Choice.* New York: Simon & Schuster, 1996.

———. *Maestro: Greenspan's Fed and the American Boom.* New York: Simon & Schuster, 2000.

———. *Shadow: Five Presidents and the Legacy of Watergate.* New York: Simon & Schuster, 1999.

Index

PHOTO © KATHERINE FREY

JOHN F. HARRIS is a veteran political reporter for the *Washington Post* who covered the Clinton presidency from 1995 through its conclusion in 2001. His work during these years earned several prestigious awards, including the White House Correspondents' Association's Aldo Beckman Award and the Prize for Distinguished Reporting on the Presidency from the Gerald R. Ford Library. Harris is a panelist on PBS's *Washington Week*. He is a graduate of Carleton College and lives with his wife, Ann O'Hanlon, and their three children near Washington, D.C.